THE
HISTORY OF
ADVERTISING

40
MAJOR BOOKS
IN FACSIMILE

Edited by
HENRY ASSAEL
C. SAMUEL CRAIG
New York University

A
GARLAND
SERIES

PRINTERS' INK
FIFTY YEARS
1888–1938

GARLAND PUBLISHING, INC.
NEW YORK & LONDON
1986

For a complete list of the titles in this series
see the final pages of this volume.

This facsimile has been made from a copy in
the Library of Congress.

Library of Congress Cataloging-in-Publication Data

Main entry under title:
Printers' ink.
  (The History of advertising)
  Reprint. Originally published: New York : Printers'
Ink Pub. Co., 1938.
  1. Printers' ink monthly—History. I. Printers' ink
monthly. II. Series.
HF5801.P74 1986   659.1'05   84-46032
ISBN 0-8240-6726-6 (alk. paper)

Designed by Donna Montalbano

The volumes in this series are printed on
acid-free, 250-year-life paper.

Printed in the United States of America

PRINTERS' INK

Fifty years
1888-1938

Printers' Ink Publishing Co.
New York
1938

FIFTIETH ANNIVERSARY ISSUE 73054

JULY 28, 1938 • *IN TWO SECTIONS—SECTION ONE* • ONE DOLLAR

PRINTERS' INK

REGISTERED U. S. PATENT OFFICE

A JOURNAL FOR ADVERTISERS

CHAPTER 867

In one of P.I's. most continued stories

1917

1938

THE fiftieth anniversary of Printers' Ink marks the twenty-second year in which The Milwaukee Journal has regularly used the pages of this publication to give advertisers the facts of the Milwaukee-Wisconsin market.

This record of consistency is indicative of the most salient characteristic of the market itself. In our first P. I. advertisement (January, 1917) Milwaukee was described as a "city which never experienced a boom and never knew a depression in which it was other than comfortably prosperous". This quality of *steadiness* persists today, and in times of "hard going" Milwaukee is one of the nation's most productive markets.

THE MILWAUKEE JOURNAL
FIRST BY MERIT

TESTIMONIAL DRAMA

Interesting Situation Between General Mills and Kellogg Comes from Latter's Radio Baseball Campaign

By Andrew M. Howe

"YOU can give Buicks to any baseball players who will accept them and you can make up a mythical Kellogg's All-American team but you can't tell the public that certain of these players enjoy great big bowls of Kellogg's corn flakes every morning for breakfast because many of the leading players have already gone on record as being Wheaties fans and we intend to see to it that these boys live up to their agreements with us not to endorse any other cereal."

President D. D. Davis of General Mills didn't use those exact words in the letter he sent to the Kellogg Company last week and to the J. Walter Thompson Company, which is handling the current Kellogg's radio baseball campaign,* but that is what he meant.

Mr. Davis' communication was friendly enough but he made himself pretty clear. He had, he said, noticed the Kellogg's baseball poll advertisements and he had no objection to the plan of picking an All-American team. In fact, he added, the players who are under endorsement contracts to General Mills will not be prohibited from accepting any Kellogg awards, should they win them. Kellogg

should understand, however, Mr. Davis continued, that it must refrain from implying directly or indirectly that these players endorse any breakfast cereal but Wheaties.

Although Mr. Davis has offered to furnish the Kellogg Company a list of the players who have signed up as Wheaties eaters, the latter doesn't intend to ask for such a list, because its plans do not in any way involve the use of testimonials from ball players for Kellogg's corn flakes. The awards are being made purely on the results of the voting of the fans. It would be nice, of course, if the winning players should also be Kellogg's corn flakes eaters but there is no intention of seeking to publicize that fact, should it be true.

The awards will be Buick cars and it is planned to have these carry some sort of Kellogg identification, but not conspicuously. "Gabby" Hartnett, for example, should he be voted the most popular catcher in the poll, may find himself in the position of driving a Kellogg's corn flakes car while he is being quoted in a General Mills advertisement.

General Mills has declined to give PRINTERS' INK a complete list of the players who are now on the Wheaties endorsement roll. A few months ago one advertisement

* See "Radio Baseball Poll," PRINTERS' INK, July 21, 1938, page 16.

contained testimonials from these twelve major league players: Joe Cronin, "Gabby" Hartnett, Charles Gehringer, Luke Sewell, Mel Ott, Louis Fette, Paul Waner, Carl Hubbell, Bob Feller, "Lefty" Gomez, Joe Medwick and Joe DiMaggio. This is not a complete roster, and furthermore the agreements with the different men terminate at various times so some of the men named here may now be free to eat Kellogg's corn flakes or some other cereal and tell the world about their preferences.

The rights of the various parties in this little testimonial drama are somewhat obscure. The General Mills agreements are between the company and the players as individuals. They agree not to endorse any other cereal. Does the acceptance of a Kellogg's Buick violate this agreement? Does the use of the player's name in Kellogg's advertising as a winner in the poll constitute a violation? Kellogg's is not a party to the agreement so what can be done to it? The player isn't a party to the selection of the All-American team so what can he, or General Mills, do about that?

Kellogg's only vulnerable point, according to one authority, is the possibility of violation of the individual player's right of privacy by using his name in advertising without permission. But is a baseball player's work on the diamond a part of his private life?

We'll probably never know the answers because this case is not likely to reach the courts. Kellogg's intentions are obviously honorable and General Mills apparently has no intentions of being unreasonable.

FRANCISCO HEADS L. & T.

DON FRANCISCO, executive vice-president of Lord & Thomas and with the firm since 1921, succeeds Albert D. Lasker as president of the agency.

Mr. Lasker, principal owner, completing his fortieth year of continuous service with the agency, will retire from active duty.

After October 1, Mr. Francisco will be located in the New York office, which becomes the headquarters of the agency. The management, personnel, and facilities of local offices remain unchanged.

Since going to California in 1916 Mr. Francisco has been actively identified with agricultural co-operative movements under which citrus and other products have been widely distributed and advertised. He has also been active in exploiting California as a tourist attraction. He is credited with the leading role in defeating Upton Sinclair in his race for Governor of California, and later managed the campaign resulting in the defeat of the special chain-store tax in that State. Mr. Francisco has served as an officer in many national and Western advertising organizations.

In addition to the new president, the following executive vice-presidents were elected: Sheldon R. Coons, New York; David M. Noyes, Chicago.

Vice-presidents are: Don Belding, Los Angeles; Mary L. Foreman, Chicago; Thomas M. Keresey, New York; Edgar Kobak, New York; Edward Lasker, New York; H. G. Little, Dayton; Leonard M. Masius, London, England; and John Whedon, San Francisco.

William R. Sachse was named secretary-treasurer.

Emotional advertising note quickens sales of strictly seasonal merchandise

As Told to William H. Bingham

By C. K. Turk

General Manager, The South Bend Awning Company

ANNUALLY, the awning industry awaits the coming of warm sunshine to sell awnings. This year was no exception. However, like many other businesses in 1938, awning manufacturers in the majority not only experienced a market with curtailed buying power, but an unusually damp and cool season as well. Both factors were slowing down the sales of awnings. Feeling the pinch of reduced sales caused by these same conditions, the South Bend Awning Company decided that increased sales efforts and improvements in its general marketing program would have to be made. Up for major consideration and revamping were the advertising methods and merchandising appeals. Here is how the company changed its newspaper advertising program which ultimately increased sales.

First, the company, in business over twenty-seven years, analyzed its present and past advertising methods as well as those of the awning industry. Essentially, it was found both company and industry were using the same kind of advertising appeal, layout and copy. Over the years, there were numerous indications that improvements in awning advertising technique had been rather slow. Little had been

done to increase the pulling power of awning advertisements. There was a tendency to use the same layouts and copy every season. General practice, year after year, was to advertise awnings as being "colorful, beautiful, decorative and well-constructed for long wear." In some instances, an advertisement carried illustrations of a striped awning with copy theme, "Our awnings are built to suit the architecture of each home to enhance its appearance, etc." Certain competitive groups with ready-made, over-the-counter merchandise sometimes advertised the old favorite appeal of price.

In any event, advertisements looked dull and unattractive, layouts and type lifeless. Illustrations and copy were without punch. Little could be found that appealed to the eye or created an urge to buy. Information was more factual than emotional. Appeals were general and not directed to fulfil specific, physical wants derived from installing awnings. However, here and there were certain pieces that had successfully pulled customer inquiries and made sales in the past. These were separated from the rest and used later in planning the new advertising program.

The next step was studying local market possibilities. The company

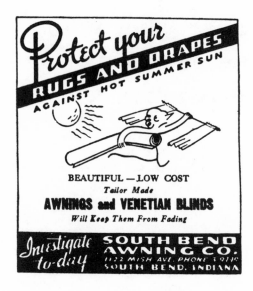

BEAUTIFUL — LOW COST
Tailor Made
AWNINGS and VENETIAN BLINDS
Will Keep Them From Fading

Investigate to-day **SOUTH BEND
AWNING CO.**
1122 MISH AVE. PHONE 3-9149
SOUTH BEND, INDIANA

wanted to learn if new ideas in building construction or changes in buying habits were influencing the buying motives to purchase awnings. Some very interesting facts developed from this investigation.

It was learned that many modern homes no longer have a wide, sweeping front and rear porch. Open terraces are now more common, requiring one or more canopy awnings for shade and protection. Awnings used in this manner provide a cool, extra summer room. Another change noted was that people were not buying awnings entirely for their homes because awnings were "colorful, beautiful, or matched the architecture of the house." Whereas this had been a motivating factor to purchase awnings in years past, it was a third and minor buying motive now. Investigation revealed that the first and strongest motive was to keep houses, porches and terraces cool.

The second influencing factor was to protect interior decorations from sun and rain. Quite naturally, the motives to buy, as well as close the sale, in practically every purchase, initiated and rested with the housewife.

Lastly, in looking for additional business, the company was aware of the new awning market opened by air conditioned homes and stores. While the present demand for awnings in this field is still small, the need is rapidly growing and awnings are being used in many places to reduce the cost of operating home and store air conditioning equipment by keeping out the hot sun. Up to the present time, little has been done to promote awning sales in this market. It is still too early for awning manufacturers to push the idea in smaller towns as the fewer number of installations compared to those in large cities will not justify the cost of advertising to this particular field.

However, the cooling effect of properly installed awnings does not keep an awning manufacturer from cashing in on the popularity of air conditioning. Considerable research by a large electrical manufacturer

6

and a university discovered the fact that awnings alone will reduce house temperatures ten to fifteen degrees in the summertime. The sun shining through window or plate glass increases inside room temperatures several degrees. Awnings prevent this, thereby adding to the efficiency of operating air conditioning equipment, or, where no equipment is used, at least keeping stores and homes cooler than outside temperatures.

The analysis of markets and buying appeals was now finished. All the evidence and information was brought together and studied. Important facts and buying motives were sifted out, studied and analyzed until the company felt they had definite conclusions around which to plan a new advertising program. Work was begun immediately on copy and layouts for newspaper display advertisements.

To gain the interest of women, some advertisements were centered around the use of awnings to protect expensive rugs and drapes from fading against the hot summer sun. Another series was on the protection they gave against rain, to keep inside decorations from being damaged during storms while the window remains open through neglect, sleep, or for allowing cool air to enter. To attract the attention of those women more interested in awnings as a house decorative fea-

ture, an emotional appeal to vanity was used, emphasizing the idea and theme "For Smart Entertaining."

Not forgetting the growing market for awnings in the air cooling field, still another series was developed on the cooling effect of awnings in reducing house temperatures ten to fifteen degrees. Copy was written to attract attention of both men and women with such captions as "Want Relief from Hot, Sticky Air," "Air-cooled Homes at One-third the Cost," "For Summer Comfort," "Sleep Coolly Tonight," and "Mother, Keep Baby Cool."

The awning season covers the months of March through July. The advertisements were scheduled to break in the local newspaper during the first week of March on the woman's page, running consistently during the five months with weekly advertisement changes. In every illustration, a humorous character was used to give life, action and a human touch to the advertisement. By showing the character enjoying

7

the benefits and protection of an awning, his actions told a story much stronger than descriptive words. This was planned with an eye to plenty of white space and a minimum of copy.

Soon after the advertising program began, inquiries started to come in, slow at first, but gradually gaining momentum until sales are now topping those made the previous year The new advertising appeals were taking hold. Results so far this season show this company's awning sales in excess of 4 per cent over last year. Advertising the benefits derived from the installation of awnings has stepped up sales in a season that would otherwise have been very dull.

FROM A VALUED ADMIRER

E. R. Squibb & Sons
New York

Editor of Printers' Ink:

Referring to your forthcoming Fiftieth Anniversary issue, I wish to congratulate you on so unique and formidable an undertaking. This history of business building through the use of printer's ink will be particularly welcome to me since I have been a constant and interested reader of your valued publication throughout the last fifty years.

Its format and typography have always been most pleasing and appetizing to me. I am sure you were wise not to follow the general modern trend and enlarge your Weekly in size. The editorial treatment of your copy has at all times been broad, independent and trustworthy. Althogether, you have every right to be proud of your long and outstanding achievement. From the start to this day you have occupied practically alone a most important field of publicity.

May the next fifty years prove equally successful to you as editors and publishers, and successful to the vast interests that you represent. These are my sincere wishes on this memorable occasion.

Theodore Weicker,
Chairman of the Board.

WASTED STAMPS

Sun Life Assurance Company of
Canada
Montreal

Editor of Printers' Ink:

In return for some of the helpful ideas I have received from other sales executives through the columns of Printers' Ink, I pass along this comment for what it may be worth.

As I go over my business and personal mail, from day to day, I often wonder why American concerns conducting direct-mail campaigns in the Canadian market place U. S. postage stamps on reply envelopes to be mailed from a Canadian address. It is not only a waste of postage but an annoyance to the person using the reply envelope.

There are four examples in my mail today. Twelve cents' worth of postage budgets wasted on just one person in one day. The odd thing is that this mail comes from substantial concerns—two large advertising agencies, a Philadelphia hotel, and one of the largest advertising novelty firms.

Seth C. H. Taylor,
Assistant Superintendent of Agencies
Sales Promotion Division.

SALES DRIVE MAKES JOBS

With 496 Communities Now Enlisted, Salesmen's Crusade Reveals Its Effect Upon Employment

By Arthur H. Little

AS the National Salesmen's Crusade moves into another week, evidence accumulates to prove that sales do create jobs.

From Texas, L. B. Merchant, Graybar's merchandise manager in Dallas, writes to the man who, in Lincoln, Nebraska, staged an experiment that has set thousands of salesmen to marching—George W. Mason, president of Nash-Kelvinator.

Mr. Merchant reports:

"There is now a permanent Crusade Office at 1616 Baker Hotel in Dallas.

"A few details will indicate what the Crusade has meant. In our Kelvinator business in Dallas we sold more units to dealers, exclusive of utility outlets, than we have ever sold in any June since we had Kelvinators.

"The Texas employment service was able to place in Dallas, during the first twenty-two days of June, 1,600 employees, or an average of seventy-four a day. During the last four days of June, which was the first 'week' of the Crusade, they placed 557 employees, or 139 a day.

"The Safeway Stores showed an 8 per cent increase in their business during the first week of the campaign. They participated actively. To handle the increased business, they took on twenty-two additional employees.

"The McGauth Hosiery Mills tied into the activity with a special Hosiery Day and, as a result, have increased their working schedule from eighteen to twenty-four hours a day. On Hosiery Day, Dallas was sold out of hosiery.

"The Brown Cracker and Candy Company tied in with the activity with a 'Smacks Day.' Their average daily sales had been sixty dozen. On the two days in which they tied in with the Crusade, they sold 2,100 dozen.

"The Hoover Company had been selling $1,600 worth of vacuum cleaners a week. With the aid of 'Sales Mean Jobs' and the story they built around it, in the first week of the campaign they sold $4,000 worth."

And meanwhile, elsewhere in America, with 496 communities planning or running local drives, these are some of the highlights that gleamed—

New York—Plans are moving forward to a permanent Crusade organization.

Chicago—Under the leadership of Oscar G. Mayer, president of the Association of Commerce, 269 firms, many of them major companies, have enlisted.

Shreveport—Having launched a crusade with a mass meeting of 6,500 executives and salespeople, this community plans to continue the mass-meeting idea. "Shreveport considers the Crusade idea one of the greatest things that has happened here since the oil-field strike of last year."

Des Moines—The Chamber of Commerce, having sponsored an initial meeting of 300 business leaders, now plans a mass meeting of consumers.

Charlotte, N. C.—The increase in business during the last three weeks has been 15 per cent.

Muskegon, Michigan—For the first time since 1937, there has been an increase in the demand for new cars and trucks. During the week of June 11, 19 dealers sold 150 units.

New Orleans—Crusade Chairman Strenby L. Drumm reports: "There already has been a 10 to 20 per cent increase in sales. Increases are reported by department stores, small retailers, manufacturers and all lines of business."

Oakland, California—In the first week of the campaign, new-car sales increased by 30 per cent. Used-car sales likewise went up.

Kansas City—It is the consensus that the crusade activity has boosted sales 18 per cent. Kansas City plans a drive to last for six months.

San Antonio—Sponsored by the Chamber of Commerce and the Sales Managers' Club, this community's drive is to be carried, by speakers, into the factories.

Portland, Maine—"Twenty thousand crusade buttons on the march! One insurance company reports collections improved. Splendid public acceptance and co-operation. Salesmen report easier approaches. Retail business much improved."

Spokane—New business pledged by the new Spending and Employment Committee of the Sales Mean Jobs campaign will exceed $500,000, reports Chairman D. Roy Johnson. He adds: "The results in the few days this committee has been working have been beyond our greatest expectations. The co-operation of Spokane business firms has been wonderful. New employment pledges are running close to 300."

TULIP BULBS AND STORE TRAFFIC

FURNITURE dealers and the furniture and bedding departments of retail stores need store traffic. Present methods of building traffic have not been very profitable. For instance, the National Retail Dry Goods Association's survey shows a 0.2 per cent profit.

As part of their fall plans, the manufacturers of Spring-Air mattresses are offering dealers a traffic building plan that is unusual. In September, two-color advertisements will break in two home magazines. In these a special offer will be made.

If the coupon at the base of these advertisements is clipped and taken with 39 cents to any Spring-Air dealer, the coupon clipper can get a $1.40 rainbow collection of twenty Dutch Tulip Bulbs. There is no obligation and nothing for the person to buy. All she is required to do is to take the coupon and the 39 cents to the dealer's store.

Spring-Air has either purchased, or has options on 5,000,000 tulip bulbs, which when packed in cartons of twenty each means that more than 250,000 cartons are available to Spring-Air dealers for distribution. The company has certified statements from the growers and suppliers that the bulbs have a retail value in excess of $350,000.

Until September 15, (when tulip planting time starts) the company's salesmen will be contacting its 4,500 dealers, taking orders for the bulbs at 39 cents per box. When a dealer places his first order, he will also receive a twenty-six piece Tulip Offer window trim, special newspaper mats and direct-mail pieces.

A MAN may be a master of elocution, oratory, and eloquence — but his after-dinner speech can still make you curse your insomnia.

A man may be a master of grammar, rhetoric, and style —but his written effort to sell your merchandise can still leave your public cold.

Advertising copy, unfortunately, is more than the arrangement of words that pleasantly and accurately describe what you have for sale.

Advertising copy is the thoughtful arrangement of those precise words that make steady sales at a profit.

Many people can write. But only a small group can write and sell!

You are interested in results from your advertising.

We share that interest.

Can you think of a better time than now to work together for that common cause?

JEROME B. GRAY & COMPANY

ADVERTISING • MERCHANDISING

TWELVE SOUTH TWELFTH STREET • PHILADELPHIA

DRI-BRITE, INC. 4443 *Cook Avenue, St. Louis, Missouri*

DRI-BRITE IS THE ORIGINAL AND GENUINE NO-RUBBING, NO-POLISHING, LIQUID FLOOR WAX

June 28, 1938.

Mr. J. R. Brady,
Chicago Daily News,
Chicago, Illinois.

Dear Mr. Brady:

You will undoubtedly be interested in the final figures concerning our recent introduction of CLICK in the Chicago market wherein the Chicago Daily News was used exclusively.

Tho CLICK is itself nothing short of revolutionary the record response to the promotion can seem almost unbelievable. However using Chicago as one of our test markets for nation wide duplicate promotions this fall...accuract figures were kept.

From prior successful CLICK promotions in comparable metropolitan markets, we estimated sample requirements as 30,000 units for Chicago. Coupons clipped from the offering advertisement of April 28th ACTUALLY WITHDREW FROM OUR CHICAGO DEALERS 49,840 CLICK SAMPLES WITHIN 3 DAYS. This means the Daily News directed 66% more CLICK minded people into our dealers' stores than we had set up as a profit-able return.

It is seldom that a manufacturer immediately starts off breaking even with a new item in a metropolitan market on a market wide advertising promotion...it is a miracle when accomplished in the black. The units sold by promotion ended up astoundingly deep in the black. Our CLICK our jobbers during the series of advertisements approximates closely, believe it or not, the number of samples given away and CLICK reorders today, though the spring selling season is over, are astounding in regularity.

We knew CLICK was a revolutionary product; we felt our advertising agency's copy intelligently presented it and we felt that for the market we were trying to reach the Chicago Daily News best serviced the interests of our dealers and the efforts of our salesmen contacting them. In short we believed from previous experiences in other test markets we would have reasonable success in Chicago. We did not expect the actual consumer stampede for CLICK that the Daily News incited.

We are glad to be able to write you of this for our final figures reflect far greater values are to be obtained from the use of the Chicago Daily News than normal investigations disclose.

Very truly yours,

DRI-BRITE, INC.

A. J. Scheu

President.

A. J. Scheu/M

THE CHICAGO

Chicago's <u>Home</u>

WITH THE MOST VALUABLE

DAILY NEWS PLAZA, *400 West Madison Street,* **CHICAGO**
DETROIT OFFICE: *4-119 General Motors Building*

How CLICK
was successfully
introduced to Chicago

SPEAKING OF YODELING!

THE ELIZABETH TOWNE COMPANY, INC.

PUBLISHERS OF *Nautilus Magazine*

HOLYOKE, MASS.

Editor of PRINTERS' INK:

Some of us wonder if such Tarzan-like yodeling as you indulge in in your editorial* in PRINTERS' INK of July 14 is an adequate way to meet the problems raised.

Ought we not rather to feel humiliated and ashamed of the vast wealth of the few when we look at the opposite side of the picture? According to the reactionary Hoover (who has done his full share to make this country what it is *not*) most of the thirteen foreign countries which he recently visited were taking better care of the under-privileged than we are.

On the opposite side of the picture of wealth which is being so loudly and boastfully presented by the tories, we find:

That we have the world's largest army of unemployed.

That one-third of our population is "ill-housed, ill-clad, ill-fed."

That we have some five million share croppers with a standard of living lower than that which obtains in the Balkans, according to Secretary Ickes, which has the lowest living standard in Europe.

---

* "Irritating, Not Fatal," page 70.

That millions of our citizens are suffering from malnutrition—so many that the government agencies are worried about the problem from the viewpoint of national defense. In some sections the percentage of sufferers from malnutrition is higher than in Germany during the World War, it is said.

Now if this vast army of unemployed and destitute were willing to starve, peacefully and patriotically, so that those of us who already live in comfort or luxury might have more, the process would soon need to be repeated. For nothing but strict government regulation will prevent the rugged individualists from producing far more than can be consumed. And soon their markets would be curtailed. And then chaos.

Only the politicians—so much derided—can prevent such an outcome. Only they can stand between the employers, the workers and the farmers and obtain something like a reasonable opportunity to live for all of them. For the first time in the history of our country, I believe, the people began to come fully into control of their own government in 1932 and I do not believe they will again let that power slip from their hands.

WILLIAM E. TOWNE,
Editor.

FIFTH YEAR FOR MIRACLE WHIP

FROM July 25 to August 7 the Kraft-Phenix Cheese Corporation will celebrate the fifth anniversary of Miracle Whip, which since its introduction has become the largest selling salad dressing. The special campaign, the largest ever put behind this product for a similar period, is built around a display program including mass, window and wall displays, dealer advertisements and a number of attention-getting stunts.

The keynote of the drive is "push quarts." Commercials on the Kraft Music Hall radio program have been featuring quarts and dealers are being told that when they push the larger size package "consumers get more for their money; they get the ideal reusable canning jar size; with plenty of salad dressing available, women use more, use it more frequently, and dealers make bigger, faster profits."

Kraft advises the trade to "get away from pint and half-pint business . . . push quarts."

IF SELLING CARS IS YOUR BUSINESS

● It will pay you to know—that today the Nebraska-southwestern Iowa Market has more registered cars than it has families—and that this rich market sold more new cars in 1937 (41,007) than St. Louis (36,671).

● In the Nebraska-southwestern Iowa Market's 107 counties, one newspaper, the Omaha World-Herald, is dominant and read by every other family. In the market's 307 largest incorporated cities, whose total population is nearly a million, 7 out of every 10 urban families read this big, state newspaper.

● With World-Herald A schedules YOU can sell more NEW cars where business has been consistently running ahead of the nation—Nebraska and Iowa.

Omaha World-Herald

National Advertising Representatives:
O'MARA & ORMSBEE, Inc.
A. B. C. Circulation 1st Quarter 1938—174,246 Daily

is for Dentifrice

...and what you *don't* know about it

A dentifrice is something you put on a toothbrush.

All the smart little boys and girls know that only 1 out of 3 Americans owns a toothbrush. That is called a "national average."

And whoever doesn't own a toothbrush wouldn't buy a dentifrice, *n'est ce pas?* (French for ain't it the truth)

The Week's News

ACCOUNTS

Italian Tourist Office

Italian Tourist Information Office, New York, has placed its account with Albert Frank-Guenther Law, Inc., that city. Media: newspapers, magazines.

"Ri-Muv" Hair Remover

The Raymond R. Morgan Co., Hollywood, is handling the advertising of "Ri-Muv" new product for the removal of unwanted hair. Media: radio, newspapers and women's magazines.

Puritan Laboratories

Richardson-MacDonald, Ltd., Toronto, is directing the advertising of Puritan Laboratories, that city, sanitation supplies.

Hood Lax

The Metropolitan Advertising Co., New York, is handling the advertising of "Hood Lax," intestinal bulk preparation of the Hood Lax Corp., that city. Media: radio.

New to Hillman-Shane

New accounts of Hillman-Shane Advertising Agency, Los Angeles, are: Esquire, Inc., beverage distributor, using radio and post-boards; "Your Hollywood Shopper," using fan magazines; Gerald M. Greenclay, apparel merchandising firm, and M. Nagel, Inc., apparel manufacturer.

Lampson, Fraser & Huth

Lampson, Fraser & Huth, New York, fur auctioneer, has placed its account with Wildrick & Miller, that city.

Kijafa Cherry Wine

Gotham Advertising Co., New York, is handling advertising of Kijafa Danish cherry wine for Jacobsens Co., Odense, Den. Media: Scandinavian papers in U. S.

Rap-i-dol

The Rap-i-dol Distributing Co., New York, is placing its advertising and merchandising with Redfield-Johnstone, Inc., that city.

Anderson, Allen & Co.

Anderson, Allen & Co., New York, investment management, has placed its account with Charles J. Cutajar, Advertising, that city. Media: newspapers, magazines.

Dunn & McCarthy

Marschalk & Pratt, Inc., New York, is now advertising counsel for Dunn & McCarthy, Inc., Auburn, N. Y., manufacturer of women's shoes. Account executive: Arthur R. Anderson.

Dal-A-No Cream Deodorant

Westheimer & Co., St. Louis, has secured the Dal-A-No cream deodorant account of Golden Peacock, Paris, Tenn. Ruthrauff & Ryan continues to handles other Golden Peacock items.

Canterbury Furniture Shops

William G. Seidenbaum, New York agency, is directing advertising and merchandising for Canterbury Furniture Shops, Inc., that city.

W. G. B. Oil Clarifier

Willard G. Myers, New York, directs the advertising of W. G. B. Oil Clarifier, Inc., Kingston, N. Y., oil filters for automobiles, effective August 1. Media: business papers and direct mail.

International Piston Rings

The International Piston Ring Co., Cleveland, is placing its advertising account with Vlchek Advertising Agency, that city. Media: trade papers and direct mail.

Callite Products

Reiss Advertising, New York, is advertising and merchandising counselor for the Callite Products division of the Eisler Electric Corp., Union City, N. J. A campaign on fluorescent tubing for display illumination will be launched in trade papers and direct mail.

Dominion Stores, Toronto

Dominion Stores, Ltd., Toronto, has placed its account with J. Walter Thompson Co., Montreal office.

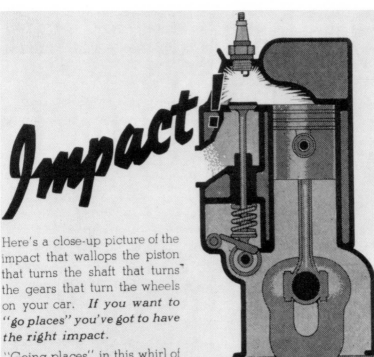

Impact!

Here's a close-up picture of the impact that wallops the piston that turns the shaft that turns the gears that turn the wheels on your car. *If you want to "go places" you've got to have the right impact.*

"Going places" in this whirl of modern business also requires the right impact. The wrong impact will backfire just as fast in your selling machine as it will in your automobile.

How can you get the right selling impact?

In the Chicago market, the Herald and Examiner in the morning and the American in the evening are offered on an optional combination plan at a dollar a line. These two great newspapers—each with a proved pulling power—deliver more than 700,000 circulation . . . deliver morning coverage and evening coverage. They deliver the right impact. *They deliver the goods.*

For added impact—for a sure-fire spark for your selling campaigns—use the Sunday Herald and Examiner, with more than 950,000 circulation.

CHICAGO HERALD AND EXAMINER *Impact!*
CHICAGO EVENING AMERICAN

National Advertising Representatives: Hearst International Advertising Service
Rodney E. Boone, General Manager

THAT CAMEL-LUCKY DUEL

● Two out of every seven packs of cigarettes sold last year were Camels. And FORTUNE this month brings you the story of R. J. REYNOLDS, biggest of the "big three", and of the running fight between Luckies ("It's Toasted!") and Camels ("Get a Lift with ..."). How the makers of Camels won back their lost sales lead, the story of Camel's $57,000,000 worth of advertising campaigns in the last five years, and the personalities behind the scenes, notably tobaccoman S. Clay Williams and adman Bill Esty. Read $57,000,000 WORTH OF WHIZZ AND WHOOZLE, page 25 of FORTUNE FOR AUGUST.

DEATH BY TARIFF... You say we have no tariffs between states? That Pennsylvania can't erect tariff walls against milk from Wisconsin? Read an analysis of the situation, by Raymond Leslie Buell, President of the Foreign Policy Association, FORTUNE p. 32.

Why didn't Hitler grab Czechoslovakia?

● Would France and England really come to the aid of the Czechs? Would the Czechs fight anyway? Why? Here are some economic sidelights, political facts, and certain weaknesses of the German position overlooked to date by the Sunday Supplements. See CZECHOSLOVAKIA, page 37 this month.

Stock exchange president, age 31

● Meet Bill Martin, ten years out of Yale, mnemonic wizard, now rocketed by reformers into the $48,000 job of simultaneously soothing conservatives, reformers, the SEC, and the wary share-buying public. Here's the story of the man they hesitated over because he was too young (and didn't wear a hat to work). See BILL MARTIN IS THIRTY-ONE, p. 47.

FORTUNE MEANS BUSINESS · FORTUNE

Fortune

FORTUNE MEANS BUSINESS · FORTUNE

9 new Fortune survey questions

- How U. S. votes on (1) cigarette preferences by brand, (2) fairness of different U. S. taxes, (3) which is making the most progress in giving the public what it wants—automobiles, radio, air transport, or movies? (Get ready for a surprise here!) These and six more questions are answered for you in FORTUNE's QUARTERLY SURVEY OF PUBLIC OPINION. See page 49 of the August issue for this newest survey.

NEXT MONTH . . . Corn Products Refining . . . Curtiss-Wright . . . U. S. Wealth . . . Morris Agency . . . Polaroid . . . Canada . . . Swedish Economic Policy . . . Business-and-Government.

USINESS • FORTUNE MEANS BUSINESS

R **August**

USINESS • FORTUNE MEANS BUSINESS

YOU'RE GOING TO CONEY ISLAND!

- Waxworks, roller coasters, shooting galleries, baby incubators, bathhouses, and bingo palaces assault the eye at dizzy angles. Hamburger, fish, onion, garlic odors greet the nose. Merry-go-rounds blare their tinny music and a million people struggle and squeal and jostle. We take Coney apart for you this month, to show you how it works. To HEAVEN BY SUBWAY, p. 61.

Did you buy a Put-Put?

- Then maybe you helped Outboard, Marine & Manufacturing Company, (which is Elto, Evinrude, and Johnson Sea Horse all at once) make their $940,000 profit last year. You may get some business ideas by reading the PUT-PUT, p. 56 of FORTUNE.

BABY RAILROAD . . . Don't laugh. (Don't even smile). You are looking at Unadilla Valley Railway's pet Mogul engine as it pushes through upstate New York weeds on its twenty-mile-long track. Spend a day with Unadilla's train crew, and see how the railroad makes its money. Page 50.

Gro-Pup Dog Food

Kenyon & Eckhardt, Inc., New York, is directing the advertising of Gro-Pup Dog Food, a new product being introduced by the Kellogg Co., Battle Creek, Mich. Media: newspapers and direct mail.

Syracuse GuildTool Co.

The Syracuse GuildTool Co., Syracuse, N. Y., is placing the advertising of its new "GuildSANDER," portable electric sanding machine, with Barlow Advertising Agency, Inc., that city.

Clark Grave Vault

Stockton, West, Burkhart, Inc., Cincinnati, is handling the advertising of Clark Grave Vault Co., Columbus, Ohio. Account executive: E. J. Hughes.

Minicamera Hobbyists

A. W. Lewin Co., Inc., Newark, N. J., is directing a campaign for Foto Graphic Services, New York. Magazines and newspaper supplements will be used.

Charak Furniture

Campbell-Lampee, Inc., New York, is handling the advertising of Charak Furniture Co., Boston, with Wallace H. Campbell as account executive. Media: magazines, trade papers and direct mail. ·

Raleigh Manufacturers

Frank B. Sawdon Advertising, New York, now directs the advertising of Raleigh Manufacturers, Inc., Raleigh clothes, Baltimore, Md. Media: national magazines, trade papers and direct mail.

Snow-Proof Co.

The Snow-Proof Co., Middletown, N. Y., manufacturer of Snow-Proof leather preserver, is placing its advertising with the Hutchins Advertising Co., Inc., Rochester, N. Y.

G. H. Bass & Co.

Badger & Browning, Inc., Boston, is handling the advertising of the G. H. Bass & Co., Wilton, Me., outdoor footwear. Media: magazines, trade and college publications and direct mail.

V. Arena & Sons

J. M. Korn & Co., Philadelphia, is the advertising counsel for V. Arena & Sons, manufacturer of "Conte Luna" macaroni.

"Oleo Saude" in Brazil

McCann-Erickson, Inc., Rio de Janeiro, Brazil, is handling the Brazilian advertising of "Oleo Saude," product of Anderson Clayton & Co., Houston, Tex., to be launched on that market shortly.

New to Ohio Advertising

New accounts at Ohio Advertising Agency, Cleveland, are: H. Blonder Co., that city, distributor of wall paper, starting production of Gold Seal brand, using newspapers, radio and posters; Rider Rubber Novelties, that city, using trade papers and direct mail.

"Treadeasy" Shoes

P. W. Minor & Sons, Inc., Batavia, N. Y., is placing its national and trade advertising account on "Treadeasy" women shoes with Stewart, Hanford & Lyddon, Inc., Rochester. Account executive: A. T. Stewart.

Walnut Manufacturers

Wallace-Lindeman, Inc., Grand Rapids, Mich., handles the advertising of the American Walnut Manufacturers Association, Chicago.

Dee-Jay Manufacturing

Whipple & Black Advertising Co., Detroit, is handling the advertising of Dee-Jay Manufacturing Co., that city, replacement grills for automobiles.

Manor House Coffee

W. F. McLaughlin & Co., Chicago, Manor House coffee, is placing its advertising with Sherman K. Ellis & Co., New York.

New to Gussow, Kahn

New accounts with Gussow, Kahn & Co., New York, are: Murray Hamburger, evening gowns, and M. Pressner, toys, both that city.

MANY GREAT INDUSTRIES HAVE BEEN
BUILT ON THEIR CATALOG

From the beginning of American business, the success of leading manufacturers has run parallel to the success of their catalogs.

When properly developed the catalog is the salesman's bible, the merchant's source of supply and the cornerstone of the business.

It was indispensable in the early days when advertising budgets were almost unknown. Today it is back on the job, assuming its old importance, inexpensively developing business with new efficiency because of improved selling technique.

The experience of producing catalogs for many of America's leading firms has given us a treasury of catalog ideas that should be helpful in making yours the best in your industry.

A phone call to MEdallion 3-3500 will bring a competent man to discuss your printing problems.

CHARLES FRANCIS PRESS
461 EIGHTH AVENUE, NEW YORK

AGENCIES

Wertheimer & Buchanan Merger

Buchanan & Co. and L. D. Wertheimer Co., New York agencies, are merging as Buchanan & Co. Erwin D. Schmerler, former president of Wertheimer, becomes vice-president of Buchanan. Other officers of Wertheimer will assume similar executive positions in the merged firm.

Stebbins Has New Duties

H. A. Stebbins, vice-president and manager of the Los Angeles office of Erwin, Wasey & Co., becomes executive vice-president in charge of all agency operations on the Pacific Coast.

J. Walter Thompson Shift

Russell Paulson, Los Angeles manager of J. Walter Thompson Co., is transferred to the St. Louis office to succeed Fred Fidler as head of the agency's office in that city. Mr. Fidler assumes an executive position at New York.

Cleveland Agency Liquidates

Richardson-Oswald, Inc., Cleveland, liquidated its business as of July 15.

Harms with B-S-H

Marvin Harms, recently an account executive with Young & Rubicam, has joined Blackett-Sample-Hummert, Chicago, in an executive capacity.

Compton Advances Edmonds

James Edmonds, formerly of the radio department with Compton Advertising, New York, becomes head of that agency's Chicago contact office.

To Open Cleveland Office

Batten, Barton, Durstine & Osborn, New York, will open an office in Cleveland this fall, with Clarence L. Davis one of the owners, in charge.

Philip Ritter Appointment

H. George Harris, former marketing and merchandising counselor with Geyer, Cornell, becomes director of marketing, research and sales promotion of the Philip Ritter Co., New York.

L. C. McElroy Succeeds Watson

L. C. McElroy, of the New York office of O'Dea, Sheldon & Canaday, succeeds K. C. Watson, resigned, as vice-president in charge of the Baltimore office.

Williams Joins Hackett

J. Loyd Williams, formerly with J. Stirling Getchell, Inc., joins M. H. Hackett, Inc., New York, as account executive.

Form Douglas-Saunders

Seymour Douglas and B. H. Saunders have formed the Douglas-Saunders Advertising Agency, with offices at 505 Fifth Ave., New York.

Winsten Changes Post

Harry Winsten, former vice-president of Kelly, Nason & Winsten, New York, will become associated with Lennen & Mitchell, that city, on August 15.

Lee Ringer Appointment

Lee Ringer, Advertising, Los Angeles, appoints Don Menke, formerly with Macmillan Petroleum Corp., as copy chief.

Erickson with Fairall

Parker H. Erickson, former radio sales manager of home appliance division of Fairbanks Morse Co., is with Fairall and Co., Des Moines, Iowa, agency.

Joins Sherman K. Ellis

George Croll, formerly with J. Walter Thompson Co., is with the New York office of Sherman K. Ellis & Co., as an art director.

Gehnrich Changes Post

Charles H. Gehnrich, formerly with *Hat Life,* joins the copy staff of Bermingham, Castleman & Pierce, Inc., New York.

Luce with Kudner

Leonard Luce, of the art staff of McCann-Erickson, Inc., will join Arthur Kudner, Inc., New York, as associate art director, in September.

Bequeathed De Rouville Firm

Horace L. Hevenor has acquired by bequest the De Rouville Advertising Agency, Albany, N. Y., formerly the property of the late George S. De Rouville. Mr. Hevenor was formerly executive manager.

Joins Clifford Broeder

George Hawkins, former advertising manager of Henry C. Hartenbach Carpet Co., joins Clifford F. Broeder Agency, St. Louis, as manager of the production department.

W. E. Pensyl in New Post

W. E. Pensyl, former Pittsburgh representative of Carson, Fletcher & Osborn, joins the copy department of Ketchum, MacLeod & Grove, that city.

Darrow Changes Agency Post

G. Potter Darrow, formerly with Al Lefton Co., Philadelphia, joins Ivey & Ellington, Inc., that city, as account executive.

In Casper Pinsker Post

Mitchell Fenberg becomes vice-president of the Casper Pinsker Advertising Agency, New York, supervising the art, research and creative department.

Harper Joins Elwood Robinson

James Harper, formerly with Radio Features, Inc., joins the publicity department of the Elwood J. Robinson Advertising Agency, Los Angeles.

ADVERTISERS

Chrysler Promotes Jacobson

C. L. Jacobson, with Chrysler Corp., Detroit, for 14 years, is appointed sales manager of the Chrysler division.

Acquires Vita-Ray Co.

Sterling Products, Inc., New York, has acquired Vita-Ray Co. of Lowell, Mass., Vita-Ray face cream.

Humes with American Bantam Car

T. L. Humes is joining the staff of the American Bantam Car Co., Butler, Pa.

Changes at Goodall

David Frankel, former sales manager of the Goodall Co., Cincinnati, is promoted to vice-president in charge of distribution. Gardner Prechtel, with the company for the last seven years, is merchandising director and Joseph Stevens, former credit manager, becomes sales manager.

Dennison Promotes Ford

The Dennison Manufacturing Co., Framingham, Mass., appoints J. J. Ford, former assistant advertising manager, as advertising manager, succeeding W. H. Leahy, who is directing the company's legal work.

To Open New York Office

The Bel Paese Sales Co., subsidiary of Societa Anonima Egidio Galbani, Melzo, Italy, is being formed with offices in New York. Robert Coedert will head the new company. The Philip Ritter Co., that city, is placing the advertising.

Changes at Celotex

Marvin Greenwood, former manager of the St. Louis branch of the Celotex Corp., Chicago, becomes assistant general sales manager, succeeding Lee Bartholomew, who is the new sales manager of Celotex, Ltd., England. Earl A. Donk succeeds Mr. Greenwood.

Hathaway Names Dodson

Roy Dodson is the new director of sales of the Hathaway Bakeries, Inc., Cambridge, Mass.

Whelan Food Firm

Howard J. Whelan, former branch manager of Canada Dry Ginger Ale, Inc., is forming the Howard J. Whelan Co., 165 Esplanade, Mount Vernon, N. Y., to specialize in food product merchandising.

Almony Has New Duties

Norman S. Almony, former manager of the Washington division of National Brewery of Baltimore, is manager of distributor sales.

Wilder to Carnegie-Illinois

T. N. Wilder, former advertising writer for Jones & Laughlin Steel Co., now writes sales literature for Carnegie-Illinois Steel Corp., Pittsburgh.

Williamson Has New Duties

Walter Williamson, manager of apparatus and supply sales, is elected vice-president of the Westinghouse Electric Supply Co., East Pittsburgh, Pa. He will carry the duties for the development of the company's apparatus and supply business, through the organization's branch houses in the field.

New Dodge Appointments

J. W. Hutchins, former manager of the New York region, and Emerson J. Poag, former director of Dodge merchandising and advertising, become assistant general sales managers of the Dodge division of the Chrysler Corp., Detroit. Donald T. Stanton, former supervisor of Plymouth sales, is the new Dodge director of sales.

Lukens Steel Promotes Simpson

W. C. Simpson, formerly with the sales development department of Lukens Steel Co., is appointed manager of the Pittsburgh sales territory.

Airtemp Appoints Snyder

A. K. Snyder is appointed advertising manager of Airtemp, Inc., air conditioning subsidiary of the Chrysler Corp. He was formerly in the sales application-engineering department.

GENERAL

New Baking Product

A new baking flour, using approximately fifteen tons of Winesaps for one ton of flour, has been developed to be blended with wheat flour to produce apple bread. The Hansen Baking Co., Seattle, will market the new loaf locally. The Izzard Co., that city, is promoting the product.

Brennan Has New Host Duties

Edward C. Brennan, secretary of the Come-to-Cleveland committee, goes to the Cleveland Convention and Visitors Bureau. He succeeds Glenn O. Glauser.

In Iron and Steel Post

Edwin C. Barringer, former editor of the *Daily Metal Trade* is now executive secretary of the Institute of Scrap Iron and Steel, Inc.

DEATHS

Louis Honig

Louis Honig, executive head of Erwin, Wasey & Co., of the Pacific Coast, died July 18 in San Francisco. He was 64 years old. In 1915 Mr. Honig founded Honig-Cooper Co., San Francisco agency. In 1929, Honig-Cooper merged with Erwin, Wasey & Co.; and Mr. Honig continued as head of its Pacific Coast operations until his death. The Honig-Cooper Co. is credited with helping set the so-called "California style" of advertising copy and layout, which later influenced the national trend of advertising production.

Bernard H. Kroger

Bernard H. Kroger, 78, founder of Kroger Grocery & Bakery Co., Cincinnati, died at Wianno, Mass., July 22. He retired after selling control in 1928. Mr. Kroker, retrieved his flooded general store in 1884 and saw it grow into a chain of 4,844 stores, 13 bakeries, 3 packing plants, 2 beverage units and a candy plant in 1,000 communities.

LeRoy Latham

LeRoy Latham, president of Latham Lithographing Co., New York, died in that city on July 25. He was 65 years old. Mr. Latham founded the firm in 1914, and was prior to that with United States Lithographing Co.

FERNANDO W. HARTFORD, 66, former publisher of the Portsmouth, N. H., *Herald*, July 22, in that city.

DANIEL S. WATKINS, 69, former vice-president of Steel Publications, Inc., July 20, at Mt. Lebanon, Pa.

GEORGE S. DE ROUVILLE, owner of De Rouville Advertising Agency, Albany, N. Y., died, that city, July 16.

HARRISON H. BAILEY, 26, former radio director of Anfenger Advertising Agency, in St. Louis recently.

COLIN HARRIS, 56, former manager of the Vancouver branch of Cockfield, Brown & Co., Ltd., recently.

"So it's my _Salesmen_ who waste our dough, eh ..."

roared the Sales Mgr. to the Treasurer ...

"think our salesmen's 'swindle sheets' are too high, do you? Claim they should spend money only on prime prospects, hey? Well then, why don't we do the same with our advertising appropriation?

"You tell me that every cigar a salesman hands out these days should bring in an order, and I'm telling you that more of our advertising money should be used to cultivate the men our salesmen have to sell. Let's use the top-notch business papers that do a real editorial job ... the ones that our prospects _have_ to read ...

the books that'll give us what we need _right now_: selling help where it counts at less cost than a cheap cigar per man.

"If you'll switch a bigger chunk of our advertising budget to the _real_ business papers reaching our markets ... the A.B.P.-A.B.C. books, for instance ... I'll confine my sales expense to the 'hot prospect' list.

"_Okay, wild man,_" said Treasurer MacTavish, "_it's a deal!_"

MEDIA–SERVICES

Promotes Robert Feemster

 Robert M. Feemster, formerly of the advertising staff of *The Wall Street Journal*, is promoted to advertising manager, with headquarters in New York. He formerly had an advertising agency of his own.

Promotes Cecil Holleran

Cecil J. Holleran, for twenty-three years with Atlanta *Constitution*, is named assistant to the editor and publisher.

Autobody Journal Changes Name

Autobody Trimmer & Painter, Cincinnati, will be known as *Autobody & Reconditioned Car* with its August issue.

Publishes Bridgeport Paper

Victor W. Knauth, former vice-president of Select Printing Co., New York, becomes publisher of the Bridgeport, Conn., *Times-Star*. John F. Bresnahan, former business manager of *Newsweek*, is chairman of the board.

Dale Patterson in New Post

Dale C. Patterson, 13 years assistant classified advertising manager of the New York *Herald Tribune*, becomes publisher of the *Florida Realty Journal*, Orlando, Fla., with the October issue.

Buys Wilmington Papers

Rinaldo B. Page, president of the Star-News, Inc., is purchasing the Wilmington, N. C., *Star-News*, morning and afternoon dailies, from the R. W. Page Corp.

Becomes "Sportswear Age"

Knitted Outerwear Age, published by The Knit Goods Publishing Corp, New York, will change its name with the August issue to *Sportswear Age*.

Steele Resigns "Inquirer" Post

George G. Steele has resigned as advertising director of the Philadelphia *Inquirer*. He was with the organization for 18 years.

Buffalo Times Sold

George H. Lyon, editor, and Earl J. Gains, business manager, Buffalo, N. Y., *Times*, assumed control of the paper last week. Scripps-Howard Newspapers bought it in 1929.

Acting Manager of KDKA

William Jackson, local sales manager of KDKA, Pittsburgh, is named acting manager pending appointment of a permanent successor to A. L. Nelson, now in New York as sales manager of the NBC Blue Network.

Heads Associated Sales Office

B. M. Ikert, educational and merchandising director for manufacturers of automotive products, now heads a new Chicago office for Associated Sales Co., of Detroit, slidefilms.

Co-Owner of "Better Fruit"

Ursel C. Narver, advertising manager of the *Oregon Grange Bulletin*, Portland, has become co-owner of *Better Fruit*. He will continue his connection with the Grange paper in addition to serving as *Better Fruit's* advertising and business manager.

Changes at Radio Sales

Murray Grabhorn resigns as vice-president and operating head of International Radio Sales, subsidiary of Hearst Radio, Inc., New York. Frank Fenton also has severed his connections with International. Loren L. Watson, former head of the transcription division, will supervise the company's time sales.

Represents Food Demonstrations

Robert Hitchings & Co., Philadephia, is representative for a series of demonstrations of food products, appliances and household items, staged in co-operation with utility companies there.

PRINTERS' INK

A Journal for Advertisers

Founded 1888 by George P. Rowell
John Irving Romer, Editor and President
1908—1933

PRINTERS' INK PUBLISHING CO., INC.
185 MADISON AVENUE, NEW YORK

ROY DICKINSON, President
DOUGLAS TAYLOR, Vice-President
R. W. LAWRENCE, Secretary
G. A. NICHOLS, Treasurer and Editor
C. B. LARRABEE, Managing Editor
R. W. PALMER, Associate Editor
ARTHUR H. LITTLE, Associate Editor
H. W. MARKS, Mgr. Readers' Service

Editorial Offices

Chicago, 6 North Michigan Avenue: Andrew
M. Howe, Associate Editor; P. H. Erbes, Jr.
Washington, 609 Carpenters' Building:
Chester M. Wright.
London, 21, St. James's Square, S. W. 1:
McDonough Russell.

Advertising Offices

Chicago
6 North Michigan Ave. ; Gove Compton, Mgr.
St. Louis
915 Olive Street; A. D. McKinney, Manager
Atlanta
1722 Rhodes-Haverty Bldg. ; H. F. Cogill, Mgr.
Pacific Coast
San Francisco, Los Angeles, Seattle, Portland
West-Holliday Co., Inc., Reps.

Subscription rates : $3 a year, $1.50 six months.
Canada $4 a year.   Foreign $5 a year.

One for the Record

Just to make the record clear—and perhaps to give a helpful hint to anybody who may be thinking about getting out an anniversary issue of some kind—we are here stating that the story of the advertiser presented in Section Two of this issue is the work of two of the younger members of our staff.

They are P. H. Erbes, Jr., and Hans von Briesen.

Mr. Erbes (Northwestern) is in his thirties; Mr. von Briesen (Harvard) is in his twenties.

Mr. von Briesen spent a year reading all the issues of PRINTERS' INK that had been put out since 1888. He had nothing to unlearn and so the notes he made were put down objectively and without bias. Mr. Erbes took this amazing quantity of data, wrote and studied for six months and then turned in his story.

Looks simple, doesn't it?

And so, after going through this anniversary experience, we pass along this bit of wisdom for what it may or may not be worth:

When you have a really big job of writing to do, assign it to some studious person who has brains and ability, who will work like a galley slave, who has vision and imagination—and who at the beginning does not know too much about the subject.

Women and Beer

In a recent Ruppert Brewery advertisement there is a picture of an attractive young woman and her gentleman friend sitting in the living room and obviously enjoying a bottle of beer—probably Ruppert's.

Now then, Colonel Ruppert is a fine, upstanding gentleman. He brews good beer and sells great quantities of it. Moreover, he runs a first-class baseball club.

But we wish he wouldn't have pictures of women in his beer advertising.

There may be nothing particularly reprehensible about it. Women, of course, drink beer—the capacity of some of them exceeding that of the men. And the picture used by the Colonel is entirely proper and nice; the girl seems to be entirely modest and dainty.

But it is the use of elements such as this that gives opponents of liquor advertising their strongest argument. Womanhood. The home. In the minds of many fair-minded people there is in these words something that just does not mix with liquor, beer and the like.

Mentioning or featuring women and the home in an advertisement of this kind is, therefore, a gratuitous slap at the sensibilities of an undoubted majority of the people—including the just and the unjust, the total abstainers, and many who do not object to a gentlemanly (or a ladylike) drink every now and then.

It is a highly unnecessary appeal, at that; just as much of the product could be sold without it.

Why, then, use it? Why create needless trouble?

If any advertiser should go out of his way to avoid the very appearance of evil, the gentleman who makes and sells a beverage containing alcohol is certainly that one.

It's Still Good

In the first issue of PRINTERS' INK fifty years ago, somebody—perhaps our departed friend Charlie Benjamin, first editor—had an editorial that holds good today.

We here quote it:

An advertisement has been defined by a careful and otherwise excellent authority to be "the public announcement of a fact." There is a pregnant, though perhaps unwitting suggestion in this definition to those who advertise; it is that whenever, wherever, and however, they make this "public announcement," and whatever be the subject of it, the matter or thing advertised should be a *fact.*

It is no greater mistake for him that has something good and genuine to sell, to leave the public to find it out for themselves than to attract people by a "taking" advertisement that lacks the element of truth. In the profession of the law, the capable yet conscientious advocate makes use of all the address and skill of which he is possessed, to present his client's side of the case in its most favorable aspect or bearing, yet he never departs from the evidence.

So with the advertiser—he should commend his wares or services to the public in the strongest and most skilfully arranged light they will bear; but the things commended should be the things he has at disposal and he should never represent them as having properties they do not possess.

Advertising has made mighty strides since that editorial was written. But there is no change in the situation that can possibly justify any argument against the statement that *truth* has been, is now and always will be the greatest and most important fundamental of advertising practice.

Costly Fireworks

When advertising and sales promotion departments clash there are likely to be costly fireworks. The rapid development of sales promotion during the last twenty years has made the chance of clash all the greater.

A number of organizations, to avoid the costly disputes that arise when two departments debate matters of jurisdiction, have tried to separate the functions of advertising and sales promotion. Where these are separated and the lines clearly drawn, advertising and sales promotion departments can work —and do work—together in a fairly happy family.

For nearly eight months PRINTERS' INK has been studying the policies of more than 100 large and medium-sized companies. The result is a Chart of Advertising and Sales Promotion Functions which, it is hoped, will serve as a definitive guide in settling jurisdictional disputes.

The chart will be published in the issue of August 4 and will be reinforced by a series of six articles explaining how it was prepared and showing striking trends that have taken place during the last several years.

P. I. Advertising Index

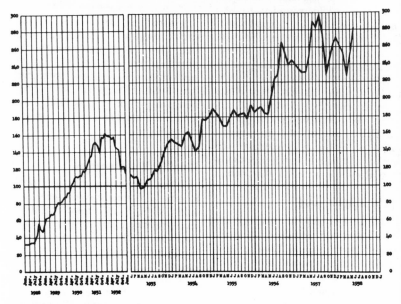

MONTHLY INDEX OF RADIO ADVERTISING (100 = Monthly Average 1928-1932 inclusive. Corrected for seasonal variation). For June, 1938, the radio index shows an advance of 12.2% over the previous month. The index for June stands at 281.0 as against 250.5 for May. The actual gross cost of time on the two principal chains is smaller for June than for May. However, the gain in the index, which has been adjusted for seasonal fluctuations, suggests that the decline in radio advertising during the summer months is becoming less severe. On the other hand, the index is down 2.9% from June, 1937. For quarterly period, April through June, the index is 1.2% below the level of the corresponding months of last year. This compares with a gain of 11.7% for the first quarter of 1938 over the same months of 1937.

(By L. D. H. WELD, Director of Research, McCann-Erickson, Inc.)

F. T. C. MOTOR ADVERTISING ORDER

WILLYS-OVERLAND Motors, Inc., has been served by the Federal Trade Commission with an order requiring discontinuance of certain statements.

The company is directed "to cease and desist from representing, through the picturization or description of a passenger automobile, in connection with a stated price, or through any other means or device, that such automobile may be purchased for $395 or any other designated price, unless such designated price is in fact the price of the automobile . . . so described."

It is also prohibited from representing "that a retail purchaser, except

for payment of . . . taxes, assessments and sales taxes, can obtain legal title to and possession of such car at point of delivery for $395 or any other designated price, unless such is a fact."

Provision is made that if the designated price does not include the cost of the accessories, pictorially or otherwise represented, any other charges except those covering freight, taxes or assessments, such designated price shall be accompanied by suitable phraseology in prominent type clearly indicating this fact.

The company has discontinued the practices referred to in the complaint.

EDITORIAL ECHOES

Seventeen editors of newspapers, magazines, trade journals, and banks and business concerns, requested permission to reprint "The Business Man Also Revolts," by Charles D. Ammon, in the June issue of DUN's REVIEW.

Similarly, other controversial articles, special business studies, industrial surveys and original findings published by the magazine have been widely commented upon and reprinted.

Such echoes reflect an appraisal of the editorial content of the magazine by readers and other editors that suggests a studied appraisal of the advertising values.

DUN'S REVIEW

Published by

DUN & BRADSTREET, INC.

ESTABLISHED 1841

NEW YORK	CHICAGO	CLEVELAND
290 Broadway	228 No. LaSalle St.	1635 E. 25th St.

REACHING CHIEF EXECUTIVES OF LARGE CORPORATIONS

COMPANY OF MEN

A composite photograph of sixty-seven employees of The Electric Storage Battery Company is being circulated by the company, manufacturers of Exide batteries, as a novel promotion piece. The purpose of the new character, called "Mr. Exide," is to show customers that the trade-mark "Exide" and the name "The Electric Storage Battery Company" represent more than a battery case, or acres of machinery and buildings. "Mr. Exide" is claimed to represent a company of men anxious to serve its customers' needs and proud of how it has served in the past.

The occasion of the photograph is the company's fiftieth anniversary, at which time it seems propitious to the directors to remind the trade of the years of experience now housed in the Exide works ready to serve the public.

Men from every department of the company's business were selected for photographs. The individual photographs were then blended into one.

A promotion folder sent out carries the following statement below the picture: . . . "this composite photograph symbolizes those members of the 'Exide Company' who serve you. As The Electric Storage Battery Company has grown in usefulness, new faces have been added to its organization. With the passage of time, others have been taken away. Yet the essential features and character of the 'Exide Company' and its batteries remain. In celebrating our Golden Anniversary, we pledge that the quality of Exide Batteries will be such as to continue to merit the approval you have accorded them in the past."

By this unusual device of a composite photograph the Exide battery people get across the reasons why their fifty years of experience are useful today.

LEFT HAMS ONLY

Eli Rush, who runs a grocery store in Wichita, Kans., has used a very common fact to give a new selling impetus to his pork sausages. Claiming that hogs usually lie down on the right side, leaving the left

Sixty-seven Exide employees

side more tender and delicate, he is advertising his sausages as coming from left hams only.

All this may sound a little far-fetched, but the truth remains that Mr. Rush is drawing customers to his store. The value of sales points which hold the interest of customers and draw attention to the business in question cannot be minimized, no matter how grotesque.

LETTER SAMPLE

When Lee - Indiana Company found itself faced with the problem of introducing a new product to automobile dealers, garages, and filling stations, it sent out a letter written on the product itself. Of course this wouldn't have been so good if the product were a grease gun, or some other item unadapted to being run through a typewriter. But fortunately, in this case, it was a sheet of tissue-paper like material for use as a wiping and polishing cloth by garage attendants.

The letter looked at first sight like a new fancy writing paper. This made the recipient more inclined to read it, which was one point in its favor from the start.

Copy in the letter itself didn't waste any time explaining the novel paper, but launched right into the selling story in the first paragraph. It read: "This letter is written on a small sample of Lee's Fibrex, an entirely new product of the Lee Manufacturing Company. It is designed to save money for you by replacing costly wiping and polishing cloths. In fact, the cost of Fibrex is actually less than the cost of laundering the cloths." Further paragraphs continued on the merchandising theme.

The letter was an attention getting novelty, but the surprise ele-

ment itself was part of the selling story on the product.

FIVE-POINT SALESMEN

Griffin M. Lovelace, vice-president, The New York Life Insurance Company, in an article in the company's magazine, *Nylic Review,* lays down five interesting specifications for a salesman. While these specifications may seem to imply more pertinently to the life insurance field, they fit pretty well any kind of salesmanship.

He says:

"If we worked as men do on the assembly line in an automobile factory, it would take a team of five men to put a policy on the books:

A prospector,
A planner,
An interviewer,
A closer,
A collector.

"Each would have to be an expert only in his one phase of the work.

"However, each life underwriter must perform the entire operation of putting a policy on the books. And he cannot produce as much business as he is capable of doing unless he schools himself thoroughly in each separate part of his work.

"It is not enough to be . . .

a good prospector,
or a good planner,
or a good interviewer,
or a good closer,
or a good collector.

"To make a real success, an agent must be . . .

a good prospector,
and a good planner,
and a good interviewer,
and a good closer,
and a good collector."

Classified Advertisements

Classified ads cost eighty-five cents a line for each insertion. Minimum order five lines costing four dollars and twenty-five cents. Classified ads payable in advance.

First Forms Close Friday Noon: Final Closing Saturday

HELP WANTED

REPRESENTATIVES WANTED

Established office supply salesmen to handle complete and profitable line of typewriter ribbons and carbon paper. Box 685, Printers' Ink.

OFFSET SALESMAN: medium sized plant in New York City with letterpress facilities, well known among buyers of quality work, has a vacancy on its sales staff. Salary or drawing to a man with following. Box 684, P. I.

WANTED—HUMOROUS WRITER

Give brief outline of experience and include a humorous commentary on one or two recent news items. Resident of metropolitan area necessary. Box 682, Printers' Ink.

Man Qualified for Job as Foreman in weekly newspaper and jobbing plant on North Atlantic seaboard. Must be able to estimate and be well recommended. Write giving experience, salary wanted, nationality, etc. Box 688, Printers' Ink.

Editorial assistant to write copy, handle layout and make-up. Prefer one with retail hardware store and trade magazine experience. State your training, experience, salary. Hardware Retailer, Security Trust Building, Indianapolis, Ind.

SPECIALTY AND PREMIUM SALESMEN. If you are accustomed to large earnings, we have openings in some exclusive territories, to sell the nationally known Meeker Line of Fine Leather Goods, for Good Will, Premium and Sales Promotion Uses. Our line is one of the most complete and best known. Over 200 numbers, in Billfolds, Letter Cases, Key Cases, Ladies' Hand Bags, Correspondence Cases, Toilet and Gift Sets, etc.
THE MEEKER COMPANY, JOPLIN, MO.

MISCELLANEOUS

12,500 ADVERTISING HEADLINES. Classified and indexed for quick reference. Clever, sales-simulating, original. Hundreds of headlines in every important classification. 157 page book, size 9x12. A great aid for advertising managers, copy writers, newspaper solicitors, and printers who develop ideas for their clients. Sent C. O. D. Return in 2 days and money refunded. Special price now $10. Write **HEADLINE IDEAS.** Dept. "P," 10 W. 47th Street, New York City.

Economy plus Speed! Newest process reproduces pictorial reprints, sales letters, ads, booklets, house organs, etc. Cuts unnecessary! 300 copies $2.50; add'l 100s 25¢. All sizes. Quantity prices less. Samples.
Laurel Process, 480 Canal St., N. Y. C.

POSITIONS WANTED

ADVERTISING SALESMAN—reliable worker, ability, successful record in national, class magazine, trade journal sales, service. (recent New York branch sales manager), Christian, high credentials, seeks connection; letters confidential. Box 686, Printers' Ink.

Experienced and Successful Space Salesman can handle one or more established Trade or Industrial papers in Cleveland terr. (Ohio, W. Pa., E. Mich.) Will be in NYC July 25 to Aug. 5 for interviews. Box 683, P. I.

EXPERIENCED ADVERTISING MAKE UP MAN DESIRES POSITION WITH PUBLISHER OF WEEKLY OR MONTHLY TRADE JOURNALS. TEN YEARS EXPERIENCE. Box 687, P. I.

ARTIST

Advertising designer of exceptional creative ability on direct mail and publication work. Roughs, comprehensives, finished art. Thorough knowledge of typography. Extensive and diversified experience qualifies this man for a responsible position. Box 689, P. I.

CAUTION!

Applicants for positions advertised in PRINTERS' INK are urged to use the utmost care in wrapping and fastening any samples of work addressed to us for forwarding. We are frequently in receipt of large packages, burst open, in a condition that undoubtedly occasions the loss of valuable pieces of printed matter, copy, drawings, etc. Advertisers receiving quantities of samples from numerous applicants, are also urged to exercise every possible care in handling and returning promptly all samples entrusted to them.

PRINTERS' INK acts in the capacity of a forwarder, as a matter of service to both subscriber and advertiser, and where extremely heavy and bulky bundles are addressed in our care, it will be appreciated if the necessary postage for remailing is sent to us at the same time.

Advertising and Sales Promotion Man for Key Position

Sales Manager

BINDERS

To make your files of the Printers' Ink Publications more accessible we sell binders at cost. The Weekly binder, holding twelve copies, costs $1.25 postpaid; is an attractive addition to desk or table.

PRINTERS' INK
185 Madison Ave., N.Y.

Advertisers' Index

No responsibility is assumed for any omission

•

CERTAIN BUSINESS MEN AT WORK

AN ambulance interne sweats near the light of a kerosene lamp to add another urchin to the thousands in Shantytown. . . . . On the third floor of a private maternity hospital a bulging socialite reserves a suite of rooms with the assurance friends may come for tea soon after the event.

In Pennsylvania three people contemplate suicide, hoping the insurance will make them worth more dead than alive to two youngsters. . . . . After paying $100 into the million dollar Louis-Schmeling gate, a well-lit pair missed all of the 124 second slug fest.

Panaceas to adjust this weird pattern of purchasing power have been more like the ruthless slashing of the cleaver than the patient, deliberate scalpel of the surgeon. But, for years *certain* business men have been employing well calculated marketing techniques to smooth out the contrasts in the distribution of wealth. They have seen the wisdom of moving goods cheaply in the market place as a means to greater volume, to higher wages, which will purchase those goods.

Certain business men are the marketing executives of America, the men found at the helm of many leading corporations. They are at work now, just as the Dorrances, Swifts, Eastmans, and Colgates of the fifty years past were at work to find the most efficient means of getting goods from factory to consumer.

Advertising to sell them the goods and services they need is at work in the pages of PRINTERS' INK MONTHLY, the dramatic source of the *certain* business man's marketing information.

PRINTERS' INK MONTHLY

A MAGAZINE OF MARKETS

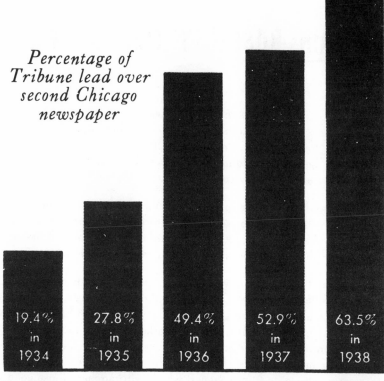

Percentage of Tribune lead over second Chicago newspaper

| 19.4% in 1934 | 27.8% in 1935 | 49.4% in 1936 | 52.9% in 1937 | 63.5% in 1938 |

5-year record of Chicago Tribune leadership in

RETAIL

ADVERTISING

LINAGE 1st 6 mos. 1934 to 1938

During the first 6 months of 1934 the Tribune led the second Chicago newspaper by 720,901 lines of retail advertising, or 19.4%. During the comparable period this year, the Tribune increased its lead over the second Chicago newspaper to 1,998,231 lines, or 63.5%.

The Tribune's percentage of lead over the second Chicago newspaper in the first 6 months of 1938 was the greatest in history.

CHICAGO TRIBUNE *the world's greatest newspaper*

Total average net paid circulation during the official six-month period ended March 31, 1938: Daily, 857,963—Sunday, 1,115,643

PRINTERS' INK

REGISTERED U. S. PATENT OFFICE

A JOURNAL FOR ADVERTISERS

FIFTY YEARS

1888

1938

1888

ON JULY 15, 1888, the sun rose over the Long Island
marshes against a delicately tinted sky. All day long, from the
bay and over the Staten Island hills, came great draughts of
bracing sea air. From dawn to sunset the day was perfect and
it was Sunday and the City of New York was one vast pleasure
ground, although many of the inhabitants, falsely warned of
oppressive heat by the Signal Service Bureau, had fled upon
suburban excursions.

On that day fifty years ago the sun saw a troubled and uneasy world. News dispatches predicted that the greatest European war would not break out in the fall after all, but
expressed confidence that the next year would surely see the
campaign's start. Nobody was "ready" for war, but Italy,
France, Germany, Great Britain and Russia were increasing
their arms. An enlarged naval appropriation was being pushed
in the United States. The summer residents of Newport were
upset about high taxes and a Congressman averred there was
something vicious and badly wrong about a system which permitted one man to earn $1,500,000 in a single year. The rail-
roads were laying their troubles at the door of low rates and
to too much regulation. The wife of the President had created
a tremendous stir by daring to appear in public without a
bustle.

On July 15, 1888, the election campaign—President Cleveland against Benjamin Harrison—was well under way. Gen.
Sheridan lay ill at Nonquitt, Mass., and the financial community was rife with rumors about the health of Jay Gould.
John Greenleaf Whittier was summering at a New Hampshire
watering place. Brooklyn defeated Kansas City, 5–4, making
three errors. There were two runaways in New York, but
otherwise the day passed without accident. The business outlook was a trifle on the gloomy side.

Under the dateline of July 15, 1888, George P. Rowell,
acknowledged in a later day as the main figure in advertising
in the nineteenth century, had placed in the mails at New
York, 5,200 copies of a new semi-monthly class magazine, which
aspired to be "a journal for advertisers."

================ Copyright, 1938, by Printers' Ink Pub. Co. ================
Vol. 184, No. 4. Weekly. Printers' Ink Pub. Co., 185 Madison Ave., New York, N. Y. Subscription $3 a year,
U. S. Entered as second-class matter, June 28, 1893, at post office, N. Y., under the Act of March 3, 1879.

GEORGE PRESBURY ROWELL
(1838—1908)
Founder of PRINTERS' INK

Foreword

THIS *is the story of the advertiser.*

The fiftieth anniversary of the founding of PRINTERS' INK is the occasion for its telling. And, appropriately enough, the data out of which this story is built were taken from the files of PRINTERS' INK itself—ranging from 1888 to 1938. It is not, however, a history of PRINTERS' INK; this paper gets its glory out of the fact that for fifty years it has faithfully chronicled, interpreted and promulgated—also to an extent developed—the unfolding of marketing in all its far-flung ramifications.

Later in this book, and incidental to the main story, will be found an account of PRINTERS' INK's founding by George P. Rowell and its subsequent development by John Irving Romer. In the later years of his life (he died in 1933) Mr. Romer frequently discussed the fiftieth anniversary number with the writer of these words. And it was his earnest wish that the present issue be built mainly around the great economic force that his paper helped build rather than around the paper itself. The present management of PRINTERS' INK is therefore happy to carry out his wishes—especially since, viewed objectively, the plan he had in mind is obviously the right one anyway.

Therefore, this story is essentially that of the advertiser.

It is the story not merely of advertising, but of the whole process of modern selling of the products of mass production. It is the story of the advertiser concept of doing business in a national market.

This is the story of fifty years in which machine distribution came to replace the old hand methods of selling, just as machine production had taken the place of the old hand methods of making goods. It is the story of the technology of distribution.

This is the story of how the manufacturer came to assume command of his own destiny, of how he established contact with the consumer and shortened the time and the distance and the cost between the factory and the market place. It is the story of how he learned to sell greater quantities of better goods at lower prices. And it is more.

For the story of the advertiser in this last half century is an integral and important part of the advance of civilization in the nation. The advertiser sold not alone breakfast foods and automobiles and electrical appliances and household furnishings. He was a salesman who traded in standards of living.

The speakers at the advertising dinners have long inclined to do their craft the disservice of crediting overmuch the achievements of "advertising." They seem to forget that advertising is simply one inseparable and illimitable expression of management policy in a modern distributive society. That without the allied forces of personal selling, merchandising and sales promotion, advertising may—and usually does—mean little.

To modern marketing practice, in its every phase, belongs the credit.

JOHN IRVING ROMER
(1869—1933)
Editor of PRINTERS' INK from 1908 until his death

And even then the immensely important contributions made by invention and technological progress and the unparalleled resources of the New World republic are not to be dismissed. These things are basic. The advertiser simply broadened their application and speeded the transmission of their benefits to the consumer.

With all these proper qualifications, the contributions of the advertiser may justly be termed heroic in their import.

By heightening consumer desires and demands and awakening new ones, the advertiser has vastly stimulated the processes of invention. He has given meaning to the machine and provided a continuing incentive to cheapen the costs of manufacture and to bring forth new products. Throughout the entire marketing channel he has encouraged and at times rendered imperative the use of more efficient, less wasteful and faster moving methods.

As products and by-products of his efforts to sell the new products of the machine at a profit, he has done much to improve the ways of life among the people.

Working hand in hand with the men of science and invention, he has lessened drudgery in the home and in business itself.

He has provided uses for the new leisure.

He has immeasurably increased the standards of cleanliness and sanitation.

He has wrought a new understanding of and desire for healthful living.

He has helped to build and maintain a body of newspapers and periodicals that stands unsurpassed, and thereby contributed to the education of the most enlightened public in the world. And he has helped to make the most informative and entertaining system of radio broadcasting that exists anywhere.

He has kept alive the desire for personal betterment.

He has played a leading role in the upbuilding of the highest standard of living in the world.

This is the story of the advertiser and it is an autobiography. It is written by Rowell and Ward and Powers and Gillam. By Romer and Dorrance and Ayer and Depew. By Hires and Lord and Curtis and Bates. By Fowler and Woodbury and Balmer and Kennedy. By Presbrey and Jones and Thorne and Pope. By Post and Liggett and Lasker and Swift.

It is written by Johnson and Wrigley and Wright and Rosenwald. By Chester and MacManus and Merseles and Sloan. By Perky and Barton and Chrysler and Erickson. By Harn and Palmer and Ingersoll and Grant. By Ford and Tew and Resor and Maytag. By Plaut and Green and Wood and McIntyre. By Kraft and Faust and Babst and Thomson. By Hartford and Hill and McCann and Deupree. By Benson and Arkell and Vail and Childs.

It is written by all these and thousands more who, by manuscript or interview, have contributed first-hand knowledge of the experiences which led to the shaping of the total course of the advertiser. By presidents, vice-presidents, sales managers and advertising executives of firms that develop modern marketing techniques; and by advertising agents and publishers and others who played a prominent supporting role on the firing line. It is written not from sideline observations but from the records left by those who made the story.

It is written, too, by the advertisers whose stories in paid space are given in this book. These organizations, in their long years of growth, have also had a prominent part in making advertising what it is today. Their stories are therefore an integral part of the general picture; they help to round out the recital into a symmetrical and historic whole.

Those records, if placed in a single volume, would occupy a bookshelf fifty feet long. They cover not far from three hundred thousand printed pages. This little story attempts to present a distillation of those records of advertiser progress, to show the significant patterns in the development of modern marketing.

This story has been conceived and built as a working tool which may have use and value to the advertiser of today. So great and complex has become the field of marketing that a true perspective of the fundamental forces which have wrought its development is almost essential to today's management decision. In the experiences of industries of the past often lies the clue to the proper course for present-day practice, for though the physical things with which we work change vastly, the minds of men and the forces of economics and society alter little and perhaps not at all.

This work aims to show the movements of marketing and merchandising through the several periods in its modern history to the underlying forces that influenced their course. It attempts to present the basis for a renewed understanding—sometimes badly needed in these turbulent days—of the fundamental workings of advertising and the related arts of salesmanship.

It is perhaps not too optimistic a guess that a reading of this tracing of the patterns of marketing may be productive of a better working knowledge of the interaction of cause and effect, of the broad essentials of progressive policies and of the basic unsoundness of certain courses which, despite the repeated showings of history, are sometimes persisted in today. Perhaps it may be a course of inspiration to those who at times find the ways of honesty and prudence to be slow in paying dividends. And it may even produce here and there a specifically usable merchandising idea, for, curiously enough, many of the "new" and successful plans of today are simply reworkings of ideas used thirty and forty years ago.

If any of these things be accomplished by this autobiography of the advertiser, then the memories of Mr. Rowell and Mr. Romer will have been honored in a way they would have liked.

THE EDITORS.

CHAPTER I

New Horizons

By P. H. Erbes, Jr.

AS the nineteenth century neared its end, the day of the frontier had ended as an important factor in the economic and social life of the nation. In 1890 the Census Report gave notice to the occurrence in this wise: "The unsettled area has been so broken into by isolated bodies of settlement that there can hardly be said to be an unbroken frontier line."

During the entire life of the republic, the frontier had, in the view of many eminent historians, conditioned the entire course of the growing republic. Westward beyond the latest line of settlement there always lay new opportunity—a new world to be occupied and exploited. There had always been room for expansion in the literal geographical sense.

It is true that for long after 1890 vast expanses of unoccupied lands lay between the more thickly settled districts and the final outposts of the frontier lines. But, as James Truslow Adams points out, the frontier was a state of mind, as well as a matter of actual pressing on beyond the successive Western boundaries of occupation. It was a psychological influence that deeply influenced the thoughts and lives of the statesmen, the business expansionists, the poor, the restless, the discontented and the ambitious.

The frontier line had passed and its passing was almost completely unmarked at the time. Little noticed likewise was the discovery at almost precisely the same interval, of a vast new realm for human expansion, a land whose wilderness had been virtually unexplored except for modest penetrations by a few bold pioneers.

This new frontier was not geographic but economic. It could be neither seen nor touched nor charted upon a map, yet the results of the crossing of it were to prove distinctly tangible, for this was the frontier of new expansion in terms of more and better things with which to live.

The machine and its handmaiden, invention, had not been without their perceptible economic effects for many years. The drudgery of toil by hand had been eliminated in many lines of manufacture. The railroads had crossed the continent. The nation was fast assuming rank as the greatest producer of iron and steel in the world.

Yet in a large degree the products of the machine had been absorbed in the processes of the nation's growth. Continuing waves of immigration, multiplication of the home population, reconstruction after the Civil War, a growing export trade and the building of the West had, together with the ordinary needs of the people as a whole, closely paralleled the growth of machine production up to this time.

Actually the life of the average person had changed little for more than twenty years. The people of the 1880's lived pretty much as had their fathers. Inventions of tremendous importance were appearing in rapid succession. G. F. Swift built the first refrigerator car in 1875, Alexander Graham Bell held the first conversation on his telephone the next year, Edison played a tune on his phonograph in 1877, Mergenthaler invented the linotype in 1886—to name a few. Yet the application of these and numerous other wonderful new and improved devices was very limited.

The only steel frame skyscraper in the world was in Chicago and it had just been built in 1885. Few homes had telephones and many business concerns were without them. Long distance telephone service did not come until 1892, when a Chicago to New York call was completed. The typewriter was in use, but only to an extremely limited degree; most business correspondence was still done by hand and copies of letters were made by a complicated arrangement involving a wringer and a press.

In the home there were gas lights —that is, in the cities there were. Aside from that little change had occurred. There were no subways in the cities and public travel was mainly by horse-drawn street cars, though a few electric powered cars were appearing toward the end of the decade. The chief mode of travel was still the horse and carriage. The safety bicycle was not invented until 1884. The incandescent electric lamp, perfected by Edison in 1878, was rare and the phonograph was not to come on the market until 1896. Packaged foods were virtually a curiosity. Practically all canning was done in the home and fresh fruits and vegetables out of season were unknown except to the very rich. An orange was a rare prize. Magazines were too expensive for the bulk of the people and an operation was seldom heard of. Family life revolved about the home which, except among the very poor in the tenements, was really a house; there were no apartments. Hard roads didn't exist and there were, of course, no automobiles and no public showings of motion pictures and no radio.

The process of urbanization, brought on by the machine's centralization of industry in the cities, was just beginning to gather real impetus in the 1880's. The capital invested in manufacturing was only $2,790,000,000 (in 1901 United States Steel alone represented a capitalization of over a billion dollars), and this figure was to be more than doubled by 1889, when it reached $6,525,000,000. About one-quarter of the population in 1880 could be called "urban" if the term were interpreted as meaning inhabitants of cities and towns of 4,000 or more.

The number of gainfully employed grew more than five million during the 1880's, attaining 22,735,-961 in 1890. Of these 9,013,336 were engaged in agriculture and mining, 5,091,293 in manufacturing and mechanical industries, 4,360,577 in domestic and personal service, 3,326,122 in trade and transportation. The total population increased from fifty to sixty-three millions.

Steam railroads were adding importantly to their transportation facilities, increasing in mileage from 83,262 in 1880 to 156,404 in 1890. In addition to the actual extension of the plant, the railroads were consolidating into better organized systems and laying the basis for providing a more effective instrument of high-speed transportation.

Education was coming to take effect in the living habits of adults. Seventy million dollars had been devoted to the establishment of free public schools in 1871 and this was beginning to bear fruit. In 1880, 17 per cent of the total population over ten years of age were illiterate—one person in every six was unable to read or write. In 1890 the proportion had dropped to 12 per cent.

From these and numerous other signs it is evident that the conditions fundamental to crossing the new frontier, to the getting of the products of the machine into the hands of the people, were beginning to take shape. Urbanization meant less self-sufficiency of the family and an increased demand for "luxury" items, things above the bare needs of life which most of us today would consider necessities. The improvement of transportation facilities brought nearly twice as many buyers within the range of the better equipped city stores. The growing number of gainfully employed and total population meant more mouths to fill and more bodies to clothe. The conquest of illiteracy meant less satisfaction with bare living and a wider reading audience.

During the 1880's there were numerous attempts by manufacturers to investigate the possibilities of advertising as a selling tool. Few of these, however, employed it in any sort of consistent and systematic way, or over a very large area.

Scarcely one business man in five hundred had any degree of faith in the proceedings, and that one had his dubious moments. The business men who summoned up sufficient courage to venture into the public prints did so with many misgivings. A "campaign" was likely to consist of two-inch, one-column space in three or four publications one time, although a plunger might take two inches in two columns for three insertions in a half dozen papers. A quarter or half page was a marvel, a full page practically a sensation, indulged mainly by an occasional patent medicine manufacturer.

The limited space prevented the presenting of an intelligent, coherent message. Illustrations were rare, and then often had little to do with the product or the message, being principally decorative in function.

Moreover, there was seldom any attempt to tie the advertisement in with the selling process. Advertising and selling were somehow regarded as things apart. Little had been done in the way of setting up a connected sales and merchandising program to capitalize upon the advertising in the trade.

The principal advertisers of this time—those who used advertising with at least a fair degree of consistency and on a reasonably large scale—included Royal Baking Powder, Sapolio, Ivory Soap, St. Jacob's Oil, Pears' Soap, Scott's Emulsion, Ayer's Sarsaparilla, Pyle's Pearline, Mellin's Food, Schenck's Mandrake Pills, Dr. Pierce's remedies, Walter Baker Cocoa, W. L. Douglas Shoes, Castoria, and Warner's Safe Cure. Scant authentic data on advertising appropriations were available in those days, as now, and the list is based in some degree upon the general impressions of those who commented upon advertising at the time. Nobody really knew how much anybody else paid for space,

10

for rates paid were a critical and secret art of advertising.

The largest advertiser at the beginning of the period was Charles A. V o e g e l e r & Company (St. Jacob's), which is believed to have spent $500,000 in 1881. At the end of the period the St. Jacob's activities had decreased and the palm had passed to the Royal Baking Powder Company, which is said to have spent an equal amount in 1891. But these were by no means typical. Both Pears' Soap and Sapolio were regarded as in the front rank of the general advertisers (that is, advertisers other than patent medicine companies), yet Pears' expenditure in 1888 was $35,000, while Sapolio's expenditure in 1885 was estimated at $70,000.

The total number of advertisers spending as much as $100,000 in a year was probably less than a dozen. And most of those were patent medicine companies.

This latter industry was, of course, the leader in use of advertising (retailers excepted) in the 1880's, as it was in the 1870's. Soap was second, baking powder third. Food products were well down in the list—also the activity in such lines as men's and women's wearing apparel, cosmetics, dentifrices and household furnishings.

Many business men considered the idea of using advertising unthinkable. They regarded it as something of a "confession of weakness." What is more, few of them thought it was necessary. And the publisher offered little encouragement or support. It was not long since it had been considered derogatory to a publication to contain advertising. Many publishers would leave advertisements in after the contract had expired, thus demonstrating to the advertiser that he was paying for space which the publisher himself considered to be of no value.

Another thing was that the advertiser had to purchase his experience first hand. There was no way of having access to the experiences of others, except in such information as the advertising agent might supply on the subjects of rates and circulation.

And so, while the art of the advertiser was perceptibly entering its formative stage in the 1880's, the real strides were yet to come. Most business news continued to go by word of mouth, unless the subject of it was a craze or fad taken up and publicized by the newspapers.

CHAPTER II
Rendezvous with the Consumer
(1888-1895)

FOR fifty years the jobber held sway in the marketing of goods. His reign was all but supreme. The manufacturer was little more than a court satellite.

The jobber told the manufacturer what he wanted made, how he wanted it made and what he would pay for it. And he was in a position to make it stick. The manufacturer set his plant in operation and did just what the jobber, or commission man, told him to do.

In the early days of manufacturing, the manufacturer had some machinery and a customer, one customer—the jobber. He needed no bookkeeper. He often did not have a stenographer. He just made goods.

As the nation grew and the machinery of production improved and the railroads spanned the continent, the manufacturer's plant and operations became larger and more complex. His list of customers increased, to several or perhaps a dozen or perhaps even more than that. But they were the same kind of customers—jobbers. The manufacturer was still dependent upon the jobber for disposal of what he made, and though the element of control was lessened, the jobber was still the head man. The specifications were perhaps less directly and abruptly issued, but the manufacturer still made what the jobber said he could sell.

Every now and then, however, some manufacturer would make a curious and interesting discovery. Perhaps by accident the public recognized the goods he made and found them satisfying and found them so again. From this circumstance, the manufacturer noticed, came materially increased orders from the commission men, and the notion struck him to mark his goods and take a little advertisement in the paper to show the public the mark and tell them about what he made. And when he did this he found that in a short time the jobber came to him and asked him what he would charge for the goods.

Or perhaps the manufacturer was a machinist or a drug store man who thought up a new device or an improved way of making some staple article. His factory was his kitchen or a corner in the basement or the barn. When he had made up some of his articles he knew no more about the channels of trade than to get out a wheelbarrow or put a basket over his arm and go from door to door to sell what he made. Then he would seek to save a few steps and ask the local storekeeper to stock his product. Perhaps he would write up something about his article and have leaflets printed and pass them around. He found his business growing, increased his production and sold to more stores. And after a time the jobbers were seeking him out to buy exactly what he made and pay the price he asked.

This, in a brief and concededly over-simplified form, is the story of the beginnings of the revolution in marketing that has taken place in the lifetime of many who live today.

The experience of neither of these nameless pioneers and their contemporaries who moved in like directions does not, however, account for the whole of the revolutionary pattern. On the one hand, so remote was the average manufacturer's position and thinking in relation to the ultimate user of his goods that instances of conspicuous demand preferences were necessarily rare and obscure. On the other, many manufactories were well established concerns and there was neither incentive nor occasion for the proprietor to get out and peddle goods. The observable and satisfying results of the tactics of these two types of pioneers were not without their influence as signboards along the new way of distribution, as will be noted in further detail at a later point. But most businesses were, in perhaps even greater degree than they are today, "different." Example alone does not account for the new turn of events.

More especially, such experiences do not explain the suddenness with which a widespread effort to keep rendezvous with the consumer came into being. In the 1880's the number of manufacturers who sought to take knowledge of their goods direct to the public and cultivate the consumer's patronage was all but negligible. There were perhaps a dozen firms outside the patent medicine business that did anything of the sort on a systematic, consistent and comprehensive basis. There were scores of manufacturers who "took an ad," as the saying went, now and then. But the manufacturer who used advertising as a planned and definite part of his management policy was a distinct exception. By 1900 the public over a large section of the country had met, become well acquainted with and added to their buying language such terms as Kodak, Heinz, Prudential, Beeman's, Coca-Cola, Ingersoll, Uneeda, Quaker Oats, Franco-American, Woodbury, Postum, 1847 Rogers Bros., H-O, Cream of Wheat and many others, with an even greater number of additions in the years immediately following.

This tremendous urge to establish a relationship, by advertising proxy, with the consumer was the product of several underlying factors of broad economic import.

Mass production! Magic term, it was a good deal more than a symbol for economists to roll around on their tongues in those days. The machines in the factories throughout the land had been gathering speed. As this century neared its end, the spinning grew faster and there were goods to be sold.

The existing distribution system was a narrow, cumbersome, slow-moving conveyer belt. The commission man, effective at the controls in his time, was facing the past. The manufacturer could make better than he could recommend and more than he could perceive demand for. The job was too big for the jobber. And his long string of dependents, ending with the retailer, were in much the same inadequate shape. The department store had come along to take a few kinks out of the tangled skein of distribution and the mail-order house was employing some timely measures. But the consumer needed talking to and somebody had to do it.

Invention! Here again the jobber moved too much with the deliberation of habit. He dealt in established demands and was slow to take up with new ones, much less those as yet unawakened by entirely new products.

New horizons! The pioneers had crossed to the Pacific. New waves of settlers had pushed in behind to build new markets. And the railroads and the new instruments of swift communication had welded a sprawling continent of settlements into a national market. Once bounded by his immediate region, the manufacturer's welding opportunity extended from one ocean to another.

There were goods to be sold, people to sell them to and the physical means with which to transport the goods to them.

In so compelling and inviting a situation, the manufacturer was not unmoved by considerations of profit. Under the old system he was virtually at the mercy of the trade, both as to the quantity and as to the price at which he might sell. If he could sell more, if he could have something to say about the price at which he sold. . . .

And then there was the matter of security. In a jobber-dominated distribution—or in a retailer dominated distribution, for that matter —the manufacturer's future was in the vest pocket of a relatively small number of trade factors. So long as he was just the maker and somebody else had full control of the selling of his goods, and therefore of the purchasing, he had virtually nothing to say about his own fate. If he could take command of his own selling process, if he could establish direct favor with those who really purchased his goods. . . .

The prospect of a rendezvous with the consumer was a promising one.

Under all these urges and incentives, and perhaps a few special ones besides, the manufacturer became more and more open-minded to the purchase of some vehicle that would bring him to the desired destination. It didn't happen over night. He didn't go to bed without the idea one day and wake up with it the next. But the consciousness grew, more slowly for some than others. The ferments of the new movement were at work.

Turning from the underlying to the overt, the final factors in the decision for this prospective buyer of a new distribution machine are to be found in the progress made on the construction and operation of the apparatus itself. Its motive power was advertising—that may be taken for granted now, though the engine and its principles of operation took some selling at the time.

The Advance Guard

THE first users of advertising were those who were nearest the consumer. The closer this relationship, the earlier the business man made advertising a part of his operating policy.

The man who sold direct to the ultimate user of his products was the man who could see, incontrovertibly and with his own eyes, that advertising made sales. The man who dealt through a series of middlemen and was, therefore, remote from what happened in the ultimate marketplace, by and large was the last to see the benefits of this sales tool of establishing his own identity in that marketplace and the last to adopt advertising. And it usually happened that the fewer were the number of middlemen, the quicker the manufacturer was to become an advertiser.

Ultimately it became possible for the manufacturer to accept the general proposition that the advertiser concept of doing business would prove resultful for him. But in the early days—and, indeed well into the present century—most advertisers were those who knew advertising worked because they had seen it work—at first hand—in the sale of their particular products.

The very first advertisers, of course, were the retailers—the men who met the consumer across the counter. Then came those who met the consumer by direct contact through the mails—the seedsmen, book publishers, sellers of novelty items and, beginning in the 1870's, the general mail-order houses. The railroads, who were retailers in the sense that they directly controlled and operated their own consumer

sales organizations, were likewise among the first.

From the Civil War on, some of the manufacturers who were just one step removed from the consumer —who sold through retailers visited by their own salesmen, began to enter the arena. The close relationship with the dealer and his problem—and sometimes the problem was very definitely shared by the manufacturer because he placed the goods on consignment—tended to result in experimentation with the methods which the retailer used in disposing of his broader range of stocks.

It is to be marked, however, that in a great many cases the manufacturer himself had sustained a personal experience in the consumer marketplace when his business was in its infancy. He had made his own goods in a limited little plant or in his home and had sold them himself, first to consumers, then to retailers and he had been on the ground to see that advertisements helped to move his goods off the retailers' shelves. As the firm grew in size and in scope of marketing operations, this understanding and appreciation of the values of the advertising persisted in the mind of the top management, even though it ultimately dealt through two or more layers of middlemen and became relatively remote from the firing line where advertising operates.

The next tendency was the penetration by industries. Once the example had been set by one company or perhaps several in a particular business, other firms in the same line, impressed by the success of their advertising rivals or perhaps acting in self defense, entered the lists.

The "my business is different" attitude did not yield so easily, however, in the transference of the advertising idea from one industry to another. It was not until the twentieth century had fairly begun that manufacturers as a whole were inclined to listen to the broad proposition that advertising as such was a potentially profitable sales tool.

There were two reasons. The first was that the leading established firms, which had the capital and the distribution to make modern marketing methods feasible, didn't think that advertising was necessary. "We are already at the head of the trade," ran the argument. "So what have we to gain by advertising?"

The advertising agents couldn't think up the answer to that one, and that was the second reason. During the 1890's, and before, the general advertising agents and their compatriots the special agents didn't, for the most part, have the organization or the basic grasp to sell the advertiser idea on a fully constructive basis. They created much new business to be sure, but they followed the lines of least resistance in going to firms in those industries where there was already an advertising precedent. And besides they had their hands fairly full dealing with the expanding activities of the volunteers who were joining the advertiser ranks.

There were other contributing reasons, of course. Experimental attempts, ineffectively managed and poorly guided, had proved unproductive for some of these firms. And there was still that old idea that maybe people would think that the

fact a firm had resorted to advertising was a sure sign it was on its uppers.

And so the tendency was for the advertiser to appear mainly from the ranks of those who had built their business on advertising from the ground, or consumer, up. The use of advertising as a projection of the general management policy of an already established concern was a later development, not much seen until the 1900's.

The question naturally arises as to why, since practically all manufacturing businesses at one time or another started in a barn or a store or a local machine shop or basement, this initial close communion with the consumer had not resulted in a universal application of advertiser methods long before. The answer, of course, lies partly in that advertising facilities were practically negligible through a greater part of the nineteenth century. But it lies also in the fact that while a close original contact was almost essential as a basic favoring condition, there were several other factors of consequence.

An important one was that the product had to be trade-markable, if there is such a word. And for many, many years the ideas of what products could be identified with the manufacturer's brand were limited. The packaged food product, for example, was almost non-existent until the 1880's and didn't really take hold until the next decade.

Some of the other factors appear in examination of the lines of business where the idea of consistent, systematic use of advertising took hold.

Number one, of course, is the patent medicine business, which dominated the advertising scene through the 1870's and 1880's and, though its relative dominance lessened, was conspicuously in the front rank in the 1890's.

First of all, the patent medicine was distinctly a specialty item. You didn't buy the product for what it was made of. You bought it for what it did, or was alleged to do. And the only way the manufacturer could relate the purported results of the product to the buying process of the shopper in the market for those results was to give the product a name. Besides, success lay not in selling one bottle but in creating continuing users. The patent medicine simply had to be trade-marked or there wasn't any patent medicine business.

Next, the consumer demand for these goods was perhaps more responsive and more widespread than any other commercial article of the time, excepting, of course, such food staples as could not be raised at home. In every new country that is sparsely settled, malaria, fevers and chills and assorted aches and ailments are prevalent, owing to exposure and lack of sanitation. Latter-day immigration Westward and settlement of new lands everywhere resulted in a tremendous demand for fever and ague remedies, liver tonics, blood purifiers, soothing syrups for children. It is to be remembered that doctors and responsible druggists were practically unknown except in a few large centers; most of the family

---

1889

BENJAMIN HARRISON inaugurated. . . . Oklahoma opened to settlement. . . . Johnstown Flood costs 5,000 lives. . . . The Dakotas, Montana and Washington admitted to the Union. . . . Department of Agriculture organized. . . . Kansas passes the first anti-trust law.

John Hooper, first advertising agent to do business in New York (circa 1845), dies. . . . *Munsey's Magazine* launched. . . . John Wanamaker is probably the largest local advertiser in the country. . . . "Advertising taught in one month, including store management"—advertisement. . . . A soap advertiser offering "Robert Elsmere" and "Criticism" by Gladstone free with each 25-cent bar. . . . Of the daily papers having over 1,000 circulation, 255 are Republican, 320 Democratic—latter leading in circulation 2,500,000 to 1,500,000.

"It is the patronage of the discriminating public that constitutes that which we call reputation"—J. Walter Thompson. . . . Number of monthly magazines increases by 108 to 1,898. . . . G. M. Hitchcock, proprietor of the Omaha *World*, purchases the *Herald* and consolidates the two papers. . . . November issue of *Ladies' Home Journal* an edition of 1,000,000 copies and costs $50,000. . . . Cocoa consumption on the increase owing to being better advertised than coffee, but "coffee dealers" are getting the idea.

medical supplies were bought at the village general store.

Then—and this is of transcendent importance—the cost of production on these medical marvels was so small, as compared to the selling price, that the proprietors could afford to take chances no other business could. Our manufacturer, for example, sold his product at six bottles for $5 and it was fully 90 per cent clear profit, the cork and the bottle costing more than the contents.

Moreover, the patent medicine entrepreneurs were shrewd bargainers when it came to advertising rates and they bought their advertising coverage at very low cost. Kilmer never used an agency. He made his own deals with publishers and never paid rates. In some cases he gave the publisher $2 worth of medicine for $1 worth of space, the publisher turning the medicine over to the local storekeeper for sale. And the practice of most of the early medical firms was much the same. They traded all sorts of commodities. S. E. Leith, who was a special agent in the heydays of the patent medicine relates that: "I traded a piano with Pinkham. I got building lots in Buffalo from Dr. Pierce. I had a block of stock in the Sterling Remedy Company from Harry Kramer. One of my publishers traded for a printing press, another for an electric dynamo and delivery wagon." Warner's Safe Cure, incidentally, got its name not from what freedom from danger the mixture may have possessed, but from the fact that its proprietor traded office safes for advertising space.

Some of the medical purveyors sent their own men through the country calling on publishers. They found what was needed and then made an arrangement whereby it could be supplied in exchange for space. The publisher had no idea what his space was worth and it was often bought by these traveling men as low as 10 cents on the dollar. Medical firms could afford to do this because of their huge profit, small financial risk and virtual freedom from product spoilage.

And the medicine man could concentrate his efforts on selling. He was free of expensive machinery, costly raw materials and real labor as problems of doing business. The business tended to attract men with an aptitude for trading and salesmanship. This, with the tremendous profit margin and breakable rate structures—leaving plenty of money to play with in catering to a responsive market, made of the patent medicine industry the number one advertiser for a good many years.

To a degree, the patent medicine man helped to show the way. The revenue contributed somewhat to the upbuilding of the publications and other media. But his value as an example of the value of the sales tactic was definitely circumscribed. Few manufacturers had any such profit margin to risk and most would have maintained and trusted that their businesses were vastly "different" from the methods which characterized a large part of the industry. Most patent medicine advertising was shamefully and flagrantly disreputable in its fake selling claims. Absolute remedial powers for cancer, consumption, yellow fever, rheumatism and other afflictions were widely claimed for preparations that had no efficacy for even the mildest ailment. Honest manufacturers were right-

A good deal has happened, in 50 years

"We believe that the spirit of craftsmanship lies at the root of all true achievement . . . that great violins, and great advertising, are created by skill and experience and devotion . . . and that there is no short cut, no royal road, no magic password to enduring success."

THE HISTORY of advertising as an economic force goes back only some sixty or seventy years. Many people now living can remember a time when there was little or no advertising . . . when it took years instead of days for a useful new product to become known . . . when many of the common conveniences of modern life were so rare and expensive that they could be enjoyed only by the well-to-do.

Many people can remember, too, when advertising as a business was looked upon with suspicion. The products promoted were, in many instances, of dubious worth. Trade practices governing the preparation and placing of advertising suggested a racket rather than a profession. '

It may not be amiss, on this golden anniversary occasion, to review some of the changes which have come about in advertising since those early days.

There has been a remarkable development in the advertising business, over the past half-century, and a constant rise in standards. Not only has advertising emerged from the chaotic competitive conditions and the era of sharp practice which marked the early years of its history; but it has also become a great and important industry,

serving many other industries, and exerting a powerful influence upon the entire economic structure of the nation.

· That advertising was able to free itself of these chaotic conditions, and to establish itself as a serious and reputable business, was due in large measure to a basic change which was introduced in the relationship between agency and publisher by F. Wayland Ayer, founder of N. W. Ayer & Son.

Prior to that time, every agency had had a list of publications which it tried to sell to the advertiser as the proper media in which to insert his advertising message. This list was promoted in each instance because the agency had an understanding with these particular publications whereby it would receive a profitable commission on all space sold.

Obviously, under this system, the advertising agency was working—not for the advertiser—but for the publications. The result was, that often the advertisement was inserted in newspapers and magazines in which it had no earthly reason to be, and the advertiser's money was correspondingly wasted. '

Mr. Ayer saw the abuses worked by this system, and he decided to do business in a different way. He adopted the principle that *the agency should work for the advertiser*, and that every publication should be selected on its merits alone, without regard to any commission, large or small, which the publication might pay.

The soundness of this principle soon came to be recognized, and the old "list system" dropped into the discard.

The results were at once apparent. As soon as advertising was freed of the incubus of badly selected media, its natural power began to manifest itself. Much advertising that had been directed, heretofore, to the wrong market, now began to pull and to sell the goods. And as soon as it was demonstrated that advertising could really increase a business, advertising itself began to have a healthy growth.

This new relationship between the advertiser and the advertising agency created a need for closer co-operation and greatly expanded service. In moving over to the advertiser's side of the fence, and embracing his interests and problems, the agency found that more diverse talents and activities were called for within his own organization.

The organization of the advertising agency began rapidly to grow. The business of the earlier type of advertising agent had been a relatively simple business. He had a list of publications, and he went around trying to peddle them. If he sold some space for a publication, he might, as an added inducement, sit down and write a piece of copy to go with it, but it was not really his responsibility.

His job was done, and his commission earned, when he had sold the space.

Under the new system, however, he assumed the responsibility of seeing to it that his client—the advertiser —got good advertising. It became *his* job to write the copy, *his* job to get it well laid out in the space specified,

and well and legibly set. *He* had to analyze markets, and sales and merchandising objectives. Instead of choosing a list of media by the simple test of how much commission he could get out of them, he found it necessary to study their circulation, readership and editorial content. And as new media were developed, it became his duty to set up the proper machinery for dealing with them, on behalf of his client, in the most effective and economical way.

All of these needs did not make themselves apparent at one and the same moment; but over a period of years they added greatly to the complexity of advertising, and of the service rendered by the well-equipped advertising agency.

The first need was for a completely objective, realistic and informed point of view in handling the problem of media selection. Thoroughgoing study and analysis were necessary in order to determine the relative value of various publications for the varied problems of advertising. This called for the services of the analytical, research type of mind; and thus was born the advertising agency Plans department, which later was enlarged to include marketing and merchandising.

But after the media were actually selected, there was found to be a complex process of negotiation with the publications, in order to secure the best possible terms, position, etc. In consequence it became necessary to set up a department geared to handle these questions, and experienced in publication methods and practices. This was the origin of the present-day Media-Contract department.

At an early stage it became evident that a well-written advertisement would sell more goods than a badly written one, and that it took a special kind of mind and a special kind of talent to write one really well. This was the beginning of the advertising agency Copy department.

After the Copy department had been, so to speak, invented, the realization followed that art and layout are equally specialized functions. So instead of having all art and layout problems handled more or less as a sideline by the copy-writer, trained artists were brought in to deal with these matters; and the Art department became a part of agency organization.

Eventually it was discovered that the buying of finished art work was a technical field in itself; and in order to leave the art directors more time for their creative work, a sub-department was created for this purpose.

Next, it came to be understood that good writing and good designing and art work were not enough. You needed good typography and a wide selection of type faces, many of which could not be carried in stock by a newspaper or magazine. Consequently the idea of the private advertising agency Print Shop came into being. This insured greater speed of production, and provided the added advantage of securing complete secrecy for the client's advertising, up to the time of publication.

Similarly, the appearance of the advertisement was found to depend so much on the quality of the plates sent to the publication, that it was found desirable to set up a special department to study engraving problems and to co-operate with engravers and publishers for better reproduction.

Finally, when the advertisement had appeared in the publication, it was found desirable to check it for position, size, date and quality of reproduction, in order to be sure that the advertiser got everything he paid for. In actual practice a Registry department of this sort was found to save thousands of dollars yearly to adver-

tisers—simply by catching mistakes and mechanical flaws in the printing of their advertisements.

When the new media of outdoor poster advertising and of radio were developed, the advertising agency had to provide suitable machinery for handling the new problems created; and the same was true in the field of publicity and public relations.

So far as we have been able to determine, N. W. Ayer & Son were, in each instance, the first to conceive and install the various types of department above-mentioned. Even today our Registry and Engraving bureaus are the only ones of their kind in existence. The records indicate, also, that many of the technical methods and practices now generally regarded as standard, originated here.

One field to which we have devoted particular attention lately is that of research and market study. The problems and difficulties of modern business place an added premium upon facts. The need for information ; . . complete and accurate information . . . is vital today in the operation both of business in general and of advertising in particular. In times like these, even the smallest guess may prove costly. Therefore we have taken measures to expand our fact-gathering and research facilities to the utmost.

In addition, our close knowledge of many businesses, gained through the years, is working to the greater advantage of all of our clients.

Underlying this skill, organization and experience is one cardinal principle which governs everything, and from the beginning has governed everything undertaken by N. W. Ayer & Son.

It is this: "Make advertising pay the advertiser."

Are we making advertising pay the advertiser?

We have good reason to believe that we are. While it would be unwise, and indeed under present unsettled conditions almost impossible, to attempt to paint a precise competitive picture of sales and advertising, we have no hesitancy in saying that in general the competitive position of our clients is strong.

That this is so may be gathered from the following fact:

Of twenty representative clients with whom we started working an average of twenty years ago, every one is the undisputed leader in his industry today.

During the past twelve months, advertising created by us has received a total of twenty awards. These are honors bestowed for technical distinction.

They consist of a total of five awards in the national Art Directors Show, including the Gold Medal for Color Illustration, the premium award of the show; five first places in the Annual Advertising Awards, including two medals; and the *Parents' Magazine* Medal given in 1938 jointly to Dr. Thomas Parran, Surgeon General of the United States, and to a radio program sponsored by a client of N. W. Ayer & Son. (This is the only radio program ever to be so honored.) Included also are ten other awards in the field of radio.

In this connection it is interesting to note that one of these awards was won in our first year of work for a new client. Another was won for a client who had been with us 38 years.

Since the founding of this House, 69 years ago, we have been privileged to grow up with the advertising business, and to share in its development. Our conception of advertising as a business function has expanded with the times. Today our conception of the function of advertising is this:

Every properly organized advertising program must (1) sell the goods; (2) create public good-will and confidence; and (3) reflect the character and ideals of the business advertised.

This is the Three-way Principle of advertising, a modern approach to the dual problem of large-scale selling and public relations.

Advertising today is not sleight-of-hand. It is not parlor magic with hats and rabbits, and it is not ballyhoo. Advertising is a scientific business based upon brains, experience and skill.

So conceived and so practiced, advertising is still a profitable undertaking; and we believe we are better equipped than ever before in our history to make it pay.

• • •

This Fiftieth Anniversary of *Printers' Ink Weekly* affords an opportune time to express our debt, and that of the entire advertising industry, to those who have managed and directed this great publication through the years. They have done a splendid work not only for advertising, but for all of American business.

We should like to take this occasion, too, to pay tribute to the many other advertising agencies who have made advertising a respected and necessary part of modern business procedure.

N. W. AYER & SON, Inc.

Washington Square, Philadelphia • New York • Boston • Chicago • San Francisco
Detroit • London • Buenos Aires • São Paulo • Toronto • Montreal

fully hesitant to associate with such charlatans in the advertising marketplace and the patent medicine tactics gave advertising a bad odor with the public that took years to overcome.

Furthermore, the industry's experience was productive of a lot of loose thinking on the subject of advertising. Some manufacturers in other lines took up the same hokum style. The spectacle of some of the medicine kings churning about the high seas in their palatial steam yachts produced the thought that extravagant expenditures and bombastic claims were the route to advertising success. In the wake came spectacular failures, in the medicine and other lines, to counteract in part whatever benefit may have laid in the experience of the successful firms.

In the 1880's the soap industry established itself as the leader among all general advertisers outside the patent medicine business. As a group, the soap advertisers were the first to make advertising a regular part of business policy for marketing a staple household article. They led the way in the use of large space, attractive ideas and copy that said something. Going into the 1890's the names of Ivory, Sapolio, Pears', Colgate, Kirk's American Family, Pearline, Packer's Tar and Siddalls' were known almost everywhere that merchandise was sold.

The soap business had an advertising tradition that went back for many years. All the first makers operated on a purely local basis. Practically all soap was made from garbage and the maker went on weekly rounds of the homes in his town. He exchanged soap for garbage, leaving two or three bars, the number depending upon the size of the family and the economy of its eating habits. Ultimately he established retailer connections and used advertising to secure a brand identity for his product, which was easily trade-marked. The advertisements, however, were entirely of the business card type.

Because soap is a rather bulky item for shipment, the business remained principally local for many years. Besides, the garbage-made product was perishable to a considerable degree. It smelled when new and as the animal oils became rancid the odor reached to the heavens. Introduction of processing vegetable oils in combination with animal oils finally eliminated the perishability factor and the makers began to explore the possibilities of regional expansion.

Through all this the soap maker remained fairly close to the consumer. As another favoring factor, his margin of profit was fairly high. The raw materials cost little and while he had no such margin as the patent medicine operators, he still had a spread which encouraged the exploration of more aggressive sales methods.

One of the greatest factors in the pioneering efforts of the industry, however, was its possession of several men of unusual sales vision. In Cincinnati there was Harley T. Procter of the second generation of the Procter family in the soap and candle works of Procter & Gamble. He was in charge of sales. A man of tremendous energy and keen foresight, he was considered by many the foremost salesman in the country.

It was Harley Procter who conceived the name of Ivory soap. The company had recently introduced a product called "White soap." Seated one morning in church, Procter found his attention diverted to commercial considerations by the recital of a passage from the Psalms: "All thy garments smell of myrrh, and aloes, and cassia, out of the ivory palaces whereby they have made thee glad." A magazine advertisement in 1882 announced the virtues of Ivory soap, and from there proceeded Procter's plans to make this new name a household word throughout the nation.

For years there was no argument in the advertising world as to which advertising was the best of all. It was Ivory soap. Endowed with Procter's enthusiasm and unshakable faith in this method of selling, each succeeding advertisement seemed to set new standards in sincere, original and attractive statement of a commercial message.

The soap industry was fortunate, too, in numbering among its ranks the great Artemas Ward (no relation to the humorist). Hired by Enoch Morgan's Sons to take charge of the advertising of Sapolio in 1885, Ward built the product into one of the most widely used articles in America by the sheer versatility of his methods. In 1891 the Sapolio proverbs were second only to Solomon's in wide publicity.

Ward's was a lively imagination and he had the true advertising touch. Perhaps one of the major factors in his success, however, was his business talent. He was the forerunner of the highest type of modern advertising executive. In a time when the preparing of advertising was considered to be an ascetic literary art, Ward made it his job to know and constantly keep in touch with every phase of the entire business of the house. Writ-

ing advertisements, he maintained, must be associated with the capacity for general business management.

Pears' soap's invasion of America with the aggressive advertising methods it had developed in England likewise helped to set the pace. James Pyle, who, carrying a basket on his arm, had led his sampling squads from door to door in the introduction of Pearline, was another pioneer, beginning advertising on a credit extended by Horace Greeley of the New York *Tribune*.

With the cumulative effect of these examples to set the course and with its inherent advantages for advertiser treatment, the soap business soon came to accept advertising as a matter of course.

The baking powder industry was another at the head of the ranks among the early general advertisers. Here the adoption was largely due to the work of a Ft. Wayne, Ind., druggist. Joseph C. Hoagland mixed up a cream of tartar preparation to take the place of the old-fashioned saleratus and other things which housewives used in their baking—the first baking powder. He began by house-to-house selling, in person, and then branched into the sampling idea. Advertising was begun and continued to grow until in 1893 Royal Baking Powder was considered the greatest newspaper advertiser in the world, using 14,000 papers and an estimated appropriation of $600,000 annually. Others had taken up the idea, including the Cleveland Brothers, Dr. Price and Horsford's Acid Phosphate, made by the Rumford Chemical Works.

The Royal Baking Powder program contributed little to the advance of copy. The advertisements

24

consisted of a display of the container and a paragraph of copy, plus the famous slogan, "Absolutely Pure." An advertisement would run unchanged over long periods, until a new policy was introduced about 1893.

However, Royal set an important example in the use of consistent insertions and widespread coverage. It continued its copy in dull times and prosperous. And H. A. La Fetra was another precursor of the modern advertising executive and an apostle of sound, orderly procedure. In 1893 he made this statement: "Millions of dollars are being squandered every year by advertisers who think they are advertising but who, in reality, are not. Good advertising is getting the facts before the public so that the public will read and believe them."

An important newcomer in the 1890's was the food industry, widespread distribution of prepared and packaged foods becoming a reality in this period. Among the prepared foods the baby foods came first. Mellin's Food, a fairly large though not always consistent advertiser in the 1880's, was perhaps the pioneer.

Then came the breakfast foods. In 1878 the American Cereal Company put Quaker Oats on the market, said to be the first packaged, advertised food product. The original founder of this enterprise, Ferdinand Schumacher, had introduced the manufacture of oatmeal in America some years before. The Quaker Oats business was developed gradually on a market-to-market basis by sampling and outdoor advertising. In 1893 the company began the use of general advertising. Numerous other oats

products came on the market—Pettijohn's, Ralston's, Mother's Oats, Hornby's Oats (H-O)—followed by wheat, barley and rice products. Prepared breakfast foods became important later in the 1890's with the arrival of Grape-Nuts, Force, Shredded Wheat and others.

In Pennsylvania, H. J. Heinz was laying the foundations for a huge food business. He began making pickles in a room in Sharpsburg and sold them to families and local grocers, delivering the goods himself in a wheelbarrow. He stressed the idea of purity both in manufacturing and soliciting, and distributed samples freely. To advertise his products he became a wide user of car cards and posters. By 1897 the Heinz plant was the largest pickle factory in the United States. Baked beans and other table delicacies were being added to the line and there was scarcely a grocery store in America but had one or more of the Heinz varieties in stock.

Among other leading food advertisers were Walter Baker & Company with their famous La Belle Chocolatiere and the Franco-American Food Company, which began selling canned soup in 1886 and devoted a fixed percentage of the business done to advertising.

The seed companies—a business adapted to mail-order selling—represented another industry in which the use of advertising was widely adopted. Leaders were the W. Atlee Burpee Company, which began business in 1876 and grew to be the largest, D. M. Ferry Seed Company, William Henry Maule and the Peter Henderson Seed Company. At first the seedsmen sold direct from advertising, but bogus concerns spoiled that. In the 1890's most companies advertised for inquiries and sold from catalogs sent to the inquirers.

Among the most unremitting advertisers in the late 1880's and the 1890's were the railroads. In 1892 the Pennsylvania was the leader, spending $230,000 in advertising its Eastern lines, the Union Pacific not far behind. In the same year Chauncey M. Depew, president of the New York Central & Hudson River Railroad, said this on the subject of advertising: "Every enterprise, every business, and I might add every institution, must be advertised in order to be a success. To talk in any other strain would be madness."

Much of the railroad effort was in huge, profusely illustrated brochures and books containing information on routes, rates and resorts. The railroads had a special penchant for quality work in this literature and many of them were truly fine examples of the printing art. They educated the public to expect artistic literature and speeded the general improvement of printed work of other advertisers. The copy, on the other hand, was inclined to be on the dull and windy side.

Much of the earlier publication advertising had been limited to rate and schedule notices. But in the '90's the roads began to enter the field of general advertising.

A premier figure in railroad advertising was Frank Presbrey, who did distinguished work for the Santa Fe and Denver & Rio Grande lines. When he entered the agency business in New York in 1893 he continued to serve importantly in the transportation field, including both railroad and steamship lines. J. M. Campbell was in at the genesis of modern railroad advertising with his work for the Burlington, and later with other lines. The Burlington was the first to break away from the practice of paying for space in passes, rather than cash, and a pioneer in advertising specifically to build traffic between certain points.

Community advertising—usually thought to be a development of recent times—was a thriving field of advertiser operations as early as 1890. The railroads, in their advertising of the attractions of the territory along their rights of way, probably set the example. But the real impetus came from the throbbing growth of new towns in the West, every one a potential metropolis in the minds of its residents. Seemingly no town was too small to entertain the hope that it would be the next Chicago, and many resorted to advertising to speed that rather confidently expected end.

The idea seems to have got a start in a small way about 1885. By 1890 at least a hundred cities and towns in the West and South were advertising with a fair show of consistency. In that year Salt Lake City raised a fund of $40,000 for this purpose, quite a sizable budget in those days.

From the new lands the notion spread back East and before long some of the cities in that section had joined the procession. A single issue of the *North American Review* in 1891 carried thirty-three pages of community advertising and such towns as Penobscot Bay and Sudbury (Ontario) were advancing their claim to fame and future growth. A number of magazines and business papers received the custom of the community advertisers, but the Sunday newspapers were generally the favorite medium. Cities of the size of St. Louis, Atlanta and Richmond accounted for a large share of the activity, of course, but one of the most energetic of all was Crowley, La.

The advertising was usually financed by a group of local public-spirited citizens who were eager to see property values increase and boom local interests generally. In some instances the town itself would vote a part of the financing. The typical advertisement displayed a picture of the town, an account of its industries and commerce, statistics and its advantages as a manufacturing site and place of residence.

Community advertising subsided in the late 1890's, then came back in a new cycle beginning around 1905.

Individually, the Eastman Dry Plate Company's activities had a material effect in spreading the advertising gospel, so sensational was its success. In 1888 George Eastman invented the portable camera and coined for it the distinctive name, "Kodak." The camera was loaded at the factory and to get his pictures developed, the user had to send the camera to Rochester, have the film taken out and developed and the camera reloaded. ("You Press the Button—We do the Rest.") Hence

1890

NELLY BLY goes around the world in seventy-two days, six hours and eleven minutes. . . . Idaho and Wyoming admitted to the Union. . . . Populist party formed in convention at Topeka. . . . Chief Sitting Bull killed while resisting arrest in North Dakota. . . . Chicago wins vote in Congress as site of World's Columbian Exposition. . . . Eleventh census shows population of 62,622,250 a 12,466,467 increase in ten years.

Imitation of labels and trade names becoming a serious problem, especially in the patent medicine industry. . . . A deaf-mute advertising solicitor, operating with pencil and paper, makes the rounds of Eastern advertisers. . . . S. C. Beckwith, New York special agent, representing thirty papers. . . . "When an advertising writer has truth enough to be generally trusted, tact enough to be generally depended upon, force enough to be wholesomely respected and business experience enough not to jump through his collar—then his happy combination of talents *may* insure him salary enough to drink Bass at his lunch"—Artemas Ward.

New York *World* netted $1,200,000—"no other newspaper in the world makes half so much." . . . Cantaloupes were muskmelons, most young men had livery bills, the hired girl drew one fifty a week and the butcher threw in a chunk of liver. . . . Chicago newspapers cease giving commission on placement of local advertising. . . . A New York concern selling space on barber shop ceilings.

A FORECAST *from the files*

On SUNDAY, July 15, 1888, in a world troubled with rumors of impending war and declining business, George P. Rowell placed in the mails at New York 5,200 copies of a new publication for advertisers—a publication destined to chronicle, shape and encourage the step-by-step progress of American business in developing the mass production and marketing technique which has given this nation the highest living standards in the world.

Under the same dateline, there were being printed in a thriving community 1,000 miles westward some 60,000 copies of a newspaper, forty-one years old and already nationally celebrated for its dissemination of information and bold courage . . . and, as a result, unusually fitted to play a leading part in making this great social and economic advance possible.

Page 4 of this 24-page Sunday newspaper was set solid with editorials on politics, business, the railroads and the tarif—hard-hitting commentaries on the livest issues of the day. One editorial on this page, however, was in lighter vein. It was about "Summer Reading":

"Luckily for those who enjoy reading in hot months and can take time for it the season is well supplied with new and capital commodities. A cheap American edition of 'Robert Elsmere,' the novel which has stirred England to its depths as none other since George Eliot wrote 'Middlemarch,' is announced. The demand for it in Chicago and through the Northwest has been constant and active since the review in the Tribune immediately after its London publication. Without desiring to suggest invidious reflections, and stating only a fact, the report of the book venders on this novel indicates how general the reading of the Tribune is among the cultivated people of the North-

western States. No other journal in the country except a weekly publication of New York has reviewed, up to this time, the most engrossing novel published in many years. The weekly alluded to contained a commentary upon it a few weeks ago, following the lines of that in the Tribune."

Set out in this long-forgotten piece is evidence of the forces already at work making available to the coming era of American business a great mass merchandising medium, delivering America's inland empire as a single market.

In these brief lines there is epitomized the editorial enterprise which fifty years ago was attracting to the Chicago Tribune a growing readership "in Chicago and through the Northwest."

TODAY the Tribune is Chicago's oldest newspaper and its youngest. While sixty other Chicago newspapers have come and gone, the Tribune and its readers have seen the frontiers disappear and Chicago grow to be the fourth largest city in the world.

Ninety-one years of action in advancing the interests of the city, region and the nation have made the Tribune a vital and intimate part of the lives of the majority of all the families in metropolitan Chicago, and of hundreds of thousands of others throughout the middle west.

Today through the Tribune the advertiser can make a direct bid for the business of the largest constant audience in the Chicago territory which is reached by any advertising medium.

On the basis of results, retailers and manufacturers depend chiefly on Tribune advertising to sell hundreds of millions of dollars of merchandise annually. To build store trafic and sales volume, they spend the greatest part of their advertising appropriations for advertising in the Tribune.

NO MATTER what you sell, to whom it sells, you can rely on the Tribune to produce the greatest volume of sales. As Chicago's first newspaper and its first advertising medium, the Tribune is the logical base around which to build your advertising program. Rates per 100,000 circulation are among the lowest in America.

Chicago Tribune
THE WORLD'S GREATEST NEWSPAPER

Average Total Net Paid Circulation During the Official Six-Month Period Ended March 31, 1938: Daily, 857,963; Sunday, 1,115,643

the consumer had to be sold the whole camera idea and Eastman set out to do it with an advertising appropriation of $25,000 for the first year. The profits in the next twelve months amounted to some $85,000.

By 1895 the word Kodak had been made synonymous with camera and part of the language. In six years it had achieved a world-wide market. Here indeed was a compelling example of how a company could use advertising to speedily create a market for a product so new that it was necessary to explain not only how it could be used but what it was.

Another whose activities made a deep impression was Richardson & De Long Brothers. The slogan "See That Hump," conceived by the advertising writer, Charles M. Snyder, and introduced in advertising of the De Long hook-and-eye in 1891, kindled a huge popularity. The subsequent success of the product was one of the most telling factors in establishing the idea that the man who made a small, low-priced article could with profit become an advertiser.

A shining proponent of persistent effort was W. L. Douglas, the shoe man of Brockton, Mass. His portrait appeared in every advertisement and his face was probably better known than that of any other man of the time, excepting only P. T. Barnum.

Douglas started advertising in 1885, although his firm was established long before. At first he dealt by mail-order, then turned to retailer distribution. Ultimately he opened retail stores of his own because he was driven to it, stores in the larger cities being unwilling to handle the line because they claimed they could realize a better profit on unknown goods.

Douglas wrote the first advertisement for his $3 shoes and continued to write a large share of those used by the firm for years. He was particularly notable for his keenly developed sense of timing. He watched weather and business conditions closely and manipulated his advertising activities accordingly. Just before the panic of 1893, he saw fit to increase his advertising and was rewarded handsomely. By 1900, Douglas Shoe was one of the largest advertisers in the country and had stood staunch witness to the point that it pays to keep advertising going.

Charles E. Hires of root beer fame started making his product in the 1870's, attending personally to manufacture and sale at first. George W. Childs, publisher of the Philadelphia *Public Ledger*, spoke to Hires on the subject of advertising in 1877 and found an attentive audience. The business grew and the advertising effort was increased and in 1888 Hires became an advertiser on a large scale, taking up good-sized space in magazines and expanding his newspaper activity. In 1892 he was reported to have invested $500,000 in advertising.

Other pioneer advertisers who led the way in what subsequently became important classifications of advertised products were Gerhard Mennen, who in 1889 began selling a special kind of talcum powder for the drug store he owned; L. E. Waterman, who invented the fountain pen in 1883 and after a period of personal sales effort entered the advertising lists; and the Regal Shoe Company, which started advertising in 1893 and in 1896 reported an eightfold increase in business.

Lines of Communication

EVEN assuming an advertiser with a complete understanding of the value of communion with the consumer and a relentless determination to consummate that end, the achievement was all but impossible throughout the greater part of the nineteenth century. The lines of communication with the consumer were sparse, uncertain and unreliable. And their keepers, when not actually hostile, did but little to welcome the advertiser as a customer.

Up to the last ten years of the century the opportunity of reaching with reasonable assurance any large proportion of the consuming public through advertising was meager. In 1888 there were 16,310 publications of all kinds—an increase of some 6,000 over 1880, yet 11,511 circulated not so many as 1,000 copies each. The total per issue circulation of all publications was (perhaps) 29,000,000 and the daily newspapers combined to offer a possible 4,500,-000. The largest magazine was *Century* with 186,257.

Newspapers and periodicals alike were largely out of the reach of the mass of the spending market on a price basis. What is more, few of them offered the type of editorial subject and treatment calculated to reach a substantial portion of the advertiser's ultimate market.

Outdoor advertising offered some further opportunity to reach the mass market, but the trade as a whole was unorganized and undependable. The excesses of itinerant sign painters in marring scenery had created a vast public antagonism, while the poster and the painted bulletin board were relatively un-developed. Car cards worked under unfavorable circumstances and had barely begun to approach their later circulation possibilities. Facilities for producing attractive direct mail matter were limited.

The use of any of these media received little constructive encouragement from their proprietors. Rates were frequently excessive and the buying process was, with rare exceptions, calculated to do anything but build confidence. Few publishers or owners of other forms of media had any real belief in or understanding of the values of advertising.

It had not been many years since all magazine publishers refused to accept advertising of any kind, and most of them still viewed it with at least a passive dislike. The majority of newspaper publishers had, by reason of their dealings with local advertisers, a somewhat more tolerant view toward advertising. But many of them looked upon the "foreign" advertiser merely as game for whatever plucking could be administered and, in a "take it or leave it" attitude, interposed such barriers against enterprising advertising practice as prohibitions against cuts and display type, or extra charges for the use of them. Moreover, many publishers of all kinds had a constitutional aversion against telling the truth about circulation totals, while others refused to give out any information whatever on this subject, asserting it was nobody's business but their own.

Whatever the medium, the chances of faithful, inviting reproduction of the advertisement were pretty remote. The equipment to do it simply didn't exist.

In the early 1890's invention came to the rescue and, coupled with the enterprise of some of the more far-sighted publishers and operators, did much to provide easy-running, dependable machines for attaining proximity with the consumer.

There was the halftone, invented in 1878 and perfected in 1885 by Frederick E. Ives, but not ready for wide commercial application until the 1890's. As late as 1889 the process engraving—either halftone or line cut—was considered inferior to the wood-cut and suitable only where quality reproduction was not necessary. Soon thereafter, however, illustrations became inexpensive and easy to prepare.

Of perhaps even greater importance was the linotype machine, Ottmar Mergenthaler's contribution to the advance of civilization. Invented in 1886, it achieved some application in the 1890's, though it did not reach a wide use until about 1905. A little earlier the stereotype had come into use on the newspaper and the application of the rotary press to magazine production began in 1884.

These devices paved the last stretch of the route toward mass production of a good publication at a low price, so far as the mechanical phases of manufacture were concerned. Other technical improvements were to come, of course, but these were basic and they vastly increased the horizons of publishing. Mass production tended to bring into being a greater sales effort to distribute its products, and it opened whole new strata of readers to the publishing business. And the competition led to the most important ingredient of all in the making of publications—better and more attractive editorial content.

Such are some of the broader aspects of the development of facilities for bringing the advertiser closer to the consumer. The ensuing paragraphs undertake to examine in further detail the developments in the individual classes of media during this period.

WRITERS about the eventful days in the newpaper world during the 1890's turn over their narratives almost exclusively to the great publishers and editors of New York and Chicago. And it is perfectly true that when you have men like Bennett and Dana and Hearst and Lawson and Medill and Ochs and Pulitzer and Reid performing in a single decade you have something to conjure with. Among them, these heroic figures set practically all the patterns that have developed the modern newspaper. The elder Bennett and Benjamin H. Day and others of earlier vintage had had something important to say about the shape of the newspaper, of course, but these eight brought the basic patterns to a point where what has come after them is largely refinement rather than innovation.

Nevertheless one may suspect that the most important development of the newspaper in this time came in the centers of lesser population. Vastly improved methods of transportation and communication had made the opportunity for a new degree of daily newspaper service in the medium-sized and small cities. And the proprietors of the papers, not infrequently borrowing from the technique of the brighter lights in the two metropolitan cities, made the most of what opportunity offered. They began the building of a daily press adapted to attracting the readership of their communities. They instituted the spread of daily newspapers over a far greater number of cities, and though the big city paper continued to grow in circulation, they lessened the previous condition of newspaper dominance by a few big city papers.

In short, the newspaper was becoming more and more available as a medium of national coverage for the advertiser. In 1888 the general advertising agencies did practically all of their business with about one-tenth of the country's fourteen thousand newspapers (of which 1,494 were dailies). Better newspapers of greater circulation were soon to change that picture. Real coverage of the cities under a million population had begun to appear.

It is a matter of recorded opinion at the time that the newspapers in the West were a good bit less provincial than those in the largest cities on the Eastern seaboard, New York in particular. Eastern papers dealt almost exclusively with affairs on the hither side of the Alleghenies and the craze for filling up the papers with local news was so great that there was room for little else. The Western papers, on the other hand, carried news of the East as well as of the West and in this respect were setting the precedent for the national horizons of the modern newspapers.

Moreover, the tendency to eliminate the physical handicaps in the use of newspaper advertising space was more marked in the West. The rules against breaking columns, use of display type and employment of cuts or the charging of a premium for such usages were, in general, more quickly done away with. As late as 1895 some of the New York papers were still placing a tax on the efforts of advertisers to make their advertisements unusual and attractive.

The influence of the metropolitan leaders in the development of journalism is by no means to be discounted, and at the head of the procession was the great Joseph Pulitzer. Coming into possession of the New York *World* in 1883, he created an actual revolution in the New York newspaper situation. Bearing the instruments of spectacular enterprise and crusading reform, he was the first to get the ear of the great mass of the public.

During the Civil War the public had developed an enormous appetite for news, which gave fresh meaning to the earlier efforts of Bennett of the *Herald* and Dana of the *Sun* in pushing the true news function in place of the elaborate essays that occupied so much of the old time newspaper's content. As a consequence of this sharpened news appetite, the newspaper attained a far more useful and respected place in society. But it had remained for Pulitzer to perceive the ways of dramatizing news in a manner calculated to win the following of large numbers of people. By 1891 the *World* had attained a circulation of 600,000 and became the first daily to boast of coverage of a substantial proportion of its market.

The inventor with his machine played no less a role than the editor with his pen. The linotype, and stereotype and constant improving of the printing press were speeding up tremendously the ability to produce better newspapers in great volume. The process engraving made possible wide use of pictures and despite the opposition of many

"All of these things we have seen and part of them we were"

Browsing through the file copies of The Milwaukee Journal, a reader of today can see the past fifty years of advertising history in Milwaukee as it is revealed through no other source. Between these covers is the story of practically every major marketing campaign Milwaukee has seen — evidence that we have been just as busy selling soap and shoes and shirts, as we have in printing the daily history of the world. Here is the 56-year record of growth of all the great retail establishments in the city and of practically every manufacturer of nationally known branded merchandise. From these yellowing pages can be compiled a Who's Who of Milwaukee and American Business from 1882 to the present.

To all of those advertisers who have had a part in making The Journal a great newspaper for Milwaukee and one of the nation's ten leading newspapers in linage — THANKS!

THE MILWAUKEE JOURNAL
FIRST BY MERIT

editors, who were inclined to resent the "cuts," illustrations had become an established thing in the dailies by 1891. They boomed circulation tremendously, and it may not be entirely a coincidence that a disposition to reveal true circulation figures began to appear just about the time the illustration came into eminence.

By 1894 there were 1,855 dailies and their combined circulation was approximately 7,000,000—not staggering viewed from a modern hilltop, but a substantial growth, being well over 50 per cent increase in six years, and significant of things to come. There can be little doubt that the final blueprints for the immense expansion of the future had been largely conceived and put to work in this period.

The arrival of the Sunday newspaper was another event of far-reaching importance, and here again Pulitzer's hand is apparent. The Sunday edition not merely established newspaper readership on Sunday, but exerted a considerable effect upon the future shape of the daily.

Prior to the Civil War none of the New York newspapers had a Sunday edition with the exception of the *Herald*. And that was the result of a whim of the elder Bennett, who happened to see a good deal of matter left on the galleys one Saturday and decided not to wait with it until Monday. The war, with important battle news coming over the week-end brought the spread of the Sunday edition, but its progress was halting for many years.

The chief credit goes to a young man who in 1900, at the age of thirty-three, had been known for years as "the father of the Sunday newspaper"—Morrill Goddard. Pulitzer had hired him and given him free rein, though at one time his

Lithographed in colors, this advertisement was instrumental in gaining sales for a widely used cleanser

alarmed associates cabled to the publisher in Europe that "This young man is ruining your business."

Goddard was the first to make the Sunday paper a separate entity. He organized his own staff of writers and assistant editors who worked for him exclusively. He had the whole *World* establishment in a turmoil in his avowed efforts to make the Sunday paper interesting, which he proceeded to do with a radical departure from the old newspaper methods—big, smashing headlines, stirring articles about things never before treated in newspapers, halftones of tremendous size. During his career as a Sunday editor (he continued his development efforts with W. R. Hearst not long after the latter purchased the New York *Journal* in 1895) Goddard introduced the Sunday magazine idea and colored illustrations.

1891

PHINEAS T. BARNUM, master showman and advertiser, dies at Bridgeport, Conn. . . . McKinley elected governor of Ohio, largely on his stand on the free silver issue. . . . Thomas A. Edison applies for patent on first motion picture camera. . . . First Empire State Express on the New York Central does New York to Buffalo in eight hours, forty-two minutes. . . . U. S. almost goes to war with Chile.

Baking powder companies conducting an advertising war over whose product is the "purest." . . . Death of S. M. Pettengill, one of the early advertising agents and E. C. Allen, proprietor of Allen's Lists and a pioneer in selling by mail. . . . At least one newspaper or periodical published in 7,152 different cities and towns. . . . "The one great golden rule in advertisement writing is to advertise one thing at a time"— Nathaniel C. Fowler, Jr., . . . Narrow columns in newspapers fast falling into disuse, owing to employment of electrotypes by advertisers.

To obtain Federal trade-mark registration it is necessary to make oath that the mark is used in commerce with foreign nations or the Indian tribes. . . . Advertising on envelopes coming in. . . . Publisher, baffled by flood of advertiser requests for position "next to reading matter," wants to know if advertisements aren't reading matter. . . . *Cottage Home* offers $175 in prizes for agents placing the most business with it and the Charles H. Fuller Advertising Agency, Chicago, takes first place. . . . Headline of Standard Shoe Tying Company advertisement: "It's knotty, but it's nice."

By 1895 the Sunday newspapers were making big inroads on the circulations of the weekly papers at every point near a railroad. The sensational weeklies, which had been so popular a few years before and in some instances had had editions of 100,000 or more, were not doing so prosperously. It was now conceded that the Sunday newspaper had come to stay. Indeed by 1898 it had reached a circulation of over four million. There were 392 Sunday papers having a circulation over 1,000—292 of them issues of daily papers, the rest independent weeklies.

It was also during this period 1888-1895 that newspaper publishers began to give greater recognition to woman's place in society and to make specific attempts to enlist feminine readership. There were snorts about "strong-minded females and new women," but in 1896 it was recorded that women's features were now an important part of the newspaper. Nearly every large paper had instituted a woman's page carrying fashions, recipes and general articles and stories catering to the interests of women.

All of which fitted importantly into the advertiser picture, for advertisers were discovering the importance of the purchasing agent of the American home. Beginning about 1890 the distaff side of the family was the subject of much discussion among those who prepared advertising, and it was asserted at this time by several writers that the woman bought at least four-fifths of all consumer merchandise. So great, in fact, was the preoccupation with this discovery of feminine importance that there was a marked disposition to ignore the male almost entirely. There came to be numerous proponents of the theory that men didn't read advertisements anyway and no purpose was served in advertising to them.

In the realm of the country weekly, the co-operative newspapers gained in importance. These were the users of "ready-prints," or patent insides. In 1863 A. J. Aikens of Milwaukee first proposed the idea of supply publishers with half-printed sheets carrying editorial matter and general advertising, the publisher to print local news and advertising on the other side. As advertising grew, it became possible to supply the ready-prints at less than the cost of production, the advertising paying the costs. In 1894 more than 7,000 of the 11,000 country papers were using these sheets.

The A. N. Kellogg Newspaper Company, Atlantic Coast Lists, Western Newspaper Union and others supplied the prints to the rural publishers and solicited general advertising. By means of this type of operation, the job of the advertiser who wanted to use a large number of small-town papers was immensely simplified. One electrotype was sufficient to cover an entire list of hundreds of papers. Postage and clerical labor were cut down materially. In addition the rates available through these channels were often much lower than could be had by dealing with the papers individually, so that in the 1890's it became more and more difficult for the general advertising agent to compete in the field with the list system.

The newspaper led all other media in volume during the period as it had for many years, but important developments were still

Service
and Age go together

CONGRATULATIONS, PRINTERS' INK, on your first 50 years of service to advertising. Throughout our 105 years, The Sun has served its readers well. In fact, The Sun's distinguished newspaper service has recently won this citation from the University of Missouri:

"To The New York Sun: For the excellence of its literary style; for its urbanity, high journalistic craftsmanship and intelligence in selecting, as well as in handling, its news; for its unqualified intellectual honesty in conducting a newspaper for a highly intelligent and discriminating newspaper audience; for its treatment of the liberal arts, political correspondence and financial and commercial news by outstanding authorities; for its Saturday issue, which in the scope, character and quality of its articles and its general informative value, is unusual among newspapers in the United States."

The Sun
NEW YORK

ahead. It was to be some years before the newspaper rose to its fullest stature as an advertising medium of national character. In many respects it was still geared primarily to the needs of the local advertiser and the accommodations for the "foreign" advertiser were far short of ideal.

As the last decade of the century opened the magazines began assembling upon the threshold of unprecedented expansion. In 1889 a magazine of 100,000 circulation was a thing to be marveled at. In 1895 the *Ladies' Home Journal* was touching 750,000, *Youth's Companion* had passed 570,000, *Ladies' World* had better than 375,000, *Munsey's* had 400,000, *Cosmopolitan* over 300,000. There were nine all told with better than 100,000 purchasers.

In a large measure the increase in the magazine reading public traced to the plain economics of lower price, which enabled new buyers to come into the market. For years the common price of magazines had been 50, 35 and 25 cents. Then came the mechanical apparatus—rotary press, linotype and process engravings—to make it possible for the publisher to lay down a magazine at a cheaper price and the scale began to move downward. *McClure's Magazine* was established at 15 cents, *Cosmopolitan* dropped to 12½ cents, then back to 15. Then came *Munsey's* with the 10-cent price in 1893, *Cosmopolitan* and *McClure's* reducing to that level in 1895.

Although circulations of a million and more have since been achieved by periodicals selling at twenty-five cents and many hundreds of thousands at higher than that, these low price levels did much of the spadework in educating people to read magazines.

Then, too, under men like Edward Bok and John Brisben Walker, magazines with a broader editorial appeal were being built. For years magazines had been made principally for those having an interest in the deeper aspects of political and literary affairs. The essay content was high. There was little of popular fiction or informative articles phrased in a popular vein. For example, a large part of the audience of *Century*, leader in circulation and advertising through the 1880's, were the leading business men.

Illustrations formed an important part of the editorial attraction of these newer magazines. As in the newspapers, the plentiful and inexpensive reproductions of pictures made possible by the process engraving found a huge and immediate public response. This brought in its wake quite a flurry of picture magazines and some of the more worrisome fretters over the future of the race were harassed, as they were to be again in 1937, by the thought that people would soon refuse to read essays and consider political arguments unless every line were accompanied by a picture. "If the average picture magazine is a criterion of the public taste," moaned one observer, "the race has developed a predominant curiosity regarding the female adorned and unadorned."

But the manufacturing of magazines was not alone in its influence. There appeared the idea that what is made must be sold. A Philadelphia gentleman went so far—and it was mighty far in those days—as to believe and publicly assert that a publisher ought to take his own medicine. His name was Cyrus H. K. Curtis and his product was *Ladies' Home Journal*, begun in 1883 as an eight-page supplement to his weekly *Tribune-Farmer.*

Curtis and his wife, who served as editor in the first years, set about putting together a readable and useful magazine, and the employment of the genius of Bok in 1889 assured further eminence for the product. But in addition to being a great publisher, Curtis was a great advertiser in the fullest modern meaning of the word. He bent every effort to selling his product and in 1889 and 1890 spent a total of $310,000 in advertising it, increasing the appropriation to $200,000 annually not long after. As a further instrument of distribution he introduced his nationwide force of youthful salesmen a little later.

Most other publishers were a little slow in grasping the point, but they came to it sooner or later. And the use of advertising and modern methods of salesmanship became fundamental in the growth of the magazine, taking first rank, once the technique of mass manufacturing had been absorbed.

Up almost to the Civil War advertising in magazines didn't exist. The magazines didn't want advertising in their pages and refused to admit it, and when admittance was granted they did little to welcome patronage. The first important landmark was the decision for acceptance by *Atlantic Monthly* in 1860 and *Harper's Magazine* in 1864, but the representation of advertisements was meager for many years. *Century,* founded as *Scribner's Monthly* in 1860 and changed to its later name in 1881, began some outright soliciting for business under Roswell Smith. Success, relatively speaking, was bountifully endowed upon the bold pioneer and *Century* quickly attained a leadership in advertising volume which it held until 1890, when *Harper's* passed it.

Most of the advertisements were small, usually eight or more to the page, though a few brave customers used space as large as a quarter or half page. The Pears' soap people gave folks something to think about when they took a full page in *Century* in 1888. Five years later, however, the palm passed to Mellin's Food which took a back cover lithographed in fifteen colors in the World's Fair number of *Youth's Companion* at a cost of $15,000; the advertisement featured a painting of a child by a French artist accompanied by a brief bit of copy. Statisticians of the time counted the words at eighty-six and managed to gulp that these goings-on represented an investment of $174 per word.

In addition to the improved advertising facilities supplied by circulation increases, the cost of advertising tended to move downward. Publishers of the new type saw fit to encourage the use of their space and larger circulation totals. Lower unit production costs enabled them to decrease the rate per thousand circulation. In consequence, advertising patrons appeared in greater numbers and explored the possibilities of larger insertions. And the results, in terms of cost, furthered the progress of the advertising proposition in the minds of the manufacturers.

The "mail-order" weekly was a particularly flourishing entity in the periodical field during the 1890's. E. C. Allen had turned from selling

Advertising and Marketing Counsel

.. Product research, on-the-ground study of markets and merchandising, and complete advertising service in newspapers, magazines, radio, and outdoor . . . . The J. Walter Thompson Company is an organization of more than one thousand people, located in twenty-five offices in the market centers of the world.

NEW YORK

CHICAGO

ST. LOUIS

SAN FRANCISCO

LOS ANGELES

HOLLYWOOD

SEATTLE

BOSTON

•

MONTREAL

TORONTO

•

LONDON

PARIS

ANTWERP

THE HAGUE

BUCHAREST

•

BUENOS AIRES

SÃO PAULO

RIO DE JANEIRO

•

CAPE TOWN

JOHANNESBURG

•

BOMBAY

CALCUTTA

•

SYDNEY

MELBOURNE

•

LATIN-AMERICAN
& FAR EASTERN
DIVISION

★

J. WALTER THOMPSON COMPANY

of recipes and merchandise by mail in the 1870's to publishing a journal for free distribution to mailing lists. The enterprise grew to become "Allen's Lists," a group of twelve papers with a circulation of more than a million.

Other mail-order journals—*Grit* at Williamsport, Pa., *Blade and Ledger* at Chicago, *Comfort* and the Vickery & Hill list at Augusta—were founded and achieved huge circulations. The advertising patronage of these papers was composed primarily of those who sold by mail or through country agents, and from their number came not a few of the general advertisers.

The religious publication was an important factor in the periodical field at this time, though showing signs of receding from its long-held position as one of the major media. In 1892 it was deemed the most favored by advertisers of all the class publications and there were 955 such papers, representing about one-eighth of the combined circulation of all publications. However, the secular magazines were beginning to supply much of the type of general material which had given the religious papers their popularity, and without the rather narrow horizons to which a religious publication must necessarily be confined. The advance in material prosperity to a considerable extent had lessened interest in spiritual reading. In addition, the aura of respectability which manufacturers thought was granted their wares by advertisements in these publications had dimmed under the practice of many publications of accepting patent medicine copy of questionable character.

"Five years ago," commented an observer of the magazine situation in 1896, "magazines did not have the enormous circulations they now claim. A magazine, half of whose pages were occupied with advertising, was undreamed of at that time." "Ten years ago," said another observer in 1906, "there were no big circulations and perhaps 80 per cent of the magazines now in existence were unborn."

FOR a time it seemed that the height of efficient achievement in the field of outdoor advertising was to emblazon the name of the product on a church steeple. This was a business in which, during the 1880's, rugged individualism reached a spectacular peak. Rare was the rock of vantage in any spot of scenic interest that did not bear the name of somebody's pills. No fence or wall was immune, for the property owner's permission was rarely sought. One enterprising firm painted a message on four-fifths of the chimneys along every line of the New York elevated system, the painters often using rope ladders to go from roof to roof.

The first important step toward eliminating these unwholesome practices came in 1891 when the responsible interests in the business formed the Associated Billposters and Distributors of the United States and Canada. In addition, subsidiary State and district associations came into existence. The national association granted franchises to bill posters, one to a city, and a forward step in advertising practice was taken with the establishment of firm rates.

The original standard posting was the three-sheet, then came the eight-sheet, then the twelve. By 1905 the sixteen-sheet poster had become the standard. Through the

1880's the theaters and other amusement advertisers were the principal customers of the poster boards. In the '90's general advertisers, finding the poster less expensive and more flexible than painted bulletins, took a greater interest in this branch of advertising. By 1905 they occupied about 80 per cent of the postings to 20 per cent for amusement advertisers, exactly the reverse of the situation fifteen years before.

"Paint," as the painted variety of outdoor advertisement was called, likewise grew in the 1890's, although up to this time it had developed faster than the poster variety. The smearing of rocks and landscapes, for which the advertiser who hired painters of his own was often responsible, abated materially under the press of public indignation and the evolution of orderly facilities for presenting messages outdoors.

"Paint" reached its greatest importance in the cities, where it could offer location and size for a display more permanent than the poster. However, it was also widely used along the railways on fences and sides and roofs of barns. The great sarsaparilla war, in which Ayer's and Hood's messages vied for attention, was a feature of most any train ride.

Some few advertisers controlled their own locations and painted their own bulletins. But most of the business was handled by the painting services of Houghtaling, O. J. Gude, Thomas Cusack, R. J. Gunning and others. "Hote," as C. J. Houghtaling was known to everybody who had anything to do with advertising, was the self-styled "king of display" and one of the most picturesque figures advertising has produced. A swaggering, expansive citizen, he was identified with nearly every large advertising success in his time. For all his bluster, Hote knew his markets.

In 1894 the poster field gained a leading spirit when Barney Link left his work for the Buffalo Bill and Barnum shows to enter the posting business at New York. He became president of Van Beuren & New York Billposting Company and ultimately owned an interest in or operated plants in 451 cities and towns. He did much to organize the medium in a way that made its use feasible on a national basis.

In 1891 came the electric sign to add a new and important facet to the outdoor medium. Electric lights had been put to signboard uses before, but only in connection with places of business—mainly theaters and hotels. Advertiser acceptance was swift and immediate and the "Great White Way" was one of the night sights of New York by 1893. A marvelous invention had made it possible to spell out the message in "letters of fire" and the large cities at night presented a carnival of lighted information about baby foods, pickles, cigars, newspapers and many other items. Especially active in the development of electrical displays was O. J. Gude, who came to be known as the "father of the Great White Way."

UP to 1888 there had been virtually no street-car advertising aside from the announcements of local merchants, owing largely to physical conditions within the car itself. But the bowing of the horse car to electric power provided a vast impetus in the next five years. In 1890 there were 1,617 miles of electric car service to 5,713 for horse cars. By 1893 Dobbin had yielded his majority, falling below 5,000 miles while the electric lines had increased to over 7,000.

The electric car not merely displaced the power of the horse, but vastly increased the extent of this mode of transportation and thereby stepped up the car-card audience. Moreover, electric cars, being far more comfortable and better lighted, improved the conditions for the presence of the advertising message. The car card offered a better value to the advertiser.

The first recorded use of the street cars as an advertising facility was in the 1860's, when the Babbitt soap people began using them on the Third Avenue line in New York, then the most populous route. The early cards were usually painted signs, often left for long periods of accumulation of dirt and illegibility. The announcement was customarily stuck straight up and down or at an angle where the side of the car met the ceiling. To lengthen its readable life, the idea of glass covered frames was introduced, and although this was effective from the standpoint of preservation, the element of light reflection frequently made the message difficult to read.

The curved rack, introduced by the street-car advertising firm of Carleton & Kissam (later George Kissam & Company) was another important step forward. It increased the value of the cards perhaps 75 per cent and did much to popularize the use of the medium among national advertisers.

A continuing difficulty in the early 1890's, however, was the labor involved in using the medium on a national basis. A considerable proportion of the car advertising facilities was in the hands of street-car men, rather than advertising men, and they had little conception of what advertising was supposed to do or how it might be applied to the advertiser's problem. Aside from George Kissam's efforts, there was little attempt to make the medium easy to use over any considerable area of the country. The advertiser often had to deal with each car company in each town, although there were a few group units covering section territories ranging up to an entire State. Organized presentation of the car card as an advertising medium was still to come.

THROUGH the great part of its national life the republic had been primarily an agricultural society. Urbanization and the rise of manufacturing began to lessen the dominant importance of agriculture in the latter half of the nineteenth century. Nevertheless the farmer has continued as a major factor in the national scheme, and, though his importance may have decreased relative to that of other economic groups, his absolute importance as a market for goods had scarcely begun before the last fifty years.

The farm press had its beginnings in the earliest days of the nation, but it was a good many years finding its rightful place in the lives of its readers. The early farm papers were little more than compilations of miscellaneous reading matter. Shortly before the Civil War, appeared the concept that a farm paper ought to talk about farm life and farm business and with that its influence began to expand. Orange Judd applied this formula to the *American Agriculturist* and the paper took the circulation lead in the late 1860's with a total of over 100,000. Among the distinguished early papers were Luther Tucker's *Country Gentleman*, a consolidation of the old *Genesee Farmer* and *The Cultivator; The Southern Planter*; D. D. T. Moore's *Rural New Yorker; Prairie Farmer*; and *New England Farmer.*

As with other publications, the greatest growth came with the new facilities for production of printed matter. Coincidentally came important events affecting the economic position of the farmer, which naturally were reflected in improved opportunities for the farm press.

By 1890 the total number of farms in the United States had reached 4,654,641 as the result of continual pressing forward against the Western frontiers. Their aggregate value was $13,279,252,649 and approximately half the country's population lived on farms.

The farmer was supposed to be largely self-sufficient, apart from his need for farm tools, so far as manufactured goods were concerned. And so, to a degree he was, but by geographical necessity rather than personal inclination. Moreover his supply of the wherewithal with which to buy goods was increasing, despite cyclical setbacks, through expansion of the national population, export trade and more efficient farm equipment and methods.

The farm paper as a market place for merchandise was pretty much limited to mail-order selling during the greater part of the 1800's. The farmer was relatively remote from the sources of supply of manufactured goods, or rather the manufacturer was remote from the retailers in the rural areas. But in the latter quarter of the century the

1892

CHARLES E. DURYEA builds the first gasoline-driven motor vehicle at Springfield, Mass. . . . Widespread labor unrest. . . . Supreme Court upholds act of Congress barring lotteries from the use of the mails. . . . Grover Cleveland elected to his second term as president.

Daniel M. Lord and Ambrose L. Thomas incorporate the long-established firm of Lord & Thomas. . . . Retailers complaining about the low margin on advertised articles. . . . Chicago *Tribune* establishes its own Eastern advertising office. . . . Halftone beginning to come into general use. . . . Advertisement: "Have you $1 and have you piles? Send us your dollar and we'll cure your piles. Or keep your $1 and keep your piles."

"The commonplace is the proper level for writing in business; in business, where the first virtue is plainness, 'fine writing' is not only intellectual, it is offensive"—John E. Powers. . . . Sweet Caporal the leading cigarette. . . . Nobody has appendicitis, wears white shoes, sprays orchards or cares about the price of gasoline. . . . John Adams Thayer and Thomas Balmer join *Ladies' Home Journal*. . . . Carpet sweeper advertised as the perfect Christmas gift.

railroads and other methods of communication began to narrow this gap and manufacturers began to use advertising to narrow it further.

By 1894 it was noticeable that the farm press was gaining in importance and circulation. It was now offering well-digested summaries of important current news as well as farm articles of a higher informative quality. It was defeating the weekly editions of the city newspapers in the competition for rural patronage by virtue of its improved, up-to-date tone.

In that year were published 189 farm papers with a per issue circulation of 3,053,457. *Farm Journal, Farm & Fireside, Farm & Home* boasted circulations in the hundreds of thousands. In the West aggressive papers of relatively recent founding like *Iowa Homestead, Hoard's Dairyman, Dakota Farmer, Breeder's Gazette* and *Wisconsin Agriculturist* came into prominence. The foundations for much greater growth were being laid. In the next ten years that expansion was to more than double the total farm-paper circulation; an important factor being the arrival of rural free delivery at the end of the century.

As a consequence of the development of the late '80's and early '90's, advertisers of general lines came to join the seed companies, farm implement firms and mail-order sellers in the advertising columns of the farm press. By 1895 these included dry goods, shoes, cocoa, soap, tobacco, books and other items.

By 1895 the business paper had struggled up from an obscure and not especially distinguished past to a position of importance and respectability.

The odds had been tremendous. The old-time business man believed in maintaining a veil of secrecy over all his movements. He was extremely jealous of competitors and the idea of publishing news concerning the flow of business was not at all relished. The pioneer business publishers had no easy time.

In the very earliest days the business periodical was represented by a handful of journals of broad editorial scope. A single paper, for example, would cover all phases of mechanical matters, another every type of manufacturing product. Lists of topics were comprehensive.

Then came new papers which addressed themselves to some specific branch of business which seemed inadequately served by the more general publications. Publications dealing with railroads, carriages, the leather business and dry goods were early in the field, the first being *American Railroad Journal*, begun in 1832 and published today as the *Railway Mechanical Engineer*.

The specialized business paper was the outgrowth of an endeavor of the "wholesale man," or manufacturer, to find his customer in a more direct manner than was possible through the daily newspaper, and it took the rudimentary form of putting his wares under the customers' eyes in an advertising circular to which was attached a thread of reading matter on some subject that might interest the readers. In other words, it was simply a house organ.

Some few newspaper men, usually of limited means and experience, took up the idea of publishing papers of their own. The conditions were not favorable for attraction of the best talent and the

48

ACME

ALLIS-CHALMERS

1888 — ADVERTISERS — 1938

AMERICAN BRASS

A. T. & T.

BABCOCK & WILCOX

BARBER-COLMAN

BETHLEHEM

BICKFORD DRILL

BRILL

BROWN & SHARPE

BUFFALO FORGE

BULLARD

CHAPMAN VALVE

CRANE

CROMPTON & KNOWLES

CUSHMAN CHUCK

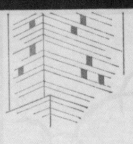

NAMES

that are

BUY WORDS

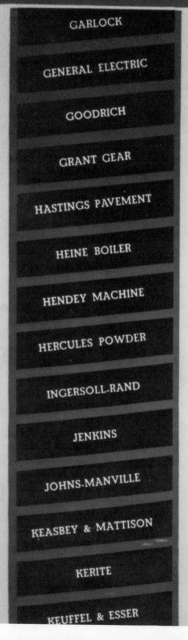

DENVER FIRE CLAY

DIXON CRUCIBLE

GARLOCK

GENERAL ELECTRIC

GOODRICH

GRANT GEAR

HASTINGS PAVEMENT

HEINE BOILER

HENDEY MACHINE

HERCULES POWDER

INGERSOLL-RAND

JENKINS

JOHNS-MANVILLE

KEASBEY & MATTISON

KERITE

KEUFFEL & ESSER

● More pay envelopes for workers — more dividend checks for stockholders — more cash reserves against adverse times — the best in salesmanship — the means to stabilize sales through diversification of customers and products —

— such are the obvious rewards of persistent advertising, achieved by these examples from hundreds of advertisers that have appeared persistently in the eight oldest McGraw-Hill publications through the past fifty-year cycle.

●

And in later McGraw-Hill publications, similarly strong names are similarly achieving — similarly adding to the national welfare —

Truly the rewards of persistent advertising reach deeply into American life.

LIDGERWOOD

LINK-BELT

a BUY WORD *it means:*

LOCKE INSULATOR

LODGE & SHIPLEY

LUDLOW VALVE

LUNKENHEIMER

MASON-NEILAN

MORSE TWIST DRILL

NICHOLSON FILE

NILES TOOL WORKS

OESTERLEIN

OKONITE

OTIS ELEVATOR

PHELPS-DODGE

PRATT & WHITNEY

RAYBESTOS

During the past 50 years leading business papers have faithfully reported the special news of business — dug deeply for the new in technical and economic developments and courageously attacked the forces of reaction within and without business — and through their advertising columns have built great names.

We are happy to acknowledge to Printers' Ink Weekly their editorial leadership and the contribution that paper has made through its advertising columns to the building of the name —

McGRAW-HILL

ROEBLINGS

SACO-LOWELL

NOT A GREAT AGGREGATION OF PUBLICATION
BUT AN AGGREGATION OF GREAT PUBLICATION

SELLERS

SIMPLEX WIRE

STANDARD OIL

STANDARD TOOL

STARRETT

ST. LOUIS CAR

STURTEVANT

SIMONDS SAW

TAYLOR-WHARTON

U. S. RUBBER

WARNER & SWASEY

WESTINGHOUSE

WESTON

WORTHINGTON

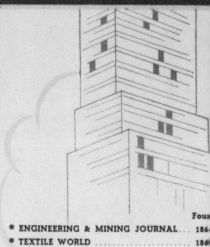

McGraw-Hill Publishing Co., Inc.
330 West 42nd Street
New York, N. Y.

possibilities of the field were not recognized. Business journals were looked upon as a luxury and support was to be had only through cultivating the vanity of manufacturers. Facts were ignored in favor of windy write-ups given in return for advertising contracts. The business paper was still a house organ, though published by proxy.

Gradually these publishers, or wiser men who succeeded them, came to learn the practical disadvantages of servility and slowly the fawning clipsheet gave way to the paper that stood on its own independent feet. It was seen that success depended upon bona fide circulation, which in turn rested with favoring the reader in terms of progressive and fearless news-gathering methods. Though the publisher who remained with his face turned toward the advertiser was still in the majority in 1890—and has not entirely disappeared to this day—the business paper which stood as the exponent of progress and guardian of sound practice in the trade it represented had made its mark.

From twenty-five papers in 1869 (half of them insurance and real estate) the field grew to nearly 800 by 1897. There were papers covering every available branch of business enterprise, from rolling mills to barbers, from shipbuilders to undertakers. In 1891 *Iron Age* had come from a three-sheet paper in 1855 to a seventy-page journal of business news. *Electrical World* was said to have made a profit of $120,000 in 1893. Higher quality of editorial writing, better type, better illustrations and better paper had been adopted by many of the publications.

The business paper was still in its formative days at this period. Its advertising, on the whole, was notoriously bad because advertisers had not been brought to see the importance of making it good. But men like David Williams, John A. Hill, James H. McGraw and Charles T. Root were at work and there was no longer doubt that the business journal had become a factor in the life of trade, rather than a parasite upon it.

IN the early eighties a change took place in theater programs. Single sheet playbills became pamphlets that carried advertising. Theater managers even in those days were advertising minded to a high degree—were, in fact, proportionately the most active advertisers in any given community. Many of the posting plants of the present day actually were born in the business offices of theaters; for theaters were the largest consumers of outdoor advertising in its infancy.

Theater programs soon came into the hands of people who recognized the real possibilities of the consistent spending circulation offered by playhouses all over the country. Development in keeping with the modern trend of advertising followed. One company in New York founded in 1884, carried this development on to magazine proportions.

IN the matter of printed material circulated by the advertiser himself there was relatively little development worthy of note at this period.

Not a few circulars were used, but for the most part they were wretchedly conceived and printed. The advertiser's main idea was to put them out as cheaply as possible.

A large proportion of the circulars was distributed by the house-to-house method. In almost every city and town there was a local distributor specializing in this work. The chief patrons were the medicine companies.

Booklets were used by some advertisers to supplement their publication advertising. These were called "primers" and were supposed to answer the questions likely to arise in the mind of the reader of the advertisements. Since the publication advertisements said little, there was plenty for the primers to do, but most of them were half-hearted efforts. However, as has been noted, the railroads were doing some really high-class work along this line.

Perhaps the greatest single exponent of well-planned printed matter was the National Cash Register Company, which depended almost entirely upon this form of advertising. The firm issued many booklets and folders and devoted considerable time and expense to continual improvement of them. Every piece carried a return card keyed by color and wording and the results which it brought were always closely checked. ·

Most lines of business put out a catalog of some kind, but these efforts, too, were in a primitive stage, both as to sales planning and quality of mechanical production. The chief users were the machinery companies, the seed companies and, of course, the mail-order companies. Even the catalogs of the latter, which represented their main sales weapon, had advanced but little. Illustrations were just coming into use and consisted mainly of crude wood-cuts. The catalog at this stage was little more than a price list and embodied no real sales appeal.

The house organ, as ancestor of the magazine and the business paper, was one of the earliest forms of printed publication. But it had not come very far since its beginning stages. One spark of life was the appearance in 1895 of the house organ based on the comic journals which were popular in the general publication field at the time. A company was formed to sell "patent insides" of comic material, often by well-known writers in the regular journals, for inclusion in the house-organ editions put out by manufacturers. Some companies adopted the comic technique for their own and built their house organs around pictures and text which satirized the weaknesses of rival concerns.

· On the whole, the evolution of direct mail and printed material lagged far behind the advertising procession. The reason apparently was that the printer was a mechanical man and his sales effort consisted of taking orders. The advertiser was left to sell himself, and he was largely pre-occupied with exploration of the fascinations of publication advertising. There was virtually no creative selling by the printer and no outside selling force took up his cause, as had the general agents and special agents for the newspapers and magazines. It was to be many years before the printer took up aggressive and constructive selling of his wares and until then the medium did not come into its own. ·

Agents in Transition

THE task of getting word through to the consumer was still a fairly difficult one in the early days of modern advertising, particularly in respect to the printed word in publications. Reaching a large number of people at a reasonable cost was an incredibly complex process, owing to the elusive indefiniteness of publication rate structures and the meager availability of trustworthy information on circulations.

The development of the services of the general advertising agency in such a way as to provide constructive assistance on these matters did much to make possible the planned and systematic use of advertising For many years this evolutionary process had been slow.

The first advertising agent was Volney B. Palmer, who began business in Philadelphia in 1841 and later extended his operations to Boston, New York and Baltimore. An almost simultaneous pioneer was John Hooper, who started business in New York in the early 1840's.

Palmer was a true agent of the publisher. He solicited business from advertisers and in return for his services received a 25 per cent commission from the papers in which the business was placed. Insofar as possible, Palmer endeavored to be the exclusive agent for the papers he represented. In many instances he was successful in this. But the lucrative new business soon made its appeal to others and before long there was considerable competition in the field. Most publishers saw no drawback in accepting any business that came to them, whatever the source,

and soon the exclusive representative idea disappeared almost entirely. The agents represented all papers without previous agreement.

In 1865 George P. Rowell set out his shingle as an advertising agent in Boston with an idea that revolutionized the business. He introduced the "list system" whereby he contracted with a number of papers to buy a large amount of space for the entire year, then turned around and sold the space in smaller units to advertisers. Since he was able to get a lower price by his quantity purchases, he could undersell other agents. Soon the business began to shape itself to the idea of acting as a wholesale dealer in advertising space.

The plan found its way to application to other media besides newspapers. In 1869 N. W. Ayer & Son in Philadelphia, and in the 1870's Lord & Thomas in Chicago, and Carlton & Smith in New York established lists of religious papers, then a very popular medium. In 1878 J. Walter Thompson took over Carlton & Smith and secured exclusive control of the advertising space in practically all the leading magazines, a move whereby Thompson became a principal factor in the development of magazine advertising.

Although the "list system" dominated the agent's practice for twenty-five years and continued as somewhat of a factor even in the 1890's, it was relatively ephemeral. But in setting up this plan Rowell created another concept of the agent's trade which was to influence profoundly its entire future development. In addition to the

1873··

The News Building in 1873.

The Detroit News

$6,000 Seized by Jewelry Store Bandits
York and Gehringer Clout Homers

··1938

Fifteen years before Printers' Ink pioneered a trade organ of inestimable value, James Edmund Scripps founded The Detroit News. 1873 was a year not very different from the present. The country was in the midst of one of its worst depressions. The Jay Cooke failure nearly swamped the little paper. Advertisers were few and had no cash, but Mr. Scripps threw all his worldly possessions into his enterprise and evolved policies and principles which have made The Detroit News to this day the home newspaper of the community.

In looking over the files 25 years later it is notable that The News was already the leading advertising medium in Detroit. Two of the advertisers who used this paper then are among the first ten advertisers in Detroit today; one is the first advertiser in Detroit and ranks with the leaders of the country both as advertiser and merchant.

Since 1873 it has paid to advertise in The Detroit News—a newspaper founded on courage.

The Detroit News

THE HOME NEWSPAPER

New York: I. A. Klein, Inc. • *Chicago: J. E. Lutz*

low price which he obtained from the papers by buying in quantities, he bespoke the established agent's commission of 25 per cent and a cash discount of 3 per cent. *In return, Rowell agreed to stand responsible for the bill and guaranteed payment whether he got anything from the advertiser or not.*

Thus the advertising agent ceased to be a representative of the publisher and became a principal, an independent contractor.

The growth of the "patent inside" and the appearance of the special agent in the 1870's contributed to the ultimate doom of the "list system." That fate was hastened and made certain by the introduction of the "open contract" plan of operation by N. W. Ayer & Son. By this method Ayer agreed to get the advertiser the lowest price it could and pass on to the advertiser the benefits of its bargaining ability and the commissions received, the advertiser to pay Ayer a percentage on the net.

In his first phase the agent had worked for the publisher. In the second he worked for himself, disposing of a commodity which he controlled. As the list system disappeared in favor of some adaptation of the Ayer idea, a new phase started. The agent appeared in the 1880's as an impartial negotiator who stood between the advertiser and the publisher.

The agent stood to the advertiser in the position of a broker, inasmuch as he did not generally undertake to contract with him that the advertising should be done in the publications, but merely attempted to get it done if he could on the conditions and at the price named.

He stood also in the position of a principal, in that he secured payment and personally guaranteed it to the publisher.

He acted as an assistant to the publisher in that he saw that the advertising was placed under the required conditions.

For the first time the agent had become an instrumentality who operated in an important degree in the interest of the advertiser. He no longer dealt primarily in what he already owned, nor performed in the employment of the seller, but acted to serve the buyer's interest in getting a low price. He found his profit not in the spread between the rate he paid the publisher and the rate he charged the advertiser, but in the commission from the publisher or a fee from the advertiser. The new way of doing business and the steady growth of competition was causing the agent to act more and more as a salesman of the principle of advertising. His future now lay in getting manufacturers already using this selling medium to use more of it and in finding new advertisers. Hence the publisher, despite the fact the agent was no longer directly in his service, was content to continue the payment of commission in recognition of these broader services.

That view was by no means universal, however. During the 1890's the agitation against paying commissions was a subject of much stirring argument at publishers' conventions, and the discontent was especially intense among the smaller papers. Pressed by competitors and aided by the absence of any real understanding anywhere of the value of advertising space, many agents battered down rates mercilessly in their fervor to get business by serving the advertiser's economical instincts. There were many irresponsible agents and many unable financially to carry out their full obligations to the publisher, while at the same time publishers had not got the idea of looking into credit matters and accepted business from any who offered it. But despite the abuses and some unfortunate experiences, the larger papers, most of them, remained convinced of the value of the agent's services in selling advertising generally and in taking responsibility for payment. The commission stood fast under this storm and the others that were to follow.

Much of the fault for the agents' practices relative to rates went back, as a few publishers saw, to the publication's own practice. There were three classes of papers with respect to rates. The first was those with an undeviating fixed schedule of charges. This group in 1890 could not be said to number as much as 1 per cent of all papers—men like Victor Lawson of the Chicago *Daily News,* Charles Jones of the New York *Times,* a young fellow named Adolph S. Ochs, who published the Chattanooga *Times,* Cyrus Curtis and a handful of others stood almost alone in adhering to their established rates. The second group consisted of those who deviated little except when the contract was especially desirable because of its amount or character. The third and by far largest was made up of those who would accept the best terms they could get, in money, marbles or chalk. With these the question of commission was often academic, since the agent could still find a profit in beating prices below his estimate to the advertiser. One root of the trouble was that

many publishers, having no understanding of advertising space except that if it wasn't filled they'd have to suffer the shame of putting out a small issue, regarded any receipt as clear profit. Another was that not one rate card in 500 was so arranged that an advertiser, agent or even the publisher himself could figure out a reasonable price on a given piece of business.

But the most penetrating factor of all was the almost complete absence of trustworthy figures on the size of the consumer audience the advertiser could get for his money. Not a few publishers refused to give out any information whatever, even in the 1890's. Most others exaggerated their figures with impressive nonchalance. This was partly the result of the practices of dishonest proprietors who told shameless lies about their distribution, and forced others in self-defense to stretch things a bit; partly the product of the general business doctrine of the time that nobody had a right to pry into somebody else's business secrets. At any rate a claimed circulation of 20,000 might mean a print order of 2,000 and a paying clientele which could be detected only under a magnifying glass. Consequently the whole basis of the price for advertising space—which in the mind of the advertiser at that time was entirely a matter of quantity—was highly elusive.

There were a few voices in the wilderness, notably that of W. J. Richards, co-founder of the Indianapolis *News,* who cried: "In the whole range of the world's wide commerce, advertising space is the only commodity which refuses the purchaser test proof of the measure given." It was Richard's contention, stated in 1889, that the right

RESEARCH
1888
1938

THE first issue of Printers' Ink fifty years ago did not mention market research. Marketing then was a local issue. Products were customary staples. Dealers (even manufacturers) knew their customers.

Marketing in 1938 is different – on a broader, national scale. The personal contact between maker and buyer is altered. Competition for markets is keener. The manufacturer who knows local market facts has the advantage.

So market research grows. Advertisers must have facts upon which to plan.

Recognition of the need for **facts** about the New

York market led The Times to organize its market research department. The use advertisers make of its findings shows that facts are wanted.

What The Times research department does is this — it finds out from retailers how advertised products sell in this market. In its first year, the department made over 20,000 calls. Its method and procedure is constantly checked by Dr. George Gallup, one of the country's foremost research authorities. Its findings have been severely checked by skeptical advertisers against their own knowledge — and have been proved, in some instances, to be accurate to within one-half of 1 per cent.

Out of all this mass of fact about the New York market, one fundamental principle of successful selling has emerged — that **advertised products, regardless of price, sell fastest where family purchasing power is high.** And in New York there are enough above-average-income families to make up a **volume** market — the one most easily and most profitably sold.

Knowing this — and knowing also that The Times reaches and sells more above-average families than any other medium — advertisers should find the next fifty years of marketing in New York a lot easier than the last fifty years — and a lot more profitable! The New York Times is always glad to help in any way it can — with **selling** facts, with a **buying** market.

The New York Times

"ALL THE NEWS THAT'S FIT TO PRINT"

of the advertiser to know the measure of his purchase is axiomatic. That hoary evil of the counting-room, false statements of circulation, furnishes the loudest demand for the rate practices of the advertising agent, he asserted. And until the circulation liar was run out of business there could be no stable rates.

Richards was perhaps the first of the publishers to speak out aggressively on a viewpoint which had previously found support only among the agents and the advertisers, and many of those rather liked the barter conditions. As one of the strongest figures in the journalism of the day, he made a considerable impression, though progress was slow for many years after.

Another important contribution was made by the San Francisco *Examiner*, first newspaper property of William Randolph Hearst. Through the energetic efforts of the *Examiner*, the California legislature in 1893 passed a bill enabling any advertiser having reason to doubt the circulation of a paper to bring the publisher into court and make him produce proofs. The bill had been introduced three years earlier but defeated in response to strenu-

1893

WORLD'S Columbian Exposition at Chicago formally opened by President Cleveland. . . . Gold reserve falls below $100,000,000, precipitating a panic. . . . Free postal delivery extended to rural communities. . . . The Cherokee Strip between Kansas and Oklahoma purchased by U. S. for $8,595,-736.12. . . . First "billion dollar" Congress adjourns.

Special agents assert business of the general advertising agencies has never been so dull as at present. . . . New York has forty-nine dailies, Chicago twenty-seven, Philadelphia twenty-two, St. Louis twelve, Boston eleven, Baltimore eight. . . . Pictures of theatrical stars being widely used in advertisements of railroads, dentifrices, cigars and medicines. . . . W. R. Hearst's World's Fair edition of the San Francisco *Examiner*, largest issue of a daily ever published, creates a sensation—120 pages, 500,000 copies, $70,000 worth of advertising. . . . Elbert Hubbard leaves Larkin Soap Company to establish the Roycroft Shop.

"The more I see of advertising, the more I am convinced of the efficacy of the 'plain tale' "—Lewis B. Jones (who this year joins the Eastman Kodak Company). . . . Frank B. White organizes an agricultural advertising agency at Chicago. . . . "The weekly illustrated magazine *Life* is a great success." . . . Agent's commission cut in some quarters from 25 to 20 per cent. . . . 259 publications of all kinds have a circulation over 25,000. . . . Dawn-of-a-new-day note: "The divorce lawyers all agree—and the evidence proves it—that there is no business for them in families that use Kirk's American Family Soap."

ous opposition by many of the other publishers in the State.

In a sense the agent's operations in seeking low rates had a measurable effect upon the final acceptance of the premise of true circulation statements, but another activity was even more important. This was the directory of publications. The first one was established by Rowell, who brought out volume one of the American Newspaper Directory (the term "newspaper" at that time covered all classes of publications) in 1869. It was a step in a direction whither no path had ever led. So meager was the knowledge of publications at that time that a mere list of the names of newspapers was a prized asset of an advertising agency. Rowell not only published such a list for public access, but undertook to penetrate the riddle of circulation estimates of the total distribution of the publications.

So important did the consideration of circulation accuracy become that in 1878 Rowell undertook to guarantee the accuracy of the circulation figures given in the directory. He invited publishers to submit signed statements of their circulations, on the thesis that a man would avoid putting his signature to a false figure. As an added precaution he set up a standing reward of $100 for disproof of such figures. Occasionally the reward was claimed—it was paid in five instances during one year—but on the whole the premise held good. However, the majority of publishers refused such signed reports and for many years most of the circulation data represented Rowell's estimates. But the consciousness of the value of guaranteed ratings grew and in 1888 these reports were much more numerous.

Other agents began to publish directories of their own soon after Rowell's beginning, the best being those of N. W. Ayer and Lord & Thomas. In 1890 there were fourteen such catalogs. They often disagreed on individual estimates and there was considerable rivalry among the sponsors as to whose was the most accurate, but the volumes did much to create a demand for and understanding of the value of true circulation figures.

In the first period of the development of modern advertising, then, the agent's principal service to the advertiser was the possession of a good list of publications and their circulations, and the knowledge and bargaining ability to get the lowest possible rates. As a subsidiary but often important claim for consideration, he relieved the advertiser of the details of placing orders, mailing electrotypes and checking papers. With the cash results to the advertiser he had little if any direct concern.

As a rule, the system worked by the advertiser sending a list of papers to a number of agencies to secure their estimates. The lowest bidder got the contract. In the 1880's the agent would often guarantee his price. But publishers soon perceived that the agent had bound himself by contract and that to obtain a big price all that was necessary was to name a high figure and refuse to move from it. And so the negotiating principle took firm hold and the wiser agents rarely undertook to contract for set prices in this way unless the advertiser was an inexperienced one and it was thought he could be switched to a weaker publication in case of trouble.

In 1893 it could be said that the

101 Preferred Brand
the Productivity of

In The News First Consumer Analysis of the Indianapolis market, consumers told their brand preferences in 101 lines of merchandise. Checking the advertising which the 101 top-ranking brands have used in this sales territory during the past five years, it is found that

95

HAVE USED NEWSPAPERS

Such a record is truly a tribute to the effectiveness of newspaper advertising.

Ask a News representative for full details of this analysis of Indianapolis' 101 Leading Brands.

THE INDIANAPOLIS NEWS

New York: Dan A. Carroll   Chicago: J. E. L⁚
110 E. 42nd St.   180 N. Michigan A⁚

in Indianapolis Prove
Newspaper Advertising!

A Remarkable Selling Record!

Of the 95 Brands Using Newspaper Advertising

91

used The Indianapolis News

72

used more space in The News than in any other Indianapolis newspaper

When America's most successful advertisers show such overwhelming preference for ONE advertising medium—their opinion can and should be accepted by <u>all</u> advertisers as a precedent for profitable advertising investment.

general agency business was on a fairly sound basis. There were fewer failures, not because the agents were making more money, but because they were exacting prompt payments and taking small risks. There were perhaps 300 such firms in the country.

In general the volume of business was increasing, yet there was developing a trend that was somewhat disturbing to those in the trade. Some advertisers, particularly the larger ones, were beginning to entertain the idea that the advertising agent, as a middleman, was an expensive luxury. Perhaps they could get just as good information and just as low prices as he could and save the fee. The greatest of the newspaper advertisers, Royal Baking Powder, was already doing just that and others sought to follow suit.

In some effort to counteract this tendency many agencies began rebating a part of the commission to the advertiser. Of the total rate, which varied, but was 25 per cent in most instances, the agent began to keep only 15 per cent for himself, sometimes as low as 5 per cent. In 1891 it was considered that the advertiser who did not get a share of the commission was not up to snuff.

This in turn produced a greater willingness on the part of publishers to pay the agent's commission to the advertiser who placed his business direct. It was felt that if the advertiser did the agent's work of buying space, he was entitled to the agent's wage. The agent's practice of rebating, in fact, forced the publisher who maintained a fixed rate structure into this policy. In effect the agent was cutting under the publisher's prices and demoralizing

his rate structure. Having so many agents on his books and despairing of dissuading all of them from the objectionable practice, the publisher adopted it himself and allowed the commission to the advertiser who applied direct.

In 1894 one agent observed that 999 in every 1,000 publishers allowed the agent's commission to the advertiser who demanded it. Without exception every one of the special advertising agents in New York made such allowances in behalf of the publishers they represented. The only known exceptions were the *Ladies' Home Journal* and the Chicago *Daily News*, both of which refused to yield even to the mighty Royal Baking Powder Company.

One immediate result was that the advertiser would go to the agent for an estimate on an advertising contract with the intention not of placing the business through the agent, but of employing it to place advertising more advantageously by direct contact with the publisher. In these instances the agent secured a fee for the data. Many thought the future course of the general agency lay in selling this advisory service to established advertisers, with its placing services limited to such new advertisers as it could sell on using advertising.

And so while the general agent in the period 1888-95 was better equipped to serve the advertiser than he had ever been before, his outlook for future expansion did not seem exactly bright. The direct advertiser and the special agent were cutting seriously into his source of revenue. To some it seemed that the day of the general agent must ultimately end in reverting to the functions of the special agent who exclusively repre-

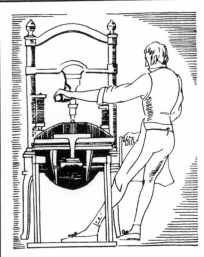

107 Years of Advertising

THIS issue of Printers' Ink is a study of advertising's progress over a half century.

The first advertisement that appeared in The Detroit Free Press, May 5, 1831, read:

"WANTED — A quick and accurate accountant who writes a good hand. Inquire at this office."

Written 107 years ago, it is still *good copy*. Moods and modes in advertising change, but basic principles do not. And this newspaper is presumptuous enough to believe that sane and sound principles of journalism with definite ideals and goals for public service are still good newspaper sense and business acumen. On that premise The Detroit Free Press has thrived for over a century, and the pace of its growth now in a rapidly shifting world is accelerating, which is important news for advertising at any time.

The Detroit Free Press

VERREE & CONKLIN, Inc., National Representatives

Member Metropolitan Sunday Newspapers, Inc. and Greater Midwest Gravure Group

sented a limited list of newspapers.

But here and there signs were appearing of an entirely new direction for the general agent's activities, signs that were little noted at the time and whose tremendous importance was not generally perceived. The general agent had entered a period not of gradual extinction but of transition toward a greater usefulness than had ever before been his.

New Kodak Cameras.

"You press the button, we do the rest."

(OR YOU CAN DO IT YOURSELF.)

Seven New Styles and Sizes

ALL LOADED WITH

Transparent Films.

For Sale by all Photo. Stock Dealers.   Send for Catalogue

THE EASTMAN COMPANY, Rochester, N. Y.

Far removed from today's attractive advertising, Kodak in the Nineties frequently confined itself to reminder copy

A China Egg may fool even the Hen, but it makes a mighty poor Omelet.

"FORCE" has been widely copied—in mere *appearance*, but there the likeness ends.

Sunny Jim

When you go to buy butter you're a little suspicious of "bargains", aren't you?
Is there any reason why you should be less particular about the quality and purity of your breakfast food?

Sunny Jim was not always cavorting over fences. Here he takes the rostrum to talk on the evils of substitution. Early days of present century

OLD KING COLE
Was a merry old soul,
A merry old soul was he;
He called for his bowl,
He called for his pipe,
He called for his S's three.

This old king was a jolly man, because he was healthy. He was healthy because he kept his blood pure. In these days it is easy not only for kings, but for the humblest subjects to keep their blood in good condition by the use of S. S. S.

All early patent-medicine advertising was not so unobjectionable as this

The Special Delivers

IN the general advertising agent the publisher had, as has been seen, a sort of free-lance salesman who undertook to represent all papers impartially. The development away from exclusive representation which had appertained with some of the earliest agents had left the publisher without anyone to represent his interests directly. Hence he had little control over his rates and business methods so far as "foreign" advertising was concerned.

To fill this need appeared the special advertising agent, who was in reality a reincarnation of such pioneer advertising agents as Palmer and Hooper, taking up as exclusive representative of the publisher where they had left off. He was first and last the agent of the publisher, as he is today, but in serving his publisher employer he rendered distinguished service for the advertiser in straightening out the channels for efficient flow of advertising.

The first special agent anywhere was J. J. Richardson, traveling representative for the Davenport, Iowa, *Democrat*. The first to establish a list of papers and operate in the manner of the modern publisher's representative—as the special agent is commonly called today —were Leander H. Crall and E. B. Mack. They were followed shortly by F. T. McFadden and J. E. Van Doren. Soon thereafter came S. C. Beckwith, who began in 1880 and moved quickly to the front rank; and in 1882 A. Frank Richardson, nephew of J. J. Richardson. A fascinating and dramatic character, Richardson became known as "the king of the advertisers" in the newspaper trade. In Chicago Henry DeClerque led the way in 1887. In 1888 Emanuel Katz came to New York to represent a list of Pacific Coast newspapers—the beginning of the Katz Agency of today—and S. C. Williams moved East from the business managership of the St. Paul *Pioneer Press* to found the firm now known as Williams, Lawrence & Cresmer.

From here on the ranks grew rapidly. By 1893 the number of well-organized firms in New York had grown from scarcely more than a dozen to about fifty, representing 250 papers. Farm papers, magazines and a few business papers had come to recognize the value of this type of representation and special agents representing these types of publications are included in this total. By 1895 the development of the business was well under way in Chicago, as Western advertising increased with the coming of Fairbank, Armour, Swift, Cudahy and others into large-scale advertising activity. Several magazines and a few Eastern newspapers were being represented in Chicago. Ultimately, of course, the special agent's field of activities came to embrace twelve important cities from Coast to Coast.

Owing to the intense trading rivalry among the general agents occasioned by growth of competition, little effective support for the establishment of stable rate structures was forthcoming from that quarter. The publisher himself, who was inclined to look on "foreign" advertising revenue as gravy, didn't contribute much to the advancement of the idea—with exceptions, of course. It was here that the special agent made his contribution. He was a principal chief influence in placing the handling of national advertising on a stable, rational and businesslike basis.

Many of the early special agents contracted to handle all the accounts outside the paper's home territory. In some cases they guaranteed the publisher a lump sum each month or a definite increase in revenue for the year. Some of them did their own billing and collecting, but they all looked after the accounts due and they got the money, sending the publishers a vast sum which never would have been collected otherwise. Some established their own rate cards. If the publisher got an order direct from the general agent it had to be sent back to the special agent for his approval and acceptance, a practice which the general agents did not relish and caused some to refuse to recognize the special agents.

The special agents brought about the discontinuance of directory advertising and trade deals covering printed material, machinery and other commodities. They encouraged the publisher to eliminate the free reading notices and the granting of special positions without pay. But more than anything else, they were largely responsible for wiping out the slashing of rates and they did this as individuals fighting to build a legitimate business for their publishers and themselves.

Many of them were in the van of the progress toward truthful statements of circulation. A. Frank Richardson, for example, for years carried on a promotional program for his papers, the keynote to which was the slogan, "Known Circulation."

In addition to improving standards of business, the special agent operated importantly in the development of new advertisers. His work was not always without flaw, for he tended to circumscribe in the mind of the advertiser the amount of advertising necessary to success by trying to show that the use of the very papers he represented would insure a thorough advertising job.

None the less in the late 1890's when the general agent was struggling with the problem of service expense and had little margin for soliciting, the special agent went out and dug up a steady flow of new advertisers. He worked with the advertiser, sometimes even helping finance him and when the account reached such size as to occupy too much of his time, would suggest a general agent. As a rule the special agent was closer to the advertiser than was the general agent. He called on the advertiser more frequently and got to know him better.

During the early 1890's the special agent was more or less in competition with the general agent. The publisher naturally tended to favor his services, and besides there was a good deal of feeling among the general agents themselves that the only solution to their destiny and that the whole tangled problem of rates and commissions could be resolved only by reverting to the idea of exclusive representation.

The Moving Finger

AS the means of communicating with the consumer became more efficient and more widely established, the advertiser began for the first time to render an appreciable degree of considered thought to the message he was to deliver.

'Leaving out wall inscriptions of Babylon and Greece and Rome and the town criers of the Middle Ages, advertising was approximately three centuries old. And in three hundred years there had been no essential change in the context of the advertisement. It was simply a vague and brief announcement, couched in general descriptive terms, of what the seller had to offer. The advertisement of the 1880's, with very few and scattered exceptions, differed from its predecessors only to the extent that the general idiom of the language had changed.

Among these exceptions, however, were the seeds of a new appreciation of the importance of what the advertiser had to say. The preparing of advertisements had long been almost exclusively in the hands of the man who bought the space. And then, in reflection of the burgeoning thought that the job might be one requiring special attention, there came into being almost overnight a new trade—the advertising writer.

In 1888 there were two independent advertising writers in all the city of New York. As an example of how business was with them it may be noted that one received his mail in care of the general delivery window and the other could be reached at a 25-cent lodging house in the Bowery. Outside New York the great John E. Powers, who had done some amazing things with the advertisements of John Wanamaker's store in Philadelphia and was already an almost legendary character, was operating. But his activities were confined at this time to retail stores.

There was a slow growth to 1891 when about a half dozen writers of some reputability were offering their services to general advertisers. From this point on the craft mushroomed. By 1894, the "ad-smiths," as was their designation for a time, numbered in the hundreds. It soon seemed that there was an advertising writer at every place where two roads crossed and a few up the country lanes. There was an ad-smith under every spreading chestnut tree. An advertising writers' competition held by PRINTERS' INK in 1896 produced no less than 851 entrants.

Powers was the first advertising writer, judged by the calendar, by achievements and by price. Few if any of his contemporaries came anywhere near him in ability. He was hailed as the "Nestor" of the advertising writers and the father of modern creative advertising. There were two kinds of advertising—"Powers style" and all the rest.

Powers, indeed, set the creative pace. He was the first to get away from the bald, dry announcement. His writing was simple and effective, terse and cogent. And it made interesting, lively reading. That is, the best of it did. Sometimes he tended to get a bit elliptical and abrupt, with the result that his message was somewhat obscure. But most of his copy sparkled with

50 Years Ago

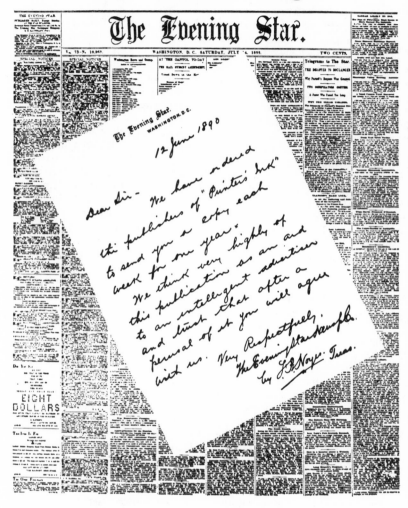

The Evening Star, Washington, D. C., in 1890 ordered several hundred yearly subscriptions to "Printers' Ink" sent to local merchants to aid them in advertising. Today the Star carries more local advertising than any other newspaper in the country.

50 Years Ago

Sworn Statement of the Circulation of The Evening Star, of Washington D.C., for 1888.

Day	Jan	Feb	Mar	Apr	May	June	July	Aug	Sept	Oct	Nov	Dec
1		26,476	26,594		26,344	25,929		25,286	28,660	25,145	26,271	30,284
2	24,148	26,437	26,439	26,091	26,284	30,287	26,149	25,270		25,105	26,136	
3	25,377	26,543	30,635	26,688	26,230		26,485	24,967	24,542	25,058	31,206	27,067
4	25,576	30,129		26,721	26,102	26,001		28,986	25,051	25,304		27,579
5	25,726		25,666	26,590	29,933	26,678	25,697		24,981	25,196	27,756	27,506
6	25,638	26,857	26,402	26,664		26,788	25,843	25,281	24,833	29,306	51,254	27,203
7	29,678	26,441	26,514	30,377	26,027	26,908	29,326	25,068	24,188		33,597	26,872
8		26,620	26,866		26,088	26,442		24,727	28,539	25,285	30,079	30,659
9	25,450	26,315	26,797	26,383	26,042	29,376	25,739	24,959		25,284	28,359	
10	25,808	25,790	31,012	26,412	26,351		25,573	25,056	25,010	25,125	31,996	26,801
11	25,943	30,853		26,427	26,009	26,072	25,603	28,838	25,058	25,279		27,017
12	25,589		26,021	26,630	29,470	26,096	25,847		25,813	25,148	26,839	26,811
13	25,517	26,457	26,702	26,678		26,130	25,973	25,188	25,598	29,565		26,601
14	30,148	26,435	27,289	30,821	25,936	25,869	29,665	25,137	25,208		26,700	26,601
15		26,334	27,321		26,167	26,223		25,119	29,528	25,256	26,741	30,392
16	25,928	26,647	27,026	26,265	26,029	29,588	25,730	24,808		25,322	26,513	
17	25,738	26,461	31,210	26,881	26,033		25,834	24,693	25,064	25,160	30,874	26,228
18	26,041	30,846		27,261	26,212	25,688	25,495	28,718	25,198	25,282		26,866
19	25,795		26,838	26,551	30,259	26,520	25,640		25,088	25,241	26,431	26,930
20	25,938	26,379	26,812	26,455		26,595	25,746	24,820	24,984	29,501	26,802	27,078
21	29,806	26,600	26,226	30,397	26,057	27,100	29,750	24,621	24,895		26,610	26,819
22		25,764	26,436		26,302	28,775		25,026	29,590	25,081	26,595	30,434
23	25,846	26,658	27,253	26,499	26,426	31,611	25,427	24,785		25,072	26,308	
24	26,312	27,624	31,114	26,754	26,500		25,580	24,933	24,899	25,333	30,736	26,828
25	26,198	31,031		26,565	26,345	31,814	25,641	28,671	24,964	25,249		26,525
26	25,934		26,684	26,484	30,154	27,627	25,765		24,921	25,338	25,623	26,525
27	25,826	27,084	26,993	26,291		26,481	25,496	24,756	25,032	29,380	26,603	26,466
28	29,806	26,147	26,740	30,023	26,173	26,517	29,640	25,004	25,077		26,556	26,751
29		26,390	26,831		26,088	26,150		24,856	28,888	26,278		29,699
30	26,324		26,916	26,250	26,765	30,126	25,236	24,839		26,177	27,015	
31	26,261		30,891		26,597		25,644	24,644		26,130		26,815
Total	658,046	679,018	742,228	679,158	721,504	713,906	659,077	689,056	645,604	700,550	720,344	688,792
Av.	26,356	27,161	27,490	27,166	26,722	27,458	26,363	25,521	25,874	25,946	28,814	26,752

Total No. Copies issued: 8,325,283. — No of Days, 310. — Average: 27,082.

City and County of Washington, } ss.
District of Columbia: I solemnly swear that the above is a true and correct statement, as set forth.

F. B. Noyes, Treasurer

Subscribed and sworn to before me this fourth day of January, A.D. 1889.

John ... Clerk, Notary Public.

Sworn statement of circulation of The Evening
Star, Washington, D. C., made by Frank B.
Noyes 50 years ago.

the illuminating simplicity of true advertising genius. Where others merely listed product specifications, if indeed they did so much as that, Powers related the article's advantages to the user's interests.

Advertising was with him not a mere matter of rhetoric, however. His distinctive style was not a mere form of words. The method of the man was behind it. And that method was to study the facts about the product before he wrote a word, to study it with exhaustive thoroughness, to go out in the trade and accumulate facts and ideas, to talk with consumers, to become thoroughly saturated with the subject on hand in every phase.

After some years in which he spent most of his time in the retail field, he offered his services to general advertisers. His terms were stiff. He first of all demanded complete control and would tolerate no interference or dictation. His price was $100 a day for which he promised nothing, that being his retainer fee. He wrote advertising for the Vacuum Oil Company and the George A. Macbeth Company, Scott & Bowne (Scott's Emulsion), Murphy Varnish Company, and numerous others. Among his works for Macbeth was one advertisement that stands comparison with any commercial notice ever written. It reads:

One of the minor troubles of housekeeping is the breaking of lamp-chimneys. Chimneys cost but little apiece, and break but one at a time. You class these little surprises among "mysterious providences," and bear them, meekly resigned.

All wrong! The chimneys are wrong; the glass was ready to pop the minute it cooled.

The maker saved 2 cents on a chimney and put this loss and annoyance on you.

"Pearl-top" chimneys do not break in use.

Great as was the Powers contribution to the technique of producing a good advertising message, it was eclipsed by the significance of his work as a champion of truthfulness. In a time when truth had few friends and practically no outspoken proponents, so far as advertising was concerned, Powers militantly advanced the cause. His sense of honesty was ingrained and he would turn down a fee rather than write something he didn't believe in.

In this connection there is an interesting Powers anecdote of his Wanamaker days. The head of the rubber goods department stopped Powers while he was prowling through the store and asked him to say something about the department in his next advertisement. "Anything particular?" asked Powers.

"Well, between you and me," said the buyer, "we have a lot of rotten gossamers which we wish to get rid of."

"All right, put a memo of what you want on my desk."

A few days later the department head reeled as he saw his advertisement. It read: "We have a lot of rotten gossamers and things we want to get rid of."

The entire lot of rotten gossamers sold that morning and Powers had a fresh example of the value of honesty.

Nathaniel C. Fowler, Jr., achieved notice for his work on the Columbia bicycle advertising and assumed rank as one of the leading writers

Yes,
Readers Commend:

- Rebuilding of eleemosynary institutions and provisions for a trained, adequate personnel.

- Woman's Institute, a week of activities for the housewife and the business woman.

- A season of summer opera in a newly completed outdoor amphitheatre.

- Farm and home improvement contest, embracing 145 counties.

- Fresh Air Fund giving 300 needy boys and girls all-expense vacation at camps.

- Free Swim Meet attracting hundreds of novices and amateurs.

- Soap Box Derby interesting school boys in creative work during summer.

- Spelling Bees in which tens of thousands of city and rural school pupils compete.

★ ★ ★

- The reader confidence ready-built by these projects greets your Kentuckiana advertising campaign, because they were made possible by active support in columns of

The Courier-Journal

THE LOUISVILLE TIMES

NATIONAL REPRESENTATIVES: THE BRANHAM COMPANY

of the day. In 1891 he sold the advertising agency which he had established in Boston subsequent to his bicycle activities in order to devote his entire time to writing advertising—an interesting sidelight on the role the advertising agency of the time played in the production of advertisements.

Fowler was the pioneer proponent of the idea that an advertisement ought to concentrate on some one central point, to advertise one thing at a time and not diffuse its fire. He scorned the prevalent vogue for cleverness. "All this poppycock advertising may look well, and, like the sensational preacher, create a tremendous stir, but the question is: 'Does it sell goods?' " Thus Fowler uttered an eternal fundamental which was virtually rank heresy in his time.

Fowler also produced the first books on the writing of advertising and advertising practice in general. In 1892 he published "Building Business," a handbook on copy and typography, which was followed shortly by the monumental "Fowler's Publicity," a thousand-page work covering in detail all phases of advertising.

In Indianapolis, as the advertising manager of The New York Store, Charles Austin Bates was doing some interesting things. As a contributor to PRINTERS' INK he exhibited a discernment and individuality of style which won him wide attention, and in 1893 he transferred his field of operations to New York. He quickly built up a large clientele among general advertisers and his "ad-writing bureau," as such businesses were often called, was soon the largest of the time.

Bates brought from his retail work the sound premise that advertising is news and to be effective must be presented in a news fashion. The viewpoint itself was news and under his energetic guidance found many followers. Another of his tenets was that the advertiser ought not merely to describe his article, but give reasons for its purchase by the reader. His "Good Advertising," published in 1896, was an important contribution to the literature of the business.

Another bright star among those who hung independent shingles as advertising writers was Wolstan Dixey, who gained fame for his Waterbury watch copy. In Chicago, E. A. Wheatley was the leader. And then there was Charles M. Snyder, a one-time newspaper paragrapher, who worked in Philadelphia writing for Hires root beer and also produced some of the St. Jacobs Oil copy. There were others of competence, of course, but those named were the only ones who achieved any particular prominence.

While Manly M. Gillam did nearly all his work in the retail field, no list of those who contributed to the art of preparing advertising would be complete without his name. It was Gillam's unenviable assignment to follow Powers at the Wanamaker store in Philadelphia and he made a tremendous success in his own right. As administrator of one of the largest advertising appropriations of the time —Wanamaker was said to spend between $300,000 and $400,000 a year —Gillam was a man whose work was to be closely attended. Consequently his sponsorship of the "common-sense," straightforward message had a deep influence on the whole practice of advertising writing.

In 1890 the writing of advertisements was hailed as a coming profession. In 1893 it had won its right to serious consideration and had ceased to be looked upon as a whimsical luxury. The term "adsmith" found its way into the dictionary. But it is to be noted, as proof of the theory that the world really does progress, that the appellation had almost completely disappeared from use by the end of the century. A new term—"copy writer"—began to make its appearance at about that time.

The advertising writer was not an unmixed blessing. Few had qualified experience. Most were prone to use reckless statements and to indulge in exuberant fancy and poetic flights. The grounding of most advertising writers was in the "literary" rather than in business and their chief standards were originality and cleverness.

Another source of impetus to preparing better advertisements came from the publishers. *Youth's Companion* early established a copy-planning department under H. H. and H. S. Sylvester, which gave attention both to writing and typography. The quality of the advertisements appearing in that magazine in the early 1890's was in marked contrast with the average run in other magazines and this activity had an important effect in establishing new standards. In the news-

1894

COXEY'S Army invades Washington. . . . President Cleveland sends Federal troops to Chicago to protect the mails in the Pullman strike. . . . Wheat and cotton reach lowest prices ever recorded—wheat at 54.5 cents, cotton at 5.56 cents. . . . Gold reserve down to $61,000,000. . . . Labor Day made a legal holiday.

Matrices just coming into use in newspapers. . . . Scott & Bowne spending $1,000,000 a year. . . . Earnest Elmo Calkins, proprietor of Calkins' Pharmacy, Ann Arbor, Mich., finds that advertising is increasing his business. . . . Sunday papers carrying as many as thirty-six pages and their bulkiness causes complaints from readers and advertisers, jokes from vaudeville performers. . . . Henry Ford makes his first motor vehicle.

Stenography is opening a new field for women workers, a young lady having taken notes at a New York Senate session "without showing the least sign of embarrassment." . . . "The pleasure of a confidential chat is heightened by the sweet breath that goes with a well-ordered system"—advertisement of Ripans Tabules. . . . Godey Publishing Company in the hands of receiver. . . . F. Wayland Ayer, president of N. W. Ayer & Son, elected president of the Merchants' National Bank of Philadelphia. . . . E. W. Spaulding resigns as advertising manager of *Cosmopolitan* to take charge of the New York office of *Ladies' Home Journal* . . . Dentifrice named Sozodid launched to compete with Sozodont.

paper field, Frank B. Noyes, manager of the Washington *Star,* saw that improvement in the advertisement would mean better results for the advertiser. Accordingly, the paper established an ad-writing bureau for the use of its customers, a move which attracted wide attention and was followed in other cities. Several papers had such bureaus in 1896. The usual basis for charge was a monthly fee, and they would do some work for advertisers in other papers.

Meanwhile the advertising agents were finding themselves occasionally faced with the responsibility of doing a piece of copy. Even prior to 1888 a young man named John Irving Romer was in the employ of the Rowell agency as a professional advertising writer; his claim to being the first agency copy man was sometimes disputed by Joseph Addison Richards, who prepared Pears' soap copy for the J. H. Bates agency. This was by no means an established part of the agent's functions, however, nor was it a full-time job. This same Richards in 1891 ran an advertisement of his services as a writer which pretty well sums up the situation at the time. The final sentence in his advertisement read: "Don't be afraid of me because I am with an advertising agent."

When called upon by a customer to prepare an advertisement, the agent would usually comply. But he rarely felt justified in assuming responsibility for the content of the space which he sold. When he did make so bold as to offer a suggestion, it was seldom received with enthusiasm by the advertiser. More often the response was outright indignation. The advertiser's main objective was to get as much

reading matter as possible in the space available.

When he did accept a copy assignment, the agent moved with discreet steps. The first, in fact the sole, principle was to find out what the client liked. The idea was not to make the best announcement possible but such a one as would be most likely to please the client. The advertiser who placed his business direct and not through an agent was at this period always the one to originate bold forms of advertising. A general agent dared not take the responsibility of introducing a new, and therefore, experimental policy.

As late as 1893 no general agency had a regularly employed copy man or considered the preparation of copy a definite part of its service. N. W. Ayer & Son probably gave more attention to copy than any other, with the J. Walter Thompson Company a close second. And Lord & Thomas and Frank Seaman were making definite efforts in this direction. From here on, things were destined to move fast.

Despite the growth of these new outside instrumentalities for preparing advertisements, many advertisers maintained a deeply founded resistance to the idea of anybody outside the factory doing the writing. They believed that only the man in the business could write a competent advertisement, because only he could know the product and the customers thoroughly. Indeed it was an expressed view of the times that a man who couldn't write his own advertisements had no business advertising. But as the more competent producers of copy perfected their methods, the value of an outside viewpoint gained recognition.

IN THE nineteenth century, it was twenty years after the first telephone exchange was built before the American people had installed a million phones. In the twentieth century, fifteen million radios were bought within ten years after the first popular broadcast.

When writing of the part Popular Mechanics has played in the people's utilization of the technical and mechanical discoveries of the twentieth century, Dr. Walter Dill Scott, President of Northwestern University, and longtime student of advertising and selling, said: "Popular Mechanics is one of the most effective of all agencies in shortening the lag-time between the discovery of important scientific phenomena and their application to promoting the welfare of mankind."

Since its *first* issue in May, 1902, Popular Mechanics Magazine has been "first" among general magazines with the news—written so you can understand it—of many mechanical developments, and thus has helped to make them everyday conveniences in millions of homes.

Popular Mechanics was first to explain automobile motors to the layman, first to give popular explanation of the Wright Brothers' flying machine, first to give an everyday commercial significance to the X-ray, to motion pictures, to radio, to stainless steel, to mechanical refrigeration, to electric welding, and to many other developments of the world's experimental laboratories.

In more than thirty-six years Popular Mechanics has not changed in name, in format, nor in editorial aim. Because of this editorial record maintained since the early days of this century, Popular Mechanics Magazine has the largest mechanically-minded man readership of any magazine—well over half a million. And because of this large, selected, mechanically-minded readership, Popular Mechanics, as an advertising medium, is a most effective agency in shortening the *lag-time* between the development of an idea and its popular acceptance on a commercially profitable scale.

Pen and Rostrum

AN essential lubricant in the development of any field of business activity is the interchange of information, ideas and experience among those who participate in it. This lubricant springs from two wells—the trade press and the organized trade group. Both made their first appearance in this opening period in the era of modern advertising.

The establishment of a press devoted to the interests of the advertiser had its beginning in 1888, when George P. Rowell established PRINTERS' INK. The journal did have a predecessor, however, in the form of the *Advertisers' Gazette*, which began in 1867 and was likewise founded by Rowell. This paper, changed in name to the *American Newspaper Reporter* in 1871, was primarily a house organ of the Rowell advertising agency.

From the very first, the editorial content of PRINTERS' INK was pointed to the interests of the man who used advertising as a means of increasing his business. The first several issues consisted largely of general discussions of advertising and selling processes, but before long, articles dealing with the specific methods and experiences of the leading advertisers of the day became a predominant feature.

The followers in the path marked by PRINTERS' INK were, to use a mild term, numerous in those early days. Up to the end of the century some 200 papers of one kind and another which professed to cater to advertisers or the advertising trade appeared. Most were of limited editorial scope and small circulation. Nearly all were short-lived. Perhaps the best were *Profitable Advertising* and *Fame* and, a little later on *Judicious Advertising*.

In 1888 the Association of General Newspaper Agents was formed in New York and this appears to have been the first organized advertising group, insofar as exclusive preoccupation with advertising affairs is concerned. A year earlier, chiefly through the promotional offices of W. H. Brearly, advertising manager of the Detroit *Evening News*, fifty-one newspaper publishers had met at Rochester, N. Y., and established the American Newspaper Publishers Association. While this group initiated and has maintained throughout its existence a close interest in advertising matters, it was and is, of course, primarily a newspaper trade organization rather than an advertising group. At the same time, however, it was at the instance of the A.N.P.A. that the agents' association came into being.

The chief purpose of the Association of General Newspaper Agents was to facilitate the process of doing business with the publishers and adjust such conflict of viewpoint and practice as might arise between the advertiser, the agent and the publisher. Eligibility for membership was extended to those agents who were financially responsible and had facilities for doing a general agency business. The total list of eligibles as drawn up by the founders comprised seventeen agencies, of which, incidentally, three—N. W. Ayer & Son, J. Walter Thompson Company and Lord & Thomas—continue in business un-

Like Old Wine...

When the first issue of Printers' Ink appeared in 1888, The Atlanta Journal was already five years old. Together the two publications have grown, progressed and improved with age . . . together they have followed the trends of the t i m e s and have kept abreast of them with their leadership. Just as Printers' Ink has chronicled all the advances in advertising . . . The Journal has paced the field in progressive publishing.

During the last two decades, The Journal's strides have been greater than ever. It was first in the South with Rotogravure in 1919 . . . a Radio Station, WSB, in 1922 . . . Wirephotos in 1935 . . . and a completely Restyled newspaper in 1938.

TODAY, THE JOURNAL LEADS ALL GEORGIA NEWSPAPERS IN DAILY CIRCULATION AND ADVERTISING LINAGE

Tune In On
WSB
THE ATLANTA JOURNAL
STATION 50,000 WATTS
— NBC —
The Voice of the South

WAGA
ATLANTA'S NEW
NBC
Blue Ribbon Nation
OPERATED BY
THE ATLANTA JOURNAL

The Atlanta Journal

The Journal Covers Dixie Like the Dew

National Representatives
O'MARA AND ORMSBEE, INC.
New York, Chicago, Boston, Detroit, San Francisco, Los Angeles, Atlanta

der the same name to the present.

The association originated the first movement toward modern principles of agency recognition. The A.N.P.A. had issued a list of forty-one recognized agents, basing its designation upon general considerations of "good standing." It was the contention of the agents' group that the forty-one ought to be pared down to their list of seventeen on the basis of proved ability and inclination to pay promptly. The agents maintained that financial responsibility ought to be a foremost consideration in any question of recognition, for the protection of both publisher and agent. The view survived the association, whose life was relatively brief, and credit standing is a matter of exhaustive and aggressive investigation in the recognition operations of every media organization today.

The first advertiser group consisted mainly of writers of advertising employed in the retail field. This was the Business Writers Association, started in Detroit in 1890. The objects were largely social, but interchange of ideas was also undertaken and all who earned their living by writing advertisements were eligible.

In 1894 came further impetus from the West. That year the Agate Club was formed at Chicago by a group of leading magazine advertising representatives, and its forums produced many stimulating exchanges of thought on the practice of the advertiser. The Agate Club lays undisputed claim to being the oldest club of advertising men in point of continuous service.

The formation of the Sphinx Club at New York in 1896 marked the first organization designed to bring together all the related interests of advertising—advertisers, agents, publishers and producers of advertising services. It developed a considerable list of non-resident members from the West and other sections of the East and, though centering its activities in New York, was virtually a national organization. Its meetings enlisted practically all of the leading advertising men of the day, from within and without the membership, as speakers, and the addresses were accompanied by spirited, open debate on the problems uppermost in advertising at that time. The first address was by Newcomb Cleveland and his subject was, "Are Advertising Rates Too High?" For constructive contributions to advertising thought the Sphinx Club's activities outshone all contemporaries.

Two other organizations of advertising media proprietors came to join the A.N.P.A. during this period. In 1891 was established the Associated Billposters and Distributors of the United States and Canada. Some of its activities have been heretofore noted.

In 1895, sixty publishers, editors and business managers of farm papers met at Chicago to form the Agricultural Press League, one of whose objectives was to keep non-payers of advertising bills from securing space in member papers.

Taken as a whole, these first steps toward building instruments for organized activity in the production of better and more orderly advertising practice were faltering and limited. Some of the groups proved impermanent and lacking in sound leadership. The conduct of constructive research and maintenance of effective organizational facilities were yet to come. None the less, these pioneer groups afforded a real contribution to the progress of the business. Wholly apart from the value of the opportunities they provided for interchange of new ideas and amplification of old ones, they helped give the practice of advertising a sense of solidity and respectability which it needed. The social contacts resultant of the meetings widened once narrow perceptions and established a basis for the mutuality of interest without which no business can progress very far.

1895

PRESIDENT CLEVELAND affirms the Monroe Doctrine as applicable to boundary dispute of Venezuela and British Guiana. . . . Anti-Saloon League founded in Washington. . . . Gold reserve after dropping to $41,000,000, finally returns to $100,000,000. . . . Morgan-Belmont-Rothschild syndicate lends treasury 3,500,000 ounces of gold coin.

W. R. Hearst, owner of the San Francisco *Examiner,* buys the New York *Morning Journal.* . . . "We agents have become educators of the business public—teaching them to advertise"— D. M. Lord. . . . National craze over the book "Trilby" finds its reflection in the merchandising world in the naming of every conceivable type of merchandise. . . . Sale of Sunday newspapers reported on the decrease because so many people are riding bicycles that day. . . . American Tobacco Company spending a million dollars for premiums.

Milton McRae joins the Scripps League, which becomes the Scripps-McRae League. . . . Manly M. Gillam leaves Wanamaker's at Philadelphia to invade New York as advertising writer for Hilton, Hughes & Company. . . . "A good deal is said about the 'cumulative' effect of advertising; yet every advertisement must stand on its own merits and ought to be not only just as good as it can be, but just as independent of the series to which it belongs as if there weren't any series."—Wolstan Dixey. . . . 2,359 new publications established in the last year, but the net increase is only 228. . . . Newspaper with the longest name: Milwaukee *Die Deutsch-Amerikanische Gewerbe und Industrie Zeitung—Fortschritt Der Zeit.* . . . Newspaper with the shortest name: Wilkes-Barre, Pa., *It.*

AUGUST 1938

5¢

SUCCESSFUL
FARMING

THE MAGAZINE OF FARM BUSINESS AND FARM HOMES

Largest
Farm Circulation
in the
World's Richest
Farm Region

MERCHANDISE

Y ★ DES MOINES, IOWA

SPREADING THE WORD

ATTENTION — this was the watchword of the advertiser in the early stage of his modern development. The beginning and, to a large extent, the end of his ambition was in some way to force, trick or cajole the reader into observing his printed notice. He felt that he had made his mark with the consumer if he had caused the latter to become aware of the name of his product—that advertising could do little more than this and little more was to be expected of it.

He had, as has been seen, come to place some degree of value on the quality of the writing of the text matter. But his prime fascination was with attracting the eye and, despite its advance in his esteem, copy was distinctly a secondary consideration.

John E. Powers, along with some others, pointed out that there was error in attracting attention without making advantageous use of it. "Advertising," he said, "is printing in an agreeable manner the facts that a buyer has to get at before he can be a buyer." And: "Advertisement readers worth having are prone to skip the instant you betray your emptiness and incompetence."

A not inconsiderable number of advertisers were coming to realize this point. But many others overlooked it. There were new temptations which were too much for them. The removal of publication prohibitions against display type and illustrations and the immense development in the quality and price of engravings were beginning to open a whole new vista of ways of smacking the public between the eyes. The memory of the exploits of Phineas Taylor Barnum and Dr. Helmbold, of Buchu fame, was fresh.

It was a day of black, glaring headlines, of advertisements printed upside down and sideways, of slangy phrases and witless puns and grotesque humor. Of rebus advertisements, of words printed backwards or forwards and backwards in alternation, of copy printed in Volapuk, then making its bid as an international language.

"Reading notices," advertisements disguised as news matter, gained great favor. This style, originated by Dr. Warner of Warner's Safe Cure, used newspaper headlines followed by regular newsprint text and set-up. The product was not mentioned until the middle or end of the article, the first part of which seldom had anything to do with the product itself. For a short period, around 1892, the "telegraph advertisement" flourished, a purported late news item which was inserted in the telegraph column of the newspaper.

It was a day when a heading like "Havana in Ashes" introduced the reader to something about a cigar. When what was considered a really special advertisement for a tailoring firm was headed: "Your Pants Are Open." (The copy below continuing: ". . . to criticism if they are not tailored at our establishment.") It was a day of poetry. Like this:

Come one, come all,
Both great and small,
And go to Chicago this Fall.
This is a rhyme—take it in time—
And go via the C. H. & D. Line.

Before breakfast (and after) titled Londoners take their exercise in Rotten Row

Have you heard this news from ENGLAND?

... Have you heard about the English magazine that offers American advertisers 4 times the coverage of LIFE?

ARE you up-to-date on England? Do you know the inside story of the amazing rise to power of Radio Times?

Here it is. The British Broadcasting Corporation controls all the radio entertainment in the country. Every Friday, complete programmes for the coming week on all stations, National and Regional, are announced in Radio Times. No other publication is allowed to print them a week in advance. Millions of listeners turn to the Radio Times for details of their radio programmes.

Issued first in 1923, today the Radio Times has a guaranteed weekly net sale of 3 million copies. This rapid growth is evidence of its usefulness and the lively interest of its readers. *One out of every four English families takes the Radio Times.*

*Independent survey, March. 1937.

What is more, 90% of its readers state that they refer to it *daily* . . . 87% look up programmes in advance; 65% are reading their copy 10 days after receiving it.* *A single advertisement in Radio Times constitutes a national campaign for a week.* And the people who read the Radio Times have money to spend, because in England radio ownership indicates good purchasing power.

The milline rate of Radio Times is only $2.46. Successful American manufacturers in Great Britain are finding it economical and effective.

To sell your product to this great family market, use Radio Times. Consult your agency, or write to: Advertisement Director, British Broadcasting Corporation Publications, Broadcasting House, Portland Place, W.1, London.

●

MR. C. M. BAKER, *President, Pond's Extract Company, states:* "Radio Times give us coverage and a type of circulation that we think excellent for our products. Its steady growth indicates, we believe, real reader interest."

Take in Dayton, Lima, Toledo and Detroit,
For I am sure you will enjoy it.

(Cincinnati, Hamilton & Dayton Railroad)

The perfecting of the technical process of reproducing pictures produced a veritable craze for illustrations. Art came in with a resounding flourish to further the objective of getting attention.

There were a number of types of illustrations in popular use. Perhaps the least prevalent was that displaying a picture of the product. Pictorial representations of the product in use or the results of its use were exceedingly rare, as were reproductions of the package.

A second type, the showing of results of not using the product, was, however, in high favor, the patent medicine companies being the chief exponents. Here was represented a disease which the product was supposed to cure, and almost inevitably the disease was in its most advanced and horrible stages. Many of these were almost unbelievably hideous and usually the portrayal was a rank exaggeration. A special ramification of this technique was the "before-and-after" picture, widely used because it told an easily comprehended story to the semi-illiterate and those of foreign birth. And it is to be noted that this device has come down to us intact. In 1890 the advertisement of a "voltaic belt" demonstrated by before-and-after pictures that the product not only improved health and posture, but combed the hair, pressed the clothes and cultivated a fine, luxuriant mustache—all in thirty days. With the more conservative ad-

vertisers the picture of the factory, of the trade-mark or of the founder—a la W. L. Douglas—were favored. But there had to be a picture. And if nothing else was available—often in preference to anything else—the advertiser used an illustration that was wholly irrelevant to the text or the product. Willowy young ladies, faultless Fauntleroys, elegant interiors of homes were reproduced without relation to the message in the widely held belief that "any cut is better than no cut at all."

A special division of the irrelevant school was the comic picture. Hundreds of engraved crimes were committed in the name of humor. The effective use of catchy drawings by Rogers Peet, Sapolio and Pearline brought on scores of inept and awkward imitators.

Going to all imaginable lengths in the stampede to get attention, some advertisers stopped at nothing. They used photographs of prominent people entirely without permission, one employing a portrait of Mrs. Cleveland, wife of the then ex-President. They used the American flag, imitations of postage stamps, money orders and other postal devices.

On a higher plane was the introduction of the idea of using pictures painted by famous artists, brought about by the Pears' soap people. Artists of the caliber of Millais (painter of the famous "Bubbles," used in 1888), Focardi and Stacey Marks were induced to permit the use of their works. These illustrations rarely had much to do with delivering a convincing sales point, but they definitely marked the path toward the use of a higher type of art in advertising. A slight setback, however, was provided by imitators, some of whom were not above making a commercial adjustment here and there in the great artist's work, such as lettering a few notes about the product on the bare back of a maiden who appeared in the picture. The more fastidious citizens, shocked no little, howled. "Nothing appears to be too sacred for the advertiser," snorted the New York *Sun*.

Came, too, the baby picture. Mellin's Food, another advertiser who did much to stimulate the advertiser's ultimate use of more attractive illustrations, was a pioneer, and its presentations of portraits of healthy babies had a definite point. Others were quick to follow, and the baby picture soon became standard equipment in the business of printed selling.

Another manifestation of the attention vogue was the rising demand for special position in newspapers and periodicals. Advertisers went wild on the subject. Top of the column, next to reading matter, was considered just about essential to success in this world, no matter how feeble the wording of the advertisement or meaningless the display.

The operations of the majority of the advertisers at this period tend to suggest certain qualities of the sheep, a characteristic which may not have been bred entirely out of the race even yet. They had little confidence in their own decisions. The new way of business was bewildering. Things were moving so fast that there seemed no time for reasoned planning of a course of action. If somebody did something that worked that was the thing to do, no matter how

much the successful one may have differed in product, in market and in resources.

Nevertheless, the basic rhythm was an upbeat. Sober minds were considering whether sheer sensationalism was any worthwhile force in attaining a stable sales success. Whether it was not important to win assent as well as attention from the consumer. And a growing number of advertisers were taking courage enough in the convictions of themselves and their more able advisers to forge ahead with temperate, reasonable advertisements. Beneath all the outward fury, advertising was becoming less of an artifice and more of an art.

The custom of sending one electrotype to all papers and letting it stand without change was disappearing. In its place was emerging an inclination to suit the message to the audience and to use an amount of space consistent with presenting a connected story.

Rudimentary attempts were being made to judge the medium by the results obtained from it. The keying of advertisements was being resorted to in an ever-increasing degree.

Several advertisers had noticed that the way you say a thing may make a difference in its influence on the reader.

It was being seen in some quarters that the mere enumeration of the things the advertiser has to offer may be effective only when presented in connection with striking price reductions. That the advertiser, in communicating with the consumer, must not think solely of his goods and his plant, but of the consumer.

A GOOD **40%** DAILY

Daily MORE THAN **4½** MILLION families
Sunday MORE THAN **6½** MILLION families

HEARST NEWSPAPERS

Albany Times-Union (Morning and Sunday) ★ **Atlanta Georgian and American** (Evening and Sunday) **Baltimore News-Post and American** (Evening and Sunday) ★ **Boston American and Advertiser** (Evening and Sunday) ★ **Boston Record** (Morning) ★ **Chicago American** (Evening) ★ **Chicago Herald & Examiner** (Morning and Sunday) ★ **Detroit Times** (Evening and Sunday) ★ **Los Angeles Examiner** (Morning and Sunday) **Los Angeles Herald-Express** (Evening) ★ **Milwaukee News-Sentinel** (Morning, Evening and Sunday) ★ **New York Journal and American** (Evening and Sunday) ★ **New York Mirror** (Morning and Sunday) ★ **Oakland Post-Enquirer** (Evening) ★ **Pittsburgh Sun Telegraph** (Evening and Sunday) ★ **San Antonio Light** (Evening and Sunday) ★ **San Francisco Call Bulletin** (Evening) ★ **San Francisco Examiner** (Morning and Sunday) **Seattle Post Intelligencer** (Morning and Sunday) ★ **Syracuse Journal American** (Evening and Sunday)

READ HEARST NEWSPAPERS

In the 15 Great Trading Areas

Represented by NEW YORK · CHICAGO · DETROIT · BOSTON
BALTIMORE · PITTSBURGH · ALBANY · ATLANTA
MILWAUKEE · SYRACUSE · SAN ANTONIO · LOS ANGELES
SAN FRANCISCO · OAKLAND · SEATTLE

and we mean

GOOD

It is a $12,679,583,734.00 market

HEARST READER FAMILY INCOMES PRESENT THE FOLLOWING IMPRESSIVE PICTURE

ALBANY	$ 75,953,390	NEW YORK	$3,707,097,404
ATLANTA	$ 193,955,385	OAKLAND	$ 154,534,250
BALTIMORE	$ 552,256,128	PITTSBURGH	$ 477,945,036
BOSTON	$1,561,950,208	SAN ANTONIO	$ 99,984,240
CHICAGO	$1,961,131,055	SAN FRANCISCO	$ 799,612,800
DETROIT	$ 943,890,997	SEATTLE	$ 212,683,984
LOS ANGELES	$1,355,471,012	SYRACUSE	$ 140,560,770
MILWAUKEE	$ 442,557,075	TOTAL	$12,679,583,734

[Computed from county averages in *Sales Management*'s estimate for 1937. In New York, the lowest county average was used for all five boroughs. Department of Commerce reports incomes for first four months of 1938 are only 6.3% below same period, 1937.]

Isn't that what your own market analysts would call good? And the 40% of trading area families becomes 60% of city zone families. That is just daily circulation. On Sunday, Hearst Newspapers reach one-fifth of all the families in the United States. And these families, by every test that has ever been made, represent *all income groups* proportionately with A DEFINITE PERCENTAGE ABOVE COMMUNITY AVERAGES.

• • •

Telephone today for one of our merchandise men. They *know* the Hearst Newspaper city trading area conditions so thoroughly that they can save your own market analysts many days of patient research.

CHAPTER III

Instruments of Conquest
(1896-1900)

THE objective held dearest by the business man of the closing decade of the nineteenth century was the conquest of his competitors. In fact, business success was largely judged by the degree to which a firm was able to confound its rivals, preferably in terms of total annihilation.

Such acceptance as advertising had achieved was largely based on its expected efficacy as an instrument for wiping out competition. A scant few advertisers had broader visions. But the great majority looked upon advertising solely as a competitive sales weapon. They viewed it somewhat as the armament of nations. Competition was believed to be the prime cause of building and manning of advertising guns, elimination of competition the only potential result.

On this premise the use of advertising increased materially beginning in 1895 and for several years thereafter. Larger guns, in the form of larger space units in the publications, and more guns, in the form of larger schedules in publications and other media, were drawn up. Advertising expenditures, particularly of the larger firms, expanded in the effort to overpower the enemy. At least 500 concerns were spending from $25,000 to $50,000 in advertising; 100 or more from $100,000 to $150,000 by 1899.

Meanwhile, however, some of the industrial generals got to thinking about another method of competitive warfare. Advertising weapons seemed expensive, slow and by no means certain in accomplishing the downfall of a good-sized rival. Would it not be a more strategic maneuver to join forces with the principal rivals and thereby concentrate control of the entire trade in a single commercial rival? "If you can't lick 'em, jine em."

Hence the trust. And hence a crisis in the development of the advertiser way of doing business.

The trust, a combination of several—sometimes a dozen or more—of the leading firms in a given line of manufacture, achieved a wide acceptance in the 1890's. Quite unlike the mergers of a later day, the trust was purely and simply an expression of the business man's desire to eliminate competition as a factor in business.

Those at the helms of these industrial giants firmly believed that advertising could be entirely done away with, although some of the more liberal conceded the value of a few occasional product notices. The same reasoning applied to all selling activities. Some observers believed the traveling salesman to be headed for ultimate doom. Since the trust controlled all the best-known and most widely sold brands, the jobber and retailer would be forced to apply to it for the goods.

Insofar as advertising was concerned, this result actually did take place in numerous instances. In almost every line in which trusts were formed, all advertising was cut off. **Competition was ended;** therefore no reason to advertise existed. It was estimated that the formation of trusts in the first six months of 1899 had caused a decrease of $9,000,000 to $13,000,000 yearly in amount spent by general advertisers—a tremendous proportion of the total. In that year was formed the baking powder trust, a shattering blow since Royal, Cleveland, Dr. Price and One Spoon were among the heaviest advertisers.

And the trusts ruled the trade with an iron hand. The American Tobacco Company, controlling all the leading cigarette brands, sold on consignment to the jobber. The jobber who handled competing brands did so at the risk of having all well-known brands taken away from him. In addition, he stood to lose certain rebates on past sales, which were forfeitable at the trust's pleasure.

The result was a virtual panic in the advertising and publishing trade. The fear that the increasing tendency to trade combinations would permanently reduce the great bulk of advertising was given expression in many quarters. Some thought that advertising would disappear completely, although others believed that the appearance of new products in new industries might extend its life for a while at least. A group of business-paper publishers met in New York in 1899 and decided that they were headed for extinction. The newspapers lamented widely.

To the remedy of this crisis, the proprietors of the advertising media were able to contribute almost nothing. The majority of publishers considered all advertising patronage as a mild form of blackmail; no one was more thoroughly convinced than the advertising solicitor of the truth of the amended adage that, "It doesn't pay to advertise." As a rule, the publisher was unable to conceive how any advertiser could ever succeed in getting his money back. He thought that the patron advertised in his paper in order to help it along, or because of interest in the fortunes of some political party. Though he constantly preached advertising, he had no real belief in its value and the idea that anybody ever got a profit out of advertising was something he simply could not comprehend.

A few publishers had no patience with the belief that advertising was a charitable contribution and stood on the premise that it was a way of spending a dollar that would get back more than a dollar. But many economists, most trust promoters and all socialists contended that the only usefulness of advertising was in a competitive market.

Almost overnight came a change. It was suddenly realized in important places that advertising is a necessary device in a modern system of distributing goods, a system by which selling could be done with far less expense than in any other way. That the hardest part of the distribution of merchandise is the distribution of the information which must precede the selling. That what the automatic machine is to making goods, the advertisement is to selling them, and as the machine thrives best where production is most highly organized, so advertising will be most extensively employed where distribution is most highly developed. That the amount of advertising called for in selling goods is related not to the number of concerns selling, but to the amount of the output. That the trust can have no more incentive

Representing a third of the country's buying power.

The twelve markets shown on the above map total $10,933,240,000 retail sales.

They alone can constitute a national business for any manufacturer. And no firm aspiring to a nation-wide business can succeed without winning them. Winning these markets is an increasingly complicated process requiring the most timely and reliable information on every phase of the marketing operation.

During the past fifty years, the population of these twelve cities has grown from 4,688,675 (1890 Census) to 19,802,847 (City Carrier Limits).

New York has grown from a million and a half to seven and a half million. Los Angeles from fifty thousand to a million and a half. Detroit from two hundred thousand to nearly two million. But merchandisingly the last twenty years have been the most rapid and vital in change.

This is an organization of men who, backed up by the individual papers they represent in these markets, have as their purpose the utmost in service, information and helpfulness to manufacturers and agencies. No other single newspaper organization affords the close personal contact and the day-to-day sources of information covering so large a part of the entire national market.

The reputation of our men and our service for unprejudiced, accurate and timely co-operation is one of our most valued and guarded assets.

HEARST INTERNATIONAL ADVERTISING SERVICE

RODNEY E. BOONE, GENERAL MANAGER

Representing

DAILY

New York Journal-American	Chicago Evening American	Detroit Evening Times
Pittsburgh Sun-Telegraph	Chicago Herald & Examiner	Syracuse Journal
Baltimore News-Post	Boston Record-American	Atlanta Georgian
Los Angeles Examiner	Albany Times-Union	Seattle Post-Intelligencer
Saturday Home Magazine	San Francisco Examiner	Saturday Comic Pictorial

SUNDAY

New York Journal-American	Detroit Times	Pittsburgh Sun-Telegraph
Boston Advertiser	Baltimore American	Albany Times-Union
Syracuse American	Atlanta American	Los Angeles Examiner
San Francisco Examiner		Seattle Post-Intelligencer

for abandoning the modern selling machine than for throwing out its most improved manufacturing apparatus.

It was seen that while the trust might temporarily withdraw all its advertisements under the misapprehension that its customers must come to it, the fact soon develops that modern business is an aggressive thing and no trust is so independent that it need not seek its customers to the extent of informing them about its product. That advertising is the motive power by which modern selling in any branch is kept up with the procession. That there will always be enough competition—active or possible—to impel the use of the best possible devices for selling goods.

And it was seen, above all, that no product of any kind had achieved its fullest possible sales. That even a trust must create new consumers.

In 1899 the trust managers were complacent, the advertising trade enshrouded in despair.

By the end of 1900 those in the advertising business had shed all signs of apprehension about the future and the trusts were examining the subject of salesmanship in an entirely new light.

Actually, of course, the underlying forces which caused the swift change were well at work even as the gloom seemed thickest.

Certain of the more farsighted and undismayed advertising agents and publishers and others were pointing out that the trust actually added further to industry's need for selling more products to more people. Their contributions were valuable. The final force to the arguments, however, was appearing in the marketing events of the time.

For one thing, the cigarette interests decided in 1896 they could get along without advertising. (The American Tobacco Company had spent nearly a million dollars in promotion, counting premiums, during 1894 and 1895, and most of this was discontinued.) Three years later it had emerged as a certainty that the savings in money effected were not entirely net. Somehow or other, smokers were seeming to get out of the habit which the manufacturers had thought was so firmly fixed it would continue undiminished. And some new cigarette companies had taken up advertising with results which were not entirely unnoticeable. Advertising was resumed.

Impressive evidence on the other side of the ledger was shown by the National Biscuit Company, a combination of a large number of firms set up in 1898 and popularly referred to as the "biscuit trust." This organization, far from diminishing its sales efforts, immediately set about advertising to obtain sales results. And, far from standing pat on established brands, it introduced a new product which by 1900 had achieved recognition as an all-time success epic in the art of modern marketing—the Uneeda biscuit.

In Philadelphia the Frank H. Fleer Company, with a new product called Chiclets, was demonstrating the vulnerability of the common trust policy. The chewing gum trust, formed in 1896 by the largest manufacturers, had abolished advertising and neither sought to develop new brands nor increase sales of old. It sold its products on the assumption it controlled the output and, except for a little billposting and some showcards and window hangers, put forth little selling effort.

Under the direction of Mayer M. Swaab, Jr., the Fleer organization moved from market to market in the East with an aggressive promotional program. Ultimately it invaded the New York market, supposed to be owned by the trust, and in less than two years Chiclets were outselling the combined trust brands. Other markets were entered until by 1906 the company's annual production had multiplied from half a million to six hundred million tablets.

In other lines new companies came and not only aggressively sold on their own merits, but also appealed outright to the anti-trust sentiment, which waxed considerable in the late 1890's. Some of the trusts had undertaken to put up prices, in line with their general theory of absolute dominance of the market. "Not Made by a Trust" became a frequent display line in the advertisements of independent companies and the public, combining the American's traditional admiration for the under-dog with dislike of the methods of certain of the trusts, responded to the appeal. By their very silence the trusts had allowed themselves, whether rightly or wrongly in individual instances, to be regarded as distributors of over-priced goods.

One by one most of those dealing with consumers resumed the ways which in the first place had built the good-will which was their chief stock in trade.

In terms of total expenditures, trust development probably slackened the rate of expansion of advertising activity in this period as compared with the preceding five years. The decade as a whole, however, showed a substantial growth. According to government census figures, advertising revenue of newspapers and periodicals was $71,243,361 in 1890 and $95,861,127 in 1900.

The more significant phase of the progress from 1896 to 1900 was in terms of the number of new recruits to the advertiser way of doing business. A large number of new advertisers appeared. Many established firms which had made only sporadic efforts to move their goods to the consumer took up systematic methods.

The largest growth in this respect was in the field of grocery products.

In 1895, C. W. Post, who was to become one of the most vigorous figures in the merchandising arena, introduced a coffee substitute called Postum, followed two years later by Grape-Nuts. In 1899 the Postum Cereal Company of Battle Creek, Mich., was well on its way toward assuming the front-rank position that it later commanded, spending about $400,000 for advertising in that year. Post, who had been a salesman for an agricultural implement house and then manager of a plow works, turned to the health food idea after suffering a breakdown in health. He came to be noted as one of the strongest believers in advertising, and always kept the advertising reins in his own hands. He once said: "I care not who manages production or sales, so long as I write the advertising." As the business grew it was not always possible for him to do the actual composition, but he read and revised all copy and wherever he might be batches of manuscript and proof were sent him for revision and approval.

At Niagara Falls, N. Y., the Natural Food Company had been organized by Henry D. Perky to

ACCOMPLISHMENT

The world looks upon Southern California as a rich market, marvels at its phenomenal growth from a desert area to a region of vast and diversified wealth and attraction... The records show that each and every project and policy responsible for Southern California's growth during the past 35 years originated with, or was strenuously and conspicuously championed by The Los Angeles Examiner, the paper that gets things done.

Represented Nationally by
HEARST INTERNATIONAL ADVERTISING SERVICE
Rodney E. Boone, *General Manager*

For more than
50 years
this has been
the leading
newspaper in
its field—

San Francisco
EXAMINER

market a new processed whole-wheat product—Shredded Wheat. Perky's entrance into the business likewise had its origin in physical ailment—dyspepsia. He had been a lawyer. Aggressively promoted and aided by a ready-made sentiment favorable to whole wheat, which had been initiated by dietetic writers of the time, Shredded Wheat caught on rapidly. It became, incidentally, one of the chief fun-poking subjects of the day, being likened by humorists, professional and otherwise, to hay, excelsior, wood shavings and so forth. But all this helped win

more attention for the new product.

The advent of these and other prepared cereals speeded the evolution of the huge industry which was being built around the American breakfast table. Producers of hot cereals—including Quaker Oats, H-O and others—expanded their activities and in 1896 there was an important newcomer in the advertising ranks, the Cream of Wheat Company.

Another arrival in the limelight was the canned food product. In 1894 C. C. Van Camp & Son had introduced pork and beans with tomato sauce. A year later the firm

1896

UTAH admitted to the Union as the forty-fifth State. . . . Gold found in the Klondike region. . . . William McKinley defeats Willian Jennings Bryan for the presidency. . . . Regulations for fourth-class mail matter enacted. . . . Woman's suffrage becomes effective in Idaho. . . . Congress contains twenty-seven newspaper editors and nine former editors.

Adolph S. Ochs acquires the New York *Times.* . . . Cyrus H. K. Curtis is the new owner of *The Saturday Evening Post.* . . . 892 department stores in the United States. . . . A Boston mercantile house, having no snow for sleigh and reindeer, sends Santa Claus through town with a fleet of donkeys. . . . Chicago retailers, indignant over high advertising rates, discuss plans for a newspaper of their own to be run at a loss, and the trade predicts success in reaching that objective. . . . First showing of a motion picture in the United States via Thomas A. Edison's vitascope.

Pettengill & Company, Boston, acquire the S. R. Niles Advertising Agency, oldest in the country. . . . War scare with Britain over the Venezuelan question brings out a rash of tie-up advertisements, one New York merchant counseling: "Don't worry about John Bull. If his fleet ever came down New York harbor, we could send down our excursion boats to meet him. *That* would settle it." . . . Metropolitan Telephone & Telegraph Company boasts 12,500 subscribers in New York City. . . . "Advertisements are printed salesmen."—Charles Austin Bates. . . . Frank Presbrey Company starts business. . . . Leading premium of the day: court plaster—an especial favorite with the accident insurance companies.

initiated advertising to support its force of house-to-house canvassers. Under Frank Van Camp the marketing program was pushed vigorously and, a little later, came widespread advertising of another Van Camp product, evaporated milk.

The year 1898 witnessed the appearance, through the Joseph Campbell Company, of a new canned product—condensed soup. The company had been in existence for some years packing a varied line of food items, including catsup, mince meat, preserves and others. It did very little advertising, for it had nothing very distinctive to feature. The new soup was seen as an advertising opportunity, a great part of the vision being supplied by a young man named John T. Dorrance. In 1899 the company ventured $5,000 in the use of car cards, adding 50 per cent more six months later. While Campbell made no great dent in the advertiser affairs of this particular period, it was soon destined to do so, for by 1905 production had grown from ten cases to twenty million cans.

In the beverage line an Atlanta firm was making itself known. In 1891 a pharmaceutical manufacturer and druggist, Asa Candler, bought a carbonated beverage syrup which was being sold at soda fountains under the name of Coca-Cola. He conceived that one of the universal and recurrent ailments of the public was the satisfaction of thirst—and, therefore, he began to merchandise the idea of refreshment. On that theme he began advertising with crude oilcloth signs and wood-cut posters. Then he added car cards and posters of more finished grade and painted signs, as well as a liberal sampling policy.

Sales grew from forty-seven gallons in the first year to half a million gallons by 1900, in which year $147,000 was invested in advertising.

The large-scale activity undertaken by the National Biscuit Company has already been noted. A number of other new arrivals made more modest beginnings and the grocery store classification — even with soap excluded—moved up to fourth place among the advertiser classifications in number of users of the sales tool. Marketing activities on soaps, by the way, were increased all along the line during the period—there was no trust trouble in this highly aggressive and individualistic field.

First place among all groups was still held, of course, by medicines, remedies and other drug-store articles. Household articles and furniture were second, wearing apparel third, construction equipment fifth.

Spotted through various industries were a number of conspicuous firms which either initiated advertiser activities in this period or materially expanded efforts begun several years before. The Ingersoll watch, for example. In 1892 Robert H. and C. H. Ingersoll were conducting a novelty shop in New York and they added to their mail-order listings a timepiece which sold at $1.50. Originally this was a small clock, but shortly later a watch movement was adopted. In a year sales rose to 40,000. The price was reduced to $1 and the company set out to develop every conceivable method of distribution, using not only jewelry outlets, but drug stores, general stores, stationery establishments and so on. The subsequent expansion of sales is well

hen PRINTERS' INK was just a lusty infant

The San Francisco **BULLETIN** was a stalwart citizen of 33 years of age when —this ad appeared in P. I. of November 15, 1888, the 9th issue!

THE CALL, equally matured in its 32nd year of publication, ran copy in P. I. of January 15, 1889—the thirteenth issue!

In 1929 these two leaders were happily joined and today

The CALL BULLETIN

is—after 83 years—alert and modern as tomorrow—and still remains

NORTHERN CALIFORNIA'S LEADING EVENING NEWSPAPER

known—by 1906 production had reached the astonishing figure of 8,000 a day—and the dollar Ingersoll, first feared by jewelers as a destroyer of the watch business—did much to establish the watch-owning habit and ultimately stimulated the sales of watches of all grades.

The famed National Cash Register Company, captained by John H. Patterson, had become practically an industry all by itself. The company instituted operations in 1884 with fourteen employees. It was not especially conspicuous as a publication advertiser, but did a large volume of high quality and well-planned advertising by mail. In many respects it was a leading pioneer in marketing methods, as will be seen later on. Sales of three thousand registers monthly were attained by the end of the century.

In the insurance field, the fire insurance companies had been active for some years, using some newspaper space, but chiefly blotters, calendars and other advertising novelties. Life insurance activity consisted mainly of pamphlets. There was some publication advertising, usually limited to annual statements and statistics, and some trade advertising. The Travelers Insurance Company had run a little sales copy on its policies. Then in the later 1890's the Prudential Insurance Company came forward as the first to employ advertising in a broad-gauged program. The famous slogan, "The Prudential Is As Strong As Gibraltar," accompanied by the illustration of that rock fortress, was placed before the public. What had been a relatively obscure Newark firm, far down in the list of companies, rose to the front rank by 1900.

The main news in the medicine field was the arrival of Omega Oil, and the methods used for introducing that product created a stir throughout the advertising business. Not one druggist had Omega Oil in stock when the advertising commenced in 1898. The company hadn't a salesman to its name. It had determined to sell through jobbers only. This was the first clear-cut case where advertising had been used to establish a market for a product on sheer consumer demand.

The campaign featured an illustration that came to be widely talked of. It was a picture of a slightly foolish looking boy with a flock of geese. The copy said: "Don't be a Goose. Use Omega Oil." Everywhere people wondered just what this was all about. The fact was that the picture had no meaning; it was just a notion of a way of attracting attention. Sales came in big volume and Omega Oil was a sensation, though it later appeared that the first several years were costly from a profit standpoint. Ultimately the business turned the corner, but as was later confessed by Bert M. Moses, who was in charge of the advertising, there had been some uneasy moments.

The apparent initial success of the company was in a way an unfortunate influence on business generally. There were a few in the advertising trade who liked to believe that advertising to the consumer was the complete answer to any marketing problem, that the dealer and the channels of trade could be ignored. All you had to do was get the consumer to ask for the product and the trade was at your mercy. The Omega Oil case seemed to support this position and the following facts did not catch up with the original impression of the

50 Years Is a Long, Long Time

THE NEW YORK MIRROR is only 14 years old as a daily and 6 years old as a Sunday newspaper. Yet today it is preferred by the second largest group of newspaper readers in New York City.

It reports international, national and local news accurately and concisely, in word and picture. It is an outstanding tabloid NEWSpaper.

GROWING IN CIRCULATION

	Daily	Sunday
1938	709,254	1,481,610
1937	608,832	1,453,550
GAIN	100,422	28,060

(From Publisher's Statement to A. B. C. for 6 months ending March 31 of each year.)

GROWING IN ADVERTISING

—the *only* New York newspaper to gain in total advertising for the first five months of 1938.

NEW YORK MIRROR

NEW YORK	CHICAGO	DETROIT	SAN FRANCISCO
235 E. 45th St.	333 N. Michigan Ave.	7-245 General Motors Bldg.	681 Market Street

company's success. At any rate, the entrancing theory of forcing distribution died a slow death and in its throes caused the waste of many an advertising dollar in the years that were to come.

Perhaps the most spectacular marketing development during the 1890's was the skyrocket career of the bicycle industry, which reached its zenith in 1896-97. In those years, according to the general impression of the times, the bicycle manufacturers spent more money in advertising than any other single product. There are no statistics to prove this, but it is certain that bicycle advertisements led all others in space in the magazines and were at least among the leaders in the newspapers and other media.

The bicycle was first made in this country in 1877, but the real development of the industry did not commence until eleven years later when the safety bicycle superseded the old high-wheeled affair. Selling through agents who commonly sold bicycles and nothing else, the industry took quickly to the use of advertising. Aided by generous publicity in the newspapers and periodicals—nearly all of the former had regular departments of cycling news —the bicycle business grew at a tremendous pace.

In 1896 there were more than a hundred bicycle manufacturers, and the manufacture of bicycle sundries was a sizable industry by itself. The number of bicycles in use had reached at least 200,000. Almost every city and town had at least one cycling club. There were thirteen papers devoted entirely to the wheel and in 1896 the *American Wheelman* put out an issue of 308 pages, hailed as the largest magazine ever issued from a printing press. In

the same year a bicycle parade was a big feature in New York. Prominent in the procession was H. M. Stanley himself and a score of Zulus, all mounted on Stanley bicycles. The annual cycle show was an event of real importance and most firms employed trick cyclists to give exhibitions around the country. There were yearly models, the shame of owning a '95 wheel in '96 was not allowed to pass unnoticed. Most of the wheels sold from $100 to $150.

The craze spread like wildfire. Never was an article of merchandise so widely publicized. Editorial writers discussed bicycle questions as gravely as they discussed the tariff. Clergymen praised or denounced the wheel from their pulpits. The bicycle was so useful a means to health and saving of time and money that surely it had come to stay.

The industry's advertising methods were generous and aggressive. Several observers, however, suggested that the copy was missing the point and "behind the times." The essential sameness of the advertisements was striking, even though from an artistic point of view there was a wide difference between them. Nearly all the copy consisted of vaporous claims which, as one observer marked, "might just as well have been applied to wheelbarrows for all the information they conveyed." They displayed neatly turned phrases which sounded pretty but brought forth no facts. "Ease of running," "strength and beauty" and such vague phrases were typical of the copy. "Buyers," exclaimed a commentator named Claude C. Hopkins, "want reasons."

In 1897 there was a slight change in direction. The advertising began

Cosmopolitan Magazine through research and promotion has revealed to advertisers, and advertising men and women, the importance of the "Age of Accumulation" and it has established the fact that most of the accumulation by families . . . in Detroit and anywhere else in the United States . . . is done before the family heads become 50 years of age . . . the 30 to 50 years of age bracket being the age range which accounts for most of the purchases being made today.

The R. L. Polk Company has made this important information on Detroit families available.

Average Age of Detroit Family Heads

Under 30	30 - 50	Over 50
8.57%	71.27%	20.16%

And the R. L. Polk Company survey revealed the fact that among the families with heads "Under 30" and between "30 to 50" years of age . . . the Detroit Times had the greatest and most thorough readership . . . only among families with heads over 50 years of age did the Times drop from first to second . . . indicating that the Times is the preferred newspaper among those who are buying today for today and tomorrow.

DETROIT TIMES
EVENING

"IN DETROIT . . . THE TREND IS TO THE TIMES"

REPRESENTED NATIONALLY BY HEARST INTERNATIONAL ADVERTISING SERVICE—RODNEY E. BOONE, GENERAL MANAGER

Used by special permission Cosmopolitan Magazine.

The Seattle Post-Intelligencer,

SEATTLE, WASHINGTON TER.

THREE EDITIONS DAILY,

SUNDAY and WEEKLY.

THE POST-INTELLIGENCER is the representative journal of Washington Territory and the only journal of general circulation in the Territory. It has also wide circulation in Alaska, Northern Idaho, Oregon and British Columbia.

The country is new and rapidly growing in every way. As yet it supplies few of its own necessities by home manufacture, so that its demands for manufactured goods and general merchandise are very large in proportion to its population.

Trade has not yet settled into regular channels, and the country affords a fine field for enterprising competition in all lines.

THE POST-INTELLIGENCER is the first and practically the only paper which goes INTO a thousand Logging Camps, Coal Mines and centres of remote settlement.

AVERAGE CIRCULATION.

The average circulation of the POST-INTELLIGENCER is as follows:

Daily,	5,500
Sunday,	7,000
Weekly,	8,500

SUBSCRIPTION RATES.

Daily,	per year, $10.00
Sunday,	" " 2.00
Weekly,	" " 2.00

Advertisers cannot reach the better part of a great constituency except through its columns, which convey to two hundred thousand readers the news of the day or week. Many of these conform their daily business to its quotations and receive their views of public matters from the POST-INTELLIGENCER.

For Advertising Rates address

THE POST-INTELLIGENCER CO.,

SEATTLE, W. T.,

ALFRED HOLMAN, General Manager,

Reproduction of the only publication advertisement appearing in the first issue of PRINTERS' INK, fifty years ago.

The Post-Intelligencer
this year celebrates its

ANNIVERSARY

1863   1938

First then and First now
with more than

100,000

daily circulation, and more than

200,000

on Sunday!

(Marching forward with Seattle)

SEATTLE
POST-INTELLIGENCER

Represented Nationally by the
Hearst International Advertising Service
Rodney E. Boone, General Manager.

to talk about flush joints, jam nuts, cushion frames, sprocket flanges, laminated rims—terms which nobody but the manufacturer or the experienced cyclist could understand. The manufacturers had not seen the possible market for bicycles among people who never rode or owned one.

When Col. Albert A. Pope, one of the leaders in the industry, began advertising the Columbia bicycle a decade before, he said very little about his own wheels as compared with others. He felt that he had to overcome the prejudice and ignorance of people concerning the new machine and point out the advantages of bicycle riding. He was one of the very first advertisers to see that: "The educating of the people is an important factor in advertising." The Colonel's wisdom got lost in the competitive shuffle, however. Most manufacturers affirmed that it would be silly to waste time and money selling cycling. The missionary work, they believed, was all done. What remained was merely to beat out the other fellow for the sales.

Thus the business went on its merry way. People were not shown how properly to ride a bicycle—a means of more or less long distance transportation in competition with the horse. Many owners overdid cycling, riding beyond the limits of their endurance, and hence soon lost interest. Proper exercise values were not taught. There was no education against reckless riding, and the indifference of some cyclists to the rules of the road caused public apathy and dislike for the wheel.

The collapse was swift in coming. In 1899, signs appeared that the business was in a languishing condition. In that year the "bicycle trust" was formed by the leading manufacturers under the name of the American Bicycle Company with the purpose, among other things, of consolidating the advertising interests of its members. So efficiently was this project carried out that advertising was all but abandoned. By 1900 the business, along with the public interest, had declined almost to the vanishing point. In 1901 the directors of the trust met in solemn conclave to face the fact that their issuance of a pretentious campaign of press notices the year before had failed. In 1902 the American Bicycle Company was bankrupt.

The contributions of the bicycle bubble to the sum of marketing knowledge were not entirely on the debit side. The manufacturers, to some extent, had shown the value of large advertising expenditures and they had led the way in the use of adequate space units. Unwittingly, they had proved for all time that public taste is fickle and suggested that while advertising might not maintain a public craze at its peak, the cessation of advertising certainly did no good. Theirs was an all-time classic example of the importance of continuing to cultivate the public interest, even in the face of generous attention from the press and of spontaneous public fascination. It was a lesson which, by the way, has been rather widely and studiously ignored through the years—the latest, apparently, being the automobile trailer industry.

Leading developments in the marketing technique during this period come under five principal headings and are noted in the sections which follow.

Fifty Years Ago

. . . there wasn't any Atlanta Georgian. We're just upstarts down this way—only thirty-seven years old. BUT—if you think we haven't become a part of the community—and a very definite and vital part!—ask any Atlanta citizen*—or better yet—ask any Georgian advertiser.

Atlanta, being very largely a distributing center, has ALWAYS been a good market for advertising. In this year of 1938, Atlanta stands out even more than usual. Here are the Federal Reserve figures, averaged for the first four months of the year, based on 1923-1925 as 100, adjusted for seasonal variations:

INDEX OF DEPARTMENT STORE SALES:

U. S.	ATLANTA
86.5	**194.3**

And, although we prefer to be modest about it, we're happy to say that today's Georgian is sharing in the linage of Atlanta's department stores—and most other advertisers! —to a greater extent than ever before.

The nearest office of Hearst International Advertising Service will give you the facts about Atlanta and the high buying power of our readers which makes it so profitable to advertise in

A HEARST NEWSPAPER

*We might just as well have said "Ask any Georgian subscriber" because mighty near all the folks you want to reach in Atlanta are Georgian subscribers.

Better and Bigger

TWO great changes in advertising copy came to the fore in this period.

The first was the use of more words—messages that were more explicit and therefore longer. The old single-paragraph advertisement of gaudy general description began to give way to definite efforts to present the advantages of the product in more striking fashion. In some few instances there were noticeable signs of a systematic attempt to build demand for the product among people to whom its use was not an accustomed one.

For years the advertisement had been at worst an outright falsehood, at its best a bald, dry announcement phrased in vague generalities. The advertiser had little esteem for the public, regarding it as something to be exploited rather than pleased.

Part of the credit for the altered viewpoint of the function of the advertising message derived from a new attitude of the publishers and proprietors of other advertising media. Many publishers had felt that their readers would pay no attention to manifest fakes in advertising copy. But in that view they had not realized that they were taking money under false pretenses.

The first step toward realization of the importance of advertising censorship traced back for many years. As early as 1859 Orange Judd, pioneer farm-paper publisher, promulgated the idea and a year later he announced that the *American Agriculturist* would exclude "deceptive advertisements, also those persons who are not reported to perform what they promise."

In 1880 Wilmer Atkinson published in the *Farm Journal* an epochal announcement—the "Fair Play" notice. Herein the publication offered to refund to subscribers any loss sustained "by trusting advertisers who prove to be deliberate swindlers."

The *Agricultural Epitomist* later followed with a similar announcement and in time the refund practice became widely adopted in the farm press. Under the policy fraudulent advertising naturally became scarce because the publisher became an expert at detecting the fakes.

Cyrus Curtis ruled out doubtful advertising even when the *Ladies' Home Journal* was far from strong. Other of the leading magazines came to realize that the elimination of the faker strengthened reader confidence and extended a strong bid for the patronage of legitimate advertisers. Newspapers, particularly the larger ones, made moves in this direction, ruling out the guaranteed cures, offers of something for nothing, fortune tellers and so on. In the outdoor field the Associated Billposters of America placed a strong ban on questionable advertisers and deceptive advertising.

While the movement could hardly be called widespread at this period, it was a definite influence. Advertisers of all kinds, finding truthfulness a prerequisite of admission in leading media, soft-pedaled the exaggerated statements and gave greater thought to forceful and persuasive presentation of facts.

Concurrently contributing to the appearance of the more explicit advertising message was a growing realization of the value of the written word. Advertisements had been keyed by some advertisers for a number of years, by the use of such phrases as "kindly mention this paper" and also by a system of running street numbers for the advertiser's headquarters which were different for each medium used. The primary object was to test the medium as to extent and quality of circulation, rather than to supply a basis for judging copy effectiveness. Nevertheless, here and there a mail-order advertiser would notice that a change in phrasing of his copy, sometimes even a change of a single word, would result in an increased response. An upstate New York advertiser of greeting cards found that large display of the word "free" increased inquiries tremendously.

These observations percolated into the general advertising field and stimulated further thought and effort with respect to what the advertisement said.

A seemingly opposing trend of the period was a widespread vogue for slogans, or "catch phrases," as they were more often called at the time. Eastman's "You Press the Button — We Do the Rest" of several years before and De Long's "See That Hump" had, by their tremendous public reception, brought on a great surge of emulation. Many advertisers accepted the belief that the absolute key to success was a compelling catch phrase—a belief that survives to this day as the general public's main conception of how to win advertising success.

The car cards, hoardings and publication pages were deluged with slogans, some of which served their owners well but most of which enjoyed results only in relation to the amount of money spent and the competition in the advertiser's particular field. These were the days of "Do You Wear Pants?" (Plymouth Rock Pants Company's famous cry), "The Beer That Made Milwaukee Famous," "Burpee's Seeds Grow," "I'se in Town, Honey," "It Floats," "Don't Be a Clam" (Siddalls' Soap), "Don't Tobacco-Spit Your Life Away (horrid word used by No-to-bac Remedy), "Pink Pills for Pale People."

The slogan by itself encouraged brief—and not infrequently vague and irrelevant—copy. But in its larger implications it served as an additional force toward focusing attention on the selection of the right word.

The selling value of the testimony of the satisfied user found wide acceptance at this time. The patent-medicine firms were the pioneers, and a number of other lines followed the example. Pears' soap set the vogue for famous names with testimonials from Langtry, Patti and others prominent in the public eye. Mariani wine attested the satisfaction of royalty and even of the Pope. Ultimately the whole thing became a competition of names and ran the cycle of abuse which has since become familiar in testimonial advertising.

So great waxed the demand for big-name testimonials that the securing of them became an organized business. The professional would submit lists from his files for the advertiser to choose from. The prospects chosen, he would send out a flattering letter about the invitation for endorsement which was being extended to "only the best people." No remuneration was offered except publicity and a free sample of the product. A series

A Salute fr

A FIFTY-YEAR BIRD'S-EYE VIEW

The Progressive Farmer—1886

Just when Printers' Ink was BORN
The Progressive Farmer was WEANED

As a slightly elder brother, therefore, The Progressive Farmer extends semi-centennial congratulations.

And in the *agricultural field* The Progressive Farmer has sought to duplicate the magnificent record and progress which Printers' Ink has made in the *advertising field*.

In this effort The Progressive Farmer has established these records among others:

1. Leading "An Agricultural Revolution" —Although it is only

52 years since The Progressive Farmer was founded, farming in 1886 was still largely dominated by superstitions borrowed from the Middle Ages. Scorning agricultural science as "book farming," many farmers waited to plant crops, kill hogs, make soap, or castrate colts until the signs of the moon or the signs of the Zodiac were "right," while all the other essentials to agricultural success were thought to have been summed up by Josh Billings in the lines—

> "He who by farmin' wood git rich
> Must rake an' hoe an' dig an' sich
> Work hard awl day, sleep hard awl nite,
> Save every cent an' not git tite."

Recognizing an agricultural revolution as "the one substantial fact upon which any really New South can be predicated,"* The Progressive Farmer, born fighting, nailed to its masthead the battleflag of "Better Schools and Better Farming." Demanding an efficient agricultural college in every state with "feeder schools in every county" (forerunners of our present Smith-Hughes vocational agriculture), Editor-Founder L. L. Polk joined Henry W. Grady, B. R. Tillman, Gen. Stephen D. Lee, Walter H. Page and other famous Southerners in a "Wake Up the South" crusade in which he never stopped fighting till he died—nor ever failed to maintain his declared ideal in founding The Progressive Farmer:

> "Serving no master, ruled by no faction, circumscribed
> by no selfish or narrow policy . . . it will fearlessly
> the right defend and impartially the wrong condemn."

2. "Equality for Agriculture:" A National Campaign—

His great work for the South winning national recognition, Editor-Founder Col. L. L. Polk next headed and led the most powerful farmers' organization in American history (the National Farmers Alliance, 2,000,000 members) in a fight for "Equality for Agriculture," nearly all its proposals having since been enacted into laws for railroad rate regulation, Federal Land Banks, production credit loans, parcel post, rural mail delivery, decentralized bank control, a better monetary system, etc.

*Sidney Lanier.

m the South

Printers' Ink—1888

3. **Farm Demonstration and County Agent Work**—The Progressive Farmer was a pioneer fighter for the establishment of farm demonstration work and county agent work, Dr. Seaman A. Knapp, national founder of this work, declaring:

> "The Progressive Farmer suits me. It is on the right track with a fast team and a good driver. I have not much time to watch the race, but I will try to be at the finish and do some cheering. Maybe they will let me tie on the ribbons!"

4. **Highly Localized Reader Service**—Recognizing the impossibility of giving effective service through a single edition to all the far-flung regions of the South from the Potomac to the Rio Grande inclusive, The Progressive Farmer was the first—and is yet the only farm publication—to establish separate editions based on adequately staffed editorial, advertising and circulation offices in each important agricultural region of the South—five separate editions having long been published by us as follows:

Carolinas-Virginia	Kentucky-Tennessee
Georgia-Alabama-Florida	Texas Edition
Mississippi Valley	

And The Progressive Farmer is the only farm publication—in the South or in the nation—that offers the combined advantages of (1) large sectional coverage and (2) strongly localized editorial service.

5. **Boys' and Girls' Club Work**—A pioneer also in promoting boys' and girls' club work and vocational education, The Progressive Farmer was the first Southern farm publication to provide Southwide prizes for 4-H Club activities, while its constant efforts to promote agricultural and home economics education were recognized years ago in the appointments of its present president to membership on the Federal Board for Vocational Education.

6. **Guaranteed Advertising**—Fighting squarely abreast of Collier's, Edward W. Bok and Dr. Harvey W. Wiley in exposing medical quacks and all forms of fraudulent advertising, The Progressive Farmer next became the first Southern farm paper to guarantee the reliability of all its advertising, and every year since has rejected many thousand dollars' worth of advertising found acceptable by many publications.

7. **First Full Time Woman Editor**—No development of the last half century has been more important than the ever-increasing recognition of woman's work and interests. The Progressive Farmer was the *first Southern farm publication* to employ a full time home economics expert as editor of our woman's department, while the farm women's clubs ("United Farm Women") organized all over Dixie under her direction were forerunners of the many thousand "Home Demonstration Clubs" now revolutionizing Southern homemaking.

8. **Some World-Famous Friends**—President Theodore Roosevelt, Gifford Pinchot, Sir Horace Plunkett, Walter H. Page, and a host of other leaders applauded crusades by The Progressive Farmer and its editors, and the first Henry Wallace, a member of the First Roosevelt's Country Life Commission (1908) declared: "The Progressive Farmer is doing as fine work as any agricultural paper that comes to my table from either North or South," while our "50th Anniversary Issue" (1936) reprinted extracts from special messages sent to us in previous years by the following world-famous figures:

President Theodore Roosevelt	Dr. Chas. W. Eliot
President Franklin D. Roosevelt	Gifford Pinchot
Admiral Robt. E. Peary	Franklin K. Lane
Thomas A. Edison	Luther Burbank
Thomas Nelson Page	Vice-Pres. Thomas R. Marshall
James Whitcomb Riley	Vice-Pres. Chas. G. Dawes
Kenyon L. Butterfield	"Red" Grange
Dr. Chas. H. Mayo	Chief Justice Hughes
Senator B. R. Tillman	Senator Carter Glass
Sen. John Sharp Williams	Walter Johnson
Ty Cobb	Edwin Markham
President Herbert Hoover	Governor Alfred E. Smith
President Taft	

9. **Foremost Living Artists, Poets, Authors**—The Progressive Farmer may not yet have realized our high ambition to become "the most beautiful rural magazine in America," but everyone will admit that it is on its way. Look at this partial list of famous living artists whose works were represented on Progressive Farmer covers in 1937, 1938:

N. C. Wyeth	Andrew Loomis
Harold Anderson	Lynn Bogue Hunt
Maxfield Parrish	Frank E. Schoonover

And not only does The Progressive Farmer say, "The best is none too good," when we go after artists but also when we go after story-writers, poets, and writers of special articles. In recent issues *Marquis James* wrote on Sam Houston, *Donald Culross Peattie* on Audubon, *Dr. E. V. McCollum* on foods, *David Grayson* on "Country Things I Love Most"; *Edna St. Vincent Millay, Edwin Markham,*

"IN THE RURAL SOUTH,

Grace Noll Crowell and *Jesse Stuart* have furnished poems, while our recent story writers have included—

Octavus Roy Cohen	Irvin Cobb
Helen Topping Miller	Ben Ames Williams
Roark Bradford	August Derleth
Norma Patterson	Archibald Rutledge

10. "Master Magazine for Farm People"—In a hundred ways

The Progressive Farmer continues to keep abreast of rural need and rural opportunity—in its 1937 year-long review of "New Sources of Farm Income"—in its long continued crusade for "Two-Armed Farming" or combining plant production and animal production in proper balance all over Dixie instead of depending on crop production alone—in its sponsorship of the "Master Farmer" movement in connection with the agricultural colleges in every state from Virginia to Texas inclusive—in its "Score Card for Blue Ribbon Farm Families" which provides for everybody a comprehensive test of progress toward Master Farmer standards—in its recent Southwide "Home Improvement Contest" with liberal prizes followed now by a similar 1938 contest for rural church improvement. The work of Editor Tait Butler has won him the coveted American Farm Bureau Award "For Distinguished Service to American Agriculture"; four southern colleges and universities have recognized Dr. Clarence Poe's editorial services (Doctor of Science, Clemson; LL.D., University of North Carolina and Washington College; Lit. D., Wake Forest) while our entire editorial staff won recognition in Alabama Polytechnic Institute's unique award to The Progressive Farmer as *"Master Magazine for Farm People."* And yet of all the tributes that have come to The Progressive Farmer in its more than 50 years' history there is none that we appreciate so much as that which plain farmers themselves originated and have repeated every year now for nearly two generations:

> "You can tell by a man's farm
> whether he reads it or not!"

✢

"Fifty years old and never before so good as now" say competent critics of Printers' Ink. And we of The Progressive Farmer rejoice that by these strenuous efforts to "keep up," the same thing is also said of The Progressive Farmer. We salute Printers' Ink and we salute the next half century in which it, like The Progressive Farmer, will find—

> "That which it has done but earnest
> Of the things it yet shall do."

"The next half century belongs to the South" which is already growing twice as fast as all the rest of America—and in the great days that lie just ahead we in our Southern agricultural field rejoice in the prospect of even closer comradeship with our great New York contemporary in the national advertising field.

PROGRESSIVE FARMER

BIRMINGHAM	RALEIGH	MEMPHIS	DALLAS

250 Park Avenue, NEW YORK   Daily News Bldg., CHICAGO

IT'S PROGRESSIVE FARMER''

of letters, carefully worked out to exploit the human desire to appear in print, would descend on those who resisted the initial invitation. The price ranged from $5 to $50 a head, depending on the eminence of the subject.

If the advertiser went after the quarry himself, the procedure involved sending a liberal, but not vulgarly lavish, collection of his wares tied up in silk ribbons. This would be placed in a Russia leather case with plush lining and a heavy engraved silver plate on the outside, stating the name of the recipient and an intimation that the gift was a tribute to his or her beauty or genius. There would be a lock on the box and the key would be sent separately by post. The method succeeded ten times in twelve, at a cost of not much more than $10 per catch. Some advertisers maintained a fancy for the endorsement of the common people, depending on large numbers of testimonials in place of fame. One ingenious medicinal cigarette company caused to be inserted in some of the packages a slip of paper on which a young lady, in a round and feminine hand, had written her name and address. The romantic

1897

KLONDIKE gold rush begins. . . . Wheat at $1.09 a bushel, highest since 1891. . . . 5,000 postmasters strike for increase in salary. . . . Floods in the Mississippi Valley. . . . Japan protests annexation of Hawaii by U. S. . . . Dingley Tariff Act signed, bringing average rates of 49.5 per cent, highest in history.

Number of publications increases 313, suggesting better times. . . . Bill before New York legislature proposes making it illegal to sell below cost. . . . Charles A. Dana, editor of the New York *Sun,* dies and is succeeded by his son, Paul Dana. . . . Seattle *Post-Intelligencer* sells 214,134 copies of special Klondike edition. . . . E. A. Wheatley, one of the top advertising writers, re-establishes headquarters in Chicago after a period in New York.

Advertising wagons, driving slowly through the streets, a familiar sight to urban residents. . . . "Sometimes I find myself wondering whether Ananias was not an advertising man"— Frederick L. Perine. . . . Forbes Munson, advertising manager of James S. Kirk & Company, given additional duties of executive management of the toilet soap department. . . . Counterfeiting of liquors and medicines is widespread. . . . Manly Gillam takes 112 brook trout in one season from streams within the limits of the new city of Greater New York. . . . The most widely talked of advertisement in years: "Pears' soap and an Anglo-American Alliance would improve the complexion of the universe."

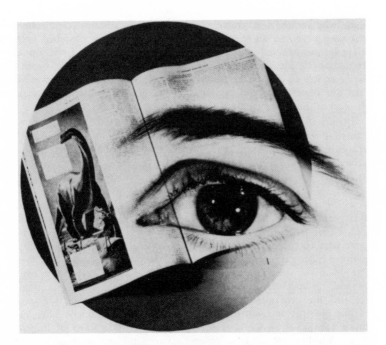

WE BUY AND SELL READERS!

Your advertisement is both a shopper and a salesman. As a shopper, it buys a countable number of readers per dollar. As a salesman, it must turn these readers into customers for the product.

We have studied this double-duty of an advertisement for 30 years. We have always respected plausible theory enough to check it against practical experience. And this method has guided us in preparing advertisements which both capture reader interest and do a selling job. Perhaps that's why our average client has been with us 10 years or longer.

May we discuss with you our method of pre-judging the selling power of an advertising campaign?

FEDERAL ADVERTISING AGENCY, INC.
444 MADISON AVENUE • NEW YORK

male who replied was answered by the young lady in an intimate and cleverly constructed letter which hinted at the pleasure which would be given her by an answer mentioning the benefits of the cigarettes. It worked fine.

Ultimately the testimonial craze caused public ridicule. Theatrical travesties on advertising were received with uproarious applause by audiences everywhere.

The second major change in advertising which became evident in this period was a definite trend to the use of larger space. The full-page idea in magazines was undergoing a remarkable growth and the size of space units in newspapers as well as periodicals was being stepped up generally.

The physical needs of the longer, more detailed copy was a factor in this. Another was the growing and better calculated employment of illustrations.

The photograph came to play a prominent part in advertising at this time, paper, printing and half-tones having improved enough to render possible a fairly respectable quality of photographic reproduction. Photographs had been used to some degree in prior years, of course, but only in limited, cut-and-dried fashion—chiefly pictures of faces or products.

In Chicago, Beatrice Tonnesen, owner of a large photographic studio, was developing the idea of using live models in her work, just as artists did. When she received an advertising order, she first created an idea and then selected a model best suited for its expression. The problem of getting a good-looking girl who would allow her face to be used was a difficult one. Those that could be dug up often

had no suitable wardrobe. But Miss Tonnesen plumbed every possible source and built up a long list of models. The work came rapidly into favor and the "Tonnesen Model" achieved a nation-wide popularity.

Other photographers offered similar services, although it was to be many years before more than a very few gave time and thought to making pictures for advertising purposes.

In paintings and drawings, as well as in photographs, the "typical American girl"—the bright-eyed, dashing maiden of sweet face and shapely figure—won and held the large share of pictorial prominence. However, the elderly gentleman began to gain considerable favor as a commercial subject. With him was associated the idea of long experience and the wisdom born of age and he was conceived to lend authority to the message. In addition he was regarded as well suited for medicine and drug copy, since the elderly man is frequently ailing.

Photography lent new impetus to the employment of children's pictures, which had already attained quite a following among advertisers. One of the most famous pictures of the time was the Wool soap twins ("My Mama Used Wool Soap"—"I Wish Mine Had"), taken from an amateur photograph of the twin grandchildren of a prominent Western poet.

The posed commercial photograph helped to set the practice of using advertising illustrations as a part of the selling story, rather than as a mere ornament or attention-catcher. And its use was encouraged by the fact that the courts were beginning to show a disposition to protect the right of privacy in photographs. The indiscriminate use of personal portraits of prominent people—hitherto a chief source of photographic illustration—was perforce on its way out.

A potent force toward not only the use of more adequate space units, but also toward a general understanding of the basic principles of advertiser practice, unquestionably came with the permeation of the fact-finding efforts of one of the greatest advertising salesmen who ever lived. His name was Thomas Balmer. A tobacco salesman with a conspicuously successful record, Balmer decided to venture into fresh fields, though at forty-five he was well on toward middle age. In 1891 he answered an advertisement run by Cyrus Curtis, then in search of a Western manager for *Ladies' Home Journal.*

Instead of plunging into a round of calls on prospects, Balmer proceeded to get to the bottom of this advertising situation, and he produced the first piece of advertising research of widespread significance. One of the things that struck him first in taking inventory of his opportunities was the fact that he found dozens of advertisers in the *Ladies' Home Journal* of the year before who had ceased advertising in the current year. He decided to find out why. He investigated 600 advertising failures, probing the causes, and after an exhaustive correspondence and study arrived at three chief causes of advertising death.

One was insufficient size of space. Nine times in ten, Balmer found, the unsuccessful advertiser had attempted to create an initial impression with less than half the space used by other advertisers to maintain an impression already created.

Some attempted to market entirely new articles in skimpy space, so that they could scarcely even begin to explain the nature of the new device to the public, much less offer arguments for buying it.

Related to this "small space disease" was the single insertion. The analysis showed that a large percentage went no farther than one insertion as a trial of advertising. The folly of the single insertion became so evident that he resolved not to accept a one-time advertisement unless it was a trial message in a series to ascertain test methods.

A third reason for failure was the lack of necessary follow-up facilities. Nobody seemed to know much about taking care of results.

Any of these defects alone, it appeared, was sufficient to bring disaster, unless the advertiser experienced an extraordinary stroke of luck.

The principles were plain, but the applying of them was not easy. Most business men who had advertised deemed that they knew all there was to know on the subject. Balmer, however, had a make-up wherein personality and magnetic force were coupled with a deep respect for facts. He deliberately made it hard for the advertiser to begin because he didn't want to see a man start before the business was ready for it, yet he put his story over with astonishing success. He helped to start the large-scale advertising of men's clothing, paints, stockings, spices, carpets and shoes by mail, and cereal foods.

As time proved out the soundness of these analyses, the acceptance of them naturally spread, and Balmer's foresighted study did much to upbuild the foundation of sound advertiser procedure.

Selling the

to America's No.1 Home

Throughout America, Philadelphia is famed as the City of Homes.

Widely known is the saying, "In Philadelphia nearly everybody reads The Bulletin."

From a small beginning, nearly half a century ago, The Philadelphia Evening Bulletin has grown steadily in the friendly interest and confidence of the people.

Men and women and children welcome The Evening Bulletin into the family circle.

It is published with *understanding* of Philadelphia home life . . .

and with reading interest for every income class.

It is edited with care for exactness in headlines and news . . . for quality in all features and departments.

Made up with studied attention value, page after page, it is a thoroughly read newspaper.

And for thirty-three years it has led all Philadelphia daily newspapers in number of readers.

With by far the largest daily circulation in Philadelphia, The Bulletin is one of America's largest daily newspapers. No newspaper

In Philadelphia — City of Homes —
nearly everybody reads

Manufacturer's Product

Market

of similar size in the nation approaches it in years of leadership.

Its position in Philadelphia and in the nation was gained without use of prizes, premiums or subscriber contests. Showing the response of the people to the things that make a careful newspaper!

The Bulletin's circulation—almost entirely within the retail trading area, reaches nearly every Philadelphia home. It gives *one-newspaper* coverage at low advertising cost, of America's largest market of individual homes!

The manufacturer's best prospects are people who live in individual, *single-family* homes.

There are more of them in Philadelphia than in any other city of America.

They are reached by the newspaper that has grown into Philadelphia's home traditions—lending to the manufacturer's message something of its own reader interest and confidence.

Your advertising agency knows the Philadelphia market . . . the economy and success of advertising to this home-loving people, by the use alone of The Evening Bulletin.

The Evening Bulletin

Beardsley and Buttons

THE attention concept of the advertising message flourished through the latter half of the 1890's as it had in the first. A new annex to the vogue, however, appeared in the use of unusual forms of advertising media.

The advertiser now became obsessed with the idea of catching the citizen off guard by confronting him with messages in places where they would be unexpected. This period produced more wild and curious advertising media than any other, before or since.

Strange more in its application than in its intrinsic form was the poster craze, which developed into spectacular proportions in 1896 after a start about two years before. The subject of the fad was a single sheet posting, used indoors as well as out, in which rather bizarre "art" effects were featured. More often than not there was no sales message and no relation of the picture to a selling point—the idea being merely to flash the product name before an eye attracted by the unusual design.

The poster form of advertising had its origin in France some years before, with Jules Cheret as the pioneer. It came to the United States by way of England, where a young artist by the name of Aubrey Beardsley had attracted wide attention by his strange designs. Beardsley was what was known as a "modern," and he conventionalized the human figure and produced unusual arrangements without attempt at correctness of drawing or accuracy of color. His posters were enthusiastically received as a revelation on the one hand and harshly condemned as a glorifier of the hideous in life on the other.

At any rate, they attracted attention and the American advertiser went in for the Beardsley style with a vengeance. All sorts of exaggerated effects and freak designs were put forth. Famous artists did not scorn to produce commercial postings. A vogue for collecting posters became quickly established and many of the choicer designs commanded a good price. They were used to a great degree by magazines and newspapers and by general advertisers of all kinds. The bicycle manufacturers were among the largest users and some of them sent poster exhibits around the country.

Not all the posters, of course, were bizarre caricatures of the Beardsley pattern. Maxfield Parrish, Louis Rhead, Will H. Bradley, J. C. Leyendecker and others produced designs which were to have a beneficial effect in advancing the standards of advertising art as a whole. But the gaudy freaks found the greatest favor among many users and before long the craze went into an eclipse.

Meanwhile the strange vogue of the advertising button was building itself up to a climax. It began at the cycle show in 1895 when a number of the manufacturers of bicycles gave away buttons bearing their trade-marks. Buttons distributed in the McKinley campaign provided further impetus, and then the craze took hold in earnest.

At the beginning the buttons bore merely a trade-mark design or a product or company name. John H. Woodbury created a new note with the inauguration of a Facial Purity League, with buttons for all the members. Then came the use of slang phrases and peppy sayings, the advertiser's name appearing below the phrase. Manufacturers issued buttons bearing such snappers as: "If you love me, grin." "Yes, darling." "Is it hot enough for you?" A great hit was made with, "I'm somewhat of a liar myself."

This was not mere child's play, mind you. There was scarcely a man, woman or youngster who did not wear an advertising button of some kind. Buttons blossomed on the lapels even of prominent businessmen. Nobody could see why people would do it, but they did. The latest button was awaited almost breathlessly, and the craze hit a downturn only when the button makers began to exhaust the supply of witty sayings.

Ingenuity ran rampant in devising new advertising mediums. There were "aeroplanes," three box kites sent up in the air with an advertising banner attached. There were wagons with signs painted on the sides or roofs, which toured residential districts and rang great gongs to attract attention. Ostriches were often used to draw the wagons. The use of bald-headed men, each with a letter of a product name or message painted on his pate and sitting in line with his likewise labeled colleagues at a theater or public gathering, became common.

A syndicate was organized to sell advertising at the circus, including space on the sides of elephants and camels and vocal announcements by the clowns. Numerous of the leading advertisers—from chewing gum to headache powders—went in for this. The advertising sailboat was practically a standard medium. It consisted of a sloop, with a message painted on its sails, which cruised back and forth in sight of people on beaches or in steamboats. The price ranged from $50 to $250 per month, depending on circulation.

Advertising hats and caps, made of canvas, became immensely popular for distribution at parades and picnics. The illustrated advertising postcard, an idea imported from Austria, was widely popular in 1899 and used by advertisers of all sizes and types. Sapolio put out a song about its product paraphrasing the popular Pinafore product and distributed copies by the million and every home rang with it until it became a national nuisance. The Rogers cloud projector, which could impress a message on clouds as high as three miles, found favor. The New York *World* had one and on clear nights the resourceful operator found a substitute screen in the side of the Times Building. On trains the train boy would place in your lap a book containing five two-cent stamps and a number of advertisements, dispensing the item to thrifty travelers for 9 cents. Tarrant's Seltzer Aperient had carefully laid plans for a system of advertising buoys running 500 miles out along the water-courses of ocean steamships and also all along the Atlantic and Pacific coasts.

Forging the Sales Tools

THE development of systematic methods of selling to stimulate the movement of merchandise through the channels of trade was relatively slow as compared to that of advertising. Many manufacturers, perhaps the majority, conceived that the power of the advertisement in dealing with the consumer was sufficient to insure maximum marketing efficiency. Salesmanship was assumed to be largely a routine, automatic performance and the creative, dynamic potentialities of the selling function were pretty much ignored.

To put it another way, the average general advertiser acted in emulation of the mail-order user of advertising. He regarded consumer advertising as sufficient unto itself in moving his goods. Salesmen, jobbers and retailers were considered little more important in the general advertiser's scheme of things than were the operations of the postoffice in delivering the mail-order merchandiser's goods to the consumer.

The earliest forms of related selling activities were those whose primary impact was upon the consumer — sampling and premiums. Both had been used to some extent for many years.

Not infrequently the pioneer advertiser—of foods and drugs especially—distributed samples of his merchandise in his house-to-house calls. He often expanded his distribution by this method.

Gradually it came to be seen that the sampling process could be made to exert an important influence upon the retailer, both in inducing him to buy an initial order of the goods and in providing the incentive for him to keep an adequate stock on hand. An interesting example is the program begun by the Coca-Cola Company about 1894. When a new market was being opened the firm asked retailers to provide lists of 100 good customers. To these it sent a letter and a ticket entitling the recipient to a free drink of Coca-Cola, the company redeeming the tickets from the retailers for the full price of 5 cents. Then men were sent on the road to distribute free drink tickets at intervals in the newer territories. Thus a constant demand upon the retailer was stimulated, with the result that he had a definite incentive to keep a supply on hand. In six years the company paid out something like $450,000 for redemption of these tickets and found the investment well worth while.

The Columbian Exposition at Chicago in 1893 provided further impetus toward the adoption of the sampling idea. There you could start out with soap and proceed through with oatmeal, biscuits, butterine, canned meat and a cup of coffee or chocolate, ending up with a glass of wine and a cigar. In the years following, food expositions became a common thing in the larger cities and many manufacturers participated in them. Most department stores followed suit and staged food demonstrations at which sampling was a feature.

As more and more canned and packaged foods came on the market, sampling assumed a prominent position and some of the operations were carried forward on a large scale. In 1896 the American Cereal Company distributed a million samples of Quaker Oats in New

From an "Oldster" of 143 years
To a "Youngster" of 50 --

GREETINGS
and SALUTATIONS

Institutions gain from the passing of the years not grey heads and stiffening joints, but wealth of experience and breadth of outlook and responsibility for leadership.

The (York, Pa.)
GAZETTE AND DAILY

(Founded 1795; Daily—1870)

recognizes this responsibility of "age," which includes a response to the changing conditions of modern life—a blending of the old with the new for the common good.

It salutes PRINTERS' INK for those same characters which make for responsive and responsible age—a living institution.

National Representatives
HOWLAND AND HOWLAND, INC.

NEW YORK	CHICAGO
247 Park Ave.	860 N. Michigan Ave.
Eld. 5-5183	State 4439

Pittsburgh, 7955 Tioga St., Churchill 8848

York and vicinity. In almost every large city there sprang up distributing organizations which made a business of providing house-to-house sampling forces.

The modern premium goes back to B. T. Babbitt, the soap manufacturer. Before the Civil War the laundry soap business was in the same class as sugar. It was bought and sold by the pound. When Babbitt brought out a soap in cake form (Babbitt's Best Soap) to overcome close competition, he found that the public, accustomed to buying by the pound and more or less irrespective of who made it, was unresponsive. To gain the interest of consumers, he conceived the idea of putting a value on the wrappers. To any person sending in twenty-five of them, he offered a panel picture and the idea took on quickly. Editions of some of the pictures ran into the hundreds of thousands.

The premium idea was adopted by a number of other soap firms. In 1888 the Larkin Soap Company began giving premiums with each $10 order. And by 1897 the premium idea had spread into a number of different fields. The chief users were the soap companies and the cigarette advertisers, who offered buttons, jewelry, pictures and novelty items upon presentation of a certain number of coupons or wrappers. Several of the cigarette companies placed the premium in the package, which was a new application. Other manufacturers at about this time adopted the idea of asking housewives and children to sell goods for premium rewards, such goods as bluing, jewelry and toilet preparations. A number of the firms dealing direct in coffees, spices and soap asked customers to solicit orders from their neighbors when ordering goods and receive a premium. Most premium procedure, however, was based on the collection of coupons, a tendency which continued strong for some years.

The idea of training the sales force to increased efficiency and effectiveness found its greatest—and almost sole—exponent of the times in John H. Patterson, president of the National Cash Register Company. In 1892 the astute Patterson sensed the coming of a business depression. He decided to do something about it other than merely reefing sails, and he set out to learn how well his salesmen were equipped for a stringent selling period. At a convention he examined salesmen on their methods to get an idea of the practices generally in vogue and to his surprise he found the men woefully deficient in arguments and methods of handling storekeeper prospects. Then followed the famous trip around the country in which Patterson and E. D. Gibbs, his advertising director, visited fifty cities in fifty-one days. A convention of agents was called in each city and Patterson and Gibbs acted as storekeepers and had their men work out selling tactics on them. These appraisals brought to light an amazing degree of incompetency and showed that the average salesman's equipment consisted largely of excuses, ineptness and bad habits.

The following year, while attending the Fair at Chicago, Patterson got the idea of a school for salesmen. While listening to the attendants at the company's booth in their expositions to visitors, he noted that what they had to say was weakly put and badly organized. He put out a "primer" for the attendants to follow in making their talks and increased crowds immediately resulted. Shortly after came the first salesmen's training school at Dayton. The men were called in for a six weeks' course. A new "primer" was devised and Patterson made the men memorize it as a means of firmly implanting the sales arguments contained. He gave examinations on the material to be sure they did so.

The Patterson methods—and in particular his "canned" sales talk, which was probably the first thing of its kind—were discounted by many and ridiculed by some. Eventually, of course, industry as a whole was to see that there was something more to selling than a pleasing personality and that modern selling demanded sales education. It was to be quite a few years, however, before the true value of this element in marketing was widely accepted and practiced.

The idea of what is currently known as "merchandising" the advertising was likewise slow in gaining acceptance. In the late 90's a few companies made moves in this direction. It was news in 1896 when one large firm adopted a plan of sending its salesmen proofs of its advertisements as they were to appear in print. Two years later a

---

1898

U. S. S. *MAINE* sunk in an explosion in Havana Harbor, with loss of two officers and 264 men. . . . War with Spain begins. . . . Admiral Dewey takes Manila. . . . Charge of San Juan Hill. . . . Cervera's fleet destroyed. . . . Santiago surrenders. . . . And the treaty of peace is signed, Spain relinquishing all claim to Cuba and ceding to the U. S. Puerto Rico, Guam and the Philippines.

A. W. Green organizes the National Biscuit Company, which begins to advertise. . . . Women advertising writers appearing. . . . New advertising medium: a cabinet, to be placed in public location, which contains a phonograph that plays a few numbers, then announces the advertiser's goods. . . . John Lee Mahin leaves Procter & Collier to form the Mahin Advertising Company at Chicago. . . . Nudity in advertisements getting a little scandalous.

Albert G. Bradford and Jarvis A. Wood admitted to partnership in N. W. Ayer. . . . Pace of modern civilization said to be making us a nation of nervous wrecks. . . . Theodore P. Roberts, formerly of Sears, Roebuck, forms his own agency at Chicago, as does J. L. Stack, formerly of Lord & Thomas. . . . Listerine, $1, being cut to 68 cents in some stores. . . . Tossing circulars out of balloons finds favor as an advertising medium. . . . New product: Caldeer's Saponaceous Dentine. . . . The timely note in advertising: "Some doubt whether America will conquer Spain, but there is no doubt that St. Jacob's Oil conquer (S)pain."

leading dry goods house concluded that proofs of company advertising were just as important a part of the drummer's equipment as his samples. A portfolio of proofs was furnished each salesman and he was instructed on how to use it in instances when the merchant claimed there was no call for the merchandise. And it was found that this procedure helped sales immensely.

Merchandising the advertising campaign direct to retailers was another innovation of the times. In 1893 Charles E. Hires had sent to dealers a single sheet, printed on both sides, calling their attention to the advantages of selling the well-known, advertised brand of root beer extract instead of unknown brands, pointing out that it insured a full profit since it was easier to sell and could be sold at the full price. This was a new idea, which at the time had no known precedent. In 1897 Hires developed the idea further and was in constant communication with every grocer and druggist who handled his product with his "Hires' Business Bringer" circulars.

By 1905 the merchandising of the advertising program had become just about an automatic part of every advertiser's activities.

In the last two years of the century, the trend to packaged merchandise transformed from a steady tide into a veritable flood. And with it came the first inklings of another consequential factor in the selling scheme—the sales power of the package.

Perhaps the greatest impetus came from the cereal companies, which for several years had vied with each other in putting out attractive packages. Twenty years

before the packaged article ha been comparatively rare. Almo every article in common use wa sold loose. The barrel and the bo> were the common containers. B 1900 the assortment of goods whicl had taken to package form was as tounding the populace—ammonia alcohol, liquors, tobacco, cigars shoe polish, baking soda, stove blacking, pins and needles, sewing silk and cotton thread, hairpins And molasses, vinegar, flour, cheese, dried apples and dozens of othc. things once regarded as staples to be sold only in bulk. Even salt which was being put up in cloth bags, and sugar which followed salt's example.

A significant role in the new surge was played by the "In-er-seal' package for Uneeda biscuit. When the National Biscuit Company was formed it had no package busines of any account. A. W. Green president of the company, discov ered that the soda cracker was the largest item of consumption and that handling in the tradition boxes and barrels did not enab' it to reach the customer in anything like its best condition. The sensa tional success of the move attracted wide attention.

The package was born of the manufacturer's urge to establish product identity with the consumer and nurtured by the housewife's growing predilection for the clear liness of packaged goods as opposed to the dirt and dust-collecting pro pensities of bulk handling. There was always the possibility that one of the boys around the stove would overreach his shot at the sawdust box.

The first packages were things of utility, labeled containers and not much more. With the latest boom

"To have great poets there must be great Audiences, too"

WILLIAM SHAKESPEARE was an accident. He lived at a time when the theatre was popular, printing possible, reading fashionable; a time midway between the mediaeval and the modern, when life was local, information limited, imaginations innocent, and the primary plots still had powerful appeal to unsophisticated people.

A century earlier, his work might never have known a stage, or it might have been lost in tattered playscripts undiscovered among the effects of dead and unimportant actors. A century later, the dramatist Shakespeare might never have emerged among the affectations of the eighteenth century English theatre.

But Shakespeare happened at a period and place that afforded him an audience . . . large enough to give him roots in English life, literature, history.

Homer, the blind chanter, came close enough to Athens' golden age to have hearers enough to want copies of his verses; copies enough to outlast the Dark Ages and let the Renaissance rediscover Homer.

Favored by their times, Virgil, Horace and Cicero passed on to posterity. But of the great engineers and inventors, Da Vinci is known only as a painter; his period provided no market for flying machines.

Successful products, much as poets, are conditioned upon recognition, reception, appreciation. Commerce as well as Art waits on an Audience.

And Audiences, too, are largely accidental, result of time and place and circumstances.

With a population as large as ours, and as rich, there is no lack of Audiences. And no lack of address to these Audiences.

For more than two hundred years, this was a raw, open country. Population originated and entered on the Eastern seaboard, trickled west in varying stages.

The long continuous struggle with nature, blotted out most other interests in the pioneers' minds. And leisure came only when crops were growing, roads made, communities established, security won.

The emigrant carries with him not only physique and coloring of his race and nation, but the habits and mind of his homeland. Every westbound wagon load and the grandchildren of its occupants bore strong but intangible ties with the East.

Mail routes followed the migrants. Necessary as nails, firearms, medicines was communication. With the mails went magazines.

Before the day of the news service and Washington

correspondent, the magazines recorded national news, the history and the course of the new nation.

The first native authors that blossomed in Boston found expression and support in the periodicals.

Godey's Lady's Book carried the crinoline to the first American women who had time and means enough to differentiate between clothing and dress.

And not the least service of the magazines to a new, raw, rich, hungry country was the news of the new products of our first manufacturers.

The magazines blazed the trail for the sewing machine salesman; sold the tin can and culinary revolution to a nation living eight months of the year on dried food, raw meats and root vegetables.

As mass production succeeded, with its cargoes of information, blue prints for better living and fiction for entertainment, the magazine was indispensable as the railroad.

As handicraft, and factory production grew beyond all local needs, the magazines found new markets for the new factories.

The trademarks, names and reputations became national. And magazine advertised commodities became standard stock in stores all over the country.

The magazines found an Audience—in the most

intelligent, enterprising, able-to-buy; the Audience that made Modern Business!

AN EMBARRASSMENT of riches in media confronts the advertiser today—innumerable avenues, innumerable audiences. But mark well this distinction:

All advertising makes sales to prospects ready to buy—*but magazines make customers!*

The magazine includes in its audience as many ready-to-buy as any medium, gives a harvest of quick sales, pays in orders, inquiries, coupons.

But *making customers* is a job that takes time and education, requires repetition and reiteration, and demands an interested and responsive audience.

Magazine advertising works long before the point of purchase; prepares the prospect that time, need and opportunity turn into the buyer.

Magazine advertising starts working on babies and keeps up to the grave; never stops educating, creating desire, identifying products.

Magazine advertising goes on building reputations, establishing preferences, seeding confidence; piling up the backlogs of future orders, pre-selling coming markets, insuring future business, assuring future dividends—as well as making sales today!

And, in time, magazine advertising makes a product part of our national life: part of our national eyes, palate, fingertip feel, sensory habit, rooted in the popular flesh and nervous system as well as in the popular mind.

Virtually every product that has national identity,

universal acceptance, has a background of magazine advertising—whatever other media were used!

And the product established by a long term of intelligent magazine advertising stands generally secure in its sales, impervious to price changes, unaffected by sporadic competition, pinnacle-high with its customers.

You can check the list of such products out of your own past experience, your present memory!

THE PAST TWO DECADES brought a vast growth of wealth, and amazing spread of advantages.

Our stock of automobiles almost equals our number of families; and our radio sets exceeds the number of families. A dozen million people patronize the motion picture theatres every day. Bridge, sports and play have become a major interest. Thicker newspapers enjoy huge augmented circulations. Books sell in greater quantities than they did twenty years ago. All of these attractions compete for people's time, money, support, compete with each other to some extent, and compete with magazines.

But remember, please, that all these phenomena are concomitants of increased means and increased leisure. And as wealth and leisure increase, *literacy increases more rapidly!* So the magazine Audience today is not less—but greater than ever before!

Magazine circulation is up over 1920 figures by some 20,000,000 copies. There are not fewer magazine readers, but more—reading more magazines.

Three magazine circulations touch 3,000,000 copies; nine others are above the two million mark.

The magazine in every field has a bigger job to do today—and does a better job.

Government and economics are essential common interests today; and magazines inform and interpret to a greater degree than ever before.

Magazines employ the graphic more, cover the world with the camera, use color lavishly and freely.

Housekeeping, cooking, child care, interior decoration, education, recreation and business concern American women today—and magazines are unflagging in catering to these concerns.

Entertaining people is a more complex, difficult job than it used to be—and the magazines supply a steady flow of brilliant, sparkling entertainment.

And in this complicated civilization of ours, more people *think* today—place more dependence on the magazine. In a world close tied by communications, with new problems, creeds and causes affecting individual conduct as well as the social scene—

IN SUMMARY THEN: The magazines enter the best homes—and best minds—in this country; reach more preferred prospects and better buying power, than ever before in their history.

The magazines interest these best millions year in and year out. They know how. They have spent a long time learning.

The magazines offer the best presentation of an advertising message; quietly, visually, to an interested, attentive recipient; in his own time, in his own mood. (An important list of attributes!)

The magazines offer color for attention, impact, or realism; offer frequency for reminding, for building impression, to make ideas and names stick.

The magazines cost less than ever before.

And incidentally, magazine advertising *sells goods!*

These are elementary facts about a major medium. You knew them all the time! But isn't it curious, in this curious business of advertising, how many advertisers seem to forget . . . ?

THIS ADVERTISEMENT for magazine advertising is signed by the Crowell Publishing Company, publishers of four great magazines, each an important advertising medium. But our business is *not* the manufacture and maintenance of advertising media, except very incidentally. We serve advertisers well— but advertisers come second.

We serve readers first and all the time. The editor is still the major figure in this publishing business; and the reader and the reading public is the boss.

From time to time, like all publishers we are under pressure from advertisers to make changes and afford cooperation that may be to our immediate advantage in revenue. And if we sometimes seem cool and unappreciative to such suggestions, it is because we feel they do not accord with our working principles, our main objectives—or yours.

Because our most important service to advertisers is the Audiences we gather and hold—great Audiences.

And without these Audiences our value to advertisers would be nil. In serving advertisers, no good publisher can do less than this—or more!

"Yankee Doodle Goes To Town"

is a thirty-minute motion picture delineating the rise of the national magazine, picturing its influence with the American public, its importance to the national advertiser. Produced by Collier's, The National Weekly, this film is available in standard and 16 mm. sizes for presentation to advertisers and their sales forces. Address the Advertising Department of Collier's.

THE CROWELL PUBLISHING COMPANY

Publishers of . . . COLLIER'S · WOMAN'S HOME COMPANION
THE AMERICAN MAGAZINE · THE COUNTRY HOME MAGAZINE

250 PARK AVENUE · NEW YORK CITY

appeared the idea of putting some salesmanship into the package.

One of the first to see the display importance of the package was the Campbell Soup Company. Most canned goods labels of the time were ugly and Campbell's design was consciously devised so that no matter how many varieties of soup a grocer might have on his shelf, Campbell, with its red, black and white color scheme, would be sure to stand out. Easy identification was also a keynote of the Uneeda design. However, very few others had caught up with this strategy by 1900, or even by 1910, for that matter.

The Uneeda package, incidentally, was one of the prominent examples of the early dual use container. Those who took their lunch to school thirty or thirty-five years ago may remember its being packed in a Uneeda package. The company advertised this point in 1901 and grocers reported it helped sales. The dual use plan was also employed in other lines. There was baking powder in glassware, tea in tea caddies, coffee in patented coffee pots, polishing powder in chamois skins.

Some attention was given at this time to developing special effects . in marketing plans. A Baltimore concern came up with a plan for selling pocket-knives and fountain pens. A customer would buy six coupons for 30 cents. He would sell the coupons to his friends for 5 cents each. The friends would secure a supply of coupons and sell them to their friends. And when all these had sold six coupons each the number one customer was entitled to a $2 four-blade, pearl-handled English steel pocket-knife or a 14-karat gold fountain pen of alleged $2 value. The company received 30 cents from the first man and 25 cents from each of his friends for a total take of $1.80 per completed transaction. If all this seems to have a familiar ring, it may be because in 1933 the same chain-letter racket and variations of it took the country by storm. In 1899 it was applied by various firms to shoes, overcoats and all manner of novelty merchandise. The "endless chain" is as eternal as its name implies. It was revived at least twice prior to 1933 and in each revival scarcely anybody ever stopped to think that on the fifteenth transaction the number of participants would have to be several times the total population of the globe.

Another new wrinkle was a program fostered in behalf of Wool soap. The Woman's Christian Temperance Union had constructed a new women's temple in Chicago, complete with mortgage. In 1898 the ladies were approached with the idea that they should confine their purchases of soap to the Wool brand and induce their friends to do the same. They were to collect the wrappers and Swift & Company would pay them a cent for each wrapper sent in and these funds could then be applied to the mortgage. The Goodwin Plan! Exactly the same idea was broached in 1933 by the Goodwin Corporation of America, except that many manufacturers were to participate and the rebates on the labels were to go to church societies. The 1898 version was a big success at the first and had the other soap manufacturers a bit worried and irritated. Apparently, however, its success was not such as to inspire an emulation more immediate than thirty-five years later.

Retailing Strides

ALTHOUGH few manufacturers had taken more than a passive interest in the retail wing of distribution, important events affecting the operations of the retailer were under way.

Chief among these was the rise of the department store. Many years before, A. T. Stewart of New York had instituted a retailing method which was to influence profoundly the course of retailing and help pave the way for the advertised brand. Stewart initiated the one-price system. For centuries the selling of consumers' goods had been a haggling proposition. Merchandise had no price other than that arrived at in the process of bargaining between the merchant and his customer. Stewart offered one price to all comers and harvested from this confidence-building measure a flourishing trade. Other merchants took notice.

John Wanamaker, Marshall Field, R. H. Macy and others came along to perfect the large department store as a distributive machine. In essence, the department store or bazaar, as it was often called, was simply an inflated version of the old-time general store, spreading the retail overhead over a large variety of items. To this, however, was added the threefold principle of liberal stocks, liberal dealing and liberal advertising—with the one-price system as the base.

The new institutions perceived the profit and public patronage to be won by selling quickly for a low mark-up. They offered a greater variety of merchandise, presented new standards of service and made it possible for the shopper to buy many things easily and comfortably under one roof. They introduced the bargain counter as a means of getting people into the store so that other things could be sold them at a profit, and to keep the bargain shelves stocked, they combed the world's close-out sources and virtually created bargain-making industries.

It has come to be that the measure of success of any retailing institution is the amount of fulminating indignation aroused among the rank-and-file retailers. By this yardstick it was quite emphatically clear by 1897 that the department store had come to stay. A great and growing sentiment against the department stores had amplified to a nation-wide roar in that year. It crystallized in the form of demand for legislation to limit the operations of the aggregated wealth and concentrated energy of the great "merchant princes." Legislative agitation was thunderous in Illinois and New York and in a number of cities. In Chicago a law was proposed which would require a store to pay a license fee in order to carry added lines, the fee to be larger than the gross profits from the expansion.

In addition there were attempts to institute retailer boycotts against manufacturers who sold to the department store octupi.

In the end the agitation died down, although it was to echo in retailers' councils and legislative halls for many years. After a time the retailers found a new dragon to fret about.

While the department stores took up the one-price system and found it good, their enthusiasm for manufacturer participation in the method proved to be less than tumultuous. The idea of an article which had a fixed price known in advance to the public did not set at all well with most of these establishments. They wanted to set their own standards of values and they strongly resisted the manufacturer's efforts to go to the consumer on his own initiative and do likewise.

In consequence the manufacturer of advertised brands found the department stores a pretty independent lot. Confident in their own consumer relations, they refused to handle manufacturers' brands in numerous lines. Where they did handle them, most refused to display the merchandise and, moreover, instructed their salespeople to offer something else and claim for it equality or superiority.

Despite the fact that the advertiser found the department store a tough customer, in the final analysis he benefited greatly from this retailing development. Ultimately the department store yielded a point in handling articles under the manufacturer's brand in many lines. From a broader standpoint, the department store taught the retail field as a whole many lessons which made it a more efficient arm of the distribution system. The more progressive of the smaller retailers realized that legislative attempts could bring no remedy, for the simple reason that people liked the department stores' way of doing business; that the one way to meet the competition of this style of retail operation was to adopt the successful methods which it had developed.

The result was a general trend to better display, improved service and the use of the persistent advertising which had proved to be so successful for the department store.

And the department store brought home some points to the advertiser. The example of these stores did much to demonstrate the value of continuous advertising and adequate space per insertion to the manufacturer. Through Powers and Gillam the Wanamaker advertising contributed to the formative stages of national advertising copy, although this "literary style," as it was known, was limited in use among retailers. Most large stores used the condensed style with listings of many items to attract bargain-seekers, and stressed the financial calamities of manufacturers and wiles of their buyers in tricking jobbers, which were represented as making possible the prices quoted.

Perhaps it was all the fuss about the department stores. Perhaps it was the increase of competition among manufacturers. Perhaps it was simply a natural growth. Whatever the reason, these final years of the century found a few alert advertisers giving thought and attention to the position of the retailer in the marketing scheme.

At the first, the advertiser was content to get his goods onto the retailer's shelf. Now it began to appear that there might be some advantage in working with the retailer to help him dispose of the merchandise in greater quantities.

What seem to have been the earliest attempts at tying-in with the merchant's selling programs are rooted in a curiously lackadaisical habit of the latter. The country dealer would often be a regular advertiser in the local paper, paying for a certain amount of space under a local contract. Having little inclination to write new copy, he would let the same announcement stand week after week. A few shrewd manufacturers spotted in this practice a neat opportunity to expand their advertising coverage. They would send to the dealer, free of charge, attractive electrotypes about their products for the dealer to run over his own name.

Indeed, it is recorded that some manufacturers went on from there and made an "allowance" to the dealer toward the cost of the space. Which would seem to be the beginning of the lively history of the advertising allowance.

Prime development of the idea of helping the dealer with his sales problem at this time came among firms selling to the dry goods trade. In 1897 the Nazareth Waist Company offered to write special dealer advertisements, each one original and done for the particular merchant, for use in conducting muslin underwear sales. In 1898 Warner Brothers Company set aside out of its general advertising fund a fair amount with which to co-operate with the dealer in his town, announcing in business-paper advertising that its department of publicity was at the command of retail dealers throughout the land. Cards, booklets, circulars, wrapping paper, showcases and stands, signs and electrotypes for display advertisements were offered. A number of other firms offered circulars for store distribution, with the dealer's name imprinted.

Shortly following the appearance of the stereotype in newspaper production, several advertisers discovered the mat as a convenient substitute for the electrotype in distributing advertising helps.

1899

UNITED STATES signs the Hague Peace Conventions for pacific settlement of disputes. . . . Horatio Alger dies. . . . In notes to Great Britain, Germany, Russia, Japan, France and Italy, United States asks maintenance of an "Open Door," in China. . . . Filipinos rebel at United States administration of the islands.

Joseph Campbell Company advertises the first canned soups at 10 cents. . . . Joseph Medill, proprietor of the Chicago *Tribune*, dies. . . . National Biscuit stages a 112-wagon parade through the streets of downtown New York. . . . G. W. Wilder becomes head of the Butterick Publishing Company. . . . Advertisements appearing on a new-fangled affair called the "horseless carriage." . . . *American Boy* begins publication.

Illinois women's clubs begin crusade against indiscriminate use of the female face and figure in advertising, claiming that it "lowers the standard of womanhood, detracts from womanly dignity and corrupts the youth of the land." . . . Advertisement: "Tho love be cold, do not despair—there's Ypsilanti Underwear."

Pardon our SUDDEN ASCENT

In polite media circles, they're not talking about advertising revenue these days. But we've just been looking over our own PIB figures, and we can't resist the temptation to let you in on them:

In our first year, 1935, THIS WEEK MAGAZINE was 24th among all magazines, with a dollar volume of $1,229,043.

In 1936, we were 19th, with $2,275,961.

In 1937, we were 17th, with $3,446,214.

In the first 6 months of 1938, we were 11th, with $1,811,085—one of the very, very few magazines to gain over the comparable 1937 period.

?

Wonder where we'll be when we're as old as Printers' Ink?

THIS WEEK *sells* BOTH *sides of the counter*

STRAIGHT THINKING
fifty years ago — and now

"JOHN, we make the finest kitchen range in the country. I'm beginning to think we ought to tell people about it."

"Great Scott, Albert ... you don't mean *advertising*? Father would turn over in his grave! And the expense! I'm told that an advertisement in Century or Harper's Weekly costs almost one hundred dollars."

"But think of all the people they reach . . . thousands of them!"

"Thousands of readers, yes ... but how many range buyers, Albert? That's what I want to know. Just because a lady enjoys reading essays or poetry or romantic stories is no sign she's likely to buy a range."

"True. I hadn't thought of that."

"But you have to think about such things, Albert, especially with business conditions as they are.

We can't afford to spend several hundred dollars a year talking about our range to people who have no reason to buy a range ... schoolmarms, seamstresses, and the like. We want to advertise to people who have homes and are chiefly interested in homes. Anything else would be sheer waste."

"Yes, you're right. But suppose there were a magazine devoted *entirely* to home subjects and home service! Then we'd be *certain* the readers were interested in home... and likely prospects for us. . ."

"Well, you look into it, Albert. Maybe there *is* such a magazine. If there isn't there certainly should be."

* * *

The American Home would have been a godsend to the shrewd, straight-thinking advertisers of fifty years ago. Witness how it *sells, sells, sells* for the shrewd, straight-thinking advertisers of today.

A *The* MERICAN HOME

sells the HOME-MARKET of America
—1,300,000 buyers for *families*

The 85 Per Cent

CIRCULATIONS of newspapers and periodicals continued to grow during the years between 1895 and 1900 at an even higher rate of acceleration. To the improved publication manufacturing facilities was added the incentive of a growing demand for larger circulations from the advertiser. For a long time advertising had been deemed as being most effective in dealing with the highest income groups, but now, with mass production reducing prices, it was being seen that the masses of the people were the buyers of advertised goods; that the advertiser should concentrate his efforts on winning the 85 per cent of the population below the wealthier class; that they not only constituted a greater total potential market, but were more interested in buying the advertised products of mass production.

Nearly all the leading magazines gained at least 50 per cent in circulation' totals during this period. There was widespread effort to increase subscription sales and subscription agents were called into service more extensively. This brought some rather lively battles with the news dealers. Some of them fought back by tearing out the advertisements in any magazine which carried a subscription agent offer, sending the torn-out advertisements to the respective advertisers who ran them, together with a card noting why this had been done. None the less, subscription promotion went ahead and added hundreds of thousands of new readers.

With the Spanish-American War, newspaper circulations reached unprecedented heights. Coverage of war events was more intensive, complete and up to the minute than had ever been offered by the newspapers on an event of such importance, owing, of course, to the improved methods of communicating news and getting it quickly on paper.

This was the time of the emergence of the so-called "yellow" journalism, the adjective deriving from cartoonist Richard Outcault's comic character whose garb was printed in yellow. The "yellow kid" appeared first in the New York *World* and attracted a huge following. Then Hearst secured Outcault's services and the character performed in the pages of the *Journal*.

Yellow journalism, whose principles were not, of course, solely applied in New York, has come down in history as something of an epithet, which has been found especially handy by politicians. It is true that the early yellow press was not entirely without its excesses. Yet with all their shrieking headlines and preposterous illustrations, the papers were honest in purpose and actually were singularly free from revolting and obscene details sometimes set forth in papers which professed greater dignity. They were always unpurchasable and they served to help keep public attention fixed on the affairs of the country. The whole movement of the yellow press was away from mere sensationalism and toward education and, by presenting public affairs in terms that interested the masses of the people, it created hundreds of thousands of newspaper readers.

It is not to be thought, however,

that the more conservative press was without progress of its own. The sedate papers which specialized in wordy essays were driven to the wall in considerable numbers. But the conservative papers which developed real news enterprise gained tremendously in circulation and influence.

With the advertiser's interest in large circulation came a new degree of curiosity as to whether he was getting the quantity he paid for. Until 1899 no serious step had ever been taken toward a union of the national advertisers for the promotion of interests common to all. In the spring of that year representatives of thirty advertisers met in New York to survey the possibilities of such an organization. From this meeting came the American Advertisers Association, with Frederick L. Perine, of Hall & Ruckel, as the first president.

The group had numerous objects, but it placed first the securing of accurate information about the circulations of publications. In the next year it set out to audit circulations, the first being the magazines of Frank A. Munsey. In three years it had conducted audits on 400 publications and made "inspection reports" on fifty-seven cities.

At about the same time a Western organization, the American Society of National Advertisers, began similar auditing work, with

1900

HURRICANE and flood devastate Galveston, Texas. . . . William McKinley defeats William Jennings Bryan for the presidency. . . . Census places total population at 76,304,799, an increase of nearly 21 per cent since 1890. . . . Boxer uprising in China.

Newspaper Representatives' Association of Chicago organized with J. E. Colby as first president. . . . Phelps Publishing Company purchases *Good Housekeeping*. . . . Manufacturing note: 4,192 automobiles produced this year. . . . *Harper's Magazine* celebrates 50th birthday. . . . The word "Free" appears in forty-three advertisements in a single issue of one farm paper. . . . Death of Daniel Sharp Ford, for forty years publisher and editor of *Youth's Companion*.

Annual sales of Montgomery Ward & Company reach $12,-000,000. . . . St. Jacob's Oil reaches the end of its meteoric trail, becoming a classic example of what happens when money spent in advertising is "saved." . . . "Stripped of all theories and of the glamor of literary or artistic skill, the advertisement writer is merely a salesman"—Henry P. Williams. . . . Henry Scripps, California newspaper publisher, dies. . . . Following in the wake of the success of Uneeda biscuit comes Uwanta beer, *Ureada Magazine*, Itsagood soap, Uandi tea and Mustapha biscuit.

THE PRINTERS' INK PUBLICATIONS

Sales, Advertising and Marketing

185 MADISON AVENUE

NEW YORK

June 15th, 1938

Mr. Raymond Bowen
New Yorker Magazine
25 West 43rd Street
New York, New York

Dear Mr. Bowen:

Thanks for your space order for our Fiftieth Anniversary issue. And if I may, I should like to suggest a copy slant you might find usable.

This issue will, as you probably know, contain a biography of marketing over the last fifty years. It will tell the year by year story of advertising, its progress and its contribution to the development of mass distribution.

It occurs to me that this offers a timely opportunity for The New Yorker to set forth its unique position as an advertising medium, and the peculiarly important role it plays in American marketing.

Starting a scant thirteen years ago, The New Yorker soon gained for itself an unprecedented readership of metropolitans. Then, without any artificial stimulation, it became a national magazine, welcomed, read, and respected by America's top-most audience. And this audience The New Yorker still holds unto itself.

Its job, then, has been to sell to this Number One market. That it has done, in good times and bad. More than that, it has sold to the mass market by selling first to those people whom others watch and emulate.

That, to me, is where The New Yorker has made marketing history.

Yours very truly,

Paul Booth

Advertising Department

Paul Booth
CSS

THE

NEW YORKER
25 WEST 43RD STREET, NEW YORK

C. W. Post as a leading spirit. Subsequently the organization merged with the A. A. A.

The A. A. A. promulgated as its definition of circulation the number of copies distributed in such a way that they were likely to be read, whether paid or not. Previously it had been considered that the number of copies printed and prepared for distribution was the only figure that could be absolutely known. Soon after it began, the A. A. A. took the further restricted definition that net-paid distribution was the important thing to be determined.

A number of the publications were themselves tending to the net-paid view. The Washington *Star,* in 1897, announced that it deducted returns from its circulation statement. The Indianapolis *News* and Chicago *Daily News* were also doing this. The *Ladies' Home Journal* and the *Ladies' World* both talked paid-in-advance circulation. The latter offered to any agent or advertiser the privilege of taking any name on the subscription list at random, whereupon it would produce the original order.

The practice of giving affidavits on circulation, while by no means widespread, was growing. The *Iowa Homestead* aggressively advertised proved circulation attested in this manner.

There was still much to be done, however. Thorough auditing of circulations was fifteen years off. The work of the American Advertisers Association was definitely a step in the right direction, but it proved to be lacking in adequacy. The method of operation was not such as to win anything like universal support.

John E. Powers has become a legend but the power of his pen will ever be evident in Macbeth copy

This was the way Royal's quarter pages appeared on back covers of magazines in 1896

CHAPTER IV

Tested and Approved
(1901-1906)

BY 1905, it could be said that the advertiser way of doing business had won the acceptance of the business community at large.

This was not true in 1900. Nor was it, as has been seen, in the years preceding. Large users of advertising had appeared. Important gains in sales and advertising technique had been made in the 1890's. But only a minority of business men were completely convinced of the value of securing identity for their wares in the mind of the consumer. Many of them were new companies. Most of them dealt in specialties—or what in those days were considered specialties.

The manufacturing world as a whole had maintained a studied indifference to advertising and such related ways of promoting sales as had been developed.

The first years of the new century saw a complete turnabout. Manufacturers everywhere manifested an intense, sometimes anxious, interest in this trade-mark business. Men who had advertising services to sell were welcomed in places where once they hadn't even been able to secure admittance. Many businessmen had felt that the whole trademark idea was a mere fad, like the bicycle craze. Now they began to see it for what it was—a permanent means of upbuilding business.

It was seen that advertising is a force that persuades the reader to pay the difference between an inferior article and one of good quality at a price which enables the manufacturer to live and over which he has a large measure of control. Quality was assuming position as a larger and larger factor in business generally, a change in business conditions wholly due to advertising linked with the trade-marked article.

And the fundamental value of the trade-mark was being better understood. The manufacturer had been accustomed to look for security in the patent. There was now conclusive evidence that the use of a trade-mark jointly with wide advertising could build up a trade and establish a degree of security not paralleled by any great patented invention. A patent, it was seen, protects only the article, has no bearing on protection of consumer demand. Whereas patents expire, demand can be maintained.

The realization that there were ways open to a manufacturer to increase the potential consumption of his goods had become firmly established. The first inklings of this came in the hey-day of the trusts, as was noted in the preceding chapter. During this later period the principle was aggressively put to work by numerous firms and it proved out in an impressive way. So long as advertising was deemed to be valuable only as a competitive tool, many companies, particularly the well-established ones, would take little or no interest in it. The new developments made it impossible to ignore the fact that the lower prices of mass-produced goods and the better facilities of distribution had brought into being a huge national market which could be cultivated beyond all previous standards of business success.

It was likewise being noticed that while mass production created advertising, the reverse was also taking place. Advertising was creating mass production. Numerous advertisers had been forced to make large expansions in production facilities to keep up with the greater demand which their consumer efforts had stimulated.

There were further increases in the buying potentials of this vast national market. Now one-third of the population was in the urban classification, as compared with one-quarter twenty years before, a factor which increased the demand for comfort and luxury articles. Continued improvement in steam and electric transportation facilities was bringing many more buyers within the range of the city stores. At the same time the farmer was definitely enlisting in the mass market. Increased use of farm machinery was lessening the drudgery of physical toil. The farmer was getting an increased income and becoming a better customer, assuming some of the buying tastes and habits of the city man. Then, too, a new era of progress and prosperity was dawning in the South, where noticeable and rapid development was under way.

The new disposition was at least partially reflected in a huge growth of advertising volume during this time. In 1900 the total advertising revenues of publications amounted to $95,000,000. In 1905 the figure stood at $145,000,000—a 50 per cent increase. It seems likely that other media showed a similar ratio of increase, for activity was stepped up in every quarter. Outdoor advertising and car cards experienced conspicuous increases.

The prime factor in the appearance of the new point of view was the success of certain trade-marked goods. To the ranks of the advertisers of the previous decade—most of whom continued to develop importantly during the subsequent years—were added a number of conspicuous new proponents of consumer salesmanship.

Of little less importance was the emergence of a new organism for serving the advertiser—or rather an old friend in an entirely new role.

A third significant element was the development of new effectiveness in the advertising message, which departed radically from previous concepts and produced greater results.

A fourth had to do with certain cleansing operations.

These and some of the subsidiary developments of the period are treated in the several following sections.

Accompanying these developments—and in a measure verifying the greatly increased interest in advertising—was the nation-wide status achieved by the organized advertising movement. From concentration almost exclusively in the two cities of New York and Chicago, the movement expanded into many other centers.

Organization of local advertising clubs began. By 1906 there was at least one advertising club in each of fifteen cities. National or regional groups included, in addition to earlier groups cited in preceding chapters, the Pacific Coast Advertising Men's Association, Periodical Publishers' Association, Advertising Club of Western New York, Banking Publicity Association and American Golf Association of Advertising Interests. The American Advertising Agents' Association was formed in 1901 but faded out of the picture after several years.

In 1904 came the establishment of the first national organization encompassing the interests of both buyers and sellers of advertising, which has come down to the present through numerous changes of name and organizational form as the Advertising Federation of America. The idea of such an organization was in the minds of a number of men during the two or three years preceding realization, and it is difficult to credit it to any one man. However, it was first publicly broached in print by S. De Witt Clough, the present president of Abbott Laboratories, who wrote a letter to PRINTERS' INK in July, 1903, suggesting that a national group would be a valuable supplement to the local clubs in the dissemination of correct advertising ideas. And C. F. Olmsted, then advertising manager of the Natural Food Company (Shredded Wheat), was active in the preliminary spadework. What was tentatively referred to as the International Federation of Advertising Interests began taking shape with H. D. Perky,

1901

TEXAS oil boom begins. . . . Carrie Nation arrested for wrecking restaurants and saloons in Kansas. . . . McKinley assassinated and Theodore Roosevelt takes the oath as president. . . . Pan-American Exposition at Buffalo. . . . Panic on New York Stock Exchange caused by struggle for control of the Northern Pacific. . . . Rural free delivery being put in operation.

Ingersoll dollar watches selling in tremendous volume. . . . United States Steel incorporated with a capitalization of $1,319,000,000. . . . Name of Milwaukee has become synonymous with the brewing of beer. . . . Paul Block opens a special representative office in New York. . . . "Buy a B. C. M. cigar instead of a drink"—advertisement by A. Lewis, Dispenser of Havana Incense as an Aid to Better Living. . . . The fictitious business paper, offering "write-ups" in exchange for orders of issues, doing a tremendous business.

H. N. McKinney, who in one year secured nearly $1,000,000 in billings, celebrates twenty-fifth anniversary with N. W. Ayer. . . . Tobacconist in New York discovers that the gift of a box of matches with each sale is a valuable advertisement. . . . James H. Bates, pioneer advertising agent, dies. . . . Alumni of Washington University decide that prosperous athletics is a great advertisement for a university and raise a fund to achieve that end. . . . A. P. W. Paper Company puts out booklets printed on samples of its product.

Biggest U. S. Grocers vote

Results of 185 surveys on request

TIME their first choice magazine

...because the news is important to them.

president of the same company, at the helm. Early in 1904 thirty-five advertisers, media men and agency men met at New York, with George H. Hazen as chairman, to discuss plans. An organization meeting was called for St. Louis to be held in conjunction with the World's Fair there that year.

One hundred and thirty-five were present at the St. Louis meeting and from it emerged the International Advertising Association. It was designed as an affiliation of the local clubs—not long after this meeting most of them joined it. Later was adopted the more descriptive name of the Associated Advertising Clubs of America.

Organized advertising at this time was not so important for its accomplishments as for providing the basis for future contributions. The same may be said of another development wherein advertising began to attract attention and study outside its own immediate sphere.

Harlow Gale, professor of experimental psychology at the University of Minnesota, had undertaken a long series of experiments to examine the value of attention features in advertisements. This was the first thorough effort to determine what general form of advertising most nearly approaches perfection in attracting the attention of the public, and having attracted that attention makes the most lasting impression upon the readers.

By far the larger proportion up to this time had attention as its main objective, as has been previously noted. To that end there was wide use of irrelevant illustration and even irrelevant text matter. Prof. Gale tested the reactions of people to various advertisements. He found that relevant text far outpulled irrelevant texts in attracting attention, that a straight dissertation on the product ranked first, and second a striking catch phrase to force the mind to recognize the article advertised.

In 1903 Walter Dill Scott made a complete study of advertising in terms of psychology, a project which attracted wide attention among advertisers and advertising men. He showed how some published advertisements conform to the laws of the human mind and become profitably effective, and he dealt with the fundamental forces of mental imagery, repetition, suggestion, association of ideas and the like. Above all Dr. Scott pointed out the value of grouping and interpreting these data on scattered phases of the effectiveness of advertisements which the advertiser had accumulated in the course of his activities.

These pioneer investigations were the precursors of what was later to be taken up by the advertiser as a normal part of marketing procedure—research.

The Ranks Expand

IN the fall of 1899 came the first halting steps of an advertiser who was to stand high in the ranks of contributors to the development of the art and science of marketing. His product at that time was regarded as a mere toy by a large section of the public, as an appalling abomination by most of the rest. In not so very many years this product was to attain recognition as a genuine economic advance in American life, to serve as the foundation of one of the largest of all industries and by its existence to exert a profound influence on several phases of distribution.

Such was the destiny that lay ahead as the first advertisements of the horseless carriage appeared in the public prints in the last year of the nineteenth century.

It was not until about 1902 that the public first began timidly experimenting with this new vehicle. A few thousand cars had been sold up to that time, of course, but the purchasers were largely of the show-off class. In 1906 it could be said that there was now no uncertainty as to its market, though not even the industry's wildest optimist dreamed of the true potentialities. It was fairly clear that the automobile was not just another bicycle fad.

Prior to 1899 there was no single building where automobiles exclusively were manufactured. Late in 1900 there were fifty-seven factories capitalized at $5,768,857. In 1905 the number of plants had increased to 136. Capital investment had mushroomed nearly 500 per cent to $23,083,860 (which was to be quadrupled three years hence), passing the tin-plate, fur and piano trades.

In that year there were 85,000 automobiles in use in the United States —one to every thousand persons.

During the first ten months of 1906 the total number of cars increased to 140,000, or 70 per cent. People could scarcely believe it, but there were 35,000 automobiles in New York State alone.

Public interest spread like wildfire. It was fanned by countless columns of motor news in the daily newspapers. Through the first part of 1899 no periodical devoted to the automobile was published. In September and October of that year five were established. Numerous others came into the field not long after. Quite a few of these magazines were class journals going to owners and prospective owners of motor cars and they gained large circulations.

Many other trades felt the industry's stimulus. The automobile created a demand for new kinds of clothes and raised real estate values around all cities. In 1906 more than a million dollars was appropriated for building better roads. All this was additional to the direct activity created by the industry in the manufacture of parts and accessories and in the establishment of servicing and repairing facilities.

The production of commercial motor vehicles during this period was negligible, but many firms were adapting automobiles to advertising purposes. For example, Swift & Company set up a great stir by equipping salesmen with automobiles. They were shipped from town to town on flat cars and used by the salesmen in calling on the trade. They were painted red and were pressed into service in parades,

Exchange Place, Providence, 50 Years Ago

Inseparable – *They grew up together!*

1888 Rhode Island Population 329,000.   Families....   71,650
Journal-Bulletin Circulation (gross)..............   36,523
CIRCULATION RATIO......................   **51%**

1898 Rhode Island Population 411,000.   Families....   90,450
Journal-Bulletin Circulation (gross)..............   50,409
CIRCULATION RATIO......................   **56%**

1908 Rhode Island Population 517,600.   Families....   113,200
Journal-Bulletin Circulation (gross)..............   64,490
CIRCULATION RATIO **57%**

1918 Rhode Island Population 601,000.   Families....   133,300
Journal-Bulletin Circulation (net)...............   80,940
CIRCULATION RATIO......................   **61%**

1928 Rhode Island Population 684,200.   Families....   159,700
Journal-Bulletin Circulation (in R. I.)............   111,084
CIRCULATION RATIO......................   **70%**

and the Journal-Bulletin Papers

Exchange Place, Providence, in 1938 © AVERY LORD

"3 out of 4"— *Dominance through Service!*

1938 Rhode Island Population 681,000.   Families.... 164,000
Journal-Bulletin Circulation (in R. I.)............ 140,983
CIRCULATION RATIO **86%**

Present coverage of 3 out of 4 Rhode Island families is the result,
not of mergers or circulation forcing, but of voluntary reader
choice. Circulation growth of 25% in the last decade, contrary
to both population and economic trends, demonstrates the current
vitality of the Journal-Bulletin, their essential service in Rhode
Island homes . . . and hence to all advertisers in this major market.

Providence Journal-Bulletin
Dominating New England's Second Largest Market

REPRESENTATIVES: Chas. H. Eddy Co., Inc., New York, Chicago, Boston, Atlanta
R. J. Bidwell Co., San Francisco, Los Angeles

street fairs and carnivals. In many towns people had never seen an automobile before. A department store which brought Santa Claus to town in an automobile that year created vast attention.

Prosperity was theirs virtually without effort, owing to the spontaneous public interest and the free attention lavished from all sides, but the leading builders continued to advertise extensively. The more stable elements in the business seemed to realize almost from the start that lasting success depended upon a constant stream of improvements in the product with a backing of consistent sales and advertising effort to implant and keep vivid the universal desire to own a car.

In the twelve leading magazines in 1905 the industry spent nearly $500,000 in advertising. The total in all media was estimated to be at least $1,000,000. In 1906 *Motor,* which then had a large circulation among motor car owners, led all the monthly magazines in advertising, its total linage in one month being almost precisely double that of the second-ranking *McClure's.*

Proportionate to the size of the industry, manufacturers of automobiles were more aggressive advertisers than any other one group.

At the first the industry was faced with the problem of surviving public displeasure. People had been accustomed to traveling six or eight miles an hour. A motor vehicle going twelve or even fifteen presented a perilous and terrifying prospect. Besides, the first cars were noisy with the explosions of the early crude internal combustion motor and its accompanying odors and smoke. In some cities laws were passed prohibiting their use except when a flagman walked an eighth of a mile ahead of the vehicle to warn pedestrians of its approach. Hence the first advertising was largely good-will in nature, aimed to sell the idea of the automobile to the public.

As people became accustomed to the strange new vehicle, the advertising soon entered a second phase. It was no longer so profitable to feature automobiles in general as to talk about the individual make. For a brief time this took the "just-as-good" angle, aimed to sell the American-made car in competition with the imported. The inferiority complex did not long remain and the cars began to stand on their own merits.

Manufacturers started to talk about performance. Stressing of spectacular driving feats became the thing. There was much talk of races, mountain climbing and endurance tests. Most companies had famous drivers in their employ whose job it was to do breath-taking things with the car for the copy to talk about.

As competition grew, makers tended to exploit various individual features of their products. They went at it with a vim that overreached its objectives. Wild and extravagant claims were made for anything that would run on wheels, including qualities that were not to be attained by the best cars of twenty years later. Freakish new models were introduced by some companies to provide further startling subject matter for the advertising.

Selling methods were in character with the advertising. The salesman would state a motor to be perfect without the slightest hesitation. As a result the real worth of the car was dwarfed by the inflated expectations of the owner, which were never realized.

During this period of advertising debauchery, manufacturing facilities were being steadily improved. Design and mechanism were rapidly bettered. The cars became more rational—this was around 1905—and so did the advertising. There was more plain, pointed selling talk, less exploiting of obscure features and devices and challenging on mechanical points. There had been a notable advance in real performance and the manufacturer could now safely talk about the car. It was no longer necessary to dwell upon specialties and attachments.

In the new advertising, manufacturers began to tell about the many uses the automobile, with its improved performance, could be put to. This was the beginning of the first utility advertising. People were told of the many benefits and enjoyments which the motor car afforded, particularly from the standpoint of pleasure. Some advertising was done which taught prospective owners to look upon the automobile as a piece of machinery requiring intelligent care and operation. Of course, the advantages of the respective makes were not neglected, and here the tendency was to sales arguments concisely and succinctly framed and modestly stated.

In 1906, while the new trend was under way, some manufacturers set off on a diversion to the lyrical quality. They spoke of "The Car of Destiny" and "The Car of Contentment" and generally tossed about florid adjectives and elegant prose. This came largely from the influx of the scalpers, who had the bicycle experience in memory. They believed the trade to be ephemeral and were out to get all they could while the getting was good. However, those with real faith in the industry proceeded on the course of sound manufacture and sound selling.

The men's clothing business had for years been dominated by old, conservative, fossilized manufacturers who made their fortunes during the Civil War selling clothing at a high profit. It was generally believed that the business could not be advertised, except to the extent of an announcement of the year in which a firm was founded. The talk of the trade was an old New York firm which had used a page one time in a New York daily. This was encouraging, but it exhausted the nerve of the partners and they settled back to spend the rest of their lives in proud contemplation of that one supreme effort of enterprise and backbone.

Late in the 1890's a radical move was made by a young Chicago firm —Hart Schaffner & Marx. The three members of the firm were of the new school—young, good merchants and game. To them went a lad named George L. Dyer, who proposed devoting himself to the impossible task of advertising a clothing house. With characteristic pluck the partners gave a cash appropriation and an office to the youngster who was ultimately with their backing to inaugurate a new era of clothes making and practically revolutionize the industry.

Hart Schaffner & Marx initiated a magazine advertising program and it was successful from the first. The firm had the medium to itself for several seasons before the rest of the trade woke up. Other manufacturers came to see that making clothes is only part of the business

A Half Century of Gr

1888

THE Spokesman-Review and Spokane Daily Chronicle greet Printers' Ink Weekly as another old timer! All three of us have been going strong for half a century or more.

The Spokesman-Review's record of service began in 1883 with the founding of the "Spokane Falls Review," which was consolidated with the Spokane Spokesman to form The Spokesman-Review in 1893. The Chronicle, a weekly in 1881, became a daily in 1883; for a time was again a weekly; changed back to a daily in 1885. For about a year it was issued as a morning daily, but on September 21, 1886, it became permanently an evening daily. Since these early days the two newspapers and their field have enjoyed phenomenal growth. The dailies' combined net paid circulation for last 12 months exceeds 110,000. Value of new wealth produced in Spokane area each year over $400,000,000!

Above: REVIEW
OFFICE 1889

Below: FIRST
CHRONICLE
BUILDING

Stages like this connected Spokane with Inland Empire in 1886

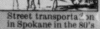

Street transportation in Spokane in the 80's

Riverside Avenue in Spokane the year Printers' Ink was born

THE SPOKESMAN-REVIEW
MORNING   **SUNDAY**

Spokane

wth in Spokane Area

1938

AND what's ahead? The year 1937 in the Spokane area showed—Agriculture best in financial returns since 1930; value of lumber higher than 1929; mining profits in the Coeur d'Alenes best in history. Business has continued good in 1938. Spokane building permits for first 4 months of the year were numerically largest for similar period in Spokane history. April Department and Apparel Store sales were 6% above April 1937. New contract for $34,442,240 let by the U. S. government in January insures continued big payroll at Grand Coulee, and eventual reclamation of 1,200,000 acres of arid but immensely fertile land. So it looks as if our first 50 years were the hardest. We stand on the threshold of a great future. Here's hoping prospects are equally bright for Printers' Ink!

Above: REVIEW BUILDING 1938

Below: CHRONICLE BUILDING TODAY

Spokane transportation today is completely motorized

One of 92 motor stages which arrive in Spokane daily from Inland Empire

Riverside Avenue in Spokane 1938

Spokane Daily Chronicle
EVENING

Washington

and there was a considerable amount of advertiser activity in the industry shortly after 1900.

Among other things, Dyer, who was later to become a leading advertising agent, invented the naturally posed illustration to displace the old fashion plate. The fashion plate was unattractive. It did not show the garment to advantage and no rational man expected to look like one, or wanted to. But the trade thought it ideal and complete, something that, like the violin, could not be improved. It seemed to Dyer, however, that an illustration ought to be a plausible picture of a suit of clothes worn by a man in a plausible attitude. His innovation was ridiculed in the trade. Retailers refused to exhibit the illustrations at first. But the public saw the point and bought the clothes.

Hart Schaffner & Marx were the first in the clothing trade—and one of the first of all advertisers—to devise ways and means of helping the retailer's business. They offered, in conjunction with their consumer program, expert retail advertising counsel and the preparation of effective advertising matter.

The bathtub came into the limelight with the institution of a broad promotional program by the Standard Sanitary Manufacturing Company. The firm had advertised for years, but first took up systematic, aggressive effort in 1902. Up to this time the bathtub was, to the consumer, simply a bathtub. Standard determined to sell beauty in sanitary fixtures and to get replacement business as well as that arising from new construction, in other words to induce folks to tear out the old-fashioned zinc tubs. The country was full of old-fash-

ioned plumbing and the fault lay in the limitations of the trade. The jobber was responsible for convincing the retailer of the value of the new products and it was up to the retailer to get in touch with the consumer. Advertising and selling effort was so far removed from the best source of information that it had little convincing power. And so Standard decided to advertise direct to the consumer.

To this purpose the company set a novel note in merchandising household equipment. Instead of merely featuring individual fixtures it set out to sell the sanitation advantages and attractiveness of "modern bathrooms." The first advertisements brought thousands of inquiries and the extent of the campaign was steadily increased. People began to demand the installations pictured in the advertisements. Accordingly the company went to the plumbers, whom it had already provided with advertising and follow-up aids, with a display contest designed to get them to exhibit such installations in their places of business. This resulted in hundreds of entries and when the plumbers saw how the displays sold goods they let them stand permanently. In the first five years of the program the sales increase brought by this creative marketing program was around 400 per cent.

The introduction of the cotton collar by Cluett, Peabody & Company opened a new chapter in the merchandising history in that field. The cotton collar was black heresy in that beehive center of the industry, Troy, N. Y. For linen was Troy's religion. From time immemorial it had been the seal and symbol of the gentleman and Troy looked with positive horror upon this audacious debasement of its sacred project. Actually from a production standpoint the cotton collar was a godsend to the industry, for it was facing a serious situation with respect to future supplies of raw materials, production of flax having fallen behind the growing consumption of linen products.

Advertising became a positive necessity in order to get the trade to stock the cotton collar at all in face of the strenuous arguments which were against it. One by one the other collar concerns fell in line, but that came later after the effects of Arrow collar advertising had been demonstrated.

The new item fell upon a market which was sadly disorganized and given to unsound practices. Some manufacturers were in the habit of doing such things as buying up stocks of competing brands and dumping them on the market through devious channels at less than cost. Dealers were accustomed to receiving tokens of the manufacturer's regard along with their stocks, the tokens ranging from showcases to special allowances for advertising that was never to be run. The dealer felt perfectly free to return any slow-moving merchandise for credit and he generally got an abject apology along with the credit. Collars represented a profitable line by reason of the honest graft which went along with them. As a merchandising proposition they were kicked into the corner.

Cluett, Peabody's advertising of the Arrow line brought into the situation an element which had never before been present except in quantities which the chemist denotes as "a trace." That element was an organized public demand

for collars bearing a certain trademark. Dealers began to appreciate that Arrow collars, wholly apart from their intrinsic merits, possessed a salability that was worth more than an extra showcase or a sub rosa discount. Thus entrenched, the firm was able to enforce a better policy of dealing with the trade. At the same time the company strongly emphasized the style appeal, while others experimented with other forms of approach, and established style as the essence of all collar advertising. Intelligently directed advertising not merely sold goods for this company, but enabled it to sell goods on a sound, equitable basis and stabilized the whole industry.

Development in the breakfast food field continued at a rapid pace, becoming what was known as the "breakfast food bubble." Lured by the success of the earlier leaders, literally hundreds of new firms flocked into the business. Most of them lacked capital and ability and soon faded. One who took up the commercial possibilities of these foods and didn't do badly at it was Will K. Kellogg, who left his post as manager of a sanitarium at Battle Creek, Mich., to organize the Kellogg Toasted Corn Flake Company. He purchased the corn flake business which had been developed at the sanitarium and began marketing the product in packages in 1906, at first using the brand name Sanitas. One of his leading principles was the building up of a crack sales force.

A wide swath in the breakfast food business at the time was cut by Force, brought out in 1902 by the H-O Company. The systematic process employed for introducing a new product set a precedent. The firm manufactured vast quantities ahead, then thoroughly distributed the goods before a line of advertising was used. The campaign broke with a concentration of large advertisements, full-page insertions in the Sunday papers for four successive weeks. The effect was not instantaneous but once started sales mounted at an astonishing pace. Incidentally, Force was perhaps the first victim of a widespread "whispering campaign." Word was bruited about that the product contained morphine, wherewith the company came out boldly and stopped the nonsense with announcement of a large cash award for conviction of the conspirators and another award to anyone who could prove the product contained any injurious substances.

Such advertising as had been used in the furniture field was mainly copy designed to influence direct sales from the factory. First to use advertising on a wide scale to promote trade through the retailer was S. Karpen & Bros. In 1901 the company had under way a program which talked quality furniture and demonstrated features which made the goods worth more, turning over the inquiries secured to the dealers, who were supplied with tie-up material.

Few business men had considered advertising more "undignified" than bankers. They had long considered it unprofessional to publish more

---

1902

CONGRESS passes act providing for construction of a canal across the Isthmus of Panama. . . . Widespread strikes in the coal industry and entire national guard of Pennsylvania is ordered to the anthracite region. . . . Permanent census office established. . . . Minneapolis motorist arrested for speeding in excess of ten miles per hour and fined $10.

Now 21,844 publications regularly issued in the United States. . . . J. K. Fraser joins Mahin Advertising Company at Chicago. . . . International Harvester Company formed by makers of McCormick, Deering, Plano, Champion and Milwaukee harvesters. . . . Advertising Novelty Manufacturers' Association organized. . . . Largest sign yet painted, occupying sides of two eleven-story buildings in behalf of Sunny Jim, appears in New York.

Calkins & Holden open up shop. . . . "A Kalamazoo Direct to You" makes its advertising bow. . . . Advertising Men's Club of Kansas City formed. . . . W. H. Kentnor takes charge of new Chicago office of the Vreeland-Benjamin Special Advertising Agency. . . . Coffee advertised as a deodorizer, disinfectant and cure for gout, nervousness, kidney and liver troubles and colds.

1905   **1938**

Established 1905

THE BUYERS' MASTER KEY
TO ALL
AMERICAN SOURCES OF SUPPLY

Member A. B. C.

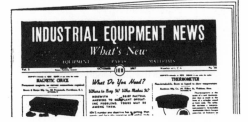

*Started
May, 1933*

*Member
C. C. A.*

*Started
Feb., 1937*

All through this anniversary issue of Printers' Ink Weekly, we are forcibly reminded that . . . times have changed continuously . . . and "reading habits" with them . . . men who specify and buy for every industry are more and more demanding **useful facts** . . . presented, as such, in **brief,** easy-to-get-at style . . . Thomas publications long ago recognized this trend and are built from the bottom up to continuously meet these changing conditions . . . and to furnish advertisers with what will always be the most obvious proof of advertising effectiveness . . . viz . . . **RESULTS** in the form of traceable buying inquiries . . . thus giving the "more-for-less" that advertising conditions, likewise changed, demand today. Proven reader interest in terms of advertising results, best describes Thomas' publications.

(*continued next page*)

Here's the History and Record of an Outstanding Development and Trend in Industrial Publishing . . .

INDUSTRIAL EQUIPMENT NEWS

The May 4th, 1933 issue of Printers' Ink Weekly carried the notice shown here recording the start of a new trend in industrial publishing . . . a trend originated and developed by *Industrial Equipment News* . . . aimed at giving useful **FACTS** to operating men in industry . . . and **RESULTS** for advertisers wanting **ACTION** from this group.

Confirmation of this predicted reader and advertiser need comes with the following high-spots from the growth of *Industrial Equipment News.*

1933 . . . original distribution 30,000 . . . addressed to attention of Plant Superintendents . . . in larger plants in all industries selected from the compilation records of Thomas' Register . . . no advertising accepted despite prompt inquiry evidence that the service was immediately being used and accepted as the spot to **look for** current and future plant needs.

1937 . . . original distribution increased to 51,440 (C.C.A. Audited) and now being directed entirely to active plant operating men who, since 1933, have **REQUESTED** that the service be sent to them every month . . . and who further indicate their regular active use of it by more than 122,368 inquiries against items appearing in it during this one year period . . . advertising capacity of 378 entirely sold out with an advertiser renewal rate of 79%.

1938 . . . distribution still climbing, 52,042 circulation . . . 12,042 *bonus* to advertisers . . . continuously directed only to those who **REQUEST** and can show need for it . . . 51.71% to plants rated at one million and over and 81.02% in plants rated one-hundred-thousand and over . . . increased buying inquiry evidence of reader usage . . . despite current conditions more than 300 advertisers in July, as basic evidence of advertising value now established.

IN SHORT . . . in only 5 years . . . *Industrial Equipment News* has, from scratch, attained outstanding leadership in the field of publications available for advertising to operating men in industry . . . highest in . . . circulation quantity and quality . . . traceable buying inquiry **RESULTS** . . . and in the number of advertisers using it . . . and **LOWEST** in cost, $79 to $85, for standard, effective advertising representation . . . Ask for "IEN PLAN".

BUILDING PRODUCTS . . . started last year . . . is applying the same proven publishing formula to reach buying and specifying factors in all branches of the building industries . . . and already showing equal promise in reader interest, as evidenced by **RESULTS** . . . 50,000 coverage for only $89 to $95 . . . Details? . . . Write for the "B-P PLAN".

THOMAS PUBLISHING COMPANY, 461 Eighth Avenue, New York, N. Y.

1900 – The Story of Thomas' Register – 1938

Away back prior to 1900 a young and ambitious Philadelphian, recently graduated from his Quaker school, was engaged on the reportorial staff of a principal Philadelphia Newspaper, and eagerly seeking some opening in the business world which would satisfy his fancy for being identified as principal with something of national scope and influence.

Among the various ideas envisioned there appeared a possible opportunity for a compendium of American Manufacturers and their products, classified to function primarily in *purchasing activities* with the same authenticity and completeness which characterize the mercantile agency guides for credit and selling functions, and other reference guides of the type which carry no advertising, but concentrate solely upon service to the user, and command from the latter the price necessary for their quality of service.

Extensive inquiry among the buyers for important organizations established the demand for such a work and willingness to pay for it. At that time, and since, the nearest approaches to such a guide were, and are, essentially advertising mediums of free distribution, with directory lists which necessarily represent a minimum of expense for completeness and authenticity.

1905 . . . Thomas' Register was launched with a determination to produce a guide based upon ascertaining what the buying powers wanted, and, to concentrate solely upon meeting their expressed requirements, charging a price commensurate with the service, and leaving advertising a secondary consideration, to fall where it would, under the above basic aim and procedure.

It was confidently assumed that in a guide of such position in purchasing activities, advertising patronage would well take care of itself.

The initial edition was a volume of 1,200 pages, 4 x 10 inches, with 80 small space advertisers. Most of them who are still in business (15) continue, and are using five times as much space as occupied by all the 80 cards in 1905.

1938 . . . After 28 years of continuous development along the lines of its original policy and procedure, with no change in name, ownership and direction, the 1938 Edition appears as a volume of 4,600 pages, 9 x 14—1500% larger than the first Edition, the largest publication of its kind in the world, and the longest established in the United States.

3129 Manufacturers are represented by 15,610 advertisements, usually of product informative character as suggested by its subscription clientele of more than 25,000 annual and intermittent subscribers in the United States, and including a major portion of the total industrial purchasing power—More than 1,500 of its subscribers are organizations in the over $10,000,000 class.

It has always maintained a paid circulation status and quality, and joined the Audit Bureau of Circulations near the start of the latter. It continues today, the only publication in its field which qualifies for membership.

Its present advertising clientele, rarely if ever half equalled in number and importance by any other trade publication, is the result of *direct buying returns* it produces—And this status of the Register fully justifies the original assumption and policy of 33 years ago, and connotes more about its value than would be shown by a mass of the usual abstract evidence.

In addition to its individual subscribers, it is kept for public reference in Boards of Trade, Libraries and Banks in more than 1,000 commercial centers in the United States, and largely used by buyers in these centers—and is the guide used by the American Consular Service throughout the world, in directing overseas buyers to American Manufacturers.

The Thomas' organization, developed along with the Register, consists of 120 persons in its home office, and 40 field men. They are all experienced and trained for their highly specialized work. The organization operates on a profit sharing basis, and changes in personnel are close to nil.

THOMAS PUBLISHING COMPANY, 461 Eighth Avenue, New York, N. Y.

than the bank's card, if they advertised at all. A marked change of attitude became evident around 1902, when a fairly respectable number of banks began employing explicit advertising messages to sell the savings idea. There had been a little of this along about 1895, but it was not until the later date that bankers generally admitted advertising to be wholly in keeping with conservative traditions, and began to look upon it in terms of methods rather than of dignity.

Pittsburgh was the home of bank advertising. The majority of the banks were advertising and acquiring national reputations through promotion of banking by mail. The idea originated with the Pittsburgh Bank For Savings and the movement worked out very well. There were many people in the rural communities who had got suddenly rich through iron and coal properties and didn't know what to do with their money. Many of the banks in small towns were weak. Advertising of Pittsburgh banks got to be a familiar sight in the magazines, and institutions in Cleveland and Chicago followed the example. This activity was a leading factor in bringing banks to see the value of advertising in their own communities and bank advertising in all media classifications grew prodigiously.

The Cremo cigar program, conducted by the American Tobacco Company, affirmed the possibilities of advertising and merchandising a 5-cent article advantageously. Pompeiian Massage Cream was suggesting the possibilities in promoting the sale of cosmetic products to women. The product was brought out for men's use by Frederick W. Stecher, who originally sold it by calling personally on barbers. It soon was apparent that the women offered a better field of prospects. He was one of the early large-space advertisers, one of the first to use a magazine double-spread. With the Calumet Baking Powder Company, William M. Wright was providing further evidence that the most strongly entrenched trust was vulnerable. The Royal Baking Powder Company with its tremendous capital had seemingly unlimited power. Wright started from scratch, began advertising in one city in 1895 and by 1906 was doing a brisk business in twelve States.

Numerous other individual advertisers came into prominence during the period to make the total accessions to the ranks the most significant of any period before and perhaps since.

A present-day advertiser was doing a persuasive job more than forty years ago.

Rastus got his position as chef before the new century's dawn—and never lost it.

Before the days of Model T. How Ford advertised
in 1905.

Enter the Service Agent

WHEN last we examined the general advertising agent he was primarily a negotiator of space contracts and secondarily an operator of machinery for distributing copy and checking papers and bills. He had virtually nothing to do with the preparation of advertising, except when specifically requested to do so by the advertiser. And even then he merely carried out the advertiser's suggestions as to what form the copy should take.

When we look at the agent again —that is in 1901—we find that in five years his shape and status have completely changed, changed in a way that not only secured his own future but also made of him a far more effective and constructive contributor to the growth of the advertiser.

The day of the "service agency" had arrived. The agent now offered expert and specialized service in planning the advertising program and preparing the advertisement. His service was still clerical in part, but it had become mainly professional. The placing of advertising remained an important part of his operations, but the creative activities—plans, copy, art, layout, typography—came first.

Competition was an important element in producing this result. As we have seen, the special agent's operations had greatly diminished the value of the general agent to the advertiser so far as ability to buy space at bargain rates was concerned. From the publisher's standpoint, the special agent had proved more valuable in the matter of soliciting direct orders for business— the field in which the general agent had so long reigned pre-eminent.

The general agent was also encountering competition at the hands of his own customers—the advertisers. It was getting so that the large advertiser could buy space cheaper, in many publications at least, than could the general agent. If he couldn't get lower rates he could retain the commission for himself. The technique of dealing with media, originated by the agent, had become rather well understood all around. Information on publications and their rates was more widely available than it had once been. Equipped with this information, the advertiser could press his bargaining advantage as the man who paid the bill.

Then there was the competition among the general agents themselves. This had continued to increase in intensity until it was clear that the only way that advertising volume could be increased was through the creation of new advertisers and greater effectiveness in results from advertising.

To put it bluntly, the general agent was all washed up as a dealer in advertising space. He was all but shorn of his bargaining advantages. Beset on all sides by competitive factors, his profit was disappearing. It is true that he might have lingered on at the old stand for some little time. For years after there were two forms of agencies—the creative agents who took an active part in planning the sales strategy of the advertiser, and the scalpers, who traded mainly on their rate bargaining ability. More and more, however, the latter were relegated to the background with the increasing stabilization of rates and of publishers' practices with regard to

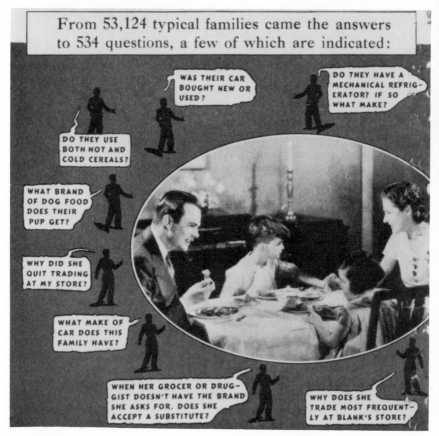
162

Announces

HOME INVENTORY

THE inventory covered an adequate cross-section sample of sixteen cities: Buffalo, Washington, Pittsburgh, Akron, Cleveland, Columbus, Cincinnati, Toledo, Indianapolis, Evansville, Knoxville, Birmingham, Fort Worth, Houston, San Diego and San Francisco.

Classifications included in the study were: food products, beverages, refrigerators, radios, furniture, cosmetics, shaving and dental aids, automobiles, tires, gas and oil, and some apparel items.

The data have been assembled by individual cities and in composite nation-wide form, and visualized in more than 4,000 charts containing a total of 17,328,389 recorded answers.

The study is available to interested firms at all Scripps-Howard National Advertising Offices.

NEWSPAPERS

NEW YORK *World-Telegram*	COLUMBUS . *Citizen*	MEMPHIS . . . *Press-Scimitar*	BIRMINGHAM . . *Post*
PITTSBURGH . . . . . . *Press*	BUFFALO . . . *Times*	MEMPHIS *Commercial Appeal*	HOUSTON . . . . *Press*
SAN FRANCISCO . . . . *News*	CLEVELAND . . *Press*	OKLAHOMA CITY . . . . *News*	FORT WORTH . . *Press*
INDIANAPOLIS . . . . *Times*	DENVER . . . . *News*	ALBUQUERQUE . . . . *Tribune*	EL PASO *Herald-Post*
CINCINNATI . . . . . . *Post*	TOLEDO . *News-Bee*	KNOXVILLE . *News-Sentinel*	SAN DIEGO . . . . *Sun*
KENTUCKY POST *Covington* edition of *Cincinnati Post*	AKRON *Times-Press*	WASHINGTON . . . . . . *News*	EVANSVILLE . *Press*

commission payment. Had the general agent not made the change that he did, he would some time or other have dropped to a position of minor consequence and perhaps complete extinction.

Over and above the questions of competition, there had arisen a real need for some type of organization to perform the services which the general agent was to assume. Throughout the nineteenth century —except for the last several years of it—the tendency of the advertiser was to concentrate in one type of medium. There were car-card advertisers, magazine advertisers, newspaper advertisers and outdoor advertisers. A leading question of the day was which medium was the best. Seldom did an advertiser use more than one medium, except in a minor and incidental way.

As the understanding of the potentialities of the consumer market became more thorough, advertisers experimented with using two or more types at the same time. This was followed by groping attempts at co-ordination. The resultant problems opened the opportunity for a new type of service to the advertiser, a counsel based on knowledge of media values as well as prices.

Furthermore, a genuine need existed for practical guidance in marketing technique. The processes of selling and advertising were still pretty much of a mystery, especially, of course, insofar as the newer advertisers were concerned. The advertiser press and the organized advertising groups, as has been noted, were disseminating the collective experiences of those who used the new art. But an operating organization which could apply the experience of others was in demand. Sooner or later some type

of organization would appear to take advantage of the opportunity.

The evolutionary process had been under way prior to 1900, of course. The first noticeable signs of it appear around 1895. Definite establishment and general recognition of the service agency concept, however, had not taken full effect until about 1905. Even so, it was not so well established but that numerous publications for years after maintained copy and layout service departments.

The so-called "old-line" agencies —Ayer, Thompson, Lord & Thomas, Batten and a few others—were leaders in the movement. The early Ayer plan described previously, of doing business so that the advertiser received the benefit of whatever rate advantage the agency might secure, was an important step in establishing the concept of serving the advertiser. It had been ridiculed by many agents at the time, but it established a basis for giving attention to other things besides getting reasonable rates. Under F. Wayland Ayer and Henry N. McKinney, a great creative salesman of advertising results, the agency's services began to develop in the new direction. J. Walter Thompson was a gentleman who had little to say about what he was up to, but he had an organization that worked hand in hand with his clients' sales forces years before it was generally understood that distribution and merchandising are an indispensable part of publicity. In 1895 Lord & Thomas were promulgating the idea that the agent should be the responsible factor who brings the manufacturer and consumer together and that writing advertisements and planning the campaign were a part of this job.

Frank Seaman was an early example of the agent who controlled patronage because he knew how to make and place an advertisement. In 1895 he said: "I do not buy space in mediums as a speculation to sell again to a customer; I am free to suggest only those publications which I regard as most valuable for the needs of each advertiser." In the same year the old Desmond Dunne Company was following the policy of appointing one man to attend to the advertising of each of its more important clients and offering its services to "entirely replace the advertising manager."

No little impetus came from a quarter entirely outside the agency field—the advertising writers. A few of these had attained a sound business footing and built up substantial organizations. Charles Austin Bates won a wide clientele of advertisers who came to him for plans and copy. Later Earnest Elmo Calkins and Ralph Holden established a copy business (1902) and served a number of the leading advertisers of the day. The George Ethridge Company gained prominence as a non-placing agency, handling the creative work for such large advertisers as Postum, N. K. Fairbank, National Cash Register and W. L. Douglas. This firm and others like it also did work for general agents. Even in the early nineteen hundreds not a few agents bought copy and designs outside.

It is interesting to note that the design function of the agency achieved its first major recognition from concerns of this sort. Bates in 1896 established the first commercial art department for advertising. A primary aim of Calkins & Holden was to have the best art department in the business.

The non-placing firms flourished until 1905. A few continued beyond that date. Although many general agents had recognized the importance of copy as a part of their job, the fact was that price competition was still so great in many instances that they had little margin left with which to finance the creative work. Consequently, many of the leading advertisers turned to the copy shops.

The importance of the message was increasing in the eyes of the advertiser. Advertising was not the runaway it had been a few years before. The advertiser's demand for ideas waxed stronger. He was seeing that the last 1 per cent taken off an estimate was not so important as what went into the space and that the proper medium was of vastly higher importance. The advertiser was asking not only for rates, but how best he could improve his methods. And the business—the better accounts—was going to those firms best qualified to create advertisements. The demand was less for the man who put the smallest valuation on his work and more for the agent whose work was really worth something.

The question of whether such service would be rendered by the general agent or by the non-placing firm was pretty well settled by 1905. The general agent won out. A few advertisers had tried the expedient of dividing the functions, appointing a general agent to place the advertisements and a non-placing organization to get them up. Some of the general agents bought plans and copy from the copy shops. But it was quickly apparent that the selection of media and the writing of copy were inseparable elements in the advertising plan as a whole,

"Good advertising should move in tune with the salesman's feet -- and salesmen are marching today in a tempo and spirit which the World-Telegram understands and faithfully portrays ..."

T. K. Quinn, President

Maxon, Incorporated

"I think the World-Telegram sparkles ... It's a provocative, well-written paper -- edited with an open mind, for open-minded people. That must be one reason for its advertising power."

Thomas L. L. Ryan, Pres.

Pedlar & Ryan, Inc.

"The World-Telegram is 'bright'. Obviously it is read by people who like that kind of a paper. They are generally 'our best customers'.

F. B. Ryan, president

Ruthrauff & Ryan, Inc.

"Advertising productivity is in direct relation to readership. Keyed to the mentally alert, better-income earners of New York the World-Telegram is a known quantity."

Russell Law
Chairman,
Executive Committee

Albert Frank-Guenther Law, Inc.

New York Wor[ld]

Local Forecast:—Increasing cloudiness with slowly

NEW YORK, W[...]

VOL. 70.—NO. 282.—IN TWO SECTIONS—SECTION ONE

BAR TRAVELERS AS PRAHA CALLS RESERVE TROOPS

Wallace Plea Is Rejected

THERE'S N[O]

Lottery Cha[...]
Filed Again[st]
Political Ch[...]

"The World-Telegram news, features and editorials have attracted a characterful quality—and-quantity of circulation that means sale$ to those who face the problem of the New York market."

H. B. LeQuatte
H. B. LeQuatte
President

H. B. LeQuatte, Inc.

"There is no substitute for newspaper circulation, if it has the type of influence which the World-Telegram provides."

J. J. Hartigan, vice-pres. and director of media

Campbell-Ewald Company

"The New York World-Telegram is a great newspaper — made so by its editorial policy, intelligent attracted good, which has buying circulation — the kind of circulation that pays advertisers."

C C Younggreen
Charles C. Younggreen, Exec. Vice President

Reincke-Ellis-Younggreen & Finn, Inc.

"The readability of your front page and the rapier thrusts of Westbrook Pegler make me reach automatically for the World-Telegram."

O. B. Winters, Executive Vice-Pres.

Erwin, Wasey & Company, Inc.

d-Telegram

rising temperature tonight and tomorrow.

EDNESDAY, JULY 0, 1938.

O DISPUTING THE STARS!

What the stars of advertising say is affirmed by the newspaper itself: The World-Telegram IS an unusual daily. It DOES reach the buy-able part of New York. It CAN help you do a bang-up selling job in the important-money sectors of New York's "cities-within-the-city."

Veto by Mayor

most efficiently handled as a centralized responsibility. The better general agents moved apart from bargain-counter competition based on space rates and expanded their creative facilities. The copy shops took on experienced space men and became general agents. Calkins & Holden followed this course not long after their establishment, as did others.

The economics of the situation were not without import in the final shape of the advertising service organism. Perhaps this was the decisive factor. The advertiser was accustomed to getting the placing service on a commission basis—the publisher paying the commission to the agent. Naturally a combined placing and copy service under the commission form of payment was easier to sell than an exclusive copy service for which the advertiser had to make a direct financial outlay. In a sense a price increase was involved. The early service agents simply refused to rebate a part of the commission received from the publishers. But it was a relatively painless increase and they had a definite selling edge over their non-placing rivals.

As the agent moved more directly into a position where he functioned more in the interest of the advertiser and less as a representative of the publishers, one might have expected to see the latter cutting off the commission. They did just the

1903

FIRST successful airplane flight by Orville and Wilbur Wright. . . . Iroquois Theater fire in Chicago causes loss of 588 lives. . . . Brigham Young dies at Salt Lake City. . . . Immigration records broken with admittance during fiscal year of 812,870 persons, an increase of 32 per cent over previous year. . . . Department of Commerce and Labor created.

Louis K. Liggett organizes the United Drug Company, establishing a combination of retail druggists to market a line of drug preparations under the Rexall brand. . . . Medill McCormick, at the age of 26, becomes publisher of the Chicago *Tribune*. . . . Gillette safety razor put on the market. . . . First automat opened in New York. . . . St. Louis Advertising Men's League formed. . . . Thomas Balmer becomes advertising manager for Butterick.

John E. Kennedy leaves Force and H-O to join the Postum Cereal Company. . . . Western Union offers its messenger service for use in delivering samples, literature, catalogs and other matter. . . . Joseph Pulitzer endows a school of journalism at Columbia University. . . . Henry Ford organizes the Ford Motor Company. . . . O. K. is a popular phrase of the day and appears frequently in advertising literature.

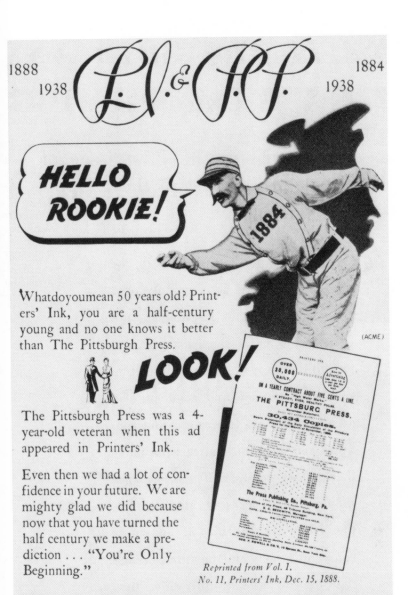

This is The 60TH ANN

CLEVELAND PR

From an Editorial in the First Issue of the Cleveland Press, First of the Scripps-Howard Newspapers:

66 We have no politics, that is, in the sense of the word as commonly used today. We are not Republican, not Democratic, not Greenback and not Prohibitionist. We simply intend to support good men and condemn bad ones, support good measures and condemn bad ones, no matter what party they belong to. . . . The newspaper should simply present all the facts the editor is capable of obtaining concerning men and measures before the bar of the public, and then having discharged its duty as a witness, be satisfied to leave the jury in the case—the public—to find the verdict. 99

opposite. The first disposition of the publisher to protect the agent's commission came with the assumption of the creative services.

It was a step founded in logic. The leading publishers noticed that a business which ceased to have an agent handle its advertising became a poorer advertiser. It lacked infusion of ideas from an outside source. They saw that the advertisers which grew most rapidly were the ones which utilized the services of a well-organized agency and that while the agent was tending to cease selling space as a specific service for a specific publication, it was upbuilding advertising volume in a broad way.

The beginnings of the agency-publisher relationship based on this viewpoint were worked out by Thomas Balmer, then Western manager of the *Ladies' Home Journal,* and C. E. Raymond, who was in charge of the Chicago office of J. Walter Thompson Company. Shortly thereafter, in 1898, the Curtis Publishing Company promulgated its agency agreement which bound the agency not to depart from card rates, directly or indirectly, and the publisher to accord the agent's commission to no one but a bona fide agent. In the early 1900's numerous magazines followed suit. The Philadelphia *Bulletin,* Boston *Globe,* Kansas City *Star,* Chicago *Daily News* and a few others of the larger newspapers announced they would give commissions to agents only. Not infrequently the policy cost money in terms of business lost, but the system stuck and in time became all but universal, though not without meeting several points at which it was put to severe test.

Thus the modern advertising agency. It was a form unique in business enterprise. It was completely a product of evolution. Probably no one could have predicted or planned the emergence of a business mechanism such as it became. But it has survived the test of fitness for nearly forty years.

Organized in this way, the agent was a more useful servant of the advertiser, particularly the newcomers. And he accomplished much more than he ever had in winning new advertiser converts, for he had something more than the negations of cheap prices to talk about.

Every Way You Figure
The NEWS
IS FIRST
in San Francisco

The RECORD of The NEWS

among San Francisco daily newspapers

SPEAKS for ITSELF

First in:

RETAIL GROCERY	since 1930	
DEPARTMENT STORES	"	1933
TOTAL RETAIL	"	1933
CITY CIRCULATION	"	1936
TOTAL DISPLAY	"	1936
TOTAL ADVERTISING	"	1936
AUTOMOTIVE	"	1937
GENERAL ADVERTISING—1st 5 months		1938*

*exclusive of affiliated advertising

Important market indices point to San Francisco as far above the average in sales possibilities. The experience of leading retail and general advertisers proves that "It Pays to Advertise" in a responsive, able-to-buy market where only one daily newspaper, The News, reaches more than half of all your San Francisco prospects, thousands more than the second newspaper.

The San Francisco News

A SCRIPPS-HOWARD NEWSPAPER

NATIONAL ADVERTISING DEPARTMENT OF SCRIPPS-HOWARD NEWSPAPERS, 230 PARK AVENUE, NEW YORK CITY   CHICAGO ● SAN FRANCISCO ● LOS ANGELES ● DALLAS ● DETROIT ● PHILADELPHIA ● ATLANTA

Rhyme and Reason

THE allusive style of advertisement, which merely sought to give publicity to the product name and was typical of all advertising effort during the preceding century, greeted the new century with its most spectacular fling. For this was the period of the great jingle craze.

The use of rhyme in advertising dated back at least thirty years and its efficacy had always been the subject of rousing argument whenever two or more advertising men met. The jingle itself—a short, catchy rhyme—had garnered something of a following in the 1890's. The most eminent ancestor was the De Long rhyming of Charles M. Snyder. Most popular example:

He rose, she took the seat and said:
"I thank you," and the man fell dead.
But ere he turned a lifeless lump,
He murmured: "See that Hump?"

The real craze, which rose about 1900 and had faded by 1903, centered, about a mythical town, an imaginary optimist and a legendary lady who still live in the memories of many—Spotless Town, Sunny Jim and Phoebe Snow.

The rhymes of Spotless Town were written by J. K. Fraser, just out of Cornell and in the employ of the producers of Sapolio, Enoch Morgan & Sons Company. The verses, used in car cards all over the nation, told the cleansing power of Sapolio in an amusing vein and caught on immediately. Soon came toys, books and plays— even political cartoons—featuring the fabled community and its residents.

Jim Dumps, or Sunny Jim, appeared in behalf of Force breakfast food. He was hailed in the public prints as "the quaintest and livest character advertising genius has ever produced." He was, in a manner of speaking, the Charley McCarthy of his time. The producing genius, incidentally, was a young lady—Minnie Maud Hanff. She was the first woman to win recognition as an advertising writer. Soon she yielded a share of the spotlight to two others, the Hoffman sisters of Chicago, who wrote and illustrated the jingles for Swift's Silver Leaf lard.

Phoebe Snow appeared under the sponsorship of the Lackawanna Railroad, which previously had been exclusively a freight line. When the road decided to solicit passenger business between New York and Buffalo, Wendell P. Colton, then advertising manager, decided to stress the cleanliness which derived from the fact that the locomotives burned anthracite and the right of way was ballasted wholly with rock. Colton invented the "Road of Anthracite" phrase and wrote a series of jingles. Then he outlined the general idea of a trade character to Calkins & Holden, and soon thereafter Phoebe made her bow. For sheer rhythm and catchiness, this series eclipsed them all, as the following example may attest:

Says Phoebe Snow
About to go
Upon a trip to Buffalo:
My gown stays white
From morn till night
Upon the Road of Anthracite.

As each of these famous three rolled up their tremendous followings, originality as represented by versification became the great hue and cry among advertisers. Questions of meter and meaning were gravely argued in the trade. There was debate on the standards of advertising poetry. Elaborated theories of mnemonics were advanced by which to weigh the power of a jingle. Imitators who thought to rhyme their way to national consumer demand came in by the dozens. And, of course, the jingle proved a mere mirage of advertising success for most. What was generally overlooked was that the jingle worked best when it followed a factual campaign; that its chief value was in keeping alive a conviction already implanted.

Even as some of the shine was coming off the jingle, a new trend in the advertising message—by far the most important yet to appear—was making itself felt. It was the direct opposite of the style whose apogee the jingle represented.

The allusive style of copy was losing its punch. In the good old days it had been enough to say that "Soandso's is the best." In effect the main distinction between competing products had been the trade name. Advertising was a game of getting the public to remember your trade name in preference to others. As competition increased this was not so easy, except by expenditures of huge sums. Trying to distinguish a commodity by mere trade name was becoming a relatively useless gesture because the competition among trade-named articles had grown to be as keen as it once was among nameless and unadvertised goods.

The rudimentary allusions and brief statements of nothing in particular began to come in for support and fuller explanations. The descriptive advertisement was born

and a start made toward giving fuller factual information. Then, around 1902, came the trend toward putting what was called "selling quality" into the advertisement. It not merely described the article, but set forth its desirability to the owner. "You" came into advertising. The advertiser sought to put into printed copy much the same thing a good salesman tells his customers face to face—"salesmanship in print," in the phrase promulgated by Lord & Thomas.

The major prophet of the new order was a former member of the Canadian Northwest Mounted Police, a man of huge physique and forceful personality named John E. Kennedy. He called it "reason-why" copy.

Men before Kennedy's time had spoken of the value of giving reasons in advertising. John E. Powers had. So had Charles Austin Bates. But it remained for Kennedy to apply the concept to the advertising process in a highly developed manner and to win a real hearing for it from the advertiser community at large. It was not until his time that any appreciable number of advertisers got away from the old publicity theory of advertising effect as the sole end and aim of the art. While he doesn't by any means deserve all the credit, he had more to do with it than anybody else.

Kennedy came into prominence as a member of the staff of Lord & Thomas at Chicago. Later he was connected with the Ethridge-Kennedy Company at New York and the Baltimore Bargain House, following which he commanded huge fees from numerous large advertisers as a writer of advertising

"Conviction is not produced by

THE DAILY OKLAHOMAN
OKLAHOMA CITY TIMES
THE FARMER-STOCKMAN

Phone 2-1211

THE OKLAHOMA PUBLISHING COMPANY

OKLAHOMA CITY, OKLAHOMA

MATURE IN ACHIEVEMENT!

YOUTHFUL IN VISION!

.. A Story of 35 Years of Effort!

Printers Ink was a year old when the Indian lands of Oklahoma were opened to white settlers in 1889. With the "Run" came thousands of ambitious farmers, business and professional men who founded and built Oklahoma City on the unbroken prairie.

Fourteen years later came E. K. Gaylord to this booming pioneer town and, with his associates, purchased The Daily Oklahoman, founded the Oklahoma Publishing Company.

Capably managed through difficult days, brilliantly edited, The Daily Oklahoman quickly became the most widely read and quoted newspaper in this new commonwealth.

In 1916, the masthead (and little else) of the Oklahoma City Times, first newspaper published in Oklahoma City, was acquired at a sheriff's sale. Today it leads all afternoon papers in the State.

Produced in a new and modern mechanical plant, these newspapers are admired for their appearance as well as their content by readers and advertisers alike.

THE SUNDAY OKLAHOMAN

Largest Sunday Circulation
in the Southwest.

THE DAILY OKLAHOMAN

Largest Morning Circulation
in the Southwest.

OKLAHOMA CITY TIMES

Largest Afternoon Circulation
in the Southwest.

Phone 2-1211

THE FARMER-STOCKMAN
THE DAILY OKLAHOMAN
OKLAHOMA CITY TIMES

THE OKLAHOMA PUBLISHING COMPANY

OKLAHOMA CITY, OKLAHOMA

THE FARMER-STOCKMAN

SERVES A Quarter-Million

Farm Families

As Oklahoma's farm population grew, the need for a medium to guide it to better agricultural methods was supplied by the weekly edition of the Oklahoman. Enlarged, redesigned, it became the Farmer-Stockman with widened scope to include every phase of farming and stock raising as well as problems of the farm home.

Edited by a large staff of recognized agricultural experts and economists, the Farmer-Stockman has become the leading force for the advancement of farming in the Southwest.

Through its columns, and after thousands of personal contacts with farm organizations and in farm homes, Farmer-Stockman editors founded and advanced, long before these projects were nationally recognized, the movements now known as:

> Diversification Projects
> Cooperative Marketing Groups
> 4-H and FFA Clubs
> Master Farmer Awards
> Terracing and Soil Erosion Prevention

Membership in the Oklahoma Publishing Company family of media has enabled The Farmer-Stockman to engage in costly, yet worthwhile and far-reaching, projects for the advancement of its farmer-readers . . . projects which have created a reader loyalty recognized by advertisers as the "plus quantity" which makes The Farmer-Stockman one of the leading sectional farm papers of the country.

THE FARMER-STOCKMAN

The Only Farm Paper with
More Than 200,000 Circulation
in Oklahoma and North Texas.

QUICK, motorized delivery service is provided
285 Oklahoma cities and towns from 2 to 12 times daily by Mistletoe
Express Service, Oklahoma Publishing Company transportation affiliate.
Developed to provide Oklahoma Publishing Company media fast, reliable
distribution to all parts of the state, it has become an indispensable service to other shippers throughout the state.

WKY RADIOPHONE COMPANY

BROADCASTING SERVICE OF THE OKLAHOMA PUBLISHING COMPANY

OKLAHOMA CITY, OKLAHOMA

OKLAHOMA'S STANDOUT STATION!

When radio was only a hobby, the Oklahoma Publishing Company was already supplying news and exploiting civic features over the amateur experimental station which was to become WKY and the third station in America to go on the air with regularly scheduled programs.

In 1928, WKY was purchased by the Oklahoma Publishing Company, became an NBC affiliate and brought Central Oklahoma its first network broadcast. A building and improvement program which started at that time has continued to this day.

A decade of efficient management and public appreciation has placed WKY in a position of unquestioned leadership in Oklahoma.

GREATEST COVERAGE   A combination of favorable frequency (900 kc.) and adequate power (5000 watts, day; 1000 watts, night) join to enable WKY to cover more of Oklahoma than does any other station.

LARGEST AUDIENCE   Surveys, both by station and advertisers, have shown WKY to have the bulk of the audience most of the time . . . shown as high as 78% listener preference.

FINEST STUDIOS   WKY's Skirvin Tower studios are among the finest, most modern in the U.S. A leading NBC executive said: "WKY's studios incorporate features which we would include in Radio City were we to rebuild today."

LATEST EQUIPMENT   A new RCA transmitter, new Truscon vertical radiator are only part of WKY's completely modern equipment. Its 200-watt mobile transmitter, portable short-wave units and ultra-high frequency transmitter, W5XAU, are all employed to render an outstanding public service.

WKY-OKLAHOMA CITY

Carries more national spot
advertising than any other
Southwestern station.

KVOR "THE VOICE OF THE ROCKIES"

OUT WEST BROADCASTING COMPANY

ANTLERS, HOTEL

COLORADO SPRINGS

A NEW PEAK

for Colorado Listeners!

A new peak in radio service came to Southern Colorado late in 1936 when KVOR joined the Oklahoma Publishing Company family. Studios were rebuilt to become probably the finest anywhere in cities of similar size. A new transmitter was installed, vertical radiator erected and a program of community service begun unparalleled in this area.

Its influence in its area is well illustrated by the remarkable results of a region-wide talent hunt just ended. In ten weeks nearly 1000 ambitious persons were given encouragement in auditions and mail-votes totalled more than 50,000.

KVOR, CBS station for Southern Colorado, is essential to coverage in this area.

KLZ BROADCASTING COMPANY

THE PIONEER STATION OF THE WEST

DENVER, COLORADO

DENVER'S FIRST RADIO STATION!

In 1935, the interests responsible for the sensational leadership of WKY, acquired KLZ, Denver. Chief among its assets were the courage and vision of its founders who had built "The Pioneer Station of the West" and established for it an enviable record of distinguished community service.

Result: Immediate construction of one of the nation's finest transmitters, completely new and modern studios, increasingly finer programming and skillful exploitation. KLZ is today Denver's FIRST station because it is:

> First in audience popularity
> First in hours of Sponsored network programs
> First in local sponsored volume
> First in hours of locally produced shows

The new CBS listening area study visualizes KLZ's tremendous influence in the Denver-Rocky Mountain region.

bare affirmation, but by proof, by inference, by argument—in short, by reason-why talk," asserted Kennedy. "Some buyers purchase, not because they are convinced of merits, but because they are curious about the product. General publicity may be well enough for a 5 or 10-cent article, but for articles costing $1 or more people won't buy unless you tell them why.

"Advertising is addressed to the most incredulous people in the world. The advertiser must avoid wind and jingle and present definite reasons why to consumers. But the claims must not fit any other lines and must be at least partially proved when stated."

An advertising campaign, in the Kennedy view, should have six cardinal points:

1. A strong pivotal feature so legally protected that it cannot be copied by imitators after the advertiser has spent thousands of dollars to make it popular and valuable. Sometimes the exclusive quality in the product can be patented, sometimes only the device for demonstrating the feature.

2. A living news interest.

3. Palpable reasons why the reader should buy the commodity. You can't just tell the reader a shoe has better leather and better workmanship. You must tell wherein and why they are better. Readers know all about the generalities of a commodity and they will not, because they need not, give much attention to empty statements.

4. Description that is condensed, containing much meaning in few words.

5. Illustrations that prove the claims.

6. Self-explained window displays. Closely linked with the "selling quality" trend in copy was the effort to get the reader to act upon the advertisement which characterized a large proportion of the advertising in this style. An essential element in selling goods by mail, it had never before achieved wide use among general advertisers. Rare in 1900, the action incentive characterized the majority of magazine advertisements and much of the newspaper copy in 1905.

Most common basis of the effort was the offer of a free booklet giving further information about the product. A few advertisers offered a booklet for a small payment. Second in preference was the sample, free or at a small charge. Other forms were the offer of an advertising novelty or premium, gratis or for labels, and the offer of a free trial of the goods for a specified period. Some method of inducement for action was represented in the advertising of almost every type of product or service, from breakfast foods to insurance, in addition, of course, to correspondence schools and mail sellers of merchandise.

Coincidentally, the corner coupon (usually triangular in shape) came into extensive favor as a means of making it easy for the consumer to respond to the offer. Almost every phase of advertising technique was credited with a "father," and here the honors are generally conceded to Ralph Tilton, who employed coupons in connection with copy he prepared for the Century dictionary in the 1890's. A host of subscription book publishers followed this lead, then the general advertisers.

Another advance was the tendency to develop small-space units and make them profitable. In the preceding period the trend to large

space had in some degree become merged into the idea that only through pages, double pages and big magazine inserts could the advertiser impress the public. By study of black-and-white effects, of processes of drawing and engraving and of type arrangement, the small advertiser cultivated individuality in his messages. In this process there was a noteworthy disposition to attempt to achieve the result along sound lines and without resort to freakish design.

It was not long before the "selling quality" movement began to assume its faddish aspects. It was widely exploited by agencies. Numerous agents and writers had their own brands of it, each brand with its own more or less appropriate name. There was a tendency to view just about every advertising problem entirely in terms of argument. Where the advertisement had once been a picture and a paragraph, it now presented long and often labored text matter with an incidental illustration. Length of copy was not infrequently confused with reasoning, elaborate statement with convincing argument. Many advertisements were "text books in subject matter and novels in length." Much copy adopted a Johnsonian complexion of rounded, elegant sentences and intricate statement. Many a wordy crime was committed in the name of reason-why and its variants.

In numerous instances reason-why was assiduously applied to selling propositions where rational processes had little or nothing to do with the purchase. There was a general tendency to assume that the buying public was a completely rational entity, whereas the buying public, by reason of its humanity, was and is irrational at least a fair share of the time. The general perception did not immediately encompass the fact that argument must be served up at the right times, on the right propositions and in the right amounts. Too little attention was given the human equation.

The Cream of Wheat Company was one of the outstanding demonstrators of the point that calculated reasoning was not the only route to advertising success. Emery Mapes reasoned that people often ate a food product not because they were argued into it but because they liked it. Although a little expository copy was used in the early years, most of the business was built on human-interest advertising. He featured human, appealing illustrations (most famous subject, of course, being the negro chef Rastus) and pulled the strings of suggestion and made it pay.

Despite the abortive uses of "selling quality" by those who did not understand it, this period marked the greatest forward steps ever taken in the realm of the advertising message, before or since. It was here that the advertiser learned the value of talking to the consumer as one person instead of as a vague, impersonal audience. He learned how better to tell his prospect what the product was and how to relate it to the consumer's need. He recognized the value of telling the consumer how to use his product—one of the widely marked events of the period being a new Ivory soap program in which a wide range of uses for the product was pointed out. Incredible as it may now seem, little had ever been done in the way of providing directions for use and suggesting new applications.

The advertiser developed a scorn for the once-worshiped gods of "cleverness" and "originality," which all too often had meant freakish presentation. He discarded the brazen tone of the street hawker, common ten years before. He learned to be calm in his address. He learned the uses of sincerity and the simple statement.

All these things the advertiser learned.

Or did he?

It must be that advertisers as a body have rather a floating intellect. For in 1905 we find the allusive assertions, the glib generalities and the raucous exaggerations in high favor once more. There was a veritable competition in, to borrow a phrase of the day, adjectival redundancy. Products were hailed as "finest," "biggest," "best," "supreme" and "most perfect" (of which the popular modern counterpart seems to be "most outstanding").

In 1906 a rampant phase of competitive snarling took a place on the stage. A number of advertisers began to wield the muck-rake, a course influenced in part at least by the "exposé" school of journalism which was then in flower in

---

1904

SERVICE pension for all Civil War veterans over 62 years of age. . . . Fire in Baltimore, largest since Chicago fire of 1871, causes loss of $125,000,000. . . . Merchant Marine Commission created. . . . Theodore Roosevelt elected to succeed himself as president, defeating Judge Alton B. Parker, 336 electoral votes to 140. . . . Russia and Japan at war.

George Batten Company, a partnership of George Batten and William H. Johns, incorporated with Batten as president and Johns as vice-president. . . . W. R. Hearst establishes the Los Angeles *Examiner*. . . . Automobile manufacturers sensitive about news reports of accidents. . . . *Everybody's Magazine* to print an index of advertisers, a move regarded dubiously in the trade. . . . Pacific Coast Advertising Men's Association organized. . . . *McClure's* leads the monthlies in linage. . . . J. M. Campbell leaves Rock Island Railroad to become advertising manager of Procter & Gamble.

C. R. Erwin and A. D. Lasker acquire the interest of D. M. Lord in Lord & Thomas. . . . Dan A. Carroll takes over the M. Lee Starke list of papers. . . . Regal introduces shoes in quarter sizes and it is said that the custom shoe maker's occupation is gone. . . . The year is establishing a precedent for large advertising expenditures in the automobile field; Waltham Manufacturing Company plans to spend $50,000 advertising Orient motor cars. . . . Hiring salesmen by bumps becomes popular as phrenological counselor firm offers its services to commercial firms.

McGuffey Readers *were in*

50 *Years Ago — when*

The old McGuffey Readers carried the torch of education to light the wilderness. McGuffey satisfied the hunger for learning; brought to the many a taste for good literature, an appreciation of ideals, morals, ethics.

And Printers' Ink has carried the torch of education to light the wilderness of advertising. In 1888 advertising was embryonic, undeveloped; today it is a mighty force! Printers' Ink has, through the years, made a great contribution to the progress of advertising and distribution.

Congratulations, Printers' Ink! As to the future—here's wishing you another fifty years of leadership and usefulness.

Charles Francis Press

every little Red School House

Printers' Ink *was Founded*

When Printers' Ink was six years old, in 1894, the Charles Francis Press was founded. In 1908 the task of printing Printers' Ink was entrusted to us—and we've been at it ever since. Printers' Ink Monthly has also been printed by us from its inception.

Charles Francis Press has grown up with its customers. We serve many of America's best known advertisers. They receive full value and quality at reasonable prices.

We offer to you the services of our large, up-to-date plant with every modern facility for the production of advertising literature, publications and general printing.

461 Eighth Ave., New York

many magazines and newspapers. Thomas Lawson's "Frenzied Finance" series in *Everybody's*, a huge reader success, had touched off exposures of most every imaginable institution in American life.

Advertisers took off hotly on the trail. Some of the more discreet raged with the fury of a campaigning Congressman at such evils as dirt, disease, toxins and garments that restrict the circulation. Others, a bit bolder, aired their commerical grudges and called their competitors names. Still others reached across the fence to take pokes at neighboring industries. "Take That Meat Away," yelled one cereal company. "The Tin Can Age Demands a Tin Can Stomach," cried another in the same field. A brewer loudly deplored the evils of coffee and "temperance drinks."

Possibly it was not irrelevant that business at the time was approaching a prosperity peak. There is no clear-cut precedent for so believing since in previous business cycles there had really been only one type of advertising copy. But there are plenty of antecedents. From 1906 forward every period of business prosperity has been marked in its last feverish gasps by a great trend to extravagantly worded general publicity copy and an accompanying tendency to knocking competitors.

When the collapse comes, the advertiser seems to roll up his sleeves and get back to straightforward, specific selling values. There must be something of the demagog in him. He matches the timber of his message to the temper of the people. When the public is in a rousing, extravagant mood, he resorts to flashy, superficial and hectic appeals. He comes back to earnestness and sincerity when the public is in deflated spirits. Or perhaps it is merely that he gets careless when the selling is easy. At any rate, this cyclical movement has persisted unfailingly to the present day.

At the same time it is equally true that a certain section of the advertiser body has consistently put to use the accumulated experience of the years. Good times and bad, they stay on the course. Those who bend to every passing fad and fancy are the more conspicuous because of the flamboyancy of the measures by which they are so easily tempted. They appear to less advantage in the list of advertisers who have been with us for many years. There the greatest mark is made by those who have quietly and unobtrusively pursued the simplicities of sound marketing methods.

Beneficent Menace

IN 1904 retailer agitation about department stores had given way to worrying about a new menace—the mail-order houses. How to offset the competition of the mail-order firms, often contemptuously called the "cat" houses, was lengthily discussed at every trade convention. The trade press published cartoons and ranting articles assailing the mail system of distribution.

Most retailers and jobbers believed that their business and that of the mail-order firms could not exist side by side. Many of them felt that they were doomed to complete extinction unless some drastic action was taken, preferably by the Government. Merchants vigorously opposed extension of the parcel post system and any postal provision for transmission of small amounts of money through the mails, although the public at large desired these. They would have abolished rural free delivery had they been able. They charged the catalog houses with misrepresentation and all manner of evil practices and threatened to boycott manufacturers who sold to them.

Selling to consumers from catalogs was not new at this time. It had first appeared more than thirty years before. But the early growth of the large mail-order houses had been slow. The great strides came after 1900.

First to enter the field on a large scale was a traveling salesman, A. Montgomery Ward by name. When, in 1869, the first transcontinental railroad was completed, Ward had the vision to foresee a great merchandising opportunity—that of selling goods to a nation-wide market by mail, then an entirely new and untried element in the merchandising scheme.

He had his plans pretty well under way when the rails met at Promontory Point, Utah. In partnership with George R. Thorne, he got together a modest stock of merchandise. Just as they were about to start, the Chicago fire destroyed everything they owned. By 1872 they had scraped together $2,400 and in a twelve by fourteen-foot room on North Clark Street in Chicago they launched the world's first mail-order business. Here the first mail-order catalog was born. It was an eight by twelve-inch single sheet which listed the small stock of dry goods the firm offered for sale. There were no illustrations, but guaranteed net prices were quoted in plain figures.

This was a revolution in merchandising which carried to the outlying districts the benefit of reduced prices, or rather of fair prices. It introduced the element of competition into the retail business in the small towns and farming communities.

In recognition of the Ward merchandising plan as a means of protecting the buyer, the National Grange arranged with Ward to buy the official supply house for the "Patrons of Husbandry."

Ward had great difficulty getting financial backing to develop his business. Finally a New York financial house extended a line of credit of $50,000, withheld at first because the house was seriously convinced that Ward's idea of substituting golden rule principles for "Caveat Emptor" was an hallucination due to overwork. With this loan the organization grew steadily

Capper

The Household Magazine
• •
Capper's Farmer
• •
Kansas Farmer
Missouri Ruralist
Ohio Farmer
Michigan Farmer
Pennsylvania Farmer
• •
Topeka Daily Capital
Kansas City Kansan
Capper's Weekly
• •
Radio Station WIBW
Radio Station KCKN

New York   Chicago   Detroit   Cleveland

❚❚ If you would know the United States, look beyond the Big Cities. Most of Our Country is <u>in the country.</u> **❚❚**

—*W. J. Cameron*

MOST of the people of the United States live "in the country" or in towns of less than 15,000 population. Half of our retail trade is from these ultimate consumers.

What Business in the United States needs today, is not more Capital nor more Labor, nor greater productive facilities—but *Markets*.

It would seem the part of wisdom, then, to cultivate to the limit, such markets as we have.

The Capper Publications, severally and combined, offer the business man—manufacturer and merchant—a direct avenue of sales approach to the homes of 4,000,000 ultimate consumers—average American families, with all the needs and wants and desires that make up the American standard of living. In and of themselves they constitute a market which if saturated with sales' effort, would be a very effective priming of the pump.

If you have wearied of waiting for the government to start things, let's do a little pump-priming ourselves.

Capper Publications, Inc.

ARTHUR CAPPER, *President*

Topeka, Kansas

Pittsburgh   San Francisco   St. Louis   Kansas City

and added new lines. In 1874 the price sheet had become an eight-page leaflet. Next year it contained 152 pages. At this time woodcut illustrations began to appear in it. In 1878 came the first mail-order fashion illustration—a picture of a single dress. The woodcuts proved such a great sales stimulus that in the early eighties the catalog was profusely illustrated. An announcement was made in the summer of 1883 that the house carried $500,000 worth of merchandise in stock. In 1896 the catalog was a semi-annual edition of half a million copies, each copy heavy enough to require 17 cents in postage.

In 1884 Richard W. Sears, telegraph operator for the Great Northern Railroad at Redwood Falls, Minn., undertook to sell a shipment of watches which the local jeweler had refused to accept. He had written to the watch company and it had agreed to let him try to dispose of the shipment by mail. What happened opened his eyes to the possibilities of selling by mail and soon his spare time work became his sole occupation. He moved to Minneapolis and started in the mail-order business in real earnest. Then he moved to Chicago and sold his business. At the age of twenty-four he had $100,000 in the bank, wherewith he entered the business in Minneapolis again and returned to Chicago in 1895.

Sears was a merchandising genius and a good judge of men. He was a shrewd buyer as well as a master salesman and believed in backing his merchandise with the broadest kind of guarantee. He built his annual sales from nothing to over $50,000,000 in seventeen years and laid the foundations for what has come down today as the largest merchandising enterprise of its kind in the world.

Numerous others entered the mail selling field—many novelty firms, some which dealt in specialty lines like women's apparel, and a few general houses. Sears, Roebuck & Company and Montgomery Ward & Company, however, continued as the great leaders.

The growth of the business was necessarily slow in the first years because the goods were sold on description and paid for before the buyer saw them. It was first necessary to educate people to visualize an article from a description or picture and then believe in the honesty of the representations made and in the willingness and ability of the seller to live up to the guarantees given. Establishing confidence was the work of years even after the public imagination had been trained to buy from the printed page.

For a long time the remittance problem was a substantial one. There were no postal money orders. Banking facilities in the small communities were limited or nonexistent. To solve the problem the Chicago houses opened account systems, giving the consumer a note on which he was paid 7 per cent interest. Goods ordered were charged against the note.

A new era of growth came when Sears and Ward ceased the practice of charging the customer for the catalog and advertised catalogs free of charge to all who wanted them. Sears had been charging ten cents, Ward fifteen. The move was made because it appeared that a firm so well known would not be likely to be the victim of curiosity seekers. When Ward issued its first free catalog in 1904 it had 2,500 employees.

Seven months later 3,500 workers were required.

The catalog houses were successful because they applied modern methods. They told something in their advertising. They dealt liberally with the customer and scrupulously lived up to their wide-open guarantees. The local merchant, on the other hand, had failed to realize that business methods had been systematized. In his advertising he merely listed the lines of articles he carried; although the city dealer was a good advertiser and knew how to make money out of it, the rural retailers usually handled advertising as though it were a charity conducted by the publisher.

The mail-order houses created new demands for merchandise, educated buyers and inspired desire for home conforts and luxuries. Rural merchants were not exposing customers to the temptations of show windows and bargain counters.

The mail-order bogey came down to the simple fact that the majority of the merchants were behind the times. The remedy, of course, was to set about catching up. That began to take place. Butler Brothers in 1905 supplied retailers with education in advertising methods and other wholesale dealers in merchandise followed suit. But for a long time, many a retailer chose—humanly, it must be admitted—to look for the fault outside himself and concentrated on demands for legislation and appeals to the sympathy of the public.

Wrigley made history while advertising itself into prominence. (*Circa* 1913)

In 1914—as before and since—Coca-Cola was consistently an advertiser

Cleaning Up

ADVERTISEMENTS of fake and worthless products were beyond all question one of the greatest deterrents to the development of advertising. Conversely, the growth of this business tool closely paralleled the routing of the fraud advertisers out of the advertising columns.

More keenly aware than ever of the value of reader confidence and of the hesitancy of the manufacturer of honest products to associate with the fakers, publishers greatly increased their efforts in purging their pages of the copy of the spurious medicine makers, the "lost manhood" preparations, the stock schemes, the mail-order cadgers and other questionable products and services. Not only were these offerings worthless, but the advertisers of them were the chief offenders in bombastic statement and sensationalism in copy and illustration. Their advertising ethics closely corresponded with their regard for the meritorious quality in their products.

By 1905 almost every publication of real rank maintained rigid standards against admission of the fraudulent product to their columns. Quite a few refused all medicine copy.

Meanwhile one publication had taken the offensive against the advertisers of spurious medicines. The *Ladies' Home Journal*, in 1904, touched off the opening attack on the fake remedies. First the actual contents of many of the alleged medicines was exposed and the fact that some of them embodied high quantities of alcohol, others deleterious drugs such as opium and morphine, was brought into public view. Then their methods of doing business were taken up. Edward Bok, who directed the campaign, enlisted the services of a young New York lawyer named Mark Sullivan, who revealed, among other things, methods of getting testimonials from Congressmen and the practice of selling letters from customers to other firms.

In 1905 *Collier's Weekly* joined the fray with a perhaps even livelier series of exposures. Robert J. Collier, with Bok's permission, employed the services of Sullivan, then enrolled Samuel Hopkins Adams in the crusade. The result was a hard-hitting unremitting campaign which gave further circulation to the public knowledge of the prevalent evils. The articles named names and took specific products and analyzed their ingredients with relationship to the benefits claimed for the remedies—including complete cure of consumption, cancer, yellow fever and meningitis.

Other periodicals and newspapers joined the cause. Closing of advertising pages to the fakes proceeded at a greater rate than ever before. And, most important of all, the public was so well awakened to the frauds practiced upon it that these activities may be said to have contributed in a major way to the passage in 1906 of the national Food and Drug Act.

The new law made it a misdemeanor to make or sell adulterated or misbranded foods, drugs, medicines or liquors and also prohibited the receipt of such goods. (Prohibition of false or fraudulent claims on labels did not come until the passage of the Sherly amendment some years later.) Dr. Harvey Wiley, chief of the Bureau of

Hyomei Antiseptic Skin Soap

Made from the fresh green leaves
of the Tasmanian Blue Gum Tree

**Contains no fats or grease to clog the
pores.**

**No dangerous alkali to dry and parch
the skin.**

Nature's own skin purifier and cleanser.

Healing. Refreshing. Beautifying.

**As much superior to the best toilet soaps
made as they are to the commonest
laundry.**

Send five cents for sample cake

Sold by all druggists, or sent by mail.
Price, 25c.

THE R. T. BOOTH CO. 40 Ave. F, Ithaca, N. Y.

Even in the early days customer was
adjured to "buy it—today."

This nude caused unfavorable comment
in 1900.

In 1902 Bon Ami was put on the
market. An example of a long-time
and constant advertiser that has not
scattered its fire.

All three of these store display pieces are twenty-five or more years old. The Berry Brothers cutout was in three panels, with floor piece and figures in foreground, all connected with muslin hinges. Buster Brown and his dog Tige were popular figures of their day. In the Ralston display, note the schoolmaster's garb and the rapture of his pupil.

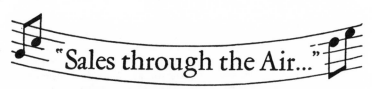

"Sales through the Air..."

How Advertising Fostered a new industry and established a national medium for the spoken word

THE peculiar bond between the speaker and his listener is as old as the first guttural sounds which human beings made to warn and attract each other, and to express their pleasure and pain.

Thousands of years ago the first efforts were made to "win friends and influence people" by the spoken word. To this day, no other method of influencing men and women is as successful as words spoken feelingly and with conviction.

Personal selling—whether in the words of an orator of Greece, the speech of a Phoenician trader, or the lofty message of an Oriental mystic—relied on the voice and the ear: transmitters and receivers of the beginning world.

The first advertising was conversational. Advertising next employed pictures and symbols. Then came visible words carved or lettered laboriously by hand. Finally, only yesterday, the printing press enabled advertisers to reach the masses with economy. Printed advertising was a boon because it had always been impossibly expensive to hire and send out enough personal salespeople to talk to every prospect.

Then came the radio, and broadcast advertising.

In less than two decades broadcasting has made available to the advertiser all the ancient and powerful attraction between the speaker and his listener. More. It has performed a unique service by multiplying incalculably the number of individual calls a single speaker can make.

The salesman who talks in a single day to 20 prospects is exceptional. But broadcasting enables a single personal salesman to speak to a thousand or a million or ten million in the space of a few minutes—and *he meets each as an individual or as a member of the intimate family circle.*

That is the peculiar miracle of advertising by radio: the speaking of one person to a million listeners as though alone and face to face with each one.

This miracle has not lessened the value of printed advertising in any of its many forms. Rather, it has added to their effectiveness by rounding out the functioning of modern advertising—by bringing to advertising the power of the well-spoken selling message directed at listeners who listen by choice and voluntarily.

Thus broadcast advertising is both a supplementary and a primary instrument in making sales. It is supplementary in that it will never take the place of any other form of advertising. It is primary in that its appeal is the appeal of a personal speaker to an individual listener, something which can be secured in no other form of advertising.

Historical Highlights

What enabled this young invention to become so quickly the nation's favorite entertainer? How did it get organized so well in a few short years that today network broadcasting is among the first mediums chosen for national advertising by the most analytical and most experienced advertisers?

Broadcasting, as we know it, is only a trifle over 17 years old. In September 1920, a department store in Pittsburgh ran an historically interesting advertisement. Desiring to sell "wireless sets," it announced that from his home Dr. Frank Conrad was broadcasting experimentally. By purchasing a receiver (hand made by a local man) one could join the select group of listeners who were participating in the delights of this new marvel of science.*

Although there were experimental broadcasts before 1920, it was not until then that the first pre-scheduled broadcast was presented to the public. Some time before election, Station KDKA announced that it would send out the results of the Harding-Cox contest on November 2, 1920. It is generally agreed that this event constituted "the first broadcast," in the modern accepted sense of the term.

Although public broadcasting began on November 2, 1920, the first program sponsored and paid for by an advertiser did not go out until August 28, 1922. This was a talk on "Jackson Heights" presented by the Queensboro Corporation, featuring the Hawthorne Court Apartments. The program was over Station WEAF, then operated by the American Telephone and Telegraph Company, and now, of course, the key station of the NBC Red Network. It is interesting to note that some of the earliest commercial programs were sold through the medium of radio itself, as Station WEAF at that time made announcements that ten minutes on the air could be purchased for $100.

The first *network* commercial program was broadcast on February 12, 1924, also over the Red Network. Its sponsor was the National Carbon

---

*From advertisement of Joseph Horne Company, Pittsburgh Sun, Sept. 29, 1920:

AIR CONCERT
"Picked Up"
By Radio Here

Victrola music, played into the air over a wireless telephone, was "picked up" by listeners on the wireless receiving station which was recently installed here for patrons interested in wireless experiments. The concert was heard Thursday night about 10 o'clock, and continued 20 minutes. Two orchestra numbers, a soprano solo—which rang particularly high, and clear through the air—and a juvenile "talking piece" constituted the program.

The music was from a Victrola pulled up close to the transmitter of a wireless telephone in the home of Frank Conrad, Penn and Peebles avenues, Wilkinsburg. Mr. Conrad is a wireless enthusiast and "puts on" the wireless concerts periodically for the entertainment of the many people in this district who have wireless sets.

Amateur Wireless Sets, made by the maker of the Set which is in operation in our store, are on sale here $10.00 up.——*West Basement.*

Company, and the program was entitled "He Knew Lincoln."

The first permanent coast-to-coast network was not established until December 23, 1928, when NBC opened its transcontinental line.

Thus nation-wide commercial broadcasting is now only in its tenth year.

Birth of the Red Network

Only through simultaneous broadcasting over several stations could two high hopes be realized: (1) making the greatest artists and entertainers available to the public, and (2) making national advertising an economical medium for the advertiser.

Only advertising revenue has enabled the editor of a national magazine to give his readers the best fiction, special articles, and illustrations. Only advertising revenue could enable broadcasting stations to give their listeners the finest entertainment the world has to offer.

Thus, in both cases, the interests of the public and the advertiser were identical.

The first stations linked for simultaneous broadcasting by a telephone line connection were WEAF of New York and WNAC of Boston. This occurred on January 4, 1923. It was not until October 14, 1923, that the first commercial "network" was constituted—by the permanent connection of WEAF and WJAR of Providence. This was called the Red Network because the lines on the telephone company's map indicating the wire connection were red.

The Red Network was operated by the American Telephone and Telegraph Company from 1923 to 1926, rapidly adding stations in key cities.

But in the meantime, the Radio Corporation of America, formed by General Electric in 1919 to foster the development of radio in the United States, had been operating WJZ New York (opened by Westinghouse in 1921) and WRC Washington. WJZ had also been hooked up on various occasions with Westinghouse stations KDKA and WBZ-A, and General Electric's WGY. It became clear that whereas the AT&T's primary interest was wired point-to-point communication, the organization with the biggest stake in the new art of broadcasting was the Radio Corporation of America. Therefore, when the new miracle of radio developed the status of an industry, AT&T retired from the field and RCA

Some "Firsts" in Broadcasting

Dec. 12, 1901—Marconi received first trans-Atlantic wireless signal.

●

Jan. 20, 1910—Caruso's voice picked up from Metropolitan Opera and transmitted experimentally.

●

Oct. 17, 1919—Radio Corporation of America incorporated.

●

Sept. 29, 1920—"Wireless receiving sets" advertised for sale to public (Joseph Horne Company, Pittsburgh).

●

Nov. 2, 1920—KDKA broadcast Harding-Cox Election Returns.

●

Oct. 1, 1921—WJZ broadcast first program.

founded the National Broadcasting Company in 1926 to engage in broadcasting nationally.* NBC took over the Red Network, broadcasting its official opening program on November 15, 1926. The Red Network then consisted of 19 stations, and there were approximately 6,000,000 receiving sets in use.**

Because of RCA's unique position as the only organization actively engaged in all phases of radio—manufacturing both transmitters and receivers, operating international and ship-to-shore communication, as well as broadcasting—NBC has had the benefit of the most complete resources of radio laboratory research and pioneering technical knowledge in existence. These facilities have in turn been used by NBC to develop its service both to advertisers and to the listening public—a mutually beneficial arrangement, financed by advertising.

Advertisers Render a Public Service

Because of its startling novelty it was enough in the early twenties to deliver to the listener almost any kind of sound; the boom of Niagara, an indifferent speech, a ragged performance of music.

Today what a difference!

A leading figure in advertising says: "Radio brings the public the finest parade of talent in the world. Just suppose it were literally a parade. Suppose that the men and women who face the microphone could be brought together on Fifth Avenue, or Michigan Boulevard, or Market Street. Swinging along in that parade would be the President of our

---

*In the announcement of the formation of the National Broadcasting Company, published in the New York Times September 14, 1926, RCA issued a statement from which the following excerpts are taken:

"The Radio Corporation of America is the largest distributor of radio receiving sets in the world. . . . It is more largely interested, more selfishly interested, in the best possible broadcasting than is anyone else.

"The market for receiving sets in the future will be determined largely by the quantity and quality of the programs broadcast. Today the best available statistics indicate that 5,000,000 homes are equipped, and 21,000,000 remain to be equipped. . . . Any use of radio transmission which causes the public to feel that the program is not the highest, that the use of radio is not the broadest and best use in the public interest, that it is used for political advantage or selfish power, will be detrimental to public interest in radio, and therefore, to the Radio Corporation of America.

"To insure, therefore, the development of this great service, the Radio Corporation of America has purchased for one million dollars Station WEAF from the American Telephone and Telegraph Company, that company having decided to retire from the broadcasting business.

National Broadcasting Company Organized

"The Radio Corporation of America has decided to incorporate that station, which has achieved such a deservedly high reputation for the quality and character of its programs, under the name of the National Broadcasting Company, Inc. The purpose of that company will be to provide the best programs available for broadcasting in the United States. The National Broadcasting Company will not only broadcast these programs through Station WEAF, but it will make them available to other broadcasting stations throughout the country so far as it may be practical to do so, and they may desire to take them. It is hoped that arrangements may be made so that every event of national importance may be broadcast widely throughout the United States.

"The Radio Corporation of America is not in any sense seeking a monopoly of the air. If others will engage in this business, we will welcome their action, whether it be cooperative or competitive. The necessity of providing adequate broadcasting is apparent. The problem of finding the best means of doing it is as yet experimental. The Radio Corporation of America is making this experiment in the interest of the art and the furtherance of the industry."

**Four years earlier—in 1922—there had been only about 60,000 receiving sets in existence. Most of them had been constructed by amateurs. Marconi, "the father of radio" visiting the United States in the early 1920's, marvelled at the thousands of schoolboys constructing home-made radios with their own hands. He declared that we were raising a nation of inventors.

country, followed by the greatest statesmen of the world, the greatest orchestras and opera companies, the outstanding stars of stage and screen, the greatest concert artists, and the leaders in sports and every other human activity. And here's the point: somewhere in that parade there would be something for everyone, no matter what his individual interests might be."

That last sentence is a reminder that the radio audience is highly selective in its "tuning-in." Its listening is *voluntary* listening. It listens only to what it likes, so its likes have had to be studied from every conceivable angle.

By their sponsorship, the national advertisers who use networks render a public service, not only with their own programs but also by making possible the presentation to the public of thousands of interesting sustaining broadcasts every year.

The advertising revenue makes it possible for the broadcasting companies to furnish the sustaining programs—music, drama, news, special events, and educational subjects. Incidentally, these sustaining programs make up 70% of all NBC network program hours.

Broadcast advertising has made American stations self-supporting, enabling them to serve listeners without taxation or fees of any kind.

Ear Magic

Before this development, advertising had appealed primarily to the eye. By sampling, the advertiser could employ sight, touch, smell, and in some cases, hearing. But the opportunity to reach people in the mass through their ears was impossible.

It is decidedly easier to listen than to read. The apparently simple act of reading actually involves the continual movement of delicate and sensitive muscles creating tensions and fatigue. Listening requires practically no muscular effort. For this reason it is said that "listening is all pleasure; there is no conscious or subconscious sense of strain or fatigue. The listener can relax completely. His mind thus becomes highly receptive."

Even the greatest writers have rarely influenced their readers so swiftly and overwhelmingly as orators influence listeners. No playwright can convey through his printed lines the force and beauty which emerge from the same lines delivered on the stage.

No salesmanager or salesman has ever been able to sell by letter or circular the way he can sell direct to listeners.

Aug. 16, 1922 — WEAF, New York, commenced operation.

•

Aug. 28, 1922 — First sponsored program (Queensboro Corporation on WEAF—10 minutes for $100).

•

Jan. 4, 1923—First simultaneous broadcasting by wire-connected radio stations (WEAF, New York and WNAC, Boston).

•

June 21, 1923—First radio address by President to people of United States (Harding on the World Court).

•

Oct. 14, 1923—Red Network established, starting with WEAF, New York and WJAR, Providence. The first commercial network.

•

Feb. 8, 1924—First coast-to-coast broadcasting hook-up (demonstration).

In broadcast advertising the personality and conviction of the speaker color his words just as these qualities color the talk of salesmen on the road or behind counters. By the emotional feeling of expressive speech supreme conviction can be transmitted from one person to another. That is what advertisers have learned from their experience with radio.

The roster of broadcast advertisers includes many of the country's great business organizations who are its most progressive advertisers.* With carefully worked-out testing methods they examine their results from every new medium they enter, and quickly retire from those which do not pay.

"Fortune's" Discovery

That the bond between speaker and listener has lost none of its ancient charm has been proved by *Fortune*. In a survey to learn America's most-enjoyed forms of recreation, here is what *Fortune* found:

Listening to the radio......................	18.8%
Going to the movies........................	17.3%
Reading magazines and books..............	13.8%
Hunting or fishing	11.0%
Watching sporting events	10.4%
Reading newspapers.......................	7.1%
Playing outdoor games	6.6%
Playing cards and indoor games...........	5.3%
Attending legitimate theatre..............	3.7%

Only three months ago, *Time* magazine announced under the heading, "And Now—Radio," that news about broadcasting would henceforth be reported regularly, being "the first major addition to Time's table of contents in 15 years." *Time* said editorially, ". . . radio is making big news 24 hours a day . . . radio is the only new service Time's always-articulate readers asked for in thousands of letters. . . ."

Radio Today estimates that $747,000,000 were spent during 1937 alone for 8,000,000 receiving sets, 40,000,000 replacement tubes, and for electricity, batteries, parts, supplies, and service.

According to the Joint Committee on Radio Research, there are (as of Jan. 1, 1938) 26,666,500 radio-owning families in the United States. This represents *homes*—not sets only. There are at least 6,000,000 additional sets in these homes. And about 5,000,000 automobiles are equipped with radios. Thus over 37,000,000 sets are owned by 26,666,500 families.**

How much are they used?

---

*In 1937, 134 advertisers invested $38,651,286 in NBC network time on behalf of 191 products. 80% of these advertisers had been on NBC prior to 1937. From these "repeaters" came 96.8% of NBC's gross income from network broadcasting. Twenty-five of these companies had been NBC advertisers for five years or longer.

The list includes Bristol-Myers, Cities Service, General Foods, R.C.A., American Tobacco, Firestone Tire, General Electric, Procter & Gamble, General Mills, Standard Brands, Pepsodent, National Dairy, Quaker Oats, Kellogg, Campana, Wander, Pacific Coast Borax, Household Finance, Lamont Corliss, G. Washington Coffee, Bayer, Carnation, Lady Esther, R. L. Watkins, Sun Oil.

**It is interesting to compare this seventeen-year growth (1920-1937) with that of home telephones and electric lights. The first home telephone was installed in 1877. Today, after sixty years, there are 12,500,000 telephone owning families in the United States. (AT&T estimate as of January 1, 1938.) Electric lights were first installed in homes in 1880, and in the fifty-seven years that have elapsed we have reached a total of 22,800,000 homes equipped with electricity. (McGraw-Hill estimate as of January 1, 1938.)

Surveys indicate that 70% or more of all radios are used daily, being turned on for an average of more than five hours. Studies made from time to time by the Columbia Broadcasting System, the Joint Committee on Radio Research, the Co-operative Analysis of Broadcasting, and the National Broadcasting Company confirm the estimate.

The Information Service of the Rural Electrification Administration reports, "Our surveys show that on all the new REA-financed lines which have recently gone into operation, the socket-power radio is the most popular appliance. In almost every case it is the first appliance purchased."

During the depth of the depression when unemployment was at its worst, families clung to their radios, preferring to make any other sacrifice rather than part with the entertainment, educational, and spiritual help they could summon at almost any hour of the day or night from this friend in the home.

America's advertisers have made all this as free as the air through which it comes!

Tremendous Response—and the Explanation

Tremendous radio response, running into hundreds of thousands, and in some cases into a million or higher, are matters of record, and familiar to most advertising men. Comparatively modest programs have secured remarkable audience response year after year and far higher returns per dollar expended than was earned from any previous advertising.

Because of this, an agency principal says, "Broadcast advertising, properly handled, is much *more* than advertising. It is something which people turn to with pleasure—and *for* pleasure. It creates, in its audience, a reaction which is primarily emotional. This makes audience response at times amazing.

"Successful use of radio, in my opinion, hinges mainly on understanding and utilizing this inherent, distinctive characteristic."

The natural desire of advertisers to evaluate broadcast advertising correctly has had a wholesale effect in stimulating fresh study of *every* advertising medium.

While coverage measurement methods have not yet been standardized,* the Joint Committee on Radio

---

Feb. 12, 1924—First network sponsored program. (National Carbon Company on Red Network).

•

Mar. 4, 1925—First nationwide broadcast of Presidential Inaugural. (Coolidge).

•

Sept. 14, 1926—Announcement of NBC's formation.

•

Nov. 15, 1926—First N B C Network broadcast.

•

Jan. 1, 1927—NBC Blue Network established.

•

April 5, 1927—NBC Pacific Coast Network established.

•

Sept. 18, 1927—First CBS program.

---

* CBS and NBC use methods which are essentially similar, though different in detail. In each case, the analysis of audience mail response is the salient factor in determining breadth and intensity of coverage. NBC, however, also introduces the factor of field strength. See "CBS Listening Areas" and "NBC Network Aireas."

Research has been engaged for some time past in a study of methods for measuring station and network coverage. This Joint Committee is composed of five advertisers, five agency representatives, and five broadcasting men. Before and since it was founded, the broadcasting organizations have supplied much valuable statistical information—quite apart from purely promotional presentations—offering this information as a contribution to all users of the medium, and they have led the way on more than one occasion with important innovations in market research.

Relationship with Other Mediums

Broadcast advertising has conformed with most of the recognized practices of the advertising business. Leading advertising agencies now make the building of radio programs quite as much a part of their regular agency function as the preparation of publication advertisements, and employ radio time buyers who operate with their Media Departments.

Broadcast advertising has been developed from the start with a sharp eye to its relationship with other mediums. Those guiding the network sales and advertising have always stressed the fact that it was not their aim to have broadcast advertising supplant other mediums, but to supplement them in a program of rounded-out advertising appeal that would increase sales. Today, broadcasting enjoys an unchallenged place among the three or four leading advertising mediums in the United States.

An important by-product of this attitude of co-operation with other forms of advertising has been the development known as "broadcast merchandising"—the active tying in of radio with other forms of advertising and promotion.*

Not One Medium Only

It is incorrect to think of broadcasting as only one medium. There are several different kinds of broadcast advertising. For one thing, local broadcasting through individual stations differs as much from network broadcasting as newspapers differ from magazines. The appeal in the first case may be concentrated on local interest, while in the case of network programs it is customary to broaden the appeal to attract a wider variety of population groups.

Even more important than the distinction between local and national broadcasting is the distinction between evening and daytime broadcasting. During the evening, radio reaches the entire family. Its broad appeal is to all ages and both sexes. During the daytime, although men are not strangers in the home, broadcasting functions quite differently. It is primarily a women's advertising medium reaching housewives. So both the pro-

*The National Broadcasting Company has always stressed the importance of this work. For five years it has published a magazine devoted entirely to ways and means of using other forms of promotion in conjunction with radio campaigns.
NBC also publishes every year an analysis of offers and contests indicating the conditions of the offer, the prizes, and other useful facts. For more than ten years NBC has maintained a merchandising consultation service which has materially helped advertisers in planning their merchandising campaigns for utmost effectiveness from their broadcasting. Thus broadcast advertising teams up effectively with almost every other recognized form of advertising or promotion.

gram and the commercial announcement are noticeably different from those used at night.

Daytime broadcasting was developed and sold aggressively by the networks and leading independent stations. They scheduled many program features expressly intended to build and develop the daytime audience. These programs included various home economics, cooking, and family welfare features, in addition to programs of a purely entertainment nature. In this work of building up they were assisted by several pioneering advertisers who bought time first "on faith," and later because they found it paid.

Daytime broadcasting soon became an increasing factor in the total National Broadcasting business, and the trend is still upward. During 1936, daytime revenue over NBC networks accounted for one-fifth of the total. By 1937 it was one-quarter. A comparative break-down of NBC Gross Revenue is interesting:

1936

Daytime. .20.09%
Evening . .75.02% *(Political shows increase evening total)*
Sunday . . . 3.09%

1937

Daytime. .26.83% *(Increase over 1936, 34.7%)*
Evening . .67.71% ("   "   "   4.1%)
Sunday . . . 5.46% ("   "   "   25.7%)

(Overall increase in NBC network revenue, 1937 over 1936, 12%)

This major division of broadcasting into (1) a general, family medium, and (2) a woman's medium, should be borne well in mind when considering the types of advertisers who use it. Whereas any comparison of local and network broadcasting emphasizes differences in *size* of advertisers, comparison between daytime and evening broadcasts involves classification of advertisers by their types of business and by their potential customers. Naturally, advertisers with products appealing chiefly to housewives, concentrate most of their effort in daytime selling.

Indicative of the growing use of radio to reach women in their homes is the fact that in 1937 a most decided upward trend was noted by NBC in "Laundry Soaps and Cleansers." The total of this classification moved ahead of "Automotive" and "Petroleum," which had ranked third and fourth respectively in 1936. Today, the largest single user of broadcasting time, Procter and Gamble, employs daytime periods almost exclusively.

Oct. 1, 1927—NBC opened its first "Broadcasting Headquarters" at 711 Fifth Avenue, New York City.

•

Apr. 4, 1928—NBC received its first television station construction permit.

•

Dec. 23, 1928—First permanent coast-to-coast network, established by NBC.

•

Feb. 1, 1929—First scheduled short-wave trans-Atlantic broadcasts, (from London).

•

Oct. 1, 1930—First direct sample offer over NBC (shortly followed by the first radio contest on the network).

•

Oct. 30, 1931—NBC commenced 120-line television transmissions from Empire State Building.

•

June 27, 1932—First price quotations in NBC network commercial announcements. (Daytime).

A New Picture in Advertising

In 1927, less than $4,000,000 were spent by advertisers with all national networks. This was but a small fraction of the advertising revenues enjoyed by the leaders among magazine publishers. But the steady growth in favor of radio advertising is strikingly shown by the following figures:

	National Broadcasting Company	Largest Magazine Group	Columbia Broadcasting System	Second Largest Magazine Group
1930	$20,088,887	$67,660,118	$ 7,605,203	$26,053,299
1931	25,607,041	51,562,381	11,895,039	23,900,166
1932	26,504,891	32,404,173	12,601,885	16,582,609
1933	21,452,732	26,120,844	10,063,566	14,918,519
1934	27,833,616	30,828,442	14,825,845	16,909,319
1935	31,148,931	31,654,924	17,637,804	19,433,788
1936	34,523,950	36,316,597	23,168,148	22,750,115
1937	38,651,286	36,394,532	28,722,118	25,464,275

From these figures it will be seen that in less than a decade the national advertising picture has changed completely. The two largest network systems are more heavily patronized than the two leading magazine publishers.

In 1937, 26 advertisers spent over $1,000,000 in magazines. Twenty of them also used networks.

In 1937, 44 advertisers spent over $1,000,000 in magazines, farm papers, and networks combined. [Printers' Ink.] Of these 27 used networks.

Of the leading 100 advertisers, 67 used network broadcasting.

Network broadcasting's share of the national advertising dollar in 1937 was approximately three times as large as in 1930.

The grand total spent for national network, regional network, local station, and national spot radio advertising in 1937 was $141,509,505—an increase of 19% over 1936. This does not include talent for which sponsors of programs spent about $40,000,000 last year.

What about Television?

No review of broadcast advertising would be complete without reference to television. The RCA engineers have produced a practical television system—NBC is now pioneering in its development as a public service.

There is little doubt that television will eventually be developed as an advertising medium. Indeed, in this country, where commercial broadcasters support the broadcasting structure, it would be impossible to develop an art like television without the aid of advertisers.

Today, television is a reality from the technical standpoint, although it remains something of a puzzle from the program and the economic sides. The expense of preparing programs is considerable, and it is not yet practicable to distribute a television program over a very wide area—hardly beyond the visual horizon. NBC broadcasts experimentally from its Empire State transmitter, with its antennae on New York's highest building, over a radius of approximately forty miles. Since this densely populated metropolitan area is a huge market in itself, this may well be the starting point of commercial television. Television development, however, will probably be restricted during the next few years, to the large centers of population.

In television, as in sound broadcasting, NBC receives the full benefit of RCA's technical facilities and laboratory research. NBC engineers and program builders are now putting the RCA Television System through its paces, in the studio and on the air. When television is ready for sponsorship, NBC will thus have both the facilities and the practical experience available for the advertiser.

Toward Tomorrow

In fifteen years, then, American business has seen broadcast advertising become, both statistically and by virtue of demonstrated results, one of the three or four major national mediums to reckon with.

It is a striking development, but probably no more striking than that which lies ahead.

The friendly but genuine rivalry existing among the major network operators—the Columbia Broadcasting System, the Mutual Broadcasting System, and the National Broadcasting Company—is certain to create still better programs and still better presentations of advertising. The work of individual stations will contribute also to this further progress.

We are witnessing the completion of a cycle. As the effectiveness of the speaker on his listeners reaches its height, a new element enters to make advertising still more effective.

"Live" visual advertising is about to be added to the persuasiveness of speech. Advertisers will have at their command an instrument as fantastic as were the inventions of Jules Verne when they first appeared in print.

The listener will also become a beholder. Every appeal to ear and eye will become possible on an immense scale.

Such selling, together with the older forms of advertising will arm the business executive, his advertising manager, and his advertising agency with equipment whose completeness leaves nothing to be desired.

It is impossible at this time, indeed, to imagine what advertising *can* desire after that!

National Broadcasting Company
Broadcasting Headquarters
A RADIO CORPORATION OF AMERICA SERVICE

Sept. 12, 1932—First price quotations in NBC evening commercial announcements.

•

Nov. 1, 1932—First national dealer meeting by radio— by Plymouth on CBS.

•

Nov. 11, 1933—NBC officially opened Radio City studios.

•

July 7, 1936—NBC gave first demonstration of high definition (electronic) television.

•

May 12, 1937—RCA demonstrated projected television picture 8 ft. x 10 ft. (IRE Convention).

•

Nov. 10, 1937—Bell Laboratories demonstrated use of coaxial cable for television (between New York and Philadelphia).

•

June 7, 1938—First television broadcast of a Broadway show. ("Susan and God" over NBC Empire State transmitter).

Chemistry, had a good deal to do with its inception and passage and he set about energetically to assure its effective enforcement. He was considerable of a showman, believing in publicity on the theory that the public should know exactly what his department should try to do. He instituted hundreds of cases and numerous firms were fined for adulteration and misbranding.

Appreciation of Dr. Wiley's efforts was not exactly universal. He drew opposition from many quarters and was accused of being a fanatic. But reputable manufacturers had reason to approve the Act and its administration and most of them did so. The public was influenced to buy better grades, confidence in advertising was raised and the advertiser was at least partially freed from the price competition of the inferior product.

Circulations of publications took a new leap forward with the establishment of rural free delivery, initiated with a few dozen routes in 1897. In its first three years, 6,009 routes were established and by the end of 1901 daily mail was distributed to more than five million homes previously dependent on distant post offices. Farm papers by 1906 achieved a huge increase which brought the aggregate circu-

1905

SUPREME COURT decision declares the "beef trust" illegal. . . . President Roosevelt orders investigation of the tobacco trust. . . . Industrial Workers of the World organized in opposition to the American Federation of Labor. . . . Supreme Court holds unconstitutional a State law limiting the number of hours of the day and week a man might work.

Street Railways Advertising Company, with Barron G. Collier as a leading factor, consolidates the principal car card interests. . . . Technical Publicity Association organized at New York. . . . Detroit *Tribune* consolidated with the Detroit *News*. . . . Cigar band collecting is the craze of the moment. . . . *Cosmopolitan* is acquired by W. R. Hearst. . . . Adcraft Club of Detroit organized; also Portland, Oreg., Ad-Men's League.

Leslie's Monthly changes name to *American Illustrated Magazine*, simplified shortly thereafter to *American Magazine*. . . . Chicago Advertising Association organized. . . . Thomas W. Lawson's "Frenzied Finance" series of articles exposing "the system" makes *Everybody's Magazine* a circulation sensation. . . . John E. O'Mara and M. H. Ormsbee establish the newspaper representative firm of O'Mara & Ormsbee. . . . S. C. Beckwith, for twenty years one of the foremost special agents, meets death in a railroad wreck. . . . Two thousand college boys, at the behest of *Success Magazine*, set out to work their way through college canvassing for subscriptions and big results are expected from this move.

lation to over six million. The new system was likewise a stimulus to newspaper and magazine circulations in rural communities. Total circulation of all publications reached 64,000,000 in 1905, as compared with 18,000,000 fifteen years earlier. The use of direct mail also experienced a big advance. It was now easy to get names of farmers from route carriers and the rural districts were flooded with booklets, catalogs and miscellaneous mailings.

The growing preference for large circulations produced numerous combinations of country weeklies, farm papers and dailies in the smaller cities. The advertiser was showing a preference for big circulation units which were easily dealt with and in response were formed the Ohio News League, the Clover Leaf Papers, the Indiana Star League and other similar combinations.

The foundations for chain journalism in the newspaper field were advanced during this period. E. W. Scripps, who had founded *The Penny Press* at Cleveland in 1878, was making rapid strides with his associates in building the present-day Scripps-Howard Newspapers. The Cincinnati *Post* was begun in 1881, the San Diego *Sun* added in 1893. From 1903 through 1906 the group underwent a major period of expansion. In the former year the San Francisco *News* and Akron *Press* were established, the Toledo *News* and *Bee* purchased and consolidated. In 1906 were started the Memphis *Press*, Evánsville, Ind., *Press*, Denver *Express* and *Oklahoma News* in Oklahoma City.

Shortly after the new century opened W. R. Hearst, having got the *Journal* well established in New York, set forth to realize upon his

vision of a nation-wide system of newspaper properties. He had begun, of course, with the San Francisco *Examiner*, the *Evening American* and the *Examiner* at Chicago and the Boston *Evening American*. The greatest expansion, however, was to come in the 1920's.

The cynosure of all eyes in the magazine field was *The Saturday Evening Post*, which in 1897 came under the Curtis aegis. At the time of the purchase this descendant from the days of Benjamin Franklin had a circulation slightly more than 2,000. Under the bold advertising policies of Cyrus Curtis and the brilliant editorship of the young George Horace Lorimer, circulation reached 325,000 in 1902, 500,000 a year later.

In the women's field, the *Delineator* was making great strides under John Adams Thayer and Thomas Balmer, who had come from the Curtis forces. Meanwhile the *Ladies' Home Journal* reached a million circulation, the first time a single edition of any publication daily, weekly or monthly had reached such a figure in paid circulation and perhaps in any kind of distribution. Development of house-to-house selling of subscriptions was a big factor in magazine growth in this period.

Color became a factor of some importance in magazines at this time. The periodicals were a long time in admitting it, but with the way opened by popular approval they quickly appreciated its commercial value. *Cosmopolitan's* use of a lithographed cover in 1896, which increased newsstand sales by 10,000 in the first month, was a principal eye opener. Also in that year came Procter & Gamble's color inserts for Ivory soap, prepared at

194

A KNOT
that holds
a **LIFETIME**

Iᴛ is said that every cartoonist, sometime in his career must draw a picture of the de luxe fisherman who didn't catch any fish and the barefooted little boy who did. Every time we see such a cartoon, we smile . . . forgetting that only yesterday the "fancy" fisherman gave his "catch" to a rich looking gentleman who failed to get any.

Fisherman's luck may be flighty, but there is nothing uncertain about the fisherman himself . . .

nor about his needs and his reading habits. The knot that holds the trout fly to the end of a leader is symbolic of the tie that holds the fisherman to his sport . . . to the products the use of which he enjoys so much . . . it is symbolic of the tie that holds him to Field & Stream.

Only the quality sportsman's magazines reach the quality readers . . . quality prospects . . . quality buyers . . . in this vast quality market of men.

Field & Stream

The Marketplace of Men

Cincinnati and shipped to the publishers for insertion in their issues, to set a new note. It was awesomely reported in advertising circles that the cost of preparing the inserts was greater than the cost of the space. By 1903, three-color process printing in magazines was available to advertisers, and although the work was not always completely satisfactory, it offered the attraction of costs lower than the lithographed inserts. In 1905 the Butterick Trio announced run-of-paper color—black and one extra. This was the first offering of magazine color which did not involve inserts or separate printing.

There had been some development of color printing in newspapers. As early as 1890 the New York *World* produced a page in two colors, both printed at one impression with one plate. Several other papers produced color work in the years following, and in 1893 the Kansas City *Journal* announced its readiness to accept orders for four-color advertisements. The real development of color in newspapers, however, did not appear until many years later.

In the realm of the car card, Artemas Ward had organized the Ward & Gow syndicate of contractors in ten large cities to sell space on a standardized basis. It did not work out very well because some of the contractors cut prices and otherwise demoralized the plan. Eventually the syndicate broke up into separate units.

Among the members of the syndicate was a young contractor named Barron G. Collier, who controlled space in a number of Southern cities. He took up some of the loose ends and acquired sales rights in a number of different cities, firm in the conviction that central, organized promotion of the medium was not only feasible but essential to its success as a tool for national advertisers. In 1905, at the age of thirty-three, he controlled the largest street-car advertising plant in the country—the Street Railways Advertising Company. At that time it included more than 11,000 cars in nearly 350 cities.

Collier's achievement opened a new era in car-card advertising and the growth of the business was largely due to him. A feature of the new phase was the tendency of advertisers to apply to car cards the advertising principles which had proved successful elsewhere. Realizing that most people rode in a car ten minutes or more, they abandoned the old formula of picture and catch phrase and turned to selling messages of thirty or forty words or more. This, too, was largely due to Collier's efforts, for he had held from the beginning that the car card need not be merely a reminder but would bring best results when it was used for a complete sales story.

A method of promotion which enjoyed a huge flurry of popularity in this period was the trading stamp or some related form of redeemable coupon. It got its first foothold in the retail field and Sperry & Hutchinson, which began issuing their famous green trading stamps in the late 1890's, had become a million-dollar corporation by 1904.

Department stores were the first users. Then smaller users took them up. Then theaters and tombstone dealers. A saloon in New Jersey commenced giving a trading stamp with each drink, while numerous Sunday schools gave up Scripture texts in favor of trading stamps as a means of encouraging regular attendance.

The fever soon percolated into the manufacturing field. Coupons or stamps were packed in almost every article that came into the kitchen. Sperry & Hutchinson introduced a plan for manufacturers, affording to the average firm a wider range of premiums than if the company attempted to redeem them individually. In addition, with its 200 premium stores from Maine to California, the trading stamp firm provided a solution to the redemption problem for the smaller firms.

In a short time the trading stamp was practically legal tender. In recognition thereof, counterfeiters got busy and produced fake stamps. As with all public crazes, the fury declined from its peak after a time. In addition, sentiment stimulated by disfavoring retailers resulted in the passage of laws in a number of States, which either forbade the stamps entirely or surrounded their issuance and redemption with varying regulations.

1906

NOBEL Peace Prize awarded to President Roosevelt for his services in bringing peace to Russia and Japan. . . . Earthquake and fire destroy greater part of San Francisco, with damage estimated at $300,000,000. . . . U. S. Steel Corporation breaks ground for the city of Gary, Indiana. . . . President Roosevelt goes to Panama, first instance of a president leaving the United States.

A group headed by George H. Hazen acquires controlling interest in the Crowell Publishing Company from J. S. Crowell, founder, who continues as vice-president. . . . Colgate & Company celebrate their 100th birthday. . . . New York advertising center migrating uptown toward Madison Square. . . . Death of William Ziegler, a founder of the Royal Baking Powder Company, which probably invested more money in advertising than any other single enterprise in the world. . . . Thomas Balmer leaves Butterick as advertising director to join Barron G. Collier and Ralph Tilton succeeds him.

Stanley Resor takes charge of the Chicago office of Procter & Collier. . . . Advertising Clubs of America formed at St. Louis, with W. M. Aubuchon as president. . . . Ambrose L. Thomas, head of Lord & Thomas, dies suddenly. . . . John H. Woodbury sells his interest in the J. H. Woodbury Dermatological Institute to devote his entire time to manufacture and sale of Woodbury's soaps. . . . Nelson Chesman, one of the early advertising agents, dies. . . . John E. Kennedy, former chief copy writer for Lord & Thomas, now a partner in the Ethridge-Kennedy Company, New York. . . . Slogan: "Schlitz—The Beer That Makes No Man Bilious."

The Fruits of

Years

$\mathcal{B}$ACK in 1840 . . . when a young enterprising merchant received a dozen pair of the latest style lace-top shoes, he would run a notice in the Memphis Appeal . . . and move them out.

In time, his business prospered because his customers came to look for his advertisements, and instead of ordering just a dozen pair of shoes, he began to buy them by the gross.

Ot course, he was just one of the many merchants who early realized the dollars-and-cents value of advertising in the Memphis Appeal—who depended on its influence and selling power.

As the city grew and the business firms became larger and more prosperous, so in equal measure did the Memphis Appeal progress. From a small upstairs print shop overlooking the Mississippi River, it has grown and expanded to its present up-to-date and efficient plant.

Through 98 years, it has stood the test of time, helping to overcome the real problems of Memphis and the great territory it serves. Today, it is the Memphis Commercial Appeal—with the largest circulation in the South. Through these many years, as Memphis and the Mid-South were pioneering and building a great city and a great territory, the advertising, news and editorial policies of the Memphis Commercial Appeal were recognized as a mirror which reflected the rapidly changing events in this rich and vast southern market.

Today . . . the Memphis Commercial Appeal is in one of the most unique positions of any newspaper in the South. It is truly an Institution. It stands alone in influence in a territorial center of more than two million people— diffusing information and the interpretation of local, national and international events— creating a strong and steady demand for the products of those who advertise in its pages.

Such are the fruits of its ninety-eight years!

MEMPHIS AND THE MID-SOUTH STATE ARE COVERED — INFLUENCED — SOLD BY

THE COMMERCIAL APPEAL

A SCRIPPS-HOWARD NEWSPAPER

National Representative—The Branham Co.

"MORE THAN A NEWSPAPER — AN INSTITUTION"

LARGEST DAILY CIRCULATION IN THE SOUTH

CHAPTER V
Consolidation of the Forces
(1907-1914)

THE utter collapse of financial affairs in 1907 was bewildering to the country at large, for business and agriculture were in a state of undoubted soundness. The effects of the banking panic spread nevertheless to all lines of economic life and early in 1908 there was a decline in advertising activity. The trough was neither wide nor deep, however, and by the summer of that year confidence was coming back. Immediately after the national elections in the fall the return to prosperous conditions was swift.

Appearing in this new period of business progress, and contributing greatly to it, was the final and most important step in completing the framework of the advertiser system of distribution. This was the hooking up of advertising and salesmanship. Advertising became recognized as a part of the sales force.

In the past the manufacturer had seldom put his publicity behind the rest of his organization. Nor had he attempted to mobilize the efforts of the sales department to the support of the advertising campaign. Advertising was considered a thing apart. It created consumer demand for the product. Selling was simply a more or less routine process of getting the goods to the merchants' shelves. That the two forces might operate to mutual advantage, had never been perceived except in piece-meal fashion. At any rate, little had been done to effect the consolidation of the forces.

Under the new order, not only was advertising linked to the selling plan but the selling plan came first. And while advertising had a definite effect in improving the conception and administration of the sales plan, this was almost as nothing compared to the effect which the selling end began to exert on advertising and the advertising business. For advertising emerged at last as a vital factor in distribution.

The salesman had in the beginning been apathetic to advertising, if not actively opposed to it. He feared that it might be a way of eliminating his services. In fact not a few of his more sanguine superiors had the same idea in mind. Hence the salesman and the sales department tended to ignore the advertising operations of the business.

Advertising, meanwhile, had been considered in many places as a virtually self-sufficient instrument. Distribution was deemed to be an auxiliary of advertising, rather than otherwise. This concept had worked pretty well so long as the competition in any given line was not great.

On the one hand, it was no longer possible to ignore the fact that advertising reduced the cost of selling by saving the salesman's time in explaining the product and the company. In such a condition advertising should naturally be geared to the salesman and vice versa.

On the other, it was becoming more and more evident that the use of advertising as a means of whipping the trade into line was a costly and roundabout way of doing business. Even when the advertiser went beyond the processes of name publicity and sought to bind the consumer to him by encouraging inquiries to his advertisements, the results had not been good enough. The fact remained that most customers went to the store to see the article. That the customer would be sure of finding it there, and under the best possible conditions, was something which events were proving to be too much for advertising alone and unsupported.

The phrase "consumer demand," in fact, had done considerable damage to advancement of advertising. The concept of advertising as a mighty steamroller which could force results and make the salesman an automaton and the dealer a slot-machine had impeded the co-operation of both. And it was false doctrine in that in a competitive field only a very small proportion of consumers actually asked for a product by brand name. It overlooked the point that a great deal of the effect of advertising was in creating a favorable impression whereby the consumer would accept the goods when dealers offered them.

The gradually evolving understanding of this latter circumstance was first given crystallized expression in the advancement of the "consumer acceptance" theory of advertising by Paul E. Faust, advertising agent, William Laughlin, advertising manager of Armour & Company, and H. J. Winsten. Detailed studies of consumer transactions at the point of sale had shown that the attitude of acceptance, exhibited by approval or veto of the dealer's brand offering, was usually present long before a positive demand for a certain brand was made upon the dealer. And that favorable frame of mind could be capitalized only with the aid of the dealer.

The whole movement to the establishment of the advertising-sales relationship was principally, of course, the product of many individual experiments in that direction, experiments often made without any particularly broad understanding of the implications involved. As a result of the great accessions to the advertiser ranks in the preceding years, the competition of advertising had increased immensely. To gain new advantage the individual advertiser would adopt some measure to improve the methods of getting his product before the consumer and the channels of distribution offered the greatest opportunity for enterprise. As one thing succeeded, he would go further and adapt to his own business similar ideas which had been found successful by others, until he saw that the entire marketing proposition depended upon dovetailing the sales and advertising ends of his business.

The true identity of advertising established, the majority of advertisers began to co-ordinate the management of the marketing function. Advertising was centered more and more in the sales operation. In many firms this took the form of placing advertising under the administration, direct or indirect, of the sales department. In others the advertising authority was expanded to include supervision of sales and not a few advertising managers became sales managers. There was a good deal of theoretical debate at the time over which should be supreme—the advertising or the sales department, but this was resolved in the practical terms of the marketing problems of the individual companies. In one way or another, the advertiser strove to place at some point the responsibility for formulating and directing a centralized distribution plan.

The change had a powerful effect on the advertising agent. The agency was called upon to act as an advisory service on selling as well as a deviser and placer of advertisements. The merchandising man came to join the copy writer and the space buyer in the agency structure. In the years immediately preceding, when copy was king, a large proportion of agency personnel was enlisted from the ranks of those who had the writing gift—journalists, newspaper paragraphers and the like. Now there came a demand for the man who had a marketing background.

Infusion of this new blood in the established firms was supplemented by the appearance of new agencies built upon emphasis on the selling function. Examples include Fuller & Smith, which stressed the importance of well-rounded business experience and research as fundamentals in the advertising picture; the Federal Advertising Agency, organized to offer the services of men trained and educated in merchandise, markets and merchants; Ruthrauff & Ryan, whose principals brought to bear upon the general advertiser's problem the tried-and-tested fundamentals of salesmanship by mail. All along the line there was a new inclination to develop methods of making advertising more certain and more profitable. Some agencies established what were known as "investigating" departments to study distribution and trade conditions.

The techniques evolved to put the new concept of marketing into practice were reflected in vast changes in the administration and operation of the sales department, in retailer relations and in consumer advertising. They are described in detail in the succeeding sections of this chapter. First, however, it is desirable to examine a new advertising development of such importance that it could be secondary only to so vital an event as the linking of sales and advertising.

This was the discovery that the uses of advertising were by no means limited to selling tangible merchandise; that advertising could be harnessed to purposes of educating the public; that it could sell ideas as well as goods.

There had been some early experiments along this line. They were confined, however, to defensive measures. In the late 1890's some unidentified tobacco interest had published a series of advertisements to counteract propaganda about the harmfulness of smoking cigarettes. In 1906 the Government's famous "beef report," which charged uncleanliness and adulteration in the packing industry without naming the offenders, brought retorts from several firms which took to advertising to right a situation wherein those employing the most scrupulous methods had suffered along with the guilty in public condemnation. The leading Chicago packers ran large newspaper advertisements calling the report untruthful in numerous particulars. The Franco-American Food Company published an open letter to President Theodore Roosevelt asking him to give individual reports on firms and right the harm done.

The summer of 1908 saw the launching of the first large-scale endeavor to carry on a constructive program of public education, aimed not at a momentary crisis but calculated to build favorable public sentiment over a long term. This was the program of the American Telephone & Telegraph Company and it was hailed at the time as an epochal event, which indeed it was. The advertising was neither planned nor written to increase business but to make known and understood the purposes, problems and policies of the system. And it educated people in the use of the telephone, telling how to get the best service. Nor did it prove to be without sales power. During the first five years the company gained over two million stations, a growth in the rate of increase.

Soon the "strange phenomenon of public service organizations assuming a friendly attitude and using advertising to make themselves understood" became quite common. Street-car companies advertised to teach the rules of the road and allay prejudices. Power companies told about electricity as a public servant. The railroads began using "safety first" as an advertising appeal.

The idea found a following among

1907

SUSPENSION of the Knickerbocker Trust Company in New York precipitates financial panic. . . . Immigration for the year' totals 1,285,349, surpassing all records. . . . Oklahoma, 46th State, admitted to the Union. . . . *Lusitania,* largest ship in the world, arrives in New York from Queenstown on first voyage, breaking previous records by making trip in 5 days, 54 minutes.

New York special agents form the Six Point League, with S. C. Williams, of Williams & Cresmer, as president. . . . Fuller & Smith established at Cleveland. . . . David L. Taylor resigns as vice-president of Lord & Thomas to become managing director of the Long-Critchfield Corporation at Chicago. . . . The "good times" panic gives immediate rise to scores of advertisements of sensational sales based upon alleged needs for ready cash. . . . Ralph Tilton, a leading figure in advertiser, publication and agency affairs, dies at New York. . . . Endless chain letter scheme revived.

Minneapolis Advertising Club and Ad-Writers' League of Louisville established. . . . Death of James S. Kirk, head of soap concern bearing his name, and of Dr. I. W. Lyon (tooth powder). . . . Des Moines takes rank as a leading publishing center, being headquarters for thirty-seven publications. . . . New York theater establishes an "escort service" for unattached ladies. . . . M. L. Wilson leaves N. W. Ayer & Son to join Frank Presbrey Company. . . . New York *Times* publishes a full page of European dispatches received by Marconi wireless telegraph. . . . Observers note that automobile copy is getting into a rut, all the advertisements seeming to say the same things.

Fifty Years of Useful Service
To the Business of Advertising

—is the admirable record of Printers' Ink, upon which it has the hearty congratulations of San Antonio Express and San Antonio Evening News.

● ● ●

Useful service to the general business community—to all producers, distributors and retailers of commodities —is also the record of The Express since 1865 and of The Evening News since 1918. It is a service of salesmanship, created and maintained by placing in the homes of San Antonio, South and West Texas newspapers of the high character and quality which inspire reader-confidence and reader-interest—so essential to success and effectiveness as advertising media.

The carefully censored advertising in The Express and The Evening News is the business and shopping guide of many thousand families who have the will and the means to buy.

Advertisers are most usefully served by concentrated circulation coverage of such homes throughout a richly productive region.

San Antonio Express
SAN ANTONIO EVENING NEWS
Texas' Foremost Newspapers

manufacturers of tangible goods and a growing body of advertising had nothing to do with goods or sales directly, dealing rather with the advertiser's organization, his business system and his integrity. It became quite the thing to issue a public statement, a court circular, phrased in stately language of an editorial character. This particular manifestation of selling ideas by means of advertising was not particularly sound or important at the time, for most of the messages were overstuffed and heavy and failed to give vital information. So far as the advertiser of a tangible product was concerned, perhaps the most important effect of the new discovery was its influence in suggesting that the services rendered by the product could be advertised. Beginning around 1910 there was a definite trend toward selling what the product did instead of what it was. The lighting fixture advertising sold illumination, filing systems were played up in terms of business profit, soap advertisers began to talk cleanliness.

To a considerable extent the educational advertising program in its primary form, was undoubtedly a reflection of the growing appreciation of the importance of good-will as a tangible asset in the conduct of business. Advertising had supplied to good-will a definiteness and measurable value which began increasingly to figure in the courts and in the financial statements of large corporations. Many firms saw an opportunity in educational or "policy of the house" advertising an opportunity to entrench the company and its products more firmly in public favor.

Yet another advertising development of basic significance was the advent of co-operative advertising.

There had been a few short-lived adventures in this direction but they were distinguished more by talk than action. Some of the lumber industries had played around with the idea a bit. In 1901 co-operative advertising of prunes had been tried by the California Cured Fruit Association with some indication of success, but inner organization difficulties brought the effort to an untimely end. Then, in 1907, the real daddy of them all, the California Fruit Growers Exchange, got into action to see what could be done about the orange business.

When the Exchange first organized as a marketing co-operative in 1903, the orange was something for Santa Claus to put in the toe of the kiddies' stockings. Joint effort in the years immediately following reduced expenses, minimized produce decay and increased the efficiency of the distributing machine until, in 1906, annual sales had been pushed up from 2,000,000 boxes to nearly 10,000,000. A new problem of over-production caused the growers to seek to widen their basic market by educating the public to the flavor and healthful qualities of their product. A $5,000 campaign was started in Iowa and the effort was continually expanded thereafter with Sunkist results which are a matter of common knowledge. In 1914 the association embarked upon an intensive program of dealer tie-up work.

With this and a few other examples, it became quickly recognized that what is beyond the capacity of one producer may be brought about by united effort. Co-operative advertising went on to become a powerful force in stimulating industry, stabilizing sales practices, lowering costs and selling better living and health habits.

From Peddling to Planning

FOR years the operations of the sales department of the average firm had centered about corralling a sufficient number of salesmen to call on the trade over as large an area as could be covered in a manner consistent with freight rates, traveling expenses and competitive distributing points. The sole object was to make big sales. The sole duty of the sales manager was to secure hustling salesmen and keep his pen hot with burning epistles of encouragement or reproach—urging, cajoling, threatening, bullying with only one object in view: to load up the customer.

When selling to the dealer, directly or through the jobber, the idea was to pile him up with a six months' or year's supply before someone else did. And there it ended. There was no thought of helping the merchant to dispose of the goods or of considering his needs, and welfare. The only creed was to sell more goods.

Competition forced a change. The only answer was to get more proficient salesmen or to take measures to improve the effectiveness of those already on the force. More intensive cultivation, smaller territories and more men became necessary.

Advertising to the consumer was making selling easier, in that the salesman found it no longer necessary to spend half his time talking quality and price. But it also increased the responsibility of the sales department because a larger quantity of goods had to be kept running smoothly through the channels of trade to an expanded number of outlets. The sales manager had to think not merely in terms of making sales but he had to think in terms of efficient distribution.

And then there was the matter of the jobber. Many an established manufacturer at this time was coming to the conclusion that the jobber was useless and a pariah of commerce, innocuous and parasitical. The new manufacturer found him an inactive and unresponsive element in the merchandising program, a hindrance to all distribution effort. The ultimate extermination of the jobber was freely predicted.

The manufacturer's attitude was not without abundant justification. As advertising awakened consumer demand and packaged goods won acceptance, jobbing methods did not prove flexible enough to adjust themselves to the new conditions. The jobber was slow to realize the profit in advertised items which moved quickly and with little selling effort. Resentful of them, he often withheld co-operation. Though he might carry the goods, and take orders for them reluctantly, he refused to show them to his customers, putting all his effort on his own brands. He stubbornly persisted in his desire to make manufacturers' profits—as he had done in the days when the manufacturer was his helpless servant—in addition to legitimate middleman's profits. He had failed to understand the economics of changes in population, selling methods and selling relationships that had come about in the last twenty years.

There was another side to the story, of course. The jobber had problems of his own, those arising from weak retailers and from the arbitrary power then enjoyed by the jobbers' salesmen who often controlled trade personally and com-

In the office of National Geographic Society's president, Dr. Gilbert Grosvenor (extreme left), are Capt. C. W. B. Knight, British trainer and big bird photographer (center), and Dr. John Oliver La Gorce, vice-president (right). James Steyn, the bird, is a trained African-born eagle.

Geography for Millions*

Thirty-three scientific men, most of whom were connected with technical branches of the government, met at the Cosmos Club in Washington on Friday, January 13, 1888, to form a "society for the increase and diffusion of geographic knowledge."

A year later the society launched a magazine as a major means toward that end.

Although the "increase" in such knowledge has been steady throughout the 50 years of National Geographic Society, the "diffusion" has come primarily since Gilbert Grosvenor became editor of *National Geographic Magazine*, in April, 1899.

First president of the society had been Gardiner Greene Hubbard. His son-in-law, Alexander Graham Bell, inventor of the telephone, succeeded him. Dr. Grosvenor, later to become Dr. Bell's son-in-law, was successively editor of the magazine, director of the work, and then president. He has served as editor for 39 years, and has been president since 1920.

But the society and its magazine have not, by any means, been a "family affair." When Dr. Grosvenor became editor, the magazine had a circulation of less than 1,000. It was a small, earnest and very technical little monthly. Its scientific readers were advised of "Geographic Methods in Geologic Investigations";

Advertisement

"The Classification of Geographic Forms by Genesis." Dr. Grosvenor, then 23, was directed to remove the technical padlock and thus to "popularize" geography.

By the time John Oliver La Gorce joined the staff of the society, in September, 1905, the circulation was 10,000. That means the membership of the society was 10,000, for each member received the official journal under the by-laws. Dr. La Gorce was 25 then. He was given a salary of $60 a month, for the organization's annual income was small, and no endowment was sought then or now.

Under the direction of these two —Dr. Grosvenor, as president and editor, Dr. La Gorce as vice-president and associate editor—membership rose continuously to 1,200,000 in 1929. After a depression dip, to 950,000, it has climbed again to more than 1,100,000.

In its work today hundreds of people participate. The governing body of the society is a board of trustees, a distinguished group of 24 men elected for life—including today Charles Evans Hughes, John J. Pershing, Walter S. Gifford, Charles F. Kettering. The editorial and research staff is large, capable, experienced. On the magazine, Dr. George W. Hutchison, secretary of the society, has served for 25 years. Raymond W. Welch is advertising director. All profits from advertising are reinvested in expanding the publication and financing field expeditions to gather original material.

About nine-tenths of the 1,100,000 who pay $3 a year as membership dues in the society are Americans. The rest reside in virtually every civilized country in the world—almost on every "island." Tanganyika has about 100 members. There are 90 in the Fiji islands. Membership in Central America today is greater than the entire roster of the society when Dr. Grosvenor took charge in 1899.

The society is conservative in its business policies. It has estimated four and a half readers to the copy, but the advertising department does not claim them. Although the current rate of $3,000 a page (black-and-white, one-time) is based on an annual average circulation of a fraction over 1,000,000, there is no formal circulation guaranty, but year in and year out the renewals average around 85%.

Those who know the *Geographic*, however, believe that its "diffusion" of geographic knowledge spreads directly each month to more than 5,000,000 people. . . There is, for example, the steady and widespread use of the magazine in classrooms, the reproduction of *Geographic* maps in newspapers. . . .

Perhaps the keystone of the society's progress has been that it has become increasingly a creative, as well as an informative force. Not content merely with reproducing discoveries and observations, it has organized many of its own world-wide surveys, and has backed financially many of the expeditions and explorations which have become news and then history in the last generation.

Journalistically, the *Geographic* has "made its own scoops." This has meant more than merely paying well for timely articles by exceptional people, though Sir Henry Stanley, writing about Africa . . . William Howard Taft on the Philippines . . . Col. Lindbergh's own descriptions of his flights . . . the paintings of birds by Louis Agassiz Fuertes . . . the photographics for which its own staff scours the world, and other features won respect and readers.

Not Profit, But Knowledge, Its Aim

Through 50 years the society has sought vigorously to break through nature's hidden frontiers, and the *Geographic* to report them. And these ventures were aided or organized without thought of financial gain. The society is not a profit-making concern. There are no stocks or bonds, no holding company. If Dr. Grosvenor or Dr. La Gorce, after more than 30 years, were to leave the society's service today, he could take with him only his personal effects. The society's "profit" comes only through adding to the sum and the spread of human knowledge.

Thus in its early years it gave substantial aid to Admiral Peary on his expedition that led to the discovery of the North Pole. It contributed $100,000 to Admiral Byrd's Antarctic expeditions. It financed and co-sponsored Dr. William Beebe when he explored underseas life off Bermuda at a record depth of 3,028 feet, and joined with the U. S. Army Air Corps in backing the stratosphere flights of Captains Albert W. Stevens and Orvil Anderson to a record altitude of 72,395 feet. . . . The world's knowledge of Alaska's "Valley of 10,000 Smokes," of New Mexico's Carlsbad Caverns, and of many another discovery and exploration has been developed largely through the efforts of the *Geographic*.

With such purposes, such an organization and career, the *Geographic,* in its business development, does not, of course, resort to frenzied competitive methods.

Circulation is built through word-of-mouth endorsement. One member nominates another. There is no circulation-building organization. The only circulation promotion is an "editorial forecast," sent to each member on expiration of his membership. The forecast, illustrated in color, is tied up with world news. Part of its business is to prepare illustrated articles on parts of the world where changes may occur, and to be ready to publish these on short notice. Months ago, for example, it began a series on Chinese cities, on Spain, on Germany. It tells its readers of coming features, quietly mentions the desirability of the *Geographic* as a gift.

The magazine has no holier-than-thou advertising censorship rules, but has always been extraordinarily conscientious as to the type of advertising which it carries. Mr. Welch estimated that about 35% of advertising which appears in "other leading magazines" is not acceptable to the *Geographic*. It carries no liquor or beer, no security advertising (except U. S. Government baby bonds); no tobacco products, except occasionally pipe tobacco; no proprietary internal medicines for self-treatment. . . . Food advertising is not desired when it carries a "medical" slant. This policy of "selected advertising" has been in effect 33 years.

National advertisers like the *Geographic* and respect it, because they feel the society's members—the "First Million"—are worthwhile, alert and prosperous prospects. Last year 65% of *Geographic* advertising was "non-travel." However, travel is the most important single classification, followed by automotive products. Next in order are insurance, cameras and optical goods, household equipment, industrial, food products, paper goods.

But more, perhaps, than in any other general magazine, the magazine's business progress is rooted in the principles of the organization which sponsors it and its editorial development.

The *Geographic* is not only scientific and "social" in its aims, but recognized as responsible in its achievement of them. It is dignified, but human, and not by any means a "stuffed shirt." It is alert. The April issue, for example, which appeared before the first of the month, carried a large color insert of the "new map of Europe," showing Austria as a province of Germany, made by the society's own cartographic department. The *Geographic* may have three or four of these map inserts in a year. Each map costs about $100,000 to produce and distribute to its readers.

The flag of the society consists of three stripes—green, brown and blue. They represent the sea, the earth and the sky. In 50 years the society has penetrated far into each of these spheres, has found and told much about each, so that millions of people could understand and enjoy.

THE NATIONAL GEOGRAPHIC MAGAZINE
WASHINGTON, D. C.

NET PAID CIRCULATION EXCEEDS 1,000,000

manded big salaries. The manufacturer had not always given the jobber the right consideration and had often set his margin at an unreasonably low figure. The private brand so indignantly resented was frequently the direct result of that very tactic.

It is also to be noted, on the jobber's side of the argument, that while the indictment might apply to a majority of jobbers, it did not fit all of them. The modern jobber, equipped and ready to operate on an up-to-date flexible basis, was appearing in some lines at least. What many mistook for the elimination of the jobber was merely the elimination of an attribute which did not belong to the jobber —the control of the manufacturer's selling processes. In time the jobber in many fields assumed a genuine importance to the well-advertised line.

Whatever the justices and injustices of the situation, numerous manufacturers were prompted by what they believed to be the jobber's deficiencies to declare their independence of him. In addition there were several possible advantages in going around the jobber which appealed to the advertiser. These included: (1) Establishment of a more permanent body of customers; when selling through jobbers the manufacturer had relatively few accounts and the loss of a single account might be a serious matter. (2) Better control of retail prices. (3) More effective work in following up inquiries and handling tie-up forms of advertising than the jobber usually provided. (4) Closer contact with the ultimate consumer and retail conditions bearing upon consumer sales.

Some firms proceeded to leave the jobber entirely out of the marketing picture. Others used the jobber for small accounts and coverage of remote areas but adopted direct selling for the larger and more accessible accounts.

To the sales department all this meant an enlarged and more complex problem of management and procedure than had formerly been the case. With the jobbing machinery, or part of it, under the manufacturer's own roof, the sales manager was forced further into engineering a broad marketing operation. Planned, intelligent selling became his direct responsibility and he had to co-ordinate and direct the effort of larger numbers of men. In addition, widening geographical distribution created the new problem of administering a decentralized zone or district form of sales organization.

In consequence sales management moved out of the herd-driving era. For one thing more emphasis was placed on training the salesmen to enable them to meet the more exacting requirements of a new day. Many firms instituted sales-training schools, conducted either at the plant or by traveling experts who taught at group meetings in various territories. Clubs in public speaking and sales technique were formed. A number of companies took up the standardized sales talk, which had been pioneered by National Cash Register, Burroughs and Toledo Scale.

The vogue for efficiency in business, which assumed the aspects of a religion around 1912, gave further impetus to more intensive development and application of sales-training methods. Attention was now turned also to the appearance and personal habits of the salesmen.

A second tendency was toward the idea of leading and inspiring the salesman to success instead of browbeating him. The process was known in those days as "gingering up" the salesman and its broad objective was to keep him looking on the bright side of things. Sales contests in infinite variety and ingenuity were employed to this end, as were honorary clubs for sales achievement. The house organ was perfected as an instrument of sustaining morale and organization spirit.

The sales convention attained wide application as an effective means both of providing instruction and arousing enthusiasm. This was a relatively new function of sales management. One of the very first sales conventions was held by the Sherwin-Williams Company back in 1881. The firm even conducted the salesmen on inspection trips through the factory—a radical move, for in those days a manufacturing plant was a secret vault where "outsiders" were not permitted to trespass.

Advertising came to occupy a place in the sales convention program. Advertisers had begun to see the value of instructing their salesmen not only in the complete details of the advertising program but in how the advertising worked and why it was planned as it was. In the past the company merely notified the salesmen about the campaign, and even that was very rare.

There was a vast advance in the use of printed aids to salesmanship, which had up to this time remained in rather a primitive state. New study was given to the proper preparation of the sales manual and teaching the salesmen how to use the principles which it set forth.

The idea of using the catalog as a sales instrument to function between the salesman's calls also came forward, both in dealer and industrial selling. The loose-leaf catalog was adopted in many lines as an economical way of keeping the catalog up to date. The sales power of catalogs generally was stepped up. Mere description of the merchandise was supplemented by expository text and illustrations showing how the product helped to increase profits, save money or accomplish some other end desirable to the prospect.

Business correspondence, which for years had been confined almost entirely to asking or answering questions about routine transactions, took a new turn. It was now seen that the letter was a potentially valuable aid in selling merchandise. The technique of writing an effective sales letter occupied a place very near the top of the list of all sales and advertising subjects in which advertisers were interested during the latter part of this period.

The sales division as a whole showed signs of moving out of the guesswork stage, a holdover from the days when markets were clamoring for goods, into a day of factual planning. In former times most manufacturers knew only the geographical distribution of their goods and had little information about the retailer and his problems. The new conditions were making it evident that no manufacturer could afford to be without such knowledge. To get it, some firms employed "sales scouts" to get information about markets and buyers.

Hands Across the Counter

OPEN, bitter denunciation of the retailer to the public was a favorite occupation of many advertisers during 1907 and for a year or more thereafter. It was aimed at the merchant's practice of substituting unadvertised goods when the customer requested an advertised brand.

Substitution was not an entirely new problem. A number of manufacturers had got excited about it around 1898 and warned the public against such practices in their advertisements. The difficulty at this time, however, was not so much a matter of the dealer openly advocating another brand when the customer asked for a certain product as it was of palming off imitations under the pretense that they were the genuine. In addition, outright counterfeiting of advertised merchandise was prevalent and presented a serious problem.

After nearly ten years' quiescence, the substitution problem came to the fore as an issue of the dealer offering something "just as good" when an advertised brand was asked for. Enraged advertisers bent their fury against the substituter in full-page advertisements attacking the retail trade in general. The retailer was assailed as a selfish, scheming villain who would do anything to wring an extra nickel's profit out of the public. It was intimated that his dishonesty knew no bounds.

The attack was enlarged then to include the non-advertiser in the target range. With this came the first emergence of the thesis that only a good product could be advertised. And some proceeded from there to the premise that a product is good because it is advertised, a sophistry which lingered on to do much harm to the sound development of advertising. The idea that advertising adds something to the value of a product and justifies a price differential over an absolutely equivalent article has come down to the present time as one of the greatest of all handicaps upon the progress of the advertiser system of distribution.

Be that as it may, the anti-substitution campaign of 1907 was not without a good deal of provocation. The merchant for many years had been accustomed to absolute rule of his own trade. His had always been the privilege of giving the consumer the kind of merchandise he thought the consumer ought to have. He resented and considered outrageous a condition wherein people came to him and told him what kind of goods they wanted to buy. His natural impulse was to refuse to tolerate such invasion of his "rights" and he sought to frustrate the hated trade-mark by introducing goods under his own label and educating his salesmen to every device of substituting his own goods for the advertised articles which consumers asked for. Hundreds of merchants seemed to get more satisfaction out of telling people they did not have the requested merchandise than they got out of any other feature of their business.

Manufacturers became genuinely alarmed. They saw valuable interests threatened because the merchant was capitalizing upon the demand which they had spent large sums to create. And so they lashed out at the seeming plotter of their downfall.

It soon became apparent, to some of the manufacturers at least, that

☆ EVOLUTION

FROM TRADING POSTS

IN 1842, Texas was a republic with Gen. Sam Houston serving his second term as President. Poverty was the rule—a cheerful, energetic brand of poverty. "Gone to Texas" had closed the accounts, in their respective communities all over the United States, of many of the most enterprising souls and some of the most reckless.

In this melting pot of rough democracy The News was born in Galveston. In appearance it resembled the Boston News Letter—more comparable, by present-day standards, to a hand-dodger than to a newspaper. Its ads, dealing mainly with shipping items, pointed to the want ads of today. There were no merchant princes. "Store shopping" was truly "trading" and the spirit of *caveat emptor* was tacitly understood.

> *Files of The News and records of its publishers, Texas' Oldest Business Institution, constitute prime material for the historian, covering 96 years of as colorful development as can be shown by any area of the New World.*

IN 1885, The News was established in Dallas to open a new epoch of Texas development at the overland gateway of immigration. Then, a town of 20,000 . . . **TO**

IN TEXAS

now, a metropolis of 325,000, Dallas has been paced by this newspaper organization which has pioneered in all worthwhile undertakings—social, civic and economic. To know The News is to understand and appreciate the Texas of 1938, with its market opportunities vital . . . its people talking and acting in terms of arts, science, industry . . . chemurgy . . . a great laboratory for the discovery of new uses for cotton . . . the development and more effective application of vast oil resources . . . a new newsprint industry based on great pine reserves . . . Trinity River canalization . . . aviation progress . . . medical research . . . education . . . amusements . . . styles . . . travel.

In The News' advertising columns are mirrored Dallas' "Fifth Avenue" stores, its institutions of popular merchandise . . . of finance and of industry.

To sell, tell The News and let it tell Texas!

MODERN MARKETS

the program of agitation against the retailer was accomplishing little or nothing. They realized that the issuance of dictatorial mandates was getting them nowhere with the retailer, who refused to scare easily and resented the calumnies aimed at him, and moreover was accomplishing little with the consumer.

What is more important, the more they thought of the substitution problem the clearer three things became—three faults which lay directly upon their own doorsteps.

In the first place, some who had studied the situation in terms of common sense instead of emotion suggested that the outcry against substitution was cloaking the real evil—lack of distribution. Few manufacturers had included the retailer in their plans. Most conceived of advertising as a big stick with which to force a helpless go-between to stock the merchandise under the old theory that if a dealer got enough requests for an item he would put it into the store. But in actual practice the dealer quite naturally sought to sell something else that he already had.

Secondly, it appeared that substitution might just perhaps, in many instances, be a reflection of ineffective advertising. Some saw that substitution grows out of weak, vague copy, that substitution fattens on the half-persuaded consumer.

Finally, the idea began to penetrate that advantage might exist in working with the retailer instead of against him.

Having failed to reform the retailer by denunciation, advertisers tried to do a little reasoning with him. Turning from coercion to conciliation, they undertook to show him that his best interests lay in selling advertised goods on the basis that, with public confidence established in advance, his actual costs of selling advertised goods were much lower than for unknown goods. He could hold his trade more easily and get better profits on the increased turnover, a way of business far superior, he was shown, to the old code of long profits on slow turnover.

The more the manufacturer looked into the retailer's interests the more he saw that to a great extent the retailer's problems are the problems of the manufacturer who, by seeking to influence consumer sales for his product, had developed a definite stake in the events taking place at the point of sale. Now it was being seen that advertising was the starting point of more harmonious and beneficial relations with the dealer, rather than a bludgeon with which to force his capitulation to the advertiser.

By 1909 there was a marked improvement in the relations existing between the manufacturer and the retailer. Advertisers were devoting study and effort to securing better distribution and recognizing the advantage of enlisting the judgment and support of the retailer toward this end. In the years immediately following a large proportion of general advertising was built around the retailer. The prime object of not a few campaigns was to impress the retailer and induce him to stock up.

To win favor and support, advertisers proceeded with great vim toward providing practical aids for the retailer to use in moving his merchandise. As time went on, they saw also that such measures served to increase the efficiency of the whole distribution machine. The advances made in that direction en-

compass almost the entire range of retailer co-operation methods as we know them today.

An important phase of the work was the supplying of physical aids for the retail selling job—electrotypes and mats for tie-up advertising, booklets and literature, statement stuffers and wrapping paper, display materials, devices and selling manuals.

The original tendency was to scatter these things broadside in huge quantities and to produce them profligately without particular reference to the dealer's needs or an integrated sales plan. But before long it was evident that the job was not merely providing material, but getting it used.

With 1913 a quality trend in dealer helps appeared. The new processes of printing, lithography and engraving came to be very much in evidence, including new effects obtained by lithography on metal, the highlight process of halftone printing for booklets, novelties in decorative material, literature printed in offset and roto-intaglio. It was recognized as important that the material must look as though it were designed, written, ordered and paid for by the merchant. The tendency was toward better helps and less of them, material which was designed for its value in the eyes of the merchant rather than to secure an effect of flashy, expensive appearance. The previous hurrah about "hitch up your store to our trade-mark" gave way to efforts to give the dealer something that would really help him sell goods as well as tie in with the national campaign.

Concurrent strides were made in improving the manner of distribution of dealer helps. The jumble of disconnected items was replaced with materials engineered to a definite plan. Numerous companies used their sales organizations with telling effect to back up the work of the advertising department. Salesmen were encouraged to turn in an advertising report on every dealer called on. As another stimulus toward getting the helps used, some firms caused the dealer to have a financial interest in them by means of either a direct or indirect charge.

To stimulate the dealer's use of newspaper advertising, some firms commenced the practice of offering special discounts on cash allowance to be used toward payment for the space.

A large amount of attention was directed to the store window as a sales promoting vehicle. In the early days of retailing, the shop window had merely been a repository for a few signs or, as was often the case in the country general stores, a storage place for excess merchandise. The idea of using the window for exhibition purposes did not appear until the 1890's, when the department stores began improving their store fronts and hiring window dressers to put in "artistic" exhibits. It was not until the new century was several years old, however, that retailers generally discovered the window display to be capable of actually making sales. A leading exponent was Truly Warner, who founded an enormously successful hat business on sales-making windows.

A few scattered pioneers among the manufacturers had ventured into this field. Almost from the start, the Coca-Cola Company had laid great stress on the window display as a promotion method, devel-

"Uncle Bill" Kaufmann's Contribution to Advertising

By G. Wm. Kaufmann
President, The Rapid Electrotype Company

IF WE make the fiftieth anniversary of PRINTERS' INK WEEKLY the occasion for asking, "Why has advertising grown so great during the past half century?", we must answer that it grew because it was able to tell the story of new inventions and better products, to a larger audience, in a more convincing manner, and in less time than the message could be carried in any other way. It follows that everyone who has helped to improve the technique of telling and illustrating the advertising story—who has invented a faster press, a quicker method of setting type or making plates, has earned a place in advertising history.

By curious coincidence the fiftieth anniversary of PRINTERS' INK WEEKLY is approximately the one hundredth anniversary of the day when John Adams, a New York woodcut engraver, made the first electrotype in America.

While we are honoring Adams perhaps we might pay our respects to those who, in our own generation, created fast electrotype production processes.

Among the latter, William H. ("Uncle Bill") Kaufmann was conspicuous; and he will likewise long be remembered for his speedy deliveries of advertising copy, in plate or mat form, to newspapers and m a g a z i n e s all over the country.

No longer ago than 1898, when "Uncle Bill" with nine helpers established a typical electrotype

© Bachrach

G. WM. KAUFMANN

foundry in Cincinnati, there were no large electrotyping plants in the country. None of these small plants was geared to serve the special requirements of national advertisers and agencies.

But no sooner was "Uncle Bill" Kaufmann launched in business than he began to consult with local and national advertisers to study their special requirements.

"Uncle Bill" quickly noticed that large advertisers and agencies launching nationwide newspaper campaigns were handicapped because they must order electrotypes made in many different cities. This meant many orders to write and many chances for mistakes.

"UNCLE BILL'S" IDEA

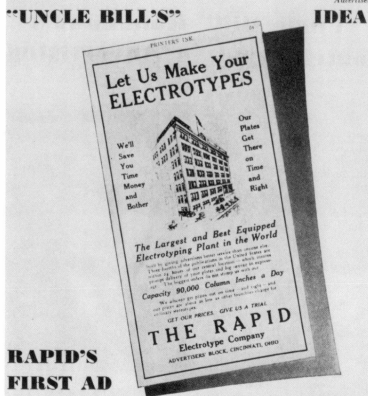

PRINTERS INK

Let Us Make Your ELECTROTYPES

We'll Save You Time Money and Bother

Our Plates Get There on Time and Right

The Largest and Best Equipped Electrotyping Plant in the World

Capacity 90,000 Column Inches a Day

GET OUR PRICES. GIVE US A TRIAL

THE RAPID
Electrotype Company
ADVERTISERS' BLOCK, CINCINNATI, OHIO

RAPID'S FIRST AD

PRINTERS' INK, SEPT. 16, 1908, LAID THE FOUNDATION FOR THE WORLD'S LARGEST ELECTROTYPE PLANT

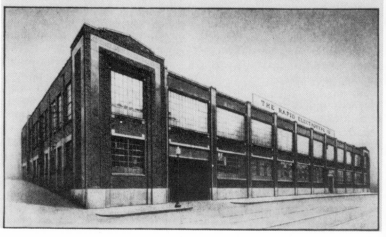

It meant electrotypes of varying quality. Some deliveries were slow and must be followed up. Some plates were made too wide and some too narrow because the column widths of the papers were not understood. Some plates were misdirected, some originals were lost. Packing was often inadequate. Responsibility for the order as a whole was divided.

By 1908 "Uncle Bill" Kaufmann had increased the facilities and organization of the Rapid Electrotype Company to such a point of size and efficiency that he could offer to handle the total electrotype requirements for the largest national campaign with assurance that he could deliver the required electros in each city where they were wanted on the exact day they were wanted.

He then presented his idea to a national advertising agency which gave him a test order. The manner in which the order was promptly filled was a surprise and delight to the agency. One by one, other agencies gave Rapid their orders calling for nationwide service.

Then "Uncle Bill" began to advertise in PRINTERS' INK WEEKLY. The first advertisement is shown on the opposite page. The bold claims of this advertisement were perfectly sincere. Rapid could, and did deliver the service. This unique service soon changed the whole picture of electrotype purchasing by national advertisers, and the Rapid Electrotype Company quickly became a national institution. Thus the company which began with nine men in 1898 and was proud when its 1908 production reached the unheard of capacity of 90,000 column inches was obliged in 1921 to build its own new plant, the largest in the world, with a capacity for 1,000,000 square inches of plates a day.

When "Uncle Bill" Kaufmann passed from the scene of his labors in 1935, he left behind him many inventions and manufacturing procedures which improved the quality of mats and electrotypes and stepped up production.

More important to advertising and to advertisers, he left behind an organization which could deliver a mat or ad plate to any newspaper anywhere in the United States in a single day. And he left to that well-equipped organization the spirit of inquiry and service which constantly studies the needs of the advertiser both as to product and service— a spirit which will continue to give birth to many new contributions during advertising's next 50 years.

oping a force of men who went from store to store trimming windows and decorating soda fountains. With skilfully designed and brilliantly illuminated displays in the windows of its branch showrooms, the National Cash Register Company had demonstrated window values as early as 1895. In 1899 Procter & Gamble had a force of window dressers on the road for Ivory and Lenox soaps, putting in displays in return for an order of a specified quantity of soap. F. H. Hoffman, general manager of the Gem Safety Razor Company, laid the early foundations of the product's success by personally demonstrating it in drug-store windows around 1901, and the company subsequently was a pioneer in the development of motion displays.

By 1911 a dozen or so manufacturers had discovered the business

1908

Taft and Sherman ticket defeats Bryan and Kern by 326 electoral votes to 157. . . . Dr. Frederick Cook claims to have reached the North Pole. . . . Former president Grover Cleveland dies. . . . Sullivan ordinance in New York City makes smoking by women in public places illegal. . . . "Twenty-three skidoo."

General Motors Corporation founded with William Eaton as president. . . . Hazen brothers seem to be taking over the magazine field: George H. is advertising manager of *Century* and *St. Nicholas* and president of the Crowell Publishing Company, publisher of *Woman's Home Companion* and *Farm & Fireside;* Josiah J. heads the advertising department of *McClure's;* E. W. heads the New York office of *Saturday Evening Post* and *Ladies' Home Journal.* . . . Charles H. Fuller, pioneer Chicago agent, retires. . . . Marco Morrow appointed advertising director of Capper Publications. . . . Death of William Emory Quinby, thirty-five years editor and chief owner of the Detroit *Free Press,* and of Murat Halstead, leader in American journalism for over a half century.

Federal Advertising Agency begins business at New York, as does the Blackman Company; Gardner Advertising Company formed at St. Louis. . . . *Christian Science Monitor* publishes first issue. . . . Butler Brothers appoint Glen Buck as advertising manager. . . . Death of George P. Rowell, who had sold Printers' Ink to John Irving Romer a few months before. . . . New York has 147 magazine advertisers, Chicago eighty-one, Boston thirty-four, Philadelphia twenty-three, Cincinnati eighteen. . . . Seattle Adcraft Association formed. . . . Dayton, Ohio, *Journal* prints 117 columns of "foreign" advertising in anniversary issue, said to be more than any American daily has ever printed in a single edition. . . . De-tan-ated Coffee advertised as being "richer in caffeine than other brands."

Last year the American Public bought over $100,000,000 worth of Compton-Advertised Products

These products are advertised by
Compton Advertising, Inc.

Barsalou Soap
Bollinger Champagne
Crisco
D. O. M. Benedictine
Fluffo
Garnier Liqueurs
Ivory Flakes
Ivory Snow
Ivory Soap
Lemon Hart Rum

Pall Mall Cigarettes
Permutit Water Softeners
Peter Dawson Scotch Whisky
Phillips Soups
P & G the White Naphtha Soap
Primex
Puritan Oil
Sweetex
Utica Club Beer
Williams & Humbert Sherry

Compton Advertising, Inc.

[FORMERLY THE BLACKMAN COMPANY]

630 FIFTH AVENUE · NEW YORK

of working up window displays for dealers to be a veritable gold mine, the efforts of the Victor Talking Machine Company, Swift & Company and Grossett & Dunlap being especially notable. From that time on the practice spread widely and at a rapid pace. Little more than a year later what had been a sporadic device had achieved general acceptance. The question was no longer one of recognition of the importance of the dealer window but of how to get goods into the window. It was noticed that a window display not only sold goods but had the interesting effect of making jobbers sit up and take notice, for here were results that he could see at first hand.

Motion displays attained wide popularity. These were usually lithographs fitted with clockwork devices. Sometimes a moving picture set-up was used. At the very first, much stress had been laid on sheer attraction of attention but this soon gave way to a tendency of sacrificing some of that element in the interest of getting across a complete selling argument in addition to name and package publicity.

Some manufacturers used elaborate displays which were loaned to the retailer for a certain period and then shipped on to another store—what is known today as the "itinerant display." These were usually placed in return for a specified order of merchandise. However, the practice of paying for store window space was followed where necessary by some manufacturers, or a special discount might be offered in return for the space. On the whole, though, the dealer was glad enough to get a well-designed display so that the charge for a window was relatively rare.

Counter displays began coming into wide use in 1914. The idea originated with the department store, which early in its career had detected the value of getting goods out of sight. Manufacturers found the counter presentation a good way of suggesting purchases and a virtually absolute preventive of substitution.

The whole question of retailer assistance crystallized into the fundamental objective of making the retailer a better customer by helping him to be a better merchant. A number of firms sent around special or missionary salesmen whose primary duty it was to give counsel on retail selling and advertising problems, in the belief that showing dealers how to sell the goods worked much more effectively than force, argument or cajolery directed to that end. Others trained their regular sales forces to teach as well as sell. Ways and means were sought of making the dealer a better credit risk and of helping him with store management problems apart from the actual selling of goods, such as how to keep track of costs and how to plan an effective store arrangement. ·

Projects in helping to educate the retail salesperson came to the fore. Here the favorite device was the retail sales manual. In a few instances these were designed to do a completely "unselfish" job in sales instruction, no mention being made of the company or its products on the premise that the helpfulness involved would create good-will. Correspondence courses in salesmanship were offered by some firms; others, whose products involved a relatively large investment, sent instructors around to hold classes at the stores or paid part of the expenses for

John B. Woodward, Inc.

Established in 1893

Representing Newspapers

In Seven of the Greatest Markets
in the United States

●

The New York Times

The Boston Globe

The Baltimore Sun

Cleveland Plain Dealer

The Minneapolis Tribune

The Dallas Morning News

The Spokesman-Review

Spokane Daily Chronicle

●

John B. Woodward, Inc.

New York	Boston	Chicago	Detroit
	San Francisco	Los Angeles	

bringing the salespeople in for a training course at the factory.

Meanwhile advertisers addressed themselves more energetically than before to selling the retailer on the proposition of the advertised brand. No longer was it considered wise to *subpoena* the retailer into service by the sheer force of advertising or to assume that the dealer was informed and interested. Most manufacturers now definitely planned to divert enough of the expenditure in the retailer's direction for him to feel the dramatic quality of the advertising program. The burden of proof of demand upon the manufacturer was growing heavier each year, as competition increased.

In order to build up dealer enthusiasm and support, the manufacturer adopted the policy of sustained, systematic advertising direct to the dealer. The trade paper was pressed into service as one means to this end. One of the secrets of the success of the Gillette Safety Razor Company was the fact that it early expended the effort to make its trade-paper copy as strong and attractive as that in consumer media. The dealer house magazine came into use as something more than a gossip sheet and was built to show how the advertising program was planned, how it worked, and to offer retail sales and advertising ideas.

Numerous other ways of binding the dealer closer to the manufacturer and his product were sought. The idea of listing dealers in manufacturer advertising came to the fore. In some fields the exclusive agency form of doing business was introduced with success, and while it sometimes restricted distribution in the community involved, it did serve to strengthen the dealer's co-

operation to a considerable degree. The Bromo Seltzer plan of selling stock to the retailer in order to induce him to push the product and avoid substitution held forth an enticing prospect and other manufacturers tried the same idea, but with considerably less success. At one point several companies, taking a cue from a fad of the times, set out to work some "new thought" angles on the dealer, getting after his mind with applications of psychotherapy to enthuse him to sell more. It didn't do much good.

In the earliest stages of the retailer-manufacturer antagonism some of the larger merchants had undertaken to fight the manufacturer by selling trade-marked products at less than cost, thus depreciating their value in the minds of the consumer and making them seem poor and cheap in quality. Vengeance gave way to the more powerful profit motive and the proposition gained in attractiveness when the department stores discovered that price-cutting on advertised brands was a business-getting measure of no small power. On ordinary bargain counter merchandise the public had to take the store's word for the value. On the advertised brand the public was educated to a value standard expressed in terms of a customary price and responded more quickly to a reduction below that price.

As the manufacturer progressed along the path to closer dealer relations he perceived the price-cutter's tactics to be a major obstacle. The rank and file of dealers were not bashful about showing disinterest in a manufacturer whose products were subjected to price-cutting, for there was little or no profit in them. Coincidental, then, with the era of cultivation of the retailer was the first strong and concerted endeavor of the manufacturer to maintain retail prices on his products.

Price maintenance was one of the most important subjects of advertiser interest throughout the period under discussion. Many an effort was made to achieve the goal, but, through the intervention of the courts, little progress of permanent significance was registered.

The Dr. Miles Medicine Company was the first to achieve an important measure of success. As early as 1903 this firm had put in effect agreements with jobbers and retailers binding them to maintain the full resale prices. Transactions were subject to check by serial numbers on all packages and suits were brought against all violators and damages collected. It was costly but effective. In 1904 the firm's remedies were sold at the full prices in 98 per cent of all cities and towns.

In 1911, after a long series of legal actions, the Supreme Court put an end to the plan, holding that under the general law the owner of unpatented goods could not sell the goods and at the same time lawfully contract to fix the price at which they would subsequently be sold. Other companies that had adopted similar plans were, of course, forced to abandon them.

Price maintenance had proved eminently popular with jobbers and most retailers, and manufacturers looked for other means by which they could effect it. In the Miles case and in certain of the trust dissolution actions the words of the courts seemed to suggest that the

Back in 1902 Packard was a conservative advertiser—featured its slogan

A testimonial from a man who was saved from an appendectomy. This was in 1900

manufacturer might maintain prices on patented articles and several plans were adjusted accordingly. Eastman Kodak, for example, withdrew price maintenance on all except its patented products, while the Kellogg Toasted Corn Flake Company used a patented carton as the basis of its plan.

The patent thesis seemed to gain support in the A. B. Dick case in 1912 when the Supreme Court held that the vendor of a patented machine could lawfully contract with purchasers for the machine (Mimeograph) to be used only with accessories and supplies furnished by the vendor. It received a sharp setback in the Sanatogen case a year later, when the Court ruled that, having sold the goods, the owner of the patent had exercised his exclusive right to sell them and could not by mere notice to the trade extend his control to cover the price at which they might be sold afterward. The Victor Talking Machine Company tried the idea of licensing its products for use in return for a stipulated royalty sum, but the Court found this to be a mere "form of expression" and applied the ruling of the Sanatogen case. Some years before, in the Bobbs-Merrill case, the Court had ruled that the exclusive right to sell copies of a book granted by the Copyright Act does not confer a right to fix and enforce a resale price. Nevertheless the decisions in the patent cases took the trade pretty much unawares.

In the meantime there had been a good deal of legislative action pro and con. In 1912 the Oldfield bill to forbid price maintenance on patented articles was introduced. In 1914 the Stevens bill to establish the right to maintain resale prices was introduced. This had the active suport of the Fair Trade League, backed mainly by manufacturers, and the energetic opposition of the National Trade Association, made up principally of department-store proprietors. Several other bills on the subject came forward, but nothing came of any of them. Certain world events were operating to make price maintenance a highly academic issue by 1915.

All the efforts at rapprochement with the retailer worked out to the distinct advantage of all concerned. The distribution machine moved forward with a vastly increased smoothness, although, of course, there was still a good deal of room for improvement. Retailers generally changed their attitude toward advertised goods from one of disapproval or disinterest to a disposition toward co-operation.

However, the thing did tend to get a little out of balance. In the keen desire to annex new dealers and woo the favors of old ones, the consumer—supposedly the party around whom all business is centered—became a pawn in the game and was almost totally ignored. Many advertising programs narrowed down to the point where they were calculated more to impress dealers. While the spread-eagle general publicity which had been displaced was no loss, concentration upon hypnosis of the dealer was now tending to swing the pendulum too far the other way.

Campbell-Ewald

PAST AND PRESENT

IN 1911, when Henry T. Ewald formed an advertising agency partnership with Frank J. Campbell, long since retired, Detroit was a fertile ground for just such pioneering abilities as the two young men possessed. All the talk in Detroit was of brakes, gears, transmissions, horsepower, mergers, gas, steam, electric, what's new, what's next, where are we going from here, and a thousand and one speculations and dreams that the world has long since forgotten.

* * *

But amid all this clamor, these two young men held to the theory that there must eventually emerge a force capable of moving automobiles out of the factories of Detroit, into the possession of the nation. And they knew of no force stronger than advertising. Henry Ewald had already had some advertising experience of his own as advertising manager of the D & C line of Great Lakes passenger boats. He had prepared and placed advertising that helped fill those boats to capacity summer after summer. So he knew that advertising did move people to

"do something" and "go somewhere." Campbell, too, had had more than a taste of advertising success. Both were agreed that their slogan would be, "We care not who makes the nation's cars, if we may write and place the nation's advertising."

And so they formed the Campbell-Ewald Company, which had as one of its clients the Hyatt Roller Bearing Company. It may be presumed that the Hyatt Roller Bearing Company was quite well satisfied with the services rendered by these two young Detroit advertising men, because Hyatt, as Hyatt Bearings Division of General Motors Corporation, is still a Campbell-Ewald client!

Very soon the new agency became the spokesman for other leading automotive manufacturers—among them, the Dayton Engineering Laboratories, Dayton, Ohio, and the Remy Electric Company, Anderson, Indiana—later merged and known as the Delco-Remy Corporation, now Delco-Remy Division of General Motors. Still a Campbell-Ewald client after all these years!

Campbell-Ewald *PAST AND PRESENT*

Other industries—other business men and business houses—watching the new agency go about its work so vigorously, decided that they wanted Campbell-Ewald to handle their advertising, too. So, alongside the early automotive accounts, grew a clientele made up of other advertisers in many lines.

One particularly striking fact is the length of time Campbell-Ewald has served many of its clients. There's a reason for that. In Mr. Ewald's own words: "We would be very short-sighted indeed if we were to neglect any thought or effort that might bring new business to us. But we would be far shorter-sighted if we were to neglect any thought or action that might help us better serve the clients we have. In brief, if we do all we can to help our present clients do *more* business, that will be reflected in *more* business for us. The advertising agency that does only what it is paid to do will soon get paid only for what it does—and that may not be enough."

THE YEAR 1918, seven years after the Campbell-Ewald Company was incorporated, was a critical one in the life of the agency. It was a successful association from every standpoint. Campbell was the writer, the dreamer, the passive partner; Ewald was the doer, the idea man, the dynamo. They had as much business as their limited staff could handle. They were making money and progress.

It was at this point that Campbell decided to give up his partnership and go abroad with a Y.M.C.A. unit. So Campbell appears no more in the story of Campbell-Ewald except for a brief moment when, on its 25th Anniversary, the Adcraft Club of Detroit feted its first president, Henry T. Ewald; and Frank J. Campbell was an honored guest.

At the Detroit Auto Show in 1921 there were 67 different makes of passenger cars displayed, which gives one some idea about the industry at that time. Today these are still manufactured: Buick, Cadillac, Chevrolet, Dodge, Ford, Hudson, Hupmobile, Lincoln, Nash, Oldsmobile, Packard and Studebaker. The others are gone the way of dreams and shadows.

It was during 1920 that Campbell-Ewald secured Buick—its first major automobile account. For 15 years thereafter, the Buick Motor Company was a Campbell-Ewald client.

In 1922, Chevrolet came to Campbell-Ewald. Then, in succession, came other General Motors cars, as well as other General Motors divisions, products and services.

THE TEN YEARS following were the busiest and maddest in America. All industry was driving furiously toward a peak, with Detroit and the automotive industry in the forefront. It seemed as if nothing could stop the upward climb to greater heights of "prosperity." It was not so much a time of planning for the future as it was for taking advantage of the present.

New forms of advertising came into the picture—such as radio; outdoor advertising became of prime importance because popular use of the motor car had multiplied circulation in this field a thousand-fold; new advertising techniques appeared, such as the widespread use of photography. But whatever they were—and whenever they showed up—the automotive industry absorbed them all and applied them to the merchandising

Campbell-Ewald *PAST AND PRESENT*

and selling of automobiles, parts and accessories.

This gave Campbell-Ewald a unique opportunity. During these years the agency not only built up a sound structure, but fortified that structure as well.

But it mustn't be inferred that Campbell-Ewald is strictly an automotive advertising agency, by any means. While a roster of its accounts shows automobiles, trucks, tires, batteries, automotive electrical systems and automotive accessories, there is also an imposing array of such products and services as adding machines, calculators, bookkeeping machines, cash registers, typewriters, posture chairs, railroads, steamship lines, resorts, hotels, toys, trade associations, footwear, luggage, golf balls, shovels, rubber sundries, building material, household products, food products, financial, cosmetics, newspapers, neckwear, and many others.

DIVERSITY of types of accounts is only logical. Campbell-Ewald had built a big advertising agency in every sense of the word. Big from the standpoint of billing, that firm foundation on which rests the financial position of any agency; big in organization, with a personnel of several hundred people, including many of America's ablest advertising and merchandising men; big in services rendered—because when you service automotive accounts, your activities reach deep into every phase of advertising and selling. And this "bigness," together with Campbell-Ewald's reputation, attracted manufacturers in many lines of business and industry.

ON "BIGNESS" Mr. Ewald is quoted as saying, "We have to be big in order to serve the accounts that have come to us. We just couldn't help it, and if 'bigness' is a crime, then I suppose we'll have to plead guilty. But what an advantage bigness is to all our clients! How else could an advertiser with a modest appropriation get *everything* an advertiser with a big appropriation gets? Take the Georgian Bay Line, for example. There's a client with a small appropriation, as appropriations go, yet it is one of the most interesting accounts we have in the house. I feel that we have been of particular service in helping them increase their patronage every year since they have been with us. We have other accounts whose appropriations are comparable, and whose results from advertising are likewise gratifying. The size of an account has little or no significance so far as Campbell-Ewald is concerned. We ask only that the product or service advertised be sound; that the business have legitimate potentialities for growth. No client of this agency ever complains of lack of personal attention on the part of the Campbell-Ewald staff. All clients have access to all the facilities of Campbell-Ewald."

The Campbell-Ewald Company is still Henry T. Ewald's most absorbing interest. When other interests call him away from the office, which they do occasionally, R. H. Crooker, Executive Vice-President, functions as Acting President of Campbell-Ewald, Detroit. Crooker has earned this honor because of years of advertising, selling and merchandising experience that reaches back to the Hugh Chalmers days. The General Manager of Campbell-Ewald is W. W. Lewis, long identified in an advertising and selling capacity with various units of General Motors Corporation. Many members of the staff have been with the agency for years—men like Loren T. Robinson and George O. Leonard, Account Executives; J. J. Hartigan, Director of Media; Eugene Zuber, Director of Outdoor, all vice-presidents of the company today; L. R. Nelson, Treasurer; and George F. Koether, Account Executive. To these might be added such men as Halsey Davidson, Art Director; Percy Atkinson, Copy Chief; and Paul Cramer, Director of Research—to mention only a few among the large personnel which is today giving point and direction to the work begun by Henry T. Ewald twenty-seven years ago. Mr. Ewald is also Chairman of the Campbell-Ewald Company of New York, Inc., of which his long-time associates, Fletcher D. Richards, is President, and L. B. Dudley, Secretary. The Chicago office of Campbell-Ewald is in charge of M. S. Charlton, another long-time associate; while the Pacific Coast offices are headed by S. S. Arnett in Los Angeles, and R. V. Dunne in San Francisco.

✦   ✦   ✦

Social and economic life in America has seen many changes since the Campbell-Ewald Company was incorporated in 1911. One can count on ten fingers the important national advertising agencies that today are operating under the same name as they were twenty-odd years ago. Some agencies have gone by the board; some have merged; there are many new agencies. All have had their ups and downs during these troublous times. It is a remarkable tribute to the soundness of the organization created so long ago by two ambitious young advertising men, that Campbell-Ewald is today as staunch as ever, with even greater facilities for serving a diversified list of clients, looking toward the future with the fervor and enthusiasm that characterized those youthful activities in the Detroit of an earlier day.

Campbell-Ewald Company

General Motors Building, Detroit

H. T. EWALD, *President*

NEW YORK · CHICAGO · WASHINGTON · LOS ANGELES · SAN FRANCISCO

Words with a Purpose

A CONSIDERABLE proportion of the advertisements of the period were built around some feature of the selling plan and specifically designed to accomplish the objective of that plan.

For one thing the advertised guarantee became far more prominent than ever before. Throughout all business the once dominant principle of the quick sale followed by the quick getaway had been displaced by the idea of making buying easy and safe. The success of the mail-order houses with their liberal and virtually unrestricted guarantees prompted emulation in the general field. The Ingersoll watch, which had got its start in mail-order distribution, was an early landmark with its unqualified guarantee to keep the watch in order for one year and exchange a new watch for an old one within the year on payment of 10 cents. In 1908 the Holeproof Hosiery Company gained wide attention and many imitators with its sensational guarantee of a new pair of hose free if the original pair developed holes in six months.

Sampling found new favor and advertising was hitched more directly to the offer, either in conducting the offer through the mails, or, if house-to-house or dealer distribution was used, in playing up the value of the product. Salesmen were for the sample, boot and horse, for it enabled them to make a big play with dealers.

Beginning around 1910 the premium, whose days were thought by many to have passed, came into more widespread use than ever before, and the offer was more directly coupled to the advertising.

Originally the value of the premium was believed to consist solely in keeping a customer buying the same brand in order to accumulate a requisite number of coupons or wrappers. In this new phase it was adapted to definite sales objectives, such as introducing a new product, removing price-cutting temptation, improving sales in a weak territory or minimizing substitution. As business conditions entered upon something of a decline in 1913, the advertising of premium offers became even more conspicuous.

Another device to emerge into the spotlight was the contest, which heretofore had had rather a curious history. Several advertisers had used contests in the 1890's, but the sole purpose lay in the value of the entries received. And almost invariably this had something to do with advertising itself. The advertiser was seeking a new slogan, original ideas to incorporate in advertising and even completely written advertisements. The one conspicuous exception was the Eastman Kodak contest of 1897, which was held to create greater interest in taking pictures. This event, incidentally, prompted several advertisers to run contests for the best photographs showing their products in use—an idea that might not go badly in a modern vogue for amateur photography.

Next came the contest whose purpose was to get proof that the advertising was being read. The Postum Cereal Company, in 1906, ran a contest for the greatest number of words made from the letters in Grape Nuts. In 1908 the limerick contest—filling in the last line of an incompleted verse—was imported from England and enjoyed a considerable vogue. This was followed by a number of puzzle contests, which in reality were lotteries, for the puzzles themselves were ridiculously simple. The idea was popular mainly in the retail field and especially among piano dealers. The post office put a stop to that with a penal code forbidding the use of mails to lottery schemes.

Soon after came the contest which had a definite merchandising reason —to secure special stimulation of sales in certain cities, to intensify interest in a certain feature of the product, to find new uses for the product, to step up dealer interest or in some way specifically influence sales. Some phase of advertising continued as the basis for the competitive element in nearly all these contests. They involved such things as providing a sentence to be used on an electric sign, choosing the best slogan from a given list, writing the last paragraph for an unfinished advertisement and writing an opinion on whether human interest or descriptive advertisements had the greatest appeal.

The linking of the sales viewpoint to advertising was by no means confined to the use of specific merchandising devices, however. Advertisers began to plan their campaigns toward objectives far more definite than winning a trade-mark following or general sales effect. Programs were now designed to develop slack season demand and create year-'round markets; to cultivate the adoption of the products for new uses; to enlist the influence of the youngsters where they might have a voice in the purchase; to increase the unit of the sale. The week sale, designed to focus the buyer's attention on the product at a specific time, became popular.

The old "omnibus" advertisement began to give way to the advertisement designed as a special tool to reach the special class of people automatically selected by the given publication in which it appeared. Much attention was given to the idea of relating copy to the medium on the idea that to hit all bulls' eyes one must use guns adapted to the different ranges.

The idea of framing the advertisement to talk in human-interest terms with a single person began to attain increased preference over the old style of talking to the crowd. And user testimony, long a favorite weapon in the salesman's arsenal, experienced a great revival beginning in 1912. Previously testimonials had been almost anathema because of the bad odor in which they had been placed by false patent medicine advertisers. Devised at this time, by the way, was the anonymous testimonial, featuring the statements of an imaginary character. This was taken up as a way of telling about the product in personal terms without risking the implications of a paid testimonial, and it has come down the years as a favorite way of telling an advertising story.

A copy trend unrelated to the main movement was the appearance of the "snobbish" appeal and its number of proponents was not inconsiderable. Here the advertisement put on airs of grandeur and ultra-smartness, deserting the usual simple, homespun language of advertising for classical allusions, elegant phrases and lofty circumlocutions. This was based largely on the psychology idea. The suppressed function of aristocracy was

WHY PRINTERS' INK
KILLED OUR PAGE...

We publishers of Promenade prepared a great tribute to Printers' Ink for this page. Great, you ask? It was as sincere as Mr. L. E. McGivena's masterpiece, *"Enteuthen Exelaunei,"* which he wrote for the 45th Anniversary Number, five years ago, but which isn't forgotten yet.

And Printers' Ink killed our page. Killed it with the gentle reminder that actions speak louder than words. So we merely report here what Printers' Ink (age 50) has done for Promenade (age 4).

As human-beings, we have relied on Printers' Ink for all advertising news, ever since we had our first jobs. Our business attitude has been largely formed by its unwavering insistence on truth in advertising.

As writers, we have written only one article about that Adamless Eden, the Promenade office. It appeared in Printers' Ink, Jan. 13, 1938.

As advertisers, we have advertised Promenade in Printers' Ink exclusively.

So what? Promenade's linage record should be of great interest to anyone who wonders what a strong old magazine like Printers' Ink can do for a strong young magazine like Promenade. Here are the figures:

1936	1937	1938
Jan.–June	Jan.–June	Jan.–June
15,090	24,552	43,629

promenade

FOR WALDORF-ASTORIA GUESTS

Martha Houston Publications, Inc., 19 E 47, New York

supposed to reside in every lowly breast and the advertisement sought to offer the product as a partial consummation of the universal yearning for social heights. And, for some products at least, it was apparently quite effective.

Advertising illustrations were very much in keeping with the main copy patterns. The purely ornamental and the "pretty picture" illustrations gave way to genuine human-interest illustrations. Natural surroundings and natural people replaced the old idealized depictions. The illustration was enrolled as a salesman to show how the product is used or how its use pleases the owner. The imagery that the skilful salesman likes to employ in getting across a point found its printed counterpart in pictorial delineations of comparative characteristics and effects. The illustrative complexion of the advertising was by no means one of ugliness, however, for the Coles Phillips school was in bloom.

The idea of showing the product in use and of injecting human interest began its mark in the industrial field as well as among consumer advertisers. Having advanced from the business-card copy style,

1909

DISCOVERY of North Pole by Robert E. Peary. . . . U. S. Fleet returns from 'round-the-world cruise. . . . Chicago, Milwaukee & St. Paul Railroad completed to Seattle and Tacoma, making seventh transcontinental line. . . . Uprising of Creek Indians suppressed by Oklahoma militia. . . . "I love my wife but oh you kid."

Condé Nast acquires *Vogue*. . . . Automobile production for the year: 127,731 passenger cars, 3,255 trucks. . . . Over a million buggies still sold annually. . . . Suffragettes in Baltimore take car cards to advertise votes for women. . . . Thomas Cusack Company acquires plant of the Gunning System. . . . Salt Lake City Ad Club established. . . . "The good advertisement is not the one you quote and talk about—it is the one you acted upon"—Earnest Elmo Calkins. . . . T. W. LeQuatte appointed advertising manager of *Successful Farming*.

Rowell's *American Newspaper Directory* acquired by N. W. Ayer & Son and merged with the *American Newspaper Annual*. . . . E. D. Gibbs, for many years advertising director of National Cash Register Company, becomes sales manager of Ketterlinus Lithographic Company. . . . J. Walter Thompson Company absorbs O. J. Mulford Advertising Agency and Lord Advertising Agency. . . . A. G. Carter is general manager of the new Fort Worth *Star-Telegram*. . . . W. H. Taylor heads David Williams Company, publisher of *Iron Age*. . . . Some product names: Wife Getter (buggy); E Z 2 Tie (neckwear); Kis-me (chewing gum); NoSmellee.

PAUL BLOCK AND ASSOCIATES

Congratulates Printers' Ink
On Its Golden Anniversary

*F*OR fifty years Printers' Ink has rendered invaluable services to the advertising profession—to advertisers, advertising agencies and publishers alike.

12 Years after Printers' Ink started up the trail, Paul Block and Associates, comprising one young man, a young lady and a boy, began its career as publishers' representatives.

Today, by following the same principles of service which has made Printers' Ink one of the outstanding magazines in its field, finds Paul Block and Associates the largest selling organization of its kind, with more than 50 efficient, experienced men, an army of assistants, located in eight advertising centers of the nation.

We now have the honor to represent
these important newspapers:

Cincinnati Enquirer
Pittsburgh Post-Gazette
Toledo Blade
Toledo Times
Worcester Telegram-Gazette
Duluth Herald & News-Tribune
Lancaster Newspapers
Bridgeport Post-Telegram
Wichita Eagle
Newark Star-Eagle

Los Angeles Herald & Express
San Francisco Call-Bulletin
Oakland Post-Enquirer
Milwaukee Sentinel
Milwaukee News
San Antonio Light

PAUL BLOCK AND ASSOCIATES
National Advertising Representatives

| NEW YORK | CHICAGO | DETROIT | BOSTON | PHILADELPHIA |
| | LOS ANGELES | CINCINNATI | SAN FRANCISCO | |

wherein the message was confined to the name of the company and the date of its establishment, industrial advertisers were finding that the attractive presentation of facts about their machines elicited an interesting response from customers.

In addition to these changes in the motivation of the advertisement, its entire complexion underwent a material change for the better. From 1911 on, a new understanding of the uses and values of sound typography became evident. The advertiser made the important discovery that readability is typography's first law and that, except in a type-specimen book, typography should not call attention to itself. He came to the conclusion that advertising which is to present important messages to the nation in space costing thousands of dollars a page must not be thrown together like an auction handbill if it is to get the results hoped for. The family idea in type gained acceptance over the old jumbled displays that encompassed a gamut of the type designer's product. And publishers, finding that the kind of typography they had to offer and the results obtained from the advertisement could influence the amount of money an advertiser might be willing to spend, were exhibiting much more concern for the appearance of the advertising page. Nor was the new tendency confined to publication advertising, for typographers and the better printers were showing the advertiser that resort to competent, professional advice would enable him to produce more effective direct-mail pieces, booklets and catalogs for the same or lesser cost.

Publishers and proprietors of advertising media gave particular attention to relating their facilities to the advertiser's sales problem where formerly they had been chiefly concerned with offering so much white space. Throughout all forms of media there was a definite trend toward digging up and presenting factual information about market potentials.

The original proponents of this tactic seem to have been the farm papers. They were active in conducting surveys to determine brand preferences and sales possibilities shortly after the turn of the century, the result, no doubt, of the fact that few advertisers had so thorough an appreciation of the rural market as they had of opportunities in urban centers.

The most notable expansion in advertising volume during the period came in the newspapers and the farm papers, although magazines and other media also showed considerable increases. The newspaper's acceptance as a national advertising medium really dates from this period and it experienced large gains in general advertising. Primary factors were more intelligent solicitation based on real encouragement and service to the advertiser and a policy of co-operating more closely with advertisers and agents. Publishers as a class began to take a greater interest in the affairs of their advertisers than at any time past. Merchandising service departments were instituted to provide practical aid and information. Newspaper advertising was interpreted in terms of marketing and advertisers were shown how it might be used to develop distribution, conduct territorial programs to take advantage of special conditions and apply extra selling pressure where needed.

Collective action figured in this effort. The special representatives, through the Six Point League of New York and other groups, got to work around 1908 to place more stress on the basic principles of newspaper advertising, less on competitive quarreling over circulation totals. Then, in 1912, came the establishment of the Bureau of Advertising by the American Newspaper Publishers Association. This organization provided a clearinghouse of creative study of advertisers' problems and market conditions and gave a great new impetus to the progress of the medium.

~The general movement of advertisers into the farm market which began in 1909 was precipitated by the financial events of the last weeks of 1907. In the preceding six years the value of farm produce had increased by almost 50 per cent. The success of the mail-order houses, which were much more keenly on the job in the rural areas, and the efforts of the farm publishers had suggested the possibilities of the farmer as a buyer of things other than farming equipment. But the clincher was provided by the fact that the country districts were almost entirely unaffected by the financial crisis in the cities. Advertisers of automobiles, household furnishings, soaps, textiles and various specialties started to cultivate rural sales in 1909 and in 1910 at least fifty more general advertisers joined in. The term "national advertiser" took on an additional, and more accurate, meaning.

Novelty or specialty advertising, which had never got much attention before, appeared on a much more diversified and widely adopted scale, doubtless as a result of the new interest in building good-will

in trade channels. Another development was the poster stamp, an idea transplanted from Europe. Collecting of advertisers' poster stamps became an enormously popular fad in 1914, then lapsed into quiescence until recent years.

Business papers circulating among retailers experienced an entirely new attitude on the part of the manufacturer, the result of his far-reaching endeavor to work closely and systematically with the retailer. Advertisers were finding that they could get an edge on their competitors by giving more consideration to business-paper advertising, that a well-planned campaign to the trade was a real aid to the sales force. At the same time the publishers were adopting more up-to-date tactics. This applied to the technical papers as well as those reaching the trade. The business press as a whole had undertaken successful measures in proving wide readership; hitherto this had been a matter of some doubt, for few publishers even went so far as to issue circulation statements.

Something else that had been holding up business-paper growth was the unpeaceful state of affairs existing between agents and publishers. The former complained of cut rates, uncertain circulation and lack of commissions. The large majority of papers paid no agent's commission. The publishers, on the other hand, resented the slight regard which the agents accorded the business-paper as an advertising proposition and felt, often rightly, that the agent was unable to handle technical accounts intelligently. About 1913 both sides began to take steps to compose the differences and two years later the Federation of Trade Press Associations established an agency relations committee to confer with agents and establish a basis for mutual cooperation.

The agency commission system as applied to consumer publications entered a serious crisis in the years from 1909 to 1913. In the former year the Standard Oil Company set about establishing an agency of its own and asked that commissions be granted to this agency. It was a crucial issue, for this was a large and powerful account and the question of observance of the spirit of the commission arrangement had never before been broached. Previously the leading publishers had stood firm in insisting that only an advertising agency could receive the agent's commission. Here the issue involved an agency true enough, but an agency established and owned by the advertiser. There were a few breaks in the ranks, but all publishers of consequence held fast.

Several years later the Association of National Advertisers declared the commission system to be an illogical way of remuneration, and expressed the belief that publishers should withdraw opposition to split commission on the theory that agents would then be free to grade their charges according to the service rendered the advertiser. The best publishers, however, took the position that what was needed was not a cutting of compensation to fit inferior service but of raising agency service to a point of value equal and more than equal to the commission.

The agents themselves recognized the pressure by exerting effort to make their services worth the differential and there was a marked improvement in the range and quality of agency service.

Appearing on the boards of large cities a week before Theodore Roosevelt's return from Africa in 1910, this poster featured the famous Gold Dust Twins and the equally well-known slogan

THE <u>WHOLE</u> FAMILY
<u>READS</u> LIFE

Reporting on the results of a quiz inserted in
every 100th copy of a recent issue of LIFE.

The WHOLE family reads LIFE

This Spring LIFE pasted a printed questionnaire into every 100th newsstand copy as it left the bindery in Chicago, mailed the same quiz to every 100th subscriber.

By this method replies to the questionnaire are almost exactly parallel to LIFE's ABC distribution both by geographic sections and by city size. Over 3500 replies have been received and 3473 of them tabulated by Forshew & Jacobus.

Some highlight findings:

FINANCIAL STATUS OF LIFE READERS:		
	Incomes over $3,000.	**55.2%**
	Occupation: BRAIN WORKERS (Executive, Professional, Proprietor, White Collar)	**78.1%**
	CAR OWNERSHIP	**84.0%**
	CARS per 1000 families	**999**

READERS PER FAMILY:		
Women 18 and over	**1.38**	
Men 18 and over	**1.34**	
Children 6 to 17	**0.55**	

Total Readers per family: **3.27**

Guest Readers		**4.98**
Outside-the-home readers (54.7% of LIFE buyers regularly lend or give their copies to someone else)		**2.51**

Total Readers per copy: **10.76**

RATIO OF READERSHIP TO MEMBERSHIP OF THE FAMILY:	
Women 18 and over	**94.4%**
Men 18 and over	**95.0%**
Young people 13 to 17	**96.1%**
Children 6 to 12	**80.7%**

NOTE: With this survey we've turned the LIFE family inside out to find out by age and sex, who reads LIFE and who doesn't. (Over 10 years of age practically nobody doesn't.) Detailed report of the survey findings on request.

A few weeks ago, questionnaires were mailed to a list of advertisers and executives of advertising agencies, asking:

> "Which of the magazines entering your
> home is read by the largest number of
> members of your family?"

In view of the findings on whole-family readership, as reported on the preceding page, the result of the 897 votes was no surprise:

LIFE	438
Time	201
Satevepost	125
Readers' Digest	114
Collier's	60
Cosmopolitan	36
New Yorker	26
American	25
Good Housekeeping	20
Liberty	18

The WHOLE family reads LIFE

Family Affairs

NEARLY all the growth in advertiser activity during preceding years had been the result of the accession of new converts to the ranks. In this period, however, a substantial part of the expansion was the result of the launching of new advertised products by established advertisers. The family of products idea came to the fore in a big way in 1910.

The new tendency was aggressively to build up a trade in a considerable number of items instead of confining efforts to a single specialty, thus taking fuller advantage of the selling organization, prestige with consumers and standing with the trade, as well as the opportunity of spreading the manufacturing overhead and filling in a seasonal lag on the established product. In some instances this took the form of introducing new products, in others of applying advertising to an old, unadvertised item.

The most spectacular manifestation of this trend was the launching of Crisco by Procter & Gamble. The program, which involved an expenditure of $3,000,000 in five years, was a landmark in planned distribution. The program was tested every step of the way and varying combinations of advertising, promotion, sampling and demonstration were tried out in different cities until the right formula was reached.

The period was not without a considerable amount of new activity, both in industries where wide development had already taken place and in several industries where advertising had been little tried.

A notable event in the food field was the packaging—and with it the advertising—of the last of the great staples, sugar. The American Sugar Refining Company had first tried out the packaging of lump sugar and the success of this, supported by a continually growing public demand for sanitary quality, led in 1912 to Domino granulated sugar in packages. Sugar began to emerge from the barrel. Not long after came Morton's salt in packages. The Morton Salt Company had previously been selling salt in bags under many different names. After a year of intensive distribution work and local advertising, it introduced the Morton packaged variety with a national advertising program in 1914.

Textiles and textile products represented a field in which there was considerable extension of activity in selling by trade-mark. Pacific Mills and Susquehanna Mills met with success in creating a consumer standing for, respectively, Serpentine Crepe and Sushana. Women's wearing of silk hosiery, then an outright luxury, received stimulus from McCallum, Onyx, Holeproof and others. Interwoven became prominent in national advertising in 1911. Paris Garter started in 1908. Numerous other advertisers of towels, handkerchiefs and underwear entered into negotiations with the consumer. With the advent of Alfred Decker & Cohn, Kuppenheimer and some twenty others, men's clothing became a leading exponent of trade-mark marketing.

The soda fountain had become a big business and around it many bottled beverages grew to fame on the wave of a tremendous public demand for "temperance beverages." Meanwhile the ice-cream soda, the soft drink and local option were making great inroads on the markets for alcoholic beverages. In an effort to stem the tide, brewers took to advertising and energetic sales methods. Their efforts centered upon developing the bottle trade and the shipping brewers — Anheuser-Busch, Schlitz, Pabst and others—moved upon the national market.

Housing was a new customer. Home construction had previously been concentrated in the hands of contractors and architects. They had all the say about building materials. In 1909 numerous manufacturers were awakening to the need of reaching the consumer, who had begun to exhibit a tendency to decide for himself on many things going into the finished home. One of the pace-setters was the American Radiator Company which had started advertising in modest space in 1902. On the theory that the best time to win notice is when business is dull, the company experimented with large space in 1908 and came out with a heavy sales increase.

Electrical appliances for home use represented still another newcomer. First to attempt to cultivate the national market was the Pacific Electric Heating Company (now the Edison General Electric Appliance Company) with its Hotpoint irons and other appliances. Previously the only advertising on such merchandise was done locally by the power companies. The Hotpoint effort introduced educational copy featuring the freedom from drudgery made possible by home use of electricity. The portable vacuum cleaner, a new product, became active around 1911, after a period in which house-to-house selling was the main reliance. Several firms were putting forward the idea of cleaning the home once a week instead of twice a year.

Additional manufacturers who had been content to go along with jobber domination of their selling came over into the advertiser way of doing business. The common experience was that each year the jobber's claims upon the manufacturer grew more insistent. He demanded further price concessions, more elaborate labels, special styles, until not infrequently the manufacturer had no alternative but to assume control of his own sales destiny. A fresh example of the benefits awaiting was provided by the Scott Paper Company, which in 1909 was making 300 different articles, the accumulation of years of doing business for the jobbers. The firm cut its line to five numbers, eliminated the jobber entirely in favor of selling direct to the retailer and advertised Scottissue towels to the consumer. One year after the change its business had increased 40 per cent.

Heartened by earlier examples, new competitors were finding courage to compete with the great trusts. Then, in the court-enforced dissolutions of several great combinations, including the American Tobacco Company and the Standard Oil Company, the trusts themselves produced new advertiser units. In time the companies which had been included in the combinations were among the leading advertisers. As a combination the American Tobacco Company had invested $10,000,000 in advertising in 1910. In 1913, after the dissolution, the successor companies expended a total of approximately $23,500,000.

One of the most interesting individual figures to rise in national advertiser ranks at this time was William Wrigley, Jr. Wrigley had started out as a jobber back in the 1890's and used premiums to get business from retailers. Once he got hold of a few dozen lamps and thinking they looked bare and empty, filled them with chewing gum. This seemed to make a hit with dealers and suggested the use of gum as a commodity.

Wrigley was close to the consumer. He went out with his sampling crews and got priceless information. He knew the trade no less intimately. He saw that his problem was to make the wholesalers want to sell to the retailers and the retailers want to buy. He offered counter scales free with $15 worth of gum, then showed the dealer how to talk, display and sell the gum. Then he offered a coffee grinder free with $38 worth of gum. The dealer sold the gum, cleaned up his profit and got the coffee mill free. Then Wrigley offered showcases, ladders, letter files, desks, chairs and other store equipment, after which he added home needs—baby buggies, silverware, lace curtains, dolls, bicycles. By 1905, though the way had not been without its difficulties, he carried a stock of $700,000 in premium goods. To get them the dealer merely had to bestir himself and sell gum.

In 1906 Wrigley set out to realize a long-cherished ambition—to market a brand of gum that would sell on a national scale. In three years he had made a national market for Spearmint. From the start he had never neglected the consumer, using car-cards and outdoor advertising to help the dealer move the gum off the counter. For the 1906 effort he enlarged his appropriation materially to $250,000 and not long after signed a million-dollar car-card contract. By 1914 his annual appropriation was $2,000,000, daily newspapers having been added to the program to the extent of $600,000. Wrigley was also a proponent of consumer sampling, conducting the largest sampling project in business history when he mailed a full package of Doublemint gum to every telephone subscriber in the country.

The resourceful and prolific William Hamlin Childs was another leading spirit of the time. He developed not one but three important advertisers—the Bon Ami Company, the Barrett Company, and the affiliated Congoleum Company. Roofing was supposed to be a product that couldn't be advertised because the materials were not the distinctive possession of any one company. Childs persisted with the idea of reaching the consumer, which had worked out rather well with the Bon Ami proposition, until the idea of advertising a "prescription" rather than the materials was developed. From this came the Barrett Specification Roof. Congoleum also was a pioneer project and its example was largely responsible for subsequent development of the advertising of other floor coverings.

The Victor Talking Machine Company had emerged as a large-scale advertiser in 1908 and it established a distributive machine of notable strength and efficiency. The musical instrument field had been a morass of discounts from the consumer up and many other unsound practices prevailed. Under Eldridge R. Johnson the company established a high degree of control over its dealer relations and introduced real marketing skill in the field.

Few events in these years attracted as much interest in the advertising trade as the large magazine advertising program launched by the National Casket Company in 1909. Although there had been some casket advertising before, this campaign was an attempt to do a public service in educating people to choose quality. There was an identifying mark on each casket and the firm took measures to identify the local undertakers with the campaign.

The most impressive events of all in the advertiser realm, however, were those taking place in the automobile industry. By 1914 the motor car had achieved second ranking among national advertisers, headed only by foodstuffs and standing in advance of toilet articles and household appliances. Automobile accessories and motorcycles were in fifth place. After farming, transportation and the textile industry, it was employing more capital and workers than any other branch of business activity.

In many respects the automobile

1910

TOTAL population now 91,972,226. . . . Boy Scouts of America organized. . . . Los Angeles *Times* building destroyed by bomb explosion in which twenty-one persons die. . . . Edward Douglas White appointed chief justice of the Supreme Court to succeed the late Melville W. Fuller. . . . Postal savings bank system established.

Robert Tinsman, one of the managers of the Root Newspaper Association, heads the Federal Advertising Agency. . . . General Motors to spend a million in advertising. . . . John E. Kennedy rejoins Lord & Thomas. . . . C. C. Winningham appointed advertising manager of Hudson Motor Company. . . . "There ought to be less watching of competitors and more attention paid to the consumer"—Thomas A. Edison. . . . Death of James B. McMahon, noted sales manager of N. K. Fairbank Company. . . . Saunders Norvell resigns as president of the Norvell-Shapleigh Hardware Company to organize the Hardware Publishing Company at St. Louis.

The completely equipped motor car is sold for the first time. . . . Eugene W. Parsons appointed advertising manager of Chicago *Tribune*. . . . F. R. Feland joins George Batten Company. . . . Cornelius Kelly establishes Kelly-Smith Company, Inc., publishers representatives. . . . Wall Street commencing to sell bonds by mail. . . . Powers & Armstrong Company becomes F. Wallis Armstrong Company. . . . Soda fountain business growing fast, while alcoholic drink sales drop $110,000,000. . . . List of new spellings announced by Simplified Spelling Board and approved by President Roosevelt and much advertising copy is now exprest in clipt words.

A LONG DRIVE TESTS A HORSE'S STRENGTH

LONG SERVICE REVEALS CHARACTER

A Chinese Proverb

FRANK
PRESBREY
CO.
Advertising since
1896

CHARLES PRESBREY...PRESIDENT

247 PARK AVENUE, NEW YORK

228 N. LA SALLE STREET, CHICAGO

ABOUT THAT
SEVENTH
SUGAR BOWL

Thirty-six years have passed since that late June day when Farm Journal received an express package from Printers' Ink. It came unannounced. In it was a handsome solid silver sugar bowl made by Tiffany. Engraved on the bowl were these words:

Awarded June 25, 1902

by PRINTERS' INK, "The Little Schoolmaster"
in the Art of Advertising, to
the FARM JOURNAL

After a canvassing of merits extending over a period of half a year, that paper, among all those published in the United States, has been pronounced the one that best serves its purpose as an educator and counsellor for the agricultural population, and as an effective and economical medium for communicating with them through its advertising columns.

In its issue of January 22, 1902, Printers' Ink had announced that it would award its seventh sugar bowl to the best agricultural paper in the country. Nominations were in order.

Those nominations flocked in. Friends of Farm Journal flooded Printers' Ink offices with unsolicited praise for their favorite farm paper. The Lecturer of the National Grange wrote: "I have noticed your Sugar Bowl offer in Printers' Ink and desire to give my testimony in favor of the gem of all agricultural papers — the Farm Journal... By all odds it is away in the lead as best serving the interests of the farmer, as a producer, a man, and a citizen."

Farmers sent messages like these: "No agricultural paper is doing so much to educate the farmer"... "Its articles go right to the heart of things"... "The real interests of the farmer (and especially of his wife) are catered to with a care, thoroughness, and withal a brevity that make the paper a model of its kind"... "Its advertising columns are a handbook for farmers' supplies that for usefulness and reliability have no equal in the world."

Cyrus Curtis wrote Printers' Ink that in his opinion Farm Journal was "the best of them all in a sense that it reaches the largest number of farmers solely on its merits, that it seems to get at the hearts of the people with its plain, homely common sense, and that farmers feel that it contains more practical information than most other publications and mixes it with a good deal of ginger."

Five hundred other agricultural papers were eligible for the honor — but when the votes were counted, Printers' Ink found that Farm Journal's friends outnumbered all the rest. So the seventh Sugar Bowl came to Farm Journal.

Farm Journal was only 25 years old then. Today Farm Journal is 61 years old. Thousands of farmers were reading it then; millions read it today with a confidence and feeling of personal intimacy that time alone can build. Farm Journal used to look quaint and old-fashioned; now it looks, and is, modern, fresh, and alive — but still serving the one basic purpose that always has shaped it. That purpose: *to help farm people get the greatest possible satisfaction out of farm life.*

Four-day writer-to-reader service is the latest step in the accomplishment of that grand purpose.

Facsimile of original heading

NOW.."THE NATIONAL NEWS MAGAZINE FOR THE MODERN FARM FAMILY"

industry showed the way in developing a unified concept of the marketing operation. With the passing of the days when a customer would pay out $100 or more in hard cash merely to gain the privilege of waiting in line to get a car, the manufacturers addressed themselves in earnest to solving the riddle of distribution. They strengthened and trained their dealer organizations, studied with keen eyes the efficiencies to be had through strategic planning of sales territories, policed dealers constantly to insure maximum effective selling effort to the consumer, exerted every possible effort toward making buying attractive in the dealer's establishment, provided the maximum possible in sales and advertising helps. They kept ceaseless tab on consumer preferences and engineered their products to the public taste. And they consistently sought to broaden the market base by forcing down price levels as rapidly as was consistent with manufacturing progress.

By all odds the dominant figure was one Henry Ford. He it was who simplified the automobile problem and gave the consumer the low-priced automobile and introduced mass production and mass distribution of motor cars. He made one car in one style at one chassis price and manufactured, advertised and sold it in such quantities as to astound not only his fellow manufacturers in Detroit, but the entire civilized world.

The common impression has it that Henry Ford's success lay entirely in his production genius. The Ford jokes helped some. And so did the Ford flair for the dramatic, publicity-winning gesture—the refunding of $50 to every person who purchased a car in 1914, the $10,000,000 gift to his employees, the raising of minimum wages to $5 a day. But the price did it. So runs the story. It is perhaps founded in part on the absence of Ford consumer advertising for some years during and after the war.

The facts are that the Ford organization embodied the greatest sales vision of the times. Credit for a good deal of it indubitably belongs to Henry Ford personally. For the rest, he had the sense and judgment to surround himself with skilled sales aides like Norval Hawkins and give them rein.

Whatever its proportionate sources, that sales vision resulted in building what by 1912 could be termed the greatest sales organization in the world. The company had more agents, more dealers, more salesmen employed by agents, more company representatives coming in contact with the public than any other in its field and few, if any, equals in any line of commercial endeavor. The planning, the organization, the system, the follow-through on the minutest detail relating to the consumer sale were without parallel.

Via the combination route the family of products idea was finding application in the automobile industry. The most conspicuous, and lasting, example was the formation in 1908 of the General Motors Corporation as a consolidation of the Buick, Cadillac, Oldsmobile and other interests. There were observers who, mindful of the history of the bicycle combine, predicted that the new project would soon go to pot because it would probably eliminate advertising. Examination of linage tabulations of a later day suggests that the forecasts were slightly deficient in accuracy.

In the wake of the automobile came many advertisers of equipment and accessories, most conspicuous of which were the big rubber companies. Among the leading entrepreneurs were Frank A. Seiberling, head of the Goodyear Tire & Rubber Company, and Harvey Firestone, both of whom became large-scale advertisers of pneumatic tires for motor cars after relatively obscure beginnings in the carriage-tire business.

The program inaugurated by the Timken companies in 1912 was a stimulating venture into the largely unexplored tactic of advertising the integral product to the consumer. After careful planning and investigation, the Timken Roller Bearing Company and the Timken-Detroit Axle Company decided, as a means of "future business insurance," to widen the reputation of their products so that they would have a distinct selling value to the manufacturer who incorporated them in his finished motor cars. The increased tendency of automobile dealers to talk bearings and axles more than they had before the campaign began demonstrated the soundness of such an advertising policy.

A new public interest in things pertaining to outdoor life, largely attributable to the automobile, created a major advance in the advertising of outdoor and sports equipment beginning with 1909. Brought into the sphere of activity were advertisers of firearms, boats, tents and hammocks, camp supplies and fishing equipment.

A forgotten episode of 1914 provided what was thought to be a threat to the future of the automobile industry. This was the career of an almost-advertiser—the cycle-car. In a country not unnoted for sudden and violent enthusiasms the cyclecar struck up a national fever which has had few equals, if any.

Here, at last, was "everyman's equipage." The cyclecar was a small, low, narrow-gauge motor vehicle, to sell at from $295 to $400. No sooner had the idea been proposed than factories sprang up everywhere. Cyclecar trade papers started. Newspapers printed huge and endless feature stories about them. There was a hysterical scramble among automobile dealers to get aboard, one manufacturer accepting deposits on more than 15,000 cars. In addition to the vast amount of free news space, there was heavy advertising by makers and agents. It was perhaps the best advertised industrial inaugural in American business history. The actual display of a completed cyclecar was an occasion for calling out the police reserves to control the crowds.

All at once the bubble burst. There were orders, but no reorders. Manufacturers soon found that they had to open up a new dealership every time they sold a car—and the vehicle sold was always a demonstrator. Before long cyclecars couldn't be given away. Bankruptcies came fast. There were warehouses containing hundreds of thousands of dollars' worth of unassembled parts for which there was no market.

The net of it all was that the cyclecar was absolutely out of joint with the transportation market and with the American people. The Ford selling at $440 was the nearest real competitor and it had a standard tread and the owner could consider himself the owner of a real automobile. The difference in

The Song that sells millions

A principle that measures the "immeasurables" in advertising

THE essence of advertising, as of life itself, is fundamentally immeasurable.

We can weigh the results of advertising. But we cannot weigh the creative vision, the sure insight, the rich treasure of experience that produce great advertising.

These are beyond yardsticks, as the genius of Shakespeare is beyond the rules of grammar. The secret of advertising success lies not in a static rule-of-thumb. It lies in a dynamic Principle of Action, a principle that includes both measurables and immeasurables — that reveals the living, spontaneous nature of creative thinking.

The essence of Salesmanship-in-print

The President of Lord & Thomas expressed this principle in an address delivered in June, 1936, to the members of the Advertising Federation of America. He said:

> "What is the essence of salesmanship-in-print? Is it purely a matter of instinct, or is it a near science open to inquiry? There is some of both in it. But this much we can rationalize:
>
> "FIRST: there must be a central idea that when lifted to the top instantly arrests the self-interest of the reader

and answers instantly the question in every consumer's mind, 'WHAT DOES IT MEAN TO ME?'

"Ofttimes the idea which intrigues the advertiser most, intrigues the consumer least.

"SECOND: having the central idea, it must...be given enticement—drama.

"THIRD: having given it drama, the presentation must be clothed with deep-felt conviction and sincerity.

"But you still may not realize all the fruits of successful advertising until you apply the final commandment of 'salesmanship-in-print' — MAKE IT SING! Make the meaning of your advertising compact —wrap up its idea, its news, its drama into a dynamic whole capable of lightning impact.

"It takes salesmanship-in-print to weld all these elements into a consummate whole—to 'Make It Sing!'"

Science plus artistry in Advertising

Thus in 1936 were summed up the discoveries and experiences that have come to Lord & Thomas during 63 years of advertising practice.

Their very success has brought wide acceptance of these fundamentals, yet their true meaning eludes many who think they can be reduced to mechanical formulas.

But seasoned advertising men know that words alone do not make the great music of advertising. Between the lines of the above quotation should be read the vital necessity of creative imagination.

Thousands of violinists, perfect in technique, never approach genius as interpretative artists. The same truth holds in advertising. The song of salesmanship is a marriage of science *and* artistry . . . of measurables *and* immeasurables . . . of market research *and* true inspiration.

Lord & Thomas, today as ever, insist upon this dual nature of the creative process. That is why "Make It Sing!" inspires growth and invention and discovery in advertising.

LORD & THOMAS
ADVERTISING

price did not compensate the prospective cyclecar purchaser for his sacrifice of pride in riding close to the ground in an imitation of the real article when the genuine could be had for approximately $100 more.

The cyclecar fever established a precept whose more conscientious observance might have saved the loss of many an industrial venture: Public curiosity is not to be mistaken for buying interest.

1911

FIRST transcontinental flight by Calbraith P. Rodgers—New York to Pasadena in forty-nine days and sixty-eight hops; total flying time eight-two hours. . . . Supreme Court orders dissolution of Standard Oil Company and of American Tobacco Company as combinations in restraint of trade. . . . Conference of Progressive Republicans meets in Chicago and adopts declaration of principles.

The Cadillac has an electric starter, developed by C. F. Kettering. . . . Crowell Publishing Company acquires *American Magazine*. . . . "Please bear in mind that advertising never added one dollar to the value of any article advertised"—Hugh Chalmers. . . . Death of Joseph Pulitzer, proprietor of the New York *World*. . . . William Wrigley, Jr., signs contract with Street Railways Advertising Company for $1,002,171.90 in space for Spearmint gum. . . .

Frank J. Campbell and Henry T. Ewald establish the Campbell-Ewald Company at Detroit. . . . Cyrus Curtis acquires *Country Gentleman*. . . . William Randolph Hearst purchases *Good Housekeeping*. . . . Standard Oil Company appoints H. K. McCann, former advertising manager of New York Telephone Company, as advertising manager. . . . James Rodgers, advertising manager for Harper & Brothers, dies. . . . United Publishers Corporation formed to acquire David Williams Company, Root Securities Company and Class Journal Company. . . . Oatmeal company points out that Boston consumes twenty-two times as much oatmeal as a certain State with low average intelligence, while in three prison schools for wayward boys only one-third of the inmates ever had oatmeal, and those rarely.

FIRST
(and only)

In 1911, when Printers' Ink was 23, Linford Smith started Oral Hygiene. The format of Printers' Ink was the inspiration for Oral Hygiene's format. But—from that point on—Oral Hygiene began to be itself.

It originated controlled circulation. It gave to the dental profession its first (and only) magazine devoted to the numerous and ever-changing *human* problems of dental practice; practice building, practice management, patient relationships, public clinic competition, unethical competition, political and social developments affecting dentistry—and the many other human problems faced by dentists daily.

It gave the profession its first (and only) magazine of controversy—its first (and only) meeting-place-in-print where dentists may freely speak their minds.

Oral Hygiene is still the *only* dental magazine of its kind—it doesn't compete for reader-interest with other dental papers.

Editorially lively, courageous, enterprising, original —it has won astonishing reader-interest. Advertisers profit by that . reader-interest. And they get the largest CCA-audited circulation in the field. So they use more space than in any other dental paper, because

ORAL HYGIENE
consistently leads in results

Oral Hygiene Publications, 1005 Liberty Avenue, Pittsburgh, Pennsylvania

LIFE-LINES of

HEARST MAGAZINES INC. celebrates its 35th year of successful publishing.

Originating new standards of excellence while adhering to sound publishing ideas, the nine Hearst magazines have each achieved leadership.

Hearst magazines tell the story of the incomparably fine American way of living — of nationally advertised products that have made the nation supreme in fashion, comfort and efficiency.

Under Hearst ownership, the story of these publications runs from the first electric lamp to air-conditioning... from the first bicycle to the automobile's automatic shift, and the transcontinental air-sleeper.

LIFE-LINES OF HEARST MAGAZINES

Founded in	Founded in
1846	1885
Town & Country	Good Housekeeping
1867	1886
Harper's Bazaar	Cosmopolitan
1868	1896
Pictorial Review-Delineator	House Beautiful
1871	1903
American Druggist	MoToR

1846
First Hearst
Magazine Founded

1907
MoToR BoaTinG

Pioneers Yesterday and Tomorrow

LEADERSHIP

The present vigor and progress of Hearst magazines is shown in the latest annual advertising linage record of Printers' Ink.

In a group of 35 magazine leaders of 1937, the gains of Hearst magazines, compared with those of the rest of the group, were substantially greater. The same comparative record for 1938 will, by every indication, show continued Hearst supremacy.

Leadership Tomorrow

The past was brilliant, but Hearst magazines are concerned with scoops to come. What novelist can best depict the stirring life of today? What illustrator, with a new, striking technique, will capture the public? What new excellence in printing can be created?

What valuable new services in fashion or utility can be advanced? What new industrialists will use the powerful merchandising influence of Hearst magazines to establish names and products in the millions of modern homes these publications serve?

Those lines on circulation and advertising charts which show through the years the upward sweep of Hearst magazines form the best tribute their staffs can pay to the creative genius of the founder of Hearst Magazines Inc., and to the early publishers whose properties he magnificently developed.

HEARST MAGAZINES Inc.

Truth—and Consequences

THE dictates of good business, as well as of conscience, had long suggested to reputable advertisers, agents and publishers the value of rooting out abuses of advertising. As has been seen, considerable progress was made in this direction, particularly by certain publishers, and this continued. In addition, with the fading of the "let the buyer beware" code of trading there was a trend to increased honesty in the conduct of general business.

The results of this pioneering work, however, were largely in terms of eliminating the more glaring abuses. And the activities were largely confined to certain classes of advertisers — the patent medicine fakes, the wildcat stock promoters and disreputable devices of one kind and another. For the most part, attention had been centered upon the totally worthless or harmful product rather than upon misrepresentation of products which had value for some purposes.

Even in the courts there had been no suggestion that an advertiser might not say just about anything he pleased in advertising an article in more or less common use.

Then came a growing belief that the character of the message should follow the patterns of honest delineation. It reached the articulate stage at the Boston convention of the Associated Advertising Clubs of America, when a strong sentiment for suppression of fraudulent, misleading, exaggerated and indecent advertising became evident with the adoption of the "Truth in Advertising" motto.

The Boston convention had come forward with no plan for action, however. John Irving Romer, editor of PRINTERS' INK, noted that fact and set to work. You can get 99 per cent of the public to agree that burglary is a very wicked thing and should be suppressed, he reasoned, but the other 1 per cent will break into your house and walk off with your silver. That is, unless there is a law which makes burglary a crime and a police force that will enforce the law.

Aroused sentiment, he pointed out, had had its beneficial effects in cleaning up the brazen transgressions. But its greatest value had been uncapitalized—namely, the opportunity which it offered for laying a firm foundation upon which might be erected a structure for making the sentiment effective. "The time has arrived," he said, "when we can do something more than *talk* about suppression of objectionable advertising."

To this end Romer engaged the services of Harry D. Nims, well-known corporation lawyer and author of the standard work "Nims on Unfair Competition," to study the possibilities of a legal attack on dishonest advertising. He examined the whole subject from the earliest time of advertising.

The potentialities of the common law were seen to be meager. Civil action by the damaged consumer was possible, but had little value in preventing fraudulent statements because damage had to be proved. And oftentimes the damage on this basis would be very small.

Statutes specifically directed against fraudulent advertising were in existence in several States. But prosecutions were rare. Only one conviction had been obtained under the New York law since its passage in 1904. In the first place, there was no agency for enforcement. In the second, the statutes were framed so that the word "knowingly" was included as a condition of the misdeed. The burden was upon the prosecution to prove that deliberate intent to mislead was in the advertiser's mind when the advertisement was written—an all but impossible task.

The Admen's Club of Atlanta had exposed a lying advertisement and caused the arrest of the advertiser. He escaped conviction on a technicality, but the incident was important in demonstrating that business men were willing to lend a hand in maintaining honest standards once something had been started.

Many felt that the responsibility for dishonest advertising rested with the publisher. But the Nims study demonstrated the necessity of getting at the prime offender. The publisher, with many patrons, was up against it to determine in every case whether an advertising statement was honest or not.

Moreover, the most honest of publishers were constantly in competition with others less scrupulous and the latter would be quick to take advantage of a mistake in judgment.

The best course appeared to be by law directed at the advertiser and the adoption of a uniform version of that law by each State. Hence the PRINTERS' INK Model Statute, which was drawn in these words:

Any person, firm, corporation or association who, with intent to sell or in any wise dispose of merchandise, securities, service, or anything offered by such person, firm, corporation or association, directly or indirectly, to the public for sale or distribution, or with intent to increase the consumption thereof, or to induce the public in any manner to enter into any obligation relating thereto, or to acquire title thereto, or an interest therein, makes, publishes, disseminates, circulates, or places before the public, or causes, directly or indirectly, to be made, published, disseminated, circulated, or placed before the public, in this State, in a newspaper or other publication, or in the form of a book, notice, handbill, poster, bill, circular, pamphlet, or letter, or in any other way, an advertisement of any sort regarding merchandise, securities, service, or anything so offered to the public, which advertisement contains any assertion, representation or statement of fact which is untrue, deceptive or misleading, shall be guilty of a misdemeanor.

However, Romer emphasized in the strongest words at his command, it was not enough merely to have a law. There must be some provision for putting it to work and keeping it effective. "We are against any law," he asserted, "unless at the same time it is made somebody's business to watch out for infractions of the laws, to collect evidence and see that the case is pressed."

To this end Romer offered the blueprints for the policing operation. Having in mind the grievance committee of the bar association, he suggested that the A. A. C. A. and the member clubs individually undertake the job of making the Model Statute a working piece of legislation wherever it was enacted into law.

The new statute was first passed in Ohio in 1913, with Minnesota close behind. Washington and New Jersey joined the ranks in the same year.

The first tangible result of Romer's emphasis on the importance of establishment of an active police power to make the statute effective was the Vigilance Committee of the Minneapolis Advertising Forum, organized in 1913. The movement spread quickly and within the year twenty-four similar committees were operating throughout the country. The A. A. C. A. formed a National Vigilance Committee to foster this development and the Advertising Affiliation recommended the same course to its member clubs.

In 1914, the Minneapolis club, under Mac Martin, expanded the move in the direction which it has ultimately taken elsewhere. A Bureau of Fair Competition was organized by the Minneapolis merchants in conjunction with the Vigilance Committee to conduct investigations of all advertisements suspected of being untruthful.

By 1915 the statute was the law in eight States, and had been passed in amended form in three States. Six others had laws based on a less effective statute, in addition to three which had similar statutes in 1911. A number of cities, including Chicago, Los Angeles, Louisville and New York, had adopted the Model Statute.

The Associated Advertising Clubs of the World (new name assumed by the A. A. C. A. in 1914) paved the way in 1915 for the transition of the policing movement from a volunteer to a paid operation. The National Vigilance Committee set about establishing local committees with paid secretaries to take charge of the work—Minneapolis, Milwaukee and Boston organizing on that basis during the year. The movement was now crystallized in its modern form and the committees began to use the improved and more accurately descriptive name of today—the Better Business Bureau.

The Model Statute was the chief factor in bringing the Better Business Bureau into existence and it became the principal weapon of the Bureaus in their ceaseless efforts in behalf of honest advertising. Ultimately the Bureau movement split off from the advertising clubs and became an independently financed and operated institution in American business life. Today fifty-six local Bureaus guard the public against fraudulent advertising and selling methods and promote integrity and confidence in all phases of business. The National Better Business Bureau, descendant of the National Vigilance Committee and established in its present-day form in 1925, deals with national cases and serves as a clearing-house for the local Bureaus.

The Model Statute is today incorporated in the laws of twenty-five States, while a number of others have modified versions of it. Unfortunately, the law will not stop all forms of dishonesty in advertising, for it deals only with statements which are untrue, deceptive or misleading. But no statute can be drawn which will achieve complete truthfulness without at the same time working injustice to a great many honest men. Dishonest statements of opinion cannot be prevented by law until some method is discovered whereby men may be made honest by legislative enactment.

Nevertheless, as administered by the Better Business Bureaus, the Model Statute has directly and indirectly saved the public millions of dollars annually by protecting the unwary against the fake advertiser, as can be verified by recourse to current accounts of the everyday activities of the Bureaus. And the value to the honest advertiser of the policing and educational activities of the Bureaus in building public confidence in advertising is incalculable.

Moving parallel with the truth in advertising sentiment was a no less vigorous demand for truth in publishers' circulation statements, and by 1912 it showed definite signs of coming to a head.

The better publishers, of course, had taken steps on their own initiative to clear up the mysteries of circulation. A number had thrown open their books to advertisers for inspection and thorough analysis, several had guaranteed rebates of the figure proved to be below that stated. But the honest publisher was still at a distinct disadvantage, for the inclination to truthfulness was by no means universal and the accurate statement was likely to suffer by comparison with those which were exaggerated.

1912

NEW MEXICO and Arizona admitted to the Union, completing the forty-eight States. . . . *Titanic,* on maiden voyage from Liverpool to New York, strikes iceberg and sinks with loss of 1,635 lives. . . . Election returns: Wilson 435, Roosevelt 88, Taft 8. . . . Act to regulate wireless telegraphy authorized.

H. K. McCann establishes the H. K. McCann Company. . . . Boston *Herald* purchases the *Traveler.* . . . Court upholds Curtis Publishing Company in refusing Winton copy which reflected on other motor cars. . . . Ruthrauff & Ryan founded by W. B. Ruthrauff and F. B. Ryan. . . Bruce Barton joins *Vogue.* . . . James Wright Brown purchases controlling interest in *Editor & Publisher.* . . . "Some follow-up systems are like the little dog running after the train—they couldn't do anything with it if they caught it"—John Lee Mahin. . . . Death of Whitelaw Reid. . . . E. F. Corbin with *Successful Farming.* . . . Harry J. Prudden appointed advertising manager of the New York *Tribune.* . . . Arthur Capper purchases *Oklahoma Farmer.*

Thomas H. Beck, former sales and advertising manager for Crisco, appointed general sales manager of P. F. Collier & Son. . . . Dr. Harvey Wiley, chief of the U. S. Bureau of Chemistry, joins *Good Housekeeping* as contributing editor in charge of the Bureau of Foods, Sanitation and Health. . . . The "I Am" craze appears as scores of advertisers imitate Robert Davis' famous "I Am the Printing Press" advertisement for Hoe presses. . . . Death of Richard S. Thain, pioneer Chicago advertising man. . . . W. W. Chapin acquires San Francisco *Call.* . . . Chamber of Commerce of the United States organized. . . . *Success* fails.

If Your Aim

IS TO PENETRATE THE DEPARTMENT STORE

YOUR MESSAGE GOES STRAIGHT AS AN ARROW
In The
DEPARTMENT STORE ECONOMIST

IF YOUR sales program AIMS at bigger business you'll score a bull's eye by advertising in the Department Store Economist. It misses no one concerned with buying and pushing your goods . . . reaches Major Executives, Merchandise Managers and Buyers, and offers the LARGEST CIRCULATION IN ITS FIELD . . . Department Store Economist not only helps you to put your line in—it helps in putting it across. Be in the one medium that gives you complete, controlled selected coverage. If you sell to and through department stores here's the magazine that goes twice monthly to a selected list of department store heads directly responsible for moving your merchandise.

DEPARTMENT STORE
Economist
A CHILTON PUBLICATION

239 West 39th Street, New York City

| Chestnut Street at 56th | 29 East Madison St. | 901 American Bank Bldg. |
| Philadelphia | Chicago | Pittsburgh |

When "Printers' Ink" first saw the light of day and was being measured for its first pair of three-cornered pants, "The Circular," was a husky 19-year-old youngster in long trousers, almost ready to vote.

Checking through our 1888 bound volumes, we find the following prominent companies then advertising—and in 1937-1938, 50 years later, the same firms still making use of the advertising pages of this leading jewelry publication:

BLANCARD & CO.
CHEEVER-TWEEDY & CO.
ELGIN NATIONAL WATCH CO.
GORHAM MANUFACTURING CO.
H. O. HURLBURT & SON
L. & M. KAHN
KREMENTZ & CO.
L. LELONG & BROTHER
NEW HAVEN CLOCK CO.
WILLIAM F. NYE

OSTBY & BARTON
PAIRPOINT MFG. CO.
D. C. PERCIVAL & CO.
WM. ROGERS MFG. CO.
 (INT. SILVER CO.)
SETH THOMAS CLOCK CO.
WALTHAM WATCH CO.
R. WALLACE & SONS
WATERBURY CLOCK CO.
J. R. WOOD & SONS

This is indeed a tribute to "The Circular," which for almost 70 years has been the authority and recognized leader of the jewelry and allied trades.

Advertisers throughout these years have chosen this publication to give their products the greatest sales dominance it is possible to obtain in any one advertising medium.

We are now looking forward to and planning for the celebration in 1944 of our 75th—Diamond—Anniversary of service to the jewelry trade.

The
JEWELERS' CIRCULAR-KEYSTONE

239 West 39th Street

A CHILTON
PUBLICATION

New York City

The American Advertisers Association had made 1,058 examinations of publishers' circulations by 1912, but it had never been successful in getting more than a few dozen advertisers to join in supporting the work. Some publishers employed auditing organizations to verify their statements, but this wasn't any too satisfactory either. At least five different organizations, co-operative and private, were offering audits, but there was no unity of viewpoint as to what constituted an audit or who was qualified to be an auditor.

The need of a properly qualified organization to make independent outside investigations and act as a clearing-house for all circulation information became more and more evident. Reputable publishers became increasingly impatient of what was described by James Keeley, then general manager of the Chicago *Tribune,* in a scathing address at the Baltimore convention of the A. A. C. A. in 1913, as the "humiliation of the honest publisher caused by the circulation liar." And Emery Mapes, of Cream of Wheat, was stirring things up a bit with a series of lawsuits demanding circulation rebates from certain publishers.

Sentiment was translated into action with the formation of two audit movements, the Advertising Audit Association in the West and the Bureau of Verified Circulations in the East. Between them they had the support of virtually all of the national advertising and publishing associations.

The advantage of coalition to the common end soon became apparent and the two groups merged, while still in the formative stage, as the Advertising Audit Association and Bureau of Verified Circulations. A. W. Erickson was named temporary chairman. Ninety days of intensive work followed and in May of 1914 the new project was launched at an organization meeting in Chicago, with Louis Bruch as the first president. Its name was simplified to the Audit Bureau of Circulations.

Into whose mind came first the idea of this co-operative effort to end the circulation mess, no one knows. O. C. Harn, then in charge of sales and advertising for the National Lead Company, was a leading figure in the Eastern movement and he has had more to do with the evolution of the Bureau than any other single person. He served seven terms as president prior to 1927, then became managing director, in which capacity he has continued ever since. Conspicuous in the Western movement was Stanley Clague, Chicago advertising agent, who served as managing director for a number of years prior to his death in 1927.

The Audit Bureau was a unique experiment in industrial self-government—the past tense of the verb signifying the fact that it has long ceased to be an experiment. It was, and is, financed principally by the sellers of advertising, the publishers. The control of its operations, however, rests with the buyers, advertisers and advertising agents.

The organization process was not an easy one. The idea had to be sold. Many perfectly honorable publishers were, humanly, reluctant about delivering their circulation affairs into the hands of an outside organization. The natural antagonism of the interests of seller and buyer had to be surmounted. And the working out of procedural techniques in the years to follow was

Make your advertising more effective

by using this information from the experience records of 18 outstanding advertising specialists of wide acceptance and recognition.

THE HANDBOOK OF ADVERTISING

Edited by

E. B. Weiss, F. C. Kendall and C. B. Larrabee

Just Published

530 pages, 6 x 9
$5.00

What this book gives you and who wrote the material

Earnest Elmo Calkins, Introduction

Harford Powel, Advertising Copy

Deane Uptegrove, Advertising Art

Laurance B. Siegfried, Type and Typography

Jack J. Boyle, Media

H. K. Boice, Radio

G. S. McMillan, Organizing the Advertising Department

Arnold Rau, Agency Organization

Frederick C. Kendall, The Advertising Appropriation

William T. Laing, Advertising Inquiries

John Allen Murphy, Industrial Advertising

L. J. Raymond, Direct Advertising

E. B. Weiss, Merchandising the Advertising

C. B. Larrabee, Packaging

Elsie M. Rushmore, Consumer Contests

Howard W. Dunk, Premium Advertising

N. J. Leigh, Window Displays

Frank R. Coutant, Testing Advertising Copy

WHAT are your questions about advertising today? Do you want touchstones for judging your copy? Are you concerned with latest trends in advertising art? Have you a problem relating to selection of proper media? Are you considering a radio program? Are you looking for a more effective way to merchandise your advertising? Are you planning consumer contests or premium offers?

Whatever your question—if it is concerned in any way with current advertising practice—this book can help you. Eighteen advertising specialists of wide experience and achievement present in this handbook brilliant treatments of current advertising problems, techniques, and principles. They offer you the benefit of their experienced views on questions within their specific specialties. As a result, this book deals with advertising as it is practiced today by the most successful advertisers.

"Complete, up-to-the-minute, and significant. Altogether, the book has a finger on the pulse of the buying public. It lives up to its title."—*Barron's*

"Every important element in the creation and production of advertising is treated by one who knows his job and is capable of setting forth its requirements."—*Wall Street Journal*

"Can be read with profit by the business man who knows nothing about advertising, by the business man who knows a great deal about it and wants to know more, by the advertising specialist and by the beginner."—*Printers' Ink*

Send for a copy on approval

McGRAW - HILL BOOK COMPANY, Inc.
330 W. 42nd St.   **New York, N. Y.**

fraught with complexities which at times seemed insurmountable in the steaming debates at the early membership conventions.

Immediately following the organization meeting, the Bureau set promptly to work, organizing a corps of auditors. First came publishers' statements, then audits were made as rapidly as possible. Many publishers held aloof from participation at first, but in time the recognition of its services became such that by far the greater part of the aggregate publication circulations in the United States—and a substantial portion in Canadian publications—came under A. B. C. audits.

Truthful data on circulation totals were not the only purpose which it served, however. From 1907 on, advertisers had begun to take an interest, scattered but growing, in learning other facts about circulation—the character of methods used in securing subscriptions, geographical distribution, percentage of newsstand and subscription circulation and other figures which might give insight into the character and quality of the circulation. To a certain degree the Audit Bureau was formed in response to a demand for more extensive, as well as accurate, circulation figures and the gathering and checking of that sort of information became an important part of its work.

The general urge toward improvement in standards and practice found expression in several important events in the field of organized advertising. This latest phase was marked by a trend to specialization, and it witnessed the founding of nearly all of the major national groups of the present day.

In 1910 the Association of Na-

tional Advertising Managers was formed with E. St. Elmo Lewis as the first president. Its primary objectives included creation of greater confidence in advertised goods, elimination of fake advertising and promotion of the conduct of educational work among retailers. In 1914 the organization changed its name to the Association of National Advertisers and embarked upon the enlarged program of research and study in advertising and sales methods which characterizes the body's work today.

The beginnings of a permanent organization of advertising agents came at the Boston convention of the Associated Advertising Clubs of America in 1911, when a resolution to form an agency association was adopted. At the Dallas convention in the following year Frank Presbrey was named chairman of a committee to further the project. For several years the work went forward on a local basis, with associations being formed in several cities. From that came the establishment in 1917 of the American Association of Advertising Agencies.

Following several years in which it had built the painted bulletin business from a relatively disorganized state to a recognized, standardized medium, the Painted Display Advertising Association became the Outdoor Advertising Association in 1914. At that time it expanded its scope to include electric signs.

To promote the interests of advertising to the farm market, the Agricultural Publishers Association was formed in 1914, with Burridge D. Butler, of *Prairie Farmer,* as the first president. The Quoin Club of New York enlarged its scope to promote magazine advertising along broad lines and publishers and

264

general managers were made eligible to what in the early days had been an organization of advertising managers. As a sub-title to its name the group adopted the words, National Periodical Association.

To make its activities more effective and more truly national in scope, the Federation of Trade Press Associations set about in 1914 to reorganize as an association of individual publishers rather than as a federation of local organizations. From this came the Associated Business Papers, Inc.

The year 1914 also witnessed a movement to the establishment of local clubs of financial advertising men. Clubs at Pittsburgh and New York were formed. These activities led to the founding of a national body in 1916—the Financial Advertisers Association.

Meantime the A. A. C. A. had been growing at a rapid rate. In 1911 there were forty-four member clubs affiliated with the association and its membership roll totaled 3,000. An educational campaign of lectures and study courses in advertising was adopted in 1913.

At the Toronto convention in 1914 delegates from a number of foreign countries were present and the organization became the Associated Advertising Clubs of the World. At the same meeting was adopted a set of standards committing members to consider the public interest in advertising, refrain from misleading statements and attacks on competitors.

It was during these years, incidentally, that a general public interest in the advertising process became manifest. Several of the magazines took cognizance of this interest and published articles describing in popular vein the theory and use of advertising. Often the articles were written by noted advertising men. Also contributing to public awareness of advertising was the fact that matters directly or quite closely related to advertising figured more extensively in the courts than at any time past as a result of numerous cases involving price maintenance, advertising misrepresentation and trademark rights. Twenty-six universities were offering some kind of instruction in advertising by 1914.

Subsequently the rising tide of commodity prices, felt especially in 1912, brought advertising into the political arena. The idea arose that advertising and the packaging of merchandise it fostered were largely responsible for the high cost of living. Legislators, intrigued by the new villain, sprang to the attack. The idea that advertising is a "tax on the consumer" received wide circulation. A committee on food supply in New York City delivered a sharp onslaught upon advertised and packaged brands, and distributed circulars in the schools urging people to break themselves of "the package habit."

A league of housewives, which did not recall the days of bulk merchandise as being so especially delightful, went on record in favor of packaged goods and protested the propaganda. Packaging came through the crisis.

The first blanket sociological indictment of advertising came in 1912 when the elder LaFollette inveighed against advertising as "the subtle peril," asserting it to be the effort of the money power to reach out its tentacles and throttle the free press. Little else along this line happened for almost precisely twenty years.

Type Marches On!

On This Occasion, the 50th Birthday of Printers' Ink, J. M. Bundscho, Inc., Now in Its 22nd Year, Takes Two Pages to Mention Some Typographic Highlights in General and a Few of Its Own in Particular.

1888 Printers' Ink, Bible of the Business, founded. *Congratulations.* Here's to another fifty years of just as valuable service to the allied industries that read you. (*P.S.*, "P. I." —In six more years, you'll only be *twice* as old as we are!)

1902 American Type Founders cut the famous Cheltenham Oldstyle.

1903 First centerspread in the *Saturday Evening Post*—Victor Talking Machine Company.

1905 American Type Founders announce the cutting of "Cheltenham Bold Condensed."

1907 First two-color centerspread in *Saturday Evening Post.*

1911 "Bodoni" and "Franklin Gothic Condensed" announced by American Type Founders. "Kennerly" by the Village Letter Foundery—and Type Marches On!

1912 Caslon continues to be most popular advertising type face in national magazines.

1914 "Cloister" brought out by A. T. F.—becomes a new favorite. ("Packard" too, remember it?)

1916 J. M. BUNDSCHO, founded by "J. M.", began business on basis of "HERE TYPE CAN SERVE YOU."

1917 Bundscho adds first Service Man, something new in typesetting establishments. (Bundscho now has 5 Service Men.)

1918 Bundscho installs its first Monotype. Starts to advertise that "Here Type Can Serve You" and runs its first ad in Printers' Ink.

1919 "Garamond" blossoms from A. T. F. — how she bloomed!

1920 Bundscho issues first Type Specimen Book. Oliver Marble Gale writes first copy for the Bundscho Blotter. (You still get one every two weeks.)

1921 Advertising Typographers of America founded in Cleveland.

1922 J. M. Bundscho dies, leaving his ideals and typographic standards as his mark on the profession.

1923 "Garamond Bold" now joins the "Garamond" family ... Bundscho opens second shop at 10 E. Pearson Street.

1924 *Post* comes out with first 4-color pages.

1925 Bundscho ownership assumed by Herbert A. Knight and E. G. Johnson.

1926 The beginning of European Type importations.

1927 Bauer brings out "Bernhard Cursive" and another new feel comes to typography.

1928 Bundscho combines both shops into "Typographical Headquarters" at 65 E. South Water Street, Chicago.

1929 Bauer picks a winner with first of the "Futura" Family and Continental another in "Kabel," and the San Serif era is on in a big way!

1930 Continental follows with the popular "Girder."

1931 Two more famous faces make their bows: "Stymie" by A. T. F., and "Weiss" by Bauer—smartly modern and modernly smart.

1932 An old stand-by, modernized, too, "Ultra Bodoni Condensed," from American, is big typographic news this year.

1933 "Trafton" by Bauer and the first One-Line Folder of type faces by Bundscho.

1934 Thirteen type faces, from "Agency Gothic" to "Ultra Bodoni Extra Condensed" from

the matrices of American and the "Corvinus" family from Bauer keep Type Marching On.

1935 Bundscho issues the biggest, thickest, most complete Type Book in the business. (We didn't say that, the book's recipients did.) Copies have gone as far as Paris, London —even Australia and the Orient.

1936 Bauer's "Beton Bold Condensed" announced. Catches many an art director's eye.

1937 Frederick W. Goudy, dean of them all, cuts his One Hundredth Type Face.

1938 J. M. Bundscho, Inc. announces its Odd Size Face Service—another exclamation point to the line "Here Type Can Serve You!"

NOTE— 1916 to 1938. As typographers, we've emphasized type faces and our type services. We've had to skip such advances as color photography, new engraving processes, metal inks, bleed and two-color pages and dozens more. All of which have worked hand-in-glove with type as "Type Marches On!"

A Little More About Ourselves

We've enlarged our premises six times in 22 years. We've bought out and absorbed three other typographic shops. We've added faces, sizes, and equipment before you asked for them—not after. We've been doing business with big and small agencies, for big and small clients in a big, yet personal way. We've created new services and we've set higher typographic standards. We're not self-satisfied but we are proud of the work we do—even though next time we'll try to do it better. That's why we say, as we said years ago—*"Here Type Can Serve You."*

J. M. BUNDSCHO, INC.

"Typographical Headquarters"

65 EAST SOUTH WATER STREET · CHICAGO, ILLINOIS

Stronger Links

DURING these years, and especially through the latter part of the period, the manufacturer was not the only one who was taking important strides in making distribution more efficient. Among other things, the chain store came forward to occupy a major role in the business scene and to revolutionize the ways of retailing.

The idea of the chain of stores was not in itself an innovation. Local or regional chains of stores dated almost back to the Civil War. The manufacturer's chain of retail units operated by the Regal Shoe Company was prominent in the 1890's. But the real growth of the chain awaited the evolution of economic conditions whereby the nation became, for merchandising purposes, one community instead of half a hundred relatively isolated and self-contained areas.

In the new century the country rapidly approached this condition. A major part of it, at least, was gradually welded together as a single trade unit and the chain stores came on with a rush. By 1914 there were 2,000 chains with an aggregate of 25,000 units, the organizations ranging in size from 300 to 900 units. The most spectacular development was the United Cigar Stores Company, headed by George J. Whelan, which had grown from eight stores in Syracuse, N. Y., at the turn of the century to 900 units of what was generally regarded then as the smoothest-running, most efficiently managed retail machine the world had ever seen. Close behind in number of stores, and much greater in dollar volume, was F. W. Woolworth's 5-and-10-cent enterprise

which had around 800 units. And of similar size was the Hartfords' Great Atlantic & Pacific Tea Company, which led all the rest in the food field. The greatest development was in the food, drug, tobacco and novelty business, but there were chains in virtually every other line of retail endeavor.

The basic principle of the chain store followed closely the pattern set by the department stores and the mail-order houses—concentration in management and buying, coupled with controlled, aggressive salesmanship. But where the department store and the mail-order house were centralized as to physical location and remote from the average retailer's place of business, the chain store operated on the same street. And, as he had upon the advent of the two earlier rivals, the retailer began once more to evoke protection from his new doom, preferably by legislation.

The chain store, in its origin, rested upon the advanced merchandising skill of some man or group of men. From that it moved to system and standardization, thence to buying in large quantities direct from the manufacturer and from there to price-cutting and promotion of private brands.

In the matter of selling, the chains gained advantage by pressing to the limit the principle of doing a lot of business at a small profit, while the independent dawdled along in the outworn practice of getting his large mark-up no matter what. Their stores were more attractively arranged and they offered a greater variety of stocks. They dealt liberally with the customer and, while they cut the un-

IMPACT

ACCORDING TO WEBSTER: The single instantaneous striking of a body in motion against another body.

ACCORDING TO YOUNG & RUBICAM: That quality in an advertisement which strikes suddenly against the reader's indifference and enlivens his mind to receive a sales message.

. . .

YOUNG & RUBICAM, INC. · ADVERTISING

NEW YORK · CHICAGO · DETROIT · HOLLYWOOD · MONTREAL · TORONTO

necessary frills of retailing to the bone, worked hard to please him. They were generous in guaranteeing goods and accepting returns, which the independent usually did grudgingly and with bad grace. Most of the chains used premium coupons at this time and urged the customer to accept them so that the premium plan could do its work of bringing the customer back again; the average retailer held his coupons back as much as possible in order to save money and thereby deprived them of much of their advertising value.

The price advantage which the chains were able to offer resulted in part from buying advantage and in part from pricing methods. The majority priced very low on a score or more advertised items having standardized values—the advertiser did much to make the chain store possible by providing such standardization. But their prices on their own brands were high. In common with nearly all retailers, they were guilty of some unfair practices. They sometimes manipulated stores or departments to carry some of them at an abnor-

1913

FEDERAL RESERVE ACT establishes the Federal Reserve Board and district reserve banks. . . . Parcels post system goes into effect throughout the country. . . . Income tax now a law. . . . Supreme Court decision affirms constitutionality of law requiring newspapers and periodicals to publish statements of circulation and ownership. . . . Department of Labor created. . . . Peace Palace at Hague dedicated.

A. W. Erickson Advertising Agency incorporated as The Erickson Company by A. W. Erickson, Newcomb Cleveland and Richard S. Childs. . . . S. Roland Hall appointed advertising manager of Alpha Portland Cement Company. . . . Jamison Handy joins the Johnson Advertising Corporation. . . . Electric self-starters now widely accepted by motor car makers. . . . George M. Burbach, foreign advertising manager of the Munsey newspapers, appointed advertising manager of the St. Louis *Post-Dispatch*. . . . Helmar offers prizes for the best love letters.

Elbert H. Baker, president of the American Newspaper Publishers Association and general manager of the Cleveland *Plain Dealer*, elected president of Plain Dealer Publishing Company. . . . F. W. Heiskell advanced to advertising manager of International Harvester Company. . . . Lee W. Maxwell named advertising manager of *American Magazine*. . . . Self-service or "cafeteria" grocery stores being tried out in several large cities. . . . William W. Ellsworth heads the Century Company, succeeding the late Frank Hall Scott. . . . American Tobacco Company giving away a bar of candy with each package of Lucky Strike cigarettes.

mally low profit and thereby discourage competition. But the chain's advantages were preponderantly legitimate and well deserved.

Doing business on a large scale, the chains could support men of large experience and talents who could divide the work and specialize. Under these men they systematized every department of the business. The average retailer knew nothing of accounting or of ascertaining costs or of pricing properly; some did things right by instinct but the majority succeeded because their competitors were no better. The chains, on the other hand, brought system to every phase of operation back of the counter. They also developed an important edge in store location. The average retailer made only one such transaction in his business lifetime. The chain was guided by a large body of experience in determining by traffic count and other criteria the best place for the store to be. Similarly the chains had scientific knowledge of the ways in which to secure maximum benefit from store arrangement.

In addition, the chains were more closely attuned to the needs and likes of the public. When prices began to soar in 1912, the A & P and others turned swiftly to the "economy store," which sold over the counter for cash with all services eliminated. The big growth in the grocery field dated from the adoption of this policy.

The effects of the new retail machine on the channels of trade were already widespread in their ramifications, although actually they were just beginning. Up to 1914 chain operation had been largely confined to the large cities. The reaching out into the small city and town communities had barely gotten under way.

Direct effect on the retailer was much more of an accomplished fact than had been the case with the earlier department store and mail-order menaces. At any rate the results were more immediately perceptible, for many of the smaller retailers were directly put out of business by chain units. Jobbers were weakened, for the chain threw out the jobber as quickly as it could and secured the jobber's discount from the manufacturer.

All this led to the formation of buying co-operatives by retailers as a means of attaining the same quantity discount advantages enjoyed by the chains. They set up their own warehouses and jobbing organizations, jointly owned, to buy direct from manufacturers. Department-store buying syndicates were organized for similar purposes. Many of the retailers in the drug field turned to membership in the so-called co-operative chains like the Rexall group sponsored by the United Drug Company and the American Druggist Syndicate.

All of which placed the jobber in further difficulties. He lost at least part of his retailer custom to co-operative syndicates and that was over and above the losses represented by gains in chain-store volume. The jobber reacted in one of two ways. He sought closer relationship with the manufacturer of advertised brands and, reversing his previous attitude, pushed them energetically. Or he began to advertise to create consumer acceptance for his own brands.

Most of the effort to meet chain-store competition was in relation to buying. Little of an organized nature was done at this time to

... H<small>E</small> *BRINGS*

T<small>ROUBLE</small> is one of the world's most plentiful commodities. Everybody has more than he wants—yet somehow our own are lightened when we know of other people's troubles . . . and how others conquered them.

A platitude . . . yes, but this simple truth is one of the principles of an *editorial technique* so different from any other that it amounts almost to psychological discovery.

Bernarr Macfadden 40 years ago realized that solution of trouble is one of humanity's primary desires—and that has always been one of his editorial principles. Today he heads a group of successful magazines. Probably one-fourth of the families of the United States is reached by them. These magazines deal with real people and their lives—their troubles, their hopes, their health, their loves.

That is the Macfadden editorial technique. It is the application to editing of principles which Macfadden learned through his own early struggles for health, happiness, and advancement—through his personal contacts with millions—through his many philanthrophies.

Macfadden knows people and he knows life. That is the simple secret of his success. His editorial technique isn't always pretty—because life isn't always pretty. His heroines aren't

ENCOURAGEMENT
to MILLIONS

An Inspired Editor Lifts People Out of Their Worries and his Genius Creates These New-Type Magazines

FORTY YEARS

1898 · · · · · · · · · · · · · · · 1938

---

always snow white Pollyannas. His heroes aren't all Fauntleroys grown up. He deals in stark realities because he knows that the real people for whom his magazines are meant, *think real thoughts, hope real hopes* and *live real lives.*

The Macfadden editorial technique is mirrored perfectly in True Story Magazine. Literally, True Story brings hope to troubled millions—lifts people above their own worries through the truthful telling of real problems and real experiences. His technique enlivens the pages of dramatic Liberty, which 2,500,000 forward-looking people purchase every week. It vitalizes every one of the magazines which comprise Macfadden Women's Group.

Macfadden's editorial technique produces magazines unlike any others in the world. Not one is an imitator. Not one appeals to an advertiser or a reader as just another magazine. Each has its own exclusive vitalities. That is why these magazines appeal so intensely to their millions of active readers.

And it is perfectly natural that these millions are so responsive to advertising in Macfadden Magazines.

PHYSICAL CULTURE · PHOTOPLAY · THE DETECTIVE GROUP

equalize the selling advantage which accrued from the chains' planned and systematic methods. Most retailers felt that all they had to do was to buy the merchandise at the same prices the chains were able to get. One of the few organizations to realize the importance of the selling factor was the wholesale house of Butler Brothers, which, under the direction of that outstanding and little publicized merchandising genius, Frank S. Cunningham, set up a separate department to help retailers solve their merchandising problems. Its activities included aid on matters of store location, store arrangement, methods of window trimming and advertising.

From the manufacturer's standpoint, the chain store was introducing problems already becoming grave and soon to be highly serious and complex. As the chain grew stronger, it waxed more imperious in its demands upon the manufacturer. The power represented by 1,000 or more—later many more—retail outlets under a single management was not to be dismissed lightly. Moreover, the chains proved to be the most enthusiastic of all the price-cutters to enter the scene. Department store price-cutting was localized. Chains nationalized the price-maintenance problem.

As to the private brand problem, previous difficulties with jobbers' brands were as nothing compared to the prospective results of the chains' invasion of the manufacturing field. The private brand of the chain had established retail distribution and the active support of the sales person behind the counter. Moreover, the manufacturer found that the smaller retailers were being forced to turn to private

brands as never before in self-defense against the low prices which the chains featured on nationally advertised brands.

These developments placed new demands upon the efficiency of the advertiser's sales organization and upon the effectiveness of the message to the consumer. Some firms, mainly in the clothing and specialty lines, sought the solution in taking control of the retailing operation. The manufacturer chain of stores began to come farther into prominence and has remained as a permanent method of operation with a number of concerns. These chain units were primarily confined to the large cities.

On the whole, however, the development of the retail chains was distinctly to the benefit of the advertiser. The chains standardized retailing methods and speeded up the entire marketing process. They set patterns of retail operation which ultimately, as the independents woke up, were to increase the efficiency of all retailing, for the many things they learned about business became public property. They made it possible for the manufacturer to secure immediate nation-wide distribution. And the cash-and-carry stores caused women to form the habit of shopping in person and thereby opened new opportunities for the advertiser's tie-up work at the point of sale.

The use of the mails as an arm of distribution expanded significantly. The focal point, of course, was the large general mail-order houses, which continued to grow at a tremendous rate. In 1909 Sears, Roebuck was doing a business of $6,000,000 a month.

Manufacturers began to sit up

and take notice of the possibilities of adapting some of the principles of mail selling to their own operations. Many of them commenced using the mail-order idea to get direct sales from consumers. In some instances this was done to get business in districts which the advertiser was unready to develop through the usual trade channels. In others it was employed as a direct means of securing ammunition with which to line up new dealers.

The big department stores, particularly in the East, decided to see what there was to this business of mail selling. Literally hundreds of stores in the principal cities established mail-order departments and issued catalogs.

Then, as the establishment of the parcel post system became imminent in 1911, the country went mail-order mad. Companies which proposed to do all of their selling by mail sprang up by the thousands. Numerous established firms saw what they deemed to be an opportunity of becoming completely independent of unresponsive dealers and arrogant salesmen.

Congress authorized the establishment of the "parcels post," as it was called then, in 1912. There had been provision for such a system since 1848 but it had never been administered in such a way as to be available for general use. Most packages were handled by the express companies. The new legislation automatically put the post-office department into the business of carrying packages on a large scale. It was not passed, however, without energetic opposition. Predictions were made that with no need of going to town, the farmer would buy only necessities. Complete upheaval of the social system.

was forecast. Distribution methods would be unbalanced. Property values around cities would be lessened or destroyed. Men would be thrown out of work.

The mail-order companies themselves were guardedly enthusiastic about the thing. They feared that small retailers would take advantage of low rates in the fifty-mile zones and go into mail-order selling. And they were apprehensive over the possibility that parcel post facilities would increase returned goods, although in the long run this proved to be more of an advantage than otherwise. They feared that the multiplication of mail houses and catalog departments would encourage mail-order buyers to do more shopping around among the different houses.

Parcel post turned out to be a revolutionary factor in business life, bringing about new conditions of sales and distribution. It was used to a wholly unexpected extent by retailers in ordering from jobbers and manufacturers and proved to be of benefit to the smaller merchants particularly. Almost every storekeeper built up with little effort a certain volume of mail-order business. For a time at least, the system was valuable in getting dealers to buy experimental lots of new merchandise and in securing more rapid distribution. Jobbers, flooded with small orders, were not so enthusiastic about it all.

The big mail-order houses established country-wide chains of depositories stocked with a limited quantity of almost every item carried to facilitate the filling of orders. Relay stations to which goods were shipped by freight, then sent out in individual orders by parcel post, were also used in many in-

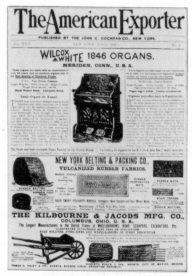

1888
When Printers' Ink First Appeared,
American Exporter Was Already 11
Years Old.

1938
Now In its 61st Year
American Exporter Carried Advertise-
ments of 575 Manufacturers in the
First Six Months.

When the first issue of Printers' Ink appeared, the
American Exporter, established 1877, had already for
eleven years been helping American manufacturers
get export business.

In 1888 exports of finished manufactures were only
$114,000,000 for the year.

They now average over a billion and a half dollars
per year.

For 61 years American Exporter advertisers have
been profitably exporting, *especially during times of
domestic depression.*

Thus in 1938 while domestic trade sagged, exports
of finished manufactures in the first four months were
actually 10.3% ahead of the same period of 1937,
largest since 1930.

Send for a copy of "Your Export Market," a valuable digest of profitable export methods.

Go After Export Trade

Over 575 manufacturers used the advertising plus foreign trade service of the American Exporter in the first six months of 1938. Several of them were advertising in its pages 50 years ago.

American Exporter advertisers' average export sales equal two months' production each year.

Their export sales cost is less than domestic, by 2-7/10%. 38% of them actually get higher prices for export than domestic.

82% of them report that export credit losses are relatively less than domestic. 63% of them did not lose one dollar last year on export credits.

American Exporter advertisers increased their export business last year by 288% over 1932. As total exports of finished manufactures increased in the same period by 159% it is clear that American Exporter advertisers get more than their statistical share of export business.

61st Year

AMERICAN EXPORTER
386 Fourth Ave., At 27th St., New York City

Reaches All Markets Every Month In English—In French—In Spanish

stances. The depositories became the foundation for the country-wide networks of branch houses now maintained by Sears and Ward.

The department stores' venture turned out to be short-lived. By 1914 many of the stores were easing up their energies in this direction. They continued to fill mail orders, but as a matter of necessity and response to regular customers, rather than as a specific effort. They had found that the mail-order business is a highly skilled operation calling for a kind of specialized buying and merchandising activity totally different from storekeeping.

Meanwhile the anti-mail-order sentiment continued in many quarters. There was a good deal of baiting of the catalog houses, things like sending for catalogs and destroying them in community fires, ordering and returning large quantities of goods, entering into worthless correspondence. On the

1914

WORLD WAR touched off in Europe as Archduke Francis of Austria and his wife are assassinated at Sarajevo. . . . Germany invades France and Belgium; Russian troops invade Germany; British forces land in France. . . . New York Stock Exchange closed in financial crisis due to war. . . . Panama Canal opened to traffic. . . . Federal Reserve system inaugurated by opening of twelve Federal Reserve banks.

"The Camels Are Coming!"—teaser campaigns herald a new cigarette. . . . William T. Jefferson and Louis R. Wasey leave Lord & Thomas to form agency. . . . Arthur Capper elected governor of Kansas. . . . William Woodhead buys *Sunset Magazine*. . . . Revival of dancing, started by Irene and Vernon Castle, stimulates silk business by increasing sales of dancing gowns . . . L. R. Greene becomes sales and advertising manager of Tuckett Tobacco Company. . . . E. F. Warner, George Jean Nathan and Henry L. Mencken purchase *The Smart Set*. . . . Francis H. Sisson elected first vice-president of H. E. Lesan Advertising Agency.

H. J. Grant, vice-president of O'Mara & Ormsbee, becomes business manager of the Milwaukee *Journal*. . . . Dante M. Pierce appointed advertising manager of Pierce's Farm Weeklies. . . . Paul E. Faust now a partner in Mallory, Mitchell & Faust. . . . Death of William Henry Boardman of the Simmons-Boardman Company. . . . George D. Buckley appointed advertising manager of *Woman's Home Companion*. . . . Richard H. Waldo joins New York *Tribune* as member of the administrative staff. . . . Cleveland candy manufacturer introduces "Votes for Women" chocolates and gives suffragettes 5 cents on each pound sold.

CHAIN STORE AGE

NUMBER 6 · 35¢ PER COPY

First

1st publication to cover the chain store field exclusively ... established 1925.

1st in quality and quantity of editorial content ... the *only* chain store magazine with A.B.P. membership.

1st in advertising volume.

1st in paid circulation ... the *only* chain store magazine with A.B.C. membership and paid circulation.

6 SPECIALIZED EDITIONS

Gen'l Mdse.-Variety Store Executives

Variety Store Managers

Druggist

Grocery Executives

Grocery Store Managers

Administration Combination

We'll be glad to furnish complete information about any of our editions and the market covered by each. Just address CHAIN STORE AGE, 93 Worth St., N. Y.

more constructive side, jobbers began to organize plans for helping the retailer do a more effective selling job. Some manufacturers adopted a policy of refusing to sell to mail-order houses.

An interesting and not too insignificant marketing development of these years was the transfiguration of the drug store. Time was when a drug store was a place that dealt in drugs. But pure drug legislation, patent medicine crusades, and the abandonment of the once popular practice of counter prescribing cut deeply into the druggist's revenue. "Doped" products, in which there was big profit, disappeared from the scene. The pill was taking precedent over prescriptions of the liquid variety, which involved herbs, liquors and a better

profit. Unless located near a hospital the druggist could no longer survive on the old-fashioned basis.

In self preservation the druggist began taking on side-lines. First cigars, then stationery. The soda fountain evolved into a means for distributing crackers, sandwiches, eggs, mayonnaise and an endless variety of soft drinks. By 1912 the average druggist would stock almost anything—flower sprinklers, bathing shoes, water wings, thermometers, whiskbrooms, watches. His stock was 25 per cent drugs and the rest specialties, from birdseed to bath cabinets. All this meant a new and more convenient outlet for many lines of manufactured products and the drug store went on to form the cornerstone of many an advertiser success.

Strength of display lines and illustrations characterized Victor's newspaper advertising in 1914. Caruso and Victor profited one another immensely

CHAPTER VI

In Times of War . . .
(1915-1918)

A GROWING feeling of uncertainty and hesitation pervaded business in the latter part of 1913. There was a shortage of liquid credit throughout the world. Some apprehension was caused by impending changes in the banking and currency system, to be brought about by passage of the Federal Reserve Act, and by the new tariff. Sales were slipping in a number of lines. The country was apparently on the verge of economic depression.

The opening roar of Europe's cannon in the summer of 1914 rocked the United States with a further sense of business insecurity. Money stringency seemed imminent. The New York Stock Exchange closed. Business men worried over the cutting off of raw material supplies and the closing down, for many, of overseas outlets for merchandise. Calamity howlers predicted the end of business. Prompted by fear of what the future might hold and in some instances by the belief everybody would be reading war news and would have no time for advertisements, many of the large firms cancelled their advertising activities. Things seemed pretty bad and a number of publications sponsored "cheer up" campaigns to spread confidence.

The immediate reaction of pessimism was relatively short-lived. During it all some of the small advertisers, imperturbed by financiers' worries about the money situation, foresaw as results of the war an enlarged home market and general business stimulation. Before long this view became general.

It soon became apparent that the forced withdrawal of European manufacturers from the American market was adding hundreds of millions of dollars to sales potentials for domestic manufacturers. Those to whom the European market had been closed saw all the more reason for increased selling effort at home. Europe's abandonment of foreign markets in South America, Asia and elsewhere suggested new possibilities for developing American export trade. And then, early in 1915 came a flood of war orders from across the seas—orders not only for arms and ammunition, but textiles, automobiles, food, iron and steel, medicines, leather, chemicals.

The war which was absorbing the energies and population of two continents profoundly changed manufacturing and distribution conditions. Whereas in the past the commercial problem had been to find a market for the world's products, fully half of the machinery of distribution was soon expending its energies to secure the products to meet the world's demand. Half of the world's manufactured products became scarce. Almost all raw materails were far short of world requirements. Prices of almost every kind of commodity commenced to rise.

Hence, although the United States was not to take part in the hostilities for nearly three years, its industrial life was predominantly influenced by the conflict abroad.

After the first unsettling shock had passed, many firms bent their energies to capitalizing trade both with the warring countries and in the overseas markets which the belligerents had abandoned. One immediate manifestation was the "Made in U. S. A." movement which came when we seemed about to inherit a goodly share of the export trade of both sets of belligerents. It was assumed that the slogan "Made in Germany" had been of overwhelming importance in building up the Empire's exports and therefore a similar slogan would be of immense service to this country. The idea was agitated with a religious fervor by associations, chambers of commerce and individuals. Meetings and speeches on the subject abounded everywhere. A few rude voices were raised in warning that the securing of foreign trade depended upon something more than passing resolutions and "standing shoulder to shoulder." At first these thoughts were dismissed as unpatriotic, but in time it became evident that unless the national trade-mark could be confined to quality products its adoption would be harmful rather than helpful to the standing of American goods abroad. The very persons who would be the first to fly to such a mark for refuge would be the makers of inferior and shoddy goods. The impossibility of making a general mark of origin carry any significance of quality finally put a quietus to the whole proposition.

Export endeavor got along pretty well without the brand. In a year of war, American trade abroad increased by a billion dollars, or more than 40 per cent.

The years saw a few develop-ments of significance to marketing practice which were unrelated to war conditions.

The Clayton Act, which supplemented the Sherman Act by declaring unlawful price discriminations tending substantially to lessen compensation or create a monopoly, went into effect and with it was launched the Federal Trade Commission as an enforcing agency.

The scare appeal came into prominence in advertising copy and proved itself successful for a number of products despite the old saw about the dangers of the "negative" appeal. In this connection, the American Chain Company, which in one of the most conspicuous campaigns of the time pictured vividly the automobile accidents that might result from failure to equip with Weed chains, drew the ire of the motor car manufacturers. The latter felt their sales were being hurt and agitated discontinuance of scare copy in all advertising, while the respondent held that it was better to bring evils to light than to ignore them.

Many manufacturers began to show a disposition to work with the jobber, who at the same time was evidencing a more tolerant view toward advertised products. The unheard of event of a jobber applying to handle an advertised line was occurring here and there. Accordingly, some firms undertook to secure the co-operation of jobbers' salesmen to insure a better presentation to the retailer. The practice of sending through jobbers the orders secured by specialty salesmen was taken up by a few firms. Here and there the old jobber-manufacturer antagonism was gradually disappearing.

There was a veritable epidemic

of co-operative marketing and advertising campaigns, encompassing just about every known type of commodity and various services as well. Diamond Brand walnuts, Eatmor cranberries and other brands entered the consumer's buying language. The florists released their famous "Say It with Flowers" slogan upon the nation and promoted telegraph delivery of flowers. Co-operative advertising was applied to sauer-kraut, apples, banking facilities, bicycles, macaroni, linoleum, raisins, tea, milk and dozens of other propositions. The majority of programs were of short duration and many fizzled badly owing to poor organization, but a number achieved important results for their sponsors.

A development of literally sensational proportions at the time (1916) was the one-cent sale, first sponsored on a large scale by the Liggett drug stores, although it had been used by other druggists a year or two before. Staggering amounts of merchandise were moved in these sales events. The idea was presented by Liggett to advertisers as a means of getting a large number of new users without actually disturbing the price structure, since the offering of an item for one cent with a purchase at the regular price tended to stress the regular price in the buyer's mind. Some manufacturers

1915

LUSITANIA sunk by German submarine with loss of 124 American lives. . . . In disagreement with Wilson over European policy, William Jennings Bryan resigns as Secretary of State. . . . Panama-Pacific International Exposition opens at San Francisco. . . . Excursion steamer *Eastland* capsizes at pier in Chicago; 852 lost. . . . Ku Klux Klan re-organized under charter grant in Georgia.

Automobile prices dropping and the industry is talking of the saturation point. . . . William Boyd appointed advertising director of Curtis Publishing Company. . . . Frank Irving Fletcher leaves Saks & Company to open his own advertising business. . . . Detroit *Tribune* merged with Detroit *Evening News*. . . . Federal Trade Commission opens up shop. . . . John E. Lutz, former Western manager of Munsey papers, joins C. George Krogness, special representative. . . . H. J. Kenner named secretary of the National Vigilance Committee.

A. D. Lasker becomes president of Lord & Thomas. . . . C. R. Erwin, previously head of Lord & Thomas, now president of Erwin, Wasey & Jefferson. . . . Death of William Rockhill Nelson, Kansas City *Star*, and of Alden J. Blethen, Seattle *Times*. . . . A. W. Gould appointed advertising manager of *Farmer's Wife*. . . . John H. Livingston, Jr., acquires Fifth Avenue bus advertising rights in New York. . . . Enter Haidees, a cigarette for women.

A GREAT NEWSPAPER COMES UP THE AVENUE OF YEARS

Sixty-five years ago, General
Chas. H. Taylor entered upon a
career as editor and manager of

The Boston Globe

that placed him among the
leaders of modern journalism in
America, and made The Globe
a family friend in the homes
of Boston and New England.

● ● ●

Through all these years, under the same ownership and management, *The Boston Globe* has looked
to the home and family for the basic inspiration of
its service to the public.

Bostonians and New Englanders know *The
Globe's* policies and respect them. Their parents and
grandparents knew and respected them. Today,
when vital questions demand sound, sane analysis,

⁺ᴸ ⁀se policies stand out more prominently than ever before.

In its presentation and interpretation of the news of the day, *The Globe* caters to no class or creed. It is clean and wholesome—*edited for thorough reading by the family in the home.* Thus it finds its way into the innermost lives of its readers—solving their problems, inspiring their thoughts, voicing their opinions.

So it is that back of the result-producing power of *The Boston Globe* there exists character and confidence, the most important appeal that can be made to ᴧhe purchasing public.

Reader respect and reader response are intangible elements, but they represent a driving, pulsing force that vitalizes circulation . . . brings people into stores . . . moves merchandise.

This reader interest, respect and response is *The Boston Globe's* greatest asset. It is something that no newspaper can buy. *It must be earned by performance.* But it is an asset that *Globe* advertisers share in building sales and prestige in the great Boston market.

The Boston Globe
A Great Newspaper in a Great Market

found this to be so and were willing to make special price allowances for such events. Others pronounced decided convictions against the practice as a demoralizer of the retail trade.

A new development in the outdoor advertising medium was the formation in 1916 of the National Outdoor Advertising Bureau as a co-operative organization for the investigation, analysis, development and placing of all forms of outdoor advertising. Twenty-three advertising agencies participated in its ownership and operation.

In response to the rapidly increasing overhead costs of agencies, publishers began to increase the commission allowance from 13 per cent, which had been the generally accepted figure, to 15 per cent. Ultimately this figure became the standard rate of compensation for a majority of media.

Apart from the events recited above, just about every other business development of the time was conditioned to a substantial degree, directly or indirectly, by the fact of war.

After the first fascinations of the export boom, attention began to center more upon the domestic market. Some firms had frowned upon export endeavor from the start, not wishing to take the risks of selling at war or under wartime conditions, and had found compensations at home.

The tremendous pace of industrial production, for export to the warring countries and elsewhere and to replace the volume of manufactured goods formerly imported, had greatly expanded the country's buying power. Wage scales were rising swiftly. This was the dawn of the silk shirt era.

An example of the new domestic sales opportunities was the appearance of the laboring man as a buyer of automobiles. That industry surpassed all previous progress. Some bold spirits saw a day when 10,-000,000 cars would be owned in the United States. To help the wage-earner finance his purchase, the industry turned to instalment selling. Up to this time the business had been on a cash basis except that some of the dealers had done a little partial financing on their own hook. In 1916 finance companies came forward to offer to handle dealer paper. Numerous manufacturers, including Reo, Buick and Cadillac issued strong statements against instalment sales. The only manufacturer advertising the instalment plan was Maxwell, which featured a "Pay as You Ride" slogan and sold cars on a 50 per cent down payment. Despite general manufacturer opposition, the financing companies went ahead with their plans and made steady progress. In a few months several of the big companies fell in line with announcements of "deferred payment" plans—the word "instalment" wasn't liked, but it was the same idea.

Numerous firms found profit in new or expanded sales and advertising effort to promote domestic products which could be substituted for similar foreign products no longer available. These included a wide range of things—soaps, perfumes, drugs, medicines, toys, wines and liquors, glassware, chinaware, gloves, hats and various specialties. The railroads, with "See America First" as their byword, set out to reap the harvest brought by the closing of facilities for European travel.

Business came easily in nearly

50 years *Plus* 1

SPORTS AFIELD was established in 1887

Without any attempt to "steal the thunder" of Printers' Ink's 50th Anniversary, it is interesting to note that among the hundreds of advertisers using space in the 1938 issues of SPORTS AFIELD . . .

Six of them were advertisers in SPORTS AFIELD in 1888.

They are: ENTERPRISE MFG. CO. (THE PFLUEGERS)
H. CLAY GLOVER
LYMAN GUN SIGHTS
HORTON MFG. CO.
LEFEVER ARMS CO.
UNION PACIFIC RAILROAD

THE DENVER RAMBLERS' TRIPLET BICYCLE.

Reprint of a wood cut used in SPORTS AFIELD
Fifty Years Ago.

SPORTS AFIELD

America's Oldest Monthly Outdoor Magazine

every line. It wasn't long before numerous firms found themselves oversold. They simply didn't have enough goods to fill the domestic demand, either because of production for sales to warring nations, shortage of raw materials, greatly increased consumption in this country or a combination of these elements. Some firms met this unusual condition by cheapening the product and thereby enhancing their ability to produce in quantity. Others simply ceased their sales efforts. But a growing number took heed of the maxim that "only the savage ceases to cultivate his crops when his stomach is full."

This point of view produced a considerable volume of what might be termed "business insurance" advertising. In common with almost everybody else, the business man felt that the war would be of short duration. The longer it lasted, the nearer the end was believed to be. On the whole the business community became acutely conscious of the ephemeral quality of war buying and sought protection against the inevitable day when business would be harder to get. Instead of curtailing their programs when the sales reason for advertising ceased to exist, leading companies maintained their appropriations but built the copy to maintain goodwill for a future period of normal relations with the consumer. No small number, convinced that money spent at this time would save heavier expenditures after the war, increased their appropriations.

The "business insurance" idea won further favor when it became plain, as soon it did, that an oversold condition enabled some competitors, including new firms, to pick up a lot of easy business and establish valuable relations with the trade. Another compelling reason for continuance of advertising was the practice of substitution among dealers, often unavoidable because the dealer had no supply of the goods requested. From the manufacturer's standpoint this indicated the advisability of keeping up contact with the consumer in order to make the switch a temporary proposition.

THE momentous declaration of April 6, 1917, turned the attention of business, as of everyone else, to the task of helping win the war in which the United States had staked its destiny. Bending of production facilities to war purposes became the imperative duty of every manufacturer whose products were in any way connected with the organization and support of an overseas fighting machine.

Advertising took an immediate part in this process. The National War Advisory Board, composed of representatives of the leading advertising, publishing and media associations, offered the Government the services of the advertising brains of the nation to aid in military recruiting and money-raising campaigns. The offer was accepted and the Board set to work in co-operation with the Council of National Defense. Nine months later the volunteer body, which had no special authority delegated by the Government, was superseded by the Division of Advertising of the Committee of Public Information. The new body was created by the Government itself and given full power to act directly for it on all matters coming within its jurisdiction. Directors of the Division included

The GREATEST MOTHER in the WORLD

Stretching forth her hands to all in need—to Jew or Gentile, black or white, knowing no favorite, yet favoring all. Seeing all things with a mother's sixth sense that's blind to jealousy and meanness; helping the little home that's crushed beneath an iron hand by showing mercy in a healthy, human way; rebuilding it, in fact, with stone on stone and bringing warmth to hearts and hearths too long neglected.

Reaching out her hands across the sea to No Man's Land; to heal and comfort thousands who must fight and bleed in crawling holes and water-soaked entrenchments where cold and wet bite deeper, so they write, than Boche steel or lead.

She's warming thousands, feeding thousands, helping thousands from her store; the Greatest Mother in the World—the RED CROSS.

Every Dollar of a Red Cross War Fund goes to War Relief.

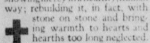

The greatest American poster produced by
the Great War

The Road To France—
He Is Keeping It Open

HE is fighting German submarines and German shells. *We can't win the war without him.* He faces the biting winds of the North Atlantic with a smile and a song—but 'way down in his heart is the knowledge that he is facing the biggest job that has ever fallen to the American Navy. . . . An ever increasing army of American soldiers in France is doing its part in a way to win the admiration of the world.

New troops must back them up. A ceaseless supply of food, guns, shells, airplanes and tanks must be sent to their support.

> We asked this man if he was downhearted. "In the words of old John Paul Jones," he said, "We've just *begun* to fight!"

THE victory of our arms—the very existence of our armies—depends upon safe transport through seas infested with submarines.

The American sailor will do his part—if we will lend him a hand. He needs money—lots of it—for ships and shells to keep open the road to France: We will not fail him.

The American Sailor Is Doing His Part—

LET US DO OURS!
BUY LIBERTY BONDS!

William H. Johns, chairman; Herbert S. Houston, L. B. Jones, O. C. Harn, W. C. D'Arcy, Thomas Cusack and Jesse H. Neal.

The Division served to co-ordinate advertising endeavor and furnish a point of contact for the Government's advertising activities. It was laid out on the lines of an advertising agency, the work being divided into major operations for working with its clients—the various Government departments—and the media. Copy departments of the leading agencies enlisted in the work and the Division distributed assignments among them. Also serving under the Division were com-

1916

COLUMBUS, N. Mex., raided by Pancho Villa and Brig-Gen. Pershing enters Mexico with troops on punitive expedition. . . . German submarine *Deutschland* arrives at Norfolk, Va. . . . Bomb hurled at Preparedness Day paraders in San Francisco; Thomas J. Mooney and Warren K. Billings subsequently convicted of the crime. . . . Woodrow Wilson re-elected president, leading Charles Evans Hughes 277 electoral votes to 254. . . . Black Tom dock explosion at Jersey City.

W. C. Durant elected president of General Motors to succeed Charles W. Nash, who has taken over the Thomas B. Jeffery Company. . . . Alvan Macauley heads Packard. . . . Death of Stephen H. Black, vice-president of Bauer & Black and one of the great sales managers of his generation. . . . Eben Griffiths leaves the city desk of the Brooklyn *Eagle* to join Vacuum Oil Company as assistant advertising manager. . . . William H. Rankin acquires John Lee Mahin's interest in the Mahin Advertising Company and becomes president. . . . Charles H. Thorne resigns as president of Montgomery Ward and Robert J. Thorne succeeds him. . . . "Advertising is not a department of business; it is only a department of the selling end of business"—F. Wayland Ayer.

Philip S. Collins advanced to general manager of Curtis Publishing Company. . . . Theodore F. MacManus and associates form Theodore F. MacManus, Inc., at Detroit. . . . Jerome D. Barnum appointed general manager of the Syracuse, N. Y., *Post-Standard*. . . . Owen B. Winters leaves Chalmers to join Carl M. Green Company. . . . National income soars to forty billions, up ten billions over 1915. . . . Merle Thorpe named editor of *Nation's Business*. . . . Henry Wallace, editor of *Wallaces' Farmer*, dies at eighty. . . . Lloyd Maxwell joins Erwin, Wasey & Company. . . . So many seaside resorts are reporting appearance of sea monsters offshore that the serpents are losing their advertising punch.

mittees of all the local advertising clubs.

The Division secured its space on the basis of contributions from advertisers and media, either in cash or space. During its tenure it used more than $1,500,000 of donated advertising facilities. This did not include all the advertising employed for wartime purposes, however, since the Division dealt primarily with activities apart from the war loan drives. These latter also employed donated facilities. Advertisers were asked to feature Liberty bonds in their regular advertisements and while media were not solicited practically all of them contributed space for this purpose.

Advertisers also helped finance the *Stars and Stripes,* official weekly newspaper of the American Expeditionary Force, which was edited by Guy T. Viskniskki. General Pershing cabled A. W. Erickson asking him to undertake to furnish 500 inches of advertising at $1 an inch for three months. Erickson secured the co-operation of the American Association of Advertising Agencies, which circularized its members for support and immediately got enough advertising to assure twenty weeks' publication.

The role of advertising and advertising methods in mobilizing the nation's resources for war was a conspicuous one. It helped enroll volunteers for military and naval service and aided in running the machinery for registration for the selective service draft. It sold the war to the working men. In September of 1917 there were 283 labor strikes, and posters and other advertising media were used to inculcate an appreciation of the seriousness of the situation. Both the Government and associations of

business men sponsored campaigns to inspire the laboring man to speed up production of needed materials. Advertising was used to raise shipyard volunteers, then to impress upon these 300,000 workers the importance of the task in which they were engaged. It was used to encourage conservation of coal and gasoline and food and other vital supplies.

The actual entrance of the United States into hostilities increased greatly the problems of advertisers in maintaining their connections with the consumer market. There were vast Government orders to be filled. Raw materials became far scarcer than before. Few companies were able to keep anywhere near the demand upon them for goods. Marketing was a question of rationing goods instead of managing to sell a year's production. In addition, with economy the watchword and keynote of American life, aggressive salesmanship was out of the question even if an advertiser did have a surplus on hand.

The proposition of wartime advertising of merchandise to consumers had two major sides, both of which resolved themselves into essentially the same thing. There was the manufacturer who had all the war business he could handle with little or nothing on the side for the general public. Then there was the firm which manufactured materials not essential for war purposes. The war order man turned to investing his usual quota toward insurance of his good-will. The man with no war orders and a nonessential market had no assured· volume. His good-will was quite as important to him as the other fellow's, but if he advertised he ran the risk of being accused of lack of patriotism and if he did not he took the chance of sacrificing prestige which had been the effort of years in building. A solution worked out in the latter case was to discontinue featuring specific products and advertise the firm as an institution.

Consciousness of future welfare continued keen in the minds of many advertisers. It was seen that the many plants created to supply war needs would have huge production facilities on their hands when hostilities ended and that these facilities would have to be turned in some way to supplying normal consumer requirements. Those who owned such plants were thinking about the problems of converting them to production of peace-time goods. Those who did not foresaw increased competition for their own lines resulting from the advent of new war-born rivals. And so, in time of war, advertisers sought to prepare for peace by keeping company and trade-mark names before the public. To that end many of these foresighted advertisers maintained their advertising volume, though changing the tenor of the advertisements, at former levels and some actually increased their campaigns.

Equal, if not greater, concern was shown over the problem of bringing the selling forces through the war in good condition. For concerns whose production had been curtailed it was a comparatively simple task to sell the decreased output. For those whose production remained near normal but whose distribution was diverted to the Government or other unusual channels the problem was much the same. Then there were the firms whose output may or may not have been restricted but whose products were semi-luxuries and were meeting with increased selling resistance. Though their immediate problem was much easier, some way had to be found of keeping the trade in line and the sales organization intact and to continue building for the future.

Many solutions were adopted. One was to broaden the line, thus giving salesmen more to do. The trend to increasing variety of stocks in retail stores which was taking place at this time made it possible for the manufacturer logically to engage in such expansion. In general the practice was to use salesmen to build up cordial, helpful relations with the trade. One firm made a list of all its former customers which had been lost without the company knowing the reason and sent salesmen to cultivate these dissatisfied buyers so that it might have a chance to sell them when business returned to normal. Other firms used their salesmen to analyze markets, to study competitive lines, to search for new ideas and to explain company policies. One well-known corporation even loaned its salesmen to other high-grade concerns, agreeing to continue paying the men's salaries provided the other house would pay their expenses. It wanted to maintain the habit of selling so that the men would be in form when normal conditions returned and, above all, to keep them in touch with the trade.

THE directly traceable effects of the war upon business and in particular the marketing end of business were to be literally enormous. It seems almost as though every

It's Simple...

to sell the

(and economical)
SOUTHEAST TOP 75% ☆

Sell the easy-to-reach market—the 19 trading areas which account for 75% of the total retail sales in the Southeast. With the daily newspapers listed here you reach 3½ out of every 5 able-to-buy families in these 19 trading areas. Families which represent the real buying power of the Southeast. In these trade areas, retail sales per white family average 27% higher than the U. S. average.   Use daily newspapers to sell the Southeast.   *Concentrate* your advertising in the 19 market areas that produce 75% of the Southeast's retail sales.

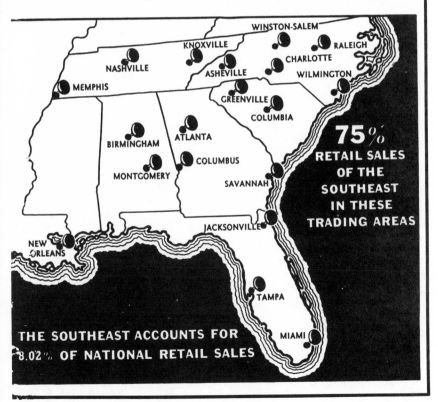

75%
RETAIL SALES
OF THE
SOUTHEAST
IN THESE
TRADING AREAS

THE SOUTHEAST ACCOUNTS FOR
8.02% OF NATIONAL RETAIL SALES

development in marketing were conditioned in some degree, directly or indirectly, by conditions which took effect during the war era. Leaving aside such issues as war debts, economic losses, international affairs, the change in moral standards attributed to war days and other general considerations, it is plain that a large proportion of the trends in markets and marketing practice in the United States were so influenced.

For one thing, the wartime employment of advertising to national ends created a new appreciation of this business force. What only advertising men suspected was given a convincing demonstration: that within certain reasonable boundaries it is possible to sway the minds of whole populations, change their habits of life, create belief in a given policy or idea by the use of the right methods of advertising. The standing of advertising with management generally was considerably improved as a consequence. And the financing of the war specifically showed bankers the value of advertising financial services, in addition to which the bonds campaigns made investors out of a great number of people.

The use of advertising messages to promote industrial harmony during the war suggested to some firms the wisdom of educational programs directed toward promoting a better understanding between capital and labor. However, this available lesson was not so universally heeded as might have been desirable.

As a means of saving on raw materials in the late stages of the war, the Government had ordered manufacturers in a number of fields to curtail their lines. Often these had developed to an unwieldy and senseless extent. In the paint and varnish business, for example, many firms were forced to keep upwards of five thousand formulas in active use and list packages in an incredible variety of sizes. Some of the big stove firms had as many as 2,500 different numbers. In the tire industry there were 287 different types of pneumatic tires and a wide range of rim sizes. The restrictions imposed caused many industries to see the advantage of standardization over the chaotic complexity which had made selling, distributing and advertising immeasurably difficult.

Simplification of lines was taken up by companies which had not been required to do so and the process continued throughout industry after the war was over. The result was an effective solution to many a merchandising problem. Efficient use of advertising became possible in numerous instances where it had not been obtained before. In addition, elimination of slow-moving models helped to induce retailers generally to operate on the basis of small stocks and quick turnover.

Costs of printed matter had mounted rapidly during 1915 and 1916. With America's participation in the war, a stringent paper shortage set in and the Government issued orders to cut down on the paper consumption of publications, catalogs and direct-mail material. In consequence attention was directed to a good deal of needless waste. The War Industries Board ordered publications to cut down on free copies and returns, and many publishers were brought to value this as a permanent policy. Advertisers, faced with the neces-

294

sity of trimming costs and conforming with Government orders, found unthought of advantage in abandoning promiscuous distribution of printed matter. Their attention was directed to the fact that catalogs had been carelessly and loosely designed. More intelligent planning, it developed, not merely conserved paper but added to the sales value of the book by making it more attractive and easy to use.

Shortage of many forms of packaging materials brought lasting changes in container design. New materials were brought into use. Ill-designed, clumsy packages were transformed into units which could be more economically shipped and more effectively displayed. There

---

1917

GERMANY begins unrestricted submarine warfare Feb. 1 and U. S. breaks off diplomatic relations two days later. . . . Declaration of war with Germany on April 6. . . . First U. S. troops land in France June 26. . . . Czar of Russia abdicates and Russia is proclaimed a republic. . . . Explosion of munition ship in Halifax harbor with 1,226 dead and 400 missing.

Henry T. Stanton and James W. Young appointed to take charge of the Chicago office of J. Walter Thompson Company. . . . L. D. H. Weld becomes manager of research department of Swift & Company. . . . C. George Krogness named general manager of Minneapolis *Tribune*. . . . Anson McKim, pioneer Canadian agent, meets death in train accident. . . . R. F. R. Huntsman elected president of the Brooklyn *Standard-Union*. . . . United Advertising Corporation formed to acquire the interests of Leonard Dreyfuss, Alfred V. Van Beuren and Samuel Pratt in sixteen outdoor advertising companies.

McGraw Publishing Company and Hill Publishing Company combine as McGraw-Hill Publishing Company, with James H. McGraw as president. . . . Henry T. Ewald becomes president of Campbell-Ewald. . . . Woolworth opens a store on Fifth Avenue in New York. . . . William M. Armistead returns to N. W. Ayer & Son. . . . A flour company advertises money back plus 10 per cent if you are not satisfied (precursor of double-your-money-back?) . . . Murray Howe establishes agency at New York. . . . A. J. Kobler joins *American Weekly*. . . . "Daylo" wins contest for a new name for Eveready flashlights. . . . George W. Hopkins named general sales manager of Columbia Graphophone Company. . . . E. Ross Gamble joins Erwin, Wasey at Chicago. . . . "Endless chain" scheme revived once more.

was a great trend to the square package.

Although sampling virtually disappeared while the United States was engaged in the conflict, the enforced restriction all through the war period brought home a telling lesson. Before economy became important, tremendous wastes had grown up in and around the sampling technique. Advertisers were brought to realize what the costs had been and future sampling operations were conditioned by this knowledge.

As restricted production made sampling uneconomic in 1917 and 1918, advertisers had their attention turned to an attribute in the printed page which hitherto had been relatively unexploited. Color in advertising had, up to this time, been valued only as a means of attracting attention. Now it was discovered that a faithful reproduction of the product in its natural colors possessed real sales power and could act as a pretty effective substitute for the sample. Recent developments in printed machinery had made high-quality color-work feasible in large runs and the year 1918 saw a large increase in the employment of color pages in periodicals and mail-order catalogs.

One of the war's strange anomalies was that while it increased the cost of nearly everything, it set in motion forces which tended to decrease the cost of retailing. The retailer took notice that the high cost of doing business was not so much in the selling as it was in the accommodation extended after the sale. He saw that much of this service, delivery and credit in particular, was superfluous for many customers, and many merchants either eliminated these services or

placed a charge on them. Meantime a Southerner named Clarence Saunders set out to do something about the cost of the retail sales óperation, and he launched the Piggly Wiggly self-service stores. The cafeteria idea in retailing spread by leaps and bounds, being spurred on by the growing shortage of labor; and while all of its effects were not permanent, many of them had a lasting influence on the shaping of events at the point of sale.

A new destiny for the passenger automobile was shaped. Throughout its career the automobile had been presented as a "pleasure car." The unprecedented war demands on business pushed the motor car into the limelight. In sheer desperation people turned to the "pleasure car" for assistance, and it proved it could meet the need efficiently as a practical time and money saver. The industry took the hint, being prompted somewhat by the fact that "gasless Sundays" and such had diminished the usefulness of the automobile as a recreational factor. It began to dispense with the talk about pleasure and picnics, which had clouded the real mission of the motor car—that of providing a new and improved means of transportation. For the first time, in 1918, the industry began systematic endeavor to sell and advertise mechanical transportation. Shortly before, by the way, the transportation possibilities had been enhanced by the introduction of the closed car, brought out first as a bid for winter business and then, having proved popular for summer use, sold the year around.

Business concerns had in 1917 begun to take up the possibilities of the automobile as a utility

296

The Wasp and the Chinaman

*Not a fable, but a true short-short on the fabulous
and inter-related history of pulp, paper, publishing,
and publicity.*

THE WORLD'S

FIRST WASP was the
world's first producer of wood-pulp paper. Her method of pulp
preparation was used, with little change, by the maker of the
paper you are now holding in your hand. The wasp still uses
the cheapest of raw materials now used in paper-making—wood.
But you can't print on her product, even if it does make fine nests.

The world's first human paper-maker—as far as we know—
was one Ts'ai Lun, a Chinese court official who lived nearly
two thousand years ago. You could have printed on his product.
But Ts'ai Lun's raw materials, cloth scraps, were expensive.
He hadn't discovered what the wasp knew by instinct—that
if wood were properly treated, it would make paper.
Neither did anyone else—for about sixteen hundred
years. And paper remained expensive—until a scant
half century ago.

When the Moslem introduced paper in Europe,
it was first scorned, then gingerly accepted
as a substitute for parchment. The Chinese, since its invention, had been
writing on paper with brushes and
printing on it with wood blocks
applied by hand — as they still
do. Europeans were using

scratchy quills for writing, so the soft Chinese-type paper was gelatinized, given a hard surface. But the surface was too hard to take impressions from the hand-applied wood-blocks first used in European printing. So the printing press was invented. Then European paper would take impressions even from the movable types invented by Gutenberg. Yet for centuries paper remained almost a luxury. Rags were, and are, high priced. At one time they were so scarce that laws were passed in some countries forbidding the export of hemp or flax, or the burial of corpses clothed in any but wool cloth. All the time the wasp was making paper out of wood, the cheapest known raw material for paper making. . . .

Paper-makers throughout the world were following the *Chinaman's* methods—had not discovered the *Wasp's!* It wasn't until the early years of the eighteenth century that any human of whom we have any record, began to consider the wasp as a paper-maker. The man who did the considering was a French scientist named René Antoine Ferchault Réaumur—and he spent twenty years at it before he published his first book on the subject. Every publisher, advertiser, every buyer of contemporary books and magazines should salute the name of Réaumur. Even if his work got little attention during his lifetime—and the practical manufacture of wood-pulp papers as we know them today did not begin until a time within the memory of living men.

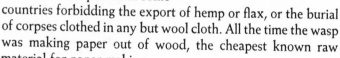

The manufacture of wood-pulp papers suitable for use in fine magazine and book work brought literature — and advertising—to the masses. The forests of the world (though only 4% of of their annual yield goes into paper) now furnish the raw

298

stuff of most paper made today. Miracle followed miracle as the pioneer pulp and pulp-paper producers enlarged manufacturing facilities, refined their products, perfected distribution methods. The mass-circulation magazine appeared. The mass magazine  carrying photo-engravings followed. Two-color work, multiple color, came in rapid succession. Then the illustrated *class* magazine—made possible by papers capable of carrying fine-screen halftones, yet produced at low costs. Cheap book papers of high whiteness and level printing surface, revolutionized book production.

Many men have contributed to the almost fabulous growth of periodical production and the accompanying development of American advertising. Prominent among them are the country's early manufacturers of pulp and paper. The names of these men and of the companies they developed, are today hardly known to the general  public which has so greatly benefited from their far-sighted experiments, research, and courageous enterprise. Only "the trade" appreciates the work of such a firm as, for example, The New York and Pennsylvania Company, Inc. Only men working in the fields of advertising, publishing, and printing realize the magnitude of The New York and Pennsylvania Company's operations, properly appraise its three-generation management record, correctly evaluate its financial responsibility in terms of service. . . .

Those who know could give you what The New York and Pennsylvania Company (with the conservatism traditional among paper-makers) will not release for publication — the

•

astounding list of America's leading publications which are printed upon The New York and Pennsylvania Company's machine - finished and super - calendered papers. That these papers are used not only by some of America's most prominent school-book and other book publishers, but by first-rank producers of labels, tablets, envelopes, and lithography as well. That the Company's history of nearly fifty years' pioneering includes many important contributions to papermaking. These date from the early days of soda pulp development to the present time, when The New York and Pennsylvania Company may claim a front-rank place in modern scientific research as to refinement, measurement, testing of surface illumination, microscopic and photomicrographic procedures, etc.

Back of all this, in terms of quality paper production, is a stability and responsibility that well reflects a commercial maxim of more than passing import in these changing times: *From whom you buy is just as important as to whom you sell.* The position of the New York and Pennsylvania Company as a supplier to leading publishers and advertisers, guarantees service far beyond the mere acceptance of an order. The New York and Pennsylvania Company will be glad to send you further information about its unusual service to publishers, advertisers, printers, and lithographers. Please address your request to the main offices at 230 Park Avenue, New York City.

vehicle. Reduction of train service in some sections, owing to war necessities, hindered salesmen from making territories as rapidly as before. Sales managers found that by using automobiles for transport of salesmen, the size of sales territories could be increased and territories reduced. The measure also made possible a more intensive degree of cultivation in the smaller towns to which, even in the best of times, infrequent train service only was available, making it necessary for the salesman to slight some dealers in order to make the train for his next point.

The motor truck gained eminence as an instrument of physical distribution. Soon after the United States entered the war the Government suggested that businessmen relieve the strain upon the railroads by employing trucks for all freight movements under forty miles. Manufacturers of advertised goods with distribution in thickly populated districts became interested in the use of trucks for direct delivery. Previously there had been a fear of prohibitive cost per ton-mile in the employment of trucks for overland distributive service. The truck was found both economical and flexible for many shipping purposes, and it won a permanent place. Results: huge increase in the sales of commercial vehicles; development of nation-wide networks of trucking services; a swifter pace of distribution for short-haul movements; a vast stimulus to the building of concrete roadways.

One of the greatest industrial changes wrought by the war was the widespread employment of women in business caused by the withdrawal of man-power for war purposes. Women were assigned to duties which had been assumed to be entirely beyond the scope of their abilities. Not only were they engaged for clerical work on a much larger scale than ever before, but were widely employed for factory work. Some houses put women on their sales forces. In many forms of routine activity women proved to be better workers than men, perhaps less accurate on the whole, but more conscientious and painstaking. To a considerable extent the new place of women in business continued to be permanent after the war had ceased.

The resultant marketing effects were to be almost endless in their ramifications. Woman became important as a personal consumer of goods as well as a purchasing agent for the home. The influx of single girls into business life was supplemented by a tremendous reduction in the proportion of women who retired from industry upon marriage.

Buying habits in matter of dress were revolutionized. The demand for freedom in women's garb doomed the fussy and voluminous garments of old. The old-fashioned corset all but disappeared. Short dresses came upon the scene. Scope replaced durability as a virtue of the wardrobe; where a woman used to buy one or maybe two tailormade suits and have them do for a season or two, she began to buy street dresses made of inexpensive stuff and would wear out several in a season. In 1914 women's shoes were made either of black leather or white canvas and about 90 per cent of all sales were in staple black shoes. Women at work demanded higher quality footwear and more variety in style, color and materials. Women had more money to spend and being out in the world every day, more incentive to improve their dress. The sale of silk hosiery boomed as never before. It was the making of the cosmetic market. And the increase in the smoking of cigarettes by the feminine sex dates from this time. The trend to working after marriage brought forth the kitchenette apartment and, it may be hazarded, a vital influence upon the sales of canned goods.

As for developments in the home, an increasing scarcity of household workers and the growing habit of economy in household management caused more and more housewives to do their own work. Immigration from all parts of Europe virtually ceased, not only because of submarine warfare but because employment was so plentiful and remunerative in the old country. The Scandinavian girls and those of Ireland, who made the best of

1918

C ENTRAL POWERS and Russia sign peace terms. . . . U. S. troops take St. Mihiel. . . . Franco-American forces launch attack in the Argonne. . . . British break the Hindenburg Line. . . . Allies reach truce with Turkey and Austria. . . U. S. troops reach Sedan. . . The Kaiser abdicates and flees to Holland. . . . Armistice signed and bugles sound "Cease Firing" at 11 a. m. November 11.

William H. Johns elected president of the George Batten Company to succeed the late George Batten. . . . General Motors takes over the Chevrolet Motor Car Company. . . . Bruce Barton and Roy S. Durstine form the Barton & Durstine Company. . . . Great scramble for woolen underwear as fuel conservation program lowers temperatures in offices and stores. . . . William Randolph Hearst purchases the Chicago *Herald* and merges it with the *Examiner*. . . . Gov. Arthur Capper of Kansas, head of the Capper Publications, elected to the United States Senate. . . . S. R. McKelvie, publisher of *Nebraska Farmer*, elected governor of Nebraska. . . . Frank S. Cunningham is the new president of Butler Brothers. . . . 600 of the 1,500 conductors on the New York surface cars are women.

Judge Robert Worth Bingham acquires the Louisville *Courier-Journal* and *Times*. . . . High price of butter brings heavy advertising of oleomargarine. . . . War Department takes over the entire output of Bull Durham tobacco. . . . S. E. Thomason named business manager of the Chicago *Tribune*. . . . Herbert F. Gunnison now publisher of the Brooklyn *Eagle*. . . . Popular sentiment against anything smacking of Teutonic origin causes changes in company names and trade-marks having a German flavor, while sauerkraut has become "liberty cabbage" and the frankfurter is a "liberty sausage."

servants, became very few in number. The opportunity for women to work in factories at wages which few housewives could afford to meet further accentuated the shortage. The hired girl, long a fixture in the majority of middle-class American homes, all but disappeared.

Once started in taking care of the home herself, the housewife, in the main, continued to do so. Thus was opened a responsive market such as had never before been experienced for manufacturers of all manner of goods capable of saving steps and making household tasks easier. This was the real genesis of the mass market for refrigerators, carpet sweepers and electrical appliances of all kinds.

The northward migration of the Negro induced a similar condition in the South. The movement had been under way for some years, but with the war, industry drew upon this source of labor to a greater extent than ever. The problem for the South became complicated by the effect of the military draft, which meant the withdrawal of thousands of Negro workers from factories and farms. Negro women went into the factories in the South; others traveled northward with their male relatives, with a resulting shortage in domestic help. With help hard to get, the Southern home was opened to labor-saving appliances, while Southern agriculture turned to power farming equipment to replace the depleted supply of cheap labor.

National daylight saving was put in effect in 1918 as a means of providing incentive for the home gardening movement and to save on electricity. Summer daylight saving continued in many centers in the succeeding years and helped to stimulate sales of golfing and other sporting equipment, of gasoline and of many other commodities pertaining to leisure life in the outdoors.

The war even affected our sleeping habits. The Government insisted on a separate sleeping unit for every soldier in the barracks. The wartime epidemic of Spanish influenza caused millions of people to favor individual beds. Whereupon followed a vast stimulus to the sale of twin beds and an influence, one way or the other, upon the activities of the divorce courts.

CHAPTER VII
Reconstruction
(1919-1921)

THE joy of victory and of peace sent business forward at a gallop immediately the warring powers affixed their signatures to the declaration of Armistice. The War Industries Board lifted its ban against certain "non-essential" enterprises, released raw materials and reversed many of its priority orders. Wartime restrictions on advertising were removed. Advertisers of practically all classes and representing almost every advertised product planned largely increased appropriations. Makers of goods with sugar as a basis, who had had very hard sledding in the closing days of the conflict, plotted big campaigns to recover lost ground. Automobile advertising resumed in large volume.

The initial enthusiasm dimmed into rather a widespread state of apprehension and hesitancy in the early weeks of 1919. Certain grave aspects of the problem of reconstruction, overlooked in the first burst of optimism, were impressed upon the consciousness of the business community and the nation at large.

War needs and war changes had wrought abnormal industrial conditions. War finance brought inflations and upward movements of prices. The markets of the world were disorganized. Products, sources of raw materials, machinery and industrial equipment had been crippled or destroyed in many countries, not a few of which were bankrupt or practically so. Though geographical position had protected the United States from the devastation and destruction which were the lot of continental Europe, many domestic product problems were bound up with the plight of the war-torn nations, for finance, loans and production are to a large extent organized on a worldwide basis. The signing of the peace treaty had not yet taken place.

Of more immediate concern, however were concrete domestic problems of labor, prices and production.

One of the biggest question marks was the returned soldier. Some four million soldiers and sailors were freed from action and places had to be found for them in the industrial life. In addition millions of men and women wage-earners in the war industries were no longer needed for war work. Labor unrest threatened as reductions in wage scales seemed necessary. In the matter of production, billions in capital, plants and equipment had become suddenly available for peace use. Every war plant, swelled to many times its former peacetime capacity, meant either great potential competition or disastrous decay. Helping these hundreds of factories shift from producing war supplies to peacetime necessities meant tremendous problems in financing. Besides, vast stores of military supplies hung over the market. Superimposed upon all these apparent difficulties was a widespread conviction that costs of commodities must go down rapidly. Consumers, retailers and wholesalers showed signs of refraining from buying in the belief that prices would have to come down at once.

The psychology of pessimism based

1919

ON April 1st, 1919, a new advertising agency hung out its shingle.

Its first advertisement, in Printers' Ink, said it was "founded on the idea of rendering superlative service to a small number of advertisers."

Its slogan was "NOT HOW MUCH, BUT HOW WELL". . . a slogan *to be lived,* as well as *talked about.*

Today in 1938, nineteen years later, finds Newell-Emmett one of the large agencies in terms of organization . . . yet serving a total of but 19 advertisers . . . and still operating under its original policy of exceptional thoroughness.

Newell-Emmett Company
Incorporated

Advertising Counsel

40 EAST 34TH STREET

NEW YORK

"NOT HOW MUCH, BUT HOW WELL"

Some highlight facts about Hardware Age—

1. It was founded 83 years ago as "The Hardwareman's Newspaper." It is still even more outstandingly the hardwareman's newspaper.

2. Its *Circulation* is at its *all-time high* following a steady six-year climb—it's now 21,106 (A. B. C.).

3. Its *Renewal Rate* has fluctuated narrowly above and below 80% for three years—that's Reader Interest.

Hardware Age is

A Chilton Publication

4. It provides *Adequate Coverage*—(there is one Hardware Age subscription to every six people employed in the trade.

5. *Over 93% of the advertisers* doing any national hardware publication advertising last year *used Hardware Age.* Hardware Age published more than 71% of the space.

6. 7 out of 10 Hardware Age advertisers did not use the competing paper—H. A. filled the bill.

7. 71% of our advertisers were *renewals* and used 87% of our total space last year—*they came back for more.*

All in all, hardware dealers and jobbers LIKE to read Hardware Age and advertisers LIKE to advertise in it.

on these considerations was short-lived, however, and it did not penetrate very deeply into the national consciousness. The year 1919 was still young when the country set upon an inflationary course unmatched in previous peacetime experience. Relief over the passing of the war emergency prevailed over preoccupation with the problems of reconstruction and helped, temporarily, to solve them. The middle and lower classes had more money than ever before. The farmer had enjoyed a period of exceptional prosperity as a result of wartime price levels. People had money. To give expression to the reaction from wartime worries and difficulties and to indulge their new taste for luxuries, they set out on one of the great buying jags of all time. Spending became the national sport.

In consequence, business moved into an intensified seller's market. The main problem was to produce enough goods to fill the orders on hand, rather than to secure orders

---

1919

VERSAILLES PEACE TREATY drawn and signed by Allied Powers and Germany but rejected by U. S. Senate. . . . Cost of war announced as $21,354,867,000. . . . Wartime Prohibition Act becomes effective; Eighteenth Amendment ratified by thirty-sixth State. . . . Navy seaplane NC-4 completes Eastward flight across Atlantic.

Crowell Publishing Company assumes control of *Collier's.* . . . Arthur Freeman, former advertising director of Gimbel's and Macy's, joins Einson Litho, Inc. . . . Thomas F. Logan enters agency business at New York. . . . Approximately twenty million smokers in U. S., of whom 40 per cent smoke cigars. . . . N. W. Ayer & Son celebrate fiftieth anniversary. . . . E. T. Gundlach in England as chairman of an American committee to investigate labor conditions. . . . Gem, Ever Ready and Star razor companies merge. . . . Printers' strike in New York temporarily holds up publication of 150 magazines and twice that number of business papers.

Clarence D. Newell, Burton Emmett and associates organize the Newell-Emmett Company. . . . E. Lansing Ray elected president of the St. Louis *Globe-Democrat.* . . . Harry J. Grant now publisher of the Milwaukee *Journal.* . . . Kerwin H. Fulton, president of the Poster Advertising Company, and associates in that firm acquire the O. J. Gude Company. . . . Howard Davis named business manager of the New York *Tribune.* . . . Edsel Ford elected president of Ford Motor Company to succeed his father. . . . Chicago Association of Commerce establishes the Advertising Council. . . . Women in many communities still bashful about buying cosmetics from male sales clerks.

to absorb the output of the war-augmented production machine. A general scarcity of raw materials helped to keep production in line with demand, while much of the surplus war stocks went abroad for relief of Belgium and other stricken nations. People kicked some about high prices, but in actuality it never before was so easy to sell merchandise.

Naturally in this state of affairs the anticipated problems of labor absorption didn't come to much and the war service men and war industry workers were taken into peacetime pursuits with comparative ease. In almost every line a scarcity of workers set in and it cost real money to get them and develop them. Even half-time jobs went begging. A number of firms actually used display advertisements to sell people on coming to work for them, describing the working conditions in glowing terms.

Selling problems received scanty attention because at the moment they seemed quite unimportant. In many fields activities in selling goods were confined to apportioning products among clamorous buyers. Retailers' shelves were swept clean by panicky waves of buying. Sales forces were relaxed in discipline and salesmen became flabby. Advertising plans and copy were approved perfunctorily because it was deemed necessary only to keep one's name before the public. In other words, it became a fixed habit of mind to concentrate upon producing goods and give to selling only such attention as was urgently demanded.

Volume of advertising increased enormously, however. The first six months of 1919 broke all records for space used and in the years 1919 and 1920 business invested more in advertising than ever before. It is a common impression that the great growth of advertising in this period is traceable to the war excess profits tax. The Government allowed advertisers to deduct advertising costs as an expense in reckoning their taxable profits. According to the popular theory, manufacturers were diverting their profits into advertising channels to escape paying the tax, thus creating good-will largely at the expense of the Government.

However, the more plausible explanation of the huge proportions to which appropriations climbed lies in the fact that advertising expenditures and sales figures are likely to run pretty close together, especially since at that time most companies figured their budgets on the basis of a percentage of sales. Moreover, many new advertised products appeared at this time as a result of conversion of huge war plants to production for normal needs. And, as previously noted, numerous advertisers prevented by war restrictions from promoting their goods in 1917 and 1918 sought to regain former momentum by increasing the intensity of their efforts.

While the excess profits tax undoubtedly accounted for a certain amount of the growth, its role was decidedly not a major one. When business fell off in 1921, advertising fell off in sympathy. When business activity went vigorously on the upgrade in 1922, advertising activity resumed. The excess profits tax was repealed on January 1, 1922, and there is nothing in the figures on advertising volume in 1922 and the years immediately following to suggest that the absence of the alleged tax incentive was any deterrent, a consideration which adds material strength to the proposition that its presence exerted a relatively minor influence.

One interesting shift in advertiser activity was brought about by the Wartime Prohibition Act, which became effective in June of 1919 and a part of the Constitution, in the form of the Eighteenth Amendment, in the following year. Faced with the problem of doing something with their huge investment in plants and equipment, many brewers and distillers entered new lines of business, including candy and kindred specialties, meat packing, evaporated milk, vinegar, butter substitutes and, of course, soft drinks and cereal beverages. A deluge of soft drinks got under way to provide consolation for a prohibition-swept nation. More imagination was shown in the naming of these new arrivals than in any other branch of business activity since the beginning of trade-marks. Among the choicer new names were Wow, Submarine Chaser, Vigoro (not to be confused with the present-day Swift & Company product for encouraging the growth of plants), Non-tox, Dan-DeLio, Flivver, Konsolation, Fizzo, O-Kid-O and Jazz.

Prohibition produced a vast increase in consumption of candy and chewing gum, producers of these stepping up their promotional activities to take advantage of sugar's popular reputation for ability to allay the craving for alcohol. Candy manufacturers were inspired to promote their product as a nourishing and desirable food, as well as an appropriate substitute for alcoholic drinks. Until this time candy had been regarded as a mere luxury and not a very healthful one at that—something for mothers to guard their children against and for the young man to haul in beribboned boxes to his sweetheart.

The banning of legal liquor also stimulated the activities of dairy companies and tea and coffee distributors. Coffee sales increased threefold in two years. More indirectly, the new legislation created a great increase in sales opportunities for equipment used in various types of sports, such as trap-shooting, golf, tennis and fishing.

Intensively cultivated for the first time in this period was the idea of stressing service features in business. Many business men were coming around to the belief that the greatest commercial success could be attained only through rendering some measure of service to the buying public, and this philosophy was widely reflected in the advertising of 1919 and 1920. Shoe companies told people how to make their shoes last longer, automobile accessory companies stressed the servicing facilities on their products, several food companies instituted domestic science departments to create household helps for promulgation through publication advertising and direct-mail literature. There was a general disposition to relate the product in some way to the idea of helping the consumer with his problems.

In retailing emerged a pronounced tendency toward widening of lines. High prices, scarcity of some lines of merchandise and the strenuous scramble for volume caused the retailer to attempt to handle anything he thought his customers might buy from him. The druggist's business centered more than ever around the soda fountain and to his line of miscellaneous specialties he added coffee, laundry soaps and extracts. Meanwhile the grocer began to handle almost as many side-lines as the drug store, including packaged drug lines, luxury toilet soaps, kitchen utensils and, in extreme instances, tires, automobile accessories and electrical appliances. The handling of drugs in grocery stores caused druggists to seek legislation limiting distribution to the pharmacies.

One branch of distribution, however, suffered a contraction. By a consent decree with the Government, the "Big Five" packers—Armour, Swift, Wilson, Cudahy and Morris—dissolved their distribution activities in grocery products and confined themselves to packing house products. They also agreed to refrain from engaging in the retail meat business. This was the result of a long conflict waged by the National Wholesale Grocers' Association, which contended that the packers through their fast refrigerator cars had superior shipping facilities for grocery sides-lines which enabled them to undersell competitors.

As with all forms of over-indul-

1920

LEAGUE OF NATIONS meets for the first time. . . . Nineteenth Amendment (women's suffrage) and Eighteenth Amendment (prohibition) go into effect. . . . Wall Street bomb explosion kills thirty. . . . Republican ticket of Warren G. Harding and Calvin Coolidge defeats James Cox and Franklin D. Roosevelt, 404 electoral votes to 127. . . . Population now 105,710,620.

Roy W. Howard resigns as president of the United Press Associations to become general business director of the Scripps-McRae League of newspapers. . . . American Railway Express Company inaugurates air express service between New York and Chicago. . . . F. J. Ross withdraws from the Blackman-Ross Company to form own agency. . . . Frank A. Munsey buys the New York *Herald*. . . . James M. Mathes and Adam Kessler, Jr., admitted to partnership in N. W. Ayer. . . . The two-pants suit is coming in. . . . Reuben H. Donnelley elected president of the Associated Advertising Clubs of the World. . . . Crowell Publishing Company appoints Lee Maxwell vice-president. . . . Manufacturer of millinery makes news by basing his entire promotion campaign around the personality of a movie star—Madge Evans.

Edwin T. Meredith, publisher of *Successful Farming*, appointed secretary of agriculture in the cabinet of Woodrow Wilson. . . . Fritz J. Frank elected president and treasurer of the Iron Age Publishing Company. . . . Santa Claus, in low favor the last five years, stages an advertising comeback. . . . W. W. Wachtel appointed advertising manager of Loose-Wiles Biscuit Company. . . . Railroads returned to private ownership and getting ready to advertise again. . . . Widespread interest in communication with the spirit world moves Ouija boards in tremendous volume.

1920
This year we entered the picture

ALTHOUGH at the newly formed Aitkin-Kynett agency, the occasion was momentous, no great consternation stirred the advertising world.

Printers' Ink had to change the subscription list . . . publication representatives made notes to call . . . and the Philadelphia Telephone Directory added the name "Aitkin-Kynett Co."

As to what part good fortune or great brilliance has played in the survival and growth of this agency, opinion, if any, differs. But it may be written as accurate history that a tenacious determination to help sell merchandise has had an important rôle.

If the policy and the philosophy of an agency could be reduced to one over-all idea, Aitkin-Kynett might be summed up as the place where it is recognized that the client is in business to make money—and the agency's job is to aid that endeavor.

The AITKIN-KYNETT Co.
Advertising
1400 SOUTH PENN SQUARE, PHILADELPHIA

gence, the buying jag was to be followed by a hangover. The first glimpses of the dawn that was to bring a morning after came early in 1920. The free competition of buyers for materials and goods often drove up price instead of increasing production, and it also depreciated quality standards to a point where first-class merchandise was extremely rare. Too many prices were being made on the basis of, "Everybody expects to pay high prices so we might as well get our share." The cost of living soared higher and higher. Strikes and social unrest began to appear. Extravagant disregard of price, although still a fairly prominent factor, became less fashionable than formerly. Sanity in buying began to return.

Soon the consumer's growing resentment against high prices commenced to take effective form. It was dramatized in the overall movement. In the South overall clubs were formed, members pledging themselves to wear overalls until clothing prices came down. Advertising in newspapers and other media was employed by consumers to promote the formation of clubs. The movement spread over that section, then northward, even to Broadway. Ministers in leading churches supported the idea and made sermons on the subject. Overalls became almost the universal attire on college campuses. The overall manufacturers were alarmed rather than pleased, however, and they tried to discourage fad buying, running advertisements pointing out that the abnormal demand raised the price of the garments and hurt the working man, who had to have them.

A general old clothes movement, unorganized but lasting, proved far more effective than the overall craze. People made their old garments do instead of buying new ones. Men had their suits turned. The half-sole enjoyed huge popularity. Now in an entirely new mood, people were demanding lower-priced goods where before they clamored for the most expensive clothing, silk shirts and the costly cuts of meats. The orgy of spending gave way to determined, almost vindictive cutting down of purchasing. Not a few storekeepers advised their customers not to buy unless they had to and some lumber dealers published advertisements advising the public not to build at this time because prices were much too high. Labor union stores were established to combat high prices of food and clothing.

All this was not long in having its effect. By May of 1920 scattering of price reductions had given way to a pronounced deflation. A wave of sensational price-cutting engulfed the country. Many department stores placed a horizontal reduction on all merchandise. Cancellations of orders came back upon manufacturers in staggering volume. The market was clogged with goods. Manufacturers curtailed production. The mail-order houses groaned under terrific inventory loads. For a time there seemed no bottom to prices, and postponed buying in anticipation of further reductions deepened the collapse. Unemployment became serious. A credit crisis set in.

The depression brought a revival of sound marketing practice. Extravagant habits contracted during the period of buying hysteria were cut down and merchandise was liquidated at replacement values to make way for normal processes. In advertising, the idea was not so much to cut down as to make sure of greater results. A notable change came quickly over the general character of advertising. Real sales argument took the place of picturesqueness. With people shopping for good values once more, reason-why copy enjoyed a comeback.

Another return to the merchandising scene was staged by the premium, which took a new and significant form. During the war the premium was outlawed as non-essential and during the subsequent easy-sale period it was all but forgotten, some observers claiming it was gone never to be seen again. In the fight to get business late in 1920 and in 1921 the premium was pressed into service once more. But this time the emphasis was on useful articles, instead of the traditional bric-a-brac, ship pictures and ephemeral novelties. Staple, useable household necessities—such as glass water sets, aluminum kitchen utensils and crockery—were offered in exchange for premium coupons, and people began to weigh values in premiums just as closely as if they were paying money for them. Sampling also returned, though without the wholesale wastes of pre-war days. A number of manufacturers turned to selling of small packages through the five-and-ten-cent stores as a means of controlled sampling.

The old reliable problems joined the old reliable advertising and selling methods on the comeback trail. The private brand, which had all but disappeared during the war owing to the inability of manufacturers to produce goods above their own requirements, moved in to do its accustomed haunting. Not all the impetus was provided by the distributors, incidentally. Manufacturers, seeking volume, went around to wholesalers with ambitious proposals whereby they would provide labels under the distributor's name in return for a large order. Some firms specialized in this and some of the largest advertisers acting in what they believed to be self-defense went in for selling private brand merchandise.

The substitution problem came to the fore once again. During the merchandise shortage it was no great breach of faith to substitute for products of standard quality. In fact it was necessary to fill many orders in this way and it was all the customer came to expect; he was glad to get almost any article that filled his need, so great was the demand. Counteracting this attitude became an important job now that business was hard to get.

The biggest issue of all in the minds of most advertisers, however, was the retailer. The current situation was demonstrating more conclusively than ever that the retail store was the neck in the distribution bottle. Many firms discovered to their loss and dismay that this neck had become so badly choked up that they were unable to get their goods into consumption. The retail clerk, careless and inefficient in the best of times, had got worse since the war. He had acquired a take-it-or-leave-it attitude in the days when merchandise was at a premium and customers could be insulted with profit, and he hadn't gotten over it. This was at least partly the fault of the advertisers, however, for during that same seller's market they had taken little trouble to interest themselves in the affairs of retailing.

To add further to the advertiser's ire and dissatisfaction, the epidemic of cancellations from retailers went from a reasonable to a frenzied stage; then buyers resumed their old tricks of demanding spe-

MEDALS
SUGAR BOWLS
AND READERS

Back in the days when such things seemed to be important The Iron Age was selected for many awards and medals. For example, silver medals at Paris in 1878 and 1889, the highest award at Chicago in 1893, and a gold medal at Paris in 1900.

Most significant of all, however, was the SILVER SUGAR BOWL awarded by Printers' Ink in 1901 to The Iron Age as "the one trade paper in the United States of America that, taken all in all, renders its constituency the best service and best serves its purpose as a medium for communication with a specified class."

Publications are no longer singled out in this way. Industrial advertisers are not interested in awards and medals. They are more interested in readers. They have, happily, more tangible means of judging publication values. Facts and figures, rather than Sugar Bowls are available to show that The Iron Age renders outstanding service to an even greater industry today.

It is still the leader in its field in influence, reader interest, and readers of the type who count when buying decisions are made.

THE IRON AGE

(MAIN LINE OF THE METAL WORKING INDUSTRY)

A Chilton 🖤 *Publication*

239 W. 39th St.   NEW YORK

al promotion discounts, pay for window space, demonstration allowances and all sorts of concessions. Some firms bethought themselves of radical remedies. The large number of factory-to-consumer surplus stock sales which had been carried on with more or less success in the liquidation furor suggested the opportunity of going past both jobber and retailer direct to the consumer. A number of concerns joined the ranks of those maintaining factory-owned retail stores in large cities, and some went into small towns as well. Some firms tried out selling by mail, though without much success. A few companies took the opposite tack of actively cultivating retailer good-will. A number of advertising campaigns featured the retailer's salespeople and place of business, telling about his service to the community. Particularly noteworthy was the Johnson & Johnson campaign of 1921, in which the company undertook to educate the public in the druggist's value to the community and at the same time cause druggists to become more thoroughly conscious of their responsibilities.

Discontent extended to the jobber system and the jobber distribution question was asked more frequently than ever before. Impressive food for thought on this count was provided by the announcement of Procter & Gamble in 1920 that, preferring to attend to their own distribution instead of leaving it to jobbers, they would divorce themselves from all wholesaling connections and distribute direct to retailers throughout the United States. The action followed experimental direct sale in the Eastern territory during the preceding year.

During the reconstruction years new developments in marketing policy and practice were few. The most important single innovation in business at large was a new attitude in the matter of employee relations —some companies saw this to be essentially a selling proposition. When the war was in progress, capital, management and labor glimpsed a new vision. During the emergency the great common purpose demanded that old differences be buried, and it was proved that the three elements could work together in harmony if the motives were strong enough. Furthermore, the value of high morale in manufacturing pursuits was clearly demonstrated in the experiences of the wartime industries and the Government industries, wherein campaigns of advertising to workers had borne fruit.

The more progressive business executives realized that the man in the factory is not a mere instrument of production, but a human being actuated by the same motives and responding to the same appeals as the rest of the public. They saw that stabilization of labor conditions could mean a reduction in costly labor turnover, that the man who was interested in his company and his task was a more efficient worker.

Many of this number went further and recognized that any sales campaign presupposes goods to sell, goods which will stand up in the competitive market, and accordingly they set out to establish a real basis for mutually co-operative employee relations. The period saw all sorts of employee welfare projects and plans for workers' representation in profits and management. Numerous firms put in plans to enable their employees to purchase company stock at a favorable price.

IN 1914, manufacturers and wholesalers alike were faced with doubt and confusion brought on by the rise of chain stores in retailing. Some advertisers saw destruction at the hands of chain operators. Retailers looked only on a dim horizon. Aroused by the seriousness of the problem, M. M. Zimmerman, then a staff member of *Printers' Ink,* was co-author in an intensive study of the significance of chain store distribution.

Sixteen years later, the chain store problem again became acute. On one side the manufacturer faced the advantages offered by chains and on the other antagonism from independents lacking the ammunition to battle in price wars. M. M. Zimmerman brought his series of interpretive, analytical, and informative articles up to date to give an impartial picture from which the manufacturer could guide his operations. Both of these series, as the years have proved, predicted the future with unerring accuracy. They enabled many a manufacturer to establish a line of action with precision and confidence.

In 1932, the food world was startled to hear that a huge circus-like retail store had opened up under the name of Big Bear in an abandoned factory. It provoked fantastic stories; outstanding of these was that it constituted a means for dumping surplus merchandise. No one believed that Big Bear was destined to play a vital part in the future destinies of the corporate chain.

It was natural for Mr. Zimmerman to watch this development. He gathered facts from every possible agency that would indicate the distributive importance of these Super Markets. When he had analyzed his facts, he was convinced that the Super Market was more than a flash in the depression pan. He found that the Super Market had established itself as a new type of retailing which would always attract a substantial percentage of the consuming public who saw sufficient savings in their food purchases to justify the sacrifice in additional service they might be getting from independents. This information was published in a series of articles of which *Printers'*

GROWTH AND INFLUENCE

Ink said in the preface: "We hesitate not at all to say that in this series Mr. Zimmerman has done perhaps the outstanding job of his career; he clarifies and makes plain a merchandising situation that fairly bristles with question marks."

In each of these successive steps, it was *Printers' Ink* which opened its pages to Mr. Zimmerman's articles and gave him the opportunity to express his almost prophetic outline of future trends. Now, after fifty years, *Printers' Ink* stands as one of the real forces in American industrial life, ever alert to the pulse of the future.

And it was this complete and authoritative background of research and merchandising which led to the founding by M. M. Zimmerman of SUPER MARKET MERCHANDISING, the only publication serving the Super Market operators. There can be no doubt of the influence exerted by M. M. Zimmerman and by the pages of SUPER MARKET MERCHANDISING in this new and colossal world of mass distribution. In its short existence of less than two years, it already has behind it a notable record of achievement. It organized SUPER MARKET INSTITUTE—it inaugurated, sponsored and successfully executed "NATIONALLY ADVERTISED BRANDS WEEK", which has become the greatest and most valuable promotion in behalf of nationally advertised brands.

Every issue of this magazine enters the office of the Super Market executive amid an atmosphere of acceptance. This same acceptance carries over to advertising in the pages of SUPER MARKET MERCHANDISING.

SUPER MARKET MERCHANDISING reaches over 9,000 mass buyers not only in the Super Market field but practically all the mass buyers in the entire field of food distribution. Every important food executive finds SUPER MARKET MERCHANDISING an absolute necessity in keeping him abreast of the constant changes in the field of self service operation and in the general field of food distribution.

For further information and advertising rate card—write

SUPER MARKET MERCHANDISING

45 West 45th Street, New York City

This was not exactly new, for Procter & Gamble had established a program for sharing company earnings with workers as early as 1887. The idea gained little acceptance elsewhere, however, until 1919. Several plans for profit-sharing or wage dividends went into effect in that year and in 1920. Many more came in 1921, as heads of businesses saw better conditions ahead and sought production efficiency and harmony by increasing employee interest in the progress of the firm.

It must be recorded, however, that by no means all of the plans for employee betterment were dictated by so far-sighted a sense of fair dealing and long-term mutual benefit. A fear of Bolshevism, or

1921

WILLIAM H. TAFT appointed Chief Justice of the Supreme Court to succeed the late Edward D. White. . . . Immigration Quota Act drastically limits immigration. . . . Five-power naval treaty signed at Washington by Great Britain, France, Japan, Italy and U. S. . . . Enrico Caruso dies at Naples.

Theodore F. Merseles heads Montgomery Ward. . . . Periodical Publishers Association re-organized to function exclusively with respect to the advertising problems of magazines. . . . Don Francisco becomes co-manager of the Pacific Coast offices of Lord & Thomas. . . . Advertising Typographers of America organized at Cleveland. . . . Frederick E. Murphy named publisher of the Minneapolis *Tribune*. . . . Art Directors Club of New York holds first annual exhibition. . . . Norval Hawkins, former Ford sales manager, becomes sales and advertising director of General Motors. . . . Death of Gen. Charles H. Taylor, forty-eight years publisher of the Boston *Globe*.

A. D. Lasker appointed chairman of the United States Shipping Board, Claude C. Hopkins succeeding him as president of Lord & Thomas. . . . Henry C. Wallace, publisher of *Wallaces' Farmer*, becomes secretary of agriculture in the Harding cabinet. . . . Courtland Smith, head of the American Press Association, named assistant postmaster general. . . . H. B. LeQuatte now president of Churchill-Hall, Inc. . . . Sudden vogue for the advertising man as a hero of magazine fiction. . . . Corporate name of Rickard & Sloan changed to Rickard & Company. . . . After many years as an advertising illustration service, the Charles Daniel Frey Company becomes a general advertising agency. . . . Some of the motor car makers are talking about streamlining. . . . William Randolph Hearst buys the Detroit *Times*. . . . John Hanrahan organizes a promotion service for publishers. . . . Taking a cue from yeast, Page & Shaw advertise vitamins in chocolate bars.

an Americanized version of it, spread through the land in 1919 and persisted for some time thereafter. Widespread strikes and the activities of the Industrial Workers of the World fed the fire, which in some industrial quarters flamed into an hysterical obsession. No small number of the plans for improvement of the condition of the worker were mere sops prompted by the opportunism of jittery employers. The plans were abandoned as the supposed crisis had passed. None the less, significant permanent gains in this field were achieved by more than a few leading advertisers who made constructive industrial relations, in one form or another, a permanent part of management policy.

In the field of advertising practice there were just two wholly new developments of special note. The American Association of Advertising Agencies made great strides in placing agency operations on a standardized basis with the adoption of a uniform rate card, form of contract and order blank, cost finding system and outline plan for handling advertising. The organization also formulated a policy for members relative to the rendering of adequate service on business-paper advertising.

A contribution to scientific space buying was made by Benjamin Jefferson in 1920 when he introduced the idea of the milline as a common denominator to show the cost per line in terms of relative circulation. The milline expresses the rate per line per million circulation, and while it, of course, takes no account of circulation quality, it affords a clearer conception of what is being paid for advertising service than had been available before. It immediately attracted wide interest in the advertising and publishing business and was quickly accepted as a common denominator for judging advertising rates.

Aside from the few developments cited, the advertiser activities of the period were given over to the preeminent considerations of getting production and marketing operations back to a peacetime basis. There was neither time nor incentive for thinking much about new directions. The main idea was to get back to "normalcy."

The late months of 1921 found the readjustment cycle on its way to completion. Money became easier and cheaper, basic commodities leaped forward in value, farm products entered upon a rising trend. Advertisers turned, without, of course, realizing quite what was up, to face the problems of an entirely new era in marketing.

CHAPTER VIII

Dawn of the Distribution Age

(1922-1929)

THE gathering forces of a new business momentum were plainly discernible in the spring of 1922. By fall, though strikes abounded and not a few factories were closed because the railroad strike hampered delivery of raw materials, many companies were behind on their orders. Wage scales began to increase. Unemployment had all but disappeared and employment agencies were advertising for workers once more. Stock prices moved up steadily.

America went to work to make good the immense shortages in its economic life. There was a six-year accumulation of construction shortage, new building having been almost at a standstill through the war and reconstruction periods. The railroads, back in private hands once more, stood in need of vast amounts of new equipment. The new opportunities confronting the automobile and the truck had barely been touched. And as to the general lines of retail commodities, the wholesale purchasing of the country had been on a short-time basis for nearly two years, producing a condition of distinctly low stocks in thousands of retail stores.

The entire economic machine responded to these primary stimulations and soon the nation careened off in high upon an unparalleled course of inflation, mental, physical, moral, spiritual and anything else you care to name. Business began to slow up a bit in the early spring of 1924, but new confidence, engendered by somewhat improved con-

dition of the farmer and the new low tax measures, soon set the wheels turning faster than ever. A wave of pessimism threatened in 1928. Profits were thinning out. Unemployment was getting on the front pages of newspapers. For two years the general commodity price level had moved within a comparatively narrow range and the trend was downward. The buying power of a large part of the rest of the world was lagging behind its normal volume and that of the American farmer was at a low ebb. The pace of production was running down. The storm signals were obscured, however, by the mounting speculative fever in the stock market and the dubiety of 1928 gave way to 1929's proclamations of "The New Era."

Real estate values in the promised land of endless prosperity underwent a $15,000,000,000 decline in the last two months of 1929 and day of reckoning succeeded day of reckoning until the tragic summation was an unparalleled economic paralysis. Mars at last demanded payment of his bill.

As events have proved, the reconstruction period of 1919-21 was a mere transition from military to civilian life. The adjustment necessitated by war's destruction and dislocation of the world economic structure had never been made. Although no physical ruination had been visited upon America and its loss in man-power was relatively small, vast outpourings of its wealth were sucked into the processes

THE
PENALTY OF
LEADER∫HIP

IN EVERY field of human endeavor, he that is first must perpetually live in the white light of publicity. Whether the leadership be vested in a man or in a manufactured product, emulation and envy are ever at work. ⟨ In art, in literature, in music, in industry, the reward and the punishment are always the same. ⟨ The reward is widespread recognition; the punishment, fierce denial and detraction. ⟨ When a man's work becomes a standard for the whole world, it also becomes a target for the shafts of the envious few. If his work be merely mediocre, he will be left severely alone — if he achieve a masterpiece, it will set a million tongues a-wagging. ⟨ Jealousy does not protrude its forked tongue at the artist who produces a commonplace painting. ⟨ Whatsoever you write, or paint, or play, or sing, or build, no one will strive to surpass or to slander you, unless your work be stamped with the seal of genius. ⟨ Long, long after a great work or a good work has been done, those who are disappointed or envious continue to cry out that it cannot be done. ⟨ Spiteful little voices in the domain of art were raised against our own Whistler as a mountebank, long after the big world had acclaimed him its greatest artistic genius. ⟨ Multitudes flocked to Bayreuth to worship at the musical shrine of Wagner, while the little group of those whom he had dethroned and displaced argued angrily that he was no musician at all. ⟨ The little world continued to protest that Fulton could never build a steamboat, while the big world flocked to the river banks to see his boat steam by. ⟨ The leader is assailed because he is a leader, and the effort to equal him is merely added proof of that leadership. ⟨ Failing to equal or to excel, the follower seeks to depreciate and to destroy — but only confirms once more the superiority of that which he strives to supplant. ⟨ There is nothing new in this. It is as old as the world and as old as the human passions—envy, fear, greed, ambition, and the desire to surpass. ⟨ And it all avails nothing. ⟨ If the leader truly leads, he remains—the leader. ⟨ Master-poet, master-painter, master-workman, each in his turn is assailed, and each holds his laurels through the ages. ⟨ That which is good or great makes itself known, no matter how loud the clamor of denial. ⟨ That which deserves to live—lives.

This text appeared in an advertisement in the
Saturday Evening Post, January 2 in
the year 1915. Copyright
Cadillac Motor Car
Company

Cadillac's most famous advertisement written
in 1914 by Theodore F. MacManus

Palmolive became favorably known because of its attractive advertising illustration and restrained copy. This was a 1924 poster

An early example of the negative copy appeal that grew in favor in the Twenties. This was a 1926 advertisement

Haltingly, in 1926, cigarette manufacturers sounded out the public's reaction to the appearance of women in their advertising

both of waging the war and partial resuscitation of impoverished Europe. To a large degree the boom fed upon fictional sales transactions with nations abroad, transactions which turned out to be gifts of our resources, for the loans upon which they were based could not be repaid. Domestically, this added to the distance of the final drop, although, of course, substantial deflation was inevitable.

While the war was at the bottom of the calamity, numerous other factors were naturally involved, factors which in complete enumeration might easily fill many volumes, and have. Booms, like floods, fires and famines, are disorganizing influences in the industrial system. They enormously increase the risks of business and the large speculative gains of the few are offset by the losses to others and the general disturbance to business. When the advances in price which they bring apply unequally to economic groups —in this instance the farmer, whose welfare so importantly figures in the country's economic health—all sorts of maladjustments and disturbances result. Moreover, the boom psychology produces staggering excesses in credit policies, in production programs, and in marketing practices, as well as abnormalities in the public temper.

This, in brief and admittedly over-simplified terms, is the economic backdrop against which the eighth phase of the development of modern marketing was staged. Obviously, the hectic events of so turbulent and abortive a period in the national life had a considerable influence upon the contemporary technique of selling and advertising. At many points the backdrop obscures what is, for the purposes of the present discussion, the main action.

Fundamentally, however, these years were portentous ones from a marketing standpoint. Though the heralded dawn of permanent prosperity was to prove illusory, this was, in quite another sense, a genuine new era in the nation's economic life. A new pioneering period had arrived.

For more than a century after the founding of the republic, ours had been an agricultural economy. Although in gestation for many years, the age of industrial production did not assume any sort of predominance until the middle 1880's and, as previously remarked, the breasting of the last frontiers was the final sign of the end of the era of agricultural pioneering. Organization of the forces of machine production then came to the fore and, concurrently, the sales function of business was developed to help carry to the consumer the news of the increasing yield of the machine.

So great was the progress in gearing up industrial production to new speeds and new quantities that in 1920 the volume of manufactured products exceeded by 95 per cent the production in 1900, while in that same interval the population increased roughly 40 per cent. Mass production, in the beginning, unleashed the forces of mass selling. Then, in turn, mass selling opened the way for further stepping up of production in quantity, establishing a profitable basis for developing and applying new economies in manufacture—an assignment for which American mechanical genius demonstrated itself to be more than adequate. Finally, the war brought a concentration of expansion in production facilities, which, in 1920, were just beginning to be turned to peace-time uses.

The advent of 1922 marked, as nearly as any evolutionary process may be tied to a precise date, the end of the production age. The machine had grown up to the point where it matched normal, basic demands upon it. It was only a matter of time, and of a very short time at that, when the machine's capacity would surpass these normal basic demands. Though in the pioneering sense the production age had ended, invention had by no means closed its books. In addition, an industry-wide movement toward manufacturing simplification, born of the Government's standardization edicts during the war, took effect in 1922 and 1923. The result was a vast saving in production costs and, through concentration of production on a relatively small number of standardized lines, a great increase in production capacity.

Stated in its more significant terms, the advent of 1922 marked

---

1922

P RESIDENT HARDING vetoes the first soldiers' bonus bill. . . . Irish Free State formed. . . . Will Hays accepts an offer to become "czar" of the motion picture industry. . . . Death of Alexander Graham Bell and of John Wanamaker.

Edward Plaut becomes president of Lehn & Fink. . . . Meredith Publishing Company starts *Better Homes & Gardens*. . . . G. B. Lambert and Milton Feasley form the Lambert & Feasley agency. . . . Death of John M. Bundscho, leading figure in advertising typography. . . . Demand for closed cars has increased until they now represent 50 per cent of total sales. . . . Don C. Seitz named publisher of the New York *World* and John F. Bresnahan becomes advertising manager. . . . Detroit *News* buys the Detroit *Journal*. . . . The flapper's ban on corsets is giving that industry plenty to think about.

Scripps-Howard Newspapers formed to take over the business of the Scripps-McRae Newspapers, with Robert P. Scripps and Roy W. Howard as principal executives. . . . J. K. Fraser now president of the Blackman Company. . . . Game of bridge is beginning to become an industry, but Mah Jongg looms as a threat. . . . Audit Bureau of Circulations decides to bar free-circulation publications from membership. . . . "Every day in every way I am getting better and better"—salesmen perking up as Emil Coue approaches American shores. . . . Richard A. Foley, prominent Philadelphia agent, dies. . . . Henry Morgenthau, Jr., buys *American Agriculturist*. . . . Jazz music said to be menacing the morals of youth. . . . Men are turning to soft collars and alarmed laundry owners are advertising the idea that the starched collar is an index of character.

We remember

we remember

LITTLE THINGS tell us that time is passing, that soon our hour-glass will be heavy-bottomed. So now on the day of the 50th Anniversary of this journal, we, too, are plagued by the nostalgic remembrance of facts forgotten. We remember...we remember, that in the fourth month of this year our renewal business was 57% above that for the fourth month of the year before. In fact, WOR renewal business for the first quarter of this year was 45% ahead of that for the first quarter of 1937...and 1937 *was* a good year. It is hard to picture cherubs and fat doves descending blithely upon us in this time of drought, but almost as good is this response of our advertisers to the lure of RESULTS in this, the 16th year of our growth and the seventh month of a great year. Thanks to the special WOR campaigns of, Bristol-Myers, Tydol, Borden, General Foods, Colgate-Palmolive-Peet, Procter & Gamble, American Tobacco, Childs Restaurants, and more than one-hundred other shrewd time-buyers whose names we'd mention if we had the space to offer. All in all, a flighty season, more larkish than we have known in some time.

Congratulations Youngster...

"*So You're* Fifty Years *old...*"

... and a fine looking lad you've grown to be ... I remember way back in '88 when you were born ... yes, and I can remember back a great deal further than that, for I'll be a hundred years old myself come next birthday ... and feeling younger every day of my life."

In November 1939 the Beacon-Journal will be one hundred years old. We are justifiably proud of our record of growth and leadership in the development of this industrial city. With a circulation of 72,524 in this rich manufacturing and retail area the Beacon-Journal provides complete, economical coverage of the Alert, Free-spending Akron Market.

FIRST in AKRON
FOR ALMOST A CENTURY
AKRON BEACON JOURNAL

ESTABLISHED 1839

Represented by Story, Brooks & Finley

the opening of a new chapter in economic·history—the inaugural of the age of distribution.

Competition brought about quick recognition of the new condition, in the actions of advertisers if not in their conscious realization. Business rivalry mounted to an intensity never before known. Brand competition multiplied prodigiously in every line. As manufacturers, driven by the necessity of finding outlets for accelerated production, widened their sales territories, invaded additional channels of distribution and expanded their lines, each of them found himself challenged by new competitive factors. It was soon sensed that the answer was to be found principally in applying to distribution the same thoroughgoing study and effort that had been given to the earlier problems of production.

In sharp contrast to the better publicized trends and fancies of the 1920's, the setting in of the age of distribution was no mere transitory phase. It was a basic economic change whose effects and implications projected far into the future —and still do. The marketing developments of the years from 1922 to 1929 were simply the beginnings of the work of adjustment to the conditions and responsibilities imposed by the new epoch.

The opening approach was a direct response to the immediate pressure exerted by the changed condition in the market place. As a group, advertisers addressed themselves to the job of rendering the marketing process a more efficient one. They sought competitive advantage in trimming down the waste and lost motion involved in the channels of trade, and considerable initiative in the same direc-

tion was put forth by retailers and wholesalers. A large share of the energy of business management rallied to the objective of cutting down the cost of distribution.

Not all the developments were on the constructive side, however. Starting about 1926, expansion of distribution became an obsession with many advertisers. An overwhelming desire for volume at all costs affected numerous organizations like a feverish disease, producing frenzied efforts to sell, sell, sell, anywhere and everywhere. Perhaps as a reflection of the national inflation psychology, sheer volume was accepted as the sole solution to the need for cutting distribution costs, although, of course, the pressure exerted by the ever-increasing amount of goods to be sold was an important contributing factor.

In every field of business there were manufacturers who were striving for a distribution to which they were not economically entitled and which they could not service adequately when and if they got it. Struggling to move the enormous unending load of merchandise dumped upon it by the manufacturing end of the business, the sales department, panic-stricken, rushed into new and untried channels of distribution and into new and distant territories. Despite slow consumption, overproduction of merchandise continued to hold manufacturing costs down, but the economies of mass production were eaten up by high-pressure distribution. Many of the annual reports began to show that profit was being sacrificed at the shrine of volume.

When territorial possibilities of expansion had been exhausted and every conceivable channel of distribution entered, the scramble for sales produced an orgy of price-cutting, discount selling, free deals, special concessions and wanton commercial bribery. Then new retail accounts of questionable or visionary value were opened. Retailers who were good for only a certain amount of credit were permitted more than their usual standing justified. Next came a lowering of credit terms. The summer of 1928 saw the selling of retail accounts which no firm in its right mind would have touched before. In some instances consignment selling was resorted to in a desperate effort to move the backed-up merchandise from the factory warehouse to the dealer's storeroom. Few thought of the inevitable day when the cost of placing merchandise on so many distant and precarious shelves would be weighed against the net returns.

In effect, the advertiser who indulged these practices was merely temporizing with a serious sales problem. But the consequences were far more severe than might merely be occasioned by the postponement of finding the true and effective solution to that problem. For in the wake of all these practices came tremendous economic waste, unstabilized local markets, ruinous price cutting. Unquestionably they contributed to the severity of the ultimate business collapse.

None the less, it was a phase which business undoubtedly would have had to go through at some time or another in moulding its approach to the riddle of the distributive age. A valuable lesson was learned, or at least exposed to view: that it had become imperative for the advertiser to equip himself with knowledge of the consuming capacity of his available markets and shape his distributing policies to the needs of the consumer.

Not the first comic-strip advertisement, but Old Gold helped set the pattern in 1928

Markets, Modernism, Mergers

RIGHT at the outset of these eventful years, the marketing process was subjected to an upheaval of major economic consequences, a vast readjustment of buying, selling and credit relationships which permanently influenced the entire distributive order. This was the advent of hand-to-mouth, or small-order, buying.

In the depression of 1920-21, many retailers found themselves stranded with huge stocks. As surpluses were finally dispersed and the turnover of new merchandise bought at the new low price levels began to replace losses, enthusiasm for the principle of turnover in selling became spontaneous and universal. Business men, brokers, Government economists, bankers, took to studying and preaching turnover. The preachments fell on eager retail ears.

Hand-to-mouth buying and its turnover ally were inevitably destined to become a part of business policy. The efficiency of the railroads, the development of truck delivery, improved methods of communication were combining to make it no longer necessary for a dealer to stock up far in advance of his more or less immediate requirements. The increased rapidity of style changes was making it inadvisable to do so. The experimentation of the chain stores with the turnover idea had already suggested the profit in the policy. However, the post-war emergency served to galvanize into almost immediate effect what otherwise would probably have been the subject of years of gradual evolution. From the standpoint of society at large and of the manufacturer interested in cutting distribution costs, hand-to-mouth buying represented a clear-cut benefit. By making goods move more rapidly from producer to consumer, it reduced the total amount of capital tied up in finished goods. The result was a smaller interest charge on the marketing process and the release of capital for other purposes.

Over and above that were many other benefits to industry. Factory production was stabilized. With the retailer buying only for immediate needs and refusing to be forced into anticipating his future wants, the manufacturer was restrained from producing to meet speculative buying and his business tended to spread throughout the year on a fairly even basis. An increase in trade resulted from the fact that under the old method the dealer either over-ordered or under-ordered. In either case he did not make the money he ought to have made and the manufacturer lost with him. Retail stocks were kept in better condition and the merchant's awareness of the demand for a given product was heightened. Salesmen, being no longer obliged to spend time attempting to keep the dealer loaded up to the guards, were enabled to spend more time taking helpful selling ideas to their accounts.

From the standpoint of the retailer, the capacity for handling a wider assortment of merchandise was increased, while the wholesaler's importance in the marketing picture was enhanced, though small-order buying tended to make his costs heavier.

"Petry's Folly"

IT is rather startling to note the similarity of the problems that faced the publishing industry during the last half of the last century, to the problems which faced the spot radio industry from 1928 to 1933. It is even more startling to note that these problems were met by the spot radio industry in much the same way.

Many publishers considered circulation figures a secret, others reached into a hat for the biggest figure they could find. Rate cards meant little since only a very few publications made more than a feeble effort to maintain the published rate. The cards themselves were so arranged that it was practically impossible to figure out a price on any given piece of business. Many agents were irresponsible and others were not financially able to meet their obligations to the publisher.

Then, in the 1870's, men like J. J. Richardson, Leander H. Crall and E. B. Mack stepped into the picture as exclusive representatives. Many publishers were dubious. Many an advertiser was skeptical and the other agents were sure this new development was in the wrong direction. Time proved their theory right, however, and soon others followed these men into the field of exclusive representation. It was these pioneers who successfully discouraged rate slashing, trade deals, free reading notices and other prevalent evil practices. They were in the vanguard toward truthful statements of circulation and did more to establish a smooth flow of business from the advertiser to the consumer than any other factor.

Now let's look at the conditions that prevailed prior to the coming of the exclusive radio station representative as we know him today.

Accurate information on "circulation" was just as difficult to obtain as it was in the publication field in the 80's and 90's.

Radio stations had no representatives whose job it was to represent their interests directly, and so had difficulty in controlling their rates and business methods on national spot advertising. The best available information came from radio brokers who did not have the interests of any particular station in a market at heart, but who listed most or all of the stations in that market for the advertiser's choice. Often three or four stations in a single market accepted business sent them from several brokers and the commission paid these brokers varied. One station favored one broker with higher commissions than others, while another station might favor a different broker. Thus a broker might receive half again as much from one station in a market as from another. Usually a recommendation was made for one station but the temptation was to recommend the station which most benefitted the broker regardless of its suitability for the advertiser.

Since the broker received *some* commission from practically all stations, he did not have the incentive to get the most accurate available information for the advertiser or to straighten out any misunderstanding between the advertiser and any particular station. It was easier to agree that the station was wrong and to switch the advertiser to another station.

"Price per inquiry" deals flourished. The station was paid nothing for time or talent but was given a fee for each inquiry, box top, or carton, turned over to the advertiser. Those that ran the offer only at the times or in the programs specified by the advertiser usually could not pull enough inquiries to justify the program costs. Many stations succumbed to the temptation to make the offer in straight announcement form many times during the day and night, and so increase the number of inquiries to the point where they were profitable. When this point had been reached the advertiser would often decide to reduce the price per inquiry. This vicious circle made it impossible for the more legitimate stations to compete.

So-called "group rates" were another evil. An advertiser was offered a list of stations to choose from. If he chose enough—say ten or twenty —he got a rebate. He couldn't tell— and his advertising agency wasn't told—which stations had cut the rates. He was supposed to pocket the money "saved," be thankful, and ask no questions!

This unstable state of affairs was holding back the progress of spot broadcasting, just as a like situation in the publishing business had retarded the growth of advertising in general prior to 1900. Various buyers of time as well as sellers of time realized and deplored the situation.

In 1932 Edward Petry decided to do something about it. All of his experience as an NBC and agency executive and buyer of radio time convinced him that the brokerage method of station "representation" was unsound; that it could not function to give proper, accurate service to advertising agencies and their clients, to sell spot broadcasting in general or the facilities of individual stations in particular. Wherever he went, he preached the doctrine of exclusive representation in radio as we know it today.

Many stations were not convinced. Exclusive representation would mean giving up all contacts with brokers from whom they were receiving the major portion of their national spot business. Many advertising agencies were interested in the idea but others were only luke warm. The general radio agent, or broker, was frankly derisive—"Petry's Folly" was their way of describing the movement.

So in 1932 Petry started a cross country trip to talk to station owners. He suggested that the unsatisfactory representation situation could be met in much the same way that it had been met by the publishing industry years before. He had nothing to sell but a firm conviction that the principle of exclusive representation, as applied to radio, would result in greater revenue to the stations, greater service to the advertiser and a rapid increase in the general use of Spot Broadcasting.

He returned from his trip in the fall of '32 with exclusive contracts signed by fourteen top ranking stations who believed in the idea of exclusive representation so strongly that they were willing to forego the revenue from (Continued on page 425)

Advertisement

An outgrowth of hand-to-mouth buying, although other factors also contributed, was the trend to handling distribution by zones. Manufacturers who distributed over large territories began to warehouse reserve stocks at strategic points as a means of getting turnover in their own operations. It was incumbent upon the manufacturer so to arrange distribution at distant points that retailers could purchase goods when they wanted them and in the quantities they needed.

Adequate physical arrangements were essential to the success of sales effort based on this policy. These took the form of, first, the branch factory, then, with further extension, the branch-house system and the use of public warehouse facilities. Warehousing of reserve stocks grew at an amazing rate from 1922 on, reflecting the many efforts at widening distribution and increasing its efficiency.

All in all the hand-to-mouth development got the marketing end of business off to a highly auspicious start. The distribution machine was well lubricated for swift action.

Despite the volume craze that was later to cause a severe hot-box, many additional sound improvements were applied to the apparatus. Aside from expansion into new markets and more intensive cultivation of establishment, which, of course, was often entirely logical, sales management responded to the challenges of the new age with measures that gave healthy impetus toward the general goal of scientific, more efficient administration of distribution. These measures come under several major headings.

Sales Organization

One of the chief developments here was in the matter of selecting and training salesmen. Reduction of turnover in the sales force received much attention, for stability was seen as a means of effecting considerable economy in sales operations. Consequently, sales managers turned more time and effort toward developing processes of selecting salesmen on a scientific basis. The training school was used to weed out applicants before their unfitness could incur expense, as well as to give finished sales education to qualified members of the force.

The system of salesmen's compensation was given an overhauling in many organizations. The majority had always used the commission plan, most of the rest the straight salary. Various plans combining the elements of incentive and control represented, respectively, by the commission and salary systems, were introduced in the effort to induce more effective effort on the part of the salesman.

In the realm of administration, numerous firms set up trading area systems of operation, breaking down political and other arbitrary boundaries into well-defined logical units based on actual marketing conditions. Effective control of sales expenditure and effort was sought also through scientific determination of sales quotas. This was an effort to replace the old criterion of comparison against the previous year's sales with a genuinely realistic measuring-stick for judging effectiveness and ascertaining weak spots.

A new organism which many firms found useful was the sales promotion department. The sales promotion division was usually conceived as a wing of the sales

HIGH-LIGHT AUTOBIOGRAPHY
OF A FIVE-YEAR-OLD • • •

March 1933	Dummy-prospectus issued during the Bank Holiday.
September 1933	Circulation experts, consulted for guidance, predict a "possible" maximum sale of 25,000 copies.
October 1933	Magazine appears as a quarterly; instantaneous sell-out of 100,000 copies.
January 1934	First monthly issue; bear stories such as "they can't keep it up" and "the next issue won't appear"; sale a trifle over 100,000 copies.
March 1934	Louis Paul's story *No More Trouble for Jedwick* published; later to win O. Henry Memorial Award.
December 1934	We record astonishment that the circulation is almost 200,000.
February 1935	Old Gold discovers the Petty girl, beginning a vogue in college dormitory decoration.
April 1935	Petty wowed 'em with "O you would, would you!" a cartoon people still talk about.
September 1935	Ernest Hemingway's *Notes On The Next War* later reprinted all over the world.
December 1935	We record astonishment that the circulation is almost 300,000.
March 1936	Emil Lengyel's article on Prince Starhemberg gets Esquire banned in Austria and written up in 900 American newspapers.
June 1936	Esquire back in Austrian favor and Starhemberg out—proving something or other.
August 1936	Ernest Hemingway writes A Farewell To Esquire under title *Snows of Kilimanjaro*.
October 1936	Cuban police confiscate Esquire and jail eight newsdealers over *Latins Are Lousy Lovers*.
November 1936	We record astonishment that the circulation is now almost 500,000; readers beginning to record astonishment at our astonishment.
December 1936	Issue totals over 300 pages; ditto over $576,000 in advertising revenue.
February 1937	*The Wench Is Not Amused* breaks all records for Sound and Fury letters.
March 1937	Terrific fuss over *Christ in Concrete* by Esquire Discovery Pietro di Donato.
April 1937	Esquire banned in Japan for saying they were about to start a war on Chinese, but weren't they?
December 1937	Esquire winds up year with 43.8% increase over 1936 in advertising revenue; total (P. I. B.) for year, $3,817,719; only four years old, but eleventh among *all* magazines.
December 1937	*World Peaceways* state advertisement run in December issue one of most successful ever published.
March 1938	Over 300 of the country's leading retailers pay $50 per seat to attend Esquire's Fashion Forum at Waldorf-Astoria Hotel.
May 1938	Edward J. O'Brien rates Esquire first among all magazines in number of distinctive short stories published.
July 1938	Esquire's national promotion of Father's Day ups sales of nation's retailers over 1937 despite unfavorable business conditions.

• • • *Esquire*
THE MAGAZINE FOR MEN

department, responsible directly to the executive in charge of sales. Generally speaking, it was assigned the duty of keeping the trade favorably inclined toward the product, all matters pertaining to personal selling being handled by the sales department and those involving consumer advertising by the advertising department. In some firms the sales promotion function was placed in the advertising department, in a few the advertising department was made a part of the sales promotion division. Whatever the arrangement, it represented an effort to concentrate responsibility for developing market information to be placed at the disposal of the sales executive for use in the more scientific upbuilding of the sales plan and for handling trade liter-

1923

PRESIDENT HARDING dies in San Francisco and Calvin Coolidge, vice-president, takes oath of office at Plymouth, Vt. . . . National Vigilance Association formed at Washington, D. C. to wage fight on the Ku Klux Klan. . . . Treaty of friendship, commerce and consular rights signed with Germany.

Briton Hadden and Henry Luce establish *Time*, weekly news magazine. . . . Edward W. Bok establishes the Harvard Awards for the best newspaper and periodical advertisements. . . . Chilton Company combines with the Class Journal Company. . . . Raymond E. Rubicam and John Orr Young form the advertising agency of Young & Rubicam. . . . Dr. Ralph E. Rindfusz appointed executive secretary of the Periodical Publishers Association to succeed Phillips Wyman, who joins the McCall Company. . . . Henry C. Marschalk and Edward M. Pratt found Marschalk & Pratt. . . . Scripps-Howard Newspapers acquire the Pittsburgh *Press*. . . . N. W. Ayer & Son win $178,000 verdict in contract suit with United States Rubber Company. . . . A new soft drink is named "Goo-Goo."

Alfred P. Sloan, Jr., heads the General Motors Corporation. . . . Hill Blackett and J. G. Sample form Blackett & Sample. . . . John F. Tims, Jr., becomes business manager of the New Orleans *Times-Picayune*. . . . 10,087 students learning advertising and merchandising in American colleges and universities. . . . Armour & Company take over Morris & Company. . . . Walter Buchen elected president of the David C. Thomas Company. . . . C. K. Woodbridge is president of the newly formed Dictaphone Corporation. . . . *The American Mercury* begins publication with George Jean Nathan and H. L. Mencken as editors. . . . Frank A. Munsey buys the New York *Globe* and consolidates it with the *Sun*. . . . Banana trade drops off as nation carols, "Yes, We Have No Bananas."

The Nashville Market is a
SALES OASIS
– sell it!

● Wholesale and retail sales indices show that the Nashville market is still buying—that it is relatively unaffected by recession elsewhere.

The reason can be found in the market's diversity of occupation—863,215 people who draw on many forms of industry and agriculture to earn an annual spendable income of *more than a quarter of a billion dollars.*

For results, follow the example of those who are selling the Nashville market *now.*

Concentrate your advertising here—in the media which gives you complete coverage of a market able to buy your goods *now.*

THE NASHVILLE TENNESSEAN *Nashville* **Banner**
Morning·Sunday   *Evening*

Represented Nationally by The Branham Company

ature, dealer promotion, house organs, display material and helps for salesmen.

In numerous lines the catalog achieved acceptance as a valuable means of standardizing, simplifying and supplementing the salesman's job. Many catalogs were designed for the salesman to use in selling to his prospect, then to perform a selling function in the interval between his calls. Since hand-to-mouth buying increased the frequency at which orders were placed and it was a physical impossibility for the salesman to make the number of personal visits required to take the order on each occasion, the catalog assumed a great deal more importance than formerly.

Even while the volume mania was exerting its most alluring fascination, which is to say in the last three years of the period under discussion, some few of the more level-headed advertisers were looking into the idea of selective selling. Analysis of costs had suggested to them that "100 per cent distribution" was not all it was cracked up to be and they began exploring the economies of dropping unprofitable dealers. In some instances this took the form of establishing minimum order rules and passing up entirely accounts that could not qualify. In others mail-order selling was substituted for personal effort on the smaller or more remote accounts.

While all these things were going on in the consumer marketing field, a great deal was happening in the precincts of selling to industry. For years the raw and unfinished material industries had neglected the marketing function, because markets had been large and growing and selling was comparatively simple. As industrial buying became more exacting and discriminating, as industrial products were judged more by quality and performance, there came a recognition of the need for sales and merchandising leadership. Manufacturers selling to industry reached the important conclusion that industrial marketing in its fundamental features is not essentially different from other lines. This new interest in merchandising matters found reflection in the creation of the National Industrial Advertisers Association as a medium of interchange of marketing experience. The advertising agent specializing in industrial accounts encountered a much wider demand for his services than before, while a number of the agencies handling consumer accounts established industrial departments.

The Sales Proposition

Heretofore business had been operated largely on the pattern of the factory producing something and then turning it over to the sales end to dispose of. Now emerged, as a direct result of marketing pressures, the principle of engineering the product for sales. In other words, considerations of what variety and quality of product the sales department could sell the most of exerted an important influence upon the planning of production.

The simplification movement of the early years of the period not only contributed to perfection of production methods but dramatized the advantage to be gained in building the product and the line as a sales proposition. Manufacturers found that simplifying their lines speeded distribution through enabling the trade to concentrate sales effort instead of spreading it out thinly over many numbers.

This strongly suggested the value of exploring other production possibilities of rendering the product easier to sell. And as management ingenuity reached the point of exhaustion in seeking new sales angles and methods, the advertiser turned more and more to the product as a source of a new message.

The growing influence of fashion served to emphasize further the importance of planning production in terms of sales. Before the war fashion changes had come slowly and it had been possible to anticipate and adjust in a more or less leisurely manner. Moreover, the changes were seldom of a drastic nature. After the war, fashion began to operate at a bewildering pace. Short skirts came in and terrorized the textile industry, but at the same time gave new prominence to hose and shoes. Fashion became preoccupied with a trend toward greater freedom—less clothes, less hair, less to put off and on, less to take care of. Fashion began to extend its influence, direct or otherwise, to just about every line of merchandise sold to the consumer, including food products.

Manufacturers who attempted to buck basic fashion trends by adhering to the old lines soon learned to their sorrow and cost that it couldn't be done. Industry in general commenced to do more of its thinking in terms of what the consumer wanted rather than what it wanted to sell to the consumer. The whole subject of product design, previously recognized only by the makers of women's dresses and to a lesser extent by those industries affected by periodic model changes, was opened up for attention.

The first tentative venture into the new realm was the application of color, limited in the past to articles of wearing apparel and personal use, to a wide range of merchandise. It was noticed that modern household equipment had given the housewife a greater amount of free time and that she was devoting more time and interest to making the home attractive instead of merely keeping it going. Color spread to almost every field in the realm of home decoration, household appliances and building materials.

A chief factor, both in the stimulation of the design movement and in its expression, was modernism. For centuries back every war has been followed by a popular urge for something new. The impulse appears in creative arts and crafts, in progressive scientific activity and in a thirst for expression. The period following the World War was no exception to this pattern.

The new spirit was crystallized in the International Exhibition of Modern and Decorative Arts at Paris in 1925. Here was an impressive mass display of the simplified, striking new beauty born of the post-war urge for something different. There were original and arresting designs, new materials and new combinations of new and old materials, expressed in all the accessories of living—furniture, home furnishings, household appliances, clothing, jewelry. Unrepresented among all the leading nations of the world was the United States, which had nothing to show. Present, however, was a group of American merchants and advertising men. They returned to carry the message of the new school of the design to the American manufacturer who, in his need for more

I N its fifty useful years Printers' Ink has chronicled many of the most important changes in America's economic history—for it has treated chiefly with the phenomenal progress, during this short span, in advertising, merchandising and distribution.

Rapid development in these three phases of the science of selling have culminated in mass production and distribution. And mass distribution, with its benefits to the mass of consumers in better merchandise and cost savings, is the basis of what the rest of the world enviously terms "The American Standard of Living."

Major role in raising the living standard of the average American family to the highest of any nation in the history of the world has been played by the chain store industry. Ancient in its conception (there is evidence of multiple store operations dating back to 200 B.C.)—but comparatively recent in its development as we know it today, chain store merchandising spread most rapidly in the United States after the World War, definitely a point at which there arose a demand for better goods at lower costs.

It's a far cry, for instance, from the old dusty cracker barrel days to this era of sanitary packaging—of refrigerated transportation of fresh fruits, dairy products, vegetables, meats and fish—of scientific production and preservation of healthful foods. It's a far cry from the days when the farmer hawked his wares in neighboring villages to today's chain food store system of offering produce, fresh and crisp from every section, in every nook and cranny of the land—of bringing practical "farm relief," by levelling gluts and surpluses, when relief is needed most.

Quantity buying, direct from the producer, eliminating middle-man's charges and unnecessary costs of multiple handling, smaller profits on a greater mass of sales, scientific distribution and precision-like organization possible only in large scale operations—these are the factors that bring tremendous savings to the consumer.

1888

THE GREAT ATLAN'

FO'

ANDARD OF LIVING

It is estimated that chain store merchandising methods last year saved American consumers an aggregate of nine hundred million dollars on the necessities and luxuries of life. Today there is hardly a home in America that does not take advantage, in whole or in part, of chain store economies.

Here is overwhelming endorsement of the chain stores by the great mass of buyers who comprise the citizenship of America—evidence of the importance they place upon this nine hundred million dollar savings which, viewed in the light of the individual family, means advantages in life that would not otherwise be enjoyed—more plentiful and more nourishing food, more money for proper medical care, education or recreation than their incomes would otherwise buy.

Here is overwhelming evidence that these millions of housewives will not tolerate the consistent efforts of an organized middleman's minority—interested in maintaining unnecessary and uneconomic piling on of costs between the producer and the consumer—to saddle on the ultimate consumer a burden of punitive chain store taxes that would wipe out the differential between the costly old order of things and present day methods.

They will not stand by and witness passively these reactionary tactics. They will not give up "The American Standard of Living."

★ ★ ★ ★ ★

Multiple outlet merchandising has been a consistent factor in building advertising volume, not only through chain stores' own purchases but through the pace they set for competitive business. Pioneering "price" advertising, they have made American business conscious of the soundness of this method of rapid merchandise turnover. The annual chain store bill for all kinds of advertising is $200,000,000. The amount of competitive advertising induced by this expenditure must amount to many millions of dollars more.

1938

WHAT CHAIN STORES MEAN TO THE UNITED STATES
(Approximate Figures)

$6,000,000,000
in purchases from manufacturers and producers.

$450,000,000
paid annually in rents to 139,810 real estate owners.

$200,000,000
paid annually for advertising of all kinds.

$475,000,000
paid annually for freight and trucking, fuel, electricity, repairs, etc.

$1,200,000,000
paid annually to 1,171,670 full and part time employees. The average weekly wage for full-time employees is $25.89.

$225,000,000
paid annually for state and local taxes.

$8,550,000,000
total spent annually by chain stores in the United States.

& PACIFIC TEA CO.

1859

attractive things to offer the consumer, was eagerly awaiting modernism without knowing it.

This was the beginning of a period of vast change in the products of the industry. It moved slowly at first, and sometimes in the wrong directions. The functional simplicity of modernism was in some quarters mixed up with bizarre, geometric ugliness and a great many unsittable chairs and repulsively designed goods of various kinds got on the market. However, the public had developed a genuine yearning for attractive design not only in bracelets but in plumbing fixtures and gradually the modernism movement took shape along sound lines, penetrating into every phase of industrial production.

The assignment of a merchandising job to the package, which hitherto had been merely a container, constituted one of the major advances in the improvement of the sales proposition. In fact it might well be said that, in the shift from passive to dynamic role, the package becomes a sales tool in its own right.

In the earlier days the advertiser did little thinking about the package. One manufacturer would accept the device gotten up for him by a container maker, who at that time was largely production-minded, and subsequent competitors would follow in the same path. Now and then, in the several years before the war, some firm would question the old form and introduce a new treatment. But most of the great consumer lines continued to suffer from lack of intelligent package design.

Slowly considerations accumulated which tended to open up the whole packaging subject. The competition of packages increased enormously. According to one estimate the number of packaged items in the drug field in 1922 reached more than 45,000, an increase from about 2,500 in just a few years. This fact alone strongly suggested that every year it was becoming more important for the package to stand out from its competitors and command the consumer's attention. The Piggly Wiggly and other self-service stores in the grocery field had brought the package more into the limelight. The general spread of the open-display method of selling throughout retailing suggested further that the package might often have more to do with selling than the retail clerk.

Since there was a constant stream of new advertisers with new products, the number of those who dared to break with old traditions was increasing and the proportion of more attractive containers in retail channels waxed larger. Some of the new entrants produced a degree of competition directly traceable, in large measure, to the package. Then again an established house would put out a new product in modern dress. Its success would raise a doubt about the old labels.

Another principal factor was the general improvement in the design of the advertisement. Many a good advertisement was ruined by the insertion of a picture of a poor package, the out-dated container looking ugly and sometimes ridiculous in modern typographical and illustrative surroundings.

Strong in the minds of many of the older advertisers, however, were two major objections to deserting an old package. The first was that

Mine Host Through The Ages

"There is nothing which has yet been contrived by man, by which so much happiness is produced as by a good tavern or inn."

Samuel Johnson

There is so much competition when it comes to writing about the value of hotels in the history of mankind that it is hard to start. When the road from Bagdad to Babylon became crowded and hospitality was overtaxed, benevolent men erected the first inns known to history. The first step forward was in Rome under the emperors. It was then the landlord became responsible for the property of his guests. None can better describe the joys of an ancient inn than Horace found in his Journey to Brindisium.

Chaucer did a job in the Middle Ages telling about the pilgrims who started from the fine old Tabard at Southwark, later put up at the Checquers of Hope in Canterbury.

Shakespeare wrote copy for the old Boar's Head in Eastcheap where proud old Sir John Falstaff sang and drank his musty ale.

Henry the Fourth, in perhaps his most famous words, marked a development in the industry. He said, "Shall I not take mine ease in mine inn." Mark the word "mine." It is important. The old inn had begun to develop into the modern hotel with its atmosphere of a man's own home.

Then there was the Maple of Barnaby Rudge, so well described by Charles Dickens. It may still be proved (if one reads Sir Walter Scott) that the Clachan of Rob Roy, kept by the Widow McAlpine, was not nearly as good a place as the Cleikum Inn where the delightful Meg Dodds was proprietress.

We give up on copy about hotels and restaurants. There is too much competition. But while PRINTERS' INK has been following the history of advertising for the past fifty years, ever since the days of Kriger's Tavern in New York in 1642, the hotel and restaurant business has been steadily forging ahead. In that development the Ahrens Publications have played an important part.

Hotel Management and Restaurant Management act as an idea exchange for hotel and restaurant operators. Hotel World Review is a combination of two of the industry's oldest hotel newspapers: Hotel World founded in 1875 and National Hotel Review founded in 1907.

Following the policy which appealed so much to Henry IV, it has been our function to help make hotels and restaurants as comfortable and satisfying as a man's home and his table, as efficient as the modern office and as profitable as the best example of industrial management. AHRENS PUBLISHING CO., INC., New York and Chicago.

the old had proved successful over a period of years, whereas a new package seemed to be a very costly gamble. Second, the old package represented a heavy investment in advertising and the advertiser tended to doubt that he would be able to carry over the good-will gained by the old package to a new one.

A few of the more courageous took the leap, nevertheless. They brought in a strange verdict. It seemed that the label could be changed without hurting either prestige or sales volume. It seemed, in fact, that business increased instead of falling off, that the new design not only held the old customers but added new ones.

The rising mass of evidence could no longer be ignored and a large proportion of industry set off on a course of package modernization. Many new labels for long established brands made their debuts. Some firms even changed the shape of their packages. Attention was given to the convenience features of the container as an added selling inducement—such factors as ease of opening or convenience while the product is being used. Dual use packages, which remained as a lasting advertisement long after the product had been consumed, became prominent.

Instalment Selling

Instalment selling was adopted as a measure of broadening the market base for many products and experienced a sensational growth. By 1927 it was literally true that, with the exception of foods and commodities of low unit price, everything from baby carriages to coffins could be obtained on the deferred payment plan. It was esti-mated in that year that at any given time over $4,000,000,000 in unpaid for merchandise was in the hands of consumers.

The original development of instalment selling was brought about by the retailer, who administered it on a more or less hit-or-miss basis of accommodation to known customers. Then some merchants evolved organized plans of handling this type of transaction. Just before the war the manufacturer was beginning to take cognizance of this sales device, but the credit mechanism was laid aside in most industries for the duration of the war and the post-war boom. In 1921, it was brought back into service and quickly was brought to a major position in the marketing scheme. Manufacturers began to urge it upon dealers in a national way and made financing connections to facilitate its operation. In the automobile industry, where manufacturers had been vigorous in their opposition a few years before, instalment selling came to occupy a part in the majority of consumer transactions. The mail-order houses turned to instalment selling to aid them in getting the big and profitable trade in the larger and more expensive goods, from which they had been largely shut out by the requirement of a full cash outlay so long an essential part of catalog merchandising. They found the rural customer a surprisingly good credit risk and extended the variety of lines in which credit accommodation might be secured.

Consumer credit naturally proved itself to be no more vicious than any other form. It became an established agency of increasing and stabilizing production, with accompanying lower production costs, and

340

Interprets
the world
we live in
to the men
and women
who mould
public opinion

Harpers
MAGAZINE

strong in influence
high in quality . . .
it commands the
most discriminating
market in America

Published since

1850

50-50

WE, TOO,

have been in business fifty years

We've seen much and perhaps we have learned something . . . One thing we do know: there is nothing we will ever cherish more than a good name.

THE KATZ AGENCY

500 FIFTH AVENUE • NEW YORK, N. Y.

for stepping up the purchasing power of the consumer. Being more or less new and sometimes in inexperienced hands, it suffered abuses. Some retail competition tended to operate on the basis of liberality of terms rather than on product quality. The hazards of the over-extended consumer are considerable. But in its soundly administered form instalment selling was essential as a means of assuring a continual outlet for mass production, a permanent part of the marketing structure.

Export Marketing

Cultivation of foreign markets was resorted to by many firms as a sales outlet for the heavy production loads. The tremendous loans abroad aided an extension of export sales of manufactured products which by 1929 mounted to more than six times the normal annual volume of the pre-war years.

Mergers

The research for distributive economy culminated in a new era

---

1924

D AWES REPARATION PLAN adopted and French troops evacuate the Ruhr. . . . Death of Woodrow Wilson at Washington. . . . Calvin Coolidge returned to office, with Charles G. Dawes as running mate. . . . Senate resolution charges fraud and corruption in execution of naval oil reserve leases and instructs the President to institute court action to cancel leases at Teapot Dome and Elk Hills.

Walter P. Chrysler develops a new motor car bearing his name. . . . New York *Tribune* purchases the New York *Herald*. . . . *Liberty* is a new weekly magazine launched by the Coloroto Corporation, of which J. M. Patterson is president and R. R. McCormick is first vice-president. . . . Associated Advertising Clubs of the World convene in London. . . . Considerable debate over the ethics of showing cocktail shakers in advertising illustration backgrounds.

Carl W. Jones appointed general manager of the Minneapolis *Journal*. . . . *Hearst's International* combined with *Cosmopolitan* under the name of the latter, with A. C. G. Hammesfahr as general manager. . . . Philip W. Lennen joins J. T. H. Mitchell, Inc., which becomes Lennen & Mitchell. . . . New York Advertising Club entertains the Prince of Wales on American tour. . . . Ellery W. Mann named president of the Zonite Products Company. . . . William A. Hart appointed advertising manager of E. I. du Pont de Nemours & Company. . . . The *Daily Mirror* is a new New York newspaper of tabloid size. . . . Headline: "Uncle Sam's Budget Program Sets an Example for Business."

of industrial combinations. In the two earlier big periods of consolidation—one beginning in 1888 and ending in 1893, the second starting in 1897 and ending in 1903—the impelling motive was economy in production. There were other considerations, including price control, freight advantage and selling considerations, but the "trusts" were primarily production mergers.

In the new period the underlying motivation was the search for increased volume of sales and lowered sales overhead, rather than desire for cheaper and more efficient production. In many cases the lower unit manufacturing costs to be secured through larger buying capacity and improved facilities was a contributing consideration. Yet more often than not the production factor was relatively negligible. (Naturally the hope of greater net earnings was never absent.)

The increased territorial scope of business operations and the intense competition caused by high production levels suggested savings in handling a group of products by one integrated sales organization. The merger brought together products traveling through the same channels of distribution. These might be related only as to class of retail outlet, as with the General Foods Corporation's long line of grocery products ranging from coffee and coconut to syrup and salt, or the Standard Brands combination of yeast, coffee and baking powder. Or they might be of the same general description with some of the acquired brands competitive and some not, as the case of the Colgate-Palmolive-Peet Company. In either case

concentration and strengthening of marketing resources was the pre-eminent consideration.

A large proportion of these distribution mergers could be more accurately described as acquisitions. Much of the advertiser development in the past was through the addition of new products. As the advertiser established one product in the trade and consumer market, he saw that with little increase in expense he could utilize the same distribution facilities for an additional product, which might be either a new item or a member of the line not previously advertised into consumer acceptance. Through the merger, however, the added product or products could be acquired without assuming the expenses and uncertainties of development of new products.

In any case, the product with an established consumer following was a fundamental characteristic of the distribution merger. In addition, most of the development centered around those products where the service of the storekeeper is the least important, items purchased frequently in small quantities.

The merger movement became prominent in 1927 (consolidation is always going on in business, of course, but a new pace was evident in this year) and reached a peak in 1929, when 1,300 concerns were involved in mergers. In the later stages some of the combinations were put together more for reasons of financial promotion than anything else. Rare indeed was the advertiser who did not receive a handsome offer (in stock) for his business.

The Pursuit of Facts

THE process of digging up factual information with which to devise a compass for setting the marketing course had never got much of a chance in prior years. When things were good, management didn't see the need of it. When things were bad, business felt it couldn't stand the expense.

What had been done in the name of research was usually carried on as a sideline of the sales department's operations. It didn't accomplish much. The scientific techniques of research were largely ignored, and they were in an undeveloped state anyway. The researchers were usually the salesmen, who were directed to get market information in slack selling seasons or to make a stab at it in conjunction with sales calls. Besides, this whole approach was fundamentally prejudicial to accurate findings because the sales department was always under the natural compulsion of guiding and interpreting the research in such a way as to uphold and justify its past methods and accomplishments.

With distribution assuming the aspects of a serious, long-term problem, the matter of eliminating haphazard guesswork from marketing activities became a mandatory job instead of a vaguely desirable luxury of business operation. In a buyer's market you had to find out what the buyer wanted or lose him to somebody who did have that knowledge, especially where that buyer's market was not a product of an acute cyclical slump but of a basic economic change.

It was seen at last, moreover, that to yield genuinely valid conclusions research must be conducted independently from any other phase of sales or business promotion. In what in many ways appears to be the most significant single advance of this entire period, scientific market research gained acceptance as a specialized function of business.

This acceptance extended far beyond the old general proposition that information is a good thing. Research began to be employed to the attainment of definite and particular objectives. Statistics of production and consumption were marshaled to produce a foundation for intelligent study of markets as a whole. Selling methods were analyzed with a view to improvement. Weak places in distribution were sought out. Sales standards were placed in specific information on territories and classes of consumers. Markets for new products were studied as the first step in drawing up marketing plans.

Enthusiasm for and interest in research reached a high pitch. In fact it became more or less of a fad and while sound development was somewhat impeded by a sudden wild, indiscriminate fever for finding out things, the process of penetrating the relatively unexplored field of techniques for market research registered material advances.

Considerable stimulus came from the advertising agency, which accepted research as a primary function. Most agencies limited themselves to the branch of research encompassing the investigative work necessary for the formulation of advertising plans. Some, however, extended their activities considerably beyond those boundaries, taking in many of the aspects of sales research.

A great amount of impetus came also from the Government. In 1922 Herbert Hoover re-organized the Bureau of Foreign and Domestic Commerce of the Department of Commerce to act as a medium of interchange of market information. Numerous studies of markets and distribution costs were contributed to the fund of marketing knowledge.

In research organized advertising found a new and important function. Exchange of information had always been an expressed objective, more honored, however, in the articles of organization than in the fulfilment. Now this objective took the form of definite projects. The Association of National Advertisers took up a plan involving study of the major media, start of a long series of research investigations. The American Association of Advertising Agencies set out on a program

1925

TENNESSEE law forbidding teaching of evolution in the schools brings Scopes trial, with Clarence Darrow pitted against William Jennings Bryan. . . . The two nine-power treaties of the Washington arms conference ratified. . . . Germany ratifies the Locarno pact. . . . Navy dirigible *Shenandoah* wrecked.

The Thomas Cusack Company, Poster Advertising Company, O. J. Gude Company and nineteen other poster firms consolidated as the General Outdoor Advertising Company with Kerwin H. Fulton as president. . . . Joseph M. Patterson and Robert R. McCormick, co-publishers and co-editors of the Chicago *Tribune* and the New York *News,* divide duties so that the former takes charge of the *News* and the latter of the *Tribune.* . . . E. R. Spaulding appointed general manager of the *New Yorker.* . . . Crossword puzzle rage is on. . . . Paul G. Hoffman elected vice-president in charge of sales of the Studebaker Corporation. . . . Charles H. Stark elected president of the Penton Publishing Company. . . . Gerold M. Lauck becomes a partner in N. W. Ayer & Son.

Walter A. Strong and associates purchase the Chicago *Daily News* from the estate of the late Victor Lawson. . . . Frank E. Tripp appointed general manager of the Gannett Newspapers. . . . Barron G. Collier, Inc., acquires Artemas Ward, Inc. . . . Lloyd Maxwell named president of Williams & Cunnyngham. . . . Louis Pedlar and Thomas L. L. Ryan establish the agency of Pedlar & Ryan. . . . A. C. Pearson named president of the Textile Publishing Company. . . . Moving picture business seeks sales appeal in naming its product; samples: "Flaming Youth," "Chastity," "Painted People," "Changing Husbands," "For Sale," "Cheap Kisses," "Single Wives," "Soiled," "Sinners in Silk."

Northwest
pedigreed printing papers

Klo-Kay Book
Mountie Book
Mountie Label
High Bulking Book
Non-Fading Poster
Titan Drawing
Northland Book
Northland Label
Northland Drawing

Ranger Book
Woodland Book
Timberland Book
Northstar Offset
Carlton Bond
Carlton Ledger
Carlton Mimeograph
North Star Writing
Northland Mimeograph

Northwoods Manila Printing
Weartext
Arrowhead Gray
Klo-Kay Index Bristol
Klo-Kay Cream Post Card
Nortex Sign
Northwest Gloss Ink Super
Nortex Utility Printing
  Papers

THE NORTHWEST PAPER COMPANY
Mills at Cloquet, Minn. Sales Offices: Minneapolis, Chicago, St. Louis, New York, San Francisco

which included qualitative analyses of circulations, buying power studies and investigation of various other marketing problems. In 1927 the International Advertising Association (now the Advertising Federation of America) set up a research program under Walter A. Strong. This took the form of a bureau of research and education which was delegated to study the economic status of advertising and co-operate in other research projects.

Accompanying all the developments in the realm of market research was a great deal of interest in another branch of the scientific investigation—industrial research. Manufacturers came to realize that the work being done in scientific laboratories had a real and important bearing upon increased sales. Industrial research provided a clearcut contribution to the solution of many marketing problems by pointing the way to broader markets through new uses, by heightening sales appeal through improvements suggested for established products and by supplying useful new products with which to cut down distribution overhead.

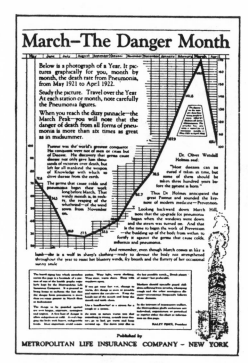

Metropolitan started a new kind of insurance advertising—designed to improve health, lessen illness and increase life's span

In 1928—only ten years ago—this layout was considered modernistic

To Many
THERE ARE FEW GREATER THRILLS
than
THE RECEIPT OF A LETTER!

THE POSTMAN'S WHISTLE! A cheery note in any home. Excitement, curiosity, the thrill of opening a strange envelope. A letter wins complete attention, no competitive advertising surrounds your <u>mailed</u> message. Of course the direct mailed message must be properly prepared . . . should be PERSONALIZED . . . EVERYONE LIKES TO BE GREETED BY NAME. Direct mail worthy of a Postman's presence is our specialty. We are the originators of Latz Letters, Giant-Grams, Personal-Print.

HARRY LATZ SERVICE
Telephone Medallion 3-0450
461 EIGHTH AVENUE · · · NEW YORK CITY, N.Y.

July 14, 1938.

Dear Printers' Ink:

Thank you for fifty years of helpfulness to advertising.

As an advertising agency, we can have no greater objective than to be as respected in our field as you are in yours.

O'Dea, Sheldon + Canaday, Inc
New York and Baltimore

Counter Concentration

THE trend to concentration of buying and selling resources in the retail field moved forward at phenomenally increased speed.

The chain store, in response to the great growth in mass production since the war, exploited its distributional advantages to the limit. By 1929 chain-store volume reached nearly $15,000,000,000, a 1,500 per cent increase since 1914. In the same sixteen years the number of store units increased 800 per cent to some 200,000 establishments. Although a period of mergers and consolidations began in 1926, the number of parent companies had reached 7,837 in 1930.

A new factor in chain retailing appeared with the entry of the two great mail-order houses—Sears, Roebuck and Montgomery Ward—into the field of over-the-counter selling.

In 1925 Sears opened a retail store in connection with its Chicago headquarters plant. Similar stores were opened at branch houses in other cities. Each was in the nature of a neighborhood department store outside the usual retail district of its city, handling for the most part the regular lines of catalog merchandise. Next came establishment of stores independent of the plants in still other cities.

The Montgomery Ward invasion of the retail-store field evolved from a different tack. In 1926 the company established a display store, or "merchandise exhibit," at Marysville, Kansas. Various lines advertised in the catalog were put on display in rotation, with attendants on hand to answer questions and take orders for delivery through the mails. First the display stores be-

gan selling the sample merchandise over the counter, then, in the early summer of 1927, they were converted into out-and-out retail stores. Meanwhile the company had also placed spot stocks of "heavy" lines, such as stoves, on retail sale at its branch houses.

The Sears development was principally in the direction of establishing of department stores in the larger cities, the small stores coming later. Ward concentrated on smaller general merchandise stores in cities and towns of lesser size. The Sears stores came to be administered as a distinct retail enterprise, merchandised more or less separately from the mail-order operation. The Ward stores continued to emphasize catalog merchandise, retail outlets serving as a supplement to mail-order distribution. Both firms expanded their retail networks throughout the nation and while some difficulties were encountered before smooth-running operation was attained, the retail business expanded their sales tremendously. It was not many years before retail volume exceeded that of mail-order, being something over 50 per cent for both companies.

Not a few economists interpreted these invasions of the retail field as a definite sign that the day of mail-order selling was over. The action had proceeded from a different view, however. The mail-order houses saw that the possibilities of great expansion in selling from the catalog no longer existed and that at the same time a new opportunity for selling at retail had come into being. The automobile had greatly increased the cruising radius of the rural consumer. As a result, the rural customer was more available to the methods of store selling. The mail-order houses simply set out to adjust their merchandising machinery to take advantage of this new potentiality, with which was combined, of course, the possibility of selling to consumers resident in the cities and towns.

For all the huge expansion of chain stores generally, the independent merchants, or rather the more efficient of them, were showing concrete evidence of strengthening their position. Despite the chains' inroads, independents were still managing to do something like 78 per cent of the total retail business, even excluding the volume of the independent department stores.

By organizing into groups, pooling his buying and adopting chain methods of advertising and display, the independent was not only counterbalancing the advantages of the chain but making more capital of the one major asset which he had always possessed—the direct personal contact with his customers. In addition, the independent was benefited by a general shift in consumer attitude toward retailing. Before the chains came, retailing consisted of lots of service and poor management. With the entry of the chains, the pendulum swung to the opposite extreme of shrewd management and no service. As a large section of the public began to exhibit a preference for the median, the independent merchant was in a better position to perform on that basis.

Many independents, desiring to meet fully the concentration advantages of the corporate chain system, turned to participation in a new form of retail distributing mechanism—the voluntary chain.

This mechanism was built from three different patterns, all aiming primarily at concentrated buying, group advertising and improved, standardized storekeeping methods, but with individual ownership of the store retained.

One was the organization created through the initiative of the wholesaler, who went out and enrolled his better customers in a co-operative system. The jobber offered pooled buying power and lower prices on staples and advertised specialties, merchandising counsel and store management assistance. In return he received low operating costs through assured volume and reduction of selling expenses, as well as an opportunity to build a market for his line of private brands.

The second type of voluntary was that evolved from a co-operative buying organization of retailers. In its simplest form, this type of operation dated back as far as 1888 in at least one instance, and it amounted to the retailers' taking over the function of the wholesaler. These early developments, however, were for a long time devoted to buying only. When retailers learned that selling had fully as much, if not more, to do with successful storekeeping, the group merchandising idea was added to the structure.

The third type is really an extension of the first, bringing into one organization a group of wholesalers as well as groups of retailers. The greatest impetus came from this type and it usually operated over a wider territory, leading representatives being the Independent Grocers Alliance and the Red & White Corporation.

The voluntary maintained the

...step forward

With the announcement of the new Midwest and Pacific Coast Color Comic Groups, *group advertising takes another step forward.*

Three years ago we set out to reorganize our existing Gravure Groups and to form new ones with the objective in mind of creating a *balanced National Coverage Pattern* in Rotogravure. This was finally accomplished with the formation of the Southern Gravure Group last September. Increased advertising patronage has been the result.

Now with the formation of these two new Comic Groups, a Group pattern comes into being in comics which is similar in scope and balance to that offered by Gravure Groups.

MIDWEST COLOR COMIC GROUP

Cincinnati Enquirer	Minneapolis Tribune
Columbus Dispatch	Omaha World-Herald
Des Moines Register	St. Paul Dispatch &
Duluth News-Tribune	Pioneer Press
Kansas City Journal-Post	Toledo Times

Circulation 1,357,257
Page Rate (4-colors) $7,440.00
½ Page Rate (4-colors) $3,950.00

PACIFIC COAST COLOR COMIC GROUP

Los Angeles Times	San Francisco Chronicle
Portland Journal	Seattle Times

Circulation 785,860
Page Rate (4-colors) $4,040.00
½ Page Rate (4-colors) $2,385.00

QUARTER PAGE RATE ON REQUEST

GRAVURE SERVICE CORPORATION

420 Lexington Avenue
New York City

Chicago　　　　　　　Detroit　　　　　　　San Francisco

great initial advantage of harnessing the full initiative and ambition of private ownership to an organization which simplified relationships with wholesalers and manufacturers and brought into effect the principle of mass distribution. By 1929 the movement, still in its early stages, encompassed 375 organizations and 55,000 retailers. Much of the voluntary's development came in the grocery field, where the chain's inroads had been strongest, but the same principle was also introduced in the drug, variety and hardware fields.

Since putting goods through retail channels at no increased cost meant real advancement, advertisers turned increasing attention to the retailer in their efforts to reduce market overhead. The steady growth of the chain store and its huge volume of business dazzled the manufacturer. In his anxiety to rush his goods through this swift-moving retail machine, visioning the elimination of many sales and advertising costs through the chains' mass buying power and efficiently organized selling equipment, he catered to the chains and tended to neglect the old dealer and jobber standbys.

The policy for a time paid dividends in terms of lowered sales expense and increased net profit. But the advertiser had not anticipated to what extent the easy volume would involve him. The chains had ideas of their own. They began to ask for lower prices, extra discounts, advertising allowances and all sorts of concessions for buying in quantities. These circumstances, plus the returning realization that the independent merchant still retained the capacity for handling the majority of the retail trade, tended to restore a balance of attention as between the two types of outlets.

The patent advantages to be gained by enlarging the retail bottle-neck in distribution caused advertisers generally to develop more intensive ways of helping out at the point of sale. The use of the service man, a representative of the manufacturer whose responsibility was to help the dealer sell instead of induce him to buy, became widely popular. A great deal of direct-mail material designed to teach retailers many things about business in general and their own in particular was pressed into service. Where the size of the unit sale justified the procedure, numerous manufacturers sent trained representatives to stores to give educational talks, often accompanied by motion picture presentations, to retail sales clerks. Business-paper copy was employed to promulgate selling ideas and show the dealer how he could make money out of the product.

Perhaps the greatest concentration of effort was in store display. The first stage of distributing display material promiscuously had, as noted in an earlier chapter, given way to the system to supplying the material only upon requests of dealers. Now the advertiser was finding that the newer idea overlooked the point that multiplicity of showings is essential to success, that thinly scattered display efforts, lacking in continuity and mass effect, are ineffective sales producers. In consequence, many advertisers joined the ranks of the few who had conducted display efforts on a systematic basis. Some established their own crews for selling dealers on the display, then installing it on the spot. Others turned to the local installation organizations, which

good-by depression No.14

One GREAT lesson we have learned in our business from 14 depressions has been NOT to lose faith in continuous advertising.

Our compliments to all media who have faithfully borne the torch carrying our message.

Modestly, may we add, a great product has meritoriously retained the confidence of its clientele to the mutual benefit and profit of all.

1826　　to　　date

 In 1935 **THE AMERICAN MERCURY'S** circulation dropped to 27,292 A.B.C. We were breathing hard. Our friends and enemies were busy writing our epitaph.  In 1936 **THE MERCURY'S** circulation went to 41,617 A.B.C.—a 52% increase over 1935.  In 1937 **THE MERCURY'S** circulation went to 62,623 A.B.C.—a 50% increase over 1936, more than 100% increase over 1935. **THE MERCURY'S** was the only important circulation gain* in the Quality field. Voluntary newsstand sales hit 40,000—greater than that of all three Quality magazines put together.  From present indications 1938 circulation will show another striking increase.  Because circulation growth has been voluntary and inexpensively obtained, advertising rates have not been increased. They are still where they were in 1935 in spite of more than a doubled circulation.  **THE MERCURY** today is a real buy for anyone who has a good idea, a Quality service, or a Quality product to sell. Write for rates today. We have no selling staff.

| *The Mercury—gained | 21,006 | Quality magazine B—lost | 3,163 |
| Quality magazine A—lost | 3,154 | Quality magazine C—gained | 5,328 |

THE AMERICAN MERCURY • 570 Lexington Ave., New York

were now offering a more reliable service than had been the case under former chaotic conditions in that field. Still others found the window display contest valuable if thoroughly promoted and intelligently planned to offer rewards to dealers of all sizes, factors which had been largely ignored in prior applications of this idea. The national week came into great favor, since it had the advantage of closely linking the display with a definite, concentrated selling campaign.

Another method of inducement was payment for space in the dealer's window or on his counter, an alternative not always voluntarily indulged since a number of the chains had instituted the policy of charging for such space.

In the designing of the material itself, a new phase appeared. Originally the display was intended merely to exhibit the merchandise. Then came the idea of the display as an advertising medium. In this latest stage of the evolution, actual

---

1926

Q UEEN MARIE OF RUMANIA makes a grand tour of America. . . . Gertrude Ederle swims the English Channel, first woman to do it. . . . Henry Ford inaugurates the five-day week. . . . Sesquicentennial Exposition held at Philadelphia.

The National Broadcasting Company established with Merlin H. Aylesworth as president and George F. McClelland as vice-president and general manager. . . . Lord & Thomas and Thomas F. Logan, Inc., consolidated. . . . Rodney E. Boone named general manager of national advertising for Hearst Newspaper Group No. 1 and Hearst Southern Group. . . . Packer Advertising Corporation formed as a merger of six outdoor advertising firms. . . . *Children, The Magazine for Parents* begins, with George J. Hecht as publisher. . . . Milton Towne elected president of the Joseph Richards Company. . . . Jagat Jit Singh, Maharaja de Kapurthala, and others of the nobility endorsing Melachrino cigarettes.

A. F. Seested, Irwin Kirkwood and associates purchase the Kansas City *Star* and *Times*. . . . William T. Dewart buys the New York *Sun* and the *Telegram* from the estate of the late Frank A. Munsey. . . . Old Gold cigarettes introduced. . . . Gordon Seagrove joins Lambert & Feasley, succeeding the late Milton Feasley. . . . Paul Block buys the Toledo *Blade*. . . . William McNamee appointed advertising director of the Chicago *Evening American*. . . . Paul Cornell forms an agency under his own name. . . . Opening sentence of a cold cream advertisement of the current lush school: "Oh, the glamor of New York in the purple dusk of twilight—what witcheries of the night as darkness falls, and Midtown, this modern Bagdad, flashes to fairyland and splendor under the myriad lights of Broadway."

salesmanship was the goal. A display that actually brought business to the dealer was the one which best suited the advertiser's broad purpose of speeding retail sales. At the same time such a display appealed strongly to the element of the dealer's advantage in using it. The result was the appearance of the tested display. The retailer was offered a unit which in preliminary trials under actual retail-store conditions had proved effective in increasing sales.

The advertiser's effort to work more closely with the retailer found its utmost expression with the revival, on a new and larger scale, of the plan of making him a part owner of the manufacturing business. By 1928 this had assumed the proportions of a definite trend, with stock offerings being made to dealers in the drug, grocery, sporting goods, motion picture, oil burner and radio fields. In that year the Beech-Nut Packing Company sold 50,000 shares of stock to the United Cigar Stores Company in an arrangement whereby the latter entered into active promotion of the sale of Beech-Nut gum and confections. In 1929, E. R. Squibb & Sons, the Vick Chemical Company, McKesson & Robbins and the W. A. Sheaffer Pen Company were among the important firms to offer distributors an opportunity to share in company profits. Some plans based the sharing on actual purchases of company merchandise, others were direct stock purchase propositions with a concession below the market price usually involved, a few were in the nature of investment trusts.

Certain of these efforts could be regarded as a counter-attack upon the retailer-manufacturer combination of functions developed in the operations of the larger chains. In a sense, they were another manifestation of the current trend toward consolidation of business interests, co-operation being brought about through closer relationship between individual distributor and manufacturer instead of by a merger of the type of distributor-manufacturer merger represented by Drug, Inc., which controlled a long line of advertised brands and the Liggett drug stores and other retailing units.

The plunge in the stock market put a damper on some of these arrangements but a few have continued along sound lines.

Starting around 1926, an old problem of retail relations came back to haunt the advertiser. Price maintenance had not been an issue of prominence for nearly ten years, having vanished from the scene at the time of the war. Now price-cutting had assumed proportions of an issue far more perplexing than formerly.

Most of the chain stores had accepted the advertised brand as an indispensable part of their merchandising operations, although in the beginning they had been basically inimical to it and had concentrated largely on substitution of low-priced merchandise. Advertising had more than kept pace with chain-store growth, however. With the post-war increase in the purchasing power of the consumer, there developed a public consciousness of quality which advertising aroused and directed to its own group of products. Buyers were no longer interested in price alone. Chains found it increasingly difficult to evade the fact that the public wanted and often demanded advertised products.

Having embraced the advertised product, the chain then concentrated on the idea of meeting an accepted demand at a price as low or lower than the customer could find elsewhere. As competition between chains themselves increased, especially in the larger cities, the advertised brand became the center of the inter-chain rivalry. With the assistance of the price concessions which many advertisers offered or felt they could not afford to withhold, price-cutting was met with price-cutting until a majority of the well-known brands had their profits cut to a point where they represented a loss. The independent dealer complained and in many instances refused to handle the advertised item whose price had been thus demoralized. The chains, in search of profit, turned once more to private brands.

In this condition, some advertisers decided to let well enough alone on the thesis that so long as price-cutting was moving a lot of merchandise, as it was in many cases, there was no point in interfering. They took the position that the power of their consumer advertising would insure continued consumer demand sufficient to nullify private brand competition and any hostility the retailer might manifest. Other firms were more impressed by the likelihood of disadvantage through loss of dealer support and debasement of product value in the consumer's mind. These began to explore once more the possibilities of devising some way of maintaining prices.

From a legal standpoint, price maintenance was still an intricate matter. A series of court decisions had by this time established pretty clearly that a manufacturer could exert his right to refuse to sell in dealing with a price-cutter, provided always that he did not exercise this right in conjunction with any price understanding or agreement between himself and his distributors and dealers. If he sold through jobbers he could not legally require or induce the jobber to refuse to sell to a price-cutting retailer, although, of course, a jobber could do so on his own initiative. Hence price maintenance activities were limited principally to manufacturers who sold direct to retailers. Even here there was much difficulty, for the price-cutter usually got the merchandise somewhere else.

Some new light was cast on the problem when, in 1926, the United States Supreme Court upheld the right of the General Electric Company to fix selling prices on electric lamps under its consignment plan of distribution. The plan had been instituted in 1912 and the litigation over it, resulting from a Government charge that of restraint in trade, had covered a considerable period of time. General Electric had adopted consignment selling because the enormous range of Mazda lamp sizes and styles to suit varying consumer needs and local conditions of current made it necessary for the average small dealer to carry a large stock—larger than the majority could afford to buy and pay for. In addition, it was desirable to protect dealers on price changes in a falling market. The point at issue in the litigation was whether the sale of lamps was made by the company to the consumer through the agent or whether it was in fact made at the time of the consignment of lamps to the agent. The court held that the distributors were genuine agents of the company and that the delivery of the stock to the agent was nothing more than a consignment to him for custody and sale as such.

Following this decision, similar consignment arrangements, sometimes called the *del credere* plan, were put into effect by other firms and the plan came into further prominence several years later.

·Paralleling the broad effort to help out at the point of retail sale was a new advertiser attitude toward that much maligned middleman who sold to the retailer. The long-standing policy of slighting the jobber gave way to a trend toward seeking his co-operation and developing his usefulness. More than one manufacturer who had cut out the jobber and gone to the retailer direct had learned that he was not altogether wise in doing so, finding by costly experience that he must choose, in certain sections at least, between doing business at a loss or recognizing the jobber. Many advertisers concluded that the jobber might not be an obstacle in the path of distribution after all. ·

Such unusual spectacles began to appear as manufacturers advertising to retailers the value of the functions performed by the wholesaler and its importance to the welfare of the merchant. Various plans for assisting the jobber to operate more efficiently were introduced. Manufacturers' specialty salesmen, calling on the retail trade for orders to be placed through the jobber, gave him a boost. Extra compensation was offered to wholesalers who did unusual selling jobs. Some firms carried on consistent programs designed to gain the friendship of jobbers' salesmen. Others inaugurated sales conventions for jobbers.

In the last two or three strenuous years of the period, talk of elimination of the jobber was renewed, and in some quarters the talk was translated into action. However, the general proposition of treating the jobber as a partner had become firmly established.

Two new forms of jobbing operations ventured into the spotlight in the 1920's. One was the cash-and-carry wholesaler, who became fairly important in some sections. He had no sales expense, except that involved by the clerks handling the orders of the retailers who came to the warehouse, and no credit risk. He was primarily a creation of the advertised brand, since he dealt in identified merchandise for which existed a definite consumer, and therefore, retailer, demand. Having a low overhead, he passed on savings which helped the independent retailer meet chain-store competition.

The second new form of operator likewise featured the cash angle, but provided lots of carry. This was the auto truck jobber, modern incarnation of the old wagon jobber, considerably stronger as to capital and more efficient in operation, however. Formerly respectable but lowly with his one horse and wagon, he now appeared as the owner of a good-sized fleet of trucks manned not by mere delivery men but by salesmen trained in helping retailers with sales and advertising problems. This type of jobber, of which there were some 10,000 operating 35,000 trucks in 1929, got his start handling perishable foods. Then he added semi-perishable lines and finally a few staples. He turned to advertised lines as soon as he learned of their easier acceptance.

For the Record

━━━

Reincke · Ellis · Younggreen & Finn
in 1938

Our company, 31 years old, salutes Printers' Ink which is 50. And for the record we take real pride in listing here our principal associates — a group that combines unusual talent and ability, and, supported by an efficient staff, serves upward of 50 accounts

───

ARNO B. REINCKE	C. N. JOHNSON
C. C. YOUNGGREEN	WALLACE MEYER
JOSEPH H. FINN	B. C. O'BRIEN
•	A. L. REINCKE
C. S. ACTON	C. A. REINCKE
H. A. BATES	A. L. SALISBURY
J. F. BROWN	L. E. SHEARS
J. J. FINN	C. C. STEVENS
J. J. FITZGERALD	GORDON TAYLOR
R. S. GHISELIN	R. B. WILLIAMS

520 North Michigan Avenue · Chicago

Emotion's Entrance

THE first advertising told the name of the product. In the second stage, the specifications of the product were outlined. Then came emphasis upon the uses of the product. With each step the advertisement moved farther away from the factory viewpoint and edged itself closer into the mental processes of the consumer. Then the cycle was completed, partly as a result of natural evolution, partly as a consequence of the demands which a distribution era made upon advertising.

Advertising entered what may well be termed the consumer stage. It began to work from the consumer's interest to the product. The advertiser commenced to talk in terms of ultimate buying motives rather than descriptive product data, although, of course, the latter remained as an important accompanying consideration. A considerable proportion of consumer advertising moved from the objective to the subjective, and the emotional appeal became an important part of the advertiser's equipment.

Copy began to deal with such things as health, happiness, comfort, luxury, sentiment, social success and the arts of winning the favor of the opposite sex. Automobiles were offered on the basis of transportation and prestige, clothing on the basis of fashion and success in business, cosmetics on the basis of sex appeal and so on all along the line. Not infrequently the advertiser started to place dominant emphasis on the subjective value, selling first the importance of the particular phase of self-advancement or gratification which

might result from the use of his product.

A good share of advertising of the period interpreted the subjective value of the product in terms of the disadvantageous consequences of not owning or using it. The advertiser portrayed the gravity of a certain physical, mental or social condition, then presented the story of the efficacy of his product as a means of banishing that state. It seems to be that this negative approach was the first form of emotional or subjective copy. The early "scare" campaigns had dealt with physical disaster of some sort and advocated the product as a way of removing the hazard. The new emotional copy simply extended the principle into broader fields of human response less tangible in nature than an actual physical accident or illness, notably failure to attain social success. From that branched off the idea, referred to in the preceding paragraph, of "selling" desirable emotional conditions.

Use of the negative slant was spurred considerably by the campaign of the Lambert Pharmacal Company in which Listerine was advanced as a product which could end the social blights occasioned by unpleasant breath—or, in the word which the company implanted in the American vocabulary, halitosis. A lingering wariness toward the value of the negative appeal was pretty well put to an end by the enormous success of this campaign, and a little later the Lever Brothers "Body Odor" campaign for Life Buoy soap just about settled the matter for all time.

Another form taken by the effort

PLEASE ÆSOP!
Not that old Elephant Story Again

We won't tell it again because we think from where each blindman stood, a rope, a wall, and a snake described the elephant pretty well . . . and that's the way with this country's business . . . it is too big to be described as good or bad! It all depends on where you sit! Down in New Orleans everything is *UP! So if your end looks bad come on down to our end! Do your selling in the prosperous New Orleans market by advertising in The Times-Picayune and New Orleans States!

*Retail sales for first four months of '38 are up 5.2%, building, payrolls and employment are up proportionately!

The Times = Picayune
NEW ORLEANS STATES

Representatives: NOEE, ROTHENBURG & JANN, Inc.

New York   •   Chicago   •   Detroit   •   Atlanta   •   San Francisco

to get closer to the consumer's problem was the widened use of the recipe style of advertising. Telling in the most definite terms what the consumer could do with the product—in other words, starting with the consumer and working back to the advertiser—this approach was not only more extensively applied to food products than ever before but was put to use in advertising of household furnishings, clothing and many types of specialties.

Since the pressure for results was not equally distributed throughout business and some industries skimmed blithely upward, a certain proportion of the advertising was of an empty, superficial quality. There was a conspicuous amount of copy that addressed its audience in high-hat terms and not a little was enrolled of the beautiful-but-dumb school.

The basic trend, however, was toward getting more salesmanship into copy. Since this buyer's market was a protracted one for many advertisers, they scrutinized the question of advertising effectiveness more closely than ever before. The business of testing copy received its first major impetus, excluding, of course, the efforts in this direction carried on for years by mail-order merchandisers.

The testing idea got its start in a very elemental way. The writer or advertiser would simply show the copy to a few friends and get their opinions on it. Some would show the advertisement to selected dealers. Then came the idea, borrowed from the mail-order people, of running a piece of copy in one publication of known pulling power with some sort of coupon or other action-impelling device to get the public reaction as compared with results on previous pieces of copy. The idea of keeping continual check on their advertising campaigns was adopted by many firms and in these years the use of coupon advertising increased greatly, one observer in 1927 estimating that coupon advertising had increased tenfold in the preceding seven years.

The growing belief that taking things for granted was a too-expensive luxury resulted in material development and increased use of the tryout campaign in a single market as a means of ascertaining the soundness of the appeal before using it on a national scale. Another development in pre-testing of copy was the laboratory method of analyzing and charting the advertisement for buying motives, psychological appeals and the like.

Contributing also to increased effectiveness of advertising was the development of a truly purposeful approach to the problems of the design and illustration of the advertisement. In the past the illustration had served a principally decorative or eye-catching function, while the art of layout had been almost entirely neglected. The exhibitions of the Art Directors Club of New York, beginning in 1921, revealed that there was really an advertising art worthy of the name and that design had become a part of the advertisement rather than a mere attachment to it.

An important event was the gradual infiltration of modernism, which in its true form of naturalism and simplicity represented a highly appropriate and useful accesion to advertising art. Its growth began in 1926 and proceeded to catch on with rapidity. There were definite signs of a fresher viewpoint,

For almost 40 years

of the 50 chronicled by Printers' Ink, W. R. C. Smith Publications have been developing manufacturing and merchandising in the South and Southwest, building worthwhile markets for advertisers.

In 1938 and in the years to come

you will find the Smith Publications effective in producing business for you in their respective fields.

COTTON
Serving the Textile Industries

SOUTHERN HARDWARE

read by 8,000 hardware dealers and distributors from Virginia to Texas.

SOUTHERN AUTOMOTIVE JOURNAL

blanketing all branches of the year-round automotive market in the 19 Southern and Southwestern states.

SOUTHERN POWER JOURNAL

3 to 1 circulation domination of power, industrial, and refrigeration plants of the South and Southwest.

ELECTRICAL SOUTH

the one paper covering all branches of the Southern electrical industry.

W·R·C·SMITH *Publications*

ATLANTA, GA.

of elimination of detail in illustration and simplified atmosphere. The camera returned from a state of relative obscurity in a new surge of originality and inventive genius wherein were featured real rather than conventional types and natural arrangements in place of the old "artistic" treatments.

The return of the camera was an unmistakable sign that advertising was getting down to every-day life and that the days of exquisite fancies in the advertising pages were being left behind. In the striving for human interest, the news-picture or "tabloid" style of advertisement, concentrating a number of illustrations on a single page, attained high favor in 1928.

In the last three years of the period the exigencies of competition produced in certain quarters a type of consumer message which was aptly termed "super-advertising." Not so blatant or so crude as the fake and hokum of forty years before, it nevertheless had a

---

1927

CHARLES A. LINDBERGH reaches Paris in non-stop solo flight from New York. . . . President Coolidge at summer camp at Rapid City, S. D.: "I do not choose to run." . . . Sacco and Vanzetti executed at Charlestown, Mass. . . . William Hale Thompson elected mayor of Chicago on promise to "bust King George in the snoot."

Ford Motor Company goes out of production for six months to make way for the Model A. . . . Columbia Broadcasting System formed under the control of the Columbia Phonograph Company. . . . John Benson appointed as permanent president of the American Association of Advertising Agencies. . . . Paul S. Willis named vice-president of the Comet Rice Company. . . . "Think of your business in terms of just one customer"—Walter P. Chrysler. . . . H. C. Macdonald elected president and general manager of Walker & Company, Detroit. . . . Scripps-Howard acquires the New York *Telegram.* . . . The iceman turns to advertising to avoid being frozen out by the rapidly growing mechanical refrigeration industry.

The Register & Tribune Company, Des Moines, acquires the Des Moines *Capital* and merges it with the *Tribune.* . . . E. F. Hummert joins Blackett & Sample, which later becomes Blackett-Sample-Hummert, Inc. . . . Fred A. Walker returns to the New York *Sun* as chairman of the executive board. . . . O. C. Harn appointed managing director of the A. B. C., P. L. Thomson succeeding him as president. . . . In a series of transactions William Randolph Hearst acquires the Pittsburgh *Sun-Telegraph* and Paul Block secures control of the *Post-Gazette* of the same city. . . . Encouraged by success with counterfeit Gordon's Gin and similar items, bootleggers turn to counterfeit advertised brands as a side-line.

● Since the first ice-cold Coca-Cola made a *pause refreshing* in 1886, Coca-Cola and Advertising have marched down the years together. The product had to be good to get where it is. And a consistent program of promotion, with monthly, weekly, daily repetition in newspapers, magazines, radio as well as on posters, painted signs, and point-of-purchase displays, ha acceptance for *the pause* ice-cold Coca-Cola. As a Coca-Cola has spread.. country to country.. arqun find Coca-Cola welcome er everybody knows that ice pure, wholesome and deli

d the years...
e *that refreshes*

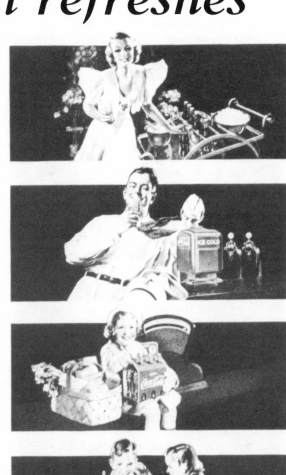

won universal
at refreshes with
sult, the fame of
on city to city..
the world. You'll
ywhere, because
id Coca-Cola is
ous refreshment.

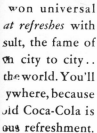

strongly reminiscent odor. Though its users represented nowhere near a sizable proportion of the total advertising, the manifestation was sufficiently conspicuous to constitute a grave threat to the credibility of all copy.

Perhaps the most acute phase of super-advertising was the tainted testimonial, which had become a critical evil in 1926 and proceeded to get steadily worse. As in an earlier outbreak of this abuse back in the 1890's but to an even more flagrant degree, testimonials were secured at a price from social leaders, shipwreck heroes, aviators and prominent athletes. Often these were wholly misrepresentative because they embodied not sincere testimony of an actual user of the product but a statement purchased for money and publicity. So intense became the competition for big-name testimony that the whole business became a patent absurdity in the eyes of the public, a threat to advertising's believability graver even than that of the element of deception. The serious issue represented by the mounting abuse became a serious one in the councils of the Better Business Bureaus, the Association of National Advertisers and other organized groups.

The misleading superlative and the exaggerated claim were lusty branches of the super-advertising tree. Here some advertisers spread their products so thickly with the butter of imagination and claimed so much that there was nothing left for the honest manufacturer of a genuinely superior product to say. The unusual was implied to be the average. If some result or

some quality was found to be desirable in the eyes of the consumer, then that result or quality was unequivocally claimed for the product. Subjective product values were distorted far beyond the bounds of reason, anything from a soap to a breakfast food being advocated for consummation of a happy marriage.

An evil of more original contriving was the doctrine of pseudo-science. Science was paraded as an expert witness for the virtues of numerous common articles. Some of the claims made in the name of science were outright falsehoods. Others were based on unreliable or wholly special test conditions, still others magnified unimportant qualities.

Such were some of the principal facets of one of the most troublesome problems which the distribution age posed to the advertiser and the advertising business. It is one thing to deal with the outright lie and quite another to put a stop to abuses which skirt the borderlines of honesty and good taste. Moreover, these abuses were more symptom than disease. They grew not from an intrinsic debasement of those responsible for shaping advertising policies but from the pressures of an intensely competitive time. And, unhappily, they were tactics which, for a while at least, produced sales results. They implied a staggering challenge to business, a challenge which, as has grown increasingly clear with the passage of time, could only be met by education of the consumer. Largely unnoticed at the time, the consumer was beginning to establish schools of his own.

New Wings for Words

IN the year 1899 they had in Budapest what was called the "Telefon-Hirmondo"—the telephone newspaper. The telephone receivers of 6,200 subscribers were hooked to a central circuit. From 10:30 in the morning until 10:30 at night news stories were sent out over the wires and to get the news of the day you simply picked up your receiver and got a connection with the central office. The stories were prepared by writers, turned over to editors for revision and then given to the man at the sending point, who was called the "stentor." In between news bulletins short stories were read over the wire and there were little dramatized playlets. There were also special features, as when Wilhelm of Germany delivered his famous toast to Hungary; a half hour after the Kaiser made his speech the verbatim text of it was read to subscribers. In the evening the opera was brought to the homes of the telephone owners, although the reproduction left a little something to be desired. Commercial establishments were offered the use of the sending facilities at the rate of one florin for a twelve-second talk.

The idea spread to other European capitals—London, Paris, Vienna. Several years later Manly Gillam, the advertising writer, attempted unsuccessfully to establish the system in the United States. He thought it would be especially good for sending out running accounts of baseball games.

In the year 1920 in Pittsburgh the Westinghouse Electric & Manufacturing Company conducted a telephone broadcast of the returns of the presidential election—but in this instance the telephone had no wires. With that event wireless telephony turned from what had been the hobby of a few thousand radio amateurs toward nationwide acceptance as a primary vehicle of entertainment and education. Previously the Westinghouse transmitter, KDKA, had conducted some broadcasts of phonograph records, but it was the election broadcast which really dramatized the magic of the new method of communication to the public at large.

For a time, few could be interested in taking up the expensive job of broadcasting. WBZ (now WBZA) at Springfield, Mass., in September of 1921, was given license No. 1. The Detroit *News* became an eminent pioneer with the establishment of WWJ, which was the first station to broadcast a comprehensive news service. Here and there others joined the ranks. Department stores, prosperous dealers, newspapers and universities set up broadcasting outfits and took their pay in prestige. Some of the manufacturers of radio receivers also became broadcasters, their compensation being a little more direct since the sale of their products depended upon maintenance of good broadcasting service.

It was not until the fall of 1922 that the wireless telephone caught up with its Budapest precursor in the matter of selling time facilities to advertisers. The American Telephone & Telegraph Company, operating WEAF at New York, offered the use of the station for advertising talks. The rate was $2 instead of one florin, for twelve seconds—

$100 for a ten-minute talk was the unit of sale. So far as dependable records reveal, the first commercial broadcast made was a ten-minute talk over this station by the Queensborough Corporation, promoter of the Jackson Heights development on Long Island, New York.

Such were the beginnings of what was to be the greatest single accession to the advertising structure since the magazine became an advertising medium many years before. The initial growth of broadcast advertising bears an astonishing parallel to the early development of advertising as a whole. To begin with, many proprietors of radio transmitters were dubious about the public reaction to the sale of time to advertisers, just as early publishers had considered that readers might deem advertisements in their pages to be an unwelcome intrusion. Before long, however, it seemed that "indirect" advertising—announcement of the name of the company sponsoring the program—might not be too objectionable. In 1922 the Department of Commerce held a conference of departmental representatives, Congressmen and radio experts at which it was decided that indirect advertising would be permissible but that direct advertising must not be countenanced. It was a matter of pretty general agreement among advertisers, agents and broadcasters that direct advertising, while perhaps immediately productive of results, would be harmful in the long run both to the station and to the advertiser responsible for it. Gradually it became apparent that the vast majority of the listeners really didn't mind so long as the advertiser contributed a good program for their enjoyment, but the erroneous conception of public psychology persisted for several years.

Operating on the assumption that only indirect advertising might be indulged, the majority of advertisers used radio purely as a good-will medium up to as late as 1928. Products were not even described. The advertiser depended upon the fact that he was presenting an enjoyable program to bring a favorable disposition toward his products. Radio was considered a means of getting name publicity and was generally thought of as having no other sound application. Here again is a similarity to the first days of advertising, for, as has been seen, name publicity was its sole end all through the 1890's.

The first forms of the radio selling mechanism likewise carried out the parallel. The radio station representative appeared and he was much like the early general agent. He usually represented all stations without specific appointment. Most broadcasters would accept business from any representative and pay him commission. As the advertising agency took up radio, the activities of the station representatives in selling the radio idea as such became a relatively less important part of their operations. The station's need became more one of specific representation, and to fill this need the exclusive representative, counterpart of the special agent in the newspaper and magazine fields, came into being.

The creating of "copy" for radio broadcasts likewise followed a familiar pattern. The stations themselves were the first to help the advertiser with this problem, maintaining departments to create and

374

(Toll Test)

WNAC	Boston
WTIC	Hartford
WEAN	Providence
WTAG	Worcester
WICC	Bridgeport New Haven
WNLC	New London
WCSH	Portland
WLBZ	Bangor
WFEA	Manchester
WSAR	Fall River
WNBH	New Bedford
WHAI	Greenfield
WLLH	Lowell Lawrence
WLNH	Laconia
WRDO	Augusta

Connecting All New England Markets

THOUGH widely separated geographically, the many markets of New England can be connected instantaneously, economically and effectively through the extensive facilities of The Yankee Network.

Fifteen stations comprise this New England-dominating group—each station situated in the urban shopping center of a major trading area. Together they provide complete, sales-producing coverage of the entire New England market.

It Works With Appendicitis
Why Not Radio?

THE symptoms are there — and your family doctor is pretty sure you've got appendicitis — but you're not satisfied with his diagnosis, you insist on the confirmation of a specialist. And the surgeon you'd choose for the carving must be a man with years of successful experience in removing appendices — a nose and throat man won't do!

We've been in radio's operating room for 15 years — before it was discovered as an organ of advertising. We witnessed the early groping for technique of treatment, those years of trial and error when a patient rarely lived beyond 13 weeks.

Hundreds of cases came under our daily observation. We began to find reasons for the high mortality rate. With facilities for perfect experiment and research—without risking the life of a patient — we developed unerring accuracy of treatment.

It is with modest pride that we point to our record of achievement since we hung out our shingle. A consultation with one of our principals will reveal the striking features of our methods.

No obligation, of course.

NEFF-ROGOW, INC.
AN ADVERTISING AGENCY
SPECIALIZING IN RADIO
30 ROCKEFELLER PLAZA
PHONE CIRCLE 7 4230

develop complete plans for broadcasting. Some of the representatives undertook to perform a similar function. Then came program bureaus which engaged in building programs, much as the advertising writing firms of old supplied a copy service. The general advertising agency was, of course, already established on a service basis for other forms of advertising, but in the main it was slow in setting up facilities for radio program planning. In 1928, according to a study made by the Association of National Advertisers, agencies prepared only 33 per cent of the leading national programs. Broadcasters were responsible for 28 per cent, advertisers for 20 per cent, program bureaus for 19 per cent.

Fundamentally, radio was attractive to the advertiser from the start. The growing number of radio enthusiasts (there were over 2,000,-000 sets in operation in 1923) represented an audience well worth reaching and the chance to deliver an audible message in the very heart of the home was too obvious to be overlooked. Wholly apart from considerations of audience reaction toward advertising on the air, however, the new medium posed serious problems which made the first growth necessarily slow. Since the beginning of advertising, its address had been entirely through the eye. This was the first mass advertising medium which made its appeal through the human ear. The technique of oral advertising had to be developed from the start, in addition to which the advertiser found himself faced for the first time with mustering the arts of showmanship to his purposes. The field was so utterly unknown that it was without sign-posts or markers of any kind. Everything had to be learned by experiment and trial and error.

By 1927 the broadcasting studio had changed from a refuge for second and third rate singers eager to inflict their meager talents upon the unseen audience to a center of a certain amount of worthwhile entertainment. The public was demanding a constantly improved service. The good old days, when the chief thrill of radio reception was in getting a new station and when any kind of a program would do to carry the mystic call letters of the stations, had passed away. Advertisers were beginning to spend real money for talent.

The fund of knowledge and experience relative to dealing with the medium was still scanty. There was a vast amount of fumbling going on, although, with some advertisers in their fourth year of sustained broadcasting, radio was no longer entirely new. There was little interchange of information among users. Most hesitated to express an opinion as to its value and such opinions as were offered were of little value because with few exceptions advertisers had failed to devise means of testing. They were drawn to radio through a general interest in it and a sense of the vast potentialities of a medium for reaching so many people at once. But having used it, they did not know whether they had used it well or wasted their opportunities.

Many advertisers had too much assurance in one respect. Although highly inexperienced as producers of public entertainment, not a few business executives undertook to dictate entertainment policies to artists and producers who had long experience in winning the favor of the public. The average program consisted merely of announcing of songs and other musical numbers, together with their rendition and the name of the advertiser and the station. Such continuity as might hold the listener's uninterrupted attention was lacking. The idea of building a program upon the basis of that employed in the preparation of a motion picture scenario or a stage show had not been grasped. Adaptability of talent to radio performance had not been analyzed.

A new factor in standardizing the medium on a national basis was in

1928

HERBERT HOOVER triumphs over Alfred E. Smith in presidential election. . . . Amelia Earhart becomes the first woman to fly the Atlantic. . . . First all-talking picture, "The Lights of New York," appears. . . . Graf Zeppelin arrives at Lakehurst, N. J., from Germany. . . . There seems to be something of a boom in the stock market.

Merger business: Chrysler Corporation takes over Dodge Brothers, Kraft Cheese Company acquires Phenix Cheese Company, Postum Company acquires Maxwell House coffee, General Mills, Inc., organized as a consolidation of Washburn-Crosby and other milling concerns, Colgate & Company and the Palmolive-Peet Company combine. . . . A. W. Shaw Company merged with McGraw-Hill Publishing Company. . . . Batten, Barton, Durstine & Osborn organized as a consolidation of the George Batten Company and Barton, Durstine & Osborn. . . . Harry Dwight Smith joins the Erickson Company as vice-president. . . . Post office department introduces the business reply card. . . . L. Ames Brown elected president of Lord & Thomas and Logan to succeed the late Thomas F. Logan. . . . Doubleday, Doran & Company starts *American Home.* . . . Hosiery manufacturers jittery over the feminine bare-leg fad.

Gen. Robert E. Wood elected president of Sears, Roebuck & Company. . . . Mortimer Berkowitz now vice-president of *American Weekly.* . . . Allen L. Billingsley elected president of Fuller & Smith. . . . W. E. Macfarlane appointed business manager of the Chicago *Tribune,* William E. Donahue succeeding him as advertising manager. . . . Death of Clarence Walker Barron, president of Dow, Jones & Company and of Doremus & Company. . . . Bragdon, Lord & Nagle Company, publisher of *Textile World,* affiliates with McGraw-Hill. . . . Scanning the vogue for special weeks, M. L. Crowther looks over the calendar and finding the second week of June, 1947, unappropriated as yet, designates it as "Mind Your Own Damned Business Week."

its first year of operation at this stage. In November of 1926 the Radio Corporation of America purchased WEAF and established the National Broadcasting Company, which proposed to make programs originating at WEAF available through stations in all parts of the country by means of telephone line hook-up It lost $500,000 in its first year, but this was not an uncommon experience in broadcasting, for out of nearly 700 stations perhaps ten could show as much as an even break between revenue from sale of time and station expenses.

In 1927 the Columbia Broadcasting System was formed by the Columbia Phonograph Company to offer a nationwide radio service through affiliated stations.

The year 1929 saw radio moving definitely toward recognition as a major advertising medium. In that year volume climbed to somewhere near $14,000,000. The Association of National Advertisers devoted an entire session at its annual convention to radio, something that would have been unthinkable two years before. The idea of merchandising the radio program to dealers appeared, as did that of advertising in newspapers, to build an audience for the program. The National Association of Broadcasters adopted a code of ethics to ban offensive and deceptive advertising from the ether.

In the preceding year or two, final proof was appearing that the listener would stand for a good deal more in the way of forthright advertising matter than had been thought. Here the parallel with early developments in advertising appears once more. It was the retailers and the mail-order sellers who showed the way in putting salesmanship into publication copy. Much of the pioneering in direct advertising over the radio was done by retailers and by a number of stations which were selling merchandise direct to consumers via radio. There were some sixty of these stations in 1928. They advertised unabashedly and, operating like a mail-order house except that the catalog was in oral form, sold something like $12,000,000 annually in mass lots of commodities like seeds, coffee, tires, plants, binder twine, overalls and so forth.

With the taking up of the direct advertising idea, the broadcast copy, or "commercial," emerged as a new problem in advertising practice. It was a routine matter to give the company name, but to devise a message that would create consumer acceptance or demand over the air was something else again. The whole question of announcements and of writing or dramatizing them was opened up for study and experiment, and it was soon learned that spoken copy has a technique often very different from that of copy prepared for the eye. This tended to bring the agency more prominently into the radio picture, since the agent had the advantage of being best equipped to fit broadcasting into its proper place in the advertiser's broad selling and advertising program, an unimportant consideration in the days of name publicity. As a result, the radio department began to occupy a place in the advertising agency structure.

Rotogravure printing was another of invention's new contributions to the array of advertising media. Its most conspicuous role was as a part of the newspaper structure in the form of supplements printed by the process, but it also achieved wide use in the printing of magazines and of catalogs, direct-mail display pieces and booklets.

Photogravure, the first form, dated back many years. This was printing from a flat intaglio plate, a hand process yielding about 800 prints from a plate. Rotogravure introduced the rotary process and high-speed printing for big runs. It appeared in America in 1913 and newspapers were quick to recognize its pictorial possibilities and develop it as a news and advertising medium, the New York *Times* establishing the first newspaper rotogravure section in 1914. Affording close approximation of the artistic values of photographic originals and exceptional depth in subject life and action, rotogravure gave the newspaper something entirely new to offer in the way of advertising reproduction.

Development was held back at first by the large investment required to equip a plant and the paucity of trained workers, as well as the difficulty of securing American-made machinery, paper and materials. These gaps were soon filled, however. By 1922 considerable progress had been made. First retailers and then national advertisers had taken to the medium. The greatest growth came in the succeeding years, however, volume moving up from $3,600,000 in 1921 to $19,800,000 in 1927.

So far as consequences immediately affecting the 1922-29 years are concerned, editorial invention even surpassed mechanical innovations in building wider audiences for the expanding market needs of the advertiser. To the newspaper field came the tabloid-sized publication with its strong emphasis upon photographic treatment of the news and brief, concise text. When Capt. J. M. Patterson and Col. R. R. McCormick of the Chicago *Tribune* established the *Illustrated Daily News* at New York in 1919 they launched an experiment new in America.

The little paper had rather a struggling time of it at first, but with a foothold once obtained, it quickly measured up to its objective of reaching the mass market. Circulation passed the million mark in a few years and the New York *News* became the largest single circulation unit among all the newspapers of the country. Other papers of the tabloid size and style were established in New York and other cities. In 1926 the list had grown to fifteen such papers, and while the standard-sized newspapers continued predominant in numbers, the tabloid had definitely won a place and added materially to the total newspaper reading public.

The newspaper field as a whole moved on to new highs in advertising volume. From $55,000,000 in 1915 daily newspaper income from national advertising rose to $260,-000,000 in 1929. Part of this is to be attributed to industrial expansion, part to continued improvement in the selling of the medium. But some credit belongs also to the development of better reproduction of the advertisement, many of the old difficulties of getting faithful reproductions of illustrations having disappeared in the face of better methods and materials.

Chain or group journalism progressed importantly in these years. By 1929 35 per cent of the total circulation of American newspapers was represented in fifty-five groups

Christian Herald

is

Sixty Years Old

♦ ♦

THE OCTOBER ISSUE will be the Anniversary Number. SPECIAL FEATURE articles will deal with the standards of living in America sixty years ago and today.

THEY WILL SHOW THAT, despite the problems which have faced government and industry during the past sixty years, the American system has given better opportunity for the development of a happy and prosperous people than any other system in the world.

THIS ANNIVERSARY ISSUE offers an ideal setting in which manufacturers may present their policies and products to a quarter of a million substantial families living in smaller cities and towns.

♦ ♦

CHRISTIAN HERALD

419 Fourth Avenue   New York City

totaling about 250 papers. The largest group was Hearst with twenty-eight papers; Scripps-Howard with twenty-five was second.

In the magazine field new developments tended to center around the new woman, as a wage-earner or a homemaker, or both. Bernarr Macfadden developed an editorial formula for attracting a mass audience for a number of new magazines which he established in this period and shortly before. The leading member of the group, *True Story*, made history in the realm of newspaper circulation, attaining in 1924, when it was little more than five years old, a monthly circulation of nearly 2,000,000 copies. Magazines catering especially to home improvement interests—notably *Better Homes & Gardens* and *The American Home*—scored phenomenal successes. The large established women's magazines—*Good Housekeeping, Ladies' Home Journal, McCall's* and *Woman's Home Companion*—stepped up the service element in their editorial contents and won ever-increasing followings. *Liberty*, established by the Chicago *Tribune* owners and later sold to the Macfadden interests, offered a popular reader appeal which quickly carried it past the million mark in the weekly field. New developments were not limited to assembling mass buying audiences, however. Such newcomers in the weekly field as *Time* and the *New Yorker* came to supply additional avenues to more selective markets.

The real advance in direct-mail advertising came in this period. Printers woke up to the importance of constructive selling of printed matter as an advertising medium. Reflecting the new interest, and contributing to it, was the establish-ment of the Direct Mail Advertising Association which evolved into broadened, independent scope from an earlier status as a department of the Associated Advertising Clubs of the World.

Outdoor advertising benefited by an increased interest built up during the war period, when posters played a major part in the loan drives and other Government advertising activities. Then came important work in the further standardization and policing of the medium as a result of the consolidation of the industry's interests when, in 1925, the Poster Advertising Association and the Painted Outdoor Advertising Association merged as the Outdoor Advertising Association of America, bringing together standardized posters, painted display and electrical display interests. The medium had been under fire from women's organizations and politicians for some years and although the abuses complained of were traceable to a reckless minority of free-lancers, the industry as a whole had suffered. The new association committed its members to a set of rigid standards of conduct in the placement of panels and displays, relative to traffic safety, considerations of scenic beauty and residential districts.

A new medium which helped to fill an advertising gap was the "Where to Buy It" service initiated by the American Telephone & Telegraph Company in the classified telephone directories of cities throughout the United States. This introduced classified listings of dealers handling nationally advertised products, so that the consumer, convinced by advertising, could readily locate a place to go for the product. In 1929 the com-

The Cheapest Salesman of All

(An editorial by J. E. Stanford Reprinted from June Issue, Southern Agriculturist)

OUR nation is generally recognized as the world's wealthiest country, and the mass standard of intellectuality is also rated the highest. This being true, it is natural that American advertising should be the most colorful and readable to be found anywhere. At the same time, it has a well-earned reputation for an unexcelled standard of truth and morality which accounts for absence of numerous advertisements in American publications that would be accepted without question by the magazines and newspapers of some other nations. There is a direct, unmistakable connection between good advertising and the general welfare which should be sufficient answer to the charge that advertising adds unduly to the price that the consumer must pay. Of course, it costs some money to sell things—a necessary charge that none of us can avoid; but advertising has always been, and still is, the cheapest salesman on the payroll. A recent survey by a New York civic association showed that the advertising chargeable to more than five dollars worth of food products purchased at retail was less than three cents. The same low rate holds approximately true for advertising costs for other things people buy. The fraction of a cent the consumer pays for advertising is usually an assurance that he is getting the kind and quality of merchandise he desires and needs. Advertisements give clues to the civic affairs, cultural accomplishments and industrial activities of a community, as well as telling of the wares for sale. An experienced person, though a stranger, can make a close estimate of the degree of community prosperity, and he can tell whether the people are progressive or reactionary, simply by reading the local advertising. A good town, like the up-and-going manufacturer or merchant, has good advertising and plenty of it. It goes without argument that a desirable, progressive town or community is always associated with good publicity. A well-planned, persistent advertising program can be as successfully used to promote the interests of the community, city, or state, as it can to increase sales of the manufacturer's or merchant's goods. The wise farmer, like the wise manufacturer, retailer, town and state, finds that advertising is his most effective worker in disposing of his well-bred livestock and high-grade, properly packed products.

pany began a national advertising program to educate consumers.

The commission system of compensating advertising agencies came in for questioning from a source outside the advertising business in 1923. The Federal Trade Commission issued a complaint charging that certain publishers' associations had unlawfully conspired to prevent advertisers placing business direct from receiving the commission that publications pay advertising agencies. Charged with participation in this "conspiracy" were the American Association of Advertising Agencies, The American Newspaper Publishers Association, the Southern Newspaper Publishers Association, The Six Point League and the American Press Association. After numerous hearings and a process of litigation which covered seven years, the Commission decided it was without jurisdiction in the case.

Institutional advertising in behalf of mail-order catalog in the early Twenties

Jantzen started the vogue for swimming suits and swimming. This advertisement shows the style of 1924

What "PRINTERS' INK" Has Done for 50 Years for Advertising

BOYS' LIFE

For All Boys—Published by the Boy Scouts of America

Has Done for 25 Years for Boys

It has co-ordinated the interests of outstanding boys in the Better Homes of the Bigger Towns.

It has, with the Boy Scouts of America, promoted higher standards of character among boys.

It has brought new interests to boys and to groups of boys.

It has established the confidence of boys in worth while products by its advertising censorship and practices.

It has provided advertisers with a responsible medium to reach young men at the formative period of their lives.

2 Park Avenue   **BOYS' LIFE**   New York, N.Y.

GUARANTEED **300,000** CIRCULATION

In the Better Homes of the Bigger Towns

Carl Byoir and Associates, Inc.

Public Relations

Carl Byoir
PRESIDENT

Gerry Swinehart
GENERAL MANAGER

V. J. Lancaster
TREASURER

George Hammond   **John Montgomery**

Jane Floyd Buck   **O. B. Motter**

Ten East Fortieth Street

New York

The New Competition

THE culmination of the competitive striving of this first episode of the distribution age was the general adoption of the concept of an inter-industry struggle for a share of the consumer's dollar—the "new competition."

In an earlier day the consumer had been left pretty much to himself to make the selection of which of his wants and desires he would attempt to fulfill with the purchasing power remaining from his purchases of the basic necessities of life. Industry had paid little attention to the fact that in many instances the consumer would have to be sold on the desirability of, say, a new paint job for his home before he would decide what brand of paint he would buy. Nor had industry seen clearly that the average consumer entertained far more needs and desires than his total income would permit him to indulge.

Essentially the new competition involved a shift from product competition within an industry to want competition between industries. The shift, of course, was in emphasis and far from absolute, since rivalry between the members of the industry remained. But there was a definite trend to mutual effort on the part of industry members toward selling their proposition as a whole and submerging at least the more overt aspects of intra-industry bickering in advertising and selling.

The ultimate in expression of this concept was the co-operative advertising campaign. The war, a gigantic object lesson in co-operation, had given an enormous impetus to the association movement. The Government had insisted on the formation of at least a temporary or war service organization in each industry and where there was an established association it was in many instances made the official point of contact between the Government and the individual manufacturer or producer. Then the industrial institute emerged as the creation of an era when the problems of distribution dominate, the institute being definitely designed to unravel the complexities of competition and selling through research in distribution.

With the recognition of the new competition, many of these associations and institutes became the focal point for joint selling effort in persuading consumers to satisfy the want to which the industry's products catered. It is to be noted that while co-operative advertising is nearly as old as advertising itself, previous applications had been limited almost entirely to fields in which the individual units were not engaged in any serious degree of competitive conflict.

The co-operative advertising movement gained fast after 1919. By 1926 more than seventy different industries were employing it as a means of meeting the competition of industries, and many of these involved participation of industries in which large manufacturing units were represented. Perhaps the most conspicuous of the newcomers was the "Save the Surface and You Save All" campaign of the paint and varnish industry, which was one of the first to bring definitely competing manufacturers into a co-operative effort.

The new competition was dramatized in its most spectacular form in 1928, when a single company challenged an entire industry in its advertising campaign. This was the famous candy-cigarette war, precipitated by the American Tobacco Company's campaign for Lucky Strikes wherein they were featured as a means of keeping from getting fat with the slogan, "Reach for a Lucky Instead of a Sweet." The pursuant events served to demonstrate just how firmly the inter-industry conflict for a piece of the consumer dollar had become entrenched, many business men up to this time having taken the new competition more or less for granted and overlooked its possible effects on their own interests. The candy industry struck back hard, first with guerrilla warfare involving individual advertisements about "coffin nails" and boycotts by employees of candy makers and distributors, then by an organized program to point out the cheapness of sugar and its wholesomeness as an article of diet.

The range of potential consumer wants increased as never before, partly through the rise of entirely new industries and partly through the entry of established industries into the consumer marketing arena. Prominent among the entirely new ones was the wireless telephone receiver. Prior to 1921 this product was represented mainly by home-constructed receivers in the hands of a few thousand wireless enthusiasts. In 1922 it was the subject of an astonishing amount of merchandising attention, reflecting, of course, the swiftness with which radio captured the public imagination. Whole departments were devoted to radio parts and assembled sets in the large stores. News-

papers were devoting entire sections to radio, and a huge advertising volume was developing. In 1928, though prices of complete receivers were still comparatively high, radio was represented by 7,300,000 receiving sets, and that was virtually the net gain in seven years.

Another young business which quickly became a merchandising giant was the mechanical refrigerator. As late as 1925 this product was news to a large section of the public. Although it had been on the market for several years, no great effort had been made to merchandise it, for it was in rather an unfinished stage from a production standpoint and was looked upon more or less as a luxury that could be sold mainly to the rich. Development of a market was also held back by lack of approval of the product by the public utilities. With the product improved and the utilities won over not only as to favor but as to active participation, the industry—whose leaders at this time were Kelvinator, Frigidaire and Servel—began to move forward. General Electric entered the race in 1927 and quickly reached the front rank. Because the industry had the courage and enterprise to apply on a big pattern the merchandising principles which the growth of the automobile had proved to be good, definitely committing itself to a policy of increasing production and lower prices, sales went ahead at an amazing rate.

The opportunity for the tremendous sales volume which the cosmetics industry has come to represent coincided largely with the entry of women into business. With the aid of advertising, a condition was reached where women would buy rouge openly, without even claiming to the druggist that the purchase was being made for a friend. The use of rouge and lipstick became regarded as quite necessary for a woman to look really well, whereas before the war no self-respecting woman would have thought of such a thing. The domestic manufacturers of complete cosmetic lines—that is, perfumes, toilet waters, rouge, lipsticks and so forth—did not appear as national advertisers until about 1923. The imported lines had done some of it, as had the large domestic makers of such products as creams, soaps

1929

K ELLOGG-BRIAND treaty pledges sixty-two leading powers to renounce war as an instrument of national policy. . . . Commander R. E. Byrd flies to the South Pole from Little America. . . . October, and public speculative fever mounts as stock market zooms to new highs. . . . Stock values decline $15,000,-000,000 in last two months of the year.

Passenger car production for the year: 4,794,898. . . . Standard Brands, Inc., formed as a consolidation of the Fleischmann Company, Royal Baking Powder Company, Chase & Sanborn. Ralph Starr Butler becomes vice-president in charge of advertising of Postum Company, Inc. . . . Fred Bohen elected president of the Meredith Publishing Company to succeed the late E. T. Meredith. . . . George G. Booth retires as president of the Detroit *News* and William Edmund Scripps take his place. . . . N. W. Ayer & Son, a partnership since 1869, incorporated with Wilfred W. Fry as president. . . . C. R. Palmer named president of Cluett, Peabody & Company. . . . The Postum Company changes its name to the General Foods Corporation.

Truman A. DeWeese leaves Shredded Wheat to join the Frank Presbrey Company. . . . William B. Benton and Chester B. Bowles organize the agency of Benton & Bowles. . . . *Youth's Companion* merged with the *American Boy*. . . . S. E. Thomason launches the *Daily Illustrated Times* at Chicago. . . . The idea of sliced bread takes hold rapidly. . . . The Booth Publishing Company changes its name to Booth Newspapers, Inc. . . . Kenyon & Eckhardt succeed to the business of Ray D. Lillibridge, Inc. . . . The *Magazine of Business* changed to a weekly and renamed *Business Week*. . . . The Blackman Company admits to partnership Richard Compton, Ray Giles, Laurence C. Meads and Mark Wiseman. . . . Fashion authorities announce return of long dresses and numerous indignant women's organizations protest that they will never give up the freedom of the short skirt.

and toothpastes. But the domestic cosmetic houses relied principally upon store demonstrations, until increasing competition brought home the value of securing recognition and acceptance through consumer advertising.

The textile industry had been backward in marketing development for years, aside from a few scattered and mainly short-lived efforts. The hosiery branch of the industry was the shining exception. Silk hosiery had been advertised to some extent before the war; then, meeting the opportunity represented by the business woman's interest in appearance, the industry stepped up its merchandising pace and completed the process of converting the product from a luxury worn only by the wealthy to virtually a necessity.

The cotton industry was provided with a lead by the experience of Wamsutta Mills. Its ancient prestige slipping, the firm was reorganized in 1919. Up to that time it disposed of its product through a selling agent to a cutter-up, who took the entire output of sheeting at a contract price and made it up into sheets and pillow cases. On part of the product he placed the Wamsutta label, the remainder going out under private brands; he set the price to jobber and retailer; neither mill nor selling agent knew where the goods went. Under the new scheme the mill took over every detail of finishing the product, redesigned its label and cut out all private brands. Advertising featuring Wamsutta percale was initiated in 1921 and, in addition to sales increases, the result was the building of a stable, year-round volume.

The Cannon Manufacturing Company became an advertiser in 1924. The business had always been a very successful one, but advantage was seen in attaching a trade-mark to the individual towels and advertising them in order that they might be identified by the consumer. The new policy had the desired result of placing the firm in complete charge of its sales interests and before long Cannon towels were being purchased by name throughout the country.

Another textile entrant came from the Pacific Coast. Carl Jantzen had in 1914 devised a new knitting stitch for producing an extremely elastic woven woolen fabric, his idea being to produce a bathing suit that would allow perfect swimming freedom. Two years later he got into production and began promoting his product on the Coast. Then, in 1921, he commenced to expand nationally in the first nationwide program in behalf of such a garment—which he chose to call a swimming suit instead of a bathing suit.

For exactly forty years prior to 1924 a nameless product had been shunted around the marts of the textile trade and the story of its rebirth and christening is one of the modern romances of industry. It was first successfully manufactured in 1884. The nearest thing it had to a name was "artificial silk." It was looked upon strictly as a substitute for silk and the public expected it to serve all the purposes and have all the qualities of silk. In 1921 the total consumption was only 15,000,000 pounds. Then the various manufacturers and distributors decided that the product ought to stand on its own merits (it had been improved considerably over the years) and should

50 YEARS AGO

no Hoyt Company executive was in the

advertising business.

Which may account for the fact that our staff

is young enough to tackle

the hard jobs of today aggressively; building sales

and *more* sales for clients

at a time when sales are not easy to make.

In the past five years our volume has tripled.

So far in 1938 we are 20% ahead of last year.

Certainly this indicates ability

to produce advertising that sells our clients' goods.

Charles W. Hoyt Company, Inc.

PLANNED ADVERTISING · NEW YORK

Established 1909

have a separate identity. At a conference in the summer of 1924 the producing and consuming industries undertook the daring experiment of inventing a word and asking the world to accept it as the generic term for the product of an entire industry. As a distinctive and easy-to-remember designation was devised the word "rayon." The new name appeared in advertising that fall and the product was presented as a fabric which in its own right filled a distinct need. From then on its career was a monumental success. Sales reached 63,000,000 pounds in 1926 and that was just a start.

Another curious bit of early product history surrounds a product related in use to the textile industry, though not a part of it. This was a device for fastening clothing, designed to take the place of buttons, hooks and eyes and other fastening methods. It first appeared on the market around 1893, and it was used for closing the vent at the back of the old-fashioned skirt. From that time until America's entry in the World War this device found other uses, but none of striking importance until it was used in connection with the soldier's money belt. After the war the manufacturer sought other uses and among the first important ones developed was for the Locktite Company as a fastener for the Locktite tobacco pouch. This led to adoption of the fastener by the B. F. Goodrich Company and that firm applied it to the Goodrich arctic, which was advertised to the trade and to the consumer as the Zipper. So successful was this product that its name threatened to become a common one for all arctics, then appeared in public

usage as the name for the closing device itself, which of course was the Talon fastener. In 1926 the Hookless Fastener Company (now Talon, Inc.) set out upon an advertising and merchandising program to establish the product definitely in the public mind and give it an identity apart from whatever product it might be used on—since which time the Talon has made its way into use on literally hundreds of different products.

An entirely new type of advertising problem was tackled by the International Cellucotton Company when, in the early 1920's, it set out to market Kotex. This was a pioneer product in a class never before advertised, and it required daring and skill to place it before a critical public. The educational advertising of the firm was so phrased as to sweep aside false reticences and the marketing venture was so phenomenally successful that a series of generous price reductions was made possible on the strength of volume production. This was an event of considerable significance, for the company was one of the first to test out the degree to which the public had outgrown its former self-consciousness and prudery regarding intimate personal functions. Not many years before, when George B. Evans made up his mind to market a preparation for neutralizing the odor of perspiration, the step was considered a bold one. The first advertisements of Mum were obscure and could merely hint at the purpose of the product. Similarly, it had for years been considered offensive to come right out and mention motherhood in print until Lane Bryant began to talk frankly in the advertising columns. These

Child Life

is edited for a Double Market

FOR CHILDREN,

Child Life means hours and hours of fun every month— new tales of adventure and mystery, teasing puzzles, thrilling make-believe games, fascinating contests, pictures that coax to be colored.

FOR MOTHERS,

Child Life means interesting food departments, a forecast of juvenile fashions, news about books and equipment for her growing family, as well as the materials for developing her children's creative talents.

● This "dual personality" makes *Child Life* magazine a splendid buy for advertisers who would introduce their products into influential, higher-income homes. (*Child Life* families average 2.5 children each.)

A RAND McNALLY PUBLICATION

538 South Clark Street,
Chicago

and other venturesome firms were beginning to establish the fact that products of an intimate or unmentionable nature could be rendered advertisable by the application of good taste and careful judgment, and the result was an important public gain in education in matters of health and hygiene.

Several of the leading insurance companies adapted advertising to their marketing programs, promotional effort in this field having been limited, with very few exceptions, to local and sectional work through printed material. One of these, the Metropolitan Life Insurance Company, launched one of the most notable advertising programs in the history of all advertising. For some years this company had been doing health promotion work, co-operating with other organizations for prevention of tuberculosis and maintaining a nursing system. As an educational endeavor designed to benefit the public and life insurance as a whole, Metropolitan embarked on a completely unselfish campaign of advertising. The messages provided helpful information on health and healthful habits and on the fight against disease in interesting, readable form. The advertisements made no attempt to sell the company's services, nor did they involve any institutional sellings except for such inferences as the reader might care to draw about a company which was performing such a welfare service.

Two entirely new methods of transportation joined the advertiser ranks at this time. Motor buses, previously confined largely to metropolitan centers, commenced to offer inter-city and inter-state service and by 1926 long-distance highway travel in common carriers was a nation-wide reality. Air transportation, advertised intermittently since 1920 (when the New York to Boston fare was $150), was well on its way to becoming a major vehicle of passenger transport by 1928. The earlier short-distance operators were being replaced by well-organized national and regional systems which turned to advertising to sell the idea of flying to the public at large.

An interesting new bid for a more prominent position on the American table was made by the cheese industry, led by J. L. Kraft & Bros. Company, now the Kraft-Phenix Cheese Corporation. In the consumer mind cheese had long been considered a rather indigestible tidbit or dessert item. Few retailers were equipped to handle it properly and only the exclusive stores carried a representative stock; retail effort to promote its sale was non-existent. J. L. Kraft, an aggressive merchandiser who got his start delivering cheese from a horse and wagon, had the ambition to promote cheese as a major food and an economical alternate for meat. He also had a new product, pasteurized—or processed—cheese, which was less subject to spoilage than bulk cheese and insured a uniform flavor and hence could be promoted in an organized manner. The company launched a campaign of extensive advertising featuring the food value and uses of cheese. The campaign was backed up by a comprehensive program of merchandising which included convenient packaging, a constantly perfected system of store delivery to insure fresh stocks and education of the dealer in methods of handling and promotion. All of which set in motion a trend whereby the per capita consumption of cheese increased significantly.

The public utilities became important advertisers at this time. In 1921 the industry was spending not more than $5,000,000 in telling its service story to the public. Five years later the activity had increased fivefold. The motion picture companies, which had been content to believe that the industry got all the promotion it needed free of charge in the news columns of the papers, turned to advertising methods of increasing public favor for their products. The oil burner industry found an opening wedge to public popularity in the great anthracite strike and in 1923 began to capitalize its opportunity as several manufacturers became consumer advertisers.

The automobile vastly enhanced its position as a fundamental factor in American economic life. The industry was now definitely merchandising by price classes. A good share of the spotlight turned to the lowest price range, with Chevrolet, now opened by General Motors, competing in the field that Henry Ford previously had almost entirely to himself. In 1927 Ford forsook the Model T and introduced the Model A with the greatest advertising effort ever exerted over a corresponding period of time. A few years before, he had abandoned advertising as an "economic waste."

It was in this period that some real attention was given the used car, which had been periodically worried about in the industry ever since 1904. Partly in response to the profit problem of the dealer and partly in recognition of the fact that the used car was in a sense a sampling proposition that helped enlarge the wage-earner market, manufacturers sought to put the used car on a merchandising basis.

It was in this period, too, that Walter P. Chrysler started the Chrysler organization toward the top rank of the industry.

The tremendous rise in the cigarette's favor is to be seen in an approximately sevenfold increase from 1914 to 1928, with the lion's share of the gain since 1920. Contributing importantly to the rise was the introduction of the blended cigarette, Camels, Chesterfields and Lucky Strikes, appearing during the war years, with Old Gold coming along in 1926. The war itself brought many young men in military life to acquire the cigarette habit. Perhaps even more important was the great advance in the custom of women's smoking. Advertising was another of the chief factors in the growth, concentrated promotion on the leading blended brands ascending far into the millions of dollars annually; Lucky Strike alone was reputed to have spent nearly $20,000,000 in advertising and point-of-sale promotion in 1928. Little direct encouragement was extended to women smokers, however, until the closing years of the period. As early as 1919 Murad and Helmar advertisements showed women smoking, but the women, despite distinct Caucasian features, were discreetly garbed in Oriental costumes and thereby not identified with the home market. But even in the late 1920's the leading brands were feeling their way on the feminine angle with extreme caution and indirection, as in the "Blow Some My Way" remark addressed by a young lady in a Chesterfield advertisement to her smoking male escort.

IN this month of July, as we congratulate *Printers' Ink* on its Fiftieth Anniversary, this agency passes its own Tenth milestone.

Because of so much recent discussion over the pre-testing and fore-analysis of advertising, it is we think significant that in our own first advertisement in *Printers' Ink* in 1928, we characterized our service to clients as "The Tested-Copy Plan in Advertising."

The past decade has had its fat years and its lean. Markets have changed. New competitions have appeared.

But one gratifying result of the consistent application of our tested-copy plan is that today—although we, of course, have added many other accounts—we are still serving, without a single break in the continuity of the relationships, the principal clients who started with us ten years ago.

Schwab & Beatty, Inc.
Advertising
386 FOURTH AVENUE • NEW YORK CITY
Telephone: AShland 4-5496

CHAPTER IX

Education in Consumption
(1930 - 1938)

IN eight and one-half years business explored the pit of an economic depression uncommon in depth and expanse, recovered to a state of qualified prosperity and spiraled once more on the downward path. From the standpoint of the economic cycle, the nation thus experienced three separate periods of change. From the standpoint of the broad pattern of business evolution, however, the years from 1930 to date (and no doubt a little beyond) may well be taken as a single and significant transitional phase of the distribution age.

Forty years had seen major gains in improving the distribution mechanism to keep pace with and lend pace to the ever widening capacity of the production machine. In the 1920's, when distribution became the central problem of business, new heights of marketing efficiency were achieved. Despite the excesses of the last hysterical boom years, the cost of the process of getting goods into consumer hands had been materially reduced.

We had learned how to make consumers want the products of the machine.

We had learned how to bring these goods to the consumer at low cost.

But we hadn't learned how to make it possible for these ready, accessible prospects to buy. We hadn't grasped the fact that modern machinery had made it not only possible but imperative that the masses should live lives of comfort and leisure, that the future of business lay in its ability to manufacture customers as well as products.

Without exactly realizing what it was up to, that section of business which embraced the advertiser method of moving goods had accomplished a good deal in this direction. By consistently expanding markets, it had helped put men to work and lower the cost of thousands of commodities. Both results meant expanded purchasing power and increased consumption, producing a standard of living unequaled —in fact scarcely even approached— in the world.

Conceivably, had it been permitted to proceed undisturbed on a course of gradual evolution, the advertiser system might have continued to take in stride the problem of distribution of purchasing power. But, along with all business, it was disturbed, and violently so.

The world-wide economic dislocation directly and indirectly caused upheavals in business and human relationships that no process of orderly development could cope with.

In the first place, the war caused the setting up of producing levels to which the distribution machinery was unequal. The pace of manufacturing merchandise outran the ability of business to manufacture customers. This, in turn, created a buyer's market wherein more thought was placed on taking customers away from somebody else than upon developing new wants and new customers, and wherein reckless, unsound selling methods contributed to destruction of purchasing power.

In the second place, the dizzy levels of fictitious prosperity based upon the post-war inflation with the accompanying obsessions of a new era of permanent prosperity tended to enshrine immediate, large profits as the sole objective of business activity. Finance got into the driver's seat and removed the steadying hand of management from the reins. A disproportionate share of the savings provided by invention and modern distribution was diverted from the channels of consumption and pumped into Wall Street. The failure of producers to share more of their profits with the buyers of their products and the men who made them, as well as with their stockholders, was a direct cause of uneconomical overexpansion in many lines. At the same time, a large part of the excessive supply of available investment money and credit was put to uses non-productive of anything but financial maladjustments.

Even in the great consumer spending year of 1929, the trend in consumer buying power had become retrogressive. The worker's share in the value created by manufacturing had declined from 42 per cent in 1919 to 36 per cent in 1929, while the share of profits and overhead increased proportionately. Those consumers able to approach the composite living standards held forth by the advertiser were far too few even in that year of seeming abundance, for 73 per cent received less than $1,300 in income.

Finally, the catastrophic collapse of the whole flimsy post-war inflation structure, with its world-wide reverberations, removed all semblance of balance between production and consumption. The national income plunged from $78,-000,000,000 in 1929 to $45,000,-000,000 in 1933. Millions lost what buying power they ever had as unemployment spread like a pestilence; millions more suffered reduced income. The machinery of production gagged on its own product. Retail sales dropped off 47.7 per cent in four years. In the midst of plentiful supplies of most necessities and many luxuries of living, a large share of the total consumer population was reduced to the level of bare subsistence.

Many individual factors contributed to the morass in which the nation found itself. Overseas were unsettled world trade relationships, growing economic warfare as country after country sought to establish itself on a basis of economic self-sufficiency, waves of currency depreciation, huge defaults on American loans, all of which not merely cut down export trade but produced disruptions of the monetary structure to which no nation could be immune. At home were the difficulties of the farmer, the widespread effects of excessive speculation, major shifts in spheres of industrial activity and employment, credit troubles. The central fact was the slack in consumer buying power. Industry suffered from no ailment which an increase in volume could not substantially cure.

Day by day it became increasingly clear that some fundamental means must be found of distributing wealth in such a way as to insure an even, expanded flow of buying power through the hands of consumers, to make incomes go further and put an end to under consumption.

FOR 44 YEARS

BEGINNING IN 1894

MAXWELL DID IT!

—STILL DOING IT

Back yonder in the "gay 90's," in the year of the first submarine, one year after Edison's first Motion Picture Machine, seven years before Wireless Telegraphy and nine years before Wright Brothers' first Motor-driven Airplane

THE FIRST MAXWELL SIGN WITH THIS CHARACTERISTIC IMPRINT APPEARED:

The R.C. Maxwell Co.

TRENTON, NEW JERSEY
ATLANTIC CITY, N. J.   NEW YORK CITY

Since its pioneer days beginning 44 years ago, the Maxwell Company has, in cooperation with all sources of national business, created, constructed and serviced all types of Outdoor Advertising Displays,

from **PAINTED WALLS, BULLETIN SIGNS, POSTER ADVERTISING** *to*

The World's Largest and Most Elaborate
Spectacular Electric Signs

The only Outdoor Advertising Company operating continuously under the same name for 44 years.

This whole contemporary period appears as a time of schooling in a hitherto unappreciated phase of the distribution function. It was, and is, a time of learning of the existence and gravity of the problem of under consumption, a problem which had never before existed as a primary responsibility of the business man.

Business was not alone in contemplation of the riddle of distribution. Since this became the central problem of all society, attempts at solution have come from other directions as well.

1930

POPULATION now 122,775,046. . . . Chief Justice William Howard Taft resigns from the Supreme Court and Charles Evans Hughes is named his successor. . . . Bank of the United States at New York City closed and many banks in the Middle West suspend business. . . . London Naval Reduction Treaty signed.

The Progressive Farmer and *The Southern Ruralist* consolidate. . . . D. M. Nelson elected vice-president in charge of merchandising of Sears, Roebuck. . . . Fuller & Smith and the F. J. Ross Company merge as Fuller & Smith & Ross. . . . The American Medical Association establishes a Committee on Foods to pass on advertisements of food products and issue an official seal of acceptance for those approved. . . . Hulbert Taft elected president and editor-in-chief of the Cincinnati *Times-Star*. . . . Death of Dr. John T. Dorrance, president of the Campbell Soup Company. . . . Says Cremo: "Spit Is a Horrid Word But It's Worse on the End of Your Cigar."

The H. K. McCann Company and The Erickson Company combine as McCann-Erickson, Inc. . . . H. K. Boice appointed director of sales of the Columbia Broadcasting System. . . . The slat-like flapper is giving way to the romantic, langorous lady who features curves. . . . Irwin Maier appointed advertising manager of the Milwaukee *Journal*. . . . *Fortune* begins. . . . James G. Stahlman elected president of the Nashville *Banner*. . . . Mark O'Dea establishes own agency at New York. . . . The nation is exhibiting a weakness for small things—midget radios, the baby Austin and miniature golf.

Orders Out of Chaos

WITH competition rendered more intense and profits more elusive by the staggering downswing of consumer purchasing power, the advertiser pursued a relentless, feverish search for methods of bringing new vitality to the selling process. Orders were fewer and harder to get, yet marketing management was faced with the problems of getting them with lower, often drastically reduced, resources of manpower and promotion money.

The usual condition of cut-throat price competition which accompanies an economic depression soon came forth to lend a chaotic note to the sales problem. First there was a strong promotional effort by retailers to break down sales resistance and get volume. The market was combed for special clearance merchandise, sales were stressed to the exclusion of almost everything else. Then came the fictitious bargain values and exaggerated advertising. Finally even the better retail outlets were affected and began to demand that the manufacturer make goods to a price.

The market was flooded by merchandise made without regard to quality and was almost demoralized for firms that tried to play fair with the consumer. The latter, forced to make a shrinking income go further, succumbed to the price lure. Though there was an eventual awakening to the dupery of price, the quality appeal suffered seriously for three long years.

At the same time advertisers found themselves facing serious losses of volume which could not entirely be laid at the door of the depression. The private brand was growing in power. For several years it had been undergoing a significant change. The old private brand was a jobber's brand and because the jobber did not advertise, it was an unadvertised brand. It was purely a price proposition and rarely even approached the advertiser's brand in quality. The new private brand was something very different. The chains had done things with it and the jobbers had learned the chains' lesson. The private brand had been endowed with a continuing identity, its quality had been improved. Certain of these brands were benefiting by an amount of advertising nearing or surpassing that of the leading manufacturers' brands, for the corporate chains, the voluntary chains and some of the leading jobbers had adopted all the modern weapons of brand promotion.

The tendency of the advertised brand to resist the trend of commodity prices had presented private brand merchandisers with an opportunity which they were not slow to grasp. They pushed the price advantage of merchandise under their own labels and began to establish an important foothold in consumer acceptance. A wave of retail price slashing an advertised brands tended to narrow the price differential, but provided an incentive for further promotion of private brands. This time the chains were not alone in their ability to cut prices. The independents had achieved a position wherein they could retaliate and the warfare reached an intensity hitherto unknown. Since the profit margin on advertised brands was thereby seriously reduced, retail distributors looked more than ever to brands which they themselves controlled for profit protection.

As was to become definitely established in the following years, the private brand was no longer just a temporary expedient for the retailer to exploit during a period of declining commodity prices. It was a formidable new competitor for consumer preference. Indeed the private brand might be said to have become a vast new accession to the ranks of the advertised brands. Moreover, some of the large distributing organizations are marketing their own brands through independent retail outlets. The Walgreen Company started doing this in 1934, Macy's department store in New York has embarked on such a policy and Sears, Roebuck & Company is experimenting with the idea for refrigerators and other items in its heavy lines.

Toward making selling efforts more effective, sales executives began spending more time in the field. Many firms abandoned the general sales convention at the home office for sectional conventions, finding in the latter lower expense and ability to concentrate on the problems of the specific territory involved. The traveling sales convention, often embodying the arts of showmanship in highly developed form toward getting across enthusiasm for the sales program, came into wide use.

The arts of visual salesmanship were applied in a far greater degree than heretofore, the practice previously having flourished mainly in direct consumer selling of large unit products. Visual methods were found to be valuable in assuring presentation of the salesmen's message to distributor and dealer in logical fashion and in removing the possibility of omission of important sales points. To these ends were adopted such devices as the photographic sales kit, various types of easel presentations and slide film and motion picture presentations.

As the depression wore on, increased attention was accorded elimination of practices which had caused distributive unrest. In a number of fields unsettled conditions, particularly regarding price, had created dealer ill-feeling which was costing money to overcome. Abuses of perfectly legitimate merchandising devices, such as the advertising allowance and the quantity discount earned the animosity of many dealers and reduced their willingness to push the product concerned. Also contributing to this state was the free deal which had been introduced by many firms to stimulate sales turnover without permanently reducing prices. Some firms began to revise their sales policies to cut down on the free deal, to place the advertising allowance on a wholly legitimate basis and to put the small dealer on a basis of discount equality. Some, particularly in the drug field, turned to consignment selling under the *del credere* factor plan in an endeavor to control the sore point of price-cutting.

Although the general tendency in the retail field was toward stabilization, there were three clearly marked trends which had some bearing on manufacturer relations with retailers. One was the improved status of the independent, the second the deceleration of chain-store growth, the third the rise of the super-market.

In the 1920 depression the chains had all the best of it, enjoying a phenomenal gain while the inde-

  **Business**

has given us **Business**

Total billings so far during 1938 on our five magazines are substantially ahead of the same period of 1937. Four of our five magazines have shown plus billings, more than offsetting the small loss shown by one magazine. We appreciate this recognition given to the southern market by sales and advertising managers.

Business conditions in the South have held up better than in any other section of the country, and many advertisers have wisely adopted the policy of extending sales and advertising efforts in the South.

The time was never more ripe for well-directed sales efforts in the South. And you'll find the Ernest H. Abernethy publications well able to work hand in hand with your salesmen, peculiarly fitted—because of the acceptance accorded them—to lift a considerable burden off your salesmen's shoulders. Further information—either about the southern market or any of the Ernest H. Abernethy publications—is yours for the asking.

★**SOUTHERN ADVERTISING AND PUBLISHING**

Dominates the advertising and selling field in the South, reaching advertisers, agencies, southern district managers of national advertisers, etc. Founded 1925.

★**SOUTHERN JEWELER**

Reaches in an intimate way retailers and wholesalers in the South. Founded 1926.

★**SOUTHERN PRINTER**

Reaches printing plants and mechanical executives of newspapers throughout the South. Founded 1924.

★**MONUMENTAL WORLD**

A National publication covering memorial dealers all over the United States; also reaching southern producers and wholesalers. Founded 1929.

★**SOUTHERN STATIONER AND OFFICE OUTFITTER**

Reaches stationers, office equipment stores, stationery departments of leading department stores in the South. Founded 1930.

EACH OF THE ABOVE PUBLICATIONS IS OLDEST, LARGEST AND MOST INFLUENTIAL MAGAZINE IN ITS FIELD IN THE SOUTH

A Ernest H. Abernethy Publishing Company, inc.

Mortgage Guarantee Building

Atlanta, Georgia

pendents lost ground. In the next depression, the independents held even and when recovery was under way tended to increase their share of the total retail volume. From 1933 to 1935 the chains' share dropped from 25.4 per cent to 22.8. The independent's course in improvement of his merchandising methods had continued and he was in a far better competitive position.

Meantime the chain store's problems had multiplied faster than the solutions. The chain had staked all of its public contact on price. When some of the independents began agitating for State laws taxing chain-store units, there was no backlog of favorable public sentiment for the chains to marshal to their cause. Reduction of the price differential between independent and chain stores had deprived them of most of their hold. The public either remained apathetic or favored the independent as State after State passed laws imposing stiff taxes on multiple unit retailers. In a few instances a belated rush at courting public favor stemmed the tide, but the taxes became law in twenty-two States. In certain of them, the added cost of doing business was so great that many of the chains had to abandon their smaller stores at least.

The super-market was a depression child, but has shown every intention of being here to stay as a permanent form of retail operation. Large-scale grocery stores were not unknown before the depression. They had reached a considerable state of development on the Pacific Coast beginning around 1927. But it was the opening of the King Kullen stores on Long Island in New York in 1931, followed by the spectacular Big Bear store near Elizabeth, N. J., a year later, that brought this form of retailing into the national spotlight. .

The price and cash-and-carry features of the super-market tended to cause the chain stores to feel its competition more keenly than the independents. This, combined with the increased tax burdens based on number of stores, has brought a chain-store trend of abandonment of small neighborhood stores in favor of fewer large units of the super-market type.

The super-market, often selling at an average mark-up of 12 per cent, brought an increase in the advertiser's price-cutting woes. This was ameliorated some by its preference for advertised brands at a time when the chains were tending to place greater emphasis on their own brands, so that in some respects the super-market appears as a desirable outlet for the advertiser.

While the general adjustments in sales policies and methods and in trade relations served an efficiency purpose, the greatest demand upon management was for salvaging as much volume as possible out of the complexities of the new economic condition. For most advertisers, mass production had to be maintained if the doors were to be kept open, and under this pressure attention was turned to development of special sales expedients. These centered mainly about four major fields of activity—freshening up the product and adding to the line; finding new markets; adopting specific forms of sales inducements; and concentrating advertising on the objective of immediate sales.

During the final gasps of the so-called "New Era," it was forgotten in many quarters that markets are not indefinitely elastic for the same

Congratulations

TO A FIFTY-YEAR-OLD
FROM A TEN-YEAR-OLD

GEARE-MARSTON

INCORPORATED

ADVERTISING

PHILADELPHIA

NEW YORK

kind of stuff. Development work slowed down and a large share of industrial research endeavor was concentrated on reducing costs, substituting materials and cutting down labor, with relatively little time spent on developing new things. Depression conditions encourage invention and this depression was no exception. To tap new sources of needed volume and profit, many firms sought to capitalize latent good-will by adding to their lines. Between 1931 and 1933 alone some 1,800 new products came on the market, some, of course, being introduced by new firms but the majority representing new entrants of established concerns. A systematic product development plan was

---

1931

S UPREME COURT upholds validity of the Eighteenth Amendment. . . . Democrats gain control of the House of Representatives for first time in twelve years. . . . Hoover moratorium on inter-governmental debts goes into effect.

Henry Ford turns out car No. 20,000,000. . . . Col. Frank Knox and Theodore T. Ellis acquire the Chicago *Daily News*. . . . Gerard B. Lambert now president of Gillette Safety Razor Company. . . . Home-rolled cigarettes coming into high favor. . . . Detroit *Free Press* celebrates its 100th birthday. . . . Death of Col. Robert Ewing, publisher of the New Orleans *States*, and of Ralph H. Booth, founder of the Booth Newspapers and U. S. Minister of Denmark. . . . Don Bridge appointed advertising director of the New York *Times*. . . . *Liberty Magazine* purchased by the Macfadden Publications. . . . Earnest Elmo Calkins retires from active agency work and Rene Clark succeeds him as president of Calkins & Holden. . . . Latest development in book publishing is to scent the volume with an aroma that creates the atmosphere of its central theme.

Robert McLean elected president of the Philadelphia *Evening Bulletin* to fill the vacancy caused by the death of William McLean. . . . R. E. Berlin named general manager of the International Magazine Company. . . . The New York *World* acquired by the Scripps-Howard Newspapers and merged with the *Telegram*. . . . Kerwin H. Fulton becomes president of the newly organized Outdoor Advertising, Inc., Burnett W. Robbins succeeding him as president of General Outdoor Advertising Company. . . . Mickey Mouse making his debut as a salesman. . . . Following the death of Col. Edward A. Simmons, Samuel O. Dunn is elected chairman and Henry Lee president of the Simmons-Boardman Publishing Company. . . . Life inmate of a State penitentiary wins first award in radio contest. The prize: a trip to Europe.

200 B. C. Frank W. Woolworth never met On Lo Kass, Chinese merchant, but both had similar ideas. Our first record of the origin of the chain store goes back to that venerable civilization of China and adds another testimonial to Oriental astuteness. Whatever Honorable Kass's visions may have been in establishing a distributive system throughout the Celestial Empire, he could hardly have anticipated a selling force so vital as that which expanded under the impetus of F. W. Woolworth's development of a chain of 5 & 10¢ stores, centuries later.

1879 It was not until Woolworth, a dry goods clerk, conceived the idea of a store with a single low-priced line that the variety stores saw the light of day. After toying with the idea in his employer's shop, he finally succeeded in his own store in Lancaster, Pa. Although his first customer did not walk in until the afternoon of the opening day, the proprietor of the "F. W. Woolworth 5 & 10¢ Store" had sold $128 worth of merchandise and ordered a duplicate of his original stock of $425 by evening. The first year he cleared $1,500, and Woolworth then began the expansion that was to put his name among the most famous of Twentieth Century merchants.

1881 It is a well known adage that imitation is a subtle form of flattery and acknowledgment of a "good thing." Woolworth's store became an inspiration to J. G. McCrory, who, aware of the reception of the first chain of "5 & 10's," started on a similar venture with an estimated capital of $550. While his subsequent expansion was not comparable to his predecessor's, his astute merchandising sense gave added impetus to the then lagging system of distribution. The more variety stores that appeared on the selling front, the more the consumer benefited.

1896 First S. H. Kress store established in Memphis.

1897 The first S. S. Kresge store was started in Detroit.

1899 By now, the low-priced idea had taken a strong foothold. In this year Woolworth and his partners had 61 stores east of Pittsburgh—a strong network of retail outlets for those days—yet merely the nucleus of what was to follow.

1906-13 During this period was seen the beginning of such major syndicates as the W. T. Grant Company, G. C. Murphy Company, J. J. Newberry Company, Neisner Bros. and the McLellan Stores Company. In 1911 various small chains were consolidated with the Woolworth interests under the name of F. W. Woolworth Co. of N. Y. It operated 594 stores including a controlling interest in a chain of the same name in England. Buying and supervision was combined under one organization.

1931 The growth of the "5 & 10" syndicates since the turn of the century had been as spectacular as their volume of business. Early in their history when the units of the largest companies were counted in the hundreds, store management was mainly controlled from a central office. With the expansion of units into the thousands and the spread over wide geographical areas, it became necessary in the late '20s to relinquish store management almost entirely to the individual store managers. The SYNDICATE

STORE MERCHANDISER was founded in this year in response to a need for a publication devoted exclusively to the problems of the store managers and their employees. Many of the features pioneered by this publication have been made a part of the standard routine of several of the largest variety store syndicates. Since 1931, it has been credited with conceiving and developing the following exclusive features: Pioneered with first series of FASHION FORECASTS by Alice Hughes, nationally known stylist. Published first of series of sales girl training articles—THINGS TO KNOW ABOUT YOUR MERCHANDISE. Inaugurated TIPS ON NEW ITEMS department. Published first running record of manager transfers and new store openings.

1932 Originated a test for selecting competent sales girls. FREE DISPLAY SERVICE DEPARTMENT developed the panel trim now used in practically all variety store window displays. Instituted a free LIBRARY LOAN SERVICE. Issued series of EMPLOYEE TALKS which were reprinted and widely used by most syndicates. Developed first FOOD AND FOUNTAIN MERCHANDISING DEPARTMENT.

1933 Introduced first day-to-day MERCHANDISING CALENDAR for variety store managers. Developed the first variety store DISPLAY BOOK. Instituted first "5 & 10" PACKAGING CONTEST AND EXHIBITION for the betterment of syndicate store packaging. Created seasonal, adjusted SALES INDEX and expanded financial department.

1934 Focused attention on the need for PUBLIC RELATIONS WORK. Sponsored a VARIETY STORE WINDOW DISPLAY CONTEST. Pioneered the OFFICIAL NEWS RELEASE of the Limited Price Variety Stores Association. Introduced the popular TRICKS OF THE TRADE feature.

1935 Introduced the TRENDS department, giving up-to-the-minute developments affecting the market. Developed individually compiled DISPLAY-IDEA FOLDERS. N. S. MacIntosh, experienced syndicate store food and fountain supervisor, appointed Food and Fountain Editor.

1936 Culminated five years' work with announcement of THE MERCHANDISER'S SALES GIRL TRAINING

MANUAL. Advocated Federal action to counteract STOLEN GOODS RACKET.

1937 READER PROBLEM FORUM introduced. HIDDEN CAUSES OF SHRINKAGE series started. Gladys Gilmore, sales training authority, started new series of SALES TRAINING ARTICLES. Forecasted trend to grading and standardized labeling. Previewed Christmas selling ideas. Created SPEECH MATERIAL

for presentation to local civic groups. Added NEW STORE EQUIPMENT section. Presented PRIMER ON TEXTILES.

1938 New pictorial presentation of MERCHANDISE ANALYSIS series. Inaugurated human interest series, ODD FACTS about the 5 & 10's. More comprehensive Fashion & Merchandise Forecast. National and Sectional PAYROLL FIGURES added to guide store managers in anticipating business conditions.

A BILLION DOLLAR MARKET
(1937 Sales of the 12 largest syndicates only — $869,165,458)

... AND HOW TO SELL IT

Executive office buyers examine, "trial-store-test" and then "list" merchandise. After that merchandise buying becomes the problem and responsibility of the individual store managers and employees only, who select and order their merchandise needs *direct from the manufacturer*. Each store manager is held personally accountable for his store's sales and net profit showing.

Managers are busy men—spend 90% of their time on their feet watching store operations. Little time for reading—must take their reading in capsule form as presented by the SYNDICATE STORE MERCHANDISER, the only publication produced exclusively for them. Its editorial features and pocket size are geared to their business; the advertising pages present a complete merchandise story.

Evidence of Reader Preference

In 1937, surveys were made in the cities of Cleveland, Pittsburgh, St. Louis, and Detroit, their purpose being to ascertain the reader acceptance and preference (if any) of the SYNDICATE STORE MERCHANDISER. Readers voted as follows:—

Preference

Total Stores	SSM	Magazine B	No Choice
242	149	46	47

Preference for The Merchandiser	61.57%
" " Magazine B	19.34%
No Preference	19.00%
	100.00%

The above has been substantiated by a survey made during the week of June 20-25, 1938, by the Ross Federal Research Co. in 32

stores in the Buffalo, N. Y., area as follows:—

Preference for The Merchandiser	50%
" " Magazine B	25%
No Preference	25%
	100%

A DEPRESSION SUCCESS STORY

The need for THE MERCHANDISER was acute and the publication filled it to the entire satisfaction of its readership as well as to the gratification of its steadily increasing roster of advertisers.

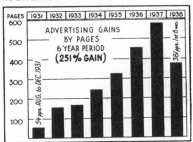

When a new publication increases its advertising linage 251% within a 6 year period and establishes itself as the definite preference of its readers, it demands the attention and consideration of careful buyers of advertising. You owe it to yourself to hear the complete story.

For further details write
SYNDICATE STORE MERCHANDISER
79 Madison Avenue, New York City

THE SYNDICATE STORE
MERCHANDISER

added to the marketing apparatus of numerous companies and there was a marked new tendency toward testing the proposed product in terms of consumer needs, dealer reception and general marketing possibilities before launching it.

For established products, times of difficult selling suggest the importance of differentiating the product in such a way that it emerges from the mass of its contemporaries with sufficient talking points to commend itself to the market. Hence, product improvement took a place near the top of the advertiser's agenda. This was expressed partly in improved performance and new features, but was even more marked in the matter of design. Good design had presented impressive evidence of paying sales dividends in the several years preceding. Now, with manufacturers in many fields forced to depend more upon the outcome of his battle with competitors for replacement volume than upon an increment of new buyers, appearance and eye appeal became an all-important consideration in many industries.

As a result, the industrial design movement spread from furniture and the de luxe lines of household equipment to almost every article from bathtubs to carpet tacks. At about this time the streamlining of airplanes, railroad trains and automobiles caught the public imagination. Soon the magic word became the keynote of all design.

The trend to better packaging reached its greatest intensity in the depression years. Since the cost of a change is seldom great—indeed actual production economies were not infrequently realized—and since a new package provides a staunch peg for newsy selling talk to trade and consumer, packaging became a favorite child of bad times. Considerable emphasis was placed on convenience, both through change in shape and the addition of various gadgets and dispenser devices making the product easier to open and to use. Previous emphasis on the appearance factor had tended to cause convenience to be overlooked. In the packaging of certain types of food items, the element of appearance took the new tack of suppressing the label so that the container might not look out of place on the well-dressed table. Cross advertising, that is the use of some part of the package to advertise other products in the line, gained new adherents, while considerable attention was given to the package insert as a sales tool.

A particularly significant development was the adoption of modern packaging principles by retail and wholesale merchandisers of private brands. Sensing that their lines were being put to disadvantage in competing with the attractive new dress of manufacturers' brands, they took the indicated action. Long backward as to packaging, many of the private brands drew up to even footing with their rivals and some of the most striking jobs of re-packing were in the private brand field.

Pervading the whole packaging scene was a pronounced trend to the use of new materials and of new adaptations of old ones. Cellophane, largely through the creative promotion of the Du Pont Cellophane Company, worked a veritable revolution in the retailing of many entire classifications of merchandise through its quality of enabling partial or total display of the package contents. In its role as a protector of the freshness of package contents, it contributed to a major trend in advertising appeal. The tin can, with the development of special linings, entered new fields, notably that of beer. Glass found its way into new applications in the food industry and elsewhere. Plastics came to play a part in the packaging of de luxe products.

The 45,000,000 boys and girls between infancy and eighteen years of age caught the eye of many an advertiser who was searching for new ways of building volume. Because children were maturing earlier than they used to and took a wider interest in the world about them, many advertisers of products whose consumption was shared by children along with the rest of the family set out after the youngsters' favor.

The developments in the technique of selling to children centered around four principal approaches. Children being born joiners, the club with a badge and a secret password found immense response. The premium was used to make the most of the congenital youthful interest in something free. The contest, with its challenge to the child's imagination, was found to exert a powerful influence. To the collector's instinct present in nearly all children were directed such devices as cutouts, pictures of athletic heroes and stories incorporated in the package design or enclosed with the product. In addition to the juvenile magazines, campaigns aimed to win child support and patronage were carried into general media, including magazines, newspaper comic sections and radio, which witnessed the appearance of a large number of serial programs built for child audiences—from fairy tales and musical programs to blood-and-thunder dramas reminiscent of the dime novel days. Special literature for distribution through stores, schools and the mails, as well as special store display material, came into extensive use.

The same eye for large figures which had found fascination in the relatively uncultivated children's market turned a vastly increased amount of attention to company stockholders. In 1914 the total number of shareholders had reached 7,000,000 and that statistic was considered mighty impressive at the time it was announced. From 1925 on, however, the spread of public ownership of corporate securities began to take on spectacular proportions. After the stock market crash, a trend from large to small investors brought a further increase of 39 per cent in three years and the number of stockholders increased to approximately 25,000,000.

Literally hundreds of companies began to solicit their "partners" to become active as sales missionaries for company products. A few concerns could point to years of effort of this kind, but the activity was a relatively new one and most of the previous work had been confined to general good-will messages. Through dividend enclosures, booklets, mailing pieces and letters, stockholders were given complete product information and urged to further their own interests by exerting sales influence with others. In some instances, special campaigns running over a period of time were conducted. There also appeared a tendency to cultivate stockholder loyalty by furnishing more complete annual reports and to enlist aid in spreading an understanding of the company and its industry.

In the search for sales effectiveness, business scrutinized its past for devices which had proved successful in the pre-boom days. These were brought back, refurbished and given new refinements, and put to work.

The premium, for example, was one of the very earliest forms of promoting the sale. It had experienced several major revivals, the last around 1912, fallen into disuse during the war and remained in a state of relative obscurity through the 1920's. Now it was not only returned to action but applied in a way that had seldom been used before. The premium proposition had always been largely confined to some sort of continuous selling. To get the premium the customer had to buy the product numerous times, saving coupons or labels and presenting them for redemption. In this latest incarnation, it was given wide employment on a single purchase basis, the buyer getting the premium on the spot from the dealer or sending in to the manufacturer for it. When the premium was of such value that the manufacturer could not afford to give it with the purchase of one or two units, the purchase premium idea was resorted to, the buyer paying part of the cost of the premium in cash.

One of the most widely adopted sales hypodermics was the consumer contest, which mounted to a tremendous popularity in 1931-32, dropped off into relative subsidence and then came back strong in 1936. In its earlier manifestations the contest was principally employed as an end in itself, a project of conducting an investigation among consumers or getting copy ideas and slogans for use in advertising. During the depression years the contest became a means to an end—immediate sales. The competitive element might be designed to focus attention on a certain sales point by soliciting essays about the product, or it might be totally irrelevant to the product, the prizes being offered for anything from solutions of puzzles to the suggestion of a name for a brown-eyed baby girl. In either event the advertiser was interested not in the content of the entries but in the volume of sales stimulated by the competition. Hitherto rarely used, the evidence of purchase—box-top, label or retailer's sales slip—was set up as a condition of entering the contest in nearly every case, although the option of sending in a "reasonably accurate facsimile" of the label was often permitted until the post office department relaxed its rules on that point.

Like the premium, the contest found its most frequent application with frequently purchased products of low unit price, the idea being to get the consumer started using the product. However, not a few contests have appeared for products of relatively large total investment, from fountain pens to automobiles. Here a visit to the dealer's establishment is usually imposed as a condition of entry.

The huge Camel cigarette contest, built around the adoption of a cellophane-wrapped package, drew nearly a million entries and keyed the first major bulge in contest use. The following deluge was so great, as more and more manufacturers increased their efforts to leave no stone unturned in the quest for more sales and new customers, that it became necessary to seek improvements in contest technique. The major one was the inclusion of con-

R. L. JOHNSON, INCORPORATED

MANAGEMENT CONSULTANTS

PUBLIC RELATIONS

INDUSTRIAL RELATIONS

PUBLICATION MANAGEMENT

•

CHRYSLER BUILDING
NEW YORK CITY

MURRAY HILL 6-2724

sideration of the role of the dealer. Previously it had been assumed that since the contest caused consumers to buy, the dealer would automatically see benefits for himself and promote it accordingly. This assumption hadn't been particularly well grounded in the first place and with an increase in the number of contests competing for interest, it collapsed almost entirely. Many of the more recent contests have sought in some way to insure that final measure of impetus and co-operation that the dealer may supply by providing special awards for him.

Another sales veteran, the guar-

1932

CONSTITUTIONAL amendment ends "lame duck" Congresses. . . . Ivar Krueger, match king, ends life at Paris. . . . James J. Walker resigns under fire as mayor of New York City and goes to Europe. . . . 20,000 bonus marchers invade Washington. . . . Franklin D. Roosevelt elected president.

"Look At All Three!" is the Chrysler keynote as the Plymouth makes an aggressive bid in the low-priced car field. . . . Sewell L. Avery elected president of Montgomery Ward & Company. . . . Cyrus H. K. Curtis retires from presidency of the Curtis Publishing Company; George Horace Lorimer succeeds him. . . . William Esty establishes agency at New York. . . . St. Louis *Star* purchases the St. Louis *Times.* . . . Lord & Thomas and Logan reverts to the former name of Lord & Thomas. . . . Dr. George H. Gallup joins Young & Rubicam. . . . C. C. Younggreen and Joseph H. Finn join Reincke-Ellis Company, which becomes Reincke-Ellis-Younggreen & Finn. . . . Agency mergers: McMullen, Sterling & Chalfant with Gotham Advertising Company; Williams & Cunnyngham with Roche Advertising Company; Albert Frank & Company and Rudolph Guenther-Russell Law. . . . Jigsaw puzzle rage is going strong and "endless chain" letters are back again.

Metropolitan Sunday Newspapers formed to sell comic section and rotogravure advertising in a number of large newspapers with A. C. G. Hammesfahr as general manager. . . . J. W. McIver appointed executive vice-president of Forbes Lithograph Company. . . . Frank Irving Fletcher and Sherman K. Ellis form Fletcher & Ellis. . . . Several firms reported to have postponed sales programs through worry over "Technocracy," new economic cult which promises national bankruptcy and chaos in eighteen months. . . . Earle J. Freeman elected vice-president in charge of advertising of the Kellogg Company. . . . Advertisement in a Chicago newspaper: "Bullet Holes Re-Woven Perfectly in Damaged Clothes."

antee, was dressed in new uniforms and given new assignments. The old-time guarantee was a closing argument in the sale of durable merchandise in the higher price ranges, the seller offering to service or replace the product if it did not prove satisfactory. In this revival it was used to a wide extent on foods and other small-price units of immediate consumption, functioning almost purely as a trial offer wherein the advertiser gambled his product against consumer satisfaction. A new attachment that went through a wave of high popularity for several years was the "double-your-money-back" guarantee. First used with conspicuous success by the Hormel Company in introducing its line of canned soups, the offer promised the unsatisfied customer not only return of his original investment but an additional contribution of similar amount as reward for his trouble and disappointment. This form of bidding for business reached its high for the period when one firm, the Pepsodent Company, launched a "triple-your-money-back" offer.

The one-cent sale was brought over from the retail field, where it had been extremely successful as a periodic store-wide sales event some years before. The manufacturer offered through the retailer two units of his own product for the original price of one plus one-cent, thus in effect offering a price reduction yet keeping the regular price in the picture. This device also went through a period of several years' popularity, having demonstrated a strong sales appeal, then died away.

Combination or related selling was another old merchandising trick, employed for years to introduce a new member of the line by offering it in conjunction with an established product at a special price. This was revived in the form of co-operation between two manufacturers of related items—as shaving cream and razors—to merge the consumer acceptance of two established products in a special sale.

One of the most intensive spheres of activity was in the matter of making arrangements at the point of sale so that the consumer would come in direct sight of and contact with the merchandise—another early sales fundamental and one which had not been fully capitalized in selling through retailers. Few advertisers were content any longer to merely get the product into the dealer's store and on his shelves. Instead they sought energetically to insure for it a position on the counter or on the sales floor. There followed much development of mass displays, floor set-ups and counter displays and dispensers. Cartons in which packaged merchandise reached the retailer were built to do double duty as display devices. A number of firms making a wide line of related products went to retailers with the idea of setting up separate shops or departments displaying the products at a central point.

In some of the household equipment and appliance lines, this new sense of the desirability of product display took the additional form of special public showings of new models and of traveling exhibits in automobile trailers. Also allied to the general trend was advertiser participation in the civic expositions, such as the Century of Progress Exposition at Chicago and the San Diego, Dallas, Fort Worth and Cleveland fairs. Here products were

not only put on public inspection but were surrounded with elaborate manifestations of the new arts of industrial showmanship, which had grown with the radio and expanded into many forms of sales activity.

In the shaping of advertising policies, production of immediate sales was placed ahead of long-term objectives of consumer acceptance. The sales viewpoint ruled advertising as never before, and in many firms advertising came more directly under the supervision of the chief sales executive.

To the pressure for quick results was added a compelling demand for greater efficiency. All business expenses were being scanned critically and intensively on the basis that they had to justify themselves and advertising was no exception. Though much progress had been made in getting away from hit-or-miss methods, there was still some holdover water from the days of easier selling that had to be squeezed out—and that quickly.

As a result, advertising progressed more in effectiveness than in any preceding period. Except in one respect, which will be noted later.

A considerable share of advertising, including radio, was built around the sales incentive devices listed above, in particular the premium, the contest and the various forms of special price inducements. (Price, once rarely mentioned in national advertising copy, attained a considerable eminence.) However, these offers were featured mainly in periodic campaigns staged at intervals for extra sales stimulation.

A principal characteristic of the general run of advertising was the return to action of that old hard-times standby, reason-why copy. The frills and fancies of the appeals to smartness and exclusiveness, where they had been indulged in the better days, were abandoned in favor of straight forward, shirt-sleeve sales talk.

As in the sales end, there was a pronounced tendency to go back to the early days for ideas and inspiration. Advertising combed its memory book for the good, old-fashioned fundamentals, a tendency which reached its most explicit manifestation when the Quaker Oats Company brought some of the old Claude Hopkins copy back to the firing line. The old tested mail-order stratagems were dusted off and put to work in general advertising.

Even the old patent medicine entrepreneur was not undisturbed in the revival of bygone formulas. But where he bespoke the ague, nervous dyspepsia and summer complaint, his new-day followers set out to free the human race of the ravages of Sneaker Smell, Paralyzed Pores, Vacation Knees, Spoon Food Face, Office Hips, Underarm Offense, Ashtray Breath and scores of similar afflictions. Where he traded in herbs and aromatics and tonics, his modern counterpart proclaimed the remedial properties of tennis shoes, face powder, furnaces, cigarettes, typewriters and English walnuts.

The backward glance was not the only source of inspiration, of course, and one of the most striking of the new developments was the adaptation of the comic strip technique to advertising copy. You can find examples of advertisements modeled after comic strips, balloons and all, in the 1890's and the idea achieved a mild burst of popularity around 1925. Newspaper editors, and to a lesser degree, advertising men had always known that most people like

Out of the West . . .

THE clarion call of "Gold" in '49 opened new vistas of enterprise for a nation that had clung timidly to the land between the Mississippi frontier and the Atlantic. Out of the East rose serpentine trails of Conestogas trudging with high hopes amid hardship toward the land of the Golden West. Gold they did find, and it made itself manifest in more than the precious metal. The land abounded in opportunity comparable to that on the Eastern shores.

No longer was there one source of culture in the country. From that humble origin, out of the West have come leading industries . . . fisheries, shipping, motion pictures, agriculture and food packing, exponents of fashion, mining, publishing. And, out of the West has come West-Holliday Company, one of the nation's leading publishers' representatives for a quarter century.

Like all successful enterprises of Western origin, West-Holliday's efforts to sell the value of newspapers as an advertiser's most effective tool have been characterized with unrestrained industry, and utmost loyalty to the publishers it has served. Now more than ever with a network of offices in the leading centers of advertising activity, we are able to promote a closer co-operation and understanding of mutual problems among the advertiser, agency and publisher.

Out of the West has come this great force, lending volume to the voices of those who say "It pays to Advertise!"

New York   Chicago   Detroit   St. Louis
San Francisco   Los Angeles   Portland   Seattle   Vancouver, B. C.

to read the funnies, but there were no reliable data on the point. The findings of Dr. George Gallup, in his reader recognition studies of the popularity of various features of the newspaper, provided a startling piece of information. It appeared that all classes of people, from corporation president to factory worker, read the comics; that next to the picture page, the comic strips were more widely read than any other part of the newspaper, including the featured news story on page one.

With its exceptional attention value resulting from long-established reading habits, its emotional hold on the public and its adaptable physical form, the comic strip technique quickly achieved a place as a part of standard advertising equipment, including considerable use in business-paper copy. The modern comic strip trades more in emotional human interest than in humor and the advertiser adopted the same formula, presenting his product story in terms of the everyday problems of everyday people.

Some of the principal copy appeals that climbed into favor at this time were: the freshness appeal, featured in terms of the cellophane wrapper and the device of dating the product for sale before a certain date; the vitamin, which had enjoyed a flurry several years before and lost its news value, then came back into much more prominence than had earlier been the case; the stressing of the dealer's establishment and his part in making the purchase.

As competition waxed more virulent, some of the old advertising abuses joined the old methods in returning to the scene, and these, too, presented refinements and ex-

pansions. Competitive knocking copy became rampant. Where attacks of this kind had formerly been confined to the merits of rival products, some advertisers made the doubtful contribution to the wavering public estimate of advertising of openly attacking the veracity of assertions made in the advertisements of competitors. In the desperate effort to impart a striking sensational note to advertising, pseudo-science was carried to new heights of magnifying simple discoveries and obscure scientific evidence.

The general disposition to subject all existing methods to scrutiny gave a decided forward impetus to all forms of market research and in particular to research concerned with the testing of copy. Perhaps the most salutary aspect in this activity was the recognition of the fact that copy testing, despite earlier enthusiasms, was still in the experimental stage, that there is no final, pre-determined answer to effective advertising, and that testing is merely one advertising tool which by itself can never replace individual ability, experience and sound knowledge of marketing principles. At the same time, considerable progress was registered in developing the various techniques, of which pre-testing for sales, though the most costly, has remained as the one carrying the most conviction. The pioneering work of Dr. Daniel Starch in analyzing inquiries has led to the establishing of many facts about pulling power, while a great deal of information about the readership of advertisements has been developed through the reader recognition method popularized by Dr. Gallup.

The liveness of advertising research is attested by the rise of in-

420

In Testimony

to the debt of all American publications, especially newspapers, to the guidance and inspiration of Printers' Ink over the past half-century and specifically to the realization of "sworn circulations", the original and long-fought-for ideal of George P. Rowell of pleasant memory, its first publisher, we hereby subscribe.

—

BRONX HOME NEWS
Evening and Sunday
373 EAST 148th STREET
New York City

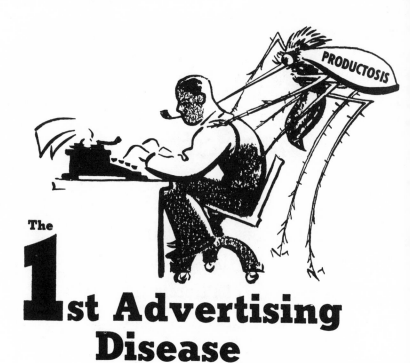

The 1st Advertising Disease

Advertising has publicized many diseases. But it has said nothing about its own disease — Productosis.

Productosis is a malady of those in close, daily contact with the "product." Advertisements, created by men suffering from Productosis, are top-heavy with "product superlatives." The prospect's self-interest is forgotten. Such advertisements cause Sales Anemia.

The preventive is detachment from the product. That is why only an outside staff, like an advertising agency, can avoid Productosis — can permanently retain the prospect's viewpoint — can create advertisements that stimulate sales.

Look at your advertisements! Are they free from Productosis? If not, let us show you how our modern "clinical methods" eradicate the First Advertising Disease from our clients' advertisements.

THE FENSHOLT COMPANY
360 N. Michigan Avenue, Chicago
Advertising ★ ★ ★

dependent research organizations operating in this field. Further progress in co-operative research projects was signalized by the formation of the Advertising Research Foundation, established in 1936 by the Association of National Advertisers and the American Association of Advertising Agencies.

The setting up of the appropriation was another phase of advertising upon which depression conditions exerted profound change. With 1930 there set in a distinct turn away from the old-fashioned method of determining the advertising appropriation on a fixed percentage of sales for the

1933

FOLLOWING numerous "bank holidays," President Roosevelt closes all banks March 6. . . . Gold redemption of currency suspended and all gold money remanded from circulation. . . . Century of Progress Exposition opens at Chicago. . . . Agriculture and industry come under Government control with passage of the Agricultural Adjustment Act and the National Industry Recovery Act. . . . Diplomatic relations with Russia resumed.

S. Bayard Colgate named president of the Colgate-Palmolive-Peet Company, E. H. Little vice-president in charge of advertising. . . . Cyrus H. K. Curtis dies. . . . *News-Week* launched. . . . John S. McCarrens appointed general manager of the Cleveland *Plain Dealer*. . . . C. P. Hanly elected president of the Ferry-Hanly Advertising Company, succeeding the late Wallace J. Ferry. . . . Legal selling and advertising of 3.2 beer begins. . . . Goodwin Corporation organized at Chicago to promote sales through ladies' church societies. . . . Glenn Griswold named publishing director of *Business Week*. . . . George M. Slocum acquires *Automotive Daily News*. . . . Inroads of new 10-cent cigarettes cause the "Big Four" to slash prices.

Death of John Irving Romer, president and editor of PRINTERS' INK. . . . Warren C. Agry appointed business manager of *Good Housekeeping* as successor to the late David LeGrand Hedges. . . . *Esquire*, a quarterly for men, appears. . . . NRA parades being held in many large cities. . . . J. M. Mathes forms his own agency at New York. . . . George S. Parker, forty years president of the Parker Pen Company, becomes chairman and Kenneth S. Parker succeeds him as president. . . . Harry Tipper named executive vice-president of the American Manufacturers Export Association. . . . Merger of the Geyer Company and the Paul Cornell Company. . . . Magicians protest that the Camel "It's Fun to Be Fooled" campaign blackens their art.

previous year. The new tendency was to look toward the future. The percentage of estimated sales and the budget based on the task to be accomplished, which had been earlier adopted by a few of the more progressive advertisers, were the methods which came into increased favor.

In the administration of the appropriation—which is to say in space buying—this period witnessed three basic changes. The first and fourth were more or less general. The other two were adopted in varying degrees by different advertisers, by some not at all, but they represent the tendency of the majority.

First. The selective attitude became paramount. Advertisers began to realize the need of a better allocation of advertising in accordance with the potential market. Advertising was specifically directed to types of markets, and in the presence of complete knowledge of sales potentials and market characteristics.

Second. Hand-to-mouth buying entered the field of advertising. In an effort to keep the appropriation as flexible as possible so that unexpected conditions might be met, many advertisers began to operate on shorter than annual commitments in planning campaigns and placing advertising. With recovery there was some tendency to lengthen the average interval, but there are many signs that planning of advertising will never return to its former universality.

Third. There appeared a marked swing away from continuity and repetition as a fundamental of advertising policy and a trend toward "spotty" schedules. Appropriations were diffused more thinly over a larger number of types of media

and a larger number of media within a given classification than was formerly the case.

An exception is to be noted on the score of progress during these years. One of the most cherished tenets of advertising has been that continuity and repetition of advertising effort is fundamental to a stable base of consumer acceptance. Though in other matters advertisers tended to dig back for the time-tested fundamentals and apply them in the light of enriched experience, many in the process loosened their grasp on the big, central ingredient of practically every advertising success since the beginning of modern advertising.

Fourth. In the flush times, much space buying had consisted of following the rule of habit in selecting media. The new tendency was to take far less for granted. Media formerly used were again examined with a critical eye to prove that they were still effective and worthy of retention on the schedule.

New developments in the media picture were plentiful. The proprietor of the advertising medium was no less energetic than the commodity manufacturer in his efforts to improve his "product."

Radio in these years came up from the comparative insignificance of its pioneering days to rank as a major advertising medium. The growth is shown graphically in the statistics of the PRINTERS' INK Index for radio advertising. From a position of thirty-two at the beginning of 1928 (100 being the five-year average of network volume for 1928-32), the curve rose to ninety in 1929, reached 160 in 1931, slacked off to a little under 100 in 1933, then climbed steadily upward to 265 at the end of 1937. Total

"PETRY'S FOLLY"

(Continued from page 329)

the radio brokers who would be barred from placing contracts with these stations after January 1, 1933.

Petry started out to build an organization with the men in the industry who were not only best qualified from experience, training and background but who saw with him the state of the industry and realized with him that something must be done to put spot broadcasting on a more sound and efficient footing. Henry Christal became associated with Petry and worked with him in perfecting his plans and setting up the new organization. Edward Voynow, a pioneer in spot and co-originator of electrical transcriptions, also became associated with the new company and was put in charge of the Chicago office. Later both Christal and Voynow became Petry's partners. Before the year was out the New York office had added two other outstanding men, H. E. Ringgold and Lawrence Field. Joe Spadea had been put in charge of the Detroit office, and Chicago had strengthened its selling organization with Robert Boniel and John Ashenhurst.

On August 15, 1933, twenty-four stations published a trade advertisement which said that they had selected the Petry Company as their sole representatives and that they had eliminated all "brokers, general representative and time selling transcription companies. Orders are acceptable only direct or through Edward Petry & Co."

In September of the same year another advertisement by the Petry stations said, "Our Time is not on the Block! We have no confidential or group rates which serve to act as an embarrassment to advertiser and advertising agencies. Our only affiliation is in having the same representative . . . plus a common interest in the betterment of spot broad-casting practices and the stabilization of radio station rates."

Letters of approval poured in to the Petry Company from advertisers and agencies. Also they "said it with orders" for Petry stations. The 4A's allowed the Petry Company to run the following line at the bottom of their trade advertising: "The principle upon which the Edward Petry & Co., Inc., operates meets with the approval of the American Association of Advertising Agencies."

The new Edward Petry Company rapidly became the most stabilizing force in the industry. Its influence was entirely on the side of a simplified but firm rate structure and the standardization of spot broadcasting methods. What was "Petry's Folly" only a few short years ago soon became the generally accepted method of spot broadcasting procedure.

Today Spot is a greater source of revenue to the radio stations of the country than all of the networks combined. Gross Spot volume is not available before 1934 but the figures have lunged from $13,000,000 in that year to $33,000,000 in 1937.

Other firms have followed the Petry Company's lead, and all those that have achieved success operate on the principles and practices advocated by Petry in 1932 and followed by his company since that date.

From time to time there have been attempts to revive some of the objectionable practices of the old brokerage system but these have usually been made by companies unfamiliar with the development of spot broadcasting over the years and have been poorly received by advertisers in general and advertising agencies in particular.

It would be no wild prediction to say that the exclusive radio representative, as we know him today, is here to stay. "Petry's Folly" has been proven sound.

Advertisement

radio advertising revenue from national advertising has passed well beyond the $100,000,000 mark. With radio manufacturers aggressively promoting the sale of receiving sets through and after the depression, the number of radio families reached 26,666,500.

A large share of the national advertising development centered around the network broadcast. The National Broadcasting Company and the Columbia Broadcasting expanded their networks to provide a comprehensive coast-to-coast coverage, with basic and optional hookups. The Mutual Broadcasting System, an outgrowth of interchange of programs among three large stations in 1934, expanded its co-operative set-up to a nation-wide basis. Numerous regional networks were established.

Spot broadcasting, in which the advertiser directed his effort through selected local stations by means of electrical transcriptions or by assuming sponsorship of programs developed by individual local stations, progressed somewhat less rapidly because the more complicated technique of operating this way was slower in being perfected. However, the elements of flexibility as to selection of market, station and time and the opportunity for localizing the message gave the method an intrinsic appeal and from about 1934 on its use has grown considerably.

Fundamental to the expansion of the medium was the fact that the advertiser and the agency suddenly began to learn a great deal about how to use radio. With the doubts dissipated as to the public's receptivity of direct selling "commercials," advertisers applied themselves to developing ways of assembling and holding an audience for the messages they presented. And they recognized at last that this element—the entertainment business—was not a matter of amateur dalliance but one requiring the enlistment and development of specialized producing skill.

The exploratory process of finding ways of cultivating public program favor tended to move in cycles. As one advertiser came up with a new idea or a new slant which proved successful, the pack took off in full pursuit. And so there were cycles of jazz, of gangsters, of amateur shows, of symphony broadcasts, of dramatic productions, of variety shows. All along, however, the base of broadcast technique was being materially widened.

For a time much of the attention was centered on the evening hours. Then daytime possibilities were investigated and here the "script show," a serial human interest drama, achieved a dominance which has continued for some time.

Another department of growing knowledge was that related to merchandising the program. Originally, if he made any effort at all to connect his broadcast to the sales campaign as a whole, the advertiser limited himself to a mere announcement and perhaps a window sticker for when the series started. As the value of tie-up was sensed, this field of effort was expanded to provide for a complete and continuing activity embodying broadsides, letters, meetings, displays, business-paper advertising, tickets for studio audiences.

Youngest of the major media, radio benefited almost from the start—that is, beginning with 1929—by a tendency to apply intensive

This Jordan advertisement of the Twenties
will go down the years as one of the high
spots of inspirational, romantic copy.

research to its workings. Entertainment values were placed on a direct basis of factual judgment through listener surveys and analysis. Through independent research organizations and such joint projects as the Co-operative Analysis of Broadcasting, the advertiser accumulated a considerable body of information on what the listener liked and why.

Although the new newspaper had become a rarity except in the small-town daily and country weekly fields, new developments in this medium have not been lacking in recent years. Progress has taken the form of new "packages" of newspaper service, developed primarily in conjunction with Sunday and Saturday editions.

Although magazine supplements had been published by many papers for some time back, the development of the *American Weekly*, distributed through Hearst Sunday newspapers, marked its advent as a national advertising medium. Though on the scene prior to 1929, the *American Weekly* has experienced greatest growth since that time. A newcomer in 1935 was *This Week*, published by the United Newspaper Magazine Corporation for distribution through a group of individually owned newspapers in a number of larger cities. *American Weekly* distribution was expanded in 1937 with the addition of newspapers outside the Hearst organization to its distributing mechanism.

These magazine supplements and similar forms of group selling—as in the several rotogravure section groups—represent a tendency to offer the advertiser the option of mass circulation in a single unit purchase. At the same time, the development embodies a specialty form of the newspaper medium in that in each case the development centers around a type of reproduction not generally available through the regular newspaper format, as four-color letter-press printing or rotogravure and color rotogravure.

The rise of the advertiser's interest in the comic strip copy technique resulted in another manifestation of group selling. In 1931 the Hearst organization began selling color advertising space in connection with *The Comic Weekly*, Sunday comic supplement of the Hearst papers. Metropolitan Sunday Newspapers was formed to offer comic section space in a coordinated list of individual papers, as was the National Color Comic Group and several regional groups.

The magazine, comic and rotogravure sections, played a part in a general newspaper trend toward offering facilities for reproducing advertisements in color. Prior to 1928, newspaper color was little more than a ripple of novelty. A half dozen or so papers had offered rotogravure color since 1922; the *American Weekly* had handled a few color advertisements. Run-of-paper color was just about nonexistent, although two-color work of this kind had been done since the 1890's and in a few rare instances retail advertisements had been printed by it. Technical advances in presses, inks and engraving methods have brought run-of-paper color to a point where some leading papers can offer four-color process work in their regular editions. Increased promotion of all forms of color and the interest of the advertiser in new ways of reaching the consumer carried newspaper color to a point where close to half of all dailies are offering at least one form.

A strange depression phenomenon in the magazine field was the rise of the large, de luxe, high-priced periodical. The two most conspicuously successful of the hard-times children were both of that character. *Fortune,* a new product of Henry Luce and the *Time* organization, was conceived as an elaborate monthly treatment of business affairs and was priced at $1 a copy. David A. Smart and William H. Weintraub followed the success of the de luxe, depression-born *Apparel Arts* as a business publication in the men's furnishings field with *Esquire,* selling at 50 cents. In addition to the high price per copy, *Esquire* featured an editorial appeal catering to men's interest, a field in which it had been "proved" by experience that no magazine could succeed. The de luxe trend was evident also among established periodicals, most of which materially stepped up the elaborateness of their editorial presentations.

While new magazines were few in the years of downturn, the first signs of recovery brought a flood of newcomers. A new direction was set by the appearance of the picture magazine. The "illustrated" magazine was quite the thing in

1934

GOLD weight of the dollar reduced to 59.06 per cent of the par fixed by the 1900 Act. . . . Drought and dust storms damage Middle Western farm areas. . . . Post office cancels air mail contracts and the army air corps carries the mail for over three months. . . . Bill providing for Philippine independence passed by Congress.

WLW opens 500,000 watt broadcast transmitter. . . . Harry M. Bitner appointed general manager of the Hearst Newspapers. . . . Chester J. LaRoche elected president of Young & Rubicam, Raymond E. Rubicam becoming chairman. . . . The Pacific Association of Advertising Agencies votes to dissolve, its members to join new Pacific Coast chapters of the Four A's. . . . Macfadden Publications buy *Photoplay.* . . . Beer in cans is appearing on the market. . . . MacManus, John & Adams formed as a merger of the interests of Theodore F. MacManus, W. A. P. John and James R. Adams. . . . Whispering campaigns alleging that certain advertisers contribute to the Nazi movement or employ lepers are being circulated in what appears to be an organized manner.

Large volume of advertising ties in with the modernization program of the Federal Housing Administration. . . . Vitamin D now included in chewing gum. . . . International Magazine Company purchases *Pictorial Review.* . . . The Burlington Zephyr becomes the first streamlined train to go into regular service. . . . The new trend in premiums: oil burner company gives away coal shovels, vacuum cleaner firm offers free brooms.

the 1890's, but the idea of carrying the formula on to primary editorial treatment through pictures had never materialized. The advent in 1936 of *Life,* another addition to the *Time* organization's line, and shortly after of *Look,* introduced by Gardner Cowles, Jr., and John Cowles of the Des Moines *Register & Tribune* organization, definitely brought the pictorial formula into what seems to be a permanent place in the magazine field.

Two principal improvements in the handling of outdoor advertising enabled that medium to reverse a declining trend in its share of the advertising dollar. The first was the establishment of a means of evaluating circulation. In 1931 the Association of National Advertisers and the Outdoor Advertising Association co-operated in sponsoring investigative research by Dr. Miller McClintock, director of research for the Erskine Bureau of Street Traffic Research at Harvard University. This culminated in the formation of the Traffic Audit Bureau, made up of representatives of the A.N.A., the O.A.A. and the American Association of Advertising Agencies, with Stuart Peabody of the Borden Company as first president. The Bureau set up principles and practices for the collection and evaluation of data and has since completed audits for a large number of markets.

The second new step was the organization of Outdoor Advertising, Inc., to act as special representative of a large number of plant owners in the solicitation of the use of the medium on a national basis. Capital stock in the new unit was assigned to the plant owners in proportion to their plant holdings. The set-up was adopted to enable the industry to place itself in proper relationship to other national media in the development of campaigns for national advertisers. Beginning in 1932, agencies recognized by the body were granted a 15 per cent commission arrangement.

Used to some extent by advertisers almost since its inception, the motion picture had never made much headway, owing to inadequate development of distributing facilities, slipshod planning of film subjects and failure to tie the film in with the general sales program. Then came a series of events which caused advertisers to look upon industrial film possibilities with fresh interest. The talking picture arrived. Two of the Hollywood producing companies initiated a movement to make sponsored short subjects and distribute them through their theater chains; protests from independent exhibitors checked this development but it got a number of advertisers started in the use of films. In 1932 a portable 16 mm. sound projector was developed, greatly increasing the flexibility of operation. And at about the same time the talking slide film was developed, providing an inexpensive device for sales and dealer training. Particularly important was the rise of producing firms specializing in industrial films and equipped to supply a creative merchandising service in planning and preparing the production.

These factors combined with the advertiser's depression disposition for trying new things to stimulate a swift growth of commercial films, the volume reaching an estimated $10,000,000 in 1937. As presently constituted the industrial film structure covers four major types: 1.

OLD AS THE HILLS......
Young as the things that grow there

The world has been told stories by pictures — ever since the world began. It re-happens with each new generation, and our Mellons spend millions for the same in later years.

G & M first made photo-engravings in 1889, and are still making them in 1938. There's been much progress in those 49 years, there are also basic principles that are old as the hills.

One of those principles is - - - no reproduction is ever finer than the plate from which it is printed, whether a simple line engraving or color process.

GATCHEL & MANNING, INC.
C. A. STINSON, PRESIDENT

Photo—Engravers

230 South Seventh Street
PHILADELPHIA, PA.

The management film, used to educate salesmen, employees, distributors and dealers in company policies and sales programs. 2. The training film, employed for specific education of the sales force distributors' salesmen and retail sales persons in selling ideas and methods. 3. The sales film used by the manufacturer's or dealer's salesman as a part of his personal solicitation. 4. The consumer film, employed as a mass advertising medium. The last-named type breaks down into two sub-classes according to the way in which its audience circulation is reached. The first is through arrangements for special advertiser showings in rented auditoriums and for showings through schools, clubs, churches and so forth. The second is through theatrical distribution. Here the film may be a one- or two-reel short, containing an institutional message but no direct selling talk, promoted through distributor channels in competition with the Hollywood product. Or it may be the currently popular "one-minute" movie, a sort of visual reproduction of the dramatized radio commercial consisting of a flash of entertainment and then a sales message. Several distributing firms handle this form and about 7,200 theaters of the total of 16,500 have contracted to show the films, usually run three on a bill with the news reels.

For several years prior to 1931 the "controlled circulation" publication, sent free of charge to a selected list of persons, had been emerging as a factor in the business-paper field. In 1931 the movement had reached a point where there was a demand for an organization to certify facts and figures about distribution of these papers. To do this job the Controlled Circulation Audit was organized by representatives of advertisers, agents and publishers.

In these complex and strenuous times the advertising agency naturally was called upon for a more comprehensive service. As advertising merged more closely than ever with the broad sales program, the agency tended to find itself sharing extensive responsibilities in connection with the planning of marketing activities as a whole. This was not a universal trend, some agencies operating on a basis of sticking closely to copy, space buying and research. But in general the agency assumed more and more of the characteristics of an all-around sales counsel, engaging in such matters as sales analysis, preparation of aids for salesmen, designing of point-of-sale material, sales training work and various sales-promotion activities.

The price of agency service also came up for examination, as it had at approximately ten-year intervals ever since the service agency first began to function. This time, however, the whole subject of advertising costs had become a pretty critical matter in the eyes of the advertiser and the renewed questioning of the commission system resulted in definite investigative action. A committee of three prominent men representing, respectively, the interests of advertiser, publisher and agency—R. R. Deupree, president of Procter & Gamble; Lee Maxwell, president of the Crowell Publishing Company; and the late A. W. Erickson, chairman of McCann-Erickson, Inc.—commissioned Prof. James W. Young to make a thorough study of the subject.

The Young report, based on a

comprehensive study of the agency since its earliest date, presented the major conclusions that the existing commission system was the best in sight for advertising as a whole and that the rate of compensation was in the main not excessive. The Association of National Advertisers viewed the report as a "real contribution" but not to be accepted as final, then made a study of its own which led to opposite conclusions. The American Association of Advertising Agencies disputed the findings of the A.N.A. report and the publishers' associations announced their favor of the commission system.

The controversy carried on from 1932 through 1935, then, with business getting better, quieted down. The net result was substantial maintenance of the *status quo*, which is that within the present framework the advertiser can get the kind of service he wants at the price he wants to pay—15 per cent commission, split commission (not supposed to be ethical but available just the same) or fee basis.

The repeal of prohibition brought two advertisers back upon the scene —beer and liquor. In substance, both were new businesses, for the merchandising world had undergone vast changes since alcoholic beverages had last been legally dispensed. Both have been hemmed in by innumerable legal restrictions as an additional handicap in getting under way.

Amazing growth has attended the advent of the electric dry shaver. In 1932 Col. Jacob Schick got into production on the Schick razor after years of experimentation and sold 10,381. By the end of 1937, with a number of others in the field, the number of dry shavers in use ex-

ceeded 2,000,000 and the makers of blade razors and shaving soaps had begun to sit up and take notice.

Frozen foods have become the focus of a new sphere of activity in the food merchandising basis. Much of the development of quick-freezing of foods had been pioneered by Clarence Birdseye for many years back and some firms had been packing and marketing frozen foods on a local basis since 1917. By 1929 the product was being sold in chain stores and other outlets in a number of cities, though little had been heard about it because none of the companies had been able to get far enough ahead of demand to indulge in aggressive promotion. In 1930 the General Foods Corporation, which had taken over the Birdseye organization, began using Springfield, Mass., as an experimental market to get complete information on the consumer and marketing possibilities of the product. Since that time, consumer marketing of packaged frozen foods has been developing at a faster pace.

An exciting interlude in the business picture was provided when the automobile trailer was suddenly discovered by the national spotlight in 1936. In that year the industry staged a miniature boom, jumping from a few scattered manufacturers to nearly 300 units, and the trailer industry was hailed far and wide as the foundation of a new society. After a while the shouting died down and a lot of hastily organized trailer companies went bankrupt and the industry found itself well able to cope with the normal trailer demand for commercial traveling and camping purposes, having demonstrated once more that the American public fancy is a wonderful and fickle thing.

The Consumer Talks Back

IN a seller's market the buyer takes what he gets and is glad to get it; in a buyer's market he tends to become particular about what he buys and critical of the methods used in selling to him. This had long been an axiom of industrial purchasing, but no similiar tendency on the part of the consumer had ever reached noticeable proportions, except on a few scattered occasions in rural areas.

In 1927 appeared a book called "Your Money's Worth," written by Stuart Chase and F. J. Schlink. It criticized sharply many of the products and most of the advertising and selling methods of American business and it achieved a considerable sale. A year later, as an outgrowth of the response to this book, the first "buying protection" organization was established by Schlink. This was an organization known as the Consumer Club which set out to publish bulletins of information and advice about various lines of merchandise.

The popularity of "Your Money's Worth" soon led to other volumes of a similar "expose" character, all of which focused most of their attacks upon advertised brands. One of them, under the dramatic title of "100,000,000 Guinea Pigs," achieved a sale and library circulation such as few non-fiction volumes had known. The Consumer Club, under the new name of Consumers Research, Inc., expanded its services to cover a wide range of products and attained a membership of nearly 50,000 subscribers. Later, in a disagreement over some labor troubles, one group broke off and formed the Consumers Union

and together the two organizations secured around 100,000 subscribers.

Because the charges made in the books were in many cases biased and inaccurate, most advertisers chose to dismiss the whole question of the consumer's attitude toward advertising and business generally. They tended to regard the consumer movement as a surface agitation by "crackpots" and "radicals."

Actually, the consumer movement was a deep-seated one springing from a number of fundamental causes, some the product of the buyer's market condition and some of independent origin. For one thing, advertising had educated people to want a higher living standard and, with buying power reduced by the economic depression, they were impelled to buy more wisely so that they might have more of the things they wanted. For another, that part of advertising which was inane, exaggerated and deceptive had created a tendency toward distrust of all advertising as a dependable source of consumer advertising. Furthermore, in some fields advertisers were failing to supply sufficient factual information about their goods, while the quality of some of industry's products, particularly under depression exigencies, was not always immune to just criticism. Finally, the sentiment as a whole was related to a growing distrust of business and the American economic system.

The self-appointed consumer protective organization was merely one phase of a broad movement. Quietly and without ballyhoo fireworks, consumer education had taken root

434

CRG

The bitterness of poor quality remains long after the sweetness of low price is forgotten.

C. R. GRAUMAN STUDIO
540 NORTH MICHIGAN
CHICAGO, ILLINOIS

in numerous soils. The schools had greatly expanded their instruction in buying. Domestic science, home-making and home economic courses had not only increased in number but had expanded in scope to include schooling in how to select foods and textiles. Health and hygiene courses had come to include instruction on buying of toothpastes, cosmetics and medicines.

Meanwhile, thousands of women's clubs had interested themselves in consumer problems and in buying standards. The literature of buying developed tremendously, both through privately published books and magazines and literature sent out by the Government.

Some of this sentiment found translation into direct action in the growth of the consumer co-opera-

1935

SAAR VALLEY returns to Germany. . . . Social Security Bill signed. . . . Supreme Court decision invalidates the National Industrial Recovery Act.

Death of Adolph S. Ochs, publisher of the New York *Times*, and appointment of Arthur Hays Sulzberger to succeed him. . . . Colby M. Chester elected chairman of the General Foods Corporation, Clarence Francis succeeding him as president. . . . W. H. Cowles, Jr., named general manager of the Spokane *Spokesman-Review* and *Chronicle*. . . . T. K. Quinn elected president of Maxon, Inc. . . . The Association of National Advertisers changes its organization plan to include a paid president and Paul B. West is named to the post. . . . Chesser M. Campbell appointed advertising manager of the Chicago *Tribune*. . . . Arthur H. Kudner establishes agency at New York. . . . Amateur hours are the big thing in radio programs. . . . N. Joseph Leigh elected president of the Einson-Freeman Company as Morris M. Einson transfers control of the business to a group of his associates.

John Cowles, Gardner Cowles, Jr. and Davis Merwin acquire the Minneapolis *Star*. . . . *This Week* begun as a weekly magazine section supplement. . . . Graham Patterson becomes president and editor of *Farm Journal*. . . . H. W. Newell joins the Geyer-Cornell Company, which becomes Geyer, Cornell & Newell. . . . Death of Lucius Long Nieman, president and editor of the Milwaukee *Journal* since its founding in 1882. . . . Harold A. Wise becomes advertising manager of *Liberty* and Carroll Rheinstrom succeeds him as advertising manager of *True Story*. . . . Santa Claus behaves outrageously in the advertising pages, smoking cigarettes, flirting with women and drinking young blended whiskey.

tive movement. By 1935 the number of co-operatives had reached 6,600, with a total membership increased by 40 per cent to 1,800,000. Total sales amounted to $365,000,000, or about 1 per cent of the country's total retail trade. The growth in volume from 1933 to 1935 was not in pace with the recovery in the general retail trade, suggesting that it might not be too significant. But then in 1937 'the rate of increase was 23.6 per cent, considerably above the rate for retailing as a whole.

Some advertisers who had been airily dismissing the existence of a real consumer movement had their eyes opened at the public hearings held in 1933 in connection with proposed revision of Federal pure food and drug legislation. Appearing in behalf of some of the unfair and dangerous elements in the early form of this legislation were not only the rabid professional protectors of the consumer but a number of perfectly respectable, honorable, upright leaders of women's organizations. Support for imposition of arbitrary grades on canned foods also came from a number of national and local women's clubs. A little later Anna Steese Richardson of the Crowell Publishing Company went on a nation-wide circuit of the leading women's clubs and came back with the report that women were not only critical of advertising but, more ominous, were inclined to laugh at much of it.

In the first organized attempt at that time to meet consumer sentiment with a constructive program, the canning industry, through the National Canners' Association, developed a new system of labeling for its products. Grade labeling, under which so immeasurable a quality as flavor would be subjected to arbitrary Government determination and identification by a set of symbols, was being actively pushed both by consumer groups and by a number of Government officials. The canners came forward with a descriptive labeling program, whereby the contents of the can would be characterized in plain, understandable and fair language. In the fall of 1937 the program became effective on a substantial portion of the industry's pack.

Individually, a few manufacturers, particularly in the textile field, began to place product information in their advertising and on their packages on a more specific base. Then, in 1937, the larger retailers commenced to take action. They sensed a real import to the consumer movement and a genuine demand for more information about merchandise. Programs of consumer education and more informative advertising and labeling were taken up in a number of stores.

Although the honest advertiser has suffered a good deal of abuse at its hands, the consumer movement may by and large be taken as a definite contribution to the problem of distribution. The merchandiser of a worthy product, straightforwardly advertised, has nothing to fear from an educated buyer. On the contrary, he is accorded a measure of protection from less scrupulous rivals. In the long view, the establishment of sound and unprejudiced machinery for consumer education appears as a valuable control upon the marketing process. It simply tends to apply in more rapid and effective form the economic law of the inevitable elimination of the unfit and undeserving seller.

There Ought to Be a Law

WITH the nation in a fear psychosis which verged on a panic in the spring of 1933, the business community was ready for Government to take a hand in solving the knotty problems of distribution. From that time forward, just about every major development in distribution has hinged in some degree upon legislature action, State and Federal. While Government showed no reluctance at extending its power broadly over business, at the same time it was a rare legislative proposal which lacked the vociferous support of at least one section of business.

One of the first moves of the Roosevelt administration was the passage of the National Industrial Recovery Act, designed as a frontal attack on both fundamental phases of the distribution problem. It proposed to increase buying power by creating employment and raising wages, to protect sound marketing practices by placing checks on the "chiseler." In return for raising wages and shortening hours, industries were given freedom from anti-trust law provisions to the extent of being permitted to unite under codes prohibiting selling below cost, loss leaders, deceptive advertising, trade bribery and other unethical and demoralizing practices of the unscrupulous minority.

The objectives were appealing and business supported the National Recovery Administration with almost unanimous enthusiasm. Admirable as it was in theory, however, putting the NRA into effective practice was not so easy. Getting the codes drawn up proved to be a prodigious task, and in the hurried process inequities and economic fallacies were not infrequent. Enforcement, despite the Governmental authority which lay behind the code once it had been adopted by an industry's majority, proved to be impossible. The law was too complex and too broad, the codes too hastily devised. Long before the Supreme Court declared it unconstitutional in 1935, the NRA had ceased to be of any great consequence.

A move to control food and drug advertising appeared in 1933 with the introduction into Congress of the Tugwell Bill, a proposed revision of the pure food and drug statute. In its original form this bill, unobjectionable in its motives, was a tyrannical expression of fanatical zeal. Under the guiding hand of the late Senator Royal S. Copeland the bill was modified into sensible channels and finally an instrument was evolved which on the whole was acceptable to decent business and which embodied desirable protection both for consumer and advertiser.

The Copeland Bill, as it became known, was in the Congressional hopper for nearly five years. Most of the delay had been caused by a disagreement between the Senate and the House of Representatives as to whether control over advertising should be vested in the Department of Agriculture or the Federal Trade Commission, the Senate favoring the former and the House the latter. The outcome was the passage in the spring of 1938 of the Wheeler-Lea Act, which gave the Trade Commission authority over

false and misleading advertising of any commodity, with a special section covering foods, drugs, devices and cosmetics.

Up to this time, the Commission had taken a considerable interest in advertising in its administration of the anti-trust laws, but in 1931 the Supreme Court ruled that it was empowered to proceed against untrue or misleading advertising only where that advertising constituted unfair competition in interstate commerce. Under the Wheeler-Lea legislation, the Commission assumes power over all unfair or deceptive acts or practices, as well as unfair competition.

1936

SUPREME COURT decision upsets the Agricultural Adjustment Act. . . . King George V of England dies and Edward VIII succeeds him. . . . German troops reoccupy the Rhineland. . . . Rebellion in Spain. . . . Franklin D. Roosevelt re-elected as President.

Wilfred W. Fry dies and Harry A. Batten succeeds him as president of N. W. Ayer & Son. . . . The Mutual Broadcasting System becomes a coast-to-coast network with the affiliation of the Don Lee Network of California. . . . Roy S. Durstine elected president of Batten, Barton, Durstine & Osborn, William H. Johns becomes chairman of the executive committee. . . . Emanuel Levi named publisher of the Chicago *Herald* and *Examiner*. . . . James H. McGraw retires as chairman of the McGraw-Hill Publishing Company and James H. McGraw, Jr., becomes his successor. . . . Time, Inc., buys *Life* and terminates the career of the fifty-three-year-old humorous magazine, applying its name to a new weekly featuring photographic content. . . . The undraped feminine form is being used to draw attention to advertising messages for a wide variety of products.

Roy W. Howard becomes chairman of the executive committee of Scripps-Howard Newspapers, as well as president and editor of the New York *World-Telegram;* William W. Hawkins succeeds him as chairman of the board. . . . Lenox R. Lohr named president of the National Broadcasting Company. . . . Mark Ethridge appointed general manager of the Louisville *Courier-Journal* and *Times*. . . . M. L. Annenberg buys the Philadelphia *Enquirer*. . . . Kenneth Groesbeck joins Ruthrauff & Ryan as vice-president. . . . Edgar Kobak becomes vice-president of Lord & Thomas. . . . *Literary Digest* poll registers 100 per cent error in predicting the presidential election, raising some questions about research samples.

Shortly after the Wheeler-Lea passage, the Copeland Bill was enacted as the Federal Food, Drug and Cosmetic Act. It expands the regulation of standards of foods and drugs and brings cosmetics under its jurisdiction, but the advertising provisions remain with the Trade Commission.

Another legislative project initiated in 1933, but of much speedier enactment was the Securities Act which set up the Securities and Exchange Commission to administer ~ulations covering the sale of :ks and bonds. The law and ¡ regulations established by the .ommission hemmed about the advertising of securities with numerous provisions so drastic that this form of advertising virtually disap-~eared. In 1935 the SEC modified ¡ regulations somewhat so that the ᴜse of advertisements became at least feasible.

From 1934 each session of Congress and the State legislatures saw ᴀn avalanche of proposals directly or indirectly affecting marketing and advertising, and these of course were only part of a general governmental expansion of regulation ᴏver business.

The passage of the Robinson-Patman Act in 1936 marked a major advance into the regulation of marketing practices. This statute, actively sponsored by independent retailers and wholesalers, was principally designed to prohibit unfair price discriminations by a seller between competing buyers, at the same time prohibiting a buyer from knowingly inducing or receiving such discrimination. It specifically bans unfair discrimination between buyers by false brokerage payment, disproportionate distribution service and disproportionate payment for such service. As an amendment to the Clayton Act, its general purpose is to insure free and fair competition in interstate trade, its immediate purpose to protect the small buyer from being put at a buying disadvantage simply because of his size. It provides for criminal penalties and for civil enforcement by permitting any party injured by its violation to file suit for triple damages.

The immediate effect was discontinuance of all advertising allowances and special discounts to retailers by most of the larger firms, although the Act was aimed only at inequitable arrangements. Since then a large percentage have gone back to advertising allowances in modified form, though they are much more cautious than formerly and check carefully to make sure the money granted to retailers for advertising and promotion is used for the actual services stipulated. Quantity discounts are again being given but are equally available to all.

Some firms have taken the law as an opportunity for permanently withdrawing from a cumbersome and increasingly dangerous situation and have refused to return to the old discount methods even in modified form.

Another legislative move of widespread effect was embodied in the State fair trade acts. In 1931 the California legislature enacted a law empowering the manufacturer to fix a resale price for his product by contract with any local dealer. The act was amended in 1933 to prevent a dealer from knowingly cutting under the price fixed by a contract made under it, even though he was not a party to a similar contract.

In 1936 in connection with suits against the California and Illinois fair trade acts, the Supreme Court held that such legislation was not a violation of the Federal Constitution. In 1911 the Court had ruled in the famous Miles case that the maker of a branded article had no interest in it and no right to stipulate its resale price after it was sold to the dealer. In the later decision, however, it took the position that while the dealer owns the commodity, he does not own the trade-mark or the good-will that the mark symbolizes; and that good-will is property in a very real sense, injury to which is a proper subject of legislation.

Meanwhile the number of States having such legislation grew rapidly until finally fair trade acts appeared on the statute books of all but five. In 1937 the national legislature passed the Miller-Tydings amendment to the Sherman Act, exempting from the provisions of that act any contract in trade that is legal in a State. This legalized the fair trade laws for purposes of interstate commerce and freed the manufacturer desiring to operate under them from establishing a branch in each fair trade State. Thus price maintenance, long forbidden except under complicated and rather risky arrangements, was placed on a completely legalized permissive basis.

The legislator's sharpening nose for revenue flushed up the marketing process as a subject for taxes. The first step was the sales tax, which has been adopted in a number of States. The burden here, of course, falls upon the retailer. Next came the idea of taxing advertising, first espoused by the late Huey Long in a measure held unconstitutional by the Supreme Court. That it was the particular law and not the proposition of the tax was demonstrated in 1938, when the high court upheld the New Mexico tax of 2 per cent on amounts received from the sale of advertising space. A serious threat, not yet a fact but the subject of bills in several legislatures, is compulsory State registration of trade-marks. A revenue-getting measure, it holds the possibility of tremendously increasing the costs and complexity of trade-mark operation.

The statutes enumerated are merely a few of the more important in the whole range of new regulatory measures affecting in some way methods and costs of distribution. Every law directed at regulating business has, of course, an indirect effect on advertiser activities, in addition to which the general uncertainty caused by the constant turmoil of proposed legislation tends to impede the flow of aggressive sales planning.

While the quota of unsound and uneconomic laws has not been inappreciable, this period of Government intervention in the distribution scene has included some action which makes for progress. In a time when a condition of under consumption exerts its temptations to the reckless seller to exceed the bounds of sane and ethical procedure, decent business gains by legislative measures which insure the maintenance of fair competition. Although it is still too early to judge how realistically they square wtih economic laws, certain of these measures have benefited the ethical majority in substantial ways.

Twenty-Five Men Had a Vision—
Their Followers Made the
Dream Come True

Tuesday, July 31, in the year 1900 was a bright, sunny day. At the old Hotel Victory in Put-In-Bay, Ohio, twenty-five men met for an outing. All were members of the Detroit Stewards' Club.

Two men had more serious things on their minds than enjoying the weather and the grand menu. The Detroit River whitefish and the Burgundy Sherbet which were excellent. Over the McLaren's cheese, the Bailey beaten biscuits and the Moet & Chandon champagne. Jacob Miller of Detroit said to S. S. Bradt, president of the Detroit Stewards' Club, "There should be a national association of stewards." The idea carried, and a meeting was called for the next year.

• • •

September 30, 1901. At Statler's Hotel during the Pan American Exposition at Buffalo, the dream of the year before became a reality.

The aims of the association were to fight against impure and adulterated foodstuffs; to work for correct weights and measures; to establish training schools for better service to the consumer; to interest American medicine in the development of better cookery for the sick.

From the very start the association started to turn these dreams into actualities. The International Steward, established a few years later in 1904, has fought over the years to make these dreams come true, and today all of them have been put into actual practice. During the course of making dreams come true it enlisted the aid of such men as President Theodore Roosevelt, who was an honorary president of the association, Senator Beveridge, Vice President Fairbanks and scores of other senators and congressmen.

• • •

Today The International Steward is the only publication devoted to the objectives of making the progressive stewards and caterers of greater service to the American public.

More than 70% of the outstanding hotels, restaurants, industrial restaurants, clubs, steamship lines and railroads have memberships in the association and subscribe to The International Steward. It offers to advertisers a class market with mass purchasing power.

The International STEWARD

304 W. 58th Street   **New York, N. Y.**

The Road Ahead

THE advertiser system of doing business is economic progressivism. Progress and progressiveness are of its essence. It breeds progress and it thrives only under conditions which permit progress.

For more than forty years this dynamic business force had played a major role in upbuilding standards of living and standards of buying. For more than forty years it had not only helped to lower the functional cost of getting goods into the hands of the consumer but had increased the ability of more consumers to buy more and better goods through making possible lower prices and wider industrial activity.

When increased production levels, worldwide economic dislocation and business greed for unreasonable profits had combined to bring a staggering catastrophe and to render acute the problem of distribution of purchasing power, a bewildered nation sought refuge in reaction.

In the first days of the growing disaster, enlightened business leaders made a courageous effort to stem the tide. They sensed the importance of maintaining the levels of consumer purchasing power and in the face of declining volume adopted a policy of refusing to cut wages. It was a heroic attempt, but the overwhelming forces of deflation and competitive inroads of opportunistic members of the business community doomed it to failure.

When the continuing inroads of deflation had reduced the nation to a state of despair, reaction set in with a vengeance. Salvation was sought not in producing ways for more people to own more goods, but in restricting production and freezing prices. Then the whole problem was turned over to Government, which, however liberal its leaders may be or profess to be, is fundamentally an economic reactionary. Government attempted to prime the flow of purchasing power with huge public funds, an essential measure in the emergency. But Government also espoused the reaction of less goods and higher prices.

Business meanwhile exhibited a distinct tendency to pursue the same course. Overwhelmed by the gravity of the economic disaster and necessity for survival expediences, business not only in many instances encouraged the restrictive phases of Governmental policy, but conducted its own operations on a similar concept. In many quarters the advertiser principle fell into disuse and abuse. Aggressive sales methods and advertising were used, true enough. But in far too great an extent they were used not to expand the broad, basic market, but to resist such expansion. Advertising was not infrequently employed as a means of forcing a higher price not justified by any superiority in the product itself, only by the fact that it was a "nationally advertised brand." And that policy has not only robbed the consumer of purchasing power, but has impeded the operation of the whole essential logic of the advertiser method—which, once more, is to pass on the benefits of mass production and mass distribution to the consumer.

THE TRUTH ABOUT JOHN JONES*...

by A. E. DUNCAN
Chairman of the Board
COMMERCIAL CREDIT COMPANY

JOHN JONES is one of millions of American wage-earners, salaried and professional workers whose annual income is more than $1,000. He occasionally purchases articles on the instalment plan

His critics would have you believe that he fosters heedless buying of luxuries, promotes extravagance, piles up debt and contributes to or prolongs a business depression. They believe that his instalment purchases are a huge proportion of all retail purchases, which is not at all true

I believe it is my duty as head of a national organization, with 4,200 employes, specializing in financing instalment sales, to tell you the truth about John Jones— *sound instalment buyer*—and to offset much misinformation which has been and is being spread about him.

Depressions are not caused by people's purchases. Purchase and consumption create *more* business, *more* jobs, *more* wealth, *more* prosperity Depressions are caused when people *stop* normal purchasing. To blame any depression on the instalment purchasers means that instalment buying must *drop off* in much greater proportion than cash or short term credit buying.

The facts shown by the recent report of the United States Bureau of Foreign and Domestic Commerce are that the estimated total instalment sales during 1937 were only 12.2% of total estimated retail sales, compared with 11.8% for 1936, 10.9% for 1935, and 13% for 1929; also, that the average amount of credit outstanding on retail instalment accounts during 1937 was about $2,900,000,000.

Total retail sales during 1937 approximated $41,000,000,000, of which only 12.2%, or $5,000,000,000, were

*A symbolical name, not that of any person.

instalment sales . . . and 87.8%, or $36,000,000,000, were for cash or on open credit. A 40% *drop* in all retail sales, during a depression, based on 1937 figures, means a *drop* of 4.88%, or $2,000,000,000, on all instalment sales; but it would also mean a *drop* of 35.12%, or $14,400,000,000, in retail sales made for cash or on open credit.

It must be obvious, then, that the drop in volume of sales for cash or on open credit, and not the drop in instalment sales, causes and prolongs a business depression. A total retail instalment debt of $2,900,000,000, which is reduced during a depression need not cause concern.

Systematic saving is one of the basic principles of accumulating wealth. Sound instalment buying encourages the budgeting of family income and systematic saving for investment in durable family possessions. It produces mass buying power and makes mass production possible, which results in much lower prices on articles generally sold on the instalment plan. It has helped build great industries—the automobile, refrigerator and radio industries. It keeps factories busy and labor employed. It has raised America's living standard far above that of any other nation. It has made yesterday's luxuries today's necessities.

Upon the above facts, I believe that all reasonable persons will find that John Jones.. *sound instalment buyer*..is not a menace. He is a worthy and valuable contributor to the prosperity of American business and to the happiness of American life.

These years of education in consumption have served to establish clearly that a prime essential of the distributive problem is to so mold the course of business policy as to constantly and unfailingly provide a flow of purchasing power into the hands of the customer. And written on the blackboard in large emphatic words is the precept that management must on the one hand so merchandise its products as to bring their prices closer to the consumer's ability to pay for them, and on the other so engineer its operations to insure a greater income for that consumer by shaping its course to smaller—but far stabler—profits.

Elusive at best, the patterns of economic development are difficult of detection at so close a historical

1937

EPIDEMIC of sitdown strikes spreads over the nation. . . . Committee for Industrial Organization breaks with American Federation of Labor and sets up rival labor federation. . . . Dirigible *Hindenburg* burns at Lakehurst, N. J. . . . Roosevelt proposal to increase Supreme Court to fifteen members sidetracked by the Senate. . . . The "Recession" begins. . . . Japan starts China "incident."

Henry B. Humphrey of Boston completes fifty years as an advertising agent. . . . New York *American* merged with the *Journal*. . . . Walter W. Templin becomes president of J. Stirling Getchell, Inc. . . . *Look* is a new picture magazine, with Gardner Cowles, Jr. as president and editor and John Cowles as vice-president. . . . Malcolm Muir becomes president of *News-Week*. . . . Frank Braucher appointed vice-president of WOR. . . . The National Advertising Agency Network is the new name of the Allied Service Agencies. . . . Robert L. Johnson leaves Time, Inc., to form a management consultant firm. . . . Joseph Wilshire becomes chairman of Standard Brands; Thomas L. Smith succeeds him as president. . . . 2,000,000 people buy $12,000,000 worth of cigarettes to compete for $200,000 in prizes in the Old Gold contest.

Joseph P. Knapp becomes chairman of the board of the Crowell Publishing Company. . . . The name of the Blackman Advertising Company, Inc., is changed to Compton Advertising, Inc. . . . L. E. McGivena, Frederic S. Suhr and Tom Varley purchase the agency of Briggs & Varley. . . . The Baltimore *Sun* celebrates 100th anniversary. . . . Guy C. Smith with the Jam Handy Picture Service. . . . Hanff-Metzger, Inc. becomes Buchanan & Company. . . . *Pictorial Review* buys *Delineator*. . . . The Dionne quintuplets, three years old, earn $861,148.39, a large share of it for recommending advertised products.

perspective. However, the signs are multiplying that this time of schooling in consumption is nearing its end and that the lessons have been well learned.

Management, always fundamentally an out-and-out progressive in its tendencies, is regaining the helm so long in the hands of inevitably reactionary finance. Certain prominent business executives have lately raised their voices in terms which speak of leadership in getting to the roots of the problem of underconsumption. There is a lessening tendency either to rely on the Government for everything or to waste precious time in merely glooming about and cussing at Governmental policies and personalities. Organized business groups, as well as individual firms, are at last beginning to pay some attention to what the consumer, through the consumer movement, has to say.

Above all, the plain everyday logic of economic laws is on the side of progressivism and it may not forever be denied.

Once the advertiser system is put to work in terms of its fullest potentialities and of the new understanding of its responsibilities, the future course of business promises well. The latent springs of the nation's consuming power have been scarcely half tapped. The prospects for everything that business has to sell—and for the many new things with which science stands ready to provide it—number in the millions.

To this new assignment, the functional side of distribution is far better fitted than ever before. The hardships of depression selling produced, as has been seen, immense gains in increased efficiency of selling methods, and most of these gains were held through the recovery period. Certain of the legislative measures introduced by Government have freed the sound and honest merchandiser from many of the handicaps imposed by the stupid minority of unscrupulous business elements. The consumer movement has contributed incentive for closer adherence to basic values in production and distribution.

To the panorama of fifty years of progress in dealing with a new economic tool, then, is brought a prospect of more effective employment of the instruments of human betterment which the advertiser system has evolved.

Such is the story of the advertiser.

*(To be continued)**

* PRINTERS' INK, Aug. 4, 1938, *et seq.*

PRINTERS' INK

A Journal for Advertisers

Founded 1888 by George P. Rowell
John Irving Romer, Editor and President
1908—1933

PRINTERS' INK PUBLISHING CO., INC.
185 MADISON AVENUE, NEW YORK

ROY DICKINSON, President
DOUGLAS TAYLOR, Vice-President
R. W. LAWRENCE, Secretary
G. A. NICHOLS, Treasurer and Editor
C. B. LARRABEE, Managing Editor
R. W. PALMER, Associate Editor
ARTHUR H. LITTLE, Associate Editor
H. W. MARKS, Mgr. Readers' Service

Editorial Offices

Chicago, 6 North Michigan Avenue: Andrew
M. Howe, Associate Editor; P. H. Erbes, Jr.
Washington, 609 Carpenters' Building:
Chester M. Wright.
London, 2 Arundel Street, W. C. 2:
McDonough Russell.

Advertising Offices

Chicago
6 North Michigan Ave.; Gove Compton, Mgr.
St. Louis
915 Olive Street; A. D. McKinney, Manager
Atlanta
1722 Rhodes-Haverty Bldg.; H. F. Cogill, Mgr.
Pacific Coast
San Francisco, Los Angeles, Seattle, Portland
West-Holliday Co., Inc., Reps.

Subscription rates: $3 a year, $1.50 six months.
Canada $4 a year.   Foreign $5 a year.

Fifty Years

The story of an organization and its accomplishments is obviously of chief interest to itself.

The foregoing history of fifty years of merchandising has, therefore, mentioned PRINTERS' INK only incidentally.

This being our Fiftieth Anniversary, however—and bearing in mind the fact that we are here devoting some hundreds of pages to the business history of the last half century—we wonder if our readers will allow us to have these three editorial pages to blow our own horn a bit.

In the first place, where did Mr. Erbes get the material out of which he built this fascinating recital?

We quote a memorandum which he sent with his final batch of copy:

"I am impressed by the fact that all the immense body of information which the total manuscript contains has come exclusively from PRINTERS' INK. I have consulted no other source. Except for a couple of paragraphs of historical background in the first chapter, preliminary to the start of the marketing story proper, every fact and every thought has come from the pages of PRINTERS' INK.

"Indeed, a very large proportion of the actual paragraphs, sentences and phrases have been taken over intact and direct from past issues. All I did was condense the material here and there and arrange it in the patterns which the mass of notes suggested.

"I am not saying that wasn't a large job, but I do want to emphasize that this whole thing is PRINTERS' INK."

All of which would seem to indicate that the editorial standard of this journal for advertisers has been consistently high through all the years and that its reporting and interpreting of merchandising trends has been accurate.

Who founded PRINTERS' INK, who built it, what has it accomplished for merchandising, and what are its objectives?

George P. Rowell started PRINTERS' INK in July, 1888. Its first editor was Charles L. Benjamin. When Mr. Benjamin resigned to take up other work, Mr. Rowell asked him to find a successor. He thereupon brought in his young friend, John Irving Romer, advertising manager of the Royal Baking Powder Company, and introduced him to Mr. Rowell. Thus Mr. Romer became the second editor, leaving later to go into general advertising work.

In 1908 busy and prosperous Mr. Rowell decided that he wanted to let up a bit; and here Mr. Romer again entered the picture, to re-

448

main until his death on August 9, 1933. Mr. Rowell sold control to J. D. Hampton, H. A. Biggs and Mr. Romer.

In the autumn of 1909 following Mr. Rowell's death in 1908, Messrs. Hampton and Biggs offered to sell out to Mr. Romer—who, by this time, had a vision (since realized) of the great merchandising power PRINTERS' INK could become. He decided to buy the paper and devote his life to it. He interested his friend Richard W. Lawrence and between the two of them they managed to consummate the transaction—a hefty one for them in those days. They bought the property, and on October 27, 1909, PRINTERS' INK announced them as the new owners. It was to be a fifty-fifty proposition. A little later on, though, Mr. Lawrence found that his other business interests demanded more and more of his attention and he told his partner:

"This is your life work and so I am going along with you as a minority stockholder."

At Mr. Romer's death, part ownership in the company—with its two publications, PRINTERS' INK and PRINTERS' INK MONTHLY, the MONTHLY having been established in December, 1919—was acquired by some of the working members of the present staff. At this time the ownership is divided among these staff men, Mrs. Katherine Romer and Mr. Lawrence.

So much for the history of PRINTERS' INK. A vast amount of human interest could be injected, but Mr. Erbes has taken up most of the space!

What are some of the things this paper has done for merchandising?

It initiated the Truth in Advertising movement and fought it through to a successful conclusion. No person other than John Irving Romer was responsible.

On September 1, 1888, it started the fight for clean circulation methods and has kept it up ever since.

It was the first to see in the chain store an outlet which would wield a great influence on advertising. It printed the first merchandising analysis of chain stores ever made by a business publication and since 1914 has printed more than six hundred articles on the subject.

In 1930 PRINTERS' INK MONTHLY was the first to predict a decline in chain-store growth and influence —a prediction that has come true.

In 1929 PRINTERS' INK made the first merchandising analysis of the voluntary chain movement. It was the first business paper to tabulate chain-store earnings by months.

It introduced the milline system —also the consumer acceptance principle, differentiating the latter from consumer demand.

In 1920 it made the first analytical study of methods for determining the advertising appropriation. Since then in the two papers have appeared more than four hundred studies on the subject, including the MONTHLY's chart for allocation of the advertising appropriation.

Always leading in the fight for decent food and drug legislation— a part of its general campaign for truth in advertising—it was the first to see the iniquities and dangers of the Tugwell Bill in 1933. Its stinging attack on the Tugwell Bill rallied advertisers in defense of their rights—with the result that today the country has the Copeland Bill, a workable and fair measure.

It started the fight against taxation of advertising.

From a s u g g e s t i o n made by

Robert Tinsman in PRINTERS' INK in 1910 came the American Association of Advertising Agencies.

It exposed the State trade-mark registration racket. Its articles and editorials attacking this altogether unnecessary tax have been used by advertisers in many States as a basis for constructive fighting in legislatures.

It made the first study of the effect of instalment selling on merchandising.

In 1919 it saw the great confusion that existed among advertisers in regard to slogans, and established a slogan clearing house which today has more than 7,500 advertising phrases and is the only file of the kind in the world.

In 1915 it began to publish articles dealing with stockholder relations showing advertisers how goodwill among stockholders could be built through the intelligent use of advertising.

It created the first table of earnings of national advertisers. This table is now published semi-annually and gives a complete financial picture of national advertising in all branches.

Another pioneering statistical work of PRINTERS' INK was the creation in 1904 of the summary of magazine advertising linage. It followed this by inaugurating a farm-paper advertising summary.

In 1927 it printed the first tabular showing of expenditures of leading national magazine advertisers and in 1934 extended its statistical service by printing the first table of linage used in newspapers by leading national advertisers.

Further to strengthen its statistical service, in 1935 it established the PRINTERS' INK Advertising Index which is the first authoritative statistical picture of advertising activities.

It started the fight for high wages as a means of maintaining purchasing power. It was the first to show that the industrial relations proposition was in large part an advertising job—an idea that has just come into its own this year.

PRINTERS' INK's service to merchandising is not confined to the pages of the two publications. Its readers' service department—established in 1909 as an information bureau for subscribers—answers each year more than 15,000 inquiries.

What about the next fifty years?

Beginning in 1888, PRINTERS' INK's most notable service to merchandising has been that of making and keeping manufacturers advertising conscious. On this firm foundation it expects to continue building.

There is a stern task ahead. This is the greatest and richest country in the world and its economy, basically sound, is going to endure.

But advertising must watch itself! It can win against all opposition, however—regardless of all the isms that are now nibbling at it—if it can at all times know the truth and thus be able to fight intelligently as well as courageously.

PRINTERS' INK will continue, as in the past, to set forth the truth and to do continuous battle to the end that advertisers shall never lose sight of the fundamentals upon which their success must always be based.

See you again—or your heirs, administrators and assigns—in 1988!

Wouldn't it be a real e v e n t, though, if all of us—including Mr. Rowell, Mr. Romer and our present readers—could drop around for a few days that summer and see what was doing!

Fifty Years of Useful Service to Advertising

ON THE EVE OF THE FIFTIETH ANNIVERSARY

OF

PRINTERS' INK

We, the members of the American Association of Advertising Agencies, in convention assembled at White Sulphur Springs, publicly extend to that worthy publication our hearty congratulations on a long and useful career as the pioneer and a leading organ of opinion in the advertising world.

We desire to record our deep appreciation of the outstanding service it has rendered advertising in presenting so much of the best thinking and authoritative writing in our field.

It has been ever alert in denouncing wrong and in championing right, in improving technique, in encouraging more and better advertising in good times and bad, in promoting and securing sound legislation in protection of reader and consumer, and in raising the standards of our business.

We commend its courage in standing by its convictions without fear or favor and in subordinating immediate to the long-run good. Even those who have at times differed from its point of view recognize the honesty of its intent, the sincerity of its statements, the wholehearted interest of its editors in the welfare of our industry.

We offer Printers' Ink our best wishes for a prolonged continuation of its useful career and have embodied these sentiments in a printed statement as a permanent record of them.

American Association of Advertising Agencies

White Sulphur Springs, West Virginia April twenty-second, MCMXXXVIII

one day last week, at a dinner party,
some one posed the question: "What is the
most important thing in life ... in people,
in business, in things?" The quality of
"BALANCE" was voted most important.

A s Advertising has grown in stature, in skill and finish, it has attained a degree of BALANCE — and it requires that same quality in its media.

Independent of it, but parallel, the New York Herald Tribune, over a period of nearly 100 years, has developed BALANCE . . . it has attracted many of the greatest names in journalism to its columns . . . it has introduced many of the devices to speed up production, to improve reproduction (the Tribune first used the linotype machine, first printed a newspaper halftone, first modernized typographic style).

Today the New York newspaper which more than any other combines the elements of great tradition and great enterprise is the newspaper which has brought them closely into balance with the full range of interests of readers and advertisers.

By every metropolitan area measurement the Herald Tribune circulation is in balance with the full potentiality of the New York Market.   **Herald** NEW YORK **Tribune**

Resolved . . *that the president of the Lithographers National Association, Incorporated, be, and he hereby is, authorized and directed to send to Printers' Ink Publishing Company, Inc., an engrossed copy of the following resolution:*

To PRINTERS' INK:

By a unanimous vote of the members of the Lithographers National Association, Incorporated, in convention assembled at Hot Springs, Virginia, on the 11th day of May, 1938, I have been asked to send to you the following message:

Fifty years ago Lithographers first organized to foster lithographic progress and to promote the observance generally of sound trade practices. Fifty years ago PRINTERS' INK began its noteworthy career.

This happy coincidence of time tempts us to send to PRINTERS' INK a message of esteem, of congratulation and of commendation, to wish it an ever larger and more prosperous future—and this equally for its own sake, and for the sake of those whose interests it serves.

For half a century PRINTERS' INK has been fertilizing, cultivating and helping to harvest a field in which the Graphic Arts have flourished.

PRINTERS' INK has been one of the outstanding students of problems; one of the great impartial voices of differing opinions; one of the finest broadcasters of new facts and truths; one of the most enthusiastic advocates of what it believed to be the right; and one of the most courageous critics of what it believed to be the wrong.

PRINTERS' INK has welcomed to its columns an expression of the thoughts of all, to the end that its readers might form judgments unbiased by its own beliefs. Because of this policy, it has attracted to itself the contributions of the ablest thinkers; the most expert technicians; and the leaders in our field.

Through half a century, PRINTERS' INK has carried a torch to light the path of progress toward improved and better processes and methods; higher standards in the field of advertising, and the eradication of evils and unethical practices . . . both by law and by the co-operation of those who had at heart the ultimate good of all concerned.

PRINTERS' INK has established itself in the confidence of all and has earned for itself the respect and appreciation of all through sincerity of purpose and unswerving devotion to the advancement of the interests and the elevation of the standards of those who are interested in the field which it serves.

Name Index

A

A. P. W. Paper Co., 143
Adams, James R., 429
Adams, James Truslow, 8
Adams, Samuel Hopkins, 192
Advertisers' Gazette, 76
Advertising Affiliation, 258
Advertising Audit Association, 262
Advertising Club of Western New York, 142
Advertising Clubs of America, 197
Advertising Federation of America, 143
Advertising Novelty Manufacturers' Association, 156
Advertising Research Foundation, 423
Advertising Typographers of America, 318
Agate Club, 78
Agricultural Epitomist, 110
Agricultural Press League, 78
Agricultural Publishers Association, 264
Agry, Warren C., 423
Aikens, A. J., 38
Akron *Press*, 194
Allen, E. C., 37, 41
Allen's Lists, 44
Allied Service Agencies, 446
American Advertisers Association, 137, 140, 262
American Advertising Agents' Association, 143
American Agriculturist, 46, 110, 322
American Association of Advertising Agencies, 264, 290, 319, 346, 384, 423, 429, 430, 433
American Bicycle Company, 108
American Boy, 132, 389
American Cereal Co., 25, 124
American Chain Co., 282
American Druggist Syndicate, 271
American Golf Association of Advertising Interests, 143
American Home, 378, 382
American Illustrated Magazine, 193
American Magazine, 193, 252
American Medical Association, 400
American Mercury, 332
American Newspaper Annual, 236
American Newspaper Directory, 59
American Newspaper Publishers Association, 76, 78, 239, 384
American Newspaper Reporter, 76
American Press Association, 384
American Radiator Co., 242
American Railroad Journal, 48
American Railway Express Co., 310
American Red Cross, (facing p. 288)
American Sugar Refining Co., 241
American Society of National Advertisers, 137
American Telephone & Telegraph Co., 203, 372, 382
American Tobacco Co., 79, 89, 92, 160, 242, 270, 388
American Weekly, 428
American Wheelman, 104
Anglo-American Alliance, 116
Anheuser-Busch, Inc., 242
Annenberg, M. L., 440
Apparel Arts, 429
Armistead, William M., 295
Armour & Co., 65, 310, 332
Armstrong, F. Wallis Co., 244
Arrow collar, 155, (facing p. 160)
Associated Advertising Clubs of America, 146, 256, 257, 258, 265

Associated Advertising Clubs of the World, 258, 265, 343, 382
Associated Billposters and Distributors of the United States and Canada, 44, 78
Associated Billposters of America, 110
Associated Business Papers, Inc., 265
Association of General Newspaper Agents, 76
Association of National Advertisers, 240, 264, 346, 370, 377, 379, 423, 430, 433, 436
Association of National Advertising Managers, 264
Atkinson, Wilmer, 110
Atlanta, The Admen's Club of, 257
Atlanta, Ga., 27
Atlantic Coast Lists, 38
Atlantic Monthly, 41
Aubuchon, W. M., 197
Audit Bureau of Circulations, 262, 264, 322
Automotive Daily News, 423
Avery, Sewell L., 414
Ayer, F. Wayland, 73, 164, 289
Ayer, N. W. & Son, 51, 54, 59, 74, 76, 164, 236, 307, 332, 389
Ayer's Sarsaparilla, 10, 45
Aylesworth, Merlin H., 357

B

Babbitt, B. T., 46, 126
Baker, Elbert H., 270
Baker, Walter & Co., 10, 25
Balmer, Thomas, 47, 119, 168, 172, 194, 197
Baltimore Bargain House, 175
Baltimore *Sun*, 446
Banking Publicity Association, 142
Barnum, Jerome D., 289
Barrett Co., 243
Barron, Clarence Walker, 378
Barton, Bruce, 259, 302
Barton, Durstine & Osborn, 378
Barton & Durstine Co., 302
Bates, Charles Austin, 72, 97, 165, 175
Bates, J. H. Agency, 74
Bates, James H., 143
Batten, Barton, Durstine & Osborn, 378
Batten, George, 183, 302
Batten, George Co., 164, 183, 378
Batten, Harry A., 440
Beardsley, Aubrey, 122
Beck, Thomas H., 259
Beckwith, S. C., 27, 65, 193
Beech-Nut Packing Co., 348, 358
Beeman's, 13
Bell, Alexander Graham, 9, 322
Bennett, James Gordon, 32, 33
Benson, John, 367
Benton & Bowles, 389
Benton, William B., 389
Berkowitz, Mortimer, 378
Berlin, R. E., 406
Berry Brothers, (facing p. 193)
Better Business Bureau, 258, 370
Better Homes & Gardens, 322, 382
Big Bear stores, 404
Billingsley, Allen L., 378
Bingham, Robert Worth Judge, 302
Birdseye, Clarence, 433
Bitner, Harry M., 429
Black, Stephen H., 289
Blackett, Hill, 332
Blackett & Sample, 332
Blackett-Sample-Hummert, Inc., 367

O

Ochs, Adolph S., 32, 55, 97, 436
O'Dea, Mark, 400
Ohio News League, 194
O-Kid-O, 309
Oklahoma City *Oklahoma News*, 194
Oklahoma *Farmer*, 259
Oldfield, Bill, 228
Old Gold cigarettes, 326, 357, 395, 446
Oldsmobile, 248
Olmsted, C. F., 143
Omaha *Herald*, 17
Omaha *World*, 17
O'Mara, John E., 193
O'Mara & Ormsbee, 193
Omega Oil, 102
One Spoon Baking Powder, 89
Onyx Hosiery Co., 241
Ormsbee, M. H., 193
Outcault, Richard, 136
Outdoor Advertising, Inc., 406, 430
Outdoor Advertising Association, 264, 382, 430

P

Pabst Corp., 242
Pacific Association of Advertising Agencies, 429
Pacific Coast Advertising Men's Association, 142, 183
Pacific Electric Heating Co., 242
Pacific Mills, 241
Packard Motor Car Co., 227
Packer Advertising Corp., 357
Packer's Tar soap, 23
Page & Shaw, 318
Painted Display Advertising Association, 264
Painted Outdoor Advertising Association, 382
Palmer, C. R., 389
Palmer, Volney B., 51
Palmolive soap (facing p. 321)
Palmolive-Peet Co., 378
Paris Garter, 241
Parker, George S., 423
Parker, Kenneth S., 423
Parrish, Maxfield, 122
Parsons, Eugene W., 244
Patterson, Graham, 436
Patterson, J. M., 343, 346, 380
Patterson, John H., 102, 126
Peabody, Stuart, 430
Pearline, see Pyle's Pearline
Pears' Soap, 10, 11, 23, 24, 41, 74, 84, 111, 116
Pearson, A. C., 346
Pedlar, Louis, 346
Pedlar & Ryan, 346
Pennsylvania Railroad, 26
Penny Press, The, 194
Penobscott Bay, Ontario, 26
Pepsodent Co., 416
Perine, Frederick L., 116, 137
Periodical Publishers' Association, 142, 318
Perky, Henry D., 94, 146
Pettengill & Co., 97
Pettengill, S. M., 37
Pettijohn's, 25
Phelps Publishing Co., 137
Phenix Cheese Co., 378
Philadelphia *Bulletin,* 172
Philadelphia *Enquirer,* 440
Photoplay, 429
Pictorial Review, 429, 446
Pierce, Dante M., 278
Pierce's remedies, Dr., 10, 18
Piggly Wiggly Stores, 296, 338

Pinkham, 18
Pittsburgh Bank for Savings, 160
Pittsburgh *Post-Gazette,* 367
Pittsburgh *Press,* 332
Pittsburgh *Sun-Telegraph,* 367
Plaut, Edward, 322
Plymouth Rock Pants Co., 111
Pompeiian Massage Cream, 160
Pope, Albert A., Col., 108
Portland, Oreg., Ad-Men's League, 193
Post, C. W., 94, 140
Poster Advertising Association, 382
Poster Advertising Co., 346
Postum Cereal Co., 13, 94, 165, 227, 233
Postum Co., 378, 389
Powers & Armstrong Co., 244
Powers, John E., 47, 67, 72, 82, 131, 140, 175
Prairie Farmer, 47
Pratt, Edward M., 332
Pratt, Samuel, 295
Presbrey, Frank, 26, 264
Presbrey, Frank, Co., 97
Price, Dr., 24, 89
Printers' Ink, 76, 222, 256
Printers' Ink Model Statute, 257, 258
Procter & Gamble Co., 23, 194, 222, 241, 315, 318, 432
Procter, Harley T., 23
Profitable Advertising, 76
Progressive Farmer, The, 400
Prudden, Harry J., 259
Prudential Insurance Co., 13, 102
Pulitzer, Joseph, 32, 33, 168, 252
Pyle, James, 24
Pyle's Pearline, 10, 23, 24, 84

Q

Quaker Oats, 13, 25, 97, 124, 418
Queensborough Corp., 374
Quinby, William Emory, 222
Quinn, T. K., 436
Quoin Club of New York, 264

R

Radio Corp. of America, 379
Railway Mechanical Engineer, 48
Ralston Wheat Food, 25, (facing 193)
Rankin, William H., 289
Ray, E. Lansing, 307
Raymond, C. E., 172
Red & White Corp., 352
Regal Shoe Co., 30, 183, 268
Register & Tribune Co., 367
Reid, Whitelaw, 32, 259
Reincke-Ellis-Younggreen & Finn, 414
Reo Motor Car Co., 286
Resor, Stanley, 197
Rhead, Louis, 122
Rheinstrom, Carroll, 436
Richards, Joseph Addison, 74
Richards, W. J., 55, 58
Richardson, A. Frank, 65, 66
Richardson, Anna Steese, 437
Richardson and DeLong Brothers, 30
Richardson, J. J., 65
Richmond, Va., 27
Rickard & Co., 318
Rickard & Sloan, 318
Rindfusz, Ralph E., Dr., 332
Ripans Tabules, 73
Robbins, Burnett W., 406
Roberts, Theodore P., 127
Robinson-Patman Act, 441
Roche Advertising Co., 414

Technical Publicity Association, 193
"Telefon-Hirmondo," 372
Templin, Walter W., 446
Textile World, 378
Thain, Richard S., 259
Thayer, John Adams, 47, 194
This Week, 428, 436
Thomas, Ambrose L., 47, 197
Thomason, S. E., 302, 389
Thompson, J. Walter, 17, 51, 164
Thompson, J. Walter, Co., 74, 76, 236
Thomson, P. L., 367
Thorne, Charles H., 289
Thorne, George R., 187
Thorne, Robert J., 289
Thorpe, Merle, 289
Tilton, Ralph, 180, 197, 203
Time, 332, 382, 429, 440
Timken-Detroit Axle Co., 249
Timken Roller Bearing Co., 249
Tims, Jr., John F., 332
Tinsman, Robert, 244
Tipper, Harry, 423
Toledo *Bee,* 194
Toledo *Blade,* 357
Toledo *News,* 194
Toledo Scale Co., 211
Tonnesen, Beatrice, 118
Towne, Milton, 357
Traffic Audit Bureau, 430
Travelers Insurance Co., 102
Tribune-Farmer, 41
Tripp, Frank E., 346
True Story, 382
Tucker, Luther, 47
Tugwell Bill, 438

U

Uandi tea, 137
Uneeda Biscuit, 13, 129, 137
Union Pacific, 26
United Advertising Corp., 295
United Cigar Stores Co., 268, 358
United Drug Co., 168, 271
United Newspaper Magazine Corp., 428
United Publishers Corp., 252
UNITED STATES
    United States, 290
    Bureau of Foreign and Domestic Commerce of the Department of Commerce, 346
    Department of Agriculture, 17, 438
    Department of Commerce and Labor, 168
    Division of Advertising of the Committee of Public Information, 288
    Federal Housing Administration, 429
    Federal Trade Commission, 282, 283, 384, 438
    National Industrial Recovery Act, 437
    National Recovery Administration, 423, 438
    National War Advisory Board, 288
    Securities and Exchange Commission, 441
    United States Liberty Loan, (facing p. 289)
    War Industries Board, 294, 304
United States Chamber of Commerce, 259
United States Rubber Co., 332
United States Steel Corp., 9, 143, 197
Ureada Magazine, 137
Uwanta beer, 137

V

Vacuum Oil Co., 70
Van Beuren, Alfred V., 295
Van Beuren & New York Billposting Co., 45

Van Camp, C. C., & Son, 97
Van Camp, Frank, 98
Van Doren, J. E., 65
Varley, Tom, 446
Vick Chemical Co., 358
Vickery & Hill, 44
Victor Talking Machine Co., 224, 228, 243, 280
Vigoro, 309
Viskniskki, Guy T., 290
Voegeler, Charles A., & Co., 11
Vogue, 236

W

WBZ, 372
WBZA, 372
WEAF, 372, 379
WWJ, 372
Wachtel, W. W., 310
Waldo, Richard H., 278
Walgreen Co., 402
Walker, Fred A., 367
Walker, John Brisben, 40
Wallace, Henry, 289
Wallace, Henry C., 318
Waltham Manufacturing Co., 183
Wamsutta Mills, 390
Wanamaker, John, 17, 70, 72, 130, 131, 322
Ward, A. Montgomery, 187
Ward, Artemas, 24, 27, 196
Ward, Artemas, Inc., 346
Ward & Gow, 196
Ward, Montgomery, & Co., 137, 190, 384
Warner Brothers Co., 132
Warner, E. F., 278
Warner, Truly, 218
Warner's Safe Cure, 10, 18, 82
Wasey, Louis R., 278
Washburn-Crosby, 378
Washington *Star,* 74, 140
Washington University Alumni, 143
Waterman, L. E., 30
Weintraub, William H., 429
Weld, L. D. H., 295
West, Paul B., 436
Western Newspaper Union, 38
Western Union, 168
Westinghouse Electric & Manufacturing Co., 372
Wheatley, E. A., 72, 116
Wheeler-Lea Act, 438, 441
Whelan, George J., 268
White, Frank B., 58
White soap, 24
Wife Getter (buggy), 236
Wilder, G. W., 132
Wiley, Harvey, Dr., 192, 193, 259
Wilkes-Barre, Pa., *It,* 79
Williams & Cunnyngham, 414
Williams, David, 49
Williams, David, Co., 252
Williams, Henry P., 137
Williams, Lawrence & Cresmer, 65
Williams, S. C., 65, 203
Willis, Paul S., 367
Wilshire, Joseph, 446
Wilson & Co., 310
Wilson, M. L., 203
Winningham, C. C., 244
Winsten, H. J., 201
Winters, Owen B., 289
Winton car, 259
Wisconsin Agriculturist, 48
Wise, Harold A., 436
Wiseman, Mark, 389
WLW, 429

Woman's Christian Temperance Union, 129
Woman's Home Companion, 382
Wood, Jarvis A., 127
Wood, Robert E., Gen., 378
Woodbridge, C. K., 332
Woodbury Dermatological Institute, J. H., 197
Woodbury, John H., 122, 197
Woodbury Soap, 13
Woodhead, William, 278
Wool soap, 118, 129
Woolworth, F. W., 268, 295
Wow, 309
Wright, Warren, 160
Wrigley, Jr., William, 243, 252
Wrigley, Jr., William, Co., 191

Wyman, Phillips, 332

Y

Young, James W., 295, 432
Young, John Orr, 332
Young & Rubicam, 332
Younggreen, C. C., 414
Youth's Companion, 40, 41, 73, 389
Ypsilanti Underwear, 132

Z

Ziegler, William, 197
Zipper, 392

Subject Index

Advertiser,
  story of the, 4-7

Advertisers,
  the first, 15-30

Advertising,
  acquires marketing background, 202
  attacked and exposed, 434-437
  building consumer demand vs. consumer
    acceptance, 201
  enters the consumer stage, 362
  first books on, 72
  first co-ordination with selling, 200-202
  first merchandising of, 127-128
  first sociological attack on, 265
  how war affected, 281-303
  merchandising it to retailers, 226
  realization of its importance as a force in
    distribution, 88-90
  sales viewpoint starts to rule, 418
  wartime employment of to national ends,
    288-290

Advertising Agency,
  accepts scientific market research, 345
  awakening to appreciation of copy, 74
  costs investigated, 432-433
  develops merchandising and marketing
    functions, 202
  early beginnings of, 51-64
  engages in sales counsel work, 432
  first house agency, 240
  first recognition by publishers, 78
  the non-placing, 165
  transition from space broker to creative
    organization, 161-172

Advertising Allowance,
  beginning of, 132
  regulation of, 441

Advertising Appropriations,
  for automobiles in 1905, 150
  in 1890 and 1900, 94
  in 1900 and 1905, 142
  methods of determining, 423-424
  newspaper, 380
  of tobacco trust before and after dissolu-
    tion, 242
  post-war increase in, 308
  some early, 10-11
  Wanamaker's in 1890's, 72

Advertising Associations,
  first national, 143-146
  formation of first, 76-79

Advertising Clubs,
  establishment of early, 78
  founding of modern national advertising,
    264-265
  organization of local, 142-143

Advertising Publications,
  first, 76

Agricultural Publications,
  See Farm Papers

Art,
  development of advertising, 364-367
  early use in advertising, 84-85

Attention,
  attracting through trick copy, 82-85
  weird media used to attract, 122-123

Automobile,
  advertising during 1922-1929, 395
  becomes second largest advertising indus-
    try, 244
  early advertising of, 147-151
  first use by salesmen, 296-301

mass production of, 248
sold as transportation, 296

Automobile Trailer,
  new industry, 433

Baking Powder,
  early advertising, 24-25

Bathtub,
  advertised, 154

Banks,
  early advertising, 156-160

Bicycle,
  marketing and advertising in its heyday,
    104-108

Booklets, called primers in early days, 49-50

Breakfast Food,
  early advertising, 25

Business,
  regulation by Government (1933), 438-442

Business Papers,
  inception of, 48-49
  establishment of advertising press, 76
  controlled circulation, 432
  consideration given to, 239
  used to merchandise advertising to retail-
    ers, 226

Buttons,
  an advertising medium, 122-123

Buying,
  hand-to-mouth, 327

Buying Power,
  depressed, 398

Cameras,
  early advertising, 27-30

Candy,
  famous candy-cigarette war, 388

Canned Foods,
  advertising in 1890's, 97-98

Car Card Advertising,
  genesis of, 45-46
  growth of, 196

Cash Registers,
  beginning of National Cash Register Co.,
    102

Catalog,
  assumes importance, 334
  birth of mail-order, 187-190
  primitive stage, 50

Censorship,
  early attempts by publishers, 110

Chain Newspapers,
  See Newspapers

Chain Selling,
  in 1890's, 129

Chain Stores,
  advertise private brands, 401-402
  come to fore, 268-274
  develop private brands, 359
  growth of, 351
  retailers fight against, 352,354
  State taxes, 404

Cheese,
  processed, 394

Chewing Gum,
  advertising during trust area, 92-94
  Wrigley's marketing methods, 243

start copy censorship, 110
start copy writing departments, 73

Mail Order,
enters chain-store field, 351
history and development, 187-191
houses advertise private brands, 402
venture of department stores and retailers
into, 275-278

Mail-Order Publications,
early position, 41-44

Market,
interest of advertisers in mass, 136

Market Research,
gains acceptance, 345-348

Marketing,
Government regulation of (1933), 438-442

Mass Production,
started by Ford, 248

Media,
development of curious, 122-123
their failure to encourage advertisers, 31

Merchandising Service Departments,
instituted by publishers, 238

Mergers,
era of distribution, 343-344

Milline,
introduction of, 319

Monopolies,
See Trusts

Motion Pictures,
use by advertisers, 430-432

Motor Bus,
advertising, 394

Negative Copy,
See Scare Copy

New Products,
development of, 406-410
launched by established advertisers, 241

Newspapers,
advertising volume, 1915 and 1929, 380
chain groups, 380-382
chain groups develop, 194
circulations grow, 136
development as a medium from 1888-1895,
32-40
early relations with representative, 65-66
start copy writing departments, 73-74
Sunday editions arrive, 36-38
Sunday editions grow, 428
tabloid-sized papers, 380
use of "ready-prints," 38
use of rotogravure, 379-380

One-cent Sales, 283
Idea adopted by manufacturers, 416

Outdoor Advertising,
development of in 1880's and 1890's, 44-45
development during 1922-1929, 382
principle improvements in 1930's, 430
See also Posters

Oversold,
advertising when, 288

Packaging,
becomes a reality, 25
era of modernization, 338
first attack on merchandise in, 265
grade labeling comes, 437
inception of, 128-129

principles adopted for private brands, 410
of staples, 241
reaches greatest intensity, 410-411

Parcel Post,
effect on distribution, 275

Patent Medicines,
beginning of Omega Oil, 102
early advertising of, 16-19

Photographs,
in advertising illustration, 118-119
news pictures in advertising, 367

Position,
rising demand for special, 85

Posters,
craze for in 1896, 122
early development, 44-45
See also Outdoor Advertising

Premiums,
as used in 1910, 233
early use of, 126
given on single purchase, 412
popularity in 1920 and 1921, 313

Price Competition,
during the depression following 1929, 401

Price Inflation,
following War, 304-307, 312

Price Maintenance,
early history of, 227-228
prices of advertised products cut, 358-360
State Fair-Trade Acts, 441-442

Printing,
early technical improvements in newspaper, 32-33

Private Brands,
advertised, 401-402
adopt modern packages, 410
arises through growth of chain, 274
developed by chains, 359
supplanted by trade-marks in textile field,
390
use by retailers, 213

Product Design,
pays sales dividends, 410
receives attention, 335-338

Production,
age ends, 322
passes distribution, 397-400
stabilized, 327

Profit Sharing,
employee, 315-318

Prohibition,
effect of, 309
repeal of, 433

Psychology,
early study of in advertising, 146

Public Utilities,
as advertisers, 395
early institutional advertising, 202-205

Publishers' Representatives,
early development of, 65-66

Radio,
development of broadcasting, 372-379
growth of, 424-428
growth of set and parts business, 388

Railroads,
early advertising, 26

Rates,
early instability, 54-55

Rayon,
development of, 390-392

Reading Notices,
popularity of in 1890's, 82

Reason Why Copy,
trend toward in 1900's, 175-180

Related Selling, 416

Religious Papers,
in 1890's, 44

Research,
early advertising, 146
scientific market, 345-348

Retailers,
co-operative buying to meet chain competition, 271
denunciation by manufacturer, 213-216
education of, 224-226
hostility to department stores, 130
hostility to mail-order, 187
manufacturer's improved relations with, 216-228
manufacturers offer stock to, 358
position improves 1933-35, 404
start organizing into groups, 352-354
take on side-lines, 309-310

Rhymes,
in advertising, 174-175

Rotogravure,
new form of printing, 379-380

Sales Conventions,
early, 212
held locally, 402

Sales Management,
rise of scientific, 206-212

Sales Methods,
start of systematic, 124-129

Sales Organization,
methods perfected, 330-334

Sales Promotion Department,
a new organism, 330-334

Salesmanship,
development of modern, 206-212

Salesmen,
training of, 330
early training of, 126-127
growing emphasis on training, 211-212
selection of, 330
use automobiles, 296-301

Sampling,
early forms, 124
replaced by color advertising, 296

Scare Copy,
development of, 362
comes into prominence, 282

Seeds,
early advertising, 25

Selling,
first co-ordination with advertising, 200-202

Service Man,
helps retailers with selling, 354

Shoes,
early advertising, 30

Side-lines,
by drug store, 280
by retailers, 309-310

Slogans,
popularity of in 1890's, 111

Small Order,
buying, 327

Soap,
early advertising, 23-24

Soft Drinks,
beginning of Coca-Cola, 98

Space,
size and its relation to advertising failures, 119

Space Buying,
agency's early role in, 51-64
by patent medicine advertisers, 18
development of larger units, 118
list system described, 51-54
new tendencies, 424

Special Agent,
See Publishers' Representative

Standardization,
of lines due to War, 294
speeds distribution, 334

State Fair-Trade Acts,
introduced, 441-442

Stock,
offered by manufacturers to retailers, 358

Stockholders,
courted by business, 411

Street Car Advertising,
See Car Card Advertising

Stunt Advertising,
early era of, 122-123

Substitution,
a problem in 1907, 213-216

Super Market,
coming of, 404

Tax,
against chain stores, 404
excess profits, 308
leveled on sales, trade-marks, etc., 442

Testimonials,
in 1890's, 111-118
use of tainted, 370

Testing Copy,
gains impetus, 364

Textiles,
an industry that developed, 390-392

Tobacco,
advertising during trust era, 92

Trade Associations,
advertising grows, 282-283
early development of in advertising field, 76-79
first advertising by, 205

Trade-Marks,
early use of, 15-30
idea of selling by, 241
manufacturer's acceptance of, 141
State tax laws, 442
supplant private labels in textile field, 390

Trade Papers,
See Business Papers

Trading Stamp,
popularity of, 196-197

Trusts,
failure of the bicycle, 108
Packers' consent decree, 310
their adverse effect on advertising volume, 88-89
their awakening to need for advertising, 88-90

Truth in Advertising,
framing of P. I. Model Statute, 256-259
fraudulent advertising exposed, 192
John E. Powers a champion of, 70

Advertisers' Index

Continued on next page

Advertisers' Index

No responsibility is assumed for any omission

Titles in This Series

9.
C. Samuel Craig and Avijit Ghosh, editors. The Development of Media Models in Advertising: An Anthology of Classic Articles. 1985

10.
C. Samuel Craig and Brian Sternthal, editors. Repetition Effects Over the Years: An Anthology of Classic Articles. 1985

11.
John K. Crippen. Successful Direct-Mail Methods. 1936

12.
Ernest Dichter. The Strategy of Desire. 1960

13.
Ben Duffy. Advertising Media and Markets. 1939

14.
Warren Benson Dygert. Radio as an Advertising Medium. 1939

15.
Francis Reed Eldridge. Advertising and Selling Abroad. 1930

16.
J. George Frederick, editor. Masters of Advertising Copy: Principles and Practice of Copy Writing According to its Leading Practitioners. 1925

17.
George French. Advertising: The Social and Economic Problem. 1915

18.
Max A. Geller. Advertising at the Crossroads: Federal Regulation vs. Voluntary Controls. 1952

19.
Avijit Ghosh and C. Samuel Craig. The Relationship of Advertising Expenditures to Sales: An Anthology of Classic Articles. 1985

20.
Albert E. Haase. The Advertising Appropriation, How to Determine It and How to Administer It. 1931

21.
S. Roland Hall. The Advertising Handbook, 1921

22.
S. Roland Hall. Retail Advertising and Selling. 1924

23.
Harry Levi Hollingworth. Advertising and Selling: Principles of Appeal and Response. 1913

24.
Floyd Y. Keeler and Albert E. Haase. The Advertising Agency, Procedure and Practice. 1927

25.
H. J. Kenner. The Fight for Truth in Advertising. 1936

26.
Otto Kleppner. Advertising Procedure. 1925

27.
Harden Bryant Leachman. The Early Advertising Scene. 1949

28.
E. St. Elmo Lewis. Financial Advertising, for Commercial and Savings Banks, Trust, Title Insurance, and Safe Deposit Companies, Investment Houses. 1908

29.
R. Bigelow Lockwood. Industrial Advertising Copy. 1929

30.
D. B. Lucas and C. E. Benson. Psychology for Advertisers. 1930

31.
Darrell B. Lucas and Steuart H. Britt. Measuring Advertising Effectiveness. 1963

32.
Papers of the American Association of Advertising Agencies. 1927

33.
Printer's Ink. Fifty Years 1888–1938. 1938

34.
Jason Rogers. Building Newspaper Advertising. 1919

35.
George Presbury Rowell. Forty Years an Advertising Agent, 1865–1905. 1906

36.
Walter Dill Scott. The Theory of Advertising: A Simple Exposition of the Principles of Psychology in Their Relation to Successful Advertising. 1903

37.
Daniel Starch. Principles of Advertising. 1923

38.
Harry Tipper, George Burton Hotchkiss, Harry L. Hollingworth, and Frank Alvah Parsons. Advertising, Its Principles and Practices. 1915

39.
Roland S. Vaile. Economics of Advertising. 1927

40.
Helen Woodward. Through Many Windows. 1926